Why? Why? Why?

Why schools fail students

A book by

Bernie Gilman

"Dedicated to the young, in whose spirit, the search for truth marches on."

Published by Createspace

Copyright © 2016 by Bernard Gilman

ISBN-13: 978-1530172023

ISBN-10: 1530172020

Contents

Acknowledgements

Any individual's accomplishment is almost always the result of a team effort, and writing this book has been something that I have been working on for ten years, as my work has always taken preference over my 'external' interests. In short, I would not have been able to complete this personal project without the support of a large number of people, something which I feel duty bound to formally recognize here.

First of all, I would like to extend my thanks to Dennis Balls, who has stuck with me throughout, and has read my various drafts with a view to correcting typographical errors and occasional lapses in my use of English grammar and spelling. He has kept me on task, despite long periods of inactivity due to work commitments, and his comments have always been totally positive, constructively critical and kept me motivated and determined to see this project through to publication.

Equally, I owe considerable thanks to my wife, Sarocha, who has not complained too much when I have shut myself away in a spare room in order to work on the various drafts. She has also kept me on task, as she has kindly appreciated the importance of this project to me personally and professionally.

Thanks are also due to Nick Newell who was one of the first people with whom I discussed my concerns regarding the hidden messages that schools so often send to students, and others, that contradict or otherwise undermine the explicit aims of schools. As always, the ensuing conversations, often over a few cold beers, were a catalyst in helping me decide to go beyond personal carping and actually put my ideas, thoughts and comments on paper in the form of a book.

Additionally, I must extend my thanks to all those teachers who have been my colleagues over the last 38 years at various schools, in different countries, as well as those I interviewed for posts but was unable to appoint. The dynamic of such interactions has taught me a great deal. Similarly, thanks must go to many parents of students, with whom I have discussed my ideas, often in direct relation to the performance of their sons and daughters.

Finally, I must thank the many hundreds of wonderful young people whom it has been a pleasure and a joy to teach, as well as being my privilege to work and learn with such a diverse collection of interesting characters. They have taught me so very much over the years, not only whilst at school, but also having tracked me down to renew contact often after many years. I find that incredibly humbling. It also brings great joy to my heart to know that some 'old' students still recall our time together, when I taught them Economics, with fond memories and even appreciation. I could mention many such students, but it would be unfair to do so, simply because I would inadvertently fail to include many more than I might be able to name here.

Special thanks are also due to Michael Segedy for his friendship and his support and assistance during the publication stages of this work – his expertise has been invaluable!

To all of the above, thank you for your help and company – intentional or unintentional, direct or indirect, even willing or unwilling – you have taught me more than I could possibly have learnt from reading numerous tomes, or by listening to the wisdom of academics in the world of education. I will never forget you or your role in my personal and professional growth and development. Thank you again!

Foreword

Few people will deny the importance and influence of compulsory education, not only for the life of every individual, but also for the life of the local community, of the whole nation, even of the world. Bernie Gilman is concerned that the education which secondary schools in the United Kingdom are currently required to provide falls far short of its potential to develop successful, confident, socially responsible young people. He believes that too many complete their formal education with a sense of failure and a lack of self-worth and personal direction in life, and this book explores his thesis that it is not our children who fail school, but it is our schools which fail our children.

When young people reach the age of majority at eighteen and enter the adult world and come to the end of their period of compulsory education, most people would agree that we would wish them, on leaving school, to have gained and to take with them into a fulfilling life ahead:

- The formal examination results, the requisite qualifications and the skills to enable them to fulfil their ambitions in Further and Higher Education or in a career.

- A clear awareness of their own particular, unique talents and strengths which will define their existence and which they can contribute to society and put at the disposal of others.

- A love of learning, a thirst for knowledge, and an enjoyment from study which will continue throughout their lives.

- Friendship, and lots of friends who will share their future lives with them and be there when needed.

- Strong moral and ethical values, knowing what is right and wrong, upholding truth, and the courage to fight injustice and exploitation and inhumanity wherever they meet it, but especially in the workplace.
- A sense of responsibility for the society, the community and the environment in which they will live, in a local, national and global dimension.
- Self-respect and self-esteem, being confident and at ease with themselves, but modest about their achievements.
- Respect for their bodies and the importance of looking after their health as they grow older.
- Love and tolerance for other people, and to have learned that if you love, trust and care for others, they will reciprocate with love, trust and care, and if you hate, distrust and abuse others, they will respond with hatred, distrust and abuse.
- A desire to develop their own faith and set of beliefs, and a spiritual dimension to their lives to provide landmarks to guide their way through life.
- A zest for life and a determination to grab opportunities and make the most of all that life has to offer.

A young person meeting such a range of success criteria can be considered to be educated, not merely schooled, for "Education is what is left when you've forgotten what you learnt."

Bernie Gilman argues that every person is entitled to expect these outcomes from their education, but that the prescriptive, target-driven, assessment-dominated, standardised direction in which secondary schools in the United Kingdom have been taken by successive governments since the early 1980's has impeded schools and teachers from providing an appropriate education for every individual child, irrespective of what their particular strength, talent and ability may be. The result is that sizeable numbers of our young people do not attain the arbitrarily prescribed academic standard of five GCSE grades A-C, including English and Maths, and leave school with a sense of failure which conditions their future life, and that is indefensible. No parent would wish to bring up their family of children in such a way that some of them leave home, having failed to identify and fulfil their particular potential.

To assess the efficacy of modern education, he invites us to consider to what extent it succeeds in fulfilling the assertion of the ancient Greek epigram that "The mind is a fire to be kindled, not a vessel to be filled."

Bernie draws on a wide experience of the world of education, as a pupil and student, as a classroom teacher, a school manager and a headteacher, and an educational adviser, both in Britain and in international schools. In this book he examines the current state of Britain's schools and casts his critical eye over most aspects of the education system – the curriculum, the assessment process, the nature of leadership and management, teacher training, the effect of political interference and the nature of modern society. His concern is for the quality of the experience to which we subject our young people in schools today and the pertinence of that experience to the digital, information age and the globalised world in which they will live their lives. This is not a book of esoteric educational theory, but rather his own critical reflection of a career spent in education, written with the heart as much as the head and written with passion, erudition, humour, humility and, occasionally, indignation. Not many people will concur with everything that he proposes, but that is not his intention. He challenges the traditional orthodoxy and the conventional wisdom about the nature and structure of compulsory education in the hope that it will encourage his readers to reflect in unconventional ways about the education which they experienced and which today's youngsters are experiencing and to consider how radical changes might lead to significant improvements, to the benefit of the future well-being of every individual and of the nation as a whole. It is therefore a book which is of relevance and interest, not only to educational professionals, but to parents and everyone affected by education, and I heartily recommend it as such.

Dennis Balls
Former Headteacher
The Guernsey Grammar School and Sixth Form Centre

Introduction: 'Who Am I to Talk?'

I first went to school in 1958, as an apprehensive five year old child, and a fetching sight I must have been: a tiny boy with sizeable and seemingly infectious, blotchy freckles ranging freely across his nose and cheekbones, wearing shorts as well as the rest of the school uniform, including the eternally ridiculous school cap! Since that day, of more than a little trepidation, I have failed to generate the thrust required to blast out of the gravitational pull of that world, and boldly go where many men and women have gone before!

After failing my eleven plus, as most of us did (indeed had to), I was duly sent off to the local secondary modern to begin my secondary schooling. I was there for only one year before my parents decided that I would be better off educationally (and probably, they would be better off without a naughty, pre-adolescent son) by being sent to a Royal Navy boarding school. In terms of my academic development, it was a shrewd move and, at the age of sixteen, I managed to confound my subject teachers by achieving averagely good pass grades at GCE 'O' level in six subjects and failing only one. The reason they were surprised and puzzled by my performance was that they were predicting only one pass grade – and that was in the subject I flunked! They were confounded with some justification, as it was my 'best' subject and the one that I enjoyed above all else with, perhaps, the exception of geography.

Given their lack of belief in my academic potential, and notwithstanding my prowess on the rugby field, as well as a flailing, south-paw boxer, the opportunity for me to stay on to take 'A' levels in the Sixth Form was subject to several limiting conditions or qualifications, if that is not too ironic. My father decided that the school held precious little faith and belief in his elder son and that my education would be better served by allowing me to return to the family home and take my 'A' levels at the local Technical College. The subjects I was to study were determined by my parents, which seemed perfectly reasonable to me, as schooling had always been determined, structured, delivered and assessed by other people – I had no decision-making role in that process and nor did I expect or anticipate ever really having one.

Given that I had never 'failed' Economics and Law before – mainly, and obviously, because I had never previously studied them – those two subjects were to be my main areas of study. Now, bearing in mind that this was in the 1970s, I would have agreed to anything if it meant that I could escape basin-bowl haircuts every three weeks, courtesy of an apparently blind and certainly unfashionable barber, and being able to grow my hair to a length that might 'Wow' the girls – a gender with which I had had very little contact at boarding school, apart from an elderly and caring matron. So, Economics and Law it was!

It was customary in those days to take three 'A' levels, and so an argument, thinly disguised as a discussion – to which I was still a largely disinterested spectator – took place to determine what 'my' third subject should be. Not for the first time, or the last, my parents had somewhat different ideas on this matter. My father was adamant that Pure Mathematics was a great idea, given its universal application and his love of slide-rules, whereas my mother, who was always the more forward-thinking parent in many ways, had one eye on Britain's impending entry into the European Community and felt that French was a better choice. They couldn't agree, and so I began my Sixth Form life taking **four** 'A' level subjects which, in view of my fairly weak, academic performance in French and Mathematics a few months earlier, was clearly an exaggerated, inflated and unjustifiable belief in my academic capability at the time.

After four, austere years at boarding school, where my actions for every waking hour of the day were determined for me – and shaped, if needs be, by the use of a cane or slipper if I dared to deviate (I was once given the slipper by the senior students in their common room, without any adult supervision, for the anti-social and unacceptable act of 'throwing a tennis ball near school buildings') – the laissez-faire life at 'Tech College', at the end of the liberal 1960's and early 1970s was a real blast! If you didn't want to go to lectures, you didn't have to. Nor did you have to do your homework, if you didn't want to. Fabulous! If you were determined to fail, then they would let you..........ah!

2

At the end of two, immensely enjoyable and hedonistic years, during which time I lost my virginity – something that I had to do for the sake of my sight – I was indeed lucky to scrape pass grades in Economics and Law, while less fortunate in French, in which I was awarded an 'O' level pass – which means I have passed that level twice! By the way, if you are wondering what happened to Pure Mathematics, well it was decided that I should 'drop' that particular avenue of study following a massive score of 4% in the mock examination at the end of the first year.

After a third year at the College, during which time I continued to grow my hair and got into a rock band, playing the drums, I failed to improve my 'A' level results in Economics and Law by more than one measly grade, and went to Teachers' Training College in Yorkshire to study a four-year, Bachelor of Education degree course.

I was about to experience a real sea-change in my academic fortunes!

I flourished, thanks to a great man called Alun Roberts who was my Economics tutor and, later, a very dear friend. He was the very first person, outside my family, who made me believe that I had academic potential as well as the skills and personal qualities to become a talented classroom teacher. He encouraged me, observed me in different settings, boosted me, nurtured me, praised me, helped me, supported me, counselled me, pushed me, challenged me, taught me and much more – I would never be able to thank him enough; he was truly a wonderfully gifted and delightful human being!

He retired the year after I graduated, although I am assured that the two events are not related in any way, and after many years living in his beloved Wales with his wonderful wife Megs, he became the *late* Alun Roberts. I still feel a deep and lasting sense of loss and grief, which brings tears to my eyes every time I think of him – which I often do. He was quite simply a dear, dear man and friend, as well as being a masterful educator in the very best sense of both the adjective and the noun!

I began teaching as a fully qualified member of the profession in secondary schools in 1976 and, from that time, I worked in various locations and organisations around the country as a secondary school class teacher, Department/Faculty Head, Adviser/Inspector of Schools, and Head Teacher at two large comprehensive schools – but, mercifully, not at the same time! I had evolved, without a great deal of conscious thought, into what was euphemistically called a 'career teacher'.

But then, in 1997, I made what many considered to be a courageous career shift, if not exactly a career change. Others felt that I was not being at all courageous, rather it was a foolhardy move to resign my relatively well-paid post as Head Teacher and become a student again. For a long time and for reasons not really relevant here, I had harboured a growing desire to live and work abroad. Suffice to say, I had always felt like a 'fish out of water' in England; a sensation of slow suffocation in an alien environment and culture. At first, I actually believed that such dissatisfaction and simmering misery with life was a natural state of affairs. After all, I had been to 'Sunday School' and was led to believe that 'Life' was another, but higher order type of test in which I had to also achieve a pass grade if I was to be admitted or permitted into 'The Kingdom of Heaven'. I was serving a life-long sentence, it seemed. But when I first started to travel overseas I gradually began to feel that it didn't matter what my passport said; I instinctively sensed that I was in the wrong place, but at the same time had absolutely no idea where I was supposed to be. The time had come to find out!

Moving On and Out

I had a sense of great release after making that monumental decision, as well as more than a tinge of anxiety and self-doubt, as I started a course of study to qualify as a teacher of English as a Foreign Language. A month or so later, I was on an airplane – my new adventure of living and working overseas as a teacher of Business English took me to Italy for a few months and then on to the land of raw herrings and Carlsberg – Denmark! After nearly two years in Copenhagen, and one depressingly dark and gloomy winter, when the use of the term 'daylight' was a fraudulent misnomer, I managed to secure my first appointment in an international school, in Kuwait – and enjoyed a return to the teaching of Economics again. Apart from the interaction with young people, mainly from different Arabic-speaking countries, it was not to be an enjoyable experience. I found it difficult to tolerate the behaviour of senior managers who sought to control through fear and favours and who, in my opinion, seemed to see the enterprise first and foremost as a money-making opportunity for themselves and the owners, rather than as a place to genuinely promote the life chances of young people, and professionally develop colleagues.

So, after a year, I was on the move again to where I discovered my true, spiritual home in the 'Land of Smiles' – namely, the Kingdom of Thailand. I worked in Bangkok for two years designing and developing business management training programs for a consulting company before becoming Head of High School in an international school-setting again, this time in Singapore, for two years.

Singapore – or 'Lego-land' as I prefer to call it – is effectively one big, heavily regulated shopping mall (with a peripheral, but world-beating zoo); a Westernised consumer's paradise. It is utterly predictable, devoid of any semblance of spirituality and, for me, a dreadfully dull place. I feel it could be true to say that if you want a good existence then go to Singapore, but if you really want to *live*, then go to Thailand. Indeed, someone once quipped that the difference between Singapore and a pot of yoghurt is that, left long enough, the yoghurt would develop its own culture.

So it was that I had an overwhelming desire to return 'home' – back to Thailand – where I fortunately secured the post of Head Teacher of a recently-established international school. And that is where I was for two more years, before moving to a post at an international school in India. This was followed by a short and sadly tragic stint living and working in Sub-Saharan Africa as Principal of an international school. After that, I was relaxed and relieved to find myself back in what I still consider to be my permanent home in Thailand – God willing and, of course, the ever fickle and inconsistent immigration authorities of Thailand.

I then spent nearly four years working as an English language consultant for a large, Thai-owned multinational company in the agro-food business, designing and delivering customised, English-language training programs for the more senior personnel, including the CEO. After that immensely enjoyable and well-paid period of employment, I accepted the post of Principal at an international school in Malaysia, but asked to be released from my contract after one year owing to micro-management on the part of the Malaysian School Director – something that is endemic in international schools it seems. I returned to Thailand and spent a year ostensibly working on this book, but actually devoted a lot of time to going to the gym, cooking and doing various part-time jobs to keep the proverbial wolf from the door.

After that highly relaxing year off, I started to look for another school post, but not as a school leader. In short, I wanted to return to that which was always my forte, and become a classroom teacher again. As Head or as a Principal, I always yearned to have more day-to-day contact with the students, and a return to the 'chalk-face', therefore, seemed a totally logical step. At the time of publication of this book, I am working as Head of Economics at a school in Peru, teaching the subject to IGCSE and IB Diploma level. I am thoroughly enjoying the experience, as are the students it seems, given their generous tributes to the way I teach.

Whilst the future will undoubtedly consist of a few more unexpected twists and turns, I continue to do as all good teachers instinctively do. I like to reflect upon what I have done before. It is important to look back and evaluate one's own performance and actions, and to learn from previous experience. Unfortunately, I rarely had time to do that in the UK, as most of my time was spent just trying to 'get on' and 'keep up' with all the new initiatives that were thrust upon those of us in education – the new things that we **had to do** – whilst continuing to do our best for the young people whom it was always a privilege to work with and for, regardless of how challenging they might be or how difficult their home and wider social (or anti-social) circumstances made them.

This book is, therefore, a reflection, now that I have succeeded in putting enough distance between myself and the professional treadmill in the UK, and found the time and inner peace to put what has gone before into some kind of personal and professional perspective. Whilst in the UK, I was so involved in pounding that damnable treadmill, that all of my time was spent running ever faster and faster and yet still failing to keep up, let alone getting ahead in any meaningful sense, so that I was unable to truly take stock. I was too busy reacting and responding to the day-to-day challenges, the short-term shocks, largely externally imposed by Central or Local Government that I simply never had the chance to reflect upon the longer-term changes that I now believe were undermining the schooling of young people, and my profession. If I hadn't jumped at the time I did, I would have surely have suffered the fate of *'the boiled frog'!*

For those of you that are not familiar with that conceptual term, please let me explain that it does not refer to a dish that one might find on the menu of some bistro in France – or Thailand for that matter! The boiled frog syndrome is an analogy that explains the demise of many large and successful business organisations over time, and it adheres to the following impeccable, scientific and yet gruesome logic, I believe. If you heat a pan of water until it is very hot and take a live frog and drop it in, the poor, unfortunate amphibian will bounce (or hop) immediately back out again – the external shock will be so sudden and dramatic that it will take instinctive remedial action with a dramatic sense of urgency, and who can blame it? On the other hand, place the same frog in a pan of cool water and very slowly heat it up, the imperceptible rise in temperature is missed by the frog living in, and for, the here and now. The frog is oblivious to the increasing temperature and will remain where it is until it is literally overcome by the heat, and dies!

So it is in the real world, that we are so involved and pre-occupied with responding to wave after wave of government and other societal initiatives – dare I say short-term 'shocks' or imperatives – that those of us in schools inevitably miss the longer-term changes that are gradually affecting and engulfing us. We inevitably fall victim to the under-currents that make our desire to truly promote the life chances of young people either impossible or increasingly difficult. We are blinded by the short-term imperative and simply do not see how the landscape is evolving – until it is also too late for us all.

To date, I have now enjoyed some forty years in education and training, and for the most part it has been an enormous privilege to have been involved in promoting the life chances of young people both in England and overseas, not only in a variety of different cultures, but also in a huge array of contrasting contexts. I believe that I have to some extent 'earned my spurs' and have the qualified right to give my opinions and views on what I passionately believe – that secondary schools in England, despite the best intentions and extraordinary efforts of many teachers, by and large fail the young people whose potential talents and gifts they are responsible for unleashing, liberating and nurturing, during what are perhaps the most defining years of their lives.

I have seen the increasing and utter failure of schools to meet the many fine and ambitious aims, as stated in their respective school brochures. Schools are incredibly busy places, but all the dedicated and often frenetic, even frantic activity seems to create a lot more heat than light, not only for teachers but also for the students!

Over the years, the enjoyment and sense of privilege had been gradually eroded as I felt myself and my valued colleagues being slowly twisted into becoming mere educational technicians, responsible for efficiently and effectively doing the bidding of civil servants and government – following a political rather than an educational agenda. This was in stark contrast to seeking to become dedicated professionals who, in concert with other talented colleagues and external agencies, are seeking to perfect the art of promoting independent learning and helping to enlighten generations of young people – *supported by* layers of government and educational administration. Sadly, when these imposed initiatives fail to match the rhetoric of the government perpetrators, as they usually and perhaps inevitably do, it is the technicians who get the misplaced and erroneous blame!

The true professionals grow ever more disaffected and disillusioned, as do the students, whose real needs remain unaddressed, ignored and latent. If that seems harsh or inaccurate then perhaps you are one of the many victims, perhaps a prisoner, of your own experience as a teacher or student. It 'worked' for you and so it is unquestionably good for everyone else.

When I told one of my nieces that I believed secondary schools failed young people, she seemed critically sceptical and expressed her doubts by saying that she had turned out, "OK". But then, mediocrity should not be confused with excellence. Why did she not feel that she had turned out as a brilliant star, and one that was capable of casting light into darkened corners of the world, as well as within her own doubtless and boundless galaxy of hidden, or yet to be discovered, innate talents!

All I ask of you, the reader, is that you consider what is obviously a subjective point of view and be prepared to pick up on any points which might possibly strike a chord within you – regardless of who you are – and then perhaps seek to refine or amend your philosophy or perception of education and, more importantly, act upon what you fundamentally believe to be right, to make matters better than they are now. If what I say makes you feel uncomfortable, ask yourself "Why?" If you feel outraged or angry then please be prepared to unpick your emotions and question the values that have guided your behaviours and thinking to date. If you utterly discount a lot of what I say, please do not reject those points with which you tend to agree or sympathise. I do not profess to be right – that would be incredibly arrogant, churlish and dogmatic – rather I just want to express my views, which I am prepared to debate and further articulate with anyone!

I do feel that the time for true and genuine educationists to fight back against the constant and relentless political interference in what is arguably, and probably, the most important area of public service and expenditure, is long overdue.

Reflect honestly upon your own experiences at school, and consider how effectively they prepared you for your life then and your life now. I always marvel at statements by many people who say that their schooldays were the best years of their lives. Whilst I like the idea that 'nostalgia isn't what it used to be' and that those people genuinely feel that sentiment, I would challenge that view by suggesting that if those days really were the best years of their lives, then perhaps they failed dismally in helping them make the most of the rest of their human existence – isn't that one of its key objectives after all?

What's it all about - really?

Nearly 20 years ago, I was asked if I could summarise my experiences of secondary school education in a couple of sentences. It didn't take a great deal of effort to recall those years – much of which was fun and worthwhile – and

9

yet two words immediately and unconsciously sprang to mind – **'Boredom'** and **'Fear'**!

I wonder what young people attending secondary schools today in England would say if asked the very same question – assuming that they felt inclined to offer a response at all. Perhaps we should ask them. In the meantime, I shall assume that the majority might be quite negative about the whole secondary school experience in England, given their behaviour in, and attitude towards school. If not negative, their sentiments might be fairly ambivalent at best, rather than full of expressions of enjoyment, wonder and passion, as well as achievement and success. For some, there would be the stock, establishment answer…..I go to school to learn! But why do they have to go to school to learn, and who decides what they learn, how they learn it, and when?

This book is a personal view as to why I believe so many secondary schools quite literally fail – fail themselves, their communities, the nation, society and more importantly, fail the young people who populate or attend them. I accept that this is a serious accusation or charge to make, but I truly feel it is a justifiable one, at least as a generality.

When I was a student at school, I was always told to use a dictionary to improve my spelling, but I find that a dictionary is of far greater use when used as a means of clarifying what is meant by the words, terms and phrases that are used every day. The Collins COBUILD English Dictionary points out that 'to fail' essentially means to be unsuccessful in achieving what one was trying to do. If a business, or organisation or system 'fails', it can mean that it becomes unable to continue in operation or in existence. If one's health or eyesight is 'failing', then it is becoming gradually weaker or less effective. If a quality or ability that you have 'fails' you, then it is not good enough in a particular situation to enable you to do what you need or want to do. To 'fail' an examination means that one does not reach the standard that is required, and so on.

The media frequently report that this school or that school is failing – or, more euphemistically and less pejoratively, being placed under 'special measures'. We hear stories about schools where too many students fail to reach external examination standards at the age of sixteen years, or even earlier. The more right-wing media outlets even like to suggest that the state system of education is failing to produce the right results or meet expected standards – whatever these might be.

Such criticisms are always hurtful mainly because no one likes to fail (which is one powerful outcome of schooling), but then surely is it not true to say that failure is a key or essential feature of effective learning and development? In my assertion that secondary schools are failing young people, it is fundamentally important to be clear about what it is that schools are supposed to be doing and whose needs they are supposed to be meeting. Next, it is only right to suggest why and in what way schools fail to achieve what it is that they are supposed to be doing. Consequently, I want to outline how I honestly believe secondary schools could be far more successful, and far more unlikely to fail their many stakeholders, and especially the young people who have the potential to bring schools to brilliant and vibrant life.

I shall argue that one fundamental error is that government initiatives in education over a number of years have served to transfer fundamental decision making away from professionally trained, experienced teachers in favour of giving it increasingly to politicians and civil servants, among others. Such initiatives also fail because they are almost always focused on the *symptoms* of the under-achievement of schools and students as opposed to the *root causes*. When Tony Blair was re-elected to serve again as Prime Minister, he said that one of the key platforms of his second term in office would be, 'Education, Education, Education!' I would suggest that a better slogan would have been, 'Initiative, Initiative, Initiative' – despite his stated aim of relieving education generally, and teachers specifically, from the more recently imposed experience of constant change!

Moreover, politicians as well as teachers ignore or are blind to the fundamental and immensely powerful hidden messages that underlie the way in which we structure, 'package' and deliver schooling. This ignorance or blinkered vision means that government initiatives are undermined by the hidden messages that have a far greater impact in practice than any amount of peripheral tinkering.

11

It is not my intention to castigate or apportion blame upon professional teachers; they are largely a highly dedicated and talented group of individuals. Teaching is a vocation of which it is both highly enjoyable and a genuine privilege to be a member. Over a number of years, however, the immense reservoir of professional goodwill has been stretched to a point where it has drained away from, if not blown apart in the case of many career-minded teachers. Governments have progressively degraded – even 'dumbed-down' – the profession, in terms of the genuine empowerment of teachers. As I have said, teachers have increasingly become mere technicians who are required to do the bidding of successive governments in putting wave after wave of initiatives into practice, and then to take the blame when these centrally determined schemes do not achieve what they are intended to – in short, when they *fail*. And, of course, failure is largely inevitable for reasons which I have outlined above, and which I shall elaborate upon further during the course of what follows.

When things go wrong in an organization, it is customary for someone – some poor individual – to take the blame, to be the scapegoat and to 'carry the can'. However, sound management research suggests that most organisational failure is usually due to the failure of systems rather than unfortunate individuals. Nick Leeson is a classic case in point; a man who effectively bankrupted the austere and reputable Barings Bank as a result of dubious, even illegal, financial dealings, and was eventually prosecuted and sent to prison for his actions – but where were the checks and balances in such an august organisation? How was he allowed to, or not prevented from, taking and making such reckless and illegal transactions? Why didn't the heads of the top management also roll? Answer - he was effectively made the scapegoat – so popular in British culture!

Similarly, if state schools fail to achieve what they are intended to, then it is the various governments over time that created the systems that should be held to account. It is governments that fail and not schools or the teaching profession!

Educationists often claim that the wider and thornier issue of the declining state of British society – in terms of the loss of genuine respect and the decline in law and order, accompanied by a rise in selfishness and greed, for example – means that schools cannot be expected to fully compensate for these societal ills, and that they should not be seen as the villain of the piece, or the cause of these problems. Whilst such an assertion is definitely valid to some extent, there is a real danger that it can all too easily be used as an excuse for inaction or the acceptance of lower and more modest expectations in schools themselves.

Later in this book, I will reflect upon these broader issues and the external forces which militate against what the school system should be seeking to achieve. But a big part of the problem is a lack of clarity about the real purpose of schools. I will begin by arguing that schools are expected to fulfil a role that they simply cannot be expected to achieve, due to this lack of clarity and the powerful vested interests that are best served by maintaining the status quo. In so doing, it is almost inevitable that, today, the destiny of secondary schooling is not exactly a rosy or an optimistic one.

So, who am I to talk, let alone judge? I am someone who cares passionately for a school system that maximises the possibility of achieving the full realisation of the potential of every human being and to liberate the talents that every person undoubtedly possesses. I want to see a school that promotes real learning and stimulates all young people to want to learn – not just whilst at school but throughout their lives. I believe that education is a fundamental human right that should genuinely seek to identify if not develop dreams within young people and adults alike, and then help provide them with the skills, knowledge and abilities to make these dreams come true. The sky is the limit in this respect!

Section A: Setting the Scene

Chapter One: 'Why, Why, Why?'

Well, if Tom Jones can ask this philosophically repetitive question of Delilah, then I intend to ask it in an attempt to uncover the real reasons which I believe explain why secondary schools fail young people so often. Let me pose just a few:

➤ Why does the government feel a relentless need to introduce wave after wave of new, often re-packaged, hare-brained, recycled, regurgitated, but hardly novel, initiatives?

➤ Why does government not allow a greater amount of time for previous initiatives to be properly tested and then to become part and parcel of everyday practice before introducing additional, over-lapping or new and contradictory ones?

➤ Why do so many of these initiatives fail to achieve the intended outcomes?

➤ Why does the government always think it knows better than the professionals who are responsible for actually delivering secondary schooling at both the strategic and operational level?

➤ Why are governments so willing to take chances with the schooling of successive generations of young people in this way?

➤ Why do so few students feel the real thrill, the joy and exciting buzz of learning?

➤ Why is school work so often seen as a chore – something that has to be done, even suffered and endured, during one's childhood and teenage years, rather than as a liberating, exciting and enjoyable, lifelong experience?

➤ Why do so many young people play truant from school?

➤ Why are so many young people being excluded – temporarily or permanently – from school?

➤ Why does the UK have the lowest staying-on rate for Higher Education in Europe?

➤ Why are girls out-performing boys in secondary schools?

- Why is it that the thrill that children in primary school usually display tends to dissipate or evaporate almost as soon as they reach secondary school – if not before?
- Why is society witnessing the worrying sense of disaffection and pessimism that young people all too often display towards their secondary schooling?
- Why is this sense of disaffection and pessimism becoming more widespread – even 'infecting' primary school education?
- Why the open negativity, even hostility, towards education that characterizes the behaviour of many parents, not just their offspring?
- Why is there an apparent cycle of disaffection and hostility towards education that is being transmitted from generation to generation?
- Why does this cycle of disaffection seem to be spreading and multiplying?
- Why are league tables for measuring the so-called performance of schools so important?
- Why do these league tables take no account of the true, often huge, value-added learning that some schools manage to help their students achieve, by taking proper account of the level of prior achievement of students when they join the school, let alone the remedial action to compensate for the adverse social and environmental factors that can so powerfully militate against achievement and success?
- Why is academic achievement virtually the only important yardstick when it comes to assessing the attainment, progress and success of schools and the students that attend them?
- Why do schools signally fail so many young people in terms of helping them to discover and nurture their aptitudes, talents and abilities that are often lost to the world, not just to the individuals concerned, which is far more tragic?
- Why do so many people not discover their real talents and abilities until they retire – if they are lucky enough to do so at that time?
- Why does the government seem so intent and determined to pander to the exclusive or specific wishes of the middle class when forming its education policies and initiatives?

➤ Why doesn't the government seek to more fully and appropriately meet the needs of the working class parents, who may themselves be disenchanted about the relevance and usefulness of schooling – very often as a result of their own negative or unfulfilling experiences?

➤ Why do these problems all seem to be getting worse or failing to be met and overcome?

➤ What is going wrong?

And finally, perhaps the most important of all questions:

➤ Why do children stop asking, **"Why?"**?

In the following chapters, I shall attempt to cast some light on why the questions above arise and remain unresolved, beginning with what is one of the central tenets of my arguments – the fact that governments, schools and teachers very often fail to consider the hidden messages that lie behind their actions – messages that often convey a totally different, even contradictory meaning from those of the many explicit statements or courses of action.

Chapter Two: Power of Hidden Messages

What Are We Saying?

People communicate in three main ways: by speaking and writing in their own language (or another language) and through the use of gesture, which is also culturally determined, but what is actually going on in these different types of communication? Why are communications sometimes so difficult, with the intended message being so frequently misinterpreted by the receiver? Do we really understand what we are doing when we seek to communicate with others?

I would suggest that we communicate largely to express our feelings, emotions, ideas and thoughts to other people, and when speaking or writing we use words. In reality, when we speak, all we are doing is expressing ourselves by making sounds – hopefully sounds that are recognisable and understandable to other people in a given community. When we want to express what we are thinking or want to say in written form, what we actually do is to turn the sounds we utter into symbols that are also recognisable and understood within a given community of people. This is not an easy process, as in the English language we only have twenty-six symbols, albeit used in many different combinations and contexts. When we are reading aloud, of course, we are engaged in the opposite process of turning combinations of symbols into sounds or noises.

We all know that words are what people say or what they write, but what is often not properly understood is how unhelpful words alone are in conducting and ensuring effective face-to-face communications. Much more important than the words we choose to use is the use of the ***tone*** of our voices as well as our ***body language***. In fact, research suggests that the dictionary definition of words alone is only responsible for a mere 7% of the actual meaning. Yeah right, as little as that? Perhaps not surprisingly, when I first heard this I thought it was absurd, laughably silly and found it almost impossible to believe, but let's consider a couple of simple illustrations that help to prove the point.

After listening to you talking for a while, I turn to you and say, *"You're quite clever."* You reply by courteously saying, *"Well thank you!"* This is a response which makes me think that you are being sarcastic in your reply, because I was certainly not paying you a compliment. Actually, I was trying to tell you that I think you are not really very clever at all, and felt the urge to share my somewhat negative view of you.

Clearly, it all depends on which word you emphasise with the tone of your voice that determines the real meaning of the speaker. If I place the stress on the word *'clever'*, then I am indeed paying you a compliment, but what I actually did do in the above example was to stress the word *'quite'* which, of course, conveys a significantly different meaning; not quite the opposite, but almost. Try saying it in the two different ways:

1. "You're quite **clever**."
2. "You're **quite** clever."

A second and more extensive illustration lies in how one says this sentence:

"I didn't say he beat his dog."

As a written sentence, with no context from which to gather its precise meaning, it does not say very much at all. It could actually have seven slightly different meanings depending upon where the speaker places the stress.

"I didn't say he beat his dog." = someone else said he beat his dog.

"I didn't say he beat his dog." = a flat denial, offering no other explanation.

"I didn't say he beat his dog." = I wrote it in a letter, or implied it by gesture.

"I didn't say he beat his dog." = I said she (or a different 'he') beat his dog.

"I didn't say he beat his dog." = I said he didn't feed it, for example.

"I didn't say he beat his dog." = he beat someone else's dog.

"I didn't say he beat his dog." = he actually beat his cat.

The words we utter play only a relatively small part in face-to-face conversations, but the tone we invest in our utterances, and the body language we employ in tandem with our speech, are far more important when it comes to communicating effectively and getting our point across. In other words, what we say is heavily dependent upon *__how__* we actually say it.

Even in face-to-face verbal communications, therefore, it is possible for the intended message to be distorted if the speaker does not say it in the appropriate way, using the right tone. What is 'appropriate' or 'right', however, is also a cultural issue. American English, for example, is different in many ways from British English, in terms of vocabulary, grammar and intonation. We are indeed two nations divided by a common language, and a very big Ocean, thankfully! The Americans pronounce the name of the capital city of the Russian Federation as if they kept farmyard animals there in damp and unkempt circumstances (Moss Cow), whereas, the British make the same word sound as if it were a type of elite, incorporated tailoring business, minus the male siblings – Moss Co.

But you do not need to traverse the Atlantic Ocean to see how important intonation, pronunciation and enunciation are. A Yorkshire man went to see the local vet and the conversation they had went as follows:

"Vetinary, I am worried about me cat; it's not well."
"Oh really, I'm sorry to hear that. Is your cat a tom?"
"No, I brought it with me, ya daft beggar!"

Regional variations in intonation and pronunciation, such as the one above, provide a rich source of humour in the United Kingdom. But, verbal communications are far from precise for another very important reason, and that is the vital role that body language plays in face-to-face communications. When we speak to people, the three elements of the words we use, our tone and body language, all have a part to play in the process, with words playing their very minor role. Your body language on the other hand is slightly more important than the tone of your voice, or your intonation in communicating effectively, when engaged in face-to-face conversation.

The words may say one thing, but your tone and, certainly, your body language, can so easily send a different message. Your words are overt and easy but your body language sends incredibly powerful messages which are far more complex in structure. In fact, most of the body language cues that we transmit are sent without us being consciously aware that we are sending them – but we mean what they say. The vast majority of our incredible arsenal of body language signs is employed unconsciously; an ability that is culturally and socially determined and learned. We have control over some of them, assuming we know which ones they are, what they mean and how to control them, but of the many thousands we use, we can intentionally influence only a relatively small number.

Body language is so powerful, that we are able to communicate very effectively without any use of words or intonation. During my long-haired, teenage years I remember my father obliquely and subtly trying to get me to have a haircut by explaining how first impressions are very important when first meeting someone – your dress, your gestures, your eye contact, your movements, your conduct, your hygiene and odour, your posture and such like. First impressions really do count! When we meet someone for the first time, it is believed that we form as much as ninety per cent of our eventual impression of them in as little as ninety seconds of first encountering them, often before they even open their mouths and speak. Some psychologists have said that first impressions might even be formed in as little as just ***three seconds***. At interview, a person's appearance, or the way they enter the room can have a dramatic impact upon whether or not they eventually get the job, after the questioning and talking is over. Your body language can effectively 'sell' you well or, alternatively, sell you hopelessly short.

One of the most popular refrains when the British travel overseas on holiday is, "Do you speak English?" This testifies to the belief that English is widely spoken around the World, in its various versions. It also exposes an appalling reluctance to learn the language of other countries, even those closest to us. We see the French as arrogant, because they quite often refuse to speak English when encountering mono-lingual English folk on holiday in France. Actually, I admire their stereotypical obstinacy because what they are really trying to say to us is, *"Make an effort and speak my language!"* I prefer to see their obstinacy as a desire to protect their culture in the face of the Anglo-Saxon tidal wave that threatens to swamp them. After all, culture is significantly and, perhaps, more powerfully expressed and communicated through our language, as well as our cuisine, sports and music, for example.

We also view our most proximate neighbours in this way because they are irritated by the Anglo-Saxon mentality which expects others to speak English, even though we are, after all, in their country…….when in Rome, as they say. Given this dreadful ability of the British in such circumstances to be able to communicate with the right words, or noises, we rely instead upon gestures – pointing, nodding, shaking our heads, etc. – as well as shouting, borne out of frustration and an erroneous assumption that the reason they do not understand English is because they are profoundly deaf, or just plain stupid!

Men and women use body language differently as well – just to add to the Venus and Mars challenges. As the Head Teacher of a school in England, I recall more than a sense of bemusement at meetings with an extended senior team of colleagues – the majority of whom were women – when throughout the meeting my female colleagues nodded enthusiastically, whilst I put forward a tricky proposal for a fairly fundamental change in the methods of teaching and learning that we should adopt. As a result, I felt assured and comforted that, if and when put to the vote, my proposals would be agreed to or carried. Not so – it was voted down, much to my disappointment and confusion. I was unaware of the fact that feminine nodding was an indication that they were listening actively, out of a feeling of involvement, rather than any actual agreement. Men, on the other hand, tend to nod only when they support or agree with what someone is saying, which is a far more reliable indicator of success when it comes to the vote!

Fortunately, there are many ways in which we employ the same body language – especially, and thankfully, in the area of sexual attraction. It is often these hidden messages – hidden from our conscious thoughts, but starkly apparent to our unconscious selves – that explain the inexplicable, such as what a very beautiful woman sees in a man who others see as fairly run-of-the-mill, perhaps dull, and certainly not handsome. Now it may be that he is loaded, but more often than not, it is because the woman is quite simply attracted by, and to him. There is, after all, a huge difference between what is beautiful and that which one finds attractive, even if one is only focussing on looks and ignoring personality and character. In Thailand, for example, many Thai women fall in love with men who do not have lots of cash and neither do they have good looks – and I should know! Instead, they are attractive for what they are, how they act, and not what they look like. The book is not judged by the cover, but by its inner substance. In Thai they refer to a man as being *'Jai dee'*, or having a good heart; something they seem capable of determining extraordinarily quickly by sensing the hidden messages that a person unconsciously transmits, or gives off. It may, of course, also and alternatively be a rather subtle form of Oriental flattery!

An example of body language employed for sexual attractiveness purposes is the 'enlarged triangle' of vision, and these are signals that one can consciously employ and read, assuming of course that one is aware of them. When a man and a woman meet for the first time, they always focus on each other's eyes, whilst they are engaged in social intercourse. Their gaze flits from left to right and right to left – or from eye to eye – not staring intently at only one eye, unless of course one of them happens to be a glass eye!

In such unusual cases, we tend to feel that to look at the false eye at all might be drawing attention to the fact, and so we find ourselves trying desperately to focus on the one, normal eye, which is actually very difficult to do, even when we are consciously seeking to do just that. Then we become conscious of the fact that the other person will surely realise that we are avoiding their unorthodox appearance and so we find ourselves torn between not wanting to look at the artificial eye, and yet feeling an almost uncontrollable urge to do exactly the opposite.

Notwithstanding glass eyes, or nervous ocular twitches, in most cases we simply transfer our gaze at irregular, but relatively short intervals from eye to eye – unless, of course, we are sexually interested in the other person, and this is where we begin to consciously or unconsciously employ the triangular visual body language. Now we continue to look from eye to eye, but also occasionally we find ourselves glancing down at the other person's mouth at an almost imperceptible speed. Some argue that this deviation from the left-right convention is indicative of our unconscious wondering what it might be like to kiss the person with whom we are engaged in social intercourse.

26

If the interest is truly aroused at this stage then we enlarge our triangular field of vision. Now, whilst keeping the eyes very much as the two main focal points, largely to be seen to be behaving ourselves and not getting out of order, we begin to glance further 'South' than just the mouth; to encompass, incorporate, even savour the rest of the body................and you don't need me to tell you why and what you might be contemplating, albeit unconsciously!

Making Ourselves Clear

These few, simple examples of the fundamental, but often overlooked importance and centrality of hidden messages translate far more powerfully in the context of education and schools. There are all kinds of well-known sayings in the English language that add weight to my belief that the hidden messages we send through the way we structure, design and deliver schooling, as well as seek to measure the success of this complex and multi-faceted, political football that we loosely refer to as 'state schooling', are often contrary to the intended ones. We know what we want people to hear and believe, but I am of the view that the reality is we actually live a whopping fib in terms of the actual effects of what we do and how we do it. How many times have you heard people resort to well-used, or well-worn, sayings such as, *"Do what I say, not as I do."* or, *"It is common sense."* or *"That's the way it is."* and so on. When a child or a student at school asks the question *"Why should I do this?"* we used to often hear the almost automatic response of *"Because I said so!"* No wonder people stop asking, *"Why?"* In other words, we all 'talk the talk' but less often, if ever, 'walk the walk'!

We need to ensure congruence between the words that profess what we are seeking to do, and the hidden messages we give through our actions or inactions so that they send the same, unerring message.

This issue of congruence is also aptly illustrated by the lack of it between words and body language on the part of students in a typical classroom. It also demonstrates how important tone of voice is in effective communication.

In the remaining chapters of this book, the overwhelming power of hidden messages will feature prominently as a recurring theme in explaining why secondary schools, as well as the government and society at large, fail children. But if we are really serious about wanting schools to enable young people to succeed and to be empowered to act as responsible and intelligent members of society, then we have to be true – true to ourselves and to those who represent our future, as well as to the other important stakeholders, such as parents, industry and commerce, universities, etc.

Are we on the same page?

As I have already noted, I have been in education and training for nearly forty years now and I can honestly say that I am monumentally unclear about what we are supposedly and fundamentally trying to achieve in schools. It seems to me that this is more than just incredibly worrying. As the saying goes, if you don't know where you are going, then any road will take you there. Clarity of purpose seems to me to be a pretty fundamental issue before one can expect to embark upon any venture, unless of course it is intended to be a 'magical mystery tour'.

What is the difference between primary and secondary schools? If there is no difference then why do we create two different phases......three, in some cases, in educational systems where there are middle schools? What are we really trying to achieve, individually and collectively? What is our real view of students at secondary school? Are they a raw material, a client, a product on a chronological conveyor belt, or a unique spirit, blessed with a range of talents that yearn to be discovered and explored?

I joined the teaching profession straight from teachers' training college and joined the treadmill that I had left a few years earlier as a student, but now I was operating from a different standpoint, with my back to the 'chalk-face', as it was called before the advent of the inferior 'white-board', spirit-based marker pens and the far from smart, Smart-Boards. I was allocated classes to teach: students studying GCE 'A' Level, GCE 'O' Level and C.S.E. courses in Economics, Law and Commerce. What was I there for? Simple! The aim was to get as many students through their examinations with the best possible grades and, thereby, become a successful teacher. To be honest, that was about it!

All the philosophy, history, sociology and psychology of education that I had studied for three of the four years at college were of some use I am sure, but I am not sure if the school really sought to harness these skills, or whether I was assumed to be inexorably putting them into practice. The truth is that I was fundamentally aimless in terms of holistic student learning, apart from helping them learn the 'stories' specified on the syllabus that would enable them to pass the final examination. I guess it was just assumed that the woolly, but well-intentioned efforts of about one hundred teachers would somehow knit together, following an invisible, seemingly self-ordained pattern, and miraculously fulfil some inevitable goal.

I did what I did without questioning the overall and fundamental aim of my efforts when taken together in concert with those of my wonderful colleagues. I had been to school and followed the same, or similar basic diet of subjects and other experiences, and so it seemed perfectly logical that the young people, whose life chances were now partly my responsibility, should undertake the same journey whilst they were at school. Examination results in academic subjects were the ultimate aim for these young people, so that they could leave school, 'preferably' go on to university and ultimately get good jobs. I was fulfilling my role if I enabled the students who worked with me to achieve good grades, and that was about it. Indeed, I got promoted after my first and second year in teaching largely because I seemed to be good at motivating the older, secondary students to achieve fairly spectacular results in their final examinations, and I hasten to add that their success was very much their achievement and not mine!

It was not until I was a Head of Department in a new school, after several years of teaching, that I can recall any requirement being placed upon us to state our school aims and objectives. This was one of the spin-offs of the drive to adopt more business-like approaches in the world of state schooling. Interestingly, these initiatives did not need to apply to independent schools.

So it was that we were subject to a surprisingly challenging initiative, namely to formulate and state our school aims in an explicit way. It was a task that we were not only too busy teaching to undertake seriously and conscientiously, but we were also ill-prepared in terms of being clear about the underlying processes and the identification of values that drove us individually and collectively to complete the process in a meaningful way.

What we did, therefore, was to take a document published by Her Majesty's School Inspectorate (HMI), which enumerated a series of aims that seemed perfectly plausible, right and reasonable to us. These were dutifully and automatically adopted and incorporated within our 'school brochure', which was another document that we were required to publish annually. The truth of the matter was that those hi-jacked, bold aims that HMI had stated, were not really consistent or congruent with the school's established modus operandi or the values of a group of staff who were far from united in terms of what the school should be essentially trying to achieve, and for whom.

Indeed, there were essentially two distinct groups within the staffroom, whose philosophies of education were fundamentally at odds with each other. On the one hand, there were those who felt that we should be catering for an academic elite, much like a grammar school. On the other hand, there were those of us who believed in the comprehensive principle, that we should provide a rich educational entitlement to all young people regardless of their academic ability. Never the twain would or did meet – mark my words!

In all honesty, we achieved neither, although the academic results we obtained were a reasonable compromise which made the school popular with its client groups of parents and their secondary-age offspring. The school was actually termed as a community school with a comprehensive intake, but for many years never lived up to that billing in any real sense. Instead it became a dual-use facility, which is in my view a far cry from what a community school could and should become. Of course, we were not helped in achieving our school name by an extreme Right-wing Conservative Government who, with customary ignorance, arrogance and lack of intelligence, insisted on viewing community education as an alien Left-wing concept – something to be eradicated and certainly not encouraged or promoted, despite asking schools to be more responsive to the needs of parents. But then, what was one to expect from a political doctrine that had led its leader to boldly claim that there was no such thing as 'society', only individual men and women and families. Mind you, that did not deter them from using collective terminology to sweeten their more disenfranchising and extreme ideological initiatives like 'the community charge' (the ill-fated poll tax) or 'care in the community' – an attempt to save money on providing adequate care for the mentally ill and disabled by closing their specialist (and expensive) care-homes, and expecting them to be 'accommodated' as if by magic in the mainstream of, dare I say it, society. More recently, the same obscene and disingenuous concept became euphemistically known as David Cameron's 'Big Society' initiative – please stop me from laughing at the gullibility of the British electorate when confronted with the not that 'old wine' in arguably 'new bottles' scenario.

With the benefit of hindsight, I have often reflected on those days of having to determine school aims with a critical eye, a process that makes me cringe a little and smile a while at our understandable naivety. When given the professional luxury of the time to properly reflect, whilst undertaking my Master's Degree during a one-year, full-time, secondment, one of my tutors asked us all to bring a copy of our school aims from our school brochures for sharing and consideration during a seminar within the 'curriculum analysis and design' component of the course. Being diligent students, we all complied with the request, although my school was in the process of rewriting the brochure, and so I arrived at the meeting somewhat embarrassingly, empty-handed.

It was an interesting seminar. Listening to the aims stated in each school's brochure, there was an amazing similarity between them all – as well as the previously mentioned HMI document. This made me wonder if it was because we were all equally clued-up and on the same wavelength, or whether this was not actually the case, and that we were all similarly clueless and in desperation clutching at helpful straws.

After the sharing was over, the tutor asked me to reflect and, without the benefit of glossy documentation, to try and summarise what the school aims were of the school where I worked. I had to admit that what I had heard from the others' contributions were essentially the same as 'my' school. But then I shocked everyone slightly by admitting that we did not do what we claimed to do, and that the hidden messages of our curriculum were not congruent at all with the grandiose aims that were elegantly and powerfully stated in the brochure, courtesy of the esteemed HMI.

31

The truth was that the school where I worked had an essentially simple philosophy, or message for the students who attended. It was as follows:

Work hard;

Look smart (i.e. wear the school uniform properly);

Behave yourselves; and this will result in

Eventual academic success!

After a short silence, I suspect of somewhat stunned and uncertain reflection, my fellow students and colleagues admitted that in all honesty those were also the guiding principles of their schools, despite the claims that they (otherwise) made.

That M.A. (Ed) course was a real revelation, enabling me to stand back and think carefully about what I had been doing for the previous 12 years as a classroom teacher and middle manager, as well as the purpose of my own schooling of an even longer period, at that time.

What also interested and surprised me at the time was the fact that there were, broadly speaking, two categories of teachers following the course. There were those, like me, who saw it as an opportunity for serious professional development – engaging in rejuvenating research, shared dialogue and a journey of discovery – and then there were others who openly admitted that they were not really interested in the joy of learning itself; rather they approached the course solely as a means of obtaining the higher degree that had become so important for any teacher who aspired to apply for and ultimately become a senior manager in a school. Such is the nature of 'academic inflation'.

This has since made me think about the fundamental concept of schooling and higher education; is it a means to an end, an end in itself, or one chapter of a life spent in the pursuit of self-enlightenment?

What are we talking about when we refer to schooling and education, and what are we really trying to achieve and for whom? Are the covert, hidden messages through which we communicate, regarding what we do and how we do it, really supporting and reinforcing our stated aims? Are they what we should really be doing, or are they contradictory to the overt purpose of formal schooling? Are we on the right track, or are we all prisoners of traditional orthodoxy?

After all, as in face-to-face communications, if the unconscious hidden messages of our body language are saying something at odds with the verbal messages we are consciously seeking to convey – that is, if they are not congruent – then people will always take the former interpretation. The result being that we fail to achieve that which we had intended!

Furthermore, I am reminded of the rather incongruous word that we use to describe much of what we do in schools – namely: *'work'*, instead of possibly more accurate and meaningful words such as 'studies', 'activities' or 'discoveries'. How often do you recall hearing the word 'work' uttered by the teachers at the school you attended? Perhaps it would be more accurate for me to ask you how many times in one day, or one lesson, did you hear that popular four-letter word? Now, reflect upon what the potential hidden messages of that might be, and what its connotations could be in the minds of those who have often been effectively press-ganged into performing it? Who is it for? The work force does not even get paid for doing a good job, unlike criminals in prison!

My edition of the Collins COBUILD English Dictionary devotes three pages in its attempt to give all of the various meanings of 'work' as a noun, adjective and verb, with perhaps the most commonly understood definition, as far as everyday usage is concerned being:

"When you work, you do the things you are paid or required to do in your job."

I find it interesting that work all too often tends to imply something that is far from voluntary or pleasurable in nature, or spiritually rewarding in its outcomes. Instead, it conjures up images of something that you are compelled to do, by others or by economic and pecuniary imperatives. It would not be a huge leap of logic to suggest that the use of 'work' for activities that should be enlightening, stimulating, challenging and enjoyable leads to less constructive or positive images of drudgery, repetitiveness, and boredom. This is a reasonable extrapolation to make, as most of what young people do at school

33

is done at the bidding of other people, and the dictionary seems to support this interpretation.

I cannot remember who it was who once pointed out that if 'hard work' was such a good and worthy thing to do and to do well, then why it is that the rich do not keep more of it for themselves?

Some Lefty Nonsense

Although, when compared to many millions of others worldwide, I have been very lucky, I have since realised that two factors, even from the outset of my formal education – or schooling – severely impaired the chances of me ever meeting my full potential, let alone discovering the true nature of my calling, or human spirit. One was the fact that I was left-handed, and the other was the pre-eminence that academe held within the entire process, as if it was the only show in town. (Actually it was, and to this day, effectively still is!) The latter impediment is something to which I shall return when considering the content of the school curriculum later, but the former is one of which most people are blissfully ignorant, mainly because they are right-handed. If they are left-handed, then like I used to be, they are possibly ignorant of the unintentional and extreme discrimination that they face every day from people, systems, architecture, design and inanimate objects. It deserves and demands attention here!

My earliest memories of being useless were at primary school, when I effectively and unconsciously learnt that I was not cut out to be a practical man, unlike my father and his father before him, who were both immensely skilled with their hands, in terms of carpentry, home decorations and mechanics for example. At the youngest age in primary school, I knew that I could not use the scissors that used to be kept in a wooden block at the front of class. This was a huge problem as we seemed to spend an inordinate amount of time cutting out shapes from pieces of paper. Perhaps it was to develop my finer motor skills – which it definitely did not do – in fact it had quite the opposite outcome. The reason being that scissors are designed for right-handed people, which interprets into 'wrong-handed' for me. I can still recall, with an almost equal amount of pain, my pathetic attempts to cut out the shapes that we were instructed to do, again without any explanation of the

34

learning outcomes such tasks were designed to achieve. In my hands the scissors, which in those days were very elementary and rudimentary pieces of equipment, only succeeded in feebly bending the trembling piece of paper between the ill-fitting blades. It was as if the paper was submissively looking up at me and saying, *"What exactly is it that you are trying to do?"*

In those days I was still willing and able to point out any inadequacies in my environment that I did not consider to be down to me. So, I told the class teacher that the scissors were blunt, which to all intents and purposes they were, and she suggested – helpfully, she thought – that I go to the front of the class and change them for another pair. I would then select another, 'better', pair of scissors from the wooden block which housed the class supply on the teacher's desk. I misguidedly thought that those with the pointed ends to the blades were necessarily sharper than the snub-nosed ones, mainly because the students sitting near to me were using them and managing to complete the task with embarrassingly considerable ease compared to me. I would return confidently to my desk, obviously expecting that all would now be well. Wrong!

Not unnaturally, I quickly came to the de-motivating realisation that I could not perform a simple task that other children could evidently complete with consummate ease; a feeling that my teacher reinforced with her subtle and strangely encouraging observation that I was simply 'cack-handed'. She would come to my table following my repeated protestations that every pair of scissors was blunt, take the offending equipment into her right hand and deftly prove me wrong in nothing more than a few, quickly-executed and expertly delivered snips!

Even my father, who despaired at my ineptness when handling tools with which he displayed skills of near craftsmanship, would tell me, when I plaintively complained that the wood saw was blunt, that 'a poor workman blames his tools'. At such a tender age, I had absolutely no idea that it was not me that was at fault – it really **was** the tools I was required to use!

My teachers and parents were also similarly unaware that such a fundamental obstacle was put in my way. So ingrained and hidden is this discrimination against left-handed – or right-brain dominant – individuals in our societies, that I too remained blissfully ignorant as to the real reason for my apparent, natural ineptitude. Even when I was married, my wife expected me to be like her father and be an excellent 'do-it-yourself' practitioner and enthusiast, especially as our first house was a residence that made huge demands on its occupiers if they were to keep it from falling down around their ears. By this time, I had already accepted that practical tasks were nearly always an insurmountable challenge for me, and that they triggered a fiery temper when my attempts at anything practical used to confound my macho-driven desire to perform them. My feeble attempts at simple 'do-it-yourself', like putting up shelves, and assembling flat-pack furniture items were also accompanied with rages of anger, the air full of the choicest bad language that anyone could have invented and put so creatively together into a tirade sponsored by sheer frustration. The only DIY home task I enjoyed, and was good at, which is why I enjoyed it, was painting – because the brush was not designed for preferable right-handed use in order to apply emulsions and glosses. Screwdrivers, screws, electric drills and other DIY paraphernalia – on (or in) the other hand – didn't work well at all, unless the other hand was quite literally the right one!

Similarly, my wife also expected me to be good at mending our second-hand car – we were both teachers on relatively low salaries and were blighted by having to buy run-down properties and unreliable forms of transportation. Similarly, I was utterly hopeless at increasingly reluctant attempts to live up to my wife's quite reasonable, and yet unreasonable, expectations. I experienced no joy, just unmitigated stress and an impending sense of personal and marital disaster on such occasions. For the sake of our marriage, my wife took on those tasks that I could not seem to perform, and I agreed to do those things I actually could do – like stripping the walls and subsequently applying fresh paint to them and woodwork in the form of skirting boards, doors and such like. I enjoyed this and loved to do it, even though I still had not grasped that it was not me that made those other tasks nigh on impossible to perform without turning the air a very dark shade of blue. It really was the tools – the scissors, the screwdrivers and screws, the electric drill with holding handle, the saws and the like that were at fault in my hands. They are all designed to be used by right-handed practitioners. In the hands of a left-hander, they were not only stubborn and frustrating practical implements, but they were also a hazard to the user. In the USA it has been estimated that an average of 2,000 people die each year in accidents operating machinery simply because they are incompatibly left-handed and subsequently endangered. In that sense, I consider myself fortunate to have escaped so lightly to date!

At primary school, these hidden messages that promoted my incompetence were legion. We used to use fountain pens, with ink wells built into the desk. The pen had a replaceable nib, which right-handed people were able to pull gracefully across the paper thanks to its design, whereas I used to try and push it from left to right, with an obstinate nib scratching the paper in protest as it went. The ink pot was embedded in the right-hand corner of the desk, which made its necessarily frequent use far from convenient, with my left-hand crossing my torso, and the desk, to recharge my pen. Needless to say, I was a slow writer, and this basic skill was one that had also to be legible. Additionally, the speed of a left-hander's writing is also slow due to the fact that we should really write from right to left, so that we can actually see what we are writing, instead of obscuring the last few letters and words with our writing hand. I can imagine that right-handed people writing Arabic script would feel the same way. This is why left-handers often look so ungainly when they write – with further taunts and jibes at being 'cack-handed' – because they either have to hold the pen slanted diagonally away from them, or rotate the paper clockwise, some 45 degrees to the right, so that what they write is still visible. This may seem frivolous, but in examinations slow-writers are always at a big disadvantage when seeking to write comprehensive answers whilst competing against the clock. After all, students with special educational needs are often given additional time in competitive examinations, in recognition of their particular challenges – but not left-handed students. Obviously, they (we) are not 'special' enough!

As the use of technology has increased, so too has the discrimination against left-handed people. I recall visiting a huge internet shop in Tottenham Court Road in London, which boasted literally hundreds of computer terminals, but not one of them was set up with the mouse on the left-hand side, and with the click buttons reversed so that people like me can use them as easily as the more numerous right-handers. More often than not it is almost impossible to move the mouse across to the left, as the connecting wires are usually too short or trapped. In any case, is it really that unreasonable to expect people to *think* to provide maybe five or ten terminals set up for the minority group in society? Not to do so is quite simply blatant 'leftism'!

My whole life has been plagued by this unintentional and largely hidden discrimination. Any turning or serrated cutting implement is designed exclusively for right-handed use – like can openers, serrated kitchen knives and corkscrews. Improved design for right-handed people is a further irritation for those who are left-biased. In Tesco's supermarket, I saw about five racks of kitchen scissors with perhaps 10 pairs on each, all with moulded angular, plastic handles to accommodate one's finger and thumb more comfortably – but not this particular 'one'. In my left hand, they are virtually impossible to use unless I am willing to accept self-inflicted, manual torture, and to add to that, left-induced incompetence.

Lefties are additionally inconvenienced by a constant and unrelenting barrage of non-verbal, almost invisible discrimination. Fixed location pens at banks and post offices are always on the right, which means that I have to drag the pen further across to the left to begin writing, often against the resistance of a spring, which results in the clerk questioning the authenticity of my signature. When bills, credit card slips and the like are presented to me for signing, in shops and hotels for example, they are always unhelpfully slanted in such a way as to make it easy for a right-handed signatory to make his or her mark. I have to move it and slant the top to the right – and then realign the original with the underlying carbon copy – before appending my signature. Similarly, in restaurants, teaspoons are always placed in a saucer to the right of the cup, thereby encouraging me to knock the cup over when wishing to reach for it to stir my drink with my left-hand. This is one reason why I gave up putting sugar in my tea or coffee…..so not entirely bad, I guess!

For some time now I have been having my work shirts tailor-made for me, but only recently have I asked for the breast pocket to be put on the right-hand side so that it is easier for me to use my left hand to access the items placed therein. I look far less clumsy and, dare I say it, 'cack-handed', now than before. Sadly, other forms of leftist discrimination prevent it from being really that useful, as the machines that take or 'read' travel cards and bank cards are all on the right-hand side. This means that if I am carrying anything, I still have to carry it in my left hand in order to leave my right hand free for inserting and retrieving my card.

The design of everything is for and usually by the right-handed user – from buildings to kitchens and furniture. Being a thinking person, I am aware of the unintentional discrimination against not only lefties, but also women, in architecture.

Have you ever thought about why it is that in theatres and public event venues, during the interval there is always a queue outside the women's lavatories, but rarely do men have to be so (literally) inconvenienced? Yes, I know that it is because women are required to sit down to do all their business, whilst men only have to do that occasionally when number two is (quite literally) pressing in a public place. In view of these differences, why can architects not cater for the particular needs of women in society and provide more space in their plans for public buildings to accommodate the female toilet area, to allow more cubicles to be made available, so that it is not 'standing room only'? I would hazard a guess that it is because the architect is almost always a man, and a female architect is so conditioned by the traditional way of designing buildings, that she rarely considers such obvious oversights. Admittedly, it could also be due to the fact that toilet space is not exactly a potential money-spinner, so any additional space is given over to a larger bar area or more seats, for example, in order to generate more revenue. What if women were given more space but then charged a fee to use the more convenient facility? On the other hand, if men were excused payment and allowed to go freely, if you will excuse the pun, then I am sure that would be deemed to be unduly discriminatory.

The discrimination against left-handed people is apparently acceptable – perhaps because we are considered relatively trivial, if we are considered at all. It is true that one or two such inconveniences are tolerable, but it is the litany of such inconveniences that taken cumulatively are so (often unconsciously) frustrating and that makes them truly unfair. The only way that I console myself that being left-handed is an advantage in general, is remembering that the left-hand side of the body is controlled by the right-hand side of the brain, and right-handers rely on the workings of the left-side of theirs, then it follows that only left-handed members of society are in their 'right' minds!

The point of that complaining digression was to illustrate how traditional ways of doing things are taken as unquestionably correct and that people do not think critically about alternative, better and often fairer ways of doing things, so that the true needs of **_all_** people can be taken account of in the way we do things. The hidden messages we send through such orthodoxy are immensely powerful, mainly because they are usually unconsciously designed and delivered, which allows them to continue unquestioned – much in the same way as the power of persuasive advertising is not the obvious message that the seller is sending, but that which appeals to our innermost and unconscious desires and weaknesses.

I honestly believe that the hidden messages that are sent through traditional schooling are equally powerful but considerably more harmful, as they can so easily and innocently damage children's trust, creativity and individuality as well as their self-esteem and confidence.

Chapter Three: What Are We Talking About?

Schooling vs. Education

Yes, we all went to school, and so we all know what school is and what it is not. Therefore, as adults, whether parents of children attending school or otherwise, we feel perfectly qualified to talk knowledgeably about what is wrong with state schooling and what should be done to put it right. Not only that, we feel we are competent to determine policy matters as well as matters concerning the day-to-day running of such enterprises.

As parents and lay people now have a greater say regarding what goes on in schools to which they entrust the education of their children, it is imperative that they do indeed act in a well-informed and, dare I say it, highly intelligent manner. Sadly, they rarely do, especially in the international school arena, in my experience. The die has long been cast, and the thirst for top grades in academic subjects for their offspring is unquenchable, and they are so single-mindedly driven that they subject their children to additional lessons, private classes and more. This places a questionable burden on the learners – their children – especially in terms of its opportunity cost, as measured by what they sacrifice or never experience as a result of the immense demands on their time and the intense focus on academic success or bust (or 'burst' even). Moreover, it promotes the view that any failure in this sole pursuit of academic achievement is almost a heinous crime, and this fear of failure can lead to some students cheating in order to avoid the parental castigation and wider stigma that 'failure' would produce.

The political thrust to give parents a potent and powerful voice in education was given great impetus when Kenneth Baker, the then Secretary of State for Education in Mrs. Thatcher's government, introduced The Great Education Reform Bill in the 1980s. It was rightly given a suitable 'pet' name – The GERBIL – and it fooled people into believing that it gave greater power over what went on in schools to parents. The truth is that it led to a massive increase in, and centralisation of, the powers that it conferred upon the government to determine the nature and shape of what they called 'education' and 'the school curriculum'. Indeed, when he launched this centralising agenda at a Tory Party

Conference, he said something along the lines of, "For far too long, education has been in the hands of the teaching profession!" What a prize idiot!

The standing ovation he received for expressing that sentiment was indicative of the failure of schools in the past – mainly independent schools, to which many of the Tory grandees and their supporters went – to encourage young people to think critically and clearly. With respect, which means I am going to be disrespectful, Mr. Baker was talking out of the top of his loaf – or possibly another orifice a lot further south. It was like saying, the Health Service has for far too long been in the hands of the medical profession, or that law and order has for far too long been in the hands of the police, and the legal profession. Well, yes, Ken! Not for the first time, a politician was interfering radically in something of which he had little, if any, real philosophical or *practical* and everyday knowledge or experience.

I am fascinated by the way in which we blindly assume that everyone shares a common and clear understanding of the terms that we use on a daily basis – but is there really a clear and shared understanding of words that we use, especially some of the more abstract terms? Do we all agree on what we mean by words such as 'schooling', 'teaching', 'learning' and 'education'? Are they synonymous and interchangeable in practice, or are they fundamentally different? If they are not the same, then what is the difference, and should we not be more careful in how we use them in public debate, and when making decisions that impact considerably upon the life chances of young people? What is it that we are actually talking about?

If you ask most people why we send children to school, the answer you get may well depend on who you ask – teachers, parents, government officials, politicians or the young people actually at school – but would they be significantly different? I have a feeling that the answers given would be only slightly at variance and that there would be quite a lot of overlap, although perhaps expressed with differing degrees of eloquence and angst. I have often asked people this question over the years – mainly of the young people who attend school – and the most common responses I have received are remarkably similar. Most respondents tend to say that they go to school:

- To learn.

- To be educated.
- To prepare us for adult and working life.
- Because we have to!

Leaving aside the last answer for now, the responses would tend to imply that school, education and learning are one and the same thing in terms of their purpose, if not their meaning, so let us consider this apparent similarity for a moment.

Being a product (or a victim) of my schooling, in cases where I need to ascertain the precise meaning of words, I again believe in referring to a dictionary – my preference being the excellent *'Collins COBUILD English Dictionary: Helping learners with real English'* – as well as the views and comments of other notable people. The latter may be partial and selective, but I still think their views are valid, and the light their past utterances cast upon the issues I wish to examine is highly relevant. So let us see what these terms might mean and to what extent they are truly synonymous.

Schooling

The dictionary offers the interpretation that, 'schooling is the education that children receive at school' – clear, precise but not really casting any light upon the purpose of the exercise. It suggests that education is a, if not 'the' fundamental part of schooling, but not the only place where it takes place, although the relationship between the education received or acquired, in or out of school is far from clear. So what does the dictionary have to say regarding the fundamental meaning of 'education'?

Education

This term is defined as being 'a process that involves teaching people various subjects, usually at a school or college, or being taught'. Again, a very traditional answer that rings true with our own experiences perhaps, and the responses listed above. It suggests that education is essentially the same as schooling, involving a recipient being taught a variety of different subjects between the ages of 5 and 21 years – for those who are willing and able to receive a university education. It focuses on teaching rather than learning, which is another interesting and rather worrying aspect of the given definition.

It has been suggested that true education is what survives when what has been learnt has been forgotten. I believe that this second offering is far more accurate, when I reflect upon my own education. Most of what I was taught at school has long since been exiled into the realms of my unconsciousness – especially algebra, geometry and much else besides. But, perhaps the whole experience is to this day unconsciously informing my thoughts, as well as my decisions, actions and behaviours. But to remain in the conscious world for a while longer, let us examine what has been said about the meaning of teaching, which according to the dictionary is a central feature in the educational process whilst at school.

Teaching

Again the dictionary gives a very traditional and a comfortably general definition of teaching as, 'the work that a teacher does in helping students to learn'. Skinner offers us a slightly more active approach, and one that tentatively emphasises a partnership between teacher and learner, when he says that 'teaching is the art of assisting discovery'. His use of the word 'art' is actually very powerful, given that defining art is also a very difficult task. After all, what is art?

Galileo went even further when he said that 'you cannot teach anyone anything, you can only help them develop it from within'. This perspective casts a very different light onto the role of the teacher – one of a facilitator and manager of learning rather than a person who delivers a pre-determined curriculum through the artificiality of distinct and separate subjects. It also suggests that the driving force should be the internal spirit or innate ability of the learner, rather than an external teacher who is obliged to follow a prescribed syllabus which is determined by yet some other, external agency.

Albert Einstein was far more damning in his view of schooling in his day, which is not that different to what we offer now, when he pointedly said:
"It is, in fact, nothing short of a miracle that the modern methods of instruction have not yet strangled the holy curiosity of inquiry; for this

44

delicate plant, aside from stimulation, stands mainly in need of freedom."

This view was strongly echoed by Carl Rogers who, I think rightly, said:
"I have come to feel that the outcomes of teaching are either unimportant or hurtful.........that the only learning which significantly influences behaviour is self-discovered, self-appropriated learning."

These views run counter to the orthodox definitions that one would expect to find in a dictionary, and they provide great food for thoughtful reflection if nothing else. I, for one, will argue that these more alternative perceptions should inform the general thrust of education in the secondary as well as the primary phase of state schooling.

If the earlier orthodox reflections on what might constitute teaching at secondary school are a little worrying, then it is worth considering the definition of lecturing (that is what we call the 'teaching' that goes on in universities and colleges) which is *"the art of transferring information from the notes of the lecturer to the notes of the students without going through the minds of either."* I am hoping that this quotation was made for purposes of humour, but then – many a true word is spoken in jest!

The alternative definitions of teaching above focus much more explicitly on the importance of learning as that which should occupy our thoughts and actions as administrators, teachers and students – we should all be learning, and not assume that it is only students who are engaged in this process. So what is learning exactly?

Learning

I began this chapter by asking if we all share a common understanding of terms that we use freely and frequently and, again, the dictionary gives a range of slightly different definitions of the term – which is quite understandable given that learning can, and should, take place in many different contexts and at different times in our lives.

The dictionary starts with a fairly orthodox and mundane view of learning as, "The process of gaining knowledge through studying." This is very partial in the sense that it ignores the discovery and development of skills and competences, as well as values for example. It also inadvertently assumes that studying is the route to acquire information, and that raises the question of what do we understand by 'studying' as well as knowledge. Moreover, given the massive explosion in this knowledge-based outcome of learning, what selection of seemingly infinite knowledge do we want young people to be exposed to and learn while at school, and does this decision not smack of potential indoctrination, notwithstanding any judgement about whether it is intentional or not?

A slightly broader definition from the Collins' English Dictionary offers the view that, "If you learn something, you obtain knowledge or a skill through studying or training." It goes on to say that, "If you learn something, you find out about it." This latter offering is in many ways less definitive as to both the content and process of learning, and for that reason I prefer it to any of the others we have referred to thus far. Indeed, it must by definition include learning that arises from negative experiences. Another view reinforces this point: "If you learn from an unpleasant experience, you change the way you behave so that it does not happen again, or so that if it happens again, you can deal with it more easily." This accords more closely with Alice Heim's definition of 'intelligence' which is what I presume we want our young people to acquire whilst they are school. This definition is given in a moment, below.

A similar definition from the dictionary says that, "If people learn to behave or react in a particular way, they gradually start to behave in that way as a result of a change in attitudes." At long last, a less oblique reference is made to the formation of values as part of the learning process, as these will inform our attitudes and behaviours.

Finally, the dictionary offers yet another definition of learning, and one that is very specific in its context: "If you learn something such as a poem or the script of a play, you study or repeat the words so that you can remember them." Although I hope that this is not the aim of formal schooling, watching many young people revise for their examinations it would appear as though this is exactly what they are doing – learning the 'stories' that we want them to learn in any particular subject, and be able to regurgitate them as and when required. Of course, we profess that we also require students to learn these stories by active learning methods, and that we also promote the development of the skills of analysis and evaluation as part of the process. But, if one considers how much of what a student revises for an examination that they are able to recall a few weeks or months after the test, it is hardly extensive. So what was the point of all the stress, the sweat, and the 'burning of the midnight oil' in the run-up to the final examinations all about? Maybe the view I mentioned earlier, that true education is what survives when what has been learnt has been forgotten, is not all that far from the mark!

In my view, it is not until we get to a definition of 'intelligence' that we come close to a view about what we **ought** to be focusing on while young people are at school. The dictionary becomes more enlightening when it offers the definition of intelligence as, "The ability to think, reason and understand, instead of doing things automatically or by instinct." Or, as the psychologist Alice Heim put it, *"Intelligence is the grasping of the essentials in a given situation, and responding appropriately to them."* It must be, therefore, that we should encourage our children to learn to be intelligent individuals whilst they are at school, so that they can continue to learn and be increasingly intelligent in their lives after school.

The focal point of all our endeavours should be student learning rather than teaching – on outcomes that promote intelligent behaviour, rather than on outdated and largely irrelevant inputs. Although this is something that many schools claim to support and deliver, they are still hamstrung by pre-determined, heavily content-laden syllabuses that drive teacher-directed learning. It is all very well to claim that we are focusing on the students' learning needs, but if what we are focusing on is largely irrelevant or pre-determined in terms of expected outcomes, then are we truly developing intelligent young men and women as individuals, or are we doing it en masse? Are we really empowering children by nurturing them to become the future generations of intelligent citizens who are capable of learning from our mistakes by not only contributing to, but also shaping the world in which they live and making it a better place for societies to thrive and survive? Or, is it that what we say we are doing does not really correspond to that which we are actually doing, in reality?

How can we really be doing this to any significant extent if the learning outcomes we chase whilst children are at school are still heavily subject based and reinforced by endless testing and checking to ensure that everyone is still 'on track'. The reality is that teachers and students will still be doing the bidding of others who externally establish the syllabus, and decide what should be learned. Moreover, given the knowledge explosion, any syllabus – as currently designed – will necessarily be partial in terms of its coverage. This is not only unhelpful it is also dangerous; leaving syllabuses open to becoming tools of inadvertent, or even intentional, indoctrination, as I mentioned earlier. This risk is heightened when government ministers start professing what should be taught to young learners, and at what age – and how!

Indeed, it is argued that this is one reason why right-wing governments in the UK had always resisted any notion of a National Curriculum, until the arrogance that arose out of the landslide win (on less than 50% of votes cast) of the Thatcher administration's second term led them to erroneously believe that the left-wing were finished and would never again mount a serious political challenge. After all, to create a National Curriculum would create the very machinery that would, as they saw it, allow the 'loony' left' to indoctrinate children with their socialist nonsense when they were returned to power.

Now, I am not suggesting such indoctrination is necessarily intentional and part of some great conspiracy, although I do believe that such powerful influences definitely can and do come into play. Additional and reinforcing forces of indoctrination occur through the hidden messages that we send by the very way that schooling is structured, packaged and delivered day-by-day, month-by-month and year-by-year by educational institutions, examining boards, and teachers. At best, these hidden messages serve to seriously undermine the explicit aims of the schooling process – making it something that is not really educational in terms of helping the growth of intelligent and creative young men and women.

Later chapters of this book will examine and illustrate these all-powerful, hidden messages in greater detail, to show how blind teachers, young people and the wider electorate are to them. Moreover, when we come to realise, identify and accept that what we might be doing amounts to little more than indoctrination, there is a tendency to believe what we are doing, and the messages we are sending are right and proper – such is the success of the system in formulating our values and beliefs, as well as our total obedience to anything that can best be described as 'common sense'.

I think it was Karl Marx who warned us to beware of people who resort to this convenient notion of 'common sense' – it is a way of avoiding critical and intelligent thought that may challenge our cosy assumptions about life and what we are all born to do, as well as how!

In the following section, I want to build upon this quick examination of what we mean by these various, inter-related terms and think critically about what the real purpose of schooling actually is – both from the perspective of what we claim it to be about, as well as to take a look at the hidden messages which I believe accompany much of the rhetoric.

I am always amazed when people say that their school years were the best of their lives; that was not the case for me. I have enjoyed my learning and life since I left school immeasurably more. I could say that my four years at college of education, where I trained to become a teacher, could stake a strong claim to be assessed in such superlative terms, but the diversity of my life experiences to date and the changing contexts that age, location and circumstances bestow, make such comparisons largely meaningless.

Chapter Four: What is Schooling For?

It has been said that what teachers do is essentially the same as the performance of an actor, the only difference being that the teacher makes up his or her own dialogue. I do not intend to get side-tracked into considering that comparison just yet, but whilst training to be a teacher, and in my first few years of teaching, I did perform in various plays. I preferred comedies to the more cerebral drama performances, mainly because I love the sound of laughter – especially when I elicit it by actions which are intentional on my part. Indeed, my favourite sound is that of people laughing – an extreme, outward expression of happiness and other positive emotions!

On a few occasions, however, I did take on more serious roles, the most notable and successful being that of 'Tom', the narrator and one of the four, main characters in the play, 'The Glass Menagerie' by Tennessee Williams. I mention this fact simply to explain why I am about to refer to a short section where Tom is talking to his friend Jim – a section that resonates with me as being even more true today than when it was written in the last century:

Tom: *I'm tired of the movies.*

Jim: *Movies?*

Tom: *Yes, movies! Look at them. All of those glamorous people – having adventures – hogging it all, gobbling the whole thing up! You know what happens? People go to the 'movies' instead of 'moving'. Hollywood characters are supposed to have all the adventures for everybody in America, while everybody in America sits in a dark room and watches them have them! Yes, until there's a war. That's when adventure becomes available to the masses! Everyone's dish not only Gable's! Then the people in the dark room come out of the dark room to have some adventure themselves – Goody, goody! – It's our turn now to go to the South Sea Islands – make a safari – to be exotic, far off! – But I'm not patient. I don't want to wait 'till then. I'm tired of the movies and I'm about to move."*

And shortly after that, Tom, who works in a shoe warehouse, continues:

"I'm starting to boil inside. I know I seem dreamy, but inside, well, I'm boiling! – Whenever I pick up a shoe, I shudder a little thinking of how short life is and what I am doing!

50

Whatever that means, I know it doesn't mean shoes.......except as something to wear on a traveller's feet!"

For those not familiar with the play, the three key themes running throughout the play are those of disappointment, escape and expectations. Tom's father left the family to escape a long time before, and Tom has the responsibility to undertake his mundane job in order to support his mother and disabled sister. The three members of the Wingfield family all have expectations and dreams of how life will turn out for them, and how situations will unfold leading to the ultimate realisation of their dreams or goals. Unfortunately, reality never meets their expectations, and this disappointment breeds unrest and dissatisfaction. The reality of their lives is too depressing and mundane, so each one finds a way to escape. For the mother it is her memories and for the daughter it is her collection of glass ornaments.

Tom wants more out of life than to work in a shoe warehouse. He craves more in life, and it is this craving that leads him to the movies every night – it is his escape. In short, Tom lives unfulfilled, as illustrated in one final extract from the play, where Tom is trying to tell his mother how it is that he feels trapped by force of circumstance:

"Every time you come in yelling that Goddamn 'Rise and Shine! Rise and Shine!' I say to myself, 'How lucky dead people are!' But I get up. I go! For sixty-five dollars a month I give up all that I dream of doing and being ever! And you say 'self' ......self's all I ever think of. Why listen, if self is what I thought of, Mother, I'd be where he is (pointing to a photograph of his long-departed father) – GONE!"

So what has this got to do with education and schooling? The answer is – everything! We all enter this world naked, with a spirit, and we depart it in essentially the same way – we just look older, more worn! I have dreams and ambitions which are largely unfulfilled – and one is to work in a school that enables young people to dream about their futures, to have a driving vision in, and passion for their lives, as well as to enable and empower them to take the responsibility to fulfil their true destinies.

When I was young, I remember being told that the world is my oyster – and I don't think they meant because it was tough and chewy. I have never been quite sure what the analogy was supposed to be. Perhaps I was supposed to be the pearl that would evolve and grow inside over time – largely in response to the continued irritation, or grit, encountered in life. Alternatively, it could have been a warning that life as a pearl was to feel trapped within a confined space, to face restricted growth!

When I was a teenager, I recall feeling a sense of great optimism about the world and the opportunity it would offer me to grow and fulfil my dreams. Despite my outward, adolescent lethargy and indifference, I felt within me a powerful driving spirit. I believed that I had a mission in life, although I had no real idea what it was to be; which was one of the great frustrations of being a teenager. I needed to understand myself better and discover my inner calling, to be enlightened as to the purpose of my being alive. In this process of self-discovery and enlightenment I needed guidance and support – but from whom and when, that was the question. To some extent it could have been, and was, my mother and father, but the tragedy that we had experienced when my natural mother was killed in an awful car accident, left us as a group trying to deal with unexpressed grief and to make 'another' life with new family members, with my father all too busy with developing his career in the Senior Service – Her Majesty's Royal Navy!

So it was that perhaps school was to nurture me and enable me to discover my true calling and mission in life. I am sure that is what my parents expected from the many years I would spend in scholarly pursuits. If they did, then like the Wingfields, we would all be disappointed.........or was it me that was the disappointment?

School for me was neither liberating nor enlightening. It was limiting, prescriptive and threatening in so many ways. In that constraining and intimidating environment, I began on the formal school – maybe life – treadmill that required me to run ever faster just to meet pre-determined and almost exclusively academic expectations that everyone seemed to have of me, although I never knew why........it was just required and expected, as if pre-ordained by some all-knowing and wise deity!

The Purpose of Schooling

What is the purpose of this multi-billion pound thing that we call 'education', or more precisely, 'schooling'? It is important that we understand what we claim the purpose of school to be, as well as what it actually is in reality, because the two things are rarely, if ever, the same. This is the competing tension between the rhetoric and the reality in so many political matters, where sound-bites and image triumph over the true substance of what we do, and the intentions that lie behind them. To give this greater clarity, the question we need to consider is, are schools intended to transform society over time, or are they really only required to transmit society's values and prepare young people for the world as it is, rather than as we would like it to be – or is it both of these things?

I have little doubt what has been the driving agenda for the forty years that I have spent in education. The claim is that schools are to transform society to make it better for us all, by encouraging young people to become enlightened and critical thinkers, but I honestly believe that that vision is nothing more than a chimera, an illusion. Schools have one major over-riding aim, and that is to obediently reflect and reinforce societal mores, norms and values. It is not truly allowed to encourage young people to challenge, question, amend and modify the powerful vested interests which require things to stay very much the same as they always were, or change only in the manner which suits their own agenda.

This is why it is blatantly unreasonable to blame schools for virtually all societal ills. I recall Margaret Thatcher commenting on the riots that erupted during a football match, which required mounted police with batons on the pitch to bring it under control. She blamed this on the laissez-faire attitude and lack of discipline in our schools, as well as the permissiveness of the 1960s, when people were allowed to do as they liked. Such a view represents the Everest of hypocrisy from a Prime Minister whose own belief in laissez-faire economics and individual liberties, not to mention her obsession with silly and impractical free-market dogma, did so much to untie family cohesiveness and divide society, as well as promote the needs of the individual over those of society as a whole. She should have been told to visit a school and see how teachers manage to control such individuals without recourse to mounted police, batons and brute force. Education is always an easy scapegoat in such circumstances, allowing politicians to dodge their true responsibilities by attending to the symptoms rather than the true systemic causes of society's ills.

Young people are pressured – or schooled – into adopting an identity, rather than being allowed the time, space and encouragement to actually create their own. True individualism is rare and all too often branded as eccentric or maladjusted – as compared to existing societal norms, maybe. Any attempt by schools to promote activities which might truly challenge and question traditional orthodoxy are quickly squashed or repressed, either by government legislation or the power of the vested interests in the media and the middle classes. I can recall initiatives to develop political education in schools, as well as peace studies, and proper sex education. They all scared the vested interests in society, as represented in the civil service, government and the 'free' press. Political education was a very hot political potato which, along with other helpful learning experiences such as parent-craft, has quietly withered on the National Curriculum and its associated political vine.

Other challenges from schools and education are dealt with by deeming them to be left-wing concepts, like the whole notion of progressive education. In his excellent book, '1 Out of 10', Peter Hyman makes this point very well, as follows:

> "Vision is more important to a party of the Left, for the Left trades in hope, in progress and the future. The Right's juices flow when they are railing against the enemy, a threat to their way of life: foreigners, high taxes, socialism, communism, asylum seekers, lone parents, gays, loony councils, young people, Europe, television, permissiveness. The Left dreams of the good society, the end of poverty, full employment, a community of equals, children growing up with life chances, trains that run on time, hospitals that cure people, schools that unleash the potential of all, foreign aid ending world hunger."

If that is a true Left-wing agenda for action, then I am necessarily placed among their ranks – or that pigeon hole – for sure!

The Right stamp on any initiative that is seen to question the status quo or their very peculiar sensitivities, in both senses of the word 'peculiar'. This is

54

why the whole issue of sex education is so badly dealt with. How does one talk about the whole issue of HIV and AIDS awareness, whilst at the same time being unable to talk about the risks associated with casual relationships, including those which are homosexual in nature? Teachers who seek to deal in reality are pilloried for seeking to promote these types of sexual encounters, which is just cheap political point scoring. The right would rather demonise unorthodox sexual preferences and homosexual practices, thereby justifying the failure to address the world which young people will have already encountered, and maybe are personally experiencing. Of course, we should recognise traditional relationships in the context of loving, heterosexual family contexts, as long as it's not incestuous I assume, but that is not the reality of the world which young people already inhabit and to which they are exposed. To pretend otherwise, and to turn a blind eye is negligent and likely to attract adolescents who wish to challenge the adult world by doing something that is forbidden and mysterious, aided and abetted by a lack of effective education.

I can recall an enlightening initiative to introduce 'peace studies' into the curriculum, when the 'Cold War' was at its height and threatening, if not promising, Armageddon. This was a notion that the 'Right' (wrongly) made sure that they crushed, through the political rhetoric espoused by Tory politicians and their vile media interests. Others sought an apparently more reasoned approach, arguing that if peace studies were to be taught, then it was only right and proper to introduce the counter-balance of 'war studies' to the school curriculum. In response to this spurious argument, one commentator argued that war studies were already firmly well entrenched and traditionally rooted within the school curriculum, carefully disguised as History'!

Another tactic, oft-employed by the Right, is to use their dominant control of the allegedly 'free-press' to ensure that the public are not encouraged to hear or believe views that challenge their traditional orthodoxy. In short they kill the messenger, very often by not publishing reports that they themselves commissioned, or otherwise discredit the source of such dangerous views.

They can do this by cutting the funding that the sources might be receiving – as Margaret Thatcher did when she axed the government grant to one economic forecasting group, The Cambridge Economic Policy Group

(CEPG), in a vain attempt to stop them from making predictions about unemployment and growth of the British economy – or the dire lack of it – as a direct consequence of adopting dubious monetarist policies. The fact that the CEPG had the best track record among the various groups that were engaged in economic forecasting was an irrelevance (or an inconvenient relevance) to the Conservative Government. Instead they diverted the money that was saved by wielding the axe in one quarter, to other forecasters who, although having a less distinguished and accurate history, were part of the machinery that was trying to quell the fears of the general public about the true and inevitable consequences of the Right's blind faith in ineffective, let alone damaging and immoral economic policy decisions. The message is clear: if you want to get on in the world, 'keep your nose clean' and 'toe the line', to use two very pertinent idioms.

Entrenched conservatism, as well as Conservatism, in the UK is a serious brake on what I shall attempt to demonstrate are necessary and long overdue progressive and radical alternatives that challenge the status quo and traditional orthodoxy in almost everything – not least schooling and education. It is purely fallacious to believe that schools in any way act so as to transform society, by properly equipping young people to effect the changes that are needed. The problem is that teachers and parents are necessarily victims of their own experience of education. In general, they have been effectively conditioned into believing that comfort with the known, tried and tested methods of organising and delivering things did well for them, and so will do equally well for their offspring, and the offspring of others. The reality is that the world has changed; it has moved on and become different, and yet by and large, education continues to stumble backwards into the future gazing longingly at the past.

Why is there so much in-bred resistance to anything being labelled as 'radical' and 'progressive'? The dictionary rightly states that radical changes and differences are very important and great in degree, and that radical people believe there should be a shift in the dominant paradigm which holds sway over shaping society to try and bring about these changes. This makes me think of immense issues such as sustainable growth, solving the inexorable rise in terrorism, ensuring environmental protection and the more equitable distribution of income and wealth, as well as other resources – like safe drinking water, decent health care and relevant and effective education. Similarly, the dictionary correctly informs us that someone who is progressive or has progressive ideas, has *modern* ideas about how things should be done, rather than *traditional* ones, and that progressive change happens gradually over a period of time. What is so unnerving about such concepts – I welcome them! Why do we allow terms, such as 'radical', 'progressive, and 'revolution' for that matter, to be hijacked by political imperatives and subjected to such blatant, pejorative and damaging misrepresentation?

It is no wonder that our young people are increasingly disenchanted and disaffected by education when they spend their time being literally schooled in a system that acts as if we live in the past, and which has precious little to do with the real world they see outside the school gates. I honestly believe that we need a democratic revolution in education – a period of radical and progressive change that is reflective of past practice, but not determined by, outdated traditions. We need to determine an agenda for significant change which is introduced gradually over time to breathe a long overdue blast of fresh air into something that is currently failing our young people and, therefore, all of us. What should be open to debate is not the need for such action, but the detail of the changes and the direction in which it might take us. As yet, however, the power and inertia of traditional orthodoxy holds us all firmly in its invisible and pervasive grasp, acting as a brake which prevents us from collaboratively accepting, adopting and embracing genuine change.

In his book, Peter Hyman echoes the point that children need the belief that they can achieve whatever they set their minds to, and that belief will drive them to have dreams and a passion in life, as well as to achieve and fulfil them. Children are no different to anyone else; they need to have a genuine belief in themselves and in their surroundings, as well as believing that people (especially their teachers) genuinely care for them, and that they *do* have a future. We need to restore that spirit of great optimism and hope that was prevalent in the 1960s. My favourite song of all times is 'Imagine' by John Lennon, only because I find myself increasingly wishing that his lyrics could come true, rather than seeing the world going in exactly the opposite direction in so many ways. It was not just the dream for peace that John Lennon sang about with which I concur, but also the *hope* that underpins that wish. Indeed, he uses the word 'hope' many times in that wonderful anthem – an abstract but very real 'tune' that seems to have abandoned most societies in the world. Instead, people act as if they believe their destiny and salvation lie in materialism and consumerism – the endless acquisition of the latest and newest gadget or product – rather than exploring their potential and liberating their unique talents, and truly living their lives.

We must all work towards enabling young people to believe in the power of education to offer real and new opportunities in life, but only if we change what schools do most of the time, as well as how they do it. In his book Peter Hyman includes the comment of a teacher who observed, rightly I believe, that children today are not used to deferred gratification and so cannot grasp an immediate win from education. We have lost children, seduced by the irresistible, capitalist treadmill which promotes the urgent acquisition of 'things'. More worryingly, they fail to discover and feel the true buzz that the discovery of their talents and inner brilliance would and could give them; a feeling that would be far more lasting, meaningful and fulfilling than merely accumulating the latest 'stuff'!

Society at large, and not just schools, must do everything they can to cultivate this self-confidence in our young people, as well as the concomitant mind-set of self-belief. Society's biggest contribution would be to allow and empower schools to adopt a transforming, rather than a largely historical, agenda for radical and progressive change, as previously defined, to provide children with genuine and not artificial or superficial life chances. As W.B. Yeats put it, *"Education is not the filling of the pail but the lighting of a fire."* The problem is that schools are never going to be so empowered as long as the collective belief that their role is to prepare young people for adult and working life – the future – by giving them tools crafted in the distant past. This aim is as redundant as it is stifling and irrelevant.

During the time of the many initiatives trying to encourage schools to link the curriculum more closely to industry and commerce, particularly in the 1980s, as a teacher of economics and business studies I was heavily involved in seeking to encourage more young people to consider careers in industry. This required forging a mutual understanding of industry's role by teachers and schools, and vice versa. The Schools, Industry Partnership (SIP) work at local education authority level was interesting and enjoyable, but it also revealed a huge clash of agenda held by the two broad groupings of partners. I recall one senior engineer from a multi-national company persistently at odds with the teachers involved in this partnership work who professed that our paramount obligation as educators was to consider the learning needs of young people. He was utterly opposed to this perspective, arguing that we were almost criminally negligent in not putting the recruitment needs of industry at the fore of all our endeavours. In his eyes, we were fundamentally wrong in regarding the needs of young people as our over-riding responsibility, and not the needs of industry and commerce.

Of course, both sides were almost forced into disagreement and conflict when the main villain of the piece was (and still is) the traditional need to view academic work as the pinnacle of human endeavour and achievement. This pre-eminence of academe is the pivotal determinant of the orthodox school curriculum – and that is just what society at large demands. Had schools sought to significantly introduce a worthwhile vocational dimension to the school curriculum, it would have been seen as watering down the academic curriculum and, subsequently, resisted. As a general rule, those people who favour the retaining or extending of grammar school education are only so inclined as long, of course, that their children are able to attend one. Comprehensive schools and a more balanced curriculum entitlement, including a greater emphasis on practical, technical and vocational types of learning, are only seen as appropriate or suitable for 'other people's children'. The skewed nature of the traditional school curriculum will be examined in more detail in the next section of this book. For now, I want to dwell a while on the misguided and damaging view that schools should be essentially preparing children for adult life.

'Us' or 'Them'?
Firstly, whose adult life are we preparing them for – ours or theirs? Are they being prepared for us or for them? It is ridiculous to suggest that we know what the world will look like in the future. The most important education that young people receive is during their formative years, and children spend more

than 10 years in school, as a general rule, now that we are seeking to keep them in full-time, formal education until they are aged 18 years, if not longer. This begs the question, "What will the world be like in say fifteen years' time?" I have no idea to be honest, except that it will be different in terms of the way we currently lead our lives. It is for this reason that we should be educating young people to think and act intelligently, in keeping with Alice Heim's view of what constitutes intelligence. Darwin is often famously misquoted as saying that successful evolution was a matter of the 'survival of the fittest', whereas what he actually said was that the species that survive are usually not the smartest or the strongest, but the ones that are most responsive and adept in adapting in a relevant and appropriate way to changes in their environment. This greater emphasis of creative problem-solving and decision-making skills has implications for the amount of content in the school curriculum, as well as how it is chosen, as will be examined later in this and subsequent chapters.

Additionally, this notion of preparing young people for adult and working lives in the future fails to acknowledge, let alone address the fact that children live in the world today and whilst growing up, particularly during adolescence, they are very often desperately trying to make sense and operate effectively and successfully in the here and now. To ignore this simple but powerful reality to such an extent is to send an even more potent hidden message to young people, and that is that they are not deemed as important or worthy until they can contribute in some material way; that their lives are an irrelevance almost. This is not the intended message, but it is one that I am convinced 'we' send without knowing. This adds to the feeling that education whilst at school is something that is **done** to them, a sentiment which is reinforced by the fact that we make the entire process, at least up to the age of 16, compulsory.

Formal schooling appears increasingly irrelevant to, and in the lives of, young people, as well as the other issues they face and experience such as the physical, emotional and chemical changes that they are currently grappling with, and of which they have to make sense. This is typified and exacerbated by society's ambiguous and muddled thinking about young people, especially those in the 13 to 17 age range. They are not adults and yet they are not children anymore, so what are they – or should I ask, "Who are they?" It seems as though we intentionally or blindly fail to try and really understand their everyday trials and tribulations and ignore their needs and life realities, seeing their inevitable challenge of the irrelevance of traditional orthodoxy as threatening, maladjusted, dangerous even. The response to this is to add more compulsion, backed by sanctions, often legal in nature, to 'persuade' them to conform and do what we expect of them. Young people are not legally seen as adults until they reach the age of majority at 18 years, and yet they are able to join the armed forces and *technically* able to go into active service and sacrifice their lives at the age of 16 years. At the same time, they cannot vote for the government that takes the country to war, for whatever reason, and cannot watch a violent and bloody portrayal of war in a film at the cinema which others have deemed to be only suitable for adults. Similarly, at the same time as the Labour government was thinking of reducing the age of consensual homosexual sex from 18 to 16 years, to give it an equal and non-discriminatory status with heterosexual intercourse, it was considering raising the age at which young people can legally buy cigarettes in the reverse direction, from 16 to 18 years of age. As one comedian pointed out, under these proposed changes, a sixteen year old can apparently be sodomised, but is not legally eligible to have a cigarette afterwards!

This utterly confused thinking about how we should treat young people during these challenging transitory years is replicated and reinforced by schools and the hidden message of preparation for some future life. Let's just get them through the difficult years so that they can be ready to fit into our imagined future world, perhaps? Secondary education in particular seems to be more about control and compulsion, rather than creating a truly liberating environment in which young people can flourish. This was classically demonstrated by another piece of Thatcherite thinking (if that is not a downright contradiction in terms) when the Conservatives demanded the inflation of the basic **3Rs** into the **6Rs** – the well-known **reading**, **writing** and 'rithmetic, plus plenty of good old **right**, 'rong and **religious education**, as if schools had been ignoring these additional and occasionally misspelt elements, or actively working in a contradictory manner, until this mind-blowing demand was made.

Such pronouncements do little to do otherwise than to reinforce the view that the true purpose of education is about gentling the masses; getting them to conform and not 'rock the boat' by challenging the conventional way of doing things. This helps keep things very much as they always have been. That is after all what conservatism means, and if you are not sure then you can check the dictionary which says, *"Someone who is conservative or has conservative ideas is unwilling to accept changes and new ideas."* This might explain, for example, why Conservative/Republican politicians in the USA are so reluctant to change the way we produce and consume goods and services and lead our lives in a way that does not add to climate change and environmental degradation.

What's the Incentive?

It has been said that 'education is a process of transmission and reception, of information flow, of delivery'. I am not going to try and refute this claim, as it seems to describe the 'education' that schools offer fairly accurately. What is important, however, is that for this delivery approach to teaching to work, learners are necessarily cast in the role of receivers, and to fulfil this usually passive role, they have to be one of three things. First of all, they have to be coerced, under the threat of sanction, into being receivers, and this is demonstrably the case for many young people, whether we like to admit it or not. Just ask them!

Secondly, they will be willing receivers if they feel extrinsically motivated through the incentive of rewards. This was particularly evident in the Thatcher years, when so much happened to undermine the cohesiveness of our society, which consequently became unstuck or unstitched, and very much for the worse. This is not a contradiction of the definition of conservatism offered above, as Margaret Thatcher's 'radical' change agenda was founded on Victorian values, as she so often and proudly proclaimed, which is hardly change with a forward-thinking and truly radical thrust. For a long time, teachers had used the lure of getting a job as the reason why children from essentially working class families should conform and study hard at school. But, in those areas hit hardest by the Thatcher 'experiment', unemployment rose significantly, and even many graduates were left high and dry on the dole. This acted to remove the extrinsic motivation or reward that teachers, parents and society could hold up as a carrot in front of otherwise reluctant receivers or learners – to obtain academic qualifications in order to get a good job as a source of income, and access to the materialist, consumerist world, stuffed full of goodies. This was the start of so much unrest and disaffection by many young people who now saw coercion as the only reason to go to school. The hope of employment was a myth in their eyes; a mirage, a lie on the part of society – even many middle class children and graduates felt the same, as if all their efforts were for nothing. The riots that erupted in London and some other major cities were not fomented by just the mindless, disenfranchised poor, but also included graduates and those who populate the middle classes amongst their ranks. Be honest and stop denigrating the deprived and the poor, most of whom adhere to the mores of society even though they have a very good reason to do otherwise.

This state of affairs was almost light years away from the third way of encouraging learners to be receivers, and that is to be intrinsically motivated to want to learn as a result of natural curiosity and enjoyment. Sadly, this most desirous reason to be motivated to receive education as currently envisaged is like a long lost dream for so many secondary school students. Educationists were once driven and possessed by the belief that education was a right – something to which everyone has an inalienable right. Now the concept has been hi-jacked to have a purely instrumental and utilitarian purpose – to prepare people for industry and commerce. If education does not contribute to wealth creation – and a purely financial and materialist notion of 'wealth' – then it has no real value. The pursuit of profit and money is the only other show in town these days, and we are the spiritually poorer for it, as well as increasingly unhappy and disenchanted with our inevitably limited lot.

Success is measured in money terms, and the world cares more about making money than caring for the welfare of people – the two are not the same, and neither is money the route to inner peace and contentment. If it were, there would be no reason why rich and famous people are so prone to harmful excesses in their use of legal, illegal and prescription drugs. To add insult to injury, the culture of celebrity, like that of consumerism and materialism which has been generated by, and copied from American culture, means that young people are more likely to emulate these (spiritually) poor role models and copy those things that apparently explain their star status – but only those to which they have ready and easy access. It is almost impossible to encourage the most economically and socially disadvantaged young people to be receivers of an irrelevant and broadly uninteresting school curriculum, given their slight chance of one day achieving academic success and securing a 'decent' job, as a route to income and wealth. This is made doubly and ironically difficult when these same youngsters see the boy who left school at 16 years of age, sitting at the school gate in a BMW 5-series car obtained on the proceeds of dealing in 'controlled substances', as narcotics are euphemistically called. This quick route to obtaining the 'trappings' of success are literally impossible for some to resist. They too become seduced into emulating the trappings of the road to nowhere!

This is not cynicism. It is an honest and realistic observation of further contradictions that society allows and actively encourages, which lay innocent and despairing schools and teachers open to false accusations of complicity if not conspiracy. Schools cannot be expected to fight the negative messages that are so powerfully transmitted by the collective actions of society. Furthermore, if children are being encouraged to be receivers as opposed to critical and creative thinkers, then it is hardly surprising that they are likely to receive the extraordinarily powerful messages that we would rather they did not receive. What chance do schools have if they are prevented from seeking to adopt a transforming agenda for change, and instead required to do the bidding of successive governments and civil servants who largely represent the middle and upper classes who, by and large, are still able to effectively motivate their offspring with the possibility of extrinsic rewards in the form of degrees, and well-paid jobs? This is especially true if their offspring went to the 'right' school or college!

In the section on the wider issues that undermine the education which is delivered whilst young people are at school, I will argue that the stranglehold that the middle classes hold over government policy decision-making works to the detriment not only of their own children, but also of children from working class and less affluent backgrounds – and to a much greater and more immediate extent. But, it is relevant here to focus on how this stranglehold has done so much to stifle the formulation of a radical and progressive change agenda for schools and their curricula.

Means or Ends?

The assumption that the main goal of formal education is to obtain academic qualifications means that all the change schools have experienced has largely been focused on the **means** and <u>not</u> the **ends** or overall goals of the compulsory experience that thousands of young people endure. I would suggest that this is one contributory factor for the failure of so many of the endless avalanche of initiatives that schools have attempted not to be buried under, or burdened by, for many decades now.

It was again the wise Albert Einstein who said, *"Perfection of means and confusion of goals seem – in my opinion – to characterise our age."* This is a fundamental cause of why state education (and private education for that matter) has failed so many young people to a greater or lesser extent. The symptoms are what successive governments have been treating and seeking to ameliorate, which is missing the point and akin to re-arranging the deckchairs on the Titanic. If that is the wrong metaphor, then they act like the orchestra that continued to play as the ship sank into the freezing waters – to an audience that were otherwise preoccupied. Their efforts and tuneful or terminal refrains went largely unnoticed I suspect.

This failure to truly question the purpose of education – the overall goals – has been the cause of wasted millions of pounds that has endlessly poured into formal education to treat the symptoms of its irrelevance to so many young people and society. A classic example is in the way that Margaret Thatcher and then Tony Blair, when Prime Ministers of Great Britain, refused to act on the advice of an impressive and virtually unanimous chorus of informed opinion recommending changing the GCE 'A' Level and AS examinations that most young people take at the age of 18 years. Margaret Thatcher put it – quite aptly I believe – when she referred to her iron-willed determination to preserve 'The Gold Standard' of the A-Level system as the main reason to ignore the considered advice of the Higginson Report which strongly recommended doing away with what had become an old-fashioned and irrelevant examination. I consider this as an apt, but unfortunate justification on Mrs Thatcher's part, because reverting to The Gold Standard at the end of the First World War was one of the main contributory factors that plunged the World economy into a massive depression, with the misery of mass unemployment and crushing poverty that it created. The reintroduction of the Gold Standard then was as much of an irrelevance and a mistake as the decision to retain the GCE 'A' Level examinations was when Tony Blair more recently followed in Mrs. Thatcher's imperious footsteps and chickened out as well – no doubt in fear of upsetting the powerful middle class.

The GCE 'A' Level is the end point of our entire system of compulsory education in the UK – it is the tarnished golden goal to which all children are supposed to aspire. The result for years has been that we fail an ever increasing number of young people from the earliest of ages, so that we can identify the minority who will 'do well' at 'A' Level and go on to university. At the same time, we wonder why the talent embodied in the residual 'failures' lies unfulfilled and untapped, with the owners totally disenchanted with the farce into which they have been press-ganged to act, or simply to observe as audience members.

I believe that this antiquated goal is a token that symbolises the folly that has become known as 'School'. As Julius Erving said, *"Goals determine what you are going to be."* This might explain why so many children do not become what they could be, because they are obliged to try and become what 'we' want them to be, or would like them to be.

Young people should be brimming with a burning passion for life and learning; they should have their own goals, visions and dreams in life, and for life. School should, therefore, be fulfilling and exciting, not a boring and frustrating chore for so many, achieved often only with the power of legal compulsion.

Education should be about freedom not prescription or compulsion; about liberating the real wealth of a child's inner spirit, not caging, chaining and constraining it. The agenda for formal education ought to be about transforming societal values and actions, not about meekly reinforcing them. It should emphasise collaboration and not competition, which means that it should be essentially inclusive and not selective. It should be fun and enjoyable as well as stimulating, but should rarely if ever be boring and dull. It should be challenging but not impossible; it should be about celebrating the successes of all rather than mourning, bemoaning or criticising the failures of the many; it should be focused on tackling the real causes of under-achievement, and not its symptoms. Above all else, it should be relevant to the needs of young people, and not some irrelevant anachronism.

A Japanese proverb says that vision without action is a daydream, but action without vision is a nightmare. When I was a child, I had dreams – daydreams – I wanted to be successful at lots of things, but the hidden message of schooling quickly made me aware of my limitations and taught me that I was a relative failure, that I was not very good at many things that adults saw as important. I genuinely believe that this unconsciously dented my self-confidence and self-esteem, as well as tarnished the attractions of my once cherished ambitions. I learnt very early on in my school life, to 'scale things down a bit – or a lot'. Never was I encouraged and truly supported to 'go for it', to 'get up and go' – except on the rugby field or in the boxing ring! I was never asked what I was interested in, I was simply told what had been decided for me to do – and adults always know best, when you are very young. Whenever I felt that I wanted to do something different from that which had been prescribed for me, then I was told that I would not be able to do it, or that I could not do it, or that I would not make a living out of it – with a dubiously materialistic definition attached to the reality of 'living'.

Today, my observations of many young people in secondary schools is that they are devoid of any driving vision or ambition, but they are intent on action nonetheless – why else be alive? More and more teenagers are devoting most of their energy and thoughts to everyday, short-term gratification, fuelled by rampant consumerism and a culture of dubious celebrity. This scenario has already become the nightmare of which the Japanese proverb warns, and yet still we persist in treating the symptoms rather than the deep-rooted and fundamental causes. Dealing with these will challenge the vested interests and their blinkered if not blind assumptions, and demand systemic, societal, political and economic change in the long-term.

It is, I think, right to say that change is inevitable, but that growth is intentional. Education has changed but not grown, because its goals are still defined by the traditional orthodoxy that has remained firmly and deeply entrenched in society's psyche. The deliberate change in education has been endlessly

67

focused on the 'means' and never really been asked to adopt new, more relevant 'goals'. The goalposts have not moved in decades – centuries even. In other words, formal education and schooling has not really changed at all, but it has certainly failed dismally to grow with the times, which is why it does not meet the needs of society anymore – which has erroneously become the urgent and relentless catalyst for even more, means-focused change. The result is that young people are on one level or plane, whereas we treat them, and school, as if things are what they were and not what they really are......is it any wonder so many youngsters resent it, or fail to see its relevance to them?

What Are We Missing?

Ashley Montagu said, *"By virtue of being born into humanity, every human being has a right to the development and fulfilment of his (or her) potentialities as a human being."*

This liberal view of education has not been in fashion since the more utilitarian and instrumentalist philosophy that has informed education policy formulation came into vogue in the 1970s. So how well have we been doing over the many years of compulsory formal education? If one approves of, and feels that we should as a society adopt such an approach, then history would seem to suggest that when Howard Kendricks said, *"Nothing is more common than unfulfilled potential,"* he had managed to hit the proverbial nail squarely on its head. In such circumstances, how can one escape the assertion that the corollary of this is that society and schools must have also failed our young people? This failure did not start when the new-wave philosophy took hold, because the main goal of schooling has always been an inappropriate one for all young people, but some much more than others.

Possibly the greatest ever mistake made was when public schools (i.e. Church and state-maintained schools) began to cater for the needs of the majority of children whose parents could not afford to send them to privately-run schools (perversely called 'public schools') in the U.K. Instead of embarking on designing a truly liberating and enlightening curriculum, these schools sought to emulate the education offered by the independent sector – both in terms of content and methodology – which saw academic success as the greatest human achievement. The young people, who went to independent or 'public' school, were being prepared for adult life just as they are today, but the difference was that the working life that was envisaged was in the professions, the civil and armed services, or politics. They were being groomed to become the ruling elite of the country and not get their precious little hands roughened or soiled in the cotton mills, the mines and factories that their emergent middle-class parents had created and owned. Given the tiny percentage of young people who attended such schools, this anti-industrial culture would not have mattered very much, but because the government maintained schools sought to offer a similar style of education, all children were to be forced through an educational sausage machine that inherently saw academic work as the only, truly worthwhile pursuit. It is not the liberal view of education or the more utilitarian view per se that is centrally important in explaining why human potential is left largely undiscovered. It is the view that there can only be one goal, and that no other type of learning is relevant or truly worth pursuing.

We see this same mistake being replicated even today, when adults who went through comprehensive schools and secured what society regards as a good job with a decent income (the two are usually one and the same thing in most people's eyes) decide that their children should attend an independent school and not, like them, go to the local 'comp'. (And notice the different destinations when I put 'attend' as opposed to 'go to'.)

Children have been leaving school – some having done well, some quite well and others extremely badly – having received a lot of information, most of which is very soon forgotten. They have either succeeded or failed on the elitist academic treadmill but I honestly believe that virtually all of them are still likely to feel as though something is missing in life – but what?

Only recently, I watched a DVD of the film entitled 'Venus', which stars the brilliant actor (the late) Peter O'Toole in one of the lead parts. He was as masterful as usual, but one line he uttered, as an aged, worldly-wise, sick and dying man, really struck a chord with me. As he looked into the middle distance, he said wistfully, regretfully and with a resigned tone: *"I'm about to die and I know nothing about myself."*

The chord it struck in my mind due to having read an outstanding book by James Hillman entitled *'The Soul's Code – in Search of Character and Calling'*, as well as to a myriad of utterances from other writers and poets, not to mention my experiences of education and life. It convinced me even more that the academically biased, formal school curriculum is hopelessly irrelevant, not only to the needs of industry and commerce, but to the essential and spiritual needs of all human beings. The main goal of our endeavours is fundamentally flawed, which means that endless changing of the means by which we seek to organise and deliver schooling will never compensate for the fact that we are heading in the wrong direction in most cases, and completely missing *the* fundamental aim in every respect.

I often reflect on the question of what is my true calling in life, by which I mean, quite literally, that which drives me, and when doing things that resonate with it, produce within me the greatest enjoyment and challenge. I am searching for the meaning of life – or perhaps more correctly and less unfathomable, my life. I want to figure out why I am here as a human being. Am I alive simply to exist and to serve my time in the pursuit of happiness and/or drudgery until I die, or am I destined to achieve something unique and special to me; to make a contribution, a difference? I am totally convinced that there is something deep inside me that already knows the answer to that question, but it is not telling me clearly and explicitly what it is that I should do to fulfil my destiny. This beneficial process of reflection necessarily demands that I not only look backwards to understand my life to date, but that I also look to the future and consider what I should do, as well as where and in what capacity. Struggling with the meaning of life should preoccupy everyone who breathes, and not just philosophers and intellectuals, because everyone is unique. This individual uniqueness manifests itself in many ways, but most powerfully, it is our inner spirituality that truly defines each and every one of us as special.

As a teacher, I once asked a group of secondary school students in assembly to consider this fundamental and defining issue by asking them the following five questions:

1. **Why** are you here?
2. Why **are** you here?
3. Why are **you** here?
4. Why are you **here**?

and

5.   Why are you here **now**?

The reaction or response was mixed, but essentially the majority were wondering if I had lost my marbles, and not those which I left in the primary school playground. This wonder was not because these young people were incapable of such philosophical thought, of that I am quite sure. I am, however, fairly certain that the reason was because they had never really been exposed to such pressing and self-defining thought processes before, and they were approaching the end of their compulsory schooling sooner or later.

Rather than try and put this in my own words, I want to refer closely to some of the points that James Hillman raises in his fascinating work which, I believe, should at least be a compulsory or core text for any aspiring school teacher, and all parents for that matter. He argues strongly and, for me, convincingly that what is lost in most people's lives and what must be recovered, is a sense of personal calling – that there is a reason to be alive, a reason which forms the essential mystery at the heart of each human life.

I have already referred to my working life as feeling as if I was running on a professional (and, ergo, an academic) treadmill and, like the luckless hamster, getting nowhere at all – no matter how hard and fast I tried to run.

James Hillman puts it as follows:

> *"To uncover the innate image, we must set aside the psychological frames that are usually used, and mostly used up. They do not reveal enough. They trim a life to fit the frame: developmental growth, step by step, from infancy through troubled youth, to mid-life crisis and aging, to death. Plodding your way through an already planned map, you are on an itinerary that tells you where you have been before you get there, or like an averaged statistic foretold by an actuary in an insurance company. The course of your life has been described in the future perfect tense."*

Please take the time to read the passage again!

He goes on to say that we dull our lives by the very way in which we conceive them, because we have stopped imagining them with any sort of romance or fictional flair. By accepting the idea that we are all the effect of a subtle buffeting between hereditary and societal or environmental forces, we reduce

71

ourselves to a result. In such a way, our lives resemble the story of a victim. For decades the argument between psychologists (and educationists for that matter) that has raged and remained unresolved, is to what extent are we the 'product' of genetic and hereditary factors, or does our environment determine what we eventually become. Clearly, both forces have a role to play in shaping our uniqueness as human beings, but they alone are not enough, offering only a partial answer. This unerring creation of a dichotomy in virtually all debates is a constraining paradigm that places those involved, very uncomfortably, on the horns of a dilemma. The debates about the virtues of child-centred versus teacher-centred learning, of political 'Left' versus 'Right', of free market economies versus planned economies, and so on not only seem to be largely unproductive in terms of achieving a consensus, let alone a lasting one. In such arguments a great deal of heat is generated, but rarely a great deal of light, mainly due to the fact that they miss the point. I am convinced that neither adversarial perspective is completely right and that they both have a role to play in terms of our actions, but they fail essentially because they are missing some fundamental ingredient – a third, even fourth dimension to the discussion.

James Hillman puts it more clearly perhaps as follows:

> "We do need to recognise at the outset that division into two (competing) alternatives is a comfortable habit of the Western mind. So this chapter will have to struggle with long-established and comforting habits of thinking in opposites that say: If behaviour is not fully the result of genetic inheritance, then what is left over can be accounted for only by environmental influences and vice versa. The introduction of 'something else' violates our mode of thought and the convenience of its habitual operations, like the proverbial elephant in the room. A 'something else' disturbs minds that mistake comfortable (and easy) thinking with clarity of thought............'something else' intervenes in human life that cannot be held within the confines of nature versus nurture."

I have come to believe that James Hillman is correct in seeing the spirit, the soul or our individual calling as the missing 'something else' in our attempts to understand the meaning of life and our true destiny. He urges the reader to try and, "envision that what a child goes through has to do with finding a place in the world for their specific calling. They are trying to live two lives at once – the one they were born with *and the one of the place and among the people they were born into."* This process inevitably creates tensions which can manifest themselves in all kinds of ways, some of which are maladaptive, delinquent and cause pain. Parents, teachers, indeed society as a whole respond by spurning, punishing and seeking to control these manifestations, seeking conformity to norms rather than trying to understand what it is that is truly provoking such behaviours. We need to regard young people differently, to **enter their imaginations** and to discover what their calling and their destiny might be. Young people for generations – probably since modern man came into being – have complained about feeling that no one and nobody seems to understand them at all. This is often seen as a way of excusing poor behaviour or conflict between them and their family members, teachers and the norms to which others in society adhere, but I share Hillman's view that it is really an attempt – often one that is in vain – by the soul to cry out. They are not excusing themselves, they are seeking to explain their actions and the tensions they feel in the only way they can. They are also motivated by the need to understand themselves! They know they have a reason to be, a calling, but they are desperately trying to discover what it is. Society sees this purely as part of growing up, rather than as James Hillman argues, a feature of the spirit trying to grow **down** into the world in which it finds itself, very much like a tree grows roots down into the soil for its very foundations, nourishment and security. The soul is crying out from the core of each and every young person to be identified, recognised and liberated, and not conditioned by the mores of the world into which it has been born. Hillman puts it thus:

> *"It (the daimon or genius within each of us) has much to do with feelings of uniqueness, of grandeur and with the restlessness of the heart, its impatience, its dissatisfaction, its yearning. It needs its share of beauty, it wants to be seen, witnessed and accorded recognition, particularly by the person who is its caretaker. It is slow to anchor and yet quick to fly."*

I recall with great sadness the incident when Robert A. Hawkins, a 'troubled' (aren't they always?) nineteen-year-old, armed with a semi-automatic rifle, shot dead a number of people, and himself, at the 'West-roads' shopping mall in Omaha. The suicide note that he left before conducting an evidently premeditated but randomly targeted homicide, included an elementary last will and testament, and the depressingly sad self-observation that he had 'been a piece of shit all his life, but now he would be famous'.

We need a fresh way of looking at our lives. The pursuit of happiness according to James Hillman becomes the pursuit of answers to the wrong questions. He argues that we are isolated because of the industrial economic system, with the effect that we have become mere numbers. He is right when he says that we live consumerism rather than community, and that loneliness is symptomatic of victimisation. We are victims of a wrong way of life and it is wrong that we should be lonely, living within our ever-expanding materialist cocoons. We need to change the system root and branch by living in a cooperative, or a commune, and working in teams that acknowledge and promote what Karl Marx called our 'species being'.

Human beings are essentially creative social creatures, and yet the result of consumerism and competitive economic doctrine results in this isolation, selfishness, greed and a lack of concern for our fellow human beings. As a result we have nothing to bond us, or give us an individual or overall, collective identity. We are driven not by our spirituality, but seduced instead by the tinsel, the glitter and the trivia of manufactured labels, brand names and become obsessed with mere possession and outward appearance. The pursuit of material happiness makes us unhappy with everything – especially with what we already have, because it is simply never good enough. This unhappiness may well go a long way to explain why so many people are also unhappy and not content with their physical appearance, which is why plastic surgery for purely cosmetic reasons is such a massive growth industry around the world.

In Thailand, beautiful brown, olive-skinned women are made to feel dissatisfied with their skin colour, their small and beautiful noses, smaller busts, and so on. They spend money they can ill afford to look like the Eurasian models that adorn the advertising hoardings as well as their television and movie screens on a 24/7 basis. The message is to be somebody or someone that you are not. You are not allowed to be satisfied or content with yourself nor what you possess. To be satisfied is to be dull, boring and worst of all unattractive. This false materialist quest detracts, and distracts us, from discovering who we truly are, let alone what we might, and could, become. We are increasingly judged by what we own and what we look like – our purchased image – and not who we really and emphatically are.

This sad triumph of style and sound-bite over substance and detail all results in the 'dumbing-down' process that has become endemic in Western, and what are euphemistically called, developed countries. This superficial irrelevance dominates our waking moments and disturbs our sleep patterns. We are effectively becoming castrated in a spiritual sense; being divided from our true inner identity by a relentless, and equally unsustainable process making us all the same in what we look like and what we buy; which is the reason why the goal is constantly being changed, so that the quest for more is perpetuated.

The manufactured attraction of modern technological gadgets such as i-pads and cell phones is another particularly pernicious way of segregating us from our true self as well as collective and harmonious co-existence. The companies who produce internet and computer games, as well as the truly anti-social mobile (now 'Smart') phones, proudly proclaim that they are connecting us, whereas they are very successfully doing the opposite – separating us from those with whom we are nearest and often dearest – even when they are standing right next to us. This technological intrusion quite literally serves to colonise and occupy human beings, as we are all swept along on a magic carpet of artificial, spurious and irrelevant consumerist choice. Divide and rule takes on an even more ominous, detrimental and mendacious demeanour.

As the economist E. J. Mishan put it in his book entitled 'The Costs of Economic Growth', we are walking on a carpet of material goods and services that is constantly being unrolled in front of us. The effect of this illusion, which is dubiously termed 'progress' and 'development', is such that we can never keep up or catch up with it and, worse still, we do not see how that same 'carpet' is being surreptitiously rolled-up behind us. This is so that we never really have time to look back and see what we have lost – such as our health, fresh air, clean water, peace and quiet; real time for ourselves and for relaxation, as well as with our friends and families – factors which together determine our true quality of life. This view was not only true of its time, but was prophetic in the way it has grown exponentially since he wrote the book in 1967.

Buying the massively promoted brands and wearing them, or showing them off, does not enable us to access the dream that the marketers are asking us to, quite literally, buy into. It is a materialist con; a lie – which is why so many people, regardless of their income level, are so unhappy with their lot.

We have to look within ourselves to find true happiness and fulfilment. We need to create a society, and an education system within it, that enables and empowers us to reclaim our true and real identity as special, free-thinking and unique human beings. We have to at least try and resist the hidden pressures to conform and turn our backs on the marketing froth of images, brands and other transient and false symbols of success. They are truly the 'trappings' of success, in that we become trapped in a materialist bubble of our own making.

We have to discover our true spiritual identity and, quite literally, live it.

What saddens me so much is that so many young people no longer display a passion for life; for discovering, responding to and fulfilling their inner talents. What preoccupies those who do display real ambition is buying into the endless diversion that is sign-posted 'making money', to join the materialist bandwagon to acquire as much as possible. This quest for money has corrupted everything. Artists and musicians now paint, not to express their inner feelings, they do it to offer it for sale for money and, hopefully, get 'rich'. Sporting endeavours have become gladiatorial, with sportsmen and women resorting to cheating, as well as damaging their health and bodies, not to mention the integrity of the competition in which they are involved. They must win at all costs – there is so much at stake. Football icons resort to tactics which are quaintly called 'gamesmanship' in order to win the glittering prizes that justify their astronomically inflated salaries. In my rule-book, diving and intimidating referees and officials amount to nothing more than cheating. When our sporting icons are let down by their chemists, they are not banned for life from taking part in the sport. After a cursory ban, against which they always appeal, they return to the sport – the penalty is lost earnings and sponsorships for a very short period of time. The punishment does not in my view fit the crime – and it is a crime, as well as grossly unfair!

The only success that is worthwhile it seems is making money, and as much as possible. Therefore, it does not really seem to matter how one achieves such success, and the behaviour of many members of the banking industry have been 'outstanding' in terms of illustrating this selfish and negative mind-set.

Our shared humanity and inner wealth should be what drives us, rather than allowing ourselves to be steamrollered into jumping onto the deviant bandwagon of materialism which has been shunted into the mainline of life. We need to encourage young people to burst the materialist bubble and discover their destiny. It is this quest to which we should surely devote all our energies, if we are to discover ourselves and find peace and happiness in our preciously short time on Earth. We must help children and adolescents identify their true substance and to rightly feel special. We should ask them how they would wish to be remembered and help them make their own unique mark on the World. They should look inward and not be distracted by what others do, or how they conduct themselves. We cannot and will not all be materially rich if this is defined by acquisition alone, but we can all become spiritually wealthy if we look inwards instead of outwards!

Society demands that schools reflect current values and norms, and looks dimly on those that seek to be different and truly educate – as opposed to condition – young people. Their soul occasionally fights back, demanding that it be listened to, so that its spiritual blueprint is fully understood and liberated. James Hillman rightly draws attention to the fact that many eminent people choose intuition over tuition. As he says: *"They quit school; they hated it; they wouldn't or couldn't learn; their teachers walked out on them; intuition at war with tuition."* In his book, he goes on to present some examples of such eminent people. Thomas Mann, who was awarded Nobel recognition largely for a novel in his early twenties, described school as 'stagnating and unsatisfactory'. Gandhi similarly reflected on his schooldays as being the most miserable years of his life, which if one considers his material welfare is a pretty damning indictment. The Nobel prize-winning physicist Richard Feynman called his early school 'an intellectual desert'. The brilliant John Lennon was expelled from kindergarten. In the case of Woody Allen, Hillman says:

> *"(He) demonstrated his abhorrence of school in some predictable ways. When he first attended school, he was placed in an accelerated class because of his high IQ, but since the strictures of the classroom did not allow him to express himself in his own way and to use his imagination in his lessons, he instead expressed himself by*

becoming a troublemaker.........he played hooky........he failed to do his homework. He was sometimes disruptive in class and rude to the teacher, who in turn lowered his grades for his behaviour." Doesn't that sound all too depressingly familiar?

He goes on to provide a timely warning to society:

> *"......we might one day vote into power a hero who wins a giant TV trivia contest and educate our children to believe that the Information Superhighway is the road to knowledge. If one clue to psychopathy is the trivial mind expressing itself in high-sounding phrases, then an education emphasising facts rather than thinking, patriotic, politically or religiously correct 'values' rather than critical judgment may produce a nation of achieving high school graduates who are also psychopaths."*

For those of you, like I was, who are not quite sure of the precise meaning of 'psychopath' it is someone who has serious, mental problems and who may act in a violent way without feeling sorry for what they have done. I can think of some recent and current political figures who display such behaviours in a very unambiguous way, not to mention mass killings in Norway, Colorado, and Columbine for unfortunate, and deeply distressing example.

It's Only a Matter of Time

When I interview teachers for a post in a school, one question that I always ask of them, usually towards the end of the selection process is, "What are you passionate about?" The reaction I get is mixed. Some people evidently become more than a little uncomfortable, even anxious about entering such emotive territory and ask what I mean, whereas others relish the question and answer with ease; although they sometimes feel the need to provide a shopping list of passions, which amounts to little more than those things in life that they like or care about. Others still, ask if I am referring to their passion at work or in their private life, as if true passion can be pigeon-holed in such a clinical or contextual way. My response to these candidates is simply to restate the question. Most people need to think before giving an answer, regardless of whether or not they have needed the question repeating.

I am often asked by candidates in de-briefing sessions, what the 'correct answer' is to that question – the teachers' obsession with knowing the right answer to everything. The truth is that there is no one, correct answer to such a personally probing question. All I want to see is some real passion in their lives……..and, sadly, I rarely see it. Yes, I get an answer, or answers, but there is rarely any spontaneity in what they say, which belies their true passion to some extent. In all honesty, I would prefer not to work with anyone who is not passionate about something. The actual passion is largely irrelevant, but a real love or quest for something should lie at the heart – or in the soul – of every person alive. Something that drives them, something that transcends mere existence and self, and explains why they live! True passion is almost like a raison d'être, underlying every breath we take – waking or sleeping. Such passion cannot be confined to a particular context, as if it could be switched on and off at will. It explains the essence of one's being, very often in a hidden and unconscious way. Hillman puts it more productively when he says:

"Passion is probably more predictive of capacity and productive of motivation than other usual benchmarks."

Another reason why I ask that question, which is probably more informing than what has gone before, is that I was once asked the very same question when I went for a job at a Higher Education institution. My response was akin to a reflex, but not impulsive. I immediately said, "Injustice!" I thought nothing of that fact at the time, but when reflecting upon it sometime later, I said to myself, "What a good question that was!" **Why?** Because it triggered what turned out to be a second, albeit parallel, interview in effect. It was as if it aroused something lying dormant in those who were on the selection panel and who, thus far, had been going through the motions of interviewing in terms of not really getting to the core of what it was that drove the candidates. To that point, the value that drove me had been invisible to me in such a stark, clear and concise way. It did a lot to explain my past behaviours and even more to inform my future actions. I dream of a world where there are no unhelpful and inhibiting constructs between people of different race, religion, sexual inclination, age and colour that form barriers to mutual co-existence, and prevent us from recognising and celebrating our common humanity. Education is surely the key to such a life, but it is as if we are all too busy or pre-occupied in playing other people's games and chasing material dreams, that we have no *time* to explore the spiritual reality of ourselves and others.

When I learnt Accounting, we were told that one's gross income was the money we received in return for our labours, but that net income was that which was left after all statutory deductions had been levied – such as income tax, social security and pension contributions, for example. This net income is seen by economists as a person's *disposable* income – that is, the income left over for them to allocate or dispose of as they wish. Such a notion is, of course, largely mythical given the fact that when various authorities have had their share of the monetary fruits of my labour, I am still obliged to allocate my hard-earned income to those things that are deemed essential to our institutionalised existence. I refer of course to such things as mortgage payments or rent on property, life assurance, car insurance, car tax, car servicing and running costs; plus food and entertainment, credit card repayments, council tax, utility charges for gas, electricity and water, as well as the telephone.............so the list of institutionally produced goods and services goes on.

After all these 'essentials' of our existence have been paid, the residue is really what constitutes the income that we are truly free to spend as we wish – let's call it *discretionary* income. The interesting question of course, is how much is our discretionary income that we can use as we think fit? I would suggest that for most people it is either zero, or even a negative figure which requires borrowing and access to various forms of credit to sustain – thereby increasing the amount that eats into our disposable income in future time periods. I also feel that the same logic applies, with perhaps more significance to the way we live our lives – our life-time!

As all mortal creatures know only too well, there are only 24 hours in every day, which, for argument's sake we can call our **gross time**. After we have had enough sleep to recharge our batteries, we are left with what we might see as our **net time** – say, somewhere between 16 and 18 hours each day – which economists would doubtlessly be tempted to call our **disposable time**. Again, however, we are not truly free to spend this time as we would ideally wish because other things get in the way. One such time bandit is called 'work', where those who are lucky enough to have paid employment seem to spend increasing amounts of time, just to make ends meet. Whether you work 8 or 12 hours a day, by the time this significant slice of time has been deducted from your disposable time, how much are you actually left with? Of course, if you are one of those lucky individuals who profess that they genuinely enjoy their work this deduction is less of a cost, but a cost it surely is. The rest then – anything from 4 to 10 hours – is ours to dispose of as we would wish? Well no. We also have to spend time getting washed, dressed and fed for work, as well as effectively waste a similar amount of time at the end of the working day. We also lose the amount of time we spend commuting to and from work, taking the children to and from school, shopping for food, cooking and eating it, keeping the house clean and tidy, and so on.

Once we have undertaken all these chores, how much time out of our supposedly disposable time can we truly view as being our **discretionary time** – the time that we have only for ourselves? Again, I would suggest that for most people it equals zero, or a minimal amount of time when we are so tired that we can hardly drag ourselves away from the television, let alone do anything worthwhile. In fact for many of us we have negative discretionary time, expressed in terms of those things we needed to do today but that we were too tired or short of time or motivation to complete. These things get put off until that convenient 'tomorrow'!

This notional discretionary time is of vital importance, however, for it is when you actually live *your* life! The treadmill which demands ever more money and time leaves us with either no time, or no inclination, to live – we are just existing, or living a manufactured life – a virtual life! I wonder if people lie on their death bed and ask themselves the question, "Was that it?" or, "What did I really achieve?" and, "What was the point of it all?" I hope that I do not find myself asking such final waking questions, but I have a feeling that I will!

I want to make a mark, to go out with a real legacy and not to tamely or meekly shuffle off this mortal coil, or spend eternity merely pushing up the daisies. I have more life to live, and more dreams to fulfil before I die!

Section B: A Curriculum

Chapter Five: The Content of the Curriculum

I referred earlier to how during my four years of specialist training to become a teacher, I do not recall any serious attempt to explain to me, as an aspiring professional teacher, what the overall purpose of schools was supposed to be. I was, however, encouraged to study the history, psychology, philosophy and sociology of education as well as how to become a competent teacher of some of the subject matter in the discipline of Economics. But, I did not ask the key question about **why** are we all doing this and, given the nature of my own schooling, who can really have expected me to ask? That investigative question of genuine curiosity had been long-since suppressed, if not entirely extinguished. The purpose of the whole endeavour, to which I would soon become a part, was simply assumed, as far as I could tell.

I do vaguely remember talking about the school curriculum, and all it really meant to me at that time was a collection of traditionally taught, largely academic subjects, plus a few 'newer' ones such as Economics. My job was to more or less simply slot in to a school and do my job in my specialist area to the best of my ability. I do not really recall any serious attempt to define the curriculum, or to analyse its content and the way in which it could be effectively delivered in practice. That was to wait until I was lucky enough to study for my Master's Degree in my chosen field of study, 'Curriculum Analysis and Design."

When I started teaching, the school curriculum didn't seem very much different to the one I had followed at school – a diet of mainly academic subjects, such as English, Mathematics, Biology, Chemistry and Physics; French, Geography and History, and so on. Additionally, there was a little bit of time allocated to more practical subjects with Woodwork and Metalwork, for us tough and rugged lads, and Cookery and Needlework for the more dainty gals. Then, of course, there was the vital importance of P.E. and Games, which were almost always competitive in nature. It was just the way it was, and the way it had been for a long time. Moreover, to create enough time for depth of study after the age of fourteen years, as well as to fit in all the new subjects that someone somewhere had decided students should be offered, children were presented with a series of option blocks, and required to choose one subject from each grouping – the infamous options! This inevitably led to certain combinations of subjects being impossible to study due to the tortuous constraints involved in timetabling.

More worryingly, it led to many students choosing a range of subjects that excluded whole areas of experience. Different students were following different subjects, so how on Earth could anyone ensure the delivery of a coherent, progressive and continuous curriculum entitlement from 11 to 16/18 for every individual learner? They couldn't and they didn't – simple!

This premature specialisation in terms of their essentially academic diet was exacerbated at the age of 16 years, when the demand for even more specialised study to determine the lucky minority who would qualify for a university place, led to students following not eight to ten subjects, but only three – or four for the really brainy ones, or 'swots' as they were known then. (Today, they are called 'boffs' – unless that term has also fallen victim to the fad of fashion change.)

Furthermore, the only realistic options for students approaching school post-16, had to be taken from the limited selection that they had chosen to follow, often for reasons that were little if anything to do with receiving a 'rounded education', whatever that was. How were students to decide on the correct choices to make at 14 and 16 years of age? Were they to make an informed choice? If so, what was to inform the selection process – personal interest, past successes and failures, the subjects that friends in their peer group were choosing, parental diktat, favourite and/or feared teachers, teacher pressure, or future careers (assuming these were known let alone definite)?

This educational lunacy went on for years, and essentially still does under the British system of education, with only minor modifications which have amounted once again to little more than tinkering around the periphery. In any case, these modest changes were usually prompted by administrative reasons like constructing a workable timetable, rather than the true educational needs of young learners. There was little in the way of structural change. So, I ask again, what was the curricular entitlement of young people and, if there was one, could it be assuredly delivered in the context of such administrative pre-eminence and complexity?

A good starting point is to consider what do we really mean by 'the school curriculum' and to revisit what should be the real purpose of schooling. Taking the first point first, according to the dictionary which supposedly mirrors current meanings of words the term is best defined as, ***"All the different courses of study that are taught in a school, college or university."*** This is a somewhat circular point of view if one thinks about it. How do all subjects contribute to a curriculum entitlement for young people? Answer: By teaching lots of different subjects.

I don't find this particularly helpful or acceptable, in trying to understand what the curriculum really is because it is surely a partial definition which fails to include so much of what I learnt at school. Some examples of these non-subject curriculum experiences are listed below:

- ✓ How to have a cigarette (we used to call it a 'fag' but, given that I was at a boarding school, such a term would be at best ambiguous and at worst erroneous) without being caught. This generated considerable innovative flair and creativity – especially after the bruising incentive of several beatings. Also……

- ✓ How to turn a demeaning event like being beaten with a cane or slipper, into a macho opportunity – which mainly involves not crying and a sustained show of bravura afterwards, when the welts turn from a greenish-yellow into a blue-black stain on the buttocks, in a pattern that any tie-dying, t-shirt designer would have been proud of.

- ✓ How to develop strategies to avoid being identified as someone who doesn't know the answer to a question posed in class – which, for me, was most of the time.

- ✓ How to make it look like I was listening and being highly attentive, even though I was usually bored stiff, and my mind wanted to drift off to somewhere else, far away.

- ✓ How to attract the teacher's attention when I <u>did</u> know the answer to a question posed in class – which used to seem as likely as discovering a mafia cache of rocking-horse droppings.

- ✓ How school was a dull, intimidating and demeaning experience – and how the forceful imposition of authority can be a very effective tool to gain and hang on to power.
- ✓ Certain areas of the school were places that I was not allowed to enter without express permission. The inner sanctum of the staffroom for example, or the 'fuehrer-bunker' as we called the-Head's study (note it was never called just an office in those days), were strictly out-of-bounds. Whose school was it anyway? It certainly wasn't mine!
- ✓ How the only effective and lasting form of discipline is self-discipline.

I could go on and on, of course – I am a teacher after all – but I think you get my point. It might be an interesting exercise for you to consider the many things that you learnt or experienced at school, which did not find themselves given the formality of a discrete subject in the 'curriculum'. These are the very, hidden messages that schools communicate so powerfully, but usually unconsciously, to the students and staff that belong to that community of people.

The reality is that the school curriculum is not what is taught, but what is learnt by students and staff. It is not simply that which is planned and intended; it is also that which is unplanned, incidental or even accidental and happens by chance. Any true curriculum entitlement cannot, and must not be oblivious to the explicit, hidden messages that are so easily and effectively transmitted, and more readily, easily and effectively learnt. To consider only the overt and easily identified messages in the school curriculum is to miss those that we inadvertently send by the way we structure, deliver and assess each child's experience. Just like our body language, not only can these hidden messages of the curriculum so easily contradict the messages we make consciously and intentionally, but they are also the ones that will be learnt and remembered.

Let me give you two simple examples, one of interesting contrast from my time as a student, and the other from when I was a Deputy Head responsible for curriculum development.

The Real and Personal Messages from Schooling

At my single-sex boarding school, I do believe that my teachers were a caring and conscientious collection of individuals, who were undoubtedly seeking to help create future citizens that would be: constructive, courteous, independent; caring, tolerant and respected, for example. These fine aims, however, were contradicted by the frequent use of physical violence by authority figures to impose their will, or the school rules; countered by a rigid system of control and time scheduling that meant that every waking hour was filled with some pre-determined activity. At least I got to dream a little when I went to bed – and that time was determined for me as well.

I was hardly encouraged to appreciate tolerance, respect, and courtesy, when most teachers sought to highlight my weaknesses rather than my strengths, my many failures rather than the less common successes. I was quickly told when I was wrong, or in the wrong, but hardly ever identified as being right, or in the right. That is hardly surprising, given that I spent most of my time trying to avoid being made to look stupid and foolish. I am sure that my contemporaries, who were more academically able than me, felt the same way, but on balance they were rarely wrong and felt safe in their knowledge. I felt vulnerable in my ignorance – hence the strategies I adopted to reduce the occasions where that vulnerability would be exposed very publicly. The teachers that I recall with great affection and a sense of love even, were those who displayed similar qualities in their dealings with students in general, and me, in particular. They were the 'good' teachers; the ones where I not only learnt what they wanted me to learn, but were without exception teachers of the subjects that I enjoyed the most, and in which I went on to be relatively more successful in terms of examination grades.

At the age of sixteen years, as I have already mentioned, I went from boarding school, where I took my GCE 'O' Levels, to the local technical college where I was to follow 'A' Levels – in a very loose sense of the word 'follow'. It was a truly laissez-faire experience, with attendance, attention, homework and the like all optional. There were very few rules and very little that I could not do. The way this experience contrasted to the previous four years was truly sensational. It was great! It was fun! It was great fun!

There was a downside, of course. There was no compensatory system for guiding us into more beneficial and less transient, hedonistic pursuits, not to mention sheer bone-idleness. Those who chose not to work did not learn that much of what was planned and taught although, as I have already mentioned, I did lose my virginity, and I can honestly say that that experience had been intended, and occasionally planned but not executed, for many frustrating years before. The difference being that it was **my** intent and not someone else's – actually, that isn't totally accurate or true, but that is another story!

The serious point I wish to make though is that the laissez-faire approach was not in my best interests either. I needed more structure and guidance. Of course, the tutors at the technical college were caring and professional individuals who wanted us all to learn self-discipline, self-study and self-reliance, but the hidden message I really got from this admirable approach was that they didn't care about me and so why should I? The reality was that for someone fresh out of a naval-run boarding school to be plunged straight into an environment of self-determination was probably more likely, if not destined to be, unsuccessful.

Please understand, that my innate survival instincts meant that I found many things to enjoy about school and learning, and I did learn a lot. I was not totally unhappy at school. My point is that the things that I learned – that I took away from the whole compulsory experience – were those like the power of teamwork, friendship and sticking together in a tight spot, and not the things I was formally and intentionally taught!

Similarly, I learnt little of lasting use to me at technical college, but it was a blast – growing my hair from the school, 'basin-bowl' look to the more fashionable and appealing style of long and hairy, getting involved with minor drugs, rarely anything more dangerous – or experimental and recreational, to use a little linguistic garnish – than marijuana. I quickly learnt to play the drums, which was not easy as a left- handed, budding musician, and quickly found myself in a rock band, which was immeasurably good for my self-confidence and esteem.

I do feel it is important to emphasise the fact that academic study presented in an optional manner at technical college could not possibly compete with the extra-curricular joy of those days, which I was able to continue during four years at teachers' training college – although to a much more modest and balanced degree.

There are two powerful lessons that I learnt from this, which have become more apparent as I have grown older and, arguably, wiser. The first is that for the first time I really lived life to the full. Yes, it was full of teenage strife involving clashes with my parents over my life-style and lack of scholastic endeavour, but it was the time in my life when I truly felt a vibrancy and a sense of urgency in my life, which has become increasingly elusive ever since, as if it had been bleeding away imperceptibly slowly, whilst my mind was dominated with getting up to speed and jumping onto the ever-accelerating treadmill of working and adult life.

The second key lesson learned from my time in tertiary education is that I was a lucky boy! I eventually got yet another opportunity, thanks to resilient and proud parents, as well as a system of state-sponsored student grants – a ladder of opportunity which governments have systematically withdrawn for the generations that followed me. I had finally found my feet in the world, and could make sense of that which I had been through since the age of twelve years. I had found a way to make my mark, to realise that I was actually good at something. My self-esteem and self-confidence was established and that has grown steadily as I have enjoyed success and failure in my life since those wonderful days. It was a lesson that I learned all by myself, taught by force of circumstance and the trial and error of my life experiences at boarding school and technical college. Where I was immensely fortunate was in the number of chances I got to fall down and 'fail' (or was it 'learn') before finding a sense of identity and worth. School did little to help me in that respect. In fact I honestly think it retarded my development – I could have got started much earlier had those intervening years not been so barren and sparsely productive. When I got to teachers' training college, I found myself in an environment that offered me a quite carefully structured environment, but with the opportunity and encouragement to flourish – this time by striking a more mature and equitable balance between work and play, in its various forms and manifestations.

Teacher training was a more structured environment than would have been the case at university, and I was fortunate to fall under the magic that was Alun Roberts, as well as a handful of other tutors like Jim Turnbull and Don Ward, who really believed in me. Those four years also gave me the opportunity to continue my artistic expression and enjoyment. Within a few weeks, I was in another rock band, although this time it was only a relatively temporary diversion.

In order to cope with the blows to my self-esteem whilst at school, I had developed a skill to recall and tell jokes and to make people laugh – my eternal thanks to the power of comedy. It was also a talent which my father displayed with considerable skill – he was a great story-teller. I learnt so much from him and have the same affinity for meeting and getting to know people from all walks of life!

My joke-telling had been a fortuitous and useful survival skill, but it was to become much more than that. Later, in my first year of teacher training, this skill was recognised when I was asked to be the compere for the annual staff, student variety show; a major event performed in front of packed audiences on three consecutive nights, which also served to raise considerable sums for charity. I can vividly recall the way in which I agreed to do it, without a moment's hesitation, as if my spirit was speaking for me, saying, "This is what you have been waiting for!"

I had been starved and deprived of opportunities to experience, let alone excel, in creative and artistic pursuits whilst at school. No drama lessons and no music lessons. I joined the school military, marching band, because I wanted to play the side-drum – but then, so did everyone.....because they were teenagers! The band-master diverted me by noting that my "good teeth" made me a perfect specimen for playing 3rd cornet, and what a short-lived experience that was. Instead of having a lot of side drummers and selecting the best to play in the band, or rotating them (not literally), he pushed me to take up an instrument that was really not for me, and playing 3rd cornet involved playing

93

the odd note here and there, as if to fill in the gaps left by those who played first and second cornet – relegated and bored again!

At boarding school I could excel in one artistic pursuit and that was an inter-house, extra-curricular 'Prose and Verse Competition'. This involved reading a passage of prose and some well-chosen poetry to a panel of judges with style, clarity and meaning…...no mean feat given a lot of the poetry that I was given to read. I won it three years in a row, and was rewarded with a book at the annual prize-giving ceremony, or 'Speech Day' as it was known. One meagre opportunity to show my true calling perhaps – what a pity it was only an annual event, held on one autumnal afternoon each year. Technical college allowed me to experience more creative and artistic success as a rock drummer – but sadly, it was again only as an extra-curricular pursuit, but one that was not limited to just once a year. My studies inevitably suffered.

At teachers' training college, it all came together, with my success in the variety show leading to lead roles in college drama productions which were also staged in places like local secondary schools and on 'The Fringe' at the Edinburgh International Festival. Such valuable and important experiences were always a bit of a side-show to the main purpose of my formal education – to achieve academic success. My creative and artistic talents were eventually given a chance to show themselves and be recognised, but always as something that was an add-on or a barely-tolerated digression to the primary aim of examination success in the really important subjects, which had held sway for over a century, although I did just manage to escape any exposure to Latin – just!

I often wonder how my life might have been more successful if I had been able to encounter artistic and creative activities earlier, and as 'subjects' on the formal, taught curriculum, rather than as extra-curricular pursuits.

I often wonder how my life might have been more successful if I had been able to choose my own prose and poetry to read, and instruments to play. I wanted to play the drums; an instrument that caters well for those who like me, are blessed with short, stubby, banana-like fingers. The band-master innocently sent me up a blind alley, and he was not the only one. Before that my parents had done the right middle-class thing and bought an upright piano and sent me for piano lessons. I think I had expressed a desire to play music, but had not had any significant exposure to a sufficient range of instruments in order to make an informed choice of my own.

My maternal grand-father had also been a concert pianist and enjoyed a career in show-business, so there may have been that legacy that led to me suffering the piano, or should I say, "the piano suffering me"!. The fact that I had not chosen to learn how to play the piano was not helped by the dull, boring and simple tunes to which my music teacher gave me grumpy exposure. As an elderly spinster with a very austere disposition, who lived in the same village as my family, she hardly infected me with the musical possibilities that playing a piano can doubtlessly provide. Again, I was the passive victim of choices made by others about what was 'right' for me.

It was not very long at all until I started playing truant from my after-school piano lessons and using the money my parents gave me, to pay for the torture, to buy cigarettes instead. I would sit in a field and light up, enjoying the forbidden pleasure of nicotine until I was expected home again. My music teacher's name was Miss Mogg. (Sometimes names just say it all, don't they?)

Why do middle-class parents always want, almost pressurise, their offspring to play the piano or violin, or some other orchestral instrument, playing classical pieces of music which, splendid though they may be, especially when played well, are not really of the here and now in the lives of young people. Schools still allow this middle-class, adult obsession to stifle the creative talents of many teenagers who would far rather choose an instrument like the electric guitar or drums to play, and who want to make the sounds of their own era and not some bygone age when men wore wigs instead of growing their own hair. Why not let young people get 'turned on' to the joys of creating and listening to music by experiencing an instrument, or instruments, of their choice and performing pieces that they want to play, if not create their own sound. Famous rock bands like Queen, and Emerson, Lake and Palmer, to name but two, composed and performed music that was inspired by classical musicians and their works. Teenagers would do far better if allowed to find their own way into classical music rather than having it rammed down their throats – or under their chin – like so much else.

The importance of creative and expressive learning experiences in the formal school curriculum are massively and dangerously under-estimated. This is why they are almost always extra-curricular in nature, or considered low status subjects in any traditional 'options block'. In a later chapter in this section of the book, I shall argue my case for these creative learning experiences to represent the **core** element of a national curriculum, if there has to be one. They are just as important, if not far and away more crucial, than Science, Mathematics and English which enjoy favoured status in the formal curriculum entitlement that most schools offer.

One Real Message in Schooling

The second example of contradictory hidden messages overpowering the intended aims of schooling arose when I had lead responsibility for developing the curriculum at a secondary school. Its roots lie in the tensions that have customarily arisen between the traditional, academic subject-based curriculum and an acknowledgement that it alone does not meet the wider personal and social development needs of young people. Over the years that I have been in education – on the delivery side – this has led to repeated attempts to introduce another subject of sorts into the school curriculum and the educational entitlement of young people. This new 'subject' has been called such things as civics, life skills and general studies, as well as PSE and more lately PSHE. This has often been alongside or instead of a range of cross-curricular themes, dimensions and core skills, such as economic awareness, health education, careers education and guidance; environmental education, work related teaching and learning and sex education programmes – all of which, teachers are supposed to skilfully weave into the subject curriculum – without, of course, diminishing or watering-down those overly-secure and precious academic standards.

The reason why personal and social education has undergone so many renaissances, re-births and re-formulations, under the guise of different names and acronyms, is indicative of a major malaise in the content and delivery of the traditional school curriculum. The fundamental problem is that it is as welcome as an educational bad odour in an academic spacesuit – it is simply not regarded as important and is, therefore, treated as an intruder which is, of course, utterly ridiculous.

Many teachers did not want to teach it, seeing it as almost an affront to their professionalism to be asked to take a teaching role in this alien territory. Some of the excuses that I have heard are:

"I am a history teacher, not a PSE teacher."

"I have not been trained to teach it."

"There are more important things to teach."

"It's a waste of time."

"It is not an examinable subject."

Such protestations were truly shocking to me as a professional educator. As a Deputy Head Teacher, responsible for the development and delivery of this curricular component I was frequently asked to justify the inclusion of PSE as a worthwhile endeavour. I was amazed! As a teacher, I would see the personal and social education of young people as one fundamental aim of schooling and, as such, I felt perfectly entitled to simply reflect such a challenge back to the reluctant teachers in question. So I would ask them to explain how the 'content-partial' History syllabus contributed to the personal and social development of the students – something that they always struggled to do, without relying on the fact that it had always been the case. Not a very satisfactory, nor a very scholarly reply, in my view.

Surely, secondary school teachers should be trained to teach children and young people first and foremost, rather than see the delivery of a narrow, pre-determined subject as their primary, if not ultimate, aim. Why should such an important topic be sidelined simply because it is not examinable? The only way to make it worthy of inclusion and equal status in the school curriculum would be to make it an examinable subject, but then it is not sufficiently academic to merit such an accolade, is it?

The hostility of teachers who had to teach PSE contributed to the negative attitude that students felt towards attending such lessons. Staff who needed students to do other things would often ask that they be excused the occasional PSE lessons. After all, it would be the ultimate sacrilege to expect them to take the time from any academic subject, mainly because they are examinable. Such action would be very much the last resort, if not unthinkable. Students would pick up on a battery of negative, and not always that hidden, messages from teachers who taught PSE. This, and the fact that they too were already conditioned into seeing academe as the only worthy use of their time, led to students saying that PSE was boring and that it was not an examination subject. Therefore, it detracted from their need to amass qualifications to get to the next stage of their 'education'.

To be fair, other non-, or less-academic elements of the secondary school curriculum have also been casualties of the pre-eminence of academe – such as P.E., and the creative and expressive arts. Teachers would fight tooth and nail to stop their students missing class in order to rehearse for the school play or musical, or to represent their school in a sporting competition. Their negative or indifferent attitude to PSE and the like can be largely explained in the same way as why my lecturers at Hull did not really ever address or talk about the overall purpose of schooling and the curriculum. Those teachers and lecturers are also products – or victims – of their own schooling and formal education. They too only ever followed a compartmentalised curriculum entitlement; one that was a seemingly random collection of subjects in elite, specialist areas – no one really sought to explicitly pull it all together for them either.

To expect schools to effectively deliver such non-academic experiences for students is grossly unreasonable, as it is the system that inadvertently militates against the successful delivery, let alone integration, of such areas of learning. If we want to effectively educate young people, we need to drastically change the educational system. Otherwise, all such educational initiatives are bound to falter sooner or later if, indeed, they do not simply hit the resistance of an ingrained institutionalised brick wall. Yet again, mankind is expending a great deal of time, effort and money on tackling the symptoms of a particular problem without recognising the need to address the underlying, often hidden causes that will always win out!

Curriculum Inertia – Moving With the Times?

Although I have already referred to the irrelevance of the school curriculum in seeking to prepare young people for adult and working life, let us for now just accept that this stated aim is indeed genuine. How far does the subject-based, academic school curriculum set about achieving this? The answer is again by tinkering at the periphery with cross-curricular themes, dimensions and skills, or demanding a return to an educational dichotomy whereby a minority of students are selected to receive a rigorous academic diet, to fit them for the professions, armed services or politics, and the sizeable rest to be given a more vocational school experience, to prepare them for more industrial white and blue-collar occupations. This can be done, by turning the clock back to the so-called 'golden age' of grammar and secondary modern schools – or horses for courses – or even both together in one school or institution.

The better and more favoured approach of adopting a balanced diet of academic and vocational learning experiences for all students – which the whole of the educational profession as well as the Confederation of British Industry and Trades Union Congress have repeatedly called for – is over-ruled by weak Prime Ministers who are terrified of upsetting the middle class parents who would see such an approach as watering down academic standards. The truth is that academic standards would be raised, as the more academically able would be encouraged and enabled to relate and apply their knowledge in real, practical and concrete ways and contexts, which would enhance their understanding as well as their employability as post-graduates.

Let us look back in time for a moment, and examine the essential structure and content of the academic school curriculum, when apart from mass instruction and indoctrination in Church Schools, where wicked and evil left-handed children were forced to convert to the world of '**Right**eousness', the only people who received any form of schooling were those 'lucky' enough to be able to afford to attend an independent or public school (a perverse title for one that prohibited entry by the public). These elite students were the children of the privileged classes or landed gentry, along with the rougher members of the burgeoning middle-class who had made their wealth in the mills and mines – often by sending other people's children into and down them!

99

Such schools followed a traditional academic, subject-based curriculum which served the interests of the few universities that existed at that time nicely, thank you! What is interesting, however, is that if one compares the list of subjects that were included, say in the school curriculum of 1890 and that of an everyday comprehensive or independent school in 2008, one would find very little to actually distinguish one from the other. The methods may have changed somewhat, but the overall goal has remained solidly and immovably in place ever since.

"So what?" you may be inclined to say, but the truth is that, although the formal school curriculum has not changed very much at all, except perhaps for the loss of Latin and Classics, the World has changed beyond all recognition since those days. Consequently, I feel justified in asking whether such an antiquated and crusty concept can possibly be expected to prepare young people adequately for adult and working life, even if that was a laudable and relevant aim in the first place.

More importantly, the greatest change in the World has occurred in the last fifty years; a time when a frightening number of students in secondary schools have become disillusioned and disaffected with what secondary school professes to be doing for, or to them! This could be a mere coincidence, especially if one accepts that changes in our capitalist and materialist society, which are fragmenting, divisive and inequitable, have certainly contributed to the seeping and spreading malaise of dislocation, social disaffection and moral decline.

Moreover, the traditional, subject-based, academic curriculum is overwhelmingly focused on the acquisition of knowledge rather than the emphasis upon the development of skills over time so that young people can discover their own knowledge. This content-laden syllabus is necessarily partial, and this bias – however unintentional – is unlikely to be relevant to the global society that young people inhabit in the here and now, let alone the future.

Knowledge has exploded immensely, and access and exposure to it has been similarly expanded through information technologies such as the internet. The students are rarely, if ever, involved in choosing the content of the subjects that they are obliged to follow; instead this is largely or completely chosen for them by the examination boards, with emphasis upon the past – we keep doing things very much the same way, with minor changes in methodology to make the experience marginally more student-centred and less didactic. But, the reality is that the dominance of partial subject knowledge, much of it spurious and irrelevant, and which has to be delivered in a short period of time, creates a sense of urgency on the part of teachers and students alike, in their desperate attempt to 'get through' the syllabus (which again implies that there is an end to learning). This lack of radical change in the way we structure and view teaching and learning makes a mockery of any serious desire or attempt to follow a more skills-based curriculum.

The clock is against the teacher and the students, as the content largely determines the contexts in which the skills should be applied and developed, assuming that there is even one at all. Hence teachers and students are inevitably pressured into 'getting through the syllabus' in time for the final examination. This is aggravated, of course, by the introduction of ridiculous league tables showing how different schools compare in their attempts to encourage students to jump through the academic hoops that are thrust in front of them.

Everyone is preoccupied with ends and not means, with cramming their minds with facts and figures, knowledge and information, to cover all the bases. League tables set school against school without taking any account of the intake of those schools, in terms of the ability and prior successes of the students they admit. This notion of competition as the best way of achieving any meaningful outcome or success is fundamentally flawed, particularly as we make no serious attempt to create a true meritocracy, which gives every young person an equal opportunity to show their undoubted and unique potential. I wish to return to these issues of equality of opportunity, meritocracy and how we assess student success in later sections of this book.

It is the way that content is allowed to dominate the syllabus that serves to pervert and distort the true learning of young people, especially but not exclusively for adolescents, as they try to establish their own identities and

101

discover their calling or reason for being in a world where they are treated with ambiguity and apparent indifference. The only time society concerns itself with their real and genuine needs is when the rabid and right-wing press or similarly prejudiced politicians stir up the concerns of the middle classes with headlines of teenage gang warfare, vandalism and other signs of their hardly surprising maladjustment. We really should question the wisdom of allowing our press and a major political party to be run and controlled by people whose parents **bought** their schooling!

If we are really serious in our desire to help children adjust, so that they can make sense of their lives in the here and now, then let us address it in a positive, unambiguous and meaningful way – and let it be meaningful to **them** and not to us. Let us not simply bemoan and punish the symptoms of our failure to help them do so. This further alienates young people, especially those who are also hugely and adversely challenged by the pressures of social and marital breakdown and deprivation, which hampers their life chances. Let us help them meet these challenges head on – the challenges they face now – and then they will be better equipped to meet the challenges that the future will inevitably throw at them.

But instead, we persist in basing the curriculum upon the acquisition of knowledge at the expense of skills – the skill to learn, for example – by selecting the content which will form the syllabus. Then the pressure of completing the syllabus, combined with the sole, myopic focus on examination success, which league tables serve to further promote, sends the hidden message to students that if they master what is on the syllabus then they have learnt 'all that they need to know' – but the truth is they haven't often actually started. You even hear them say this now in schools. When a teacher seeks to broaden their horizons and understanding by discussing a particular topic, they will often enquire, "Is this on the syllabus?" The honest (in its strictest and narrowest sense) teacher will say, "No," to which the student will say, "Well I don't need to know it then!" When I have heard that from a young person, every fibre of my being wants to scream out, **"Yes you do!"** I want them to question, challenge and query everything and to extend their knowledge through critical curiosity – but it is too late, the damage has largely already been done, and a long time ago, by the school 'sausage machine'.

I used to feel the same way as they do now, but these days I want to awaken within them the thrill, the joy and pleasure that can be gained from lifelong learning – the learning of anything new and relevant to help 'me' understand not only the World we live in, but also to help them understand themselves in relation to it. All schools profess to want to develop life-long learners, but the system militates against this worthy aim.

The selection of the content that any learning must incorporate is, therefore, of utmost importance if we are to avoid charges on indoctrination. After all, you cannot learn skills in a vacuum; the process of doing must include something, in much the same way as you cannot just have lunch without some food on your plate. It is in this area of content selection that I have considerable fears.

Those who select content will be forced to rely on either traditional orthodoxy (so no change there) or on their own views regarding that which it is worthwhile to learn, and to learn about. This is often driven by asking ourselves **_what_** it is that we feel young people should know. I am not sure that the issue of **_why_** young people should know it is ever seriously entertained at all. Such selection is necessarily driven by the values and beliefs of those who select – values which unconsciously will govern our behaviour and actions, even though we may consciously try to resist them. True objectivity is not possible, and so the values of a select few, who are allowed to make the decision for generations of young people, will by definition guide the selection of the content. Why not let students themselves choose the content, and let **their** core values explore and make sense of the world in which they live. After all, indoctrination can occur not only through the content that we include, but also because of the mass of information that is necessarily omitted!

Sometimes, the selection of content is rigged from the start – in other words with political intent – hence the perpetual torrent of government initiatives requiring schools to do this and not do that, and even telling them how they should do it – so much for professional integrity and judgement. I can also refer to a very significant event of political values being allowed to shape the content selected for students to learn. In view of the fact that it still rankles with me, I feel impelled to recount it here.

The 'Right' Content

During the reign of Margaret Thatcher, her Secretary of State for Education, Kenneth Clarke, commissioned a thorough review and re-write of the GCE Advanced Level syllabus for Economics that all examination groups would then be obliged to follow. To undertake this review, and to make it a more manageable task, three separate groups were formed – one to look at the content of what should be taught, one to consider the methodology of how to teach it, and another to examine issues of assessment.

At that time, I was working as a Local Education Authority (LEA) Adviser, with a wide-ranging brief which also included responsibility for helping schools with the delivery of economic awareness and business education within the curriculum. One day, a telephone call from a Professor of Economics who I knew well in a professional capacity, made me aware of this initiative, when he asked me if I could join the 'Content' review group, of which he was the Chairperson, as his adviser. I was flattered that he thought to ask me of all teachers of Economics and I happily agreed. As soon as I accepted, he then gave me the reason why he felt he needed me to assist on the group.

The group was quite large in number, with academic economists making up all but one member. This sole, isolated figure was a teacher of Economics, who just happened to work within the same LEA as me. The problem was that this one practising teacher had a view very much at odds to the rest of the group about how the content should be chosen – after all, here was a golden opportunity to change the Economics syllabus to make it more challenging, relevant and interesting, as he saw it, to students studying for 'A' Level. I was there to provide a counter-balance to his apparently radical views.

In the interests of fairness and being prepared for the first meeting which I was to attend, I arranged to meet this 'renegade' teacher at his school to see the work of his Department and also to find out what his perspective was on this issue. He explained that all the university academics on the panel all represented one school of Economic thought – namely, 'neo-classical' in their view of the subject matter. He felt, rightly in my opinion, that this was a somewhat biased approach, given that there were many other schools of thought, with differing perspectives of economic issues and policy-making. Without wishing to stray into specialist territory, these schools of thought, such as the neo-Keynesian, neo-Ricardian, Hayekian and Radical (Marxist) all hold sometimes very different views about how the economy functions and the causes of intractable problems such as inflation and unemployment and, therefore, the best way of tackling and resolving them, for example.

The errant teacher felt that the best way of 'educating' as opposed to 'schooling' (in more than one sense of the word) students of Economics at such a crucial stage in their lives, would be to adopt a *multi-perspective approach* rather than focus the content on a single perspective, and particularly one that was claimed to inform the economic decision-making of a particularly dogmatic, inflexible and entrenched Conservative Party.

In this way, young people would be encouraged to take an issue, such as unemployment, and examine the differing perspectives about its causes and possible solutions, taking due account of evidence and logical thought. After all, John Maynard Keynes said that Economics was not 'a doctrine immediately applicable to policy; rather it was a technique of thinking, an apparatus of the mind that enables the possessor to draw correct conclusions'.

By taking different views of difficult and highly relevant topics such as unemployment, students would be enabled to judge the merits and demerits of each argument and form their own view of the issue, such as one based on their own interpretation of the evidence available. In such a way, maybe one of them would go on to provide a new and more effective set of solutions for governments to adopt that would lead to making the lives of the unemployed, and society as a whole, so much better. This is in the spirit of Albert Einstein's suggestion that to solve today's problems, we need to adopt different methods of thinking than those that created the problems in the first place.

I duly attended the meeting and, contrary to the reasons for my invitation, supported the teacher's contention that a multi-perspective approach would be a good way forward. We were then both branded as radical – radical because we could not support a biased traditional orthodoxy that represented a dominant political view at the expense of all other perspectives that students could examine, analyse and evaluate. To let students decide, by seeking to present all points of view for them to study and consider, is the antithesis of indoctrination.

Needless to say, I was not invited back to any further meetings in an advisory capacity, because my advice did not match the way that everyone was going to go – wrongly, I felt – and this is still my view today. As I left the meeting, two key members of the Economics Association, who had been unusually quiet during the meeting, took me to one side and kindly pointed out that if we were to go the multi-perspective route, Kenneth Clarke would never agree to it!

The lesson I learnt was that in order to get on in life, you must toe the line and not cross it! What a lesson for young people to be unwittingly but effectively taught!

Chapter Six: The Process and Methodology

Divide and Rule

When I was thinking about writing this book, I contacted a possible publisher who seemed potentially interested, and I was asked to submit a synopsis for initial consideration. It was an expected response, and so I set about preparing writing one, and then, after a short time, I stopped! Why?

A synopsis is in effect the same thing as a syllabus – a summary of the main content along with established pre-specified objectives, albeit set by myself, but which by nature would set the parameters for what I felt I wanted to say before I really started on the book itself.

I was overcome with a feeling of passionate annoyance – with myself – for having even entertained writing a synopsis at all. It is, after all, one of the things that perturbs me about the way in which we school young people, as opposed to educate them. Education is a life-long voyage of self-directed discovery, and the joy of student-centred learning is not so much about the final achievement, as it is the curiosity of not knowing where it might take one. The whole point of discovery is that the process involved is perhaps much more important than the end product. As was pointed out in the previous chapter, *learning is in my view all about using what you know to find out what you don't know – when you need to know it*!

I wanted to write a book that would essentially be a personal view on why and how it is, in my view that schools fundamentally 'fail' children by not focusing on ways to enable them to unleash their inner giftedness and talent – their spirituality even! Schools are all about prescription, even indoctrination, and not at all about liberation. They are more about control rather than genuine freedom, and increasingly so, due to the pressures exerted by central government.

So when I considered what it was that I was doing, I realised that I had no definite idea where I would end up, and what I would eventually write; not until I had written it anyway, and so any synopsis would have to be written retrospectively and not in advance of the exercise. What I did not want to do was to constrain myself by summarising what it was that I was about to say, or write.

I am reminded of a powerful lesson that I learnt about writing when watching one of my favourite films, 'Finding Forrester' starring the timeless Sir Sean Connery, who played William Forrester, a one-time Pulitzer Prize Winning author who helps a young man liberate his love of literature by writing about his thoughts and feelings. As part of the story, the young man is sitting at a typewriter and entering each word in a slow and mechanical fashion, as if concerned about issues of accuracy and spelling, structure and content. Forrester who is pacing the room behind him asks, "What's the problem? The young man (Jamal Wallace) replies, "I'm thinking!"

Forrester's response is memorable; he says, *"No! Thinking – that comes later. You write the first draft with your heart, and rewrite with your head."* Forrester's view is that the key to creative writing is first of all to write and not to think. This way your innermost feelings are allowed to find expression before you think too much about what you want to write, and how to express it.

Jamal is not easily able to follow such advice, and continues to enter the letters in a slow, laborious manner. The advice he gets from an increasingly irritated Forrester is: *"Punch those keys for God's sake!"* He tells him to feel and not think too much – to get ideas down on paper first and then see what he has written before giving it too much conscious thought.

The example from 'Finding Forrester' is also interesting because if someone really wants to write, why do they often find it very difficult to express themselves. Is this word-block because schools tend to promote the need to get things 'right' first time and, therefore, when there is no 'right' version we falter in our actions?

The delivery of the subject or formal curriculum of most schools is divided and compartmentalised to a ridiculous extent. To begin with the seamless cloak of knowledge is split up into artificial academic subjects, which means that more creative, physical, vocational and practical dimensions of learning only really find their way into the mix if they are made into subjects, preferably with an academic bent to them, as a means of justifying their place it seems, by seeking to give them greater credibility – as if they needed it! Alternatively, they can feature by being tagged on to the end of the formal school day on an optional basis, like an afterthought, as extra-curricular activities. The truth is that their place is equally as valid as purely academic types of learning. In fact, it is my belief that aesthetic and creative types of learning lie at the very heart of all human endeavour and so, should be given a *central* role in the school curriculum from the earliest of ages, as I have already said.

This fragmented curriculum delivery means that many subjects do not feature, or are not part of every young person's educational entitlement whilst at school. It also means that if another perspective or dimension of learning is required, then a whole new subject is created, which has to compete for its place within the knowledge-based and essentially academic curriculum. This is why some schools try and create options in subjects such as philosophy, psychology, media or film and television studies. This is to miss the point very often in my view, as all that might be needed is a psychological perspective on a particular topic or topics, delivered elsewhere in the overcrowded subject curriculum, from time to time. Why does this result in the creation of a separate subject rather than incorporating the psychological element into the study of a relevant topic in whatever area it is needed?

As with the example of PSE above, the answer that is so often given to this inappropriate response is to say that a psychological perspective, for example, is not on the syllabus of the other subject, or that the teachers consider themselves not trained or (academically) qualified to teach it. This professional demarcation is nonsensical to the type of holistic learning that we very often profess to be trying to achieve for the young people conscripted to attend school, but again it is an outcome of how they have been schooled and, in my view, narrowly educated.

It only requires better teacher training – or different teacher training – and the use of adults other than teachers to help in these areas. The teacher can take responsibility for facilitating and assisting student learning, but that does not mean s/he has to be the only human resource involved, or that the only place where schooling can be delivered is inside the school building – usually in a specialist classroom. The school could become effectively little more than a focal point for community-based learning, which could be designed to benefit all stakeholders in the process of a child's education at school. A school could become a learning hub, with networks of others in the local, national and global communities helping young people learn in imaginative and innovative ways. The internet and modern methods of communication make such an approach more possible than ever before! I shall talk more about the power of what I call 'community schooling' in later chapters.

The compartmentalisation of knowledge into subjects promotes exclusive and fragmented learning. To make matters worse, any particular subject, or area of knowledge and understanding is itself divided into a partial syllabus of topics and areas to be covered, which is also highly exclusive in terms of what is left out. And, as if to make matters worse, all students are required to learn the same things at the same time. So much for individualising or personalising learning! The constraints that this places on any type of self-enquiry and discovery into areas that are interesting and relevant to a particular learner are obviously significant. In effect, what happens is that all students get the same diet of content knowledge, prescribed in sometimes quite stiflingly fine detail.

The hidden message that is powerfully and relentlessly sent is that knowledge is not related or inter-related in reality. It can be looked at in isolation; indeed it should be, if it is to be truly academic and pure – untainted by other considerations. The emphasis is on objective learning, leaving subjective issues and perspectives for the artistic and creative subjects, as well as the good old extra-curricular activities. Students do not see the obvious links and overlaps between subject knowledge and are, therefore, prevented from applying knowledge in different contexts and areas; applications that would reinforce their understanding in both areas – that is the one in which they learnt it, and the context(s) in which it was subsequently applied. The links cannot be made because the delivery is not linked, and the teachers themselves are products of a fragmented and compartmentalised, academic curriculum. They are blissfully unaware of what is taught in other subjects, so how could they easily make the links even if they knew where they were? Consequently, in an already overcrowded curriculum, the practitioners who bemoan the lack of time to cover their own syllabus actually spend time duplicating what is taught in other areas. They cannot even use the overlap to reinforce learning in other areas, because of this blinkered curricular ignorance. There are, for example, economic perspectives in every other subject, and there are perspectives from all other subject areas that are relevant to a study of economics – but never the twain shall meet! Professional jealousy reinforces this artificial, exclusive approach to relevant and useful learning.

This separatist form of study makes most subjects dry and dull for most if not all young minds, or perhaps for enquiring minds, regardless of their age. Their study is mechanical and rigidly systematic, with knowledge seemingly sterile and not intrinsically useful to the learner. They do it because they have no choice, or in order to get better exam results than others and, by assumption, better-paid jobs…unless they go into teaching, of course!

This is not to say that there is never a place for detailed and in-depth study within a particular subject area, as clearly there is – but not as a general and universal approach to learning at all times. What about the romanticism of learning that can spawn a genuine desire for a more structured and disciplined approach to the willing acquisition of knowledge and skills?

Moreover, each subject is also divided when it is actually delivered, into lots of separate lessons spread over impossibly long time periods, which does little, if anything, to help sustain keen and motivated young learners whose time horizons are relatively much shorter-term in nature. Students find it extraordinarily difficult to remember what they were taught in the last lesson, let alone in the previous term or year. This is neither progressive nor continuous, and hardly coherent!

This is why, as the final examinations loom, students are forced to burn the mid-night oil (not by clubbing or surfing the 'net' this time), but revising madly to try and remember all that they have forgotten, in readiness for the exam. Then once the exams are over, they can conveniently forget most of it again – and possibly for good! It is not relevant to them or anything much else, and neither is it useful, therefore, and so it withers on the vine through lack of application and regular use. It is not memorable or helpful to the learner in most cases, and in **all** cases for some students, which is why so many young learners come to resent school and much of what they are required to study, rather than appreciate and relish the process.

The subject syllabus itself, apart from being only a fraction of the knowledge that students could learn in that area, is also sub-divided into sections that are separate – topics, theories, aspects and such like. The GCE Advanced Level Economics syllabus, for example, is presented in two main parts: microeconomics, which studies the economic behaviour of individual people, markets or firms, and macroeconomics, which examines how aggregates affect the economy as a whole – such as inflation, unemployment and economic growth. Some teachers start with the microeconomic element and move on to the bigger macro issues, whereas others prefer the opposite order. Which is right? I don't think it really matters, as either approach is flawed and can confound a beginning student of the subject, as the two are inextricably inter-related and interdependent. The dichotomy of course is an artificial, economic one, as the behaviour of individual citizens, consumers and businesses can affect the national economy, and vice versa. They need each other to provide a real and full sense, and to allow real relevance, that is applicable in practice.

To deliver a formal school curriculum that is so partial, irrelevant, fragmented and compartmentalised in every way possible is bizarre. In other words, knowledge is very much a seamless cloak – but not at school, OK!

A More Radical Educational Direction
The school curriculum is determined by political parties and other vested interests, but rarely in the interests of young people who are essentially the clientele and the new and future generations of our society. Whether you feel this is right or wrong, and I think you know my view on this, it further and powerfully reinforces the fact that education whilst at school is largely done **to** students and **not for** them (and certainly not **by** them), to make them conform and not to question or challenge those things that interest and fascinate them. I am quite sure that this is rarely an intentional action on the part of teachers but, again, this happens in an unconscious way – through a powerful, hidden message which more than offsets any conscious attempt by teachers to present a less biased and partial approach.

The dominance of content-laden syllabuses demands that the curriculum, as well as teaching and learning, inevitably respond accordingly. As a result, the multitude and diversity of talents and individual interests that generously endow our young people are all too often left undiscovered – hidden or constrained by the pre-determined path that we have created, and which we systematically lay out before them.

After all, a railway locomotive is impartial with regard to the direction that it will follow – very much like a student at secondary school – but if someone puts down the tracks, then that is the way the train will unquestioningly and unerringly go!

If we are to realise the immense potential that lies within every individual young person – diverse and different in nature though that may be – this requires an individual or personalised response surely? So why do we insist that all children follow the **same** content within the subject-based curriculum at the **same** time? This must have the effect of largely, if not totally superseding and often smothering the individual interest and initiative of the young people.

Instead of doing things this way, why don't we determine the curriculum as a set of more loosely-defined learning outcomes which are more skills based, and then allow students to choose the real-world *contexts* in which to develop them? Who knows, they may even choose something that interests them, and from that gain a curiosity to investigate things that *we* think they need to know about. After all, if these adult interests, or interests based upon traditional thinking and an orthodox curriculum, are so intrinsically important and valuable, then students will soon discover that they need to learn such things for themselves, surely? The important difference is that it should be *their* curiosity and discovery that leads them in that direction; it should not be something that we tell them that they need to know.

This truer form of learning will enable them to follow their individual interests by researching and gaining knowledge that is relevant to them, as well as applying it in different situations. I honestly believe that effective learning is an important concept which is also very simple to define: it is *"using what you know to work out what you don't know."* The intrinsic motivation that arises from self-directed and self-instigated learning is the key to such a process. Let us truly start with where the individual student *actually is* at any given moment in time and not what, and/or where, we would like them to be.

I can recall one such example from my days as a school inspector and adviser – one that resonated with me given my interest in rock music, and made me wish that I could have had a music teacher when I was a student at school, such as the one I had the pleasure and privilege to observe. Indeed, I wish I had had a music teacher in the first place – full stop!

The class involved students working on composing their own music, with the students having chosen an instrument(s) of their choice. Most of the boys in this class of fourteen-year-olds had not surprisingly been attracted to the electric guitar. Some were working collaboratively in interest groups sharing their ideas, while a few were working individually. I watched with interest as the teacher moved around the class listening to the music as well as the conversations, offering input and general direction as necessary. He was very involved in what all students were doing, and yet was not an intrusive force or obvious presence as far as the students were concerned. He was guiding, enabling and facilitating. He was not teaching in any orthodox, obvious or traditional way. The students were all very much on task, working on things that interested and excited them. Then he walked past a boy who was playing the electric guitar on a low volume, in one section of a large open-plan room. He was a rock clone – his hair was straggly, and yet his manner was surprisingly intense and focussed.

As the teacher walked past, the young man was playing a particular guitar riff over and over again – a sequence of chords that he was determined to improve upon, although it sounded very interesting to me. The conversation between the two of them went something like:

T: "That's a great sound, Peter, that's your own creation, yes?"
S: "Yeah. It's OK but I want to make it more interesting so that it really does what I want it to do. Do you know what I mean, sir?

T: "Do you mean that you want it to be more sophisticated in its structure?

S: Yeah…..maybe, just so that I can get more into it.

T   "I think I know what you mean. (Slight pause, a brief thought and then the following suggestion) Just listen to this a minute."
       (The teacher then went to the piano and played a relatively rapid series of simple notes that bore a striking similarity to what the student had played, despite being equally different. The student was immediately impressed and fascinated.)

S: "Wow, that's really cool sir! Did you write that?"

T: "No, it was another musician – I'm not that good."

S: "Who was it?"

T: "Mozart."

S: What…..wasn't he one of those classical guys – you know, the geezers what wore wigs and that?"

T: "Yes, that's right."

S: 'Wow! Have you got any of his stuff, sir?"

T: "Yes, lots. You'll find it in the music library in the resource area – go and have a look if you want. If you want to borrow any of the CDs of orchestral music that he composed, or the movie about his life, you can sign them out and take them home to listen to."

S: 'Brilliant! Thanks sir!"

At that point, the student left his guitar propped up against the amplifier and went straight to the music resource area and began his search. I noted that he was soon listening to the superb music of Mozart on the headphones and, at the end of the lesson, left with a parental consent form which allowed him to borrow and watch the movie entitled 'Amadeus', as well as one CD that he had been listening to.

I was surprised, interested and delighted by the zeal with which he followed the lead the teacher had given to this budding rock guitarist, but also by the way in which the teacher's intervention had sent the boy off to learn more about 'geezers who wore wigs' rather than grow their own hair! If the teacher had begun that lesson by telling all the students they were to learn the music of a classical musician called Mozart, the starting point would have been less inspirational and motivational or relevant. It could even have been a major turn-off for some; making his agenda very difficult to meet, given the attendant behavioural problems that might well have ensued.

It also made me think about rock music, like that of Emerson, Lake and Palmer that I liked when a little older than the student in the example above. I had never thought very much about the influences that helped them write and perform innovative rock music, but wish that I could have been pointed in the right direction by having someone make the link **explicit** to me – to make me aware of it. I now see the obvious link between Bohemian Rhapsody by Queen and it being effectively an operatic piece – just played in a rock music style.

We tend to terminate these easy avenues to excite and stimulate young people in such a way that they are eager to take responsibility for their own learning. I often think how the teacher in the case above did not *tell* the student what piece of music by Mozart his example was taken from; nor did the student feel the need to ask – he was too keen to go and look, and find out for himself. The key is to start with what motivates and interests the student, and then find the key that generates an interest in the individual or group which provides the incentive to explore the links between different types of music – or knowledge for that matter. All the 'good' teacher did was to see the opportunity and then to point the student in a new direction by making the link explicit; thereby opening-up a new dimension to the young man's musical knowledge, as well as his creativity.

Moreover, if the use of Mozart had not been an appropriate example or illustration, the skilful teacher may have sought to use another classical composer or some other source of music to give the young student the prompt and the direction he might have needed. In short, if there is a real need for young people to know about classical musicians, the Roman Empire, the Pyramids and such like, then students will themselves find a need to know, when it is appropriate for them as individuals. The task of the teacher is to **guide** students to find answers to questions; to **facilitate** their learning by exposing them to such content that we traditionally consider to be important.

116

The teacher should work mainly to enable and manage the self-determined learning of the individual student!

Subject curricula are obsessed with having pre-specified objectives – clear and established outcomes after usually two years' study, whether at GCSE or GCE 'A' Level (or the IB Diploma Program). Such pre-specified objectives are all well and good as long as they do not stifle imaginative, critical and creative thought and the development of skills, rather than an excessive emphasis on a somewhat linear and routine acquisition of knowledge.

Again, the curriculum offered by most secondary schools is laden with pre-specified knowledge that students are required to study, and this knowledge is based on that which traditional orthodoxy and adults deem to be suitable and appropriate. As a result, students are required to study issues and concepts that do not necessarily interest them, and which have limited application in the real world – or at least the one that they inhabit. This in turn, adversely affects their intrinsic motivation and desire to apply themselves, let alone the knowledge that we expect them – or demand them – to acquire. The motivation that young learners feel, if any, is more likely to be essentially *extrinsic* in nature – i.e. some form of some external benefit, such as examination success and a 'decent' job, rather than something that is intrinsically of interest to the student.

Now, it may seem as if I am dead set against pre-specified objectives, but that would not be entirely true. As an interim stage, I believe that pre-specified objectives are all well and good as long as they are fundamentally *skills-based* and not so heavily content-based. Sadly this is not the case, and within the current educational paradigm it does not seem likely to be adopted or applied.

The reason why we do not make this simple change of focus in terms of the educational objectives we adhere to, is perhaps to ensure conformity, but it is certainly to ensure that testing to identify the lucky minority of more academic students is very easy (and cheap) to standardise and, thereby, grade and rank. Why do we not take the harder as well as more challenging and expensive option when students' life chances are so fundamentally at stake?

An Economics Heretic!

Later on in my teaching career, when I was a more seasoned teacher of Economics, I decided to stop giving students the examination syllabus they required – or craved – until after the first term in their second year. The students, and their parents, were more than puzzled by this decision, and occasionally their response bordered on mild outrage. They expected and claimed it was their right to have a copy of the syllabus so that, as they put it, "we know **what** we need to know to pass the final exam," and so they could see when they had covered, 'all they needed to know'. I responded to this by saying that I was not going to teach them to 'pass the examination', which was enough to have them believe that I was worthy of being sectioned under The Mental Health Act!

They responded by saying that it was my job to, "get them through the exam." My unswerving retort was to explain to them that my main objective was to help them become good economists, and then they would pass any examination in Economics. Although they were not at all sure about this (in their eyes) radical and potentially delinquent approach, my excellent track record at having guided many scores of students to examination success in the subject at GCE Advanced level and GCSE (and before that, at GCE Ordinary level and the CSE) led them to invest in me enough trust to know what I was doing, and to go along with it, albeit a little reluctantly.

I used to start by pointing out what the great economist John Maynard Keynes had said about Economics (and although I have mentioned this before, it merits repeating here). He had said that the subject matter was not a doctrine, a body of facts immediately applicable to policy; rather it was a technique of thinking, an apparatus of the mind that enabled the possessor to draw correct conclusions. Keynes knew what he was talking about, not because he was an economist, because he was not! He was a graduate of Mathematics – not Economics – but his work in the Treasury as a civil servant inevitably led him to become interested in the subject of Economics, as the British and World economies sought to find a way out of the Great Depression that followed the First World War, and which persisted until the outbreak of the Second. He figured it out for himself, through being involved, interested and stimulated to discover why the free market did not use its 'invisible hand' to turn slump into boom, as it always had in the past. He stood conventional economic wisdom on its head in his treatise, 'The General Theory'. The World had changed and we needed new solutions to the familiar problems that we had let market forces resolve by keeping governments well away from its magical powers. Classical economists viewed Keynes' work and his new approach to economic management as economic negligence because he advocated a role for government intervention if the economy got stuck in a period of high and persistent unemployment, at a time when there was little or no social welfare net. They insisted that market forces would eventually move the economy out of the severe slump and into growth and prosperity, but that this would happen only in the long run. Keynes' response was to point out that in the long-run, we are all dead!

It is so sad that no end of persuasive, powerful and logical argument will shake us out of what John Kenneth Galbraith called our 'conventional wisdom'. It is only force of circumstance that provides any incentive to change the old-fashioned or ingrained habits of orthodoxy. For example, Keynes argued that the inter-war slump was due to the fact that private consumers and investors were not spending enough to provide the stimulus for necessary growth in the production of goods and services and, therefore, employment and incomes. He argued that in such cases of deficient total spending or demand within the economy, it was down to the government to increase its own, public sector expenditure and, at the same time, to provide a further stimulus to the spending of private sector consumers and producers by making cuts in levels of taxation. This would boost demand in the private sector and generate an expectation that things were going to get better, so that the private sector would feel more optimistic and confident in providing the kick-start needed to get the economy growing under its own steam again. In short, Keynes said that the government should engage in deficit financing – in other words, spending more on various government projects than it was receiving in the form of taxation on incomes and expenditures.

Why was this resisted so effectively, when he suggested it? Simple because it was to break with the traditional economic orthodoxy or 'wisdom' that the government had no role to play in the operation of the free market, and therefore, it should always seek to balance its own books – i.e. to ensure that they spent no more than they 'earned'. (This was the same lunatic thinking that informed Margaret Thatcher's policy making – when she set about trying to cure unemployment and inflation by a series of swingeing cuts in levels of public-sector spending by local and central government; whilst cutting the levels of taxation on the incomes of the wealthiest people in society, of course.) Her government was using a false and subsequently discredited economic argument that was nothing more than a naked act of politically-motivated redistribution of income and wealth from the least well-off in society to the wealthiest, under the fig-leaf of providing incentives for economic growth and prosperity for all. The result was akin to the Great Depression – with very rapid growth in unemployment, with the only growth industries being those of crime and social despair. That negative agenda is now being more maliciously and rigorously pursued by David Cameron's Conservative government, which we now call 'austerity' economic policy measures, and the result is exactly the same – the public deficit gets bigger, necessitating further cut-backs, and unemployment rising (notwithstanding the spread of 'zero-hours' employment contracts), with the living standards and economic welfare of the majority continuing to decline – regardless of the spin the government seeks to use to gloss over these defects in their 'thinking'.

Keynes tried to argue that although the government should spend more than it was receiving in the form of income from taxation this was in no way imprudent or reckless. He claimed (rightly, in my view) that as the economy expands and grows, the number in work would rise and incomes would grow. This would mean less expenditure on social payments to the unemployed, and the alleviation of poverty and social despair, whilst allowing the government to automatically increase its tax revenues, as people earned and spent more, and businesses made more profit. This would mean that when the private sector took over the 'engine for growth baton' again, the government would, again automatically, find itself returning to a position of a balanced budget. It was well-argued and right, but it was utterly resisted owing to the conventional wisdom that prevailed in the inter-War period.

He was not able to be proven right until the outbreak of the Second World War, when the government of the day found itself forced into making massive increases in expenditure, and borrowing to finance the shortfall, by the aggressive actions of the Nazi regime and its allies. Unemployment disappeared overnight and there was no massive surge in prices either, as there were so many idle resources that could be brought into use as the demand for goods and services rose!

The post-war period heralded a new approach to macroeconomic management, with governments of all political hues acting to take counter action at times when private sector spending was growing too fast and threatening to push inflation up too much, by cutting its own expenditures and raising taxation. Then when unemployment threatened to get out of control, and the economy was looking like it was going into recession, governments spent more, cut taxes and borrowed to finance the shortfall – along the lines that Keynes had advocated. It was no longer radical or reckless 'thanks' to the intervention of a major war challenging conventional wisdom. If it was good for the government to be **forced** to deficit finance and increase public-sector borrowing to make products to prosecute the war effort, then it was equally reasonable to do the same to promote employment, incomes and economic growth by producing goods and services that people wanted to buy in peace-time!

It might also be of interest and relevance to point out that if you see any similarities between what I have just said, and the causes and mooted solutions for the severe economic financial crisis that we are were recently experiencing in 2008/9 and beyond, then you are right. Will we ever learn that the pursuit of free, unfettered market economies is a wicked and deceitful irrelevance? Probably not!

Back to the Heretic
After that somewhat lengthy digression, in order to illustrate a key point, I can return to my argument of deliberately setting out not to teach my students to merely pass the A-level exam.

Prior to relenting and giving them a copy of the syllabus during their second year of study, and at a time when they had enough subject knowledge to make sense of its professional prescription, I felt obliged to make my point. I would give them an essay title to do for homework, about why farmers might prefer

121

bad harvests to good ones. The response from the students was that it was too easy as they had mastered price theory (relatively speaking) in the first year. So, I pointed out that it would be useful revision to keep it fresh in their minds. Every year, the students got superb marks for answers of real quality and style, and their modesty in achieving such scores was demonstrated in their feelings that their success was due to it being something which they understood only too well. So, I would ask them where they thought the question came from, Naturally enough, they all believed that the question was taken from a past GCE Advanced level paper, but they were wrong. It was, in fact, a question that had appeared on an Institute of Bankers examination paper – a post-graduate course. They were amazed, but I reminded them of what I had said about not teaching them just to pass the exam, and my point was effectively made – *and by them*!

Schooling, like most things, is held firm in the grip of conventional wisdom concerning the best and right way to educate our young people while they are at school, and it needs to be challenged and radically changed, if we are to avoid delay and wait for the whole system to hit the buffers with schools collapsing to a greater extent than they already have in so many cases.

We need to escape and break away from the traditional orthodoxy that maintains that only academic learning is truly worthwhile, by adopting and developing a truly balanced school curriculum for all young people. The balance can be flexibly adjusted to take account of emerging talents, interests and aptitudes by individual students at different times as their learning progresses. The answer is not to have vocational schools and academic schools, as this misses the point that **all** young people need a balanced curriculum entitlement. It also prevents creating divisive and unhelpful tiers within secondary schooling, which would trap students into mainly one type of learning for as long as they remain at school – and by the time they leave, the die has been cast, so to speak.

All schools should be equipped and/or organised to offer this desirable degree of breadth and balance in their curriculum offer to the students who attend them. We need to design a school curriculum which promotes academic excellence, of course, but also excellence in technical and practical, vocational and physical areas of learning, which should be inter-related and inter-woven to more closely mirror and replicate true learning, along with the fundamentally important aesthetic and creative area of learning. In this way, we will stand more chance of motivating the young and creating more intelligent and intellectual people, who are well-equipped to tackle life and its many and growing challenges in the here and now, as well as the future.

Of course, the usual riposte is that such schools would be too expensive to set up and it is more cost-effective to have specialist schools. Now, putting aside arguments along the lines of under-investing in education and failing to see the importance of effective schools, the solution is to be creative. Why should students only go to one secondary school in their area? (I would argue that this is usually for ease of administration and allocating finance, as well as creating competition between neighbourhood schools – again the system (and league tables in particular) prevents us from doing the right thing, or at least trying out new approaches to secondary schooling.)

Moreover, why should students only learn these things at a school? Why can we not have community networks with others getting involved in facilitating and guiding students' learning, all under the management of a qualified teacher if necessary? (Possibly because the Professional Associations that represent teachers would see that as a weakening of the status of teachers and, of course, the power of the professional associations themselves – more vested interest!)

This would require breaking the mould of conventional wisdom in many respects, requiring businesses, voluntary agencies and other private and government organisations to become actively involved in the process of education. This would require a shift in the conventional wisdom that has led to the modern production of goods and services being subject to excessive specialisation. Hospitals treat people who are sick, schools educate our children, the police and the law courts are responsible for law and order, and so on, and within each of those areas there is greater specialisation among doctors and nurses, specialist subject areas for teachers, etc.

Clearly, there are benefits to be accrued from such specialisation, but in the case of education and schooling, premature specialisation by allowing students to 'drop' major areas of learning experiences at a relatively early age is unwise if not potentially damaging. Furthermore, we can still have schools as long as they adopt a true community approach to the way in which they seek to educate young people. But will this be politically possible given the furore that erupts whenever there are attempts to abolish selective grammar schools, or to significantly change the current and dreadfully outmoded examination system? My view is that it simply and just has to be possible, and that it needs to be done urgently through the application of genuine political leadership. This translates as doing the right things, and not merely following populist politics that sees government tugging their elected forelock to the middle class interests that so dominate much of what government does and doesn't do.

One example I would like to give at this point is prompted by an article that appeared in the Guardian newspaper on the 25th March 2008, which reported Lord Kenneth Baker (previously, Secretary of State for Education under Margaret Thatcher's government, and who was responsible for ushering in the Great Education Reform Bill that introduced the National Curriculum for England and Wales, among other white elephants) talking about the fate of the City Technology Colleges (CTCs) that were set up during his time in Office.

He commented upon the fact that the experimental CTCs, designed to offer a more technological curriculum by including more vocational types of learning, although very successful, had really only become conventional secondary schools. He was quoted as saying, *"What strikes me is many secondary schools will have difficulty delivering vocational diplomas, because they haven't got the kit."* Whilst I agree with him about the issue of not enough 'kit' or resources and equipment to deliver such courses, which is understandably expensive, I feel that he has like so many other commentators (which is what he is now) missed the more pertinent causational factors.

During his time in Office, Kenneth Baker was responsible for promoting the notion of parent power, whilst at the same time introducing other regulations that led to a significant centralisation of power in the area of schooling, despite the rhetoric about devolving decision-making to parents, or the 'consumers'. This rhetoric effectively pushed decision making closer to the powerful and elaborately articulate middle-class parents who aspire to the elite positions in the traditional-style society that is the UK. There was no way that those parents, whose children went to CTCs, so that their children could be in new schools with lots of new resources to learn with, would allow any watering-down of academic standards and pre-eminence by having their children spend time on vocational pursuits. After all, such activities (like the old secondary modern schools) were for other people's children; not theirs! This desire by the government to address the lack of vocational education at secondary level was destined to fail due to this vested interest and the fact that it went about it in entirely the wrong way. The radical shake-up that education at school needs is never going to occur as an outcome of simple, token gestures that fail to tackle the academic hegemony. It is not possible to be 'a little bit pregnant' as they say!

The solution is to incorporate a mandatory vocational element into the educational entitlement of all children, and the same goes for the other dimensions or areas of learning that were referred to above. CTCs failed because they suffered the same fate as any old, stale and tasteless wine that is simply transferred into new and glitzy bottles. The conventional wisdom will always drag us back to the status quo.

How to Decide Upon Curriculum Content

I have argued strongly for any pre-specified learning objectives to be framed in terms of the development of **skills, values and attitudes** rather than allowing the dominance of partial content, which is often irrelevant to the inquisitive young minds of students that attend school, and which lends itself to indoctrination rather than education in its broadest sense. The stated outcomes need to be liberating and not indoctrinating or constraining.

That is not to say that no content can be specified – not if we wish to maintain the integrity of academic studies, which I honestly believe we must do, but most definitely **not** at the expense of other equally valid and important dimensions of, or perspectives on, learning. I can recall the work of EcATT (an organisation that was centred mainly on London University's Institute of Education and Manchester University) that sought to help schools develop the 'cross-curricular theme', as it was then categorised, of *economic awareness*.

Their approach was to avoid specifying any content elements at all, so as not to be guilty of unintentional indoctrination that can easily arise from presenting partial content as 'the syllabus'. Whilst I now applaud their sensible and unique approach – unique in terms of the rest of the secondary school curriculum – teachers were left perplexed, particularly as it was to be delivered by non-specialist trained teachers.

I should perhaps clarify at this stage that this cross-curricular theme of economic awareness was not the same as the subject of 'Economics' – well it was, but not in terms of aims, method and syllabus – it was designed to ensure that all students left school with a basic understanding of their economic role as citizens, producers and consumers, and not just those who chose Economics to study for external, national examinations. (Yet another example of an indirect admission by the 'powers that be' that the National Curriculum left out more than it could possibly incorporate in terms of enabling people to understand, and make sense of the society in which they live, as well as to act intelligently now and in the future.)

The reason why the syllabus of every subject is only ever going to be partial is due to an endless amount of knowledge that could be acquired and the finite amount of time for discovering it ……..sorry, being taught it. This is true in an entire life-time, and so it has to be even more of a pressing issue for the short amount of time that young people attend school. So what is my point?

Well, the problem lies in the way that we frame the content of the curriculum. We need to approach it differently, so that we have less content and more skills-based learning, and enable and allow the learner to have the greatest say in the selection of the content that interests them. We need to break down the boundaries between knowledge in the way that the traditional school curriculum is delivered. The process of teaching and learning is far more important than their respective content. But if the traditional, content-loaded curriculum is guilty of being partial, and not telling anything like the 'whole story', how can an approach as outlined above, with even less prescribed content, be an improvement?

The answer to this enigma is essentially as simple as it is elegant and powerful. Every subject is founded for its academic integrity upon a set of **core concepts** which, taken together or separately, underpin most other worthwhile knowledge within any subject area or broader dimension of learning. In Science, for example, the core concepts include matters such as power, energy and matter .... for that matter! In my specialist subject area, the core concepts include issues such as scarcity and the margin, the multiplier, wealth creation and distribution, etc. Indeed, the problem of endless knowledge and the finite amount of time that we have at our disposal to study and understand it (let alone discover new knowledge) is itself indicative of the fundamental economic problem of scarcity.

EcATT was right in wanting to avoid specifying what would have to be partial knowledge, but their approach of specifying the skills that should be developed left non-specialist teachers, and many specialists as well, utterly perplexed – including me, at that time. This was because they had all become so used to, and dependent upon, being given a content-laden syllabus – and one that takes a lot of effort if it is to be completed within the finite amount of time allowed....as if it could ever be fully completed. "Tell us *what* to teach," they pleaded? "No!" said EcATT.

At the time, I was critical of what I now admit was their 'correct' approach, and my argument for some content guidance led me to point out that we must have a content – it cannot be just a process. EcATT were not, however, saying that there should not be any content; it was just that they resisted the calls to prescribe it for teachers and the students in schools. It was for the teachers and the students to decide what content was interesting and relevant, but that still left a void about how to be sure that such self-selection 'touched all the bases' so to speak, in terms of giving students a worthwhile perspective.

At this time, I was studying for my Masters' Degree in Education, and my primary focus was on the issue of 'curriculum analysis and design'. I had to choose a topic for my dissertation and so I decided to examine the whole issue of 'Economic Awareness and the Entitlement Curriculum', as my dissertation was rather grandly and, necessarily academically entitled.

I spent a long time trying to get my head around the myriad of similar titles that had cropped-up over the years to represent this strand of a student's learning entitlement at school. I wondered whether or not the distinctions in nomenclature were in any way relevant in terms of representing any significant difference. I eventually came up with a linear development model, which started with **'economic awareness'**, leading to the higher level of **'economic understanding'**, and later to the highest achievement of **'economic competence'**. It seemed logical to me that awareness was essentially a starting point, in that someone can be simply *aware* that there is such a thing such as inflation, but not understand what it really is, what causes it, or how to deal with its adverse effects on them and the overall economy, if it gets out of hand. After all, some inflation is a positive and beneficial thing, as modestly rising prices act as an incentive to investment, consumption and, in turn, economic growth. I felt a sense of minor triumph and significant achievement, at having apparently cracked that troublesome nut, as this meant that at long last I was able to start writing the 30,000 words, within what was a very tight timescale – not much changes does it? My semi-euphoria arising from this personal 'Eureka' moment was, however, short-lived.

At one of our 'field of study' meetings, which was attended by a small group of others working within the curriculum analysis and design area, one of the other teachers, who was a musician, disagreed with my model when I took my turn and presented my dissertation topic and my general idea to them. He argued, very convincingly, that in his opinion true *'awareness'* was of a higher order than mere competence, in that if one was truly aware then they had a grasp of things that was superior to the mere ability to act. He had a very good point – bugger!

At the end of the session, my field of study tutor, who I found to be an excellent guide and critical friend, could see that I was feeling more than a little deflated at having had the balloon that represented the central tenet of my dissertation so decisively pricked. As the others left the room, he asked me to stay behind for a few minutes, which I felt would be useful, although I had no idea how. He did not tell me the solution to my dilemma, as that would have been presumptuous and overly directional, but he did offer one way out. He simply told me to go away and read Bruner – which I did, and experienced yet another and more powerful Eureka moment in my life!

This is yet another example of a really good teacher at work, as he was effectively pointing me in the right direction when I clearly needed him to facilitate and guide my learning.

The important point here is that in my error of thinking lay a major learning experience – as is always the case! I was a victim of thinking that any structure had to be linear, with, by definition, a starting and a finishing point with 'economic awareness' and 'economic competence' respectively. The solution lay in the notion of core concepts that could be applied in a variety of different contexts that grow ever more complex, sophisticated and interesting. This led me to adopt a *spiral* curriculum development methodology, which meant that the economic awareness, understanding and competence acquired in a relatively simple context, progressively led to a higher level of economic awareness, which required a more complex context to be chosen, and one that interested and was, therefore, chosen by the learner, guided by his/her facilitator. This would allow students to choose different contexts, negating the need for all students to study the same thing at the same time. They would instead, be studying what they wanted and could progress at their own rate, producing an ever widening spiral, the vortex of which would effectively suck in greater amounts of knowledge and enable the students to acquire and develop the skills associated with, and involved in, self-directed learning. This was possible, of course, because there was no external examination that required and necessitated a prescribed syllabus – a freedom to learning which was (and is) a huge strength, or a blessing of such an approach, and in no way a weakness.

This spiral curriculum model allows learners to take control of the content that consciously interests them. It would also enable them to really take responsibility for their own learning, encouraging them to take risks and make mistakes – two necessary ingredients of any learning that is to be truly effective. In this, the students would be guided by their teachers, who would now be known as learning facilitators, as well as other adults and their peers, who would be acquiring different types of knowledge, whilst developing the

129

same learning skills in many different contexts simultaneously. Imagine the dynamic of the collaborative learning that could develop within a school in this way. I find it truly uplifting and genuinely exciting!

The teachers in a school could then be called upon by individual students or groups of students at different times – no need to timetable the allocation of teachers, although their time would need to be differently managed. Teachers could then be joined and supported by other adults who have specific skills, knowledge and competences that students need. Schools could become the centre of learning networks or webs in the community, involving teachers, other adults and the students, but with the individual student as the spider who effectively spins the design of his or her own cobweb. Teachers and other adults would also be learning much more; acquiring new knowledge and perspectives, as well as honing their own skills by working more flexibly, constructively and imaginatively with young learners. Why not?

Perhaps more importantly, the selection of what context to work and learn within next would also be guided by the **spirit** or **soul** of the learner, the calling within every human being, which encapsulates and drives the innate and uniquely individualised talents, capabilities and idiosyncrasies of the individual learner. It would **not** be determined by politicians, middle-class parents or teachers, and certainly not by the bureaucrats who inhabit external examining bodies. This kind of 'stakeholder-intrusion' into what schools do makes a mockery of the education that currently takes place when learners are at school, given the different and usually competing agenda of these different interest groups. What about the real and far more legitimate and relevant interests of the individual learner – it is their education after all, as well as their life! What we get now is effectively educational colonisation by everyone except for the true client – the child, the adolescent, the student!

In this brave new world of schooling which promotes liberalised and liberated learning, external examination groups would have to find new ways of assessing the array of learning outcomes – if indeed they really need to be externally assessed at all. Historically and currently, other people and interest groups 'own' what students learn, how they learn, when they learn, the time allowed for their learning, and the outcomes of their learning. But, it should rightly, necessarily and fundamentally be all **theirs** and not ours. Let's stop trying to standardise that which is not and cannot be uniform in nature, as well as forcing students, schools and teachers to compete. Learning could become far more collaborative, with all involved feeling the pleasure, the joy and the synergy of genuine sharing and teamwork. Prescription replaced by a greater sense of personal freedom in one's learning – wonderful!

All of the above would reduce the current shackles that the system places upon what young people learn as well as how, when and fundamentally **why** they learn it, and create a climate where failure is seen as a positive thing because it becomes an inevitable, necessary and integral part of every individual's learning. Students will learn because they want to learn, because they are intrinsically motivated to discover for themselves – not because they are required and pressured into learning what many others determine for them.

This will do a great deal to promote, enhance and develop creative thinking and learning, because students will feel free to experiment, without fear of their performance always being judged against that of others in their peer group, by people other than themselves. And this brings me to the whole issue of assessment and testing.

Chapter Seven: Assessment and Testing

An Introduction: Schooling vs. Education Revisited

One of my favourite activities, that I like to undertake with fellow teachers in training sessions, is very simple to conduct and yet immensely revealing and surprising – some would say sobering, if not shocking. It has two purposes. The first is the one that it had when I was a participant in the activity myself, and the other is the one that has intrigued me about the way in which people follow and interpret a few, very basic instructions.

This is what the activity involves. First of all, I give each person a blank sheet of A3 paper and two marker pens, of different colours. I then give them the following instructions:

1. Draw a cross on the left-hand side of your piece of paper, and put your date of birth next to it. Then:
2. Draw a cross on the right-hand side of the sheet of paper, and put today's date.
3. Now draw a line that connects the two crosses.

You see, I said it was a very simple activity, but there is more, of course!

What the participants would have drawn was effectively their 'life line'. They were then asked to think of moments or times in their lives to date when they can remember learning something truly memorable, important or significant; a time when they felt a considerable sense of pride in their achievement or accomplishment. Next they were required to plot these key learning events on their lifeline by placing a cross at the approximate point in time when they happened – i.e. in relation to their date of birth and 'today'. At that point, all they had to do was to name or identify the learning events that they could easily recall.

Most participants are able to identify a few (or more) key learning experiences, although some struggle initially, as if it is difficult to identify a time when they actually learnt or achieved something really significant and genuinely memorable. Once they have done this, however, they are then asked to draw a vertical line from the top to the bottom of their sheet of paper at the point on, or in, their life line when they actually left school, and another when they ended their 'formal' education.

What is revealing about this activity is that most, if not all, of the key learning experiences that are identified are those that occurred *after* they had left school, and in most cases again, after they had finished their higher education at university or college. Furthermore, for the small number of participants who manage to identify one or two key learning opportunities that occurred whilst they were at school or university, it was usually the case that these events happened at times when they were not actually at school or university, or when they were with the school on a field trip or exchange programme.......but very rarely in a formal classroom environment.

This initial outcome is usually something of a surprise to most participants, although for others it seems as if they already knew that school had not taught them much at all – and that use of the word 'taught' is also significant. This is because they were mainly *taught* at school. They did not, sadly, *learn* much about anything worthwhile – anything that was really relevant and useful to, or memorable for them.....or not obviously so!

I then ask the participants to spend a little time to identify what it was about those key learning experiences in their lives to date, that made them memorable, special and outstanding. In other words, what was the task, who chose it, who were you working with and where; who decided upon the intended outcomes and how you were going to achieve them, and by when? After this initial brainstorming session, I then ask them to share their individual experiences in small groups and draw up an overall group list of points that they have in common, or with which they can all agree.

The feedback sessions are always equally revealing, and also immensely useful. The most common points that are made during the feedback sessions are that they were in control of their own learning (or felt as if they were), often because it was their own initiative. In other words, they possessed a true sense of ownership of their learning. Other contributory factors that are commonly given are that they:

133

- ✓ Worked with others in loose, flexible teams or groups which were formally or informally arranged;
- ✓ Also worked individually when it was appropriate;
- ✓ Were confronted with real-life challenges, but were determined to overcome them;
- ✓ Were able to decide when they would do the task;
- ✓ Felt immersed, wrapped and almost consumed by the challenge – by a desire to achieve their goal;
- ✓ Benefited personally from what they had achieved – i.e. it was relevant and useful to them.
- ✓ Were able to think of creative solutions to problems that they faced, and so on.

Would it not be genuinely wonderful if we could achieve that same spirit, desire and thirst for achievement in the classrooms of our secondary schools on a daily and consistent basis – but then the classroom is very often itself a major constraint on young people being able to experience memorable and important learning experiences.

One final point that I want to relay to you, the reader, is that the hidden message from this activity is also revealing. Look back at the three initial questions or sub-tasks that I asked the participants to perform. When I look at their sheets of paper, virtually every single person will have placed their two crosses in the *middle* of the left and right-hand edges of their sheet of paper, and then drawn a *straight* line connecting the two. Why do they do this? I didn't tell them where on the edge of the sheet they have to put the cross, and neither did I give any indication that I wanted them to draw a straight line. I would suggest that they do it in that common way because they have been well *schooled* to conform and to do certain things in set or conventional ways. It is always a rare gem of an experience for me when someone dares to break the 'mould' and locate the two crosses randomly, and draw an undulating or zigzag line between the two. It does happen, but all too rarely, sadly.

At this point, I want to make a small, but important digression to illustrate again that I believe that teachers, and then their students, are **victims** of their own formal education. This is due to the generational adherence to what was once called 'the sabre-toothed curriculum' and which, in truth, has remained largely unchanged in terms of its structure, its content or the way in which what is taught is selected or decided upon. I am not alone in this observation. Let me include at this point a small excerpt from the excellent book entitled *What They Don't Teach You At Harvard Business School (notes from a street-smart executive)'*, written by Mark H. Mc Cormack. I did not know, until I happened across this wise and truly learned text, that he was the founder of the International Management Group (IMG), which is a successful multi-billion dollar, international business organization. This is what he says in the introduction to his book:

"Much of this advice (in the book) is unconventional, not just to be different, but because I believe dependence on conventional wisdom — on old ideas and antiquated methods — is the biggest problem with American business today. Running a company is a constant process of breaking out of systems and challenging conditional reflexes, or rubbing against the grain. People want to work but policies suffocate them, and it would be impossible to write a responsive book that didn't address this problem and the many disguises it wears.

Business demands innovation. There is a constant need to feel around the fringes, to test the edges, but business schools, out of necessity, are condemned to teach the past. This not only perpetuates conventional thinking — it stifles innovation. I once heard someone say that if Thomas Edison had gone to business school we would all be reading by larger candles.

My main purpose on writing this book is to fill in many of the gaps — the gaps between a business school education and the street knowledge that comes from day-to-day experience of running a business and managing people.

Over the years we have hired many MBAs from Harvard and elsewhere to work for us. In fact, in my more impressionable days I guess this was one of my own conditional reflexes: If you have a problem, hire an MBA. As we grew and got to areas in which we had less confidence or expertise, I reasoned that by virtue of their education the MBAs were the best people to run these areas for us.

*What I discovered was that a Masters in business can sometimes block an ability to master experience. Many of the early MBAs we hired were either congenitally naïve or **victims*** (my highlights) *of their business training. The result was a kind of real-life learning*

135

disability — a failure to read people properly or to size-up situations and an uncanny knack for forming the wrong perceptions."

This resonates very well with the basic tenets of the arguments that I am trying to make here. The notion of conventional wisdom still determines what is taught, how it is structured and delivered, and how young people at school are assessed. This conventional structure is stifling their creativity and innovative flair, as well as what are currently considered to be the 'more legitimate' and 'relevant' achievements of young learners. Similarly, teachers are the victims of their training, which these days consists of a nine-month crash course after three years at university, during which they have been following other subjects – again, in a largely conventional way. How much has it really changed, and how well are we really enabling all students to become truly educated and enlightened, and to think in new and different ways?

What Do We Mean By Assessment?

Another surprising issue that I often encounter is the lack of a shared understanding of what the term 'assessment' actually means, and the fact that it is so often confused with testing. Indeed, the two terms are sometimes used in an inter-changeable manner, and yet they are not synonymous by any means. This lexical confusion is rife among all stakeholders in the school system, whether in the private or public systems of education. This lack of agreement on the meaning of the terms we use in schools is more worrying to me than it is surprising, so let's see if we can partially solve it here.

Again I turn to my trusty dictionary, and I look up the terms 'assessment' and 'testing'. This is what I find: First of all, there is the view that, *"When you assess a person, thing or situation, you consider them in order to make a **judgement** about them."* It follows, therefore, that, *"An assessment is a consideration of **someone** or something and a judgement about them."* Another dictionary definition of the term 'assessment' points out that, *"When you assess the amount of money that something is **worth** or should be paid, you calculate or estimate it."* A person who is responsible for making an assessment is an assessor, and this is defined as, *"someone who **judges** the performance of someone else, for example in an exam, at an interview, or at a sporting event."*

These definitions are inter-related, and I am more than a little concerned about the possibility that there may be a cross-contamination of one definition with another, to form a hybrid perspective in the unconscious thoughts, if not the 'eyes', of many people. Are we not effectively creating a conscious or unconscious mind-set that encourages people to view assessment as **_judging the worth of someone_**? I would argue that there is indeed a lot of evidence which suggests that this is exactly how people view the notion of assessment in schools – 'separating the wheat from the chaff' in the context of young people's life chances, so to speak. Why else the pressure that so many parents, particularly from the middle class, place on teachers and schools when end of term or mock/practice exam grades are assigned to their precious offspring? Only a grade 'A' will suffice, as less than that implies lesser value or worth, and the teacher is held to account, as their human asset has not appreciated as much as their high – often unrealistic and ill-founded – expectations demand.

I am very concerned that we are effectively and inadvertently judging the worth of someone when we assess them, and this is the antithesis of all notions of viewing everyone as having equal worth and value in society. In the personal and social education 'curriculum' there certainly used to be an emphasis on helping young people understand and appreciate that everyone has an equal worth or value, and yet the hidden message of the assessment part of the curriculum does not exactly support this version of equality.

I believe that it is the term 'assessment' itself whose value or worth should be carefully judged, as well as the processes involved and the people who conduct these judgements of young people and others, as well as how.

Then we come to the whole idea of tests and testing; what does the dictionary have to offer in shedding some light on this area of judging people? The Collins Cobuild English Dictionary offers twelve different, but related definitions of the word *'test'*. The one that most fits the context of schooling young people and measuring their achievement is, *"If you test someone, you ask them questions or tell them to perform certain actions in order to find out how much they know about a subject or how well they are able to do something."* Alternatively, the dictionary also states that, *"a test is a series of questions that you must answer or actions that you must perform in order to find out how much you know about a subject or how well*

137

you are able to do something." Yes, well that's the theory in terms of its educational application, but the practice is flawed by the process or method by which tests are performed. The whole issue of the methodology of assessment and testing will be examined separately later.

Other definitions of the word 'test' are also worrisome for me. For example, *"if you test someone, you intentionally make things unnecessarily difficult for them in order to see how they react."* Why do this to young learners who are in the early stages of their lifelong and joyful journey of discovery and learning? This notion of testing is hugely counter-productive, as I will also examine later.

Also of interest is the definition of 'test' that states, *"If you are tested for a particular disease or medical condition, you are examined or undergo various procedures in order to find out whether you have that disease or condition."* In other words, this idea of testing would seem to suggest it is more concerned with trying to find out if you have what we are looking for, as opposed to looking to find out what you actually do have – after all, if you do not test for it, or look for it, then you are highly unlikely to find it! Moreover, there is also the idea that usually a medical test is to find out what is **wrong** with you, rather than what is right about you.

Although the definitions that I have chosen to refer to here are technically different, they have quite a lot that is in common, which is quite telling. Again, I find this worrisome, because there is scope for yet further cross-contamination of one by the others, such is the power of hidden messages, and lack of knowledge of the importance of semantics, in the lexical resource of most people – even those in the teaching profession. We need to be careful when we use words. We need to think about the power of the meaning that can be invested (and vested) in particular words, assuming they are being interpreted as the speaker or writer precisely intended. If not, then we are extremely likely to be on slightly (or very) different wave-lengths, which does little for the cause of effective communication on the topic.

In addition to the strong possibility of cross-contamination between the different meanings of 'assessment' on the one hand, and among various definitions of 'testing' on the other, there is also a much more real danger of cross-contamination between the two terms themselves. The definitions and perceptions regarding the meaning of assessment and testing are all too often fused into one overall process – that of *'assessment __and__ testing'*. Even though educationists seek to distinguish the two terms and profess that they are not the same thing, they are largely trying to clarify the meaning of terms that are already deeply, and quite likely incorrectly, entrenched in the psyche of the general population.

Might these issues relating to the way we define, view and conduct assessment and testing be the reason who so many school leavers feel *'worthless'*, I wonder? Because many young school students do show signs of feeling worthless and of no use, which may be why they seek credibility and value in the eyes of their contemporaries by engaging in what is designed as the anti-social, maladjusted or delinquent behaviour of a sub-culture.

Why Do We Assess the Learning of Young People and What Do We Assess?

In view of what has just been aired, this question becomes far more difficult to answer, owing to the dichotomy created by the basic tenet of my argument. The question of why we assess the learning of young people, and what we are actually seeking to assess, should really be examined from two very differing perspectives. On the one hand we need to critically examine, "What do we *currently* assess with regard to young people's learning, and why?" Then we really need to ask what should we *actually* be assessing, and why?

As mentioned already in earlier sections, students at secondary school have been sub-consciously indoctrinated into a way of thinking that has reduced all educational endeavour undertaken at school to a single, over-riding mission – that of passing examinations, obtaining paper qualifications or credentials to hopefully enable them to progress up the academic ladder. As I have already argued, this leads students to discount anything that they encounter that is not on the official syllabus as being irrelevant, unhelpful and not worthwhile.

This indoctrination (which I honestly believe it to be) is hardly subtle. It is the simple product of a competitive society with limited places at university and in the well-paid job market, coupled with the constant emphasis placed upon passing exams and tests, getting good grades, and coming 'top' in class. As a result there is simply too much emphasis on passing the test rather than on learning for learning's sake, something that would truly enrich, enlighten and empower us all.

Equally damaging is that this excessive emphasis on learning things for the test or examination means that young people do not understand, appreciate or acquire the knowledge, skills and attitudes to know how to use, apply and reinforce or deepen what they have learnt in new and different contexts. In a recent survey conducted into the teaching and learning of Mathematics at GCSE level, the most worrying finding showed that although the examination results were increasing, the candidates' actual understanding of, and ability to apply mathematical concepts was declining! This is due to an obsession with the outcomes of 'learning' rather than the means by, and contexts in which learning occurs. In other words, the joys of engaging in the process of learning through an activity are subordinated to the simple notion of completion of the task in question. This finding about Mathematics did not come as a surprise to me at all.

The over-emphasis on achieving success and avoiding failure in external examinations, largely for the acquisition of a piece of paper with a grade attached to it, has been allowed to debase real learning for far too long. The need to identify an academic elite who are capable of going to university – and the 'best' universities at that – drives the whole school system down a blind alley for the majority of young people, who either accept lower grades or run-away from this academic circus by truanting from school or opting out of lessons by adopting often seriously disruptive and distracting behaviour. As mentioned earlier, we then tend to condemn this latter group of youngsters as misfits for displaying maladjusted behaviour. Who, or rather, what is maladjusted – the young people or the monolithic system of compulsory schooling that provokes and encourages such behaviour? As always, when the system fails, we tend to blame somebody, and not change the system – and one which has not substantively or structurally changed in some 150 years or more.

We should stop seeking to separate the academic wheat from the chaff, and the systemic by-product of failure or inadequacy that it promotes (if not requires). We need to seriously ask why schooling is not exciting and stimulating for an increasing number of 'disaffected' young people. There is also another group who go along with the system, and yet they do not really enjoy the process in which they are involved. This is because they (or their parents) are living in the hope that they might break into, or clamber their way up the graded and highly competitive academic hierarchy. At the same time, however, schooling is not adequately serving their real needs, but then what alternative is there currently – home schooling?

The culture of academe and selecting elite minorities pervades the school life of young people, and the pandemic fever for grades has long since begun to infiltrate and infect the work of primary schools, where children used to really enjoy their learning. This is not the case so much these days, owing to the introduction of competitive league tables and the imposition of national testing of students as young as seven years of age. This is plain dangerous as much as it is damaging – allowing children to feel the fear of failure (rather than seeing it as an opportunity to learn) in their early years at school. It also forces teachers to focus more on meeting prescribed benchmarks of pre-ordained types of achievement, rather than allowing them to enable and facilitate the more self-directed discovery of their students.

A recent report by Cambridge University, entitled 'Community Soundings', following research using a very large representative sample of primary students and their parents, concluded that national tests for seven and eleven-year olds are putting children under stress and feeding into a *"pervasive anxiety"* about their lives and the world they are growing up in. This supports my view that the claim that we are preparing young children and teenagers for adult and working life is unrealistic, inappropriate and misguided, as well as damaging to young people. The report clearly shows that young people (more than ever before) are concerned about the big global and local issues that they see and experience all around them in the here and now, and not in some unknown version of a different future world.

One by-product of this primary stress, according to the report, is forcing some middle class parents to pay for a *"parallel"* education system, by employing private tutors to get their children through their exams, even before the age of eleven years. Some students who were surveyed said that the tests were *"Scary"* and made them nervous. This is further evidence of the sickness of secondary education and the competitive school system seeping down to pollute and spoil the enjoyable learning waters of primary schools.

Children are already more aware and concerned for the state of the world they inhabit now without the need to add to the stress they feel about issues such as violent crime and traffic accidents, let alone global warming, international terrorism and environmental degradation and destruction. These issues which are technically outside of the school gates are more than enough for them to worry about, without the need to introduce facile national tests to appease the middle class critics of state schooling – the generations who helped create these massive and (young) life-threatening monsters.

The researchers, not surprisingly, found that the youngsters in schools which tackled the problems they actually worried about, such as those schools with eco-clubs and recycling schemes, were much happier. The researchers found that, *"Where schools had started* **engaging** *children with global and local realities as aspects of their education they were noticeably more upbeat. In several schools, children were involved in environmental projects and the sense that 'we can do something about it' seemed to make all the difference."*

To do this is eminently sensible, as it empowers and "engages" young people in their own learning – learning about the things that they are concerned about and not the things we tell them they need to know. Who knows, the innate creativity within young minds may find new and effective solutions to the problems they, and all of us face? This creativity can grow and find more sophisticated solutions if only similar methods were deemed acceptable and really encouraged in secondary schools, before the academic sausage machine grinds it out of them in the cause of traditional orthodoxy, and educational standardisation. I also found the phrase 'we can do something about it', in the above quote as very telling indeed. The idea that children are more engaged, motivated and comfortable when **they** feel they are in control of **their** learning!

The report is music to my ears, as it suggests that schooling as it is currently organized and administered may actually be rather detrimental to the personal and educational development of young people. This is indeed why the number of discerning parents who are opting out of 'the system' to have their children learning at home and not at school is growing noticeably, and not just in the UK.

Stay At Home!

A study entitled 'How Children Learn at Home' by Alan Thomas and Harriet Pattison, which was reviewed in the Guardian newspaper on the 18th August 2008, is also very revealing. They interviewed and observed twenty-six families who educated their seventy children at home. Some of those interviewed had been out of school for only a couple of years, whereas others had never been inside a school. Many of the parents in the survey kept their children out of school because they believe formal education starts too early (in the UK), and that it is restrictive, with a misplaced emphasis on testing. Some others worry that their children may be bullied (usually by their dissatisfied, disaffected and 'maladjusted' peers).

The authors discovered that the children involved absorbed information mainly by *"doing nothing, observing, having conversations, exploring, and through self-directed learning."* What I find particularly interesting is that they went on to liken the *"chaotic nature"* of informal learning to the process that leads to scientific breakthroughs, the early stages of crafting a novel, coming up with a solution to a technical problem, or the act of composing music. This finding is of huge interest to me, as these things are all ***creative*** in nature – which I believe is central to all learning, but which is so often either squeezed out of the traditional secondary school curriculum by the power and false urgency of the all-powerful academic imperative, or it is shunted into the extra-curricular sidings of the school system. But more on this very special and important matter later.

Thomas and Pattison had more to say about this important finding of their study. They noted that with this informal learning, *"Its products are often intangible, its processes obscure, its progress piecemeal. There are false starts, unrelated bits and pieces picked up, interests followed and discarded, sometimes to be taken up again, sometimes not…. Yet the chaotic nature of the informal curriculum does not appear to be a barrier to children organising it into a coherent body of knowledge."* This **coherence** in what they learn is one of the bold aims of the secondary school curriculum, but its fragmented and disjointed delivery effectively militates against achieving it for most, if not all young people. This point was also commented on in the survey by Thomas and Pattison, when they noted, *"In some ways, it may be an advantage because, rather than presenting knowledge in neat packages, the informal curriculum forces learners to become actively engaged with their information – to work with it, move it around, juggle ideas and resolve contradictions…. It is not a static thing contained in a series of educational folders. It is alive and dynamic."*

Thomas and Pattison's observations and findings are also student specific, as well as general in nature. For example, they marvel at the way one girl learned Mathematics by *"helping with the cooking and shopping, and collecting supermarket-trolley money."* They noted that the girl in question *"came to appreciate the value of material goods, but she did not see it like that. She saw only the concrete activity. If she did sometimes count money or do sums in her head, it was her decision, sparked by her emerging understanding, or simple curiosity about numbers."* They go on to point out that most of the mathematics that is acquired at primary school can be learned as an integral part of everyday concrete activities. In school, however, it seems as though mathematics has to be divorced from the dynamic realities of everyday life. Another young learner, able to learn at home whenever he felt like it, and without the restrictions of a curriculum, was seen by Thomas and Pattison as being *"much more efficient"* than studying at college. The young man in question made a very important and key observation about these experiences when he said, *"The main difference between my informal education at home and my formal education at college has been that at home* **I can focus on what I want to learn, when I want to learn it.***"* Hear, hear!

Another mother took her eldest daughter out of school at the age of five years because she decided that her daughter was not ready for a day that finished at 3.30pm, and felt that her daughter was losing the ability to occupy herself. If schooling delivers a set diet unto you, where is the motivation to want to find out for yourself? The daughter in question went on to be awarded 'A' grades for most of her GCSE and 'A' Level examinations, and later to graduate from university with a fine arts degree. The mother home educated all three of her daughters by taking them to museums and allowing them to play with others their age. She noted that they amused themselves to a large extent, and that there were never any lessons at home, or anything structured for more than a couple of weeks.

All of this begs the question why nearly all that is formally assessed in school is what the architects of the formal curriculum are looking for, and then judged by their partial and subjective standards and measurement criteria. Why do we not really try and find ways to find out what the learner can demonstrate or do that is different, new and interesting? Is this because it is too difficult to standardize it and interpret it to make it fit an examination grade that will serve as an entry requirement to university?

It seems to me as if the real purpose of assessment and testing is little more than an end in itself, rather than a serious attempt to reward and celebrate individual achievement, as a staging post along the road of genuine life-long learning. This process of jumping through pre-specified hoops is not sufficiently focused on the application of knowledge which requires the student to apply skills and demonstrate competence. Instead, students can often achieve a significant degree of academic success through their ability to recall what they have been told or what they have seen.

Surely, the real purpose of assessment and testing methods at school ought to be to ascertain a young person's attainment, and not their ability; aiming to actually **discover** their achievements or accomplishments, as opposed to 'judging' them. Greater emphasis should be placed upon recognising, categorising and celebrating individual attainment – no matter how diverse – rather than assessing their achievements against rather narrow, pre-specified objectives and always and endlessly in comparison with others, whether intentional or not.

If students were free to learn via self-discovery whilst in formal education (as I would prefer to call the time spent at school), then perhaps it would be reasonable to assess them on what they had discovered, in terms of what is **_new_** in what they know, understand and can do. Instead the school sausage machine takes the pure, clean and diversely talented raw material inherent

145

within each and every young person, processes it all in the same way, and then churns out so many bland, conditioned and unimaginative school leavers. These processed products of schooling are so often incapable of applying much if anything of what they were taught when they 'get out into the real world', which is what they were supposedly being (wrongly, in my view) prepared for in the first place. And yet at the same time, they are still blessed with unique talents which often lie dormant, possibly frustrated and further buried beneath a mound of pre-determined or required 'learning' – most of which is subsequently and soon forgotten. What on Earth is the point of that?

And when the middle classes start bleating more loudly about 'falling standards' – which they never cease to do – the government (that is responsible for the mess in the first place) are required to 'do something about it', which they do by structuring the school system and its modus operandi even more tightly and rigidly – with more testing and refined, new or repackaged pre-specified objectives. Talk about not learning through, and from, past mistakes!

What young people and their genuine education have suffered from is a regime of curriculum-led assessment, whereby they are judged according to what they were required to study and learn. What would be far more liberating, if fully implemented, would be to turn that regime upside down and have an assessment-led curriculum, whereby what a young person achieves and learns, is used to determine what they go on to study in the future – and when they want. This is an anathema to a structured, standardized and pre-specified formal curriculum, which is excessively focused on the content of what students are required to learn to pass their exams.

There are educationists who recognise, and are troubled by the curriculum-led assessment of the past 150 years, and who quite genuinely want to move towards placing greater emphasis on a more assessment-led curriculum. They talk about new and welcome concepts such as an approach that is based on 'assessment *for* learning' rather than the current, more simplistic and crude 'assessment *of* learning'. In essence, this approach argues in favour of using assessment mainly as a tool to guide and chart the speed and direction of a student's learning within the overall formal school curriculum, paying greater attention to recognising the achievements of the young learner no matter how small they may be in comparison with their peers. This approach is to be applauded and welcomed. However, I remain sceptical about the extent to which their good intentions will be realised in actual practice, in terms of how it really impacts the genuine learning of young people.

My doubt is based on the fundamental concern that these educationists are again seeking to re-arrange the deckchairs on The Titanic, or tinkering around the periphery. The fact remains that these people are also the product (or innocent 'victims') of the current educational system. Are they not, to a greater or lesser extent, also the innocent 'victims' of their own education, who may be (possibly unconsciously) seduced or enamoured with the 'rightness' of schooling as it is currently organised? I fear that too many educationists have a professional investment in the perpetuation of the school system, and that the power of traditional orthodoxy in the form of the academic, fragmented, subject-based formal school curriculum, that is deeply rooted and embedded into the psyche of all the stakeholders of schools, will always act as a brake on new, more progressive methods of education, if not an actual obstacle to their successful practical implementation. The attitude of, 'well if it was OK for me, then it is OK for them' prevails, certainly in the eyes of parents and, perhaps, many teachers.

One further constraint is surely the enormous difficulty of measuring the achievement of young people which is qualitative and subjective, as opposed to being more conveniently objective and quantitative in nature. To illustrate this point I would like to refer to the fantastic film, *'The History Boys'* which was written by the literary genius that is Alan Bennett. In the play, a select cohort of potential Oxbridge students is being tutored mainly by an older and unorthodox teacher, as well as a younger teacher who is more interested in the substance of learning than being inspirational. The older teacher is definitely inspirational because he challenges the status quo in terms of both the content and methodology of his lessons. But the Head Master comments on this to another teacher by saying, *"Sure! He gives them inspiration, but how do I quantify that?"*

In many ways, the qualitative aspects of learning are a greater achievement in terms of motivating continued learning than any amount of the more quantifiable 'stuff', but the difficulty of measuring them tends to relegate them to being ignored at worst, or treated as something of an entertaining side-show at best, in the grand scheme of student assessment and testing. This problem is perhaps more to do with government demands that the success of schools be measured in the form of standardised league tables, and the publication of the results obtained by students in the infamous and fatuous national tests, in addition to the external, infernal external examinations, than anything that the professional teacher deems to be worthwhile. The pernicious influence of government initiatives will be examined in *a lot* more detail later.

How Do We Assess Student Learning?

I can recall the National Curriculum debate about how to best assess students at school, especially when taking terminal examinations such as the GCSE (General Certificate of Secondary Education) which students usually take at the age of sixteen years. At that time, I remember being in total agreement with the idea that examinations should be designed to find out what students know, rather than these terminal assessment tools being better at discovering what the examinees did *not* know, and could not do. At that time, however, I did not give a lot of thought to how that could be done, as that was for the 'experts' on the assessment committee led by Professor Paul Black. More recently, it occurred to me that the best way to increase the chances of finding out what students do know, understand and can do, is by telling them the questions they were going to be asked *in advance* of the examination itself. This would truly help them to prepare and to give of their best.

When I shared this simple idea to my colleagues, they were aghast at my naivety, or some said 'stupidity' and suggesting, somewhat forcefully, that to do such a thing was tantamount to cheating. I was (and am) not swayed by such conventional and immature responses, as I personally experienced this idea when I took my final B. Ed examinations. For one of the twelve, final three-hour papers, we were given a long list of broad topics at the beginning of the year and told to choose just **two** that interested us. Note that: Things in which we were interested! We were then told to research and study them in greater depth than was normal for one particular topic, so that we could

148

answer a fairly general question about our two choices in the final paper. I picked 'adult illiteracy' and the issue of 'maladjusted' youngsters at school. No further guidance or pointers were given, and so this required us to use our curiosity and find out as much as we found stimulating – which was a lot in my case. I thoroughly enjoyed the **freedom** to delve into important and highly relevant concepts that I had chosen, and really learnt a great deal. This was heightened given that these issues were very much 'new' to the agenda of educationists at the time. In the three-hour examination we had to use what we had learnt to answer the two questions that were set on the topics I had selected.

The point is, telling students the question before they sit the examination is perfectly acceptable if one then sets the 'bar' higher, so to speak, by expecting a better quality answer in terms of content, analysis, evaluation and structure.

As a Head Teacher in schools, I eventually started to do the same thing when selecting staff by means of competitive interview. Having been an interviewee on many occasions for teaching and advisory posts, I had often found that the sole or final interview did not really address the kind of areas or topics that I had expected, given the nature of the post in question. This means that I often left the interview room feeling a little mystified, puzzled and perplexed with regards to why I was asked the questions I was in some cases, and what information the questions were really designed to elicit, and for what purpose. As my career has developed, I have spent increasingly more time as an interviewer than an interviewee, and felt that it was only reasonable to make the process of staff selection and interview more of an enjoyable and transparent process, so that candidates would hopefully feel more at ease than would otherwise be the case, and also clearer about the overall direction the interview would take prior to the actual experience.

I now routinely explain to staff that in the interests of equal opportunity, they will all be asked the same main questions during interview, with only follow-up questions and questions relating to their CV being different, for obvious reasons. I also usually tell the candidates undergoing final interview that if they speak to my personal assistant or secretary 30 minutes before their allotted time for interview, she (and on one occasion, he) would give them an envelope

149

in which would be a copy of the main, open-ended questions that they would be asked. These were obviously designed to help evidence the items listed in the job and person specifications which they had received at the time of application.

After all the interviews are over, I offer a de-briefing session for unsuccessful candidates, as a matter of professional courtesy, where I explain the positives of their interview and offer some advice on how they might increase their chances in subsequent interviews for similar positions. However, in reality, we (me and others on the interview panel) usually found that the reason most people were unsuccessful was simply that their personal 'fit' did not quite match what the school was looking for, and not as a result of any weaknesses in their technique or answers. This is perhaps obvious, otherwise why were they being interviewed at all? What was interesting in our feedback conversations was that, without soliciting any comment on the matter, they all said how unusual it was to be given the main interview questions in advance, but that they had found it very helpful in giving them a little time to compose themselves and to, as more than one person has put it, *"get my head around where I would be going."*

Let's be honest, offering the candidates thirty minutes to read through ten to twelve largely open-ended questions does not allow them the time to prepare elaborate answers, but only to jot down a few notes so that they do not omit any key points in the inevitable emotional stress that a job interview usually entails for most people. Moreover, I have also found that it makes the interview time more efficient, effective and reliable in eliciting interesting answers from candidates, which then enables me and the panel to select the right person for the job, with unsuccessful candidates feeling that they were given a good opportunity to state their case and, hopefully, impress.

I feel that students should know what they are going to be asked in an external examination, and be given the opportunity to question the examiner to find out exactly what they mean by the question before they seriously attempt to answer it. After all, in most examinations the questions are in writing, which is the **least** effective way of communicating, so why do we deprive young people of the opportunity to sensibly clarify what precisely the examiner is looking for in the question. They would then be better placed to answer, surely?

Schooling is not really about individuals working in a partnership with their peers, plus a teacher (or teachers) and other adults helping and facilitating their learning. It is not at all about the joys of collaborative working in teams on specific tasks of mutual interest. Instead it is all about competition, working and being assessed as an individual, with only the 'winners' feeling the triumphant joy of topping the pile. Winners they are, which by default means that the also-rans are 'losers'. I can recall how it felt to be a loser – it hurts – there is no joy or feeling of achievement when you don't make the winner's podium to receive your medal of achievement or token of worth. 'Losing' occasionally, when doing something that you really want to do and enjoy doing can be incredibly motivational, but repeated failure when doing tasks of little or no obvious relevance to the learner is soul-destroying. They are told what they have to know and then are told they are not that good at it, according to the judgment of others.

Being a loser in such a system makes one even more resentful, especially if one is always 'a loser'. I used to mark students' essays out of 20 or 25, as was the expected norm, and give them a few comments on how they could have improved their answer, but it was always interesting that the students who get a good mark are motivated and justly proud of their achievement. They eagerly show their marked work to their parents, and their peers, for further commendation and praise. There is nothing wrong with that at all; indeed, I encourage it wholeheartedly – but the counter-point is illustrated by the students who 'fail' to get a 'good score'. They usually feel utterly demoralized and de-motivated and conveniently *'lose'* their lowly-scored and marked work in the back of their exercise books or folders – or sometimes in a dustbin somewhere. They feel a sense of being a loser, a failure as they have nothing to boast about, and are therefore not in a position to receive the plaudits received by the medal winners. The more often and inappropriately we test, assess and judge them (and their feelings of self-worth), so their feelings of discouragement and disillusionment will accumulate. What are they supposed to do? Work harder? Compete more fiercely? Try harder next time? The plain simple fact is that we cannot all be winners in a competition – or any inter-personal competition for that matter, so how is this mad-cap system supposed to develop a passion for learning throughout one's lifetime?

Real education (and schooling), learning and assessment of achievement, should be far more collaborative – involving students as active participants in these processes, and not relegating them to feelings of being a passive, press-ganged and motley collection of individuals, from a resentful and potentially mutinous crew. I think it was Michael Jordan who said:

"Talent wins games, but teamwork and intelligence win championships."

As you can tell, I honestly believe that we place far too much emphasis on competition, and way too little on the greater successes and joys associated with collaborative learning and teamwork. Most, if not all great individual achievements are the product teamwork, involving a supportive network of others, each doing their own specific part or component. In the world of work, everyone recognizes the immense power of teamwork. People in unison provide a blend of talents, abilities and knowledge all coming together to produce uncommon results, as a result of the dynamics and synergy created through effective teamwork. But in schools, young people usually work individually or, more importantly, are assessed and tested individually. Sure, they can work collaboratively on a team project, but when the assessment or judging takes place there is a need to identify each individual's actual contribution to the team, measured against syllabus outcomes. How sad that these outcomes rarely, if ever, focus on the individual's ability to work effectively and constructively in a team situation. A good analogy is a football team. If a team wins a game 5-0, who usually receives all the plaudits – the person who scores the most goals, with little or no emphasis placed on the wonderful defensive players who manage to keep a clean sheet and get the ball out of defence quickly. More so perhaps the midfield player who makes a telling defence-splitting pass which leads to a goal being scored. This is why there is so often a 'man of the match' award for the player who is adjudged to have contributed most to the overall team success. ***But how do you assess individual worth when everyone has a very different role to play and does so with their individual flair and style?***

In schools, however, individual contribution is all that matters when the time for a more-formal assessment or the external examination arrives. No man of the match award here – this is left for the teachers to nominate school awards for the student who has contributed most to the general life of the school. Teachers are great at finding awards to make at the school awards' evening for those students who have achieved real success given their level of academic ability, or in other important fields such as community work, for example. But the system is less concerned with recognizing such a broad range of success unless it is through a straight or full flush of 'Grade A's in the final academic examinations. Their successes supersede all others, with even those getting into Oxbridge putting the other good graders into the relative shade. This is elitist, damaging and fundamentally unjust, in my opinion. Why else was the A-Star grade introduced for the GCSE examinations in England and Wales, if not to identify the better or best Grade 'A' student?

For goodness sake, what does a Grade A tell you about what an individual student obtaining it did so well as to deserve one – just that *'it'* was higher than a student with a lower grade. Two students may both score 98% in an examination, but this does not really tell you what they did the same or differently – or does it? Are they not likely to have both got the same score for different reasons?

Another good analogy to illustrate this point further is a symphony orchestra – another joint venture of individual performers who, quite literally, in concert with others produce music of beauty and splendour; music that evokes strong emotions for the audience members – another collection of individuals. They enjoy the music for different reasons – but how do you assess what it was about the performance that provoked such a strong and positive feeling?

Furthermore, how do we assess the performance of the individual musicians in the orchestra, afterwards, when we had all enjoyed it for quite different reasons? Some people adored the brass section, others the strings and, me, the percussion, and so on. And who was the best in the brass section? Was it the 'first cornet' because s/he had the most notes to play, or the 'second' or 'third' cornet player who seemed relegated to pick up the less glamorous pieces, or the notes that the 'first cornet' player didn't want to play?

153

In any case, the competitive nature of so much of what students do whilst at school militates against the notion, let alone the benefits of teamwork. The explicit and hidden competitive messages of the process send far more powerful signals than the less often collaborative ones about what they should be doing. You very often can see this manifest itself, for example, that when students are supposedly working together in teams, some individuals are anxious to be the best or most impressive member – or recognized as being the main contributor to the success of their joint endeavours. On the other hand, when there is a team failure they try to make it seem as though this is due to a failure of other team members. In other words, they find **_sharing_** successes and failures very difficult, which explains why the team dynamic is deficient, and maximum synergy is often so difficult to achieve, without a great coach!

To make matters worse in the final examination process, why do we place so much faith in the ability of the examining boards and their lowly-paid markers to correctly assess the ranked order of student achievement? An article published in 'The Observer' newspaper on the 10th May 2009 illustrates this important concern very well. If I were to paraphrase, using an American colloquialism, the system is really more of a 'crap shoot'!

The article focuses mainly on the work of Professor Dylan William, who at that time was the Director of the Institute of Education, and a specialist adviser for the government's Schools Select Committee, and his conclusion that each year **_thousands_** of students are given the wrong grade in external exams because the system is not sufficiently reliable to reflect their abilities. That is a pretty significant margin of error. Indeed, Professor William pointed out, *"People who manage and produce tests have a responsibility to be honest about the margins of error and report them. By pretending exam results are completely reliable, we have encouraged people to rely more on them. Exam grades are not oracles of truth and must be used wisely."* He went on to show that many candidates given B grades could just as well have been awarded 'A's with a different paper and a different marker. However, this deficiency is not communicated to the public (including the students who sat the examination) owing to, what the Guardian called 'the conspiracy of silence' among, *"consenting educationalists in private"*

154

Professor Williams went on to argue that so much depends on the number of questions that examination candidates are given to choose from by saying, *"If you want the candidates' scores to reflect their knowledge rather than how lucky they are, then you have to ask a reasonable number of questions, probably at least five and possibly as many as 10."* He explained that the more questions asked, the more accurate the assessments because performance was less likely to rely on chance that the "right" questions came up. He put it very succinctly by noting that *"candidates can get lucky two or three times, they can't get lucky 20 times."* That, in itself doesn't sound too difficult, but he went further by stating that making an exam truly accurate had major administrative and logistical problems, because it could involve *"making the test up to **eight** times longer."*

The article goes on to quote Dr. Christopher Wray, the Head of Manchester Grammar School who pointed out that his very able candidates were often given C or D grades for GCSE and A-level modules. I particularly liked the case he gave which provided a significant piece of anecdotal evidence regarding the unreliability of external examinations. It involved the 'brightest' boy in the school who was given a D grade for an A-level History module. What is interesting is that the boy in question had already secured his place at Oxford University because they had seen his work completed during the course. The school, sensibly, had his A-level paper remarked and his grade was subsequently and miraculously elevated to an 'A'. The reason given for this dramatic change in his grade was that the examiner had ***"missed the subtlety of his argument."*** This begs the question, who should be assessing whom, exactly?

Professor Williams articulated this point more generally by saying that very able students could fall victim to the increasing use of mark schemes designed to promote consistency between examiners. He said: *"To remove subjectivity, we tell examiners what to give points for and what not to give points for. So someone who finds an imaginative way of solving a problem which was not envisaged by the mark scheme gets a low grade because they did not fit the preconception."* This is another illustration of how individualism and creativity are inadvertently and unconsciously discouraged, if not over-looked, by convenient pre-specification and standardization!

As someone who, over time, was employed as a marker for different examining boards for external school examinations at different levels, including GCE 'A' Level, I often look back at those experiences and wince in painful recognition of what I was actually complicit in doing. Putting aside the content and breadth issue of the examination papers, and the reliability of these spurious assessments, just the process itself should be a matter of further concern.

My main worry was that the assistant examiners, as we were usually called, were sent hundreds of examination scripts, each one requiring us to mark several essays or some combination of short answer questions and essays. These came whilst school was still in session, and so in addition to my normal work load, I was required to plough through these papers, paying due regard to the mark scheme, and all within a very tight timescale. This meant working late in the evenings and all weekend during this frenetic period. It was rarely fun!

There were occasional enjoyable moments, however, when a student had written a really high quality paper which was a pleasure to read, as well as easier and quicker to mark. Equally enjoyable and easy to mark, although for rather different reasons, were the 'funny' ones, where the student had obviously long since 'given up the ghost' and was only sitting the paper because they had already been entered for the examination and was, perhaps, avoiding the need to reimburse the school for failing to turn up as required. Thus they would entertain themselves (and me, subsequently) during the tortuous duration of the exam by writing obviously silly answers to the set questions. These cases were also very sad, but in view of the farcical nature of what the system puts them through, who can really blame them? So why did I volunteer to undertake this annual torture?

Two good reasons come to mind, and I not sure which one is the more meritorious. The first is the money, by which I mean the opportunity to earn a pittance per script, which when multiplied by the high number of papers sent, provided a much needed income supplement – hence the motivation! The other was that it did enable me to better prepare the students I taught, at the same examination level when the time came for them to sit the end of course external examination. Why? Well, because it gave me a valuable insight into the secret garden of the process, enabling me to know what 'the examiner' was looking for! In light of what I (and others) now know about the whole exam process, this latter justification strikes me as worrying rather than helpful. *'What the examiner is looking for'* – think about that for a moment or two!

The whole issue of unreliability is not aided when one considers that each slavish assistant examiner is feverishly marking a large number of exam papers, often in their limited 'free' time, for a small financial reward, and all within a very short timescale. It is difficult to maintain a high level of concentration in such circumstances after all. Also, I have never understood why it was that the marking schemes we were given were to be treated as strictly confidential, as the assistant examiners do not see or use them until after the examination in question has been set. But, secret they were!

Sooner Rather Than Later

When I was a trainee teacher, one of my favourite areas of study was the psychology of education, as it was called. I often recall pearls of wisdom that were based on sound research as well as my own experiences of formal education, and reflected on the reality of what happens in schools where we rarely practise what we preach. Let me take just one example – the knowledge of results. It is well known that positive feedback is infinitely better than negative comments made about your performance, and that the students need to know the outcome of their work as soon as possible after its completion. This is why so many youngsters in school badger a teacher asking if their homework has been marked yet, and how well they have performed (admittedly, it was usually only those students who normally scored well that displayed such anxiety). This proximity of the assignment to finding out the result is powerful as a motivational factor and as a diagnostic tool. In my experience, the students I worked with were always eager to know how they had performed (usually the mark only, and not how it had been achieved), and I was no different as a freckled schoolboy.

Now let us consider the dreaded external examinations, which in the UK are taken mainly in the summer months, sometimes starting as early as April, in cases where practical exams are involved. The bulk of exams are over by the end of June and then the students wait for their results…. And they wait and wait, until the middle or end of August before they find out their results, and then all they get to know is a largely meaningless letter grade. They never get to find out why they did better or, in my case, worse, than they thought they had performed, or how they arrived at such a 'score'. After two months or more of painful apprehension, they get nothing more substantive than a letter on an official piece of paper. Then they conveniently forget most of what they were taught and had revised for the examination. They then prepare to move on to the next level of largely redundant and transient 'learning'.

The external examination bureaucracy leads to a massive gap, between actual performance even if it is deemed relevant to the needs of the learner, and the students finding out how they fared in the grading league, although nothing else which might facilitate and guide their future learning. In my view, the best way to assess a student's performance is to allow them, their peers and their teachers to do this. They are often their own sternest critics when it comes to their achievements. This is not done for the simple reason that it would be impossible to standardize the performance and assessment judgments nationally. How would employers select the 'right' people for training and employment? How would universities identify the students who they want to study with them? Well, my answer would be, interview them carefully and imaginatively and introduce more diverse selection methods and criteria, rather than just sitting people in a room and asking them to talk about more pre-specified questions. Make the process more active, so that the candidate can demonstrate what they can do, and then ask them to talk about it and explain why they did things in certain ways. In this way, they can show what they have really learnt – what they know, understand and can do, as well as how they might further improve upon and apply the things they can do already. Yes, this would be more time consuming and place a greater onus on employers and universities than it does today, but it would be far more reliable for their specific needs.

Instead we make the learner jump through irrelevant hoops to achieve a grade which tells the employers and universities very little that is useful, insightful or meaningful. If this were the case, then perhaps employers would not bleat about how young people with academic qualifications cannot actually apply what they are supposed to have learnt, and how they so often lack the necessary skills to be truly employable. To do things like this though, would also require schools to teach and assess students in a similar way – something to be welcomed surely?

In short, the whole edifice of official schooling is founded on principles of dubious convenience, financial limitations. speed and traditional orthodoxy, and because the main purpose of schooling is all too often considered to be about meeting the needs of industry, commerce and higher education, and all too rarely the genuine interests and needs of **the individual learner**.

Instead of letting the examination system largely determine the way we assess student achievement and progress in schools, let it be the other way around. Let's start with the needs of the learner, and then devise a method of assessing their achievement so that they can truly demonstrate a whole range of inter-related achievements.

Above all, let the learner have ownership of their own learning, please!

When I was at secondary school and later in tertiary education, more often than not, I felt acutely disappointed, equally disillusioned and downright awful when my teachers or lecturers would return my homework, which they had allegedly 'marked'. I usually felt useless and frightened of failing everything, and I know it often made me feel like giving up altogether. The feedback from my tutors was virtually never positive and constructive in nature. Negative feedback was easier, quicker and possibly more satisfying for the teacher – scrawling the word 'WRONG' in large red inked letters all across the page takes no time at all. It does no positive good either, apart from allowing the poor teacher to vent his spleen and frustration at my failure to understand his wonderful but mono-dimensional and singular exposition in class.

Why is it that teachers so often don't get the fact that telling someone something in one particular way does not mean they will understand it. How could it when I would more than likely forget it? This was because *I* hadn't actually done it, and so was prevented from being able to internalize and remember what I could have experienced for myself. This negative feedback didn't, and still doesn't do anything to address the fundamental problems of what was wrong precisely in a piece of work, and more importantly, **why**. Again, I was never given the opportunity, or felt the bravery to question or challenge the verdict which even at a relatively tender age I knew was unhelpful, but then who was I to know? If I received a mark of 8 out of 20, where exactly did I earn those marks, given that my work was usually a mass of red crosses and negative or damning one-word comments? What did I need to address, omit or include in order to be awarded the other 12 marks? I was always too timid and intimidated to ask for such helpful and potentially developmental clarification. Was this my failure, because it felt like it was, or was it theirs? I received no explanation as to why I had scored a low mark, presumably because the teacher had already told me once in class, along with everyone else.

It is such a great shame that young people are so afraid of being wrong and making mistakes. We claim that we are trying to encourage our students to learn for themselves – i.e. by inevitably and necessarily making mistakes – and yet the power of external assessment and testing, combined with peer ranking and parental pressure in some cases, sends the opposite message so much more powerfully and effectively, therefore. The outcome is to further discourage genuine learning – to be condemned to listening and not doing for oneself. I also feel its greatest damage is to at best, stifle and at worst, strangle the uniqueness of the human spirit, as well as its appetite for, and propensity to be creative and special.

This whole notion of creativity is of crucial importance and will, therefore, be looked at in more detail later. However, it is important to note that for students to be creative, imaginative and innovative, they must be fundamentally **active** in demonstrating what they know, understand, and can do. They also need to be able to appreciate how all perspectives of learning – the aesthetic, human and social, technological, mathematical, linguistic and scientific – inter-relate to create an understanding of the world of today and the future, as well as to cast light on the individual and collective problems that mankind faces on a daily basis.

Unfortunately, this is not what examinations actually do. Most examinations – with the notable exception of 'practical' examinations which usually only feature in subjects that are, in themselves, deemed to be 'creative' in nature, such as art, music, drama, and dance – contain no really practical element that attempts to assess the students' holistic knowledge and appreciation of the inter-relatedness and interdependence of knowledge. This somewhat perverse treatment is mainly due to the fragmentation of the holistic nature of learning, with the curriculum and external examinations delivered and conducted in separate and discrete subjects. It is also for convenience, as well as to ensure that all examinations are capable of being standardized, and not too expensive to administer. At no time are students assessed to see if they have understood the holistic synergy that this rag-bag of subjects is allegedly intended to provide when taken together. This is almost certainly due to the fact that its content and/or delivery mechanism is not intended for such realistic and useful purposes, if one is brutally honest about it. One partial exception is in the IB Diploma program, which at least has the 'Theory of Knowledge' element within it – but still taught and examined separately, just like any other 'subject'.

The people who are being assessed are required to prove how much of a prescribed content that was formally taught, they have actually retained by the time the exam season comes around. Moreover, this is usually achieved exclusively by mass sessions of public examinations in which the 'learners' are required to perform – without actually moving much! I remain to be convinced that the whole process really serves any other more worthy personal use or meaningful purpose – other than achieving the passport-like bits of paper that the 'successful', 'better', 'more academically able' candidates are fortunate enough to merit, to access further study or (apparently) higher-paid types of employment.

These deficiencies are compounded when one considers the fact that learning is best achieved by the learner being actively involved in what interests and positively challenges them, and yet most assessment methods are purely passive in nature. Young people are sat in a large or small room and told to act **unnaturally**: sit in silence; do not communicate with anyone (and that can mean avoiding eye contact with other examinees, rather than risk it being misconstrued and classed as 'cheating'); remove all reference materials and course notes from your table, so that you are not able to refer to any helpful materials; interpret the questions correctly, without having the opportunity of clarifying the question at the outset; and write an acceptable answer – acceptable that is to a faceless examiner – according to a mainly pre-determined and standardized answer plan.

This is not typical of how they learnt in the first place – where the emphasis is supposed to be on encouraging students in schools to collaborate and work in teams, to refer to appropriate resource materials and seek other guidance and advice from those who are more knowledgeable and skilled in the area or areas concerned. Neither is it typical of how they will be expected to work in most occupations, where team work, collaboration and cooperation are the way in which work-related assignments and problems are most usually undertaken and solved. It seems oddly perverse to me that we still insist on placing unnecessary obstacles in the path of examinees, whose life chances can so powerfully rely on the outcome of these so-called terminal assessments. The adjective 'terminal' is an important one because it tends to send the hidden message that it represents an end to the learning process, rather than encouraging young people to view it more as a staging post on an otherwise lifelong journey of curiosity and discovery – an aim that many schools purport to be trying to achieve, apparently.

At this point we need to refer back to why we are assessing young people, what is its purpose in theory and to what extent is the rhetoric matched by the practical outcomes?

When the examination results are published, we wonder why many young people feel frustrated when they 'discover' that their grade is not as good as they had expected and hoped for. In such cases they often and understandably want to know why this was – but that remains a closely guarded secret, under the more respectable guise of confidentiality. On the other hand, students who perform better than expected rarely want to know why they exceeded their own expectations – after all, such feedback could be useful to them, so that they know what to emulate and focus upon in future. Instead, they understandably focus on just celebrating their success – meritorious though that sentiment may be.

Assessment ought to be active, with the student demonstrating what they know, understand and can do, and by asking them to explain what they know and understand **_orally_**. They should be allowed to use visual aids to assist any explanation of what they are doing and why, rather than almost exclusively communicating all of this just in writing, which is the most difficult and least effective form of communication. What does this prove? Who is the better/faster writer?

Active and oral assessments would effectively draw the student into a discourse with the examiner(s) which focuses on the actual assessment of what is done and /or said. This would allow the teacher – after proper training – to assess the student on a continual basis, perhaps leading to more effective learning as well. I would argue that using such a conversational format in assessing students' performance or abilities would not only be more effective in unearthing student achievements, it would also be a more motivational and a much fairer process. After all, the teachers, such as classroom teachers, form or homeroom tutors and heads of year are the people who have the most comprehensive and intimate knowledge of the basic strengths and limitations of the young people that they work with and for. Assessments using these resources would be more effective and reliable of a young person's abilities because it is first-hand, ongoing and direct. It is also relatively stress-free which will make the communication more open, focused and ultimately effective – or fit for the purpose intended. It is relevant to their lives now and in the future, when they will spend 'the lion's share' of their time using their vocal chords and facial apparatus to communicate meaning. Only when communication is two-way can it be easily and readily effective. It is quicker and enables the speaker to check that the listener has understood the exact and often subtle meaning of the words, tone and body language employed. It was allegedly George Bernard Shaw who said:

> **"The greatest problem with communication is the illusion that it has occurred."**

The main criticism of the teacher assessment process lies in arguments that it lends itself to favouritism on the part of teachers who, in wanting to show their students in the best possible light, might be tempted to inflate the grades or otherwise distort the reliability and validity of the assessment process. This is of course made increasingly likely now that schools are being unfairly ranked in a similar way thanks to the introduction of 'league tables' based on a school's students' performance in external examinations. One solution would be to abandon open enrolment and the whole notion of league tables, but that of course would now be seen as dismantling mechanisms of 'choice' and 'fairness'; arguments that are shallow and designed to appease the middle classes so that they get to choose the 'best' school for their children. Whilst this is utterly understandable, it is predicated on the understanding that those children whose parents do not have the means or the acceptable type of lexicon to exercise this false notion of 'choice', or those parents who take little or no interest in their children's education, perhaps lacking the necessary parenting skills to enable their children to see the benefits of school (as they are at present), can go hang. They remain in schools which are impoverished further by dint of losing their 'better' or more academically-able counterparts, and then those schools are assessed by OFSTED and placed under 'special measures'.

Another way to deal with the risk of 'favouritism' is to introduce checks and balances into the system, by way of moderation procedures. This is very much akin to the system that is currently employed for the standardization of examination coursework, which is marked and graded initially by the classroom teachers of the young people in question, before being sent to the relevant examination board for scrutiny. This is not going to 'water-down' standards or any other such bogey words and phrases that right-wing lunatics put about to scare the middle class into retaining the status quo, and voting en-masse against any political party who dares to fiddle with the system that has served them so well for centuries; enabling them to hold on to the reins of real economic, social and political power.

Instead, we are stuck in the conservative frame of mind that says 'if it ain't broke, don't fix it'. Well, I am arguing that the whole thing is a mess of potage and is desperately in need of true and radical reform so that all young people are enabled to succeed in life, regardless of who their parents are. I am a passionate believer in a truly comprehensive model of schooling, so that it is more likely to represent real education, and the enlightenment and liberation of generations to come. Let's aim high and look to operate a true meritocracy, where people do indeed succeed on the basis of their own effort and ingenuity and creativity by providing them with real opportunities in key areas such as health and education.

I also have never really understood why we do not have a school examination system in which everyone could in theory fail a particular examination, or why it is not possible for everyone to achieve a grade 'A', if everyone scored over the threshold percentage score to merit the highest accolade. If, for example, the threshold in question is any score over 75%, and everyone scored between 75 and 100%, then what would happen? The examination board would introduce grade boundaries within that 25 percentile so that there is a normal curve of distribution for the final grades awarded. They would reintroduce a ranking system – but why? The answer is simple: to ensure we can maintain our 'horses for courses' system of young people effectively knowing (or being told) their limitations and their place in life. It would also not happen as traditional orthodoxy, enforced through generations of following the same madness in assessing young people's life chances, would force the cynics, the small and mean-minded, to scream and rant about how 'standards are falling'. We are trapped in this outmoded, parsimonious and ill-serving paradigm that demands norm-referenced assessment criteria.

I can recall when I was at teacher training college it was widespread knowledge that in one year, all the students failed to achieve a pass grade in the final examination for a particular subject. People were aghast that no one had passed the exam, because they were trapped in the paradigm which would have surely led to the pass grade threshold being lowered so that 'some', 'a reasonable' number passed the exam in that ill-fated year.

As I later discovered, the college examinations adopted a criteria-referenced assessment approach, where the benchmarks for a pass grade were clearly stated and agreed upon. It followed, therefore, that to pass the exam with the standard expected, it was necessary for a student to demonstrate that what they knew, understood and could do matched the established and agreed criteria. If they all surpassed that grade then they all passed and, conversely, if they all fell short of being able to demonstrate the criteria, then they all failed.

165

In Thailand, the entrance examinations to some universities and colleges require aspiring students to meet a certain score in order to be admitted. One year recently, it was reported in the press that following the series of entrance examinations, an insufficient number of young people had met the entrance criteria, so that some courses were uneconomical to run. The solution was easy – make the exam easier. It was a simple and effective solution, which led to very little in the way of public outcry. If the 'establishment' is so adamant that standards should be, at least, maintained, if not raised over time, then how come the lack of indignation when two universities (cited in these two anecdotes) did the opposite without real protest and indignation. The anger was effectively provoked by the fact that the exam must have been too difficult for the customary 'acceptable' number to make the grade.

I mention these two stories to try to show how under a norm-referenced system of assessment, this type of ambiguous behaviour occurs, and yet under a criteria-referenced methodology, it shouldn't. No one seemed interested in really finding out by asking the right questions as to why it was that so many examination candidates failed to make the grade. Instead, it was the fault of the universities/colleges for trying to maintain their customary high standards, or the fault of Thai schools and students for not preparing themselves adequately. But why did no one ask – perhaps the reason why no one, or not enough had passed was perhaps caused, at least in significant part, by the **way** students at school had been taught, or that the **way** in which they were being assessed was faulty.

This takes me back to a point made earlier: when something goes 'wrong' in an organization the tendency is to blame the individuals; a sort of collective scape-goat and finger-pointing. The reality is that it is usually the system that is at fault – demonstrating that it is definitely broke and does indeed need fixing in today's society. People have changed due to changes in the way we lead our lives, and due to technological 'advances' and a whole array of factors which mean that things are very different today to how they were over one hundred years ago. The system should be changing accordingly, in tandem with, if not ahead of the changes themselves. We should stop trying to squeeze today's young and older learners through the old sausage machine, based upon

166

spurious slogans of maintaining standards and 'what was good enough for me is good enough for you'!

When Do We Assess Student Learning?

These historic anomalies are exacerbated and matched by a similar legacy in the timing of these terminal, external examinations. Why do we need terminal examinations at all? Surely there is a need for assessment to be ongoing and permanent as well as non-threatening. It should be congruent with the nature of the continuous learning that schools allege they are trying to enable young people to appreciate, enjoy and thereby achieve. There should be no expectation of achieving a set level, at a set date and at a set age, in the form of an external examination taken under such alien conditions. As I have said, and do not apologise for repeating here, this process sends a contradictory hidden message to young people that learning is not continuous and it is not something to be enjoyed. It is a necessity that you have to follow if you want to be successful in life – or within the system if we are being honest. If learning was the focus, incorporating ongoing assessments, with the student and teacher working in a kind of partnership together to achieve some common and agreed target or goal, surely levels of performance and true learning would correspondingly rise. If we allowed the learner to be intrinsically motivated by the spirit and excitement of discovery, finding solutions and achieving self-determined goals and challenges we would not need this antiquated system of extrinsic motivation. A system which adopts a simple 'sticks and carrots' approach, based on the fear of failure (rather than the thrill of success) and promises of financially rewarding (if not meaningful and spiritually rewarding) employment in later life.

In place of real learning, we prefer what we insist on seeing as the 'tried and tested' method of terminal assessments with all their imperfections to 'assess' our young people on set dates and on content that is determined by faceless others. We then compound all of these imperfections by having these supreme terminal tests at the end of the third or 'summer term', at a time of year when students are least inclined to be stuck indoors revising and being tested, thanks to the longer days and often pleasant sunny and warmer weather. They are also held at a time of year when an increasing number of people are likely to suffer

167

from hay-fever and asthma attacks. This is frankly daft, when young people are essentially active creatures; we again encourage or force them to be passive.

Why are these examinations always taken at this time? Is it something to do with maturation or educational psychology? No! It is because we have a three-term school year (or 'academic' year as many still like to call it – which is an exclusive term for the many other equally valuable types of learning). Furthermore, the rationale for the end of the tri-semester school year being in mid-July, is another anachronism. It is based on the fact that when we were a largely agrarian economic society, we needed the children to be allowed out of school to help their parents in the fields, harvesting the crops. Yet another nonsensical and irrelevant legacy of past practice which creates another set of obstacles to effective learning. It is interesting to note that this practice was relevant some 150 years ago, the same time as the public school system and its archaic curriculum was also in its 'hey day'; and one that state schools mistakenly sought to emulate when they came into being.....and with which we are stuck today as well.

It is also interesting to note the three terms in the school year are named after the seasons, but wait! We have four seasons (in theory anyway) but only three terms: the 'autumn term' (OK, I'll give you that), then the 'winter term' (or to solve the numerical disparity, the more optimistically titled 'spring term'), and the final 'summer term'.

More importantly, we are stuck with three terms based on seasons, and because of traditional orthodoxy, and not in order to promote effective student learning. This results in a long and tiring first term for students and teachers alike, at a time of year when it is increasingly cold and dark and another seasonal, and disruptive, problem of colds and influenza with the concomitant need for absence from school (which implies the cessation of learning). It is way too long, and this is recognised, which explains why there is a week-long half-term holiday placed in the middle, which also serves to disrupt the flow of learning at a pre-determined time. We then have a very short and much-awaited ten-week second term, also with a one-week break in the middle, although I am not sure why. Habit, I guess.

Finally, there is the arduous, (quite literally) testing and overly long summer term when all students take external examinations (and interim school-administered end of term exams) all at different and overlapping times and of different lengths. This results is one or two weeks for those students not taking examinations being left with little 'academic' 'work' to do, which usually results in schools either punishing them by starting the next year's work at a time when they have just finished the year, or by excitingly different and enjoyable other types of learning in what are called a variety of terms as if to justify their inclusion. Titles such as enhancement or activities week are the norm in many schools at this time of year.

Then comes the long summer holiday, which is too long. This leads to young people being bored because they are inactive and seemingly have nothing to do. This is also too long a time for their parents who really want them back at school and conveniently looked after by others. This is in itself a scandal, because it largely demonstrates the social and psychological reliance, dependency on, or addiction to, the school system. What about the idea of schools promoting 'life-long' and 'self-directed' learning – whatever has happened to that?

The answer is that it was always a myth – an educationist's dream; not a liberating and practical reality; all thanks to the way we do things and the timing of the school terms.

For nearly as long as I can remember, educationists have been arguing for a four-term school year. Traditional wisdom, however, still prevails, making everyone continue with the same outmoded, long three-term system, possibly because of the upheaval involved in changing the timing of external examinations and subsequent university entrance. This is another way in which the influence of academically biased universities dictates the pattern of schooling that is received by all young people in the UK. The hidden message in this is that education at school is based on the need for familiarity and convenience for parents and the established interest groups, and not in the best interests of effective teaching and learning of generations of young people.

Where Do We Assess Student Learning?

Everyone knows the answer to this question, because we have all experienced it. Students are sat in a large school hall and/or in a myriad of separate classrooms which are strictly monitored to ensure that totally unrealistic 'examination conditions' are followed and obeyed. Examination boards even carry out spot-checks to ensure that schools are strictly applying all aspects of the standard modus operandi. It is a huge investment of time, money and people; time that could be better spent being involved in teaching and learning and assessing students in a more realistic setting, and in a more relevant way.

In the same way that teachers teach and students learn in a place called 'school', so it is that the essentially academic accomplishments of all young people are tested and assessed in that same environment. Why is student learning not conducted in the multi-faceted environment called the 'community', which is where what the students have learnt at school is supposedly going to be applied? Is it because it would be too difficult to control – as opposed to manage – or too complex to standardise – instead of celebrating the diversity of human talent and ability?

The result is, that for a growing number of young people, what they are taught in school, the way in which it is taught and ultimately assessed are all a tedious irrelevance that gets in the way of them being enabled to learn those things in which they are personally and genuinely interested. The counter-argument to this might be that young people these days do not know what they want to learn. This could be valid, because I can recall recalcitrant students complaining that what they were doing in class was boring. My response was a question: What do you want to do instead? The answer was often a belligerent "Nothing" or, more frequently, "Dunno." If a student wants to do nothing, then let them. They will soon get truly bored whilst others are being involved and engaged with differing degrees of success. The more common of the two disaffected retorts above that they did not know what they wanted to do is equally worrisome, but I would ask is this because they have been 'schooled out' of determining the direction, nature and intensity of independent learning for themselves. The way schools are run and the purpose they serve is too pre-specified and too prescriptive; it rarely encourages young people to determine their own learning and to explore the diversity of their innate interests, curiosities and talents.

The Effects of Assessment

All of this serves as a pervasive and often corrosive influence on student learning and the development of a habit of motivated, enjoyable and challenging life-long learning for the rest of their lives. The external examination system and the imperative of national testing of students is now distorting the curriculum and the necessary diversity of learning opportunities that students can encounter so that they can all feel the thrill of discovery for themselves – and that includes the discovery of previously hidden talents that lie within each and every one of them. Education at school should be more about littering their paths with quality learning opportunities, to enable and genuinely empower young people to find out what interests them, which is usually that in which they are able to excel. The things that we, as responsible adults, feel that students should, need to or must know about is usually founded on false consciousness and traditional orthodoxy; it is rarely premised on what students themselves really want and need to know more about, so that they can become active and constructive citizens.

This thirst for assessing student learning and holding schools and teachers accountable for their success in sustaining the unsustainable is undermining true and relevant student learning, and its pervasive and corrosive effects are creeping down to undermine the exciting work and good practice that used to characterise most primary schools. To end this section on assessment, I want to refer to an excellent article which appeared in the Guardian newspaper entitled, **'Study reveals stressed out 7 – 11 year olds'**, by Polly Curtis on 12th October 2007.

"National tests for seven and 11-year-olds are putting children under stress and feeding into a "pervasive anxiety" about their lives and the world they are growing up in, according to an intimate portrait of primary school life (Cambridge University report, 'Community Surroundings')."

The report was based on a series of detailed and in-depth interviews with 700 primary school children, as well as their teachers and parents. It showed that primary-aged children worry on a daily basis about world issues such as global warming and terrorism, and in a more localized but equally fundamental context, they are also worried about their friendships and passing the next exam. In short, these terminal assessments stress children out; and unnecessarily so.

The report found that subjecting these children to national tests results have some unsavoury outcomes. In addition to leaving most children stressed, they also effectively coerce some middle class parents into paying for private tutors to get their children through these examinations. Remember, these are children who have not yet reached secondary school age and already the disease of external examinations has infected the joy of learning for learning's sake, and panicked parents into what the report calls *"parallel learning"* with private tutors. The report also found that these primary school students actually feared the world outside the school gate, especially those who lived in urban areas who were found to be overly anxious about violent crime. Interestingly enough, their parents were more stressed about their children being involved in traffic accidents. This is effectively parents who drive their children to school to reduce the risk of being hit by a car – possibly driven by a parent taking his/her child to school!

The article in the Guardian also went on to note that the General Teaching Council for England was opposed to the national testing of seven, 11 and 14-year-olds, where the results were published in the additional educational malaise of league tables, which were scrutinised by parents when choosing a school for their children. It would seem as if parents would be better advised to scrutinize the type of curriculum that (sadly) 'rival' schools had designed to meet the needs of young people, as opposed to the stress-inducing examinations. Needless to say, the recommendations of the GTC for England were ignored by government ministers in England who were adamant these national tests would remain firmly in place. This was despite the fact that better counsel had prevailed in Wales, where the tests had been scrapped!

In conclusion, is it hardly surprising that the way student learning is assessed is probably adding to the growing and spreading disaffection of so many young people in the alleged 'education' that they receive whilst at school, and who then register this disillusionment by adopting negative and potentially damaging behaviours such as truancy and disruption and maladjustment?

Is this really the best we can do for the education of our future generations? Is this, indeed, the direction we should be going in? I think not!

Chapter Eight: The Centrality of the Creative Curriculum

"We've got to show in the next few years that we can break the cycle of deprivation. For these children, our job is to fill their pockets with confidence."

Tim Brighouse (when at the Department of Education)

In this chapter, there are essentially two issues that need to be taken together so that they mutually bestow on each other a greater sense of importance and urgency. The first is that the whole issue of the curriculum – the learning experiences that young people receive, whether intentional or unintentional, planned or unplanned, or explicit or implicit – should be at the absolute *heart* of all decision making within the school. The second issue is that the central element or dimension of the curriculum should be the ***creative and aesthetic***, as partly embodied in the ***visual and performing arts*** for example.

Creativity in all curriculum areas should also be promoted almost above all else and certainly **not** shuffled off into the curricular periphery that is all too often euphemistically called 'extra-curricular' or 'co-curricular activities'. By being pushed into this marginal territory, or seen as best delivered in the province of the aesthetic, less or non-academic subjects, the ***hidden message*** is that such endeavours are somehow a luxury and not a necessity when compared to those pursuits that are essentially academic in nature. My argument, along with far more notable others, is that this intentional or unintentional priority is, like most of the current high school system, utterly backward and back to front – actually 'arse backwards' was the phrase that initially sprang to mind!

The creative and aesthetic dimension is the most eminently powerful one that truly allows and enables young people to express themselves – something that teenagers, in particular, are desperate to do. It also works powerfully to enable young people to find the self-belief and self-esteem that undoubtedly gives them the 'pocketfuls of confidence', to which Tim Brighouse rightly refers above. In so doing, we empower young people to feel confident enough to cope with the rigours of the more academic curriculum with which so many young people feel intimidated and consequently disinterested. By changing the central focus of the school curriculum, I believe that over time we can make major inroads into the cycle of deprivation that is so deeply rooted in a lack of opportunities, as well as in feelings of powerlessness and impotence. These negative forces can effectively, directly and powerfully be tackled by engendering feelings of individual, collective or community self-belief, and the hope of a better future. The motto is definitely – *believe, achieve, succeed* – and in that order – but we have to create the conditions, opportunities and context in schools and education that motivate, liberate and enable young learners to adopt this mantra in a very personal and purposeful way.

The current focal point of the curriculum: that of achieving examination success in pre-specified academic pursuits is, in my opinion, to try and start with the outcomes or outputs, and ignore the underlying individual and essential inputs; the pre-conditions that are so vital to enabling *achievement* in a range of pursuits.

As Charles Handy rightly put it so long ago, in two of my favourite quotations:

"We should train ourselves not to ask, "How intelligent is s/he", but "Which intelligence does s/he have most of?"

It follows, therefore:

"Instead of a national curriculum for education, what is really needed is an individual curriculum for every child."

Gloria Steinem puts the same notion even more simply, in this incredibly powerful way:

"If the shoe doesn't fit, must we change the foot?"

I love that quotation, because it defines one of the central motivations for writing this book, and deftly putting it in a nutshell.

These points demonstrate that the views about secondary schooling that I have acquired through experience, critical reflection and intuitive thought over many years as a professional teacher and educator are not exactly new or original. They have, in fact, been made before by others, albeit in different ways. For this reason I consider the words attributed to others in the form of quotations as being helpful, illuminating and thought-provoking. Sadly, it seems as though such quotes are only really worth taking into consideration if they are attributed to famous or 'successful' personalities; such is the power of

175

our adopted celebrity culture. I am willing to think about and consider quotations made by anyone who is thinking, regardless of their status, reputation or background. Wise words are wise words whoever utters them, surely? After all, I have learnt a great deal from the utterances of young people in schools where I have been fortunate to have worked, or visited.

Before looking at why I believe in this centrality of a 'creative' curriculum, I should point out that it is not the only element needed to break the cycle of deprivation and disadvantage that infects current models of schooling. Social policies that promote education (not necessarily schooling), health and economic opportunities to those who are born disadvantaged are also enormously important in achieving such a, hitherto, elusive goal. In short, the real way to end this damaging and wasteful cycle of deprivation and disadvantage rests on action that is **both** *private* (via empowering people and communities through real and relevant educational opportunities) and *public* (in the sense of an enabling and supportive government policy, and action to develop infrastructure in its widest sense) in nature. We must stop seeing the solution as being either one **or** the other, when in fact it requires a real partnership between the two. Unfortunately, the way in which 'party politics' currently operates in the UK serves to perpetuate and accentuate the economic, societal and political divide that results in social ills such as poverty, disenfranchisement and deprivation. Until such time as there is a 'cross-party' consensus, and action replaces this seemingly perpetual difference, these significantly damaging ailments will remain a disgrace for, and a moral stain upon our allegedly 'civilised' society. Surely, if we cannot find any common ground in this willingly adversarial political system on important matters such as health care and education, then I would argue that this represents a massive indictment of the educational and political paradigm that is so dominant in the UK; not to mention it also being so stupendously and ridiculously out of date, childish and unhelpfully divisive.

Furthermore, the school needs to re-think its notion of what they all tend to call 'the curriculum' and focus on what is the *real* curricular **entitlement** of every young person who attends these traditional institutions. This entitlement needs to be comprehensive, clearly defined and offered to all from the age of 11 to 18 years. It also needs to be defined in terms of the broad types of learning experience that we want young people to explore, discover and enjoy – and not defined by 'core' and 'foundation' subjects which are politically and economically determined according to the needs of industry, work and adult life, as perceived by the established, controlling elite. In most cases, the current aims of schooling fail miserably to meet the innate needs, passions and interests of young people for the world that they will actually face, (as opposed to the world as it is *now*, which will be history and defunct by the time these 'school-children' actually escape their compulsory, overtly enforced and essentially divisive educational diet).

"Everybody is a genius, but if you judge a fish by its ability to climb a tree,
it will spend its whole life thinking that it is stupid."
(Albert Einstein)

Yet again, Einstein's genius pinpoints the sheer stupidity of the system, whereby the individual is 'blamed' for the inadequacy of the school curriculum, and where academe and the cognitive is effectively the only facet of human intelligence that is seen as important, relevant and useful.

The Creativity Issue

"Without creativity there is only repetition and routine. These are highly valuable and provide the bulk of our behaviour – but creativity is needed for change, improvement and new direction."
(Edward de Bono)

Edward de Bono has been writing, talking and training people about creativity – or lateral thinking ('outside of the box') – for longer than I can remember, but what puzzles me is why his ideas have yet to permeate the seemingly impregnable bastion, the traditional orthodoxy that surrounds schooling. It has, however, been the focus of much training and change in industry for example. Perhaps the lack of creativity in the curriculum that has existed for over one hundred years explains why the people who make the policy decisions are so against changing the paradigm to meet the real-world needs we have been facing in the 21st Century – or the previous century for that matter?

On the topic of lateral thinking, de Bono posits that it is the creativity concerned with changing ideas, perceptions and concepts that is crucial. He argues that:

> *"Instead of working harder with the same ideas, perceptions and concepts, we should seek to change them."*

Furthermore, and what I think is a crucial, if not critical point, he argues that this type of *'idea creativity'* is not the same as *'aesthetic creativity'*, which is why the term 'lateral thinking' came into being. This distinction is fundamental in the context of education, as de Bono believes that 'idea creativity' can be taught whilst 'aesthetic creativity' cannot. So is the latter something we are born with and which should be viewed as something that some of us have, whereas others do not?

Before I look in more detail at this question, however, it is important to ask that if de Bono is right, and idea creativity can be taught, why is there so little evidence of lateral thinking being consciously developed within young people whilst they are at school? Where is it embedded in the entitlement curriculum of all young people from the earliest of age – if it even exists at all? My view on this is that young people (and adults) see making mistakes as a bad thing, and so the learner seeks to give the answer that they think the teacher wants, rather than the one they think is right – or ***possible***. Instead, conformity and standardisation are the norm and the practice that is almost universally evident in the secondary schools that I have visited, or in which I have worked. A quotation that I am unable to attribute to anyone on the grounds that its author is apparently unknown, rightly points out that:

> *"A graduation ceremony is an event where the commencement speaker tells thousands of students dressed in identical caps and gowns, that individuality is the key to success."*

Whilst this may be apocryphal rather than genuine, the fact that it rings so true suggests that it deserves to be attributed to someone, if only to verify its origin, originality or invention.

De Bono maintains that educational establishments totally under-estimate the importance of 'possibility'. To illustrate the way this happens and the associated danger it entails, he refers to China two-thousand years ago. At that time, China was scientifically and technologically way ahead of the West, as evidenced by the fact that they had gunpowder and rockets, but their relatively advanced progress ground to an abrupt halt. De Bono says that this was because the Chinese thought they could move from 'fact to fact, rather than developing hypothesis which took account of **possibility**. He goes further by offering a more contemporary illustration of this same malaise, as a result of the *"excellence of computers"*. He says that, today, people are starting to believe that the collection and analysis of data will in itself help us to make decisions and policies and strategies which can guide us in the future. This will, however, lead to the same grinding halt to mankind making progress, which he describes as *"an extremely dangerous situation"*. What is missing is the application of creativity to interpret data in new and different ways, as well as knowing where to look for data to form new and life-changing hypotheses.

> **"Our culture and habits of thinking insist that we always move towards certainty. We need to pay equal attention to possibility."**
> (Edward de Bono)

We certainly and desperately need young people to think far more creatively as well as analytically, with perception, intuition and imagination!

As far as schooling is concerned (or 'education' as it is more commonly called), I do not wish to dwell further on the issue of lateral thinking or idea creativity, important though it is, except to say that it **must** be developed in schools and become a 'way of thoughtful life' in all areas of the school curriculum.

Instead, I wish to focus on the issue of **'aesthetic creativity'** which is something that I believe we all have in some way and to a greater or lesser extent – if indeed it can actually be quantified in any meaningful way at all. (It is rather sad that all forms of human achievement and expression have to be measurable and quantifiable in some way or another in order to appease the demands for accountability.) I believe that the school system in its orthodox and conventional wisdom crushes the learner's spirit and their creative passion until they become more standardised and prioritised, in terms of what they think, know and are led to believe they should do with their lives. Arguably, this makes them more malleable, controllable even; more easily shaped and usable by the old 'industrial age' paradigm that Stephen R. Covey refers to in his book 'The 8th Habit', and for which public education was created to quite literally **serve**. In simple terms, they are less likely to question – so that education replaces religion as a way of 'gentling the masses'!

To put it more strongly, I feel that schools emasculate, if not destroy the creativities that are undoubtedly inherent within the human spirit, or the individual essence that defines our uniqueness. In short, parents and teachers, often for all the right, loving and caring reasons, interfere with the liberation of the creative instincts that all children are born with; preventing them from truly finding themselves and achieving their destiny in life.

> *"All children are born geniuses; 9,999 out of every 10,000*
> *are swiftly, inadvertently degeniusized by grown-ups."*
> (Buckminster Fuller)

To **remain** questioning individuals from the time we were infants, when the question **'Why?'** is on the lips of every eager learner, of course requires confidence and curiosity within the individual if it is to be steadfastly maintained; the confidence to take risks, to challenge simplistic answers and to make mistakes. It also demands breaking the existing paradigm governing schools so that young people are challenged, encouraged and enabled by adults to do what they want to do, rather than what adults traditionally 'know' is right and good for them – or think they do, often mistakenly. I have often heard adults saying that school was 'OK' for them, and so it follows that it must also be 'OK' for those who follow them within the classrooms and corridors of 'education'. I am irresistibly tempted to ask, once more: "So, **'OK'** is good enough, is it?"

I have seen young people unimaginably energized and motivated by getting involved in aesthetic and creative pursuits, which although non-academic have led those students to not only amazing their parents and other adults, but more importantly, surprising themselves with what they are capable of achieving, and how genuinely alive, valued and empowered they feel in so doing!

I often recall an interesting visit to a primary school in Lagos, Nigeria, when I was in the process of setting up a new international secondary school in that fascinating country; a country of so many contradictions, but an incredibly resilient and friendly population which defines the considerable majority.

During my preliminary visit of two weeks, prior to taking up the post of founding Principal, I was invited to help 'market' the school and visit one of the main primary schools from which the fledgling school was hoping to attract students. Given that the 'school' I was to help establish had not been built at that time, despite having been given a name, in addition to my unshakeable belief that a school is essentially a community of people who are to work together in a learning partnership, what could I realistically say about this scholastic intention in the making?

I arrived at the primary school and the Head Teacher asked me to speak to a small group of Year 6 students (aged 10/11 years) in order to "tell them all about the (new) school". I instinctively and politely declined that agenda, preferring instead to talk *with* the twelve students whom I was lucky enough to meet, and find out more about them, and what made them 'tick', as it were. I began by asking them a pretty standard question concerning what were their favourite subjects in the school curriculum. The answers elicited, from a very charming and interesting audience were hardly surprising. They all had different 'subjects' that they said they liked best, which one might reasonably expect from a diverse group of pre-teens. In fact, there was very little duplication. (This may explain why teamwork is such an effective way to achieve outstanding results in any organization, because the process of collaboration – often so alien to and in schools – enables people of different strengths and weaknesses to cooperate and pool their discrete knowledge and capabilities, which they have learnt in isolation in the narrow, academic school curriculum.)

I then asked those wonderful youngsters in Nigeria a more open-ended question, about what it was that they liked to do in their free time. One might reasonably expect an equally huge diversity of responses in this area, but their answers were most interesting and revealing: gymnastics, art (more than once), music, playing the drums, playing the guitar, dance and ballet, drama, games and sports. I quickly noted that although they had all given very different 'formal' curriculum subjects as their preference, their pastimes were all in what one might call the **_aesthetic and creative_** domain. Furthermore, nobody said they found any one academic subject so interesting that they wanted to pursue it in their 'free-time'. I found this contrast in their responses to the two questions perplexing but equally fascinating. I decided to share my curiosity with them by pointing out that there was a diversity of interest in their individually preferred 'subject', but a universal attraction to aesthetic, creative and certainly non-academic personal interests, undertaken when they were free to do what they liked and enjoyed. I asked them why this was. Yet again, their answers were so illuminating and perceptive. One boy said that he thought this was because they were all "allowed" (an interesting choice of words I thought) to follow pastimes that enabled them to 'just' express themselves. It was an obvious point upon hearing, but nonetheless a brilliant, revealing and interesting response, I thought. No sooner had he uttered those memorable words than a girl sitting behind him emphatically said, "Yes, and also there is no right or wrong!"

I was enthralled and captivated by this revealing and significant learning experience for me. Perhaps what they said struck a chord in terms of my own 'over-looked' interests in the aesthetic and creative domain (music and drama especially) when I had been 'at school', whilst in those days learning so little about myself and my own destiny. Maybe their innocent and honest answers had recognized, expressed and reinforced my own latent frustration at not being given a more formal opportunity to allow my spirit free rein either at school or 'at home', as my genuinely wonderful and caring parents felt it was right that they made all of the 'major' decisions for me. For that, I thank them and lovingly condemn them in equal measure for not enabling me to explore the talents of my spirit, my personal calling and reason for being alive, but our mutual love and my cultural deference to 'those who know better' won the day, and I tried to conform to the pre-destined path that society and the ruling paradigm wished me to follow.

I have also seen the immense motivational power of aesthetic and creative activities at first hand, following the best appointment I ever made as a Head

Teacher of a secondary school where the student population came mainly from a socially and economically deprived catchment area. I needed a Curriculum Leader for the aesthetic and creative learning experiences within our school curriculum, and appointed a dance specialist and a quite exceptional person to the post. Not only was she a hugely effective manager of such a key curriculum area, but she also set the school alight with dance; dance relevant to the young men and women in this 11-16 comprehensive school. Her name was Karen Healey!

Prior to that time, the Arts within the school had been dismal in terms of reach, involvement and the standards of excellence expected and achieved. It was frankly embarrassing. I can vividly recall being invited as Head Designate to visit the school as a guest at their annual drama production, an event which proved to be eminently forgettable for all the right reasons. Its only positive was that it did involve a significant number of students from various year groups, but the quality of what was on show was, sadly, dreadfully poor. The title of the performance escapes me now, and I often wish that the squirming embarrassment I felt for the young people (and the audience) on that occasion could also be so readily expunged from my memory. It was uncomfortable being in the audience to witness that event, as the quality of what was presented was so far below reasonable expectations.

The new 'dancing curriculum leader' worked magic with those who were already keen artists and actors, as one might expect, but the most amazing transformation came with the widespread and almost immediate involvement of some of the more disaffected, truculent and challenging boys and girls at the school. Moreover, this human dynamo quickly enlisted the active support and involvement of youngsters from our main partner primary schools, and all within such a short period of time. Starting dance for the first time in the school in September, I recall Karen informing me that there was to be an evening event in late November which was ambitiously and enticingly called *'Dance Explosion'*. My earlier memories of embarrassment came back to torment me; to make me wonder what lay ahead for the assembled throng on this future occasion.

I need not have worried, as the entire evening involved so many young men and women, including those of primary school age dancing their way into the hearts, minds and souls of the immensely lucky audience. I do not exaggerate when I say that the number of people involved in the dancing, stage management, lighting and sound, was significant, but the quality of what was presented would have graced any stage in the West End of London! I sat with tears in my eyes watching so many students who had already been branded as 'failures' at school, certainly in their own eyes if not those of the 'establishment', produce such wonderful entertainment and self-expression. I was not alone in being so spiritually and emotionally moved, as those sentiments were without exception mirrored in the eyes and hearts of a packed auditorium. (Actually, that is to rather over-state the grandeur of the actual venue – a school hall.)

What also amazed me – and taught me a powerful lesson – was the fact that many of the most challenging and truculent young men and women willingly became involved, and found for once that they could earn the appreciation and admiration of others through diverse self-expression, albeit via the medium of dance and theatre. Their involvement was at odds with the lack of engagement in the rest of the traditional school curriculum, as was the success and concomitant boost to their self-esteem that arose from their aesthetic and creative achievement. It proved to be instrumental in allowing so many previously disaffected young people to engage again with the less glamorous elements of the curriculum, and with school in general. Student attendance improved, as the 'dancing truants' knew that to be absent from school would result in not being entitled to participate in that which gave them so much credibility and self-confidence. Similarly, some of those who were already known to the local constabulary and the law courts for criminal actions began to clean up their act – quite literally!

This development within the school and its community was most definitely instrumental (alongside and in tandem with other initiatives) in leading to a significant improvement in external examination results over time, thanks to the taste of success that was achieved by these young people whose prior experience within the fragmented school curriculum had been one of relative or even absolute failure. I would not have believed it had I not witnessed it with my own eyes. Truly remarkable – as was Karen Healey, the teacher who served as the catalyst in providing the opportunity and inspiration for the liberation of hitherto inner giftedness and talent that I believe all young people have in and for the Arts!

It is with profound sadness, therefore, that at the time of writing this, I read of actions of the coalition government in the UK, under the self-serving leadership of Messrs. Cameron and Gove, ably assisted by a compliant Mr. Clegg. The two proudly announce the new E-Bacc (English Baccalaureate) examination system which serves to thrust the education that takes place in schools back to the dull and distant days of 'horses for courses', by openly – even cheerfully – recognising that there will be more students "failing" under the new monolithic academic examination system that the new 'Laurel and Hardy' in government seem to prefer for the children of other people. It is worth noting that this 'new' initiative – effectively old wine in new (opaque) bottles – has been proposed without due consultation with the education profession who will be ultimately responsible for its delivery in practice, and doubtlessly judged upon its overall success or failure.

Since that very personal experience of the power that the aesthetic and creative dimension of learning has in motivating young people to become involved more fully in their learning at school, by being able to find new ways of demonstrating their self-worth and achieving success, I have, somewhat belatedly, come across similar views expressed by eminent people such as Sir Ken Robinson. He has been arguing a similar point of view far more publicly and effectively than I, with his clarion call for at least an equally important role and status for creativity within the school curriculum as that which is customarily afforded to literacy and numeracy. For those who have yet to hear him speak on the TED talks that can be found on-line, I can only suggest that you are missing a real treat, not to mention a very important line of argument that urgently needs more serious consideration in terms of the recommended action that is so long overdue. The essence of much of what he says can be captured in the following quotation, taken from his first TED talk:

"Too many people never connect with their true talents and therefore don't know what they're really capable of achieving. In that sense, they don't know who they really are."

For me the fundamental question centres on why it is that such passionate, rational and widely accepted arguments, by people such as the immensely articulate and persuasive Sir Ken Robinson, have yet to break the stranglehold that the traditional paradigm of the education that takes place at school has over the curriculum offered by most schools worldwide? As previously commented on, the nature of the subjects on offer, and the way in which they are structured, packaged and delivered via the school timetable has remained largely unchallenged and definitely unchanged. As a result, schools emasculate, if not destroy the creativities that are undoubtedly inherent within the human spirit – and that which essentially defines our uniqueness! This palpably stupid situation must be changed as well as challenged, so as to not only value the importance of the aesthetic and creative dimension of learning, but move it from the optional periphery to which it is so often assigned nowadays, to the very heart of every school's curriculum and every student's curricular entitlement.

The Centrality Issue

I am aware that to argue for such a central role to be afforded to experiences and types of learning currently viewed by many as irrelevant or optional extras to that which most schools have on offer may be rather bold, if not perceived as dogmatic, but I strongly believe this to be justified for the following reasons, among others. The first of these is to make the point that the omission of such learning perspectives in the past needs to be recognised by a healthy dose of positive discrimination, at least initially. Furthermore, it also makes up for the lost opportunity of past generations, by giving more generously to future cohorts of young people than those who have gone before. This is not as frivolous as it may seem at first. For change to be effective, it must significantly change behaviours; behaviours of students and their parents, especially with the latter group exerting such a powerful influence on the subject 'choices' that their children make and take from the ages of 14 to 18 years particularly. I would argue that the educational benefit and sheer joy that involvement in the expressive and performing arts can bestow needs to be demonstrated to those parents who still cling to the outmoded notion that academe is all that matters, so that they do not stand in the way when their offspring wish to make and take their own life choices and pursue their own interests, dreams, ambitions and goals. This need for parent education is pressing, but will not be entirely

186

achieved whilst universities and, in turn the government, still exert such a hugely negative influence (from the point of view of the Arts) on what is learnt in schools, as well as why and how it is learnt!

Another reason for this proposed centrality of the arts, as opposed to any type of learning experience, is related to the fact that children so often demonstrate their divergence and difference when it comes to those subjects on the formal curriculum that they enjoy and, in which, they also excel. But when it comes to the 'other, non-academic things' that they pursue, often in their own and out-of-school time, they demonstrate a convergence and a togetherness of enjoyment in the expressive and creative arts, which I also take to encompass various sporting endeavours. Another way of looking at this commonality is that there are so many different ways of expressing ourselves through these aesthetic and creative outlets; it offers a kaleidoscopic scope that effectively accommodates the inevitable and immense diversity of the human spirit, as well as our common humanity.

Moreover, the simple nature of the visual and performing arts, in that they are avenues in which everyone can find personal and spiritual expression, and in such a diversity of ways, enables them to experience a much more meaningful dimension through which to develop their self-esteem and self-confidence without their efforts being subjected to arbitrary definitions of being 'right' and/or 'wrong'. This justification for the centrality of the arts is strengthened, given the evidence that academic research and empirical data provides, that involvement in such pursuits does much to improve the results that so many students achieve in the more traditional, academic arena. This surely merits a central role for such ubiquitous, all-encompassing and important types of learning experience.

A further justification lies in the contention that creativity is needed in all other learning perspectives: the human and social, the linguistic, the mathematical, the scientific and technological, and so on, and for this reason its centrality is also justifiable. After all, we do not need more scientists, engineers and architects; we need **_more creative_** people in such, and other, occupations; people capable of finding new solutions to current problems in imaginative, new and different ways. The focus should be placed more fully on quality

187

rather than just quantity, in the vain hope that more of the same might be the salve to remedy today's issues, challenges and concerns. Furthermore, the aesthetic and creative learning perspective lends itself for possibility (rather than certainty) to be welcomed and entertained, which relates to the cognitive creativity to which Edward de Bono refers. It also readily accommodates learning which focuses on 'could be' (rather than 'is') questions as Guy Claxton argues in his excellent and thought-provoking book '*What's the Point of School? – Rediscovering the Heart of Education*'. The essence of both 'possibility' as well as 'could be' questions in all aspects of the school curriculum allows for the expansion of knowledge and learning; the development of curiosity and imagination, as well as more self-directed and interesting forms of enquiry for the learner, as opposed to the teacher and the education system. Such approaches are far more likely to both engage and enthuse young people; to encourage them to be more actively involved in their studies and to motivate them to strive to find out new answers to current problems, and to view mistakes and set-backs as valuable learning opportunities as opposed to a sign of failure, disappointment and a lack of success.

It must be universally known by now, that schools do a very good job in convincing young learners that mistakes are bad things which, of course, is the opposite of the truth. To illustrate this, I used to play a simple game with my tutor group to illustrate the negative mind-set that making mistakes and 'being wrong' is a barrier, rather than a potential and essential stepping stone to achievement and success. The game was essentially very simple. I would choose a number between 1 and 1,000 and the students had twenty questions to determine the number I had in mind. As was always required, I had to write the chosen number on a piece of paper prior to starting the game, so that I could not cheat by changing the number in the event of someone guessing it correctly. Once the game started, the students took it in turns to ask me questions to help identify the number in question, let us say it was **_825_**, and this is when the exercise became very revealing. There was always one student who would randomly try and guess the precise number in the first few questions, as if misguided bravado was urging them to believe that by some miracle or stroke of extreme fortune they would hit the nail on its numerical head, thanks to sheer pot luck! Such questions were always wrong, and elicited an understandable and justifiable groan of disapproval from the rest of the class for having effectively wasted a precious question. Usually, students would ask the more intelligent questions, such as, "Is it (the number) between 1 and 700?" to which, in this example, I would have replied, "No." This negative or 'wrong' answer again elicited a groan from the rest of class, in a highly disapproving way, despite the fact that the answer meant that the number that they had to identify was in the smaller range of 300 (i.e. between 700 and 1000) as opposed to a possible 700 numbers, had I answered differently. This 'wrong' answer meant that the students had significantly *increased* their chances of finding the correct answer with their remaining questions. The countervailing power of the word *'wrong'*, on the other hand, was always demonstrated when a subsequent question would be something along the lines of, "Is it between 1 and 500?" to which I had again to say, rather obviously one might have thought, "No." The more useful information gained by the previous *'wrong'* answer had been immediately discarded by some (rarely all) of the students present – quite amazing! The report on that school in terms of facilitating student learning should be, "Could do better!"

One final reason that I would like to offer to justify the central role of the visual and performing arts in school is that the methodology used is necessarily active and student-focused. This goes a long way to explain why so many students thrive when working in this curriculum domain. The success of these more active methods of teaching and learning can be used by teachers in other subject areas of the curriculum to similarly engage, enthuse and involve young people in their more academic learning pursuits. In this way, aesthetic and creative learning can be used to demonstrate the way in which more active, student-centred and student-directed teaching and learning approaches bring out the best in all students, and this can then be adopted or emulated to good effect in other subject areas. In other words, these expressive types of learning can act as a positive role model throughout the rest of the school curriculum, by reassuring often sceptical teachers that they can still cover a content laden syllabus in more imaginative and active ways, and students will probably achieve or gain better examination results as a result. More importantly, they will certainly enjoy their learning and their time in school to a much greater and personally-fulfilling degree. Such active teaching and learning methodology also has the benefit of promoting collaboration and teamwork amongst students, which can help create a true *synergy of learning*, with individuals benefiting from the amazing group dynamic that can and usually does develop.

Placing the aesthetic and creative dimension of learning at the very centre of the school curriculum would, I believe, make massive inroads into tackling the problems of student under-achievement, truancy and disaffection with school, as well as many of the other 'Why, Why, Why?' questions in the first chapter of this book, which have concerned and troubled many educationists – as well as a plethora of various others – for a long time now.

Young people are born geniuses, with what Roger Mc Gough (my favourite poet) calls 'a poetic sensibility' that is knocked out of them by well-meaning adults. He argued that children make disparate links and that they see things that we, as adults, do not normally see in our interactions with the world around us. In other words, children make connections between things all the time, and they use words in a more creative, flexible and imaginative way. The example which I simply adore that Roger Mc. Gough uses is when a child observed, "Look Dad, the candle is crying." In adult-created learning environments, these creatively gifted individuals are taught *'out'* of such wonderful and revealing ways of thinking. There is no time for day-dreaming, no time for letting your mind wander in any way, so as to see where it goes and where it takes you. Instead, the creative child is brought (quite literally) crashing back down into the concrete world of certainty, by being told that the candle is not crying, rather it is the heat of the flame that is agitating the wax molecules so that they turn from a solid into a liquid. Ah, thanks for putting me right, Dad, in your infinite wisdom!

How to Break the Mould?
As I see it, there are essentially two ways in which attitudes and behaviours can be changed: one is by a radical reform which overhauls the very nature of schooling and education, and the other is through more incremental change over a longer period of time. Although I truly believe that we need a radical shake-up in the way we view learning, the way we recognise the different types of intelligence and the way in which we help realise the many talents that young people all have in varying combinations and degrees, I am sufficiently pragmatic to accept that such dramatic and major change is unlikely to get to

190

the starting line, given the powerful way in which the traditional educational paradigm holds sway. Consequently, the need is to change the system from within, without making changes that would cause the middle classes to take flight and panic. The risk of a more gradualist agenda for change is that the power of the existing culture and vested interest groups who are in favour of maintaining the status quo, can act as a brake on any serious attempt to make the required change. In other words, custom and habit will militate against the incremental change, and prevent any serious move away from the conventional wisdom in the way we educate our young people.

So, how to square this challenging change circle? Perhaps it is worth trying a moderate degree of radical change, accompanied by a process of incremental change that at least starts to take us, in some determined and serious manner, in the new direction which we would ideally prefer to go. Change that genuinely provides a new direction capable of effectively countering the many overt or hidden messages that do so much to undermine attempts to make the schooling we offer all young people become truly educational and relevant to their real needs in the here and now, as well as in the future. We might perhaps structure and deliver the entitlement curriculum of our educational institutions in a way that is more enlightening and which liberates the inner giftedness that every new generation possesses in abundance, and which we currently squander pretty ruthlessly, and all in the name of schooling.

-- -

Section C: The Structure of the Curriculum and its Delivery

Chapter Nine: A Reason to Be

"For what is lost in so many lives, and what must be recovered, is a sense of personal calling, that there is a reason to be alive."

(James Hillman)

Before suggesting possible ways in which we might go about squaring the circle of wishing to promote the aesthetic and creative elements of learning and the curriculum on the one hand, whilst on the other hand comforting and reassuring the middle classes as well as others, that their unerring belief in the supreme rightness of the traditional academic orthodoxy would also be preserved, I want to look back at the issue of why the aesthetic and creative dimension of learning is so vital. I want to do this by asking you to consider the formidable opportunity cost of failing to give it an equal, if not a pivotal role in all that we do in schools.

Some personal perspectives on life

In the opening chapters of this book, I recounted my own schooling experiences, and how they had been shaped by the concern and directives of my loving, caring parents and the inevitable academic orthodoxy that determines the school system. As a result, I followed a route that was well-charted, pre-determined and delivered by others with little or scant regard to what might be my actual calling in life – the very reason for my being. I now know that my soul was calling me to become an actor and an entertainer of some sort, given my self-directed and historical pursuits of things musical and thespian, which did so much to distract me from the somewhat manufactured purpose of my academic endeavours whilst at school. But, believe me, they distracted me in such an engaging, enriching and empowering way because they represented the real me; the 'me' who wanted to be; the 'me' who wanted to live and feel alive!

In many ways, I have been extremely fortunate to have had a career as a teacher in schools and, more recently, as a corporate trainer; fortunate as being the facilitator of others' learning which has given me ample opportunity to entertain the assembled learners, and to do my best to make their prescribed learning engaging, interesting and fun, as much as possible. Nonetheless, I also feel as if I have missed my whole reason for being alive, and this has caused me to reflect on whether things might have been somewhat different had my natural mother not been killed in that car accident when I was so young, and when my dear sister and brother were even younger. Such reflection, however, is undertaken with a sense of immense trepidation and assumed guilt, as it implies that I believe my life may have turned out to be more fulfilling, or 'better', had I been able to receive the guidance that my natural mother could arguably have been able to provide, as opposed to that of my truly and genuinely wonderful second Mum or step-mother, who did so much more than anyone else to support my artistic interests and endeavours.

As if to avoid rightful admonishment for impertinently questioning my step-mother's love, guidance and care, let me start by making it clear how incredibly lucky I believe I was to have someone who was as supportive in her recognition and encouragement of my innate abilities, interests and drive in the artistic arena. It was she who persuaded my reluctant father to buy me my first ever drum set for the princely sum of £25 back in 1970, which replaced the substitute cardboard boxes that I 'played' in my bedroom to the accompaniment provided by my favourite band of the time – The Who and their spectacular drummer, Keith Moon – using my Mum's knitting needles as drum sticks. It was my step-mother who would travel from Somerset to Hull in Yorkshire by car, despite snow and adverse weather conditions to see me perform at College of Education, as well as to virtually every other occasion when I trod the boards in theatrical productions, both at college and in my first teaching post in Essex. She was a hugely important rock of support and motivation, as well as being full of courage and loving determination in taking the lead role in offering a genuinely maternal role for three 'damaged' young children who had been cruelly robbed of their natural mother; something that they themselves could not rationalise or comprehend in any way whatsoever. I could not have been more fortunate in what were otherwise very unfortunate circumstances, and that I know to be true from the very depths of my heart. So, who am I to risk being condemned for being churlish, or bordering on the scurrilous by seeking to reflect or question if things may have turned out 'better' or 'different' had my natural mother lived a more fulsome life? The truth is that such reflection, however unpalatable it may seem, is also equally inevitable and irrelevant, as I would be the first to admit that the theoretical outcome would have been 'different' rather than 'better', so as to avoid impossible inter-personal comparisons and unintended judgements.

My natural mother was herself an actress and the only child born to her parents, who were also professional entertainers. Her father was a concert pianist and his wife an operatic singer. They performed together in the world that was, and still is, loosely termed 'show-business'. My father had met her during the days of national service, when he was starting a career in Her Majesty's Royal Navy and she was serving in the Royal Air Force. I hope that I may be forgiven for wondering if, given her more intimate involvement in the performing arts, as well as her background and that of her parents, I might have been more encouraged to explicitly, more actively and openly explore my seemingly innate affinity for the performing arts; whether or not she may have had contacts in the business, who she could have called upon to further her son's natural inclinations and passion. Of course such questions are effectively as redundant as they are rhetorical, as there is no way of knowing, only a sense of wondering, tinged with more than a little regret and a tsunami of sadness and remorse.

To move away from an uncomfortably risky personal reflection of what alternative life chances might have arisen and been pursued, I feel compelled to incorporate similar issues of a more generalist nature to lend weight to my insistence on the central role of the creative curriculum, following an article that appeared in the Guardian newspaper on the 1st February, 2012, entitled the *'Top Five Regrets of the Dying'*. Upon reading the title, I was immediately struck by a sense of genuine sadness that anyone who was about to die had **any** regrets whatsoever. Does that not strike you as worrying or peculiarly odd, at least? The end of one's life ought to be a real celebration of considerable and deeply-felt accomplishment and contribution over the course of one's life span, however long or short that may have been. But to lie on one's death bed and have regrets is a profoundly troubling thought for me; one that I can hardly contemplate, but believe I am able to comprehend in equal measure. I was intrigued to read the article, not out of any morbid fascination, but as a way of identifying if others felt the same as me about lost life opportunities, and the wish that things had been, and could have been, different. It was a revealing read, but first some background.

The article was based upon the 'work' and research of Bronnie Ware, an Australian nurse who worked for several years in palliative care, caring for, and counselling people in the last twelve weeks of their lives. Working so closely with people during their final few weeks alive, she was struck by the fact that her patients so often had regrets about the way they had, or hadn't, lived their lives. So much so, in fact, that she eventually wrote a book which contained her observations entitled *'The Top Five Regrets of the Dying'*. One might have expected such revelations to be either trivial – such as wishing one had enjoyed a ride in a helicopter or been able to see The Niagara Falls – or perhaps incredibly diverse, given the number of different people who expressed their regrets but, in fact, neither was the case. Their regrets had so much in common, in terms of resonance, and were also deeply profound, moving and thought provoking on a very personal level.

One of the interesting features of Bronnie Ware's observations was that people who were rapidly approaching the end of their lives acquired a phenomenal clarity of vision; they were people who were able to reflect on the whole of their lives and could identify certain common themes or common regrets. The most common one of these was: *"I wish I'd had the courage to live a life true to myself, not the life that others expected of me."* These people were able to identify how many of their dreams, or how much of their real destiny, had gone unfulfilled as a direct result of decisions that they had either made, or not made, as the case may be. Bronnie Ware makes a very powerful point in relation to this most common regret when she notes that, *"Health brings a freedom very few realise, until they no longer have it."*

Linked to this, the second most common regret came particularly from the male patients who all wished that they had not worked so hard during their lives, wishing instead they had spent more time with their young children and their partners, rather than spending so much of their lifetime on the treadmill of work and being the major (or sole) breadwinner. The third most common regret was: *"I wish I'd had the courage to express my feelings."* The patients who gave this response talked about the fact that they had suppressed their feelings so as to keep the peace with others who might disagree. Many of these people had even made themselves ill due to the resentment and bitterness that was a direct product of their settling for **mediocrity in their lives**, and therefore failed to become that which they were truly capable of becoming. This point could perhaps be seen as being synonymous with the first and most common regret, albeit expressed somewhat differently. The final two most common regrets were wishing that one had stayed in touch with one's friends, which is not surprising as we all come to miss our friends as we get older, particularly, I can imagine, when one is dying, and the very simple wish: *"I wish that I had let myself be happier."* Bronnie Ware points out that many people do not realise that happiness is a life *choice* that one can make, and that one does have the power to change one's life so that there is so much more joy, difference and excitement in one's everyday and immensely special existence. It is all too easy for people to become prisoners trapped into living a familiar life pattern – one that leads to a person getting stuck in a rut of well-known habits, patterns and practices. As Bronnie Ware puts it:

"Fear of change had them pretending to others, and to their selves, that they were content, when deep within, they longed to laugh properly and have silliness in their lives again."

When I read of these regrets of life, I was deeply saddened, shocked but not surprised, and I was struck by the resonance that each one of the five most common regrets had with each other, as well as the power that a more rounded, relevant and truly liberating education whilst at school might have enabled them to live their lives differently and in more personally fulfilling ways. I have talked a lot in previous chapters about the 'treadmill' of one's formal education; its predictability, its sameness and its failure in providing us with the tools that we need to live more spiritually meaningful and honest lives. Honest, that is, to ourselves and to others. This mirrors exactly the regrets of the terminally ill at a time when there is no opportunity for them to act upon the yearned for changes that they know, with the splendid benefit of hindsight, they should have made, and the different choices that they could, and should have made. The power of education, especially when at school, when life plans, attitudes and outlooks on life are so often determined, should not be under-estimated, and we absolutely must make sure that we enable every young person to identify *their* calling, *their* destiny and *their* purpose in life. We must ensure that we enable them to discover and pursue *their* true dreams, so that they achieve spiritual and emotional intelligence, as well as the purely cognitive aptitudes, and are able to lead intelligent lives. And I refer again to my preferred definition of this slippery concept of intelligence as:

"The grasping of the essentials in a given situation and responding appropriately to them."

(Alice Heim)

A Little Philosophy of Education

Before I suggest a better way of organising our system of schooling young people, so that the way we do things more effectively promotes education in the sense of enlightenment and enabling every learner to discover their true, innate talents, I would like to consider the wonderful advice given by Steven Covey in his book 'The 7 Habits of Highly Effective People', and start with the end in mind. In some ways, to do this may seem inappropriate in that we are hopefully encouraging young people to have the appetite and ability to become life-long learners. In other words, there is no 'end' that we can use as our starting point; it is most fundamentally, necessarily and veritably a continuous process. But, upon reflection, the end that we need to have in mind is precisely the fact that there *is* no end to learning. The best learning that young people can engage in is that which will help them to become more self-confident, and to become independent, self-directed learners; learners who are not dependent on waiting to be told, but learners who are inquisitive, creative and imaginative, and learners who have the knowledge and skills that allow them to explore their true innate talents to the full, so that they, quite literally, feel fulfilled. In so doing, no matter how long or short their lives may be, the only regret they may harbour is that they did not have even more time in which to make their mark on the world, or to leave a more powerful and impressive legacy. I can imagine this is how the late, great David Bowie might have felt, given that he had further albums and music that he wanted to complete and release at the time of his passing. It really is not pie in the sky romanticism that forces me to say such things, as I honestly believe that although we will probably never achieve the 'perfect' education system, we can and must do so much better in future, so that all schools are able to achieve their *'stated'* aims

201

of creating life-long learners who can truly identify and unleash their boundless potential.

At this stage, I would like to dwell a little longer by looking at some of the ideas that Steven Covey believed, and which he espoused in his more recent publication entitled *'The 8th Habit – From Effectiveness to Greatness'*. If you have not read it, I would strongly urge you all to get hold of a copy and immerse yourself in the tremendous wisdom which the author shares with us – albeit at a modest price. It is most definitely worth it!

Many of the truly telling points that Steven Covey raises in his book are related specifically to the world of work and organisational culture, as well as the way in which the systems of operation in many businesses currently fail to take any real account of the latent capabilities of their workforce. Moreover, he talks a lot about what he calls, *"the timeless reality that lies in the voice of the human spirit, as well as destiny and achieving one's true calling in life by revealing the soul's code."* In this respect, what he is talking about is at one with the writings of James Hillman, to which I have already made reference in earlier chapters.

The whole essence of *'The 8th Habit'* is defined by Covey as twofold: finding what he calls your **own** 'voice' and then inspiring others to find **their** voice. What I really like about Covey's work is the way in which he can encapsulate what he is seeking to share in such a clear and succinct statement such as this. However, achieving this two-pronged target is far from straightforward, although he explains why we need to change our approaches to organisational leadership, systems and cultures, as well as how to go about achieving the desired outcomes. I will refer again to these issues in the following chapter, when I turn my attention more precisely to the way in which schools need to organise and manage themselves differently if they are to achieve the lofty aims that they publish in their school mission and vision statements, and which they also purport to be adhering to in actual practice. The following chapter on school management will, to some extent, explain how schools, as organisations, can help all stakeholders find their own voice, but for now, I want to say a little more about how Covey describes the concept of 'voice', before moving on to explain how the school curriculum might be structured and delivered so as to help young people discover their own.

Covey's concept of 'voice' can be found at the point where *four* aspects of 'self' overlap or correspond to, and with, each other: namely, your *talent* (your innate giftedness), your *passion* (the things which energise, excite, motivate and inspire you), your *needs* and your *conscience* (the inner voice that tells you what is the right thing to do). He goes on to make the eminently logical point that when you find yourself involved in activities – whether at work or in your private and social life – that enable you to achieve all four of these aspects to be met and fulfilled, then you will have found your voice, your calling and your soul's code. This seems on first reading to be something that is essentially quite easy to achieve, but it is my view that the essential ingredient upon which this meeting of the four aspects relies is that of genuine and unfettered freedom: the freedom to follow your natural instincts; the freedom to make choices (rather than just notional opportunity) and the freedom to make your own decisions and take your own direction in life. I fear, however, that these freedoms are the antithesis of what state or private schooling seeks to promote. Indeed schooling informs the way in which we live our lives, the direction in which we go in life, and the things that we spend our precious lifetimes doing, supposedly and hopefully with the intention of achieving happiness.

Steven Covey argues that each one of us has to choose between two very different directions or routes to follow in our lives, one of which is, *"the broad, well-travelled road"* that leads to mediocrity, whereas the alternative leads us, *"to greatness and meaning."* In essence, what Covey argues is that the former route will limit and 'straitjacket' our potential to fulfil the promise of our own, unique inner giftedness; it is clearly the easier and more convenient path to tread. Following this easier direction condemns us to a life that is thwarted by, *"ego, indulgence, scarcity, comparison, competitiveness and victimism"*, and as a result, we are following the wrong culturally-determined compass that leads us to never discovering our true selves – nor our 'voice'.

On the other hand, however, the route that leads to greatness requires us to become the **creative** force in our own lives, to allow our true inner self to grow down into the world which we inhabit. This is the direction we should follow if we are to, as Covey puts it, find our 'voice' and to go even further by enabling and inspiring others to find theirs as well. The route or direction we choose is, therefore, crucial if we are to evade the potential risk of allowing mediocrity to lead us to our death-beds with thoughts of failure and regret, as opposed to true and worthwhile accomplishment and having fulfilled our destiny – our reason for being here in the first place. What is so very important, however, is that this relatively simple freedom to choose which path to follow is, according to Covey, something that arises from and is an outcome of 'self-awareness'. And it is the vital role that the expressive, creative and performing arts can play in helping us to achieve this self-awareness and self-belief that provides the courage to choose the harder, more fulfilling road to greatness. This is fundamentally why we must place these types of learning experiences at the very centre of the curriculum that we design as an entitlement for every young person when they attend school, in whatever country they might live!

Covey's work in 'The 8th Habit' goes on to add further weight to the importance of the aesthetic and creative dimension of the curriculum, I feel, when he identifies the four intelligences or capacities of our nature. He refers to not only the mental intelligence of our minds, but also to the emotional intelligence of the heart, the physical intelligence of the body, and the spiritual intelligence of our unique spirit. He makes an important point when he argues that, *"Spiritual intelligence is the central and most fundamental of all intelligences because it becomes the source of guidance of the other three."* Furthermore, our unique potential as human beings is best unleashed when all four intelligences are brought together in our thoughts and actions. He also quotes my favourite person when it comes to commenting brilliantly on education, Albert Einstein, who said, *"Imagination is more important than knowledge."* So, why is it then, that so little time or emphasis is allowed during the formal activities that constitute schooling to giving genuinely free rein to imagination and the willingness to entertain possibility, rather than current knowledge and certainty? This central role of spiritual intelligence demands that much more time is devoted to recognising and developing it, rather than the over-emphasis that traditional orthodoxy demands we spend on mental intelligence and the needs of the mind alone, or IQ, when it comes to the vital importance of determining the school curriculum.

Covey goes on to claim that, ***"Most of us don't envision or realise our own potential,"*** with the result that so much of our human energy, our inner genius and giftedness is left unexplored, untapped and undeveloped. This is why it is so important that schools focus far more on allowing young people to dream, to think differently and to identify, to follow and develop their passions – and inordinately more than we do nowadays. In comparison, much of what is delivered in schools is a boring, spiritually unchallenging and restricting 'mush' of old knowledge which we attempt to thrust into the minds of a largely passive and modern audience. Far greater emphasis needs to be placed on helping young people to develop their own vision of themselves, so that they possess a true sense of destiny and the honest belief that their lives have a purpose, as well as a real meaning that only they can make during their very special lifetimes.

Before I reluctantly move away from the insights that Steven Covey offers to those of us who manage schools and the more important focus of managing student learning, I want to delve a little further into this vital 8th Habit of finding one's own voice, and helping others to find theirs. Covey also makes an important distinction between a person's skill and their talent, in order to clarify that they are definitely **not** the same thing at all; indeed they are most definitely not the same beast, although talents clearly do require and depend upon skills.

As I have previously mentioned, Covey's work is focused on helping our understanding of how to lead and manage business organisations, and he develops this distinction between talent and skill by pointing out that people are very often employed and, therefore, spending most of their lifetimes in work that requires skills and knowledge that have no relation to, or bearing upon, their actual innate talents. As a result, employers will suffer the wasted opportunity of never being able to tap into the true passions – or the 'voice' – of their employees. As a result, when there is this disparity between the job that people undertake and their real inner talents, their performance is not intrinsically motivated, and is likely, therefore, to require some form of *external* supervision to ensure that they do the job to an acceptable standard, or at all. Covey goes on to point out that, where people are required to perform a job that is in line with, and appeals to their passions, then they will not require such external oversight. Indeed, *"They will manage themselves better than anyone could ever manage them,"* because, *"Their fire comes from within and not from without."* I really love the way he articulated this fundamental point!

This eminently sensible view maintains that if people spend their lives performing jobs for which, and in which, they have a real talent and passion, then they will do them brilliantly well and with alacrity, clearly relates to what goes on in so many schools. If young people are required to follow heavily prescriptive content in which many of them, if not all of them, have no innate interest, talent or passion whatsoever, then it is hardly surprising that they will probably only do it in the presence of some form of coercive extrinsic motivation, namely the obligation to obtain grades and examination passes, or with constant external supervision of a teacher who is charged with essentially 'imparting' existing knowledge. This will obviously do precious little to engender a love of, and a joy for, independent learning, the thirst for which will continue for a lifetime. Even worse, the unfulfilling and irrelevant 'learning' that schools seek to force on young people, and which fails to recognise their innate spirituality, talents and passions, is most likely to be followed by the obligation to earn a living in an occupation that is equally at odds with their 'voice'. In view of this, is it really all that surprising that so many people die with the regrets that Bronnie Ware encountered in the hospices of Australia?

My final reference to Steven Covey's work, on this particular topic, is to include this following brilliant nugget that goes a long way to explain the cruel irony that young people fail at school or, more accurately, are failed by schools, largely because:

> *"People cannot be held responsible for results if they are given the methods."*

So, what then does this say about the work that schools do, and the damage they can, and do, unintentionally inflict upon young people and potential lifelong learners, if we do not fundamentally review the very essence of schooling, and radically change what students are required to spend their school life doing, as well as how, where and when? How are we to find the way of marrying what students do at school with their true talents and passions, so that they can find their own 'voice', and genuinely prepare them for life in the future, as well as in the here and now? Surely, this is the only true and effective way of ensuring that what they do in school is going to be to the benefit of industry and commerce in their future working lives. They need to know what their true talents and passions actually are, and have had plenty of time to discover, nurture and develop these whilst actually at school, so that there is more of a likelihood that they will be able to function as a 'round peg in a round hole' when at work, so that the work they do becomes an extension of who they really are, and is less likely to be a dull, boring drudge that is a waste of so much of their lifetimes. The massive problem or dilemma, however, is how to incorporate this mutual round peg into the square hole that represents the traditional orthodoxy that informs the way in which we design and deliver the school curriculum?

This issue is fundamentally about how to manage and effect change. My own view is that we need to release the stranglehold with which traditional orthodoxy currently asphyxiates genuine learning that is creative, imaginative and enjoyable – even when the going gets tough – and this requires us to break the mould, incorporate radical change and fundamentally start again. Sadly, this is never going to happen as conventional wisdom dictates that it is better the devil you know than the angel who promises you so much more, if only you would listen. What it really boils down to is a very pragmatic approach based on what is currently 'doable' as opposed to what would be far more effective, if schools are not to be replaced by 100% home-schooling. At the moment, in the right hands, home-schooling appears to be the only better alternative, and to which more and more parents are turning – and not due to misplaced ego. Rather, home-schooling tends to be less prescriptive, more liberating and learner-centred, and allows young people to learn what interests them, as opposed to what others say they should or must learn.

The following two chapters will, first of all, seek to outline not only the more pragmatic approach that fits more easily into the modus operandi of most secondary schools, and is, therefore, eminently 'doable'. And then, secondly, a more detailed coverage of the more radical, liberating alternative way of structuring and delivering teaching and learning, and one that I feel is far more worthwhile, pressing and educationally sound, even if it demands more of a substantial shift away from the traditional orthodoxy that currently dictates the nature of secondary schooling.

Chapter Ten: Alternative Curriculum Structure

A Pragmatic Approach

The hidden message of the way in which the current school curriculum is usually designed and delivered is that subjects are discrete units of knowledge, and this hugely powerful message suggests that what one learns in one subject area has no relevance to, or bearing upon, what is learnt in any of the others. This compartmentalisation of knowledge, instead of viewing it as the 'seamless cloak' that it most definitely is, contributes powerfully to students being unable to use or apply what they learn in one subject area in other subjects even within the same broad curriculum area. In other words, on the one hand, students do not see any link between what they learn in, say, Geography, with what they learn in, say, Science, but on the other hand, they also seem incapable of making any meaningful link between what is learnt in Geography with other Humanities subjects, such as History or Economics, for example. This is, of course, utterly ridiculous and just plain wrong, as the overlap between all of these is considerable and important to recognise, but this is what happens in actual practice because teachers are also 'victims' of their own schooling. They too seem to be largely unaware of the inevitable links that can and should be made, and the bridges that can and are capable of being built across this unhelpful, artificial and damaging subject divide. In other words, they are largely incapable, and/or rarely encouraged, to make the obvious links explicit so as to capitalise upon them and to enhance, broaden and extend what students learn in each convenient and familiar 'box'. What to do?

Well, whilst any fragmentation of knowledge is unhelpful and, therefore, largely unwelcome, it is possible to arrange subjects together in terms of the type of **perspective on learning** and reality that they provide. This, in turn, provides a smaller number of subject areas – or 'bits' – that need to be inter-related or linked together. Most schools have some form of faculty structure which brings together subjects, or 'birds of a similar feather', into larger organisational groupings, but this is mainly done to make overall school management easier and more effective, rather than to promote an integrated curriculum entitlement for the young people who attend school. I personally prefer to see the faculty-type set-up as a structure that, with a few modifications and a change of outlook by some of the teachers who staff them, is one way in which schools could move towards a more integrated and meaningful curriculum entitlement for students in secondary school.

Typically, one might expect to find the following faculty structure and, within each, some of the subjects that schools may decide to offer in each organisational block:

Expressive, Creative Arts & Technology	Humanities	Languages	Mathematics	Science
Art and Design Dance Design Technology Drama Food and Nutrition Graphics Music Physical Education	Business Studies Economics Geography History Politics Psychology Religious Studies Sociology	English (1st and 2nd Language) French German / Spanish Mandarin Russian	Additional Maths Mathematics Statistics	Biology Chemistry Combined Science Double Science Physics

I have intentionally listed the faculties and subjects in alphabetical order so that I do not fall into the trap of listing subjects in the traditional way with the high status, traditional academic subjects first with the 'lesser' subjects following and the arts listed last in the pecking order of being worthwhile. This more favourable alphabetical ordering also means that one very small, but significant, step can be taken to rectify decades of the Arts being condemned to an inferior status. This is why I prefer to see the Expressive and Creative Arts or, better still, the Aesthetic and Creative subjects coming first, which is one reason why I never categorise such learning experiences as the Visual and Performing Arts. This is, as I have previously alluded to, one time when I feel that a little positive discrimination is totally justifiable.

Some schools, of course, will have a slightly different arrangement for these broader faculty areas, although the tendency is for there to be five broad faculty areas in most schools that divide and parcel-up the formal school curriculum in this rather traditional way. After all, the benefits of this type of organisational rationalisation are diluted, if not largely defeated, by having too many separate faculty units. Regardless of the final groupings and titles that different schools decide upon for their various teaching and learning faculties, such organisational niceties all have one thing in common: they represent the edifice that illustrates the artificiality of the way in which we present the learning or acquisition of knowledge to young people.

The names attached to the customary five-faculty model may vary, as noted above with the Expressive and Creative Arts. Some schools prefer to link Technology with Science or perhaps Mathematics, whereas some even make it a separate curriculum area altogether. Similarly, some schools link Science and Mathematics together, and others may refer to English and Modern Foreign Languages instead of just 'Languages'. They may also list subjects offered in Year 10 and post-16 option blocks, as previously mentioned, according to their 'status' in the perverse world of traditional academic orthodoxy, or in terms of an equally unhelpful and ridiculous distinction between core and foundation subjects and areas, all of which send hidden messages to young people and other school stakeholders about the relative importance of some subject areas compared to others.

It is not only the terminology to be attached to particular faculties that can come to represent an area of difference between schools, nationally and internationally, but also deciding upon which subjects should be accommodated within particular faculties can also be an area of considerable debate and further variety. One such example, which I always find interesting, lies in the subjects of 'textiles' and 'ceramics', or 'needlework' and 'pottery' for the more ancient amongst us. In which faculty area would you feel they 'fit' most comfortably? Some may say that they are inherently creative and so should fall within the Expressive and Creative Arts, whilst others may feel they are better suited to be viewed as subjects within Technology, given that they deal with the production of artefacts from various non-resistant materials. It could, of course, be argued that they could also be quite 'at home' within the

Humanities subjects, as archaeologists always seem to be unearthing various forms of 'pottery' upon which they can base theories about how advanced a particular civilisation was and how people in earlier times lived their lives. Similarly, the clothes that people wore can tell us much about matters as diverse as climatic and other geographical (or scientific) conditions and social hierarchies at particular times in History. The very important subject of 'Food and Nutrition', or 'Cookery' as it was called when I was in secondary school – and prevented from choosing on the grounds of being of the 'wrong' gender – has within it very strong elements of Science and Technology, and also lends itself readily to the Expressive and Creative domain of the curriculum, as well as the Humanities again. Some schools used to include Business Studies in Technology, thanks to Conservative governments who saw the production of artefacts as a preliminary pursuit that is to be naturally followed by being able to market and sell such outputs in the business world for a financial profit. Whatever happened to the production of artefacts and outcomes, paintings and pieces of music, motivated entirely for reasons of self-expression and spiritual satisfaction? Must everything be 'financialised' and geared to having a monetary value in order to justify it being a worthwhile pursuit? Capitalism has done so much to prostitute the arts in every meaning of the word, and this is something that I find dreadfully unappetising, not to mention depressingly and deeply sad. Pre-specified objectives, which in this case amounts to producing something that lends itself to being marketable and of pecuniary advantage wins out over self-expression and the spiritual joy of so doing.

This issue of where do various subjects most naturally 'fit' within a faculty structure in schools is further open to question when one considers subjects like P.E. (Physical Education) and, more esoterically, Philosophy. Personally, I prefer to see PE as being mainly about self-expression, whether this is in dance, football, gymnastics, and so on, but I willingly recognise notable elements of science, mathematics, the humanities as well as language within these, and the latter is not in humorous recognition of the wonderful epithets and nouns that football players (as well as other sportsmen and women) so generously attribute to the referee or umpire, as well as their opponents and, occasionally, team-mates. On the other hand, one could well argue, and a philosopher certainly would want to, that Philosophy could be placed within the Humanities, but the problem of even these broader faculty curriculum blocks, is that once any subject is placed within a particular box, it is often presumed that it can only rightly and properly be delivered (or 'taught') by the teaching staff who are assigned to that area of the curriculum. Clearly, such compartmentalisation is not only erroneous, but it is also dangerous, due to the inter-applicability and the transfer of knowledge that should be being promoted within and across all areas of teaching and learning.

This issue is given greater import and relevance when one considers learning experiences which are already seen as cross-curricular in nature, such as PSHE (personal, social and health education) and ICT (Information and Communication Technology), not to mention the even broader accomplishments of literacy and numeracy. I have often argued that teaching ICT as a separate subject is nearly as anachronistic as was the teaching of hand-writing when I first went to school. Surely, the best way to acquire the knowledge, skills and competences sought in ICT is by learning to discover, use and develop them in all subjects and curriculum areas, as and when it is helpful and useful so to do. If there is a need for students to acquire formal qualifications in ICT, such as GCSE, then they can always sit for the examination and achieve success, but without ever having had to attend a specific class in the subject, even if it is, indeed, 'a subject'.

At this point, however, let us take whatever groupings schools decide upon, and the names they ascribe to particular faculties as given, and turn our attention to the key question of how to work, with the constraints that these artificialities impose, in a way that promotes and develops an understanding and appreciation, in the minds of both teachers and students, that what is learnt in one subject is essentially linked to, and can extend, reinforce, enrich or enhance what is studied in many other subject areas to a greater or lesser extent, and that knowledge is fundamentally interrelated and necessarily interdependent in nature.

One possible way forward in this respect is to encourage staff and then students to view faculty and subject titles as representing *different perspectives on learning*, and different perspectives on one and the same reality, as Einstein argued in relation to his theory of relativity. All that this requires is a change in the titles of a school's teaching faculties, and a realisation of what this change actually signifies, and why it is of vital and central importance in allowing young people to see the links between what they learn in one area, and at what time, to what they have learnt, or will be learning in other subjects at a different (or the same) time. To see how the more likely faculty areas that schools choose to adopt can be renamed and viewed differently is illustrated in the table below:

Expressive, Creative Arts & Technology	Humanities	Languages	Mathematics	Science
or	or	or	or	or
Aesthetic and Creative, & Technological	Human and Social	Linguistic	Mathematical	Scientific

The change in nomenclature is not in itself significant, if it does not permeate the daily discourse of teachers, students, parents and others in a meaningful and well understood and informed way. We all have to stop thinking about 'subjects', even if they are to be retained as the way to demonstrate that more integrated teaching and learning will enhance, reinforce and extend student accomplishments, and start seriously thinking about *'perspectives on reality'*. Furthermore, this perspectives approach lends itself far more effectively and readily to being much more inclusive of a whole range of other or different types of learning, that are often omitted from the so-called formal curriculum in most schools, such as social, practical and technical, the vocational, as well as moral and political considerations with which students are to engage themselves (and, note the presence and meaning of those two words: 'engage' and 'themselves'). There is no artificial limit to what can be learnt, and no barrier to what can be incorporated or included.

To move in such a direction, small and relatively straightforward as it is in actual daily practice, is in no way a major leap into the unknown, after all, it is only what was suggested in an HMI document: 'A Framework for the Curriculum' back in 1980. Even such a small departure from the traditional orthodoxy or the status quo, however, will have to be undertaken in a few important interim steps, if it is to stand a realistic chance of being successful in a relatively short period of time.

Clearly, the first step is to ensure that there is an organisational readiness for the modest change that I am proposing. This means that the staff have to be encouraged, cajoled and persuaded to 'buy into' the idea, as the Americans might say; in other words, this means that those responsible for making it happen in practice, understand *what* is required, *why* it is necessary and *how* it is to be achieved. Furthermore, they have to reach the stage where they feel a sense of genuine 'ownership' of the change, and to feel excited about it, and the potential it offers to substantially improve student learning in all their subject areas. This also requires staff to change the language they use to refer to the structural elements of the change. They need to talk and think about 'curriculum areas' and 'perspectives of learning' and not 'faculties' and 'subjects'. In effect, staff have to stop seeing themselves as custodians of some written gospel that demands to be protected at all costs from any form of cross-contamination from other subject areas, in the interests of some sort of academic purity. Such an approach is not only limiting and restrictive, it is also fundamentally sterile in terms of promoting the transferability of both skills and knowledge. This is why students leaving university are so often highly qualified academically, but employers bemoan the fact that such people seem unable to apply what they have learnt, and what they know, in the inter-related, multi-dimensional and multi-perspective context of the real world. Instead, subject teachers have to see how the proposed change in the way they deliver the curriculum can improve not only students' grasp of their own subject, by making its relevance clearer and more meaningful, but how it can also lead to improved student understanding, appreciation and performance in all other subject areas. In effect, this is no different to the manifestly greater benefit of team work in organisations as compared to the same individuals working on their own in splendid isolation. In the same way that team work creates team dynamics that lead to a synergy within the team, where their combined output is far greater than the sum of the output of all the individuals taken together, so it is quite sensible and logical to presume that a 'team' approach in the delivery of the curriculum in practice might lead to a genuine *'synergy of learning'*. This synergy of learning in theory means that what students know, understand and are able to do is far greater and more useful in everyday life

215

than what they might have learnt in each separate subject under the current regime that prevails in most schools, and which has done so for more than one century already.

It is also very important to recognise that all types of team take time to develop, passing through several quite troublesome and tricky stages, until they reach what is often referred to as the 'performing' stage, when this beneficial synergy is evident and can be identified, felt and even measured. During this initial step of ensuring organisational readiness, it is vital that those involved in its implementation are fully aware of the fact that the promised benefits of a multi-perspective approach to the curriculum will also take time to materialise, and that there is no 'quick-fix' route that can be adopted; there is no effective 'short cut'. Equally, the practitioners need to understand and be prepared for challenges that will inevitably arise en-route, so to speak. There will be failures to be learnt from, obstacles and set-backs to be overcome and remedied. This is the stuff that one is bound to encounter on the road to achieving anything that is truly worthwhile. If all of this was going to be easy, then where would be the 'buzz' that the sense of real accomplishment would provide?

The initial step, or preparatory work of achieving organisational readiness before the initiative is begun, also demands that the parents of those attending the school understand what is being done, and why. They too need to be able to appreciate the benefits that such a combined and more integrated approach to learning offers their sons and daughters, not only now, but also in the future. They need to be supportive of the initiative, or at least sceptical spectators who are standing on the touchline waiting to see if their offspring will in fact respond well to the game plan, and that they are involved and able to engage positively and constructively with the style of play being demanded by their 'coaches'. Parents need to see for themselves, if they are unable to be convinced by the logic of the rationale for change, that this 'new' approach will enable their children to engage more fully with what they are learning, and with a greater sense of cohesion and determination, as well as genuine interest. This is also why teachers have to be fully aware, committed and 'on-side' in terms of what it is they are seeking to achieve with this somewhat new approach, so that the school has several leaders and spokespeople in this process of similarly 'educating' and subsequently reminding parents as to the wisdom of the modest additions being made to the way in which the subject-based curriculum is being presented to their children whilst at school. It also enables parents to play their part in relating what is learnt in one subject to what is being taught in other subjects and the real world.

All learners, however, display a range of ability at any given time, and teachers and parents are also learners in this new outlook on curriculum delivery. Some will grasp what is being proposed and the inherent potential for maximising learning that this promises over time before others, and to greater or lesser degrees at any given time. As a result, there is no need to wait for all players to be fully supportive of the need for change. Moreover, there is no reason to wait for full parental support before the teaching staff begin to undertake and implement the first elements in the change. Some can start on the second step of implementation before others – so that they too can become change-agents within their own school, helping other, 'less-able' colleagues with the process.

This second step in effecting the desired change lends itself to a gradualist introduction, with different teams within the school, starting at different times, once they feel ready. At this stage, each of the five or six curriculum areas within the school has to begin to explore the links that exist between the various subjects that are linked together within their particular area. Taking the Human and Social curriculum area as one case in point, this would involve those responsible for teaching the subjects such as History, Geography, Economics and Business Studies, for example, working together to identify the many areas of overlap in terms of the content that they aim to teach, as well as where what they are required or seek to cover complements that which the syllabus obliges their colleagues to deal with. This would provide possibly more useful topics of professional conversation in team meetings; focussing on what students are required to learn (and how this might be better 'packaged') rather than on more mundane administrative issues, such as completing requisition forms, etc., which are better left to support staff to undertake anyway.

As these professional conversations lead teachers to a shared understanding of how 'their' subjects contribute to the learning perspective that they are responsible for leading, then this can begin to be formalised in terms of designing, delivering and evaluating joint schemes of work, which promote a more integrated and complementary approach to the teaching and learning in their curriculum area. Following on from the evaluation of, and careful reflection on, the effectiveness and efficiency of these joint or combined schemes of work, as they are delivered and subsequently developed over time, so each team colleague can refine, improve and develop their programmes of study, as any professional teacher would normally be expected to do. Only this time, this process would be done jointly, as opposed to individually or within each separate subject area, and would focus on ensuring not only greater cohesion and relevance, but would also foster real continuity and progression.

This team approach would contribute to a synergy of learning developing over time on a micro level – within their curriculum area – and help nurture the skills and attitudes necessary to take this way of working to the next level – that of integrating, as well as linking the delivery of content and skills across the curriculum as a whole, and in a complementary and contrasting way, by involving all the different perspectives on learning together. The process for this far more challenging third step would be a mirror-image of that which took place within each curriculum area. The school organisational structure and management system within those schools embarking on this multi-dimensional approach to teaching and learning, would have to be such that the necessary professional conversations within and between curriculum areas were both enabled and encouraged. This is something that will be looked at in a little more detail in the chapters that follow on school leadership and management.

The question that remains for this third step, in the development of a more inter-related and meaningful curriculum entitlement for all students, however, is, what is the motivation for such a complementary curriculum? What is to be the substantive glue that will give it a raison d'être and hold it all together at the design and delivery phase in actual practice? One possible solution is not as radical as one might imagine, although it may be a relatively alien concept to most secondary or high schools. On the other hand, however, colleagues teaching in primary schools are well versed in organising the curriculum in this way, and that is by using a thematic approach, and one that explores various perspectives in the way that young people explore particular themes so that they learn from them in an integrated, complementary and supplementary way. **There is indeed a great deal that secondary teaching staff can learn from the interesting and sound practice that is readily undertaken by their colleagues working in primary schools; colleagues who not only devise themes to be studied but also create or generate the learning materials to be utilised.**

The themes to be used can be relatively small in potential scope or indeed more comprehensive in nature. They can be covered in a relatively short period of time, or they could provide an opportunity for multi-disciplinary learning over a much longer period. Furthermore, if teachers are genuinely interested in giving students more of a lead role in their own learning, then they should be prepared to negotiate the themes with the students. In this way, it is possible to combine the content needs of the ever-present examination syllabuses, which provide details of the knowledge and skills that the teachers are obliged to help acquire and develop, and with which teachers are highly familiar, with the interests of the students in a particular class or year group. This is especially true if teachers have already successfully developed integrated study and complementary schemes of work with their colleagues in their own curriculum areas.

It is also important to appreciate that students are very concerned about many issues that they know will become more acute as they grow older and that they will have to solve or at least contend with. In my experience, students are interested in and concerned about major global issues, such as international terrorism and religious extremism, as well as global warming, resource depletion and mankind's degradation of the environment. At present, schools largely ignore the magnitude of such issues, often only being included in the peripheral arena of extra-curricular activities. These issues would form excellent themes that might engage students and make what they learn in their various subjects more meaningful, pressing and relevant to them. It might help address the stress that many students feel as a result of worrisome matters of which they are aware, but do not fully understand. Such issues or themes could be more focused by considering the needs of the syllabuses of various subjects, as well as the more precise interests and concerns of the students.

Furthermore, there is no reason at all why the themes or topics arrived at via negotiation should be problematic in nature. I for one have always been interested in taking a long-term theme that lends itself wonderfully to all areas of the curriculum, and that is *'civilisation'*. The opportunities for inter-related, inter-disciplinary and complementary learning this topic provides in all curriculum areas are considerable, albeit to a greater or lesser extent, and could be continuously developed over many years in secondary schools.

It is vital, of course, that the management and organisational systems within the school are such that the leaders of the main curriculum teams, or learning areas that contribute to, and form, the entitlement curriculum for students, are enabled to meet regularly so that they may have further professional conversations about how they might work in this more valuable and collaborative way, by designing shared schemes of work that are focused on developing the chosen themes within the classroom. This will enable students and their teachers to incorporate, draw upon and explore all of the various learning perspectives as and when they are relevant in the development of a particular theme or topic. It is then possible, over time, for teachers operating in one particular curriculum area to make explicit links forward and backward in time to what their students will be studying in the future, or have already studied in the past. In this way, the students' learning is simultaneously building on, and directly related to, what has already been learnt in other curriculum areas, or that which they will be encountering at some definite and identifiable later date. Moreover, to make these links more specific and explicit, teachers need to be able to share with their students exactly when they learnt or will be learning something relating to the chosen theme, as well as in what curriculum area it was or will be studied. It should also be possible to name subjects and the teachers who will be involved at such times in this process. For such an approach to work, however, demands that teachers are willing and ready to develop what I consider to be a more interesting and educationally worthwhile way of meeting the demands of externally-determined programmes of study, or examination syllabuses.

There are advantages arising in such an integrated approach to teaching and learning for the school as a whole. It is not only more effective in helping students fully grasp what it is they are required to learn, but also a far more efficient way of going about this. It saves time by avoiding needless and repetitive coverage of the same, or similar, subject matter that features in more than one subject area. For example, a great deal of what students learn in a subject like Business Studies, is also covered in subjects like Economics, History and Geography, as well as in Design Technology. Similarly, what young people learn, when studying something like 'climate' in Physical Geography is also covered again in Science, albeit at different times, in different ways and under a different guise. This unnecessary duplication can be avoided if teachers are able to relate learning in one area to that which occurs elsewhere in the curriculum in such a way that students are encouraged to make the links and to integrate what they are learning. It also means that any overlap or repetition is planned rather than random, incidental or accidental, and that it promotes the consolidation and reinforcement of prior learning.

If such an approach is successfully developed, a true synergy of learning can occur so that what students learn is far greater than the sum of what they would have learnt in their individual subject studies when taught in splendid isolation. Indeed, it is also quite possible that, in time, the learners will become more adept at searching for, identifying and exploring the inevitable and diverse links between knowledge, so that the learning becomes more truly and honestly **theirs**. In this way, students are surely far more likely to become the type of independent and self-directed, lifelong learner that all schools profess to be seeking to promote and develop, as grandly stated in their aims, goals and mission statements.

Unfortunately, there are, however, other obstacles of a more systemic nature that will need to be overcome if such a pragmatic approach to integrating and relating what students learn is to ever get past the drawing board stage, and these are the current assessment regime that is currently followed in schools, and the way in which schools determine the actual delivery of their curriculum, via the timetable.

Taking the current assessment regime, there will be a need for a corresponding adjustment in the way in which we decide to examine students at the age of 16 and 18 years. It is not easy to see how the current reliance on terminal

221

examinations in every separate subject could possibly accord with a multi-perspectival and inter-disciplinary curriculum. This would require examination boards, and the government, to see the advantages and benefits of the different curriculum approach, and work to produce new forms of external examinations. But then again, if we are to allow the context or themes which teachers and students use to explore the different perspectives to be negotiated, to allow greater freedom and make learning more intrinsically motivating for young people, this would be very difficult, if not impossible to incorporate within the remit of an external examination paper. There are two ways to solve this assessment hurdle. The first is for the exam boards to offer examinations in which students are limited to choosing from a prescribed list of agreed themes or contexts. After all, we are always being told that it is better, as well as being more educationally sound and appropriate to implement curriculum-led assessment methods, whereby we assess what students have learned, rather than allowing the final assessment 'tail' to wag the curriculum 'dog' by relying on an assessment-led curriculum. The second way of overcoming this terminal assessment hurdle is to not allow it to be an obstacle in the first place and simply do away with terminal examinations altogether. This is an option which I would prefer to see, largely on the grounds that they are not very effective, reliable or valid assessment instruments. This is not as heretical as it may seem, if one were to replace terminal examinations with something more meaningful, relevant and potentially motivational. Why don't we let the people who decide upon the contexts or themes to also determine how to assess their outcomes – i.e. allowing teacher and peer-group assessment?

This would require *'system re-design'*, a term coined by educationist David Hargreaves, and to which I will refer in a little more detail as part of the concluding section of this book. To allow teacher and peer group assessment to replace terminal examinations would mean it would be impossible to use standardised terminal examinations as a selection device to be used by universities and potential employers. Quite so! They will have to find their own ways of assessing who they wish to admit for higher education or to employ, rather than expect schools to do their dirty work for them, as they do now. The curriculum and its assessment should surely be designed to meet the needs of the learner, much in the same ways as the doctor's diagnosis and treatment regime is tailored to meet the needs of the individual patient. To do otherwise would be negligent, unreasonable or downright stupid, surely!

The second significant systemic change that would be needed if schools were to adopt the multi-perspective and more inter-disciplinary learning that I have suggested as being the pragmatic solution (surprisingly now that it might involve terminating terminal assessments that are subject-based) lies in the way in which we currently organise the school day, week or term into small units of discrete subject teaching, of very limited duration. Whilst this is not such a 'make or break' type of associated dilemma, it would require some creative thinking on the part of school leaders and their teacher colleagues to ensure this new approach can be accommodated and effectively, as well as efficiently delivered in daily, weekly and termly practice. It may be that, instead of short bursts of discrete subject-specific teaching and learning, longer units of time are assigned to the completion of a particular, multi-disciplinary theme, for a particular class or year group. This would make delivery much easier and more effective, as it would negate the need for teachers to make forward and backward, time-referenced links between what the students are learning in the various subjects in order for them to appreciate the curricular coherence that is afforded through inter-related and inter-dependent teaching and learning. What is more, such an approach would allow students to experience team teaching methodologies, whereby teachers representing different dimensions of learning deliver a set of negotiated themes or contexts to a large group of students in these longer blocks of time.

This may be ambitious, and take time to design, develop and implement, but it is eminently doable and, therefore, certainly worthy of a try. After all, this integrated approach is one way that learning can become more meaningful for students, but I believe there is a better, more liberating, exciting and enlightening way to organise teaching and learning in schools; one that would be seen as being even more radical which would also require a fundamental shift in the way subject syllabuses are designed as well as how we assess and measure student accomplishment. The following chapter explores this more radical, but more educationally-sound, alternative.

Chapter Eleven: New Curriculum Structure

A Radical Approach

In the previous chapter, I proposed an easier way of achieving a more integrated and stimulating curriculum entitlement for all young people attending secondary school, and to some extent, the upper years of primary schooling, or Key Stage Two. It represented a way of moving forward, taking account of the traditional school curriculum, and the convenience and familiarity afforded by 'subjects', that would not prove too much of a wrench to the way schools are currently organised and administered, although there were serious constraining influences on its adoption owing to the current use of terminal assessments in subject-specific examinations, and the need to change the structure of the school day and the timetable. Nonetheless, it was still only very much 'a half-way house', in that it still leaves many deficiencies of schooling as it is currently perceived, untouched and intact. For example, the emphasis is still on the predominance of academe, with a curriculum stuffed full of pre-specified content objectives that teachers have to address, or hoops that students have to jump through, much like performing animals in a circus. As I think should be abundantly clear by now, I do not see the status quo as something to be stuck with any longer than is absolutely necessary, unless we wish to continue to squander, and leave untapped, the inner talents that all young people have in abundance. We need to do far more to enable them to find their 'voice' so that they are capable of helping others find theirs.

Removing the Shackles

I intend to recommend and propose that more radical change is needed if schooling is to become truly educational in nature, as opposed to something that so many young people are forced to endure. What I would prefer to see introduced is a curriculum which is more negotiated, that places the needs and interests of the individual student at the very centre of what happens in school; a curriculum that liberates learning to a far greater degree. At the same time, however, I do believe that far more radical change can still occur using the current framework of school subjects, but which cuts out the obsession with pre-specified content, and allows students a greater degree of choice or

224

freedom to select that which they want to learn. What follows may be seen as being excessively radical by many readers, but what I am proposing is based very much on the work of outstanding educational thinkers such as Jerome S. Bruner and David Hargreaves, and many others who argued something similar before it ever even occurred to me.

In his excellent and landmark book, *'The Challenge for the Comprehensive School – Culture, Curriculum and Community' (1982)*, David Hargreaves suggested that the main aim of secondary education could be the promotion of dignity, which he defined as, *"a sense of being worthy, of possessing creative, inventive and critical capacities...... of having the power to achieve personal and social change."* But how is this possible without throwing off the shackles that the school curriculum currently requires students to 'wear' when at school, and which leads so many young people to feel disenchanted, indifferent and even hostile to what schools require them to do. If students are effectively prevented from learning things that they regard as useful and interesting, things which they are then encouraged and able to apply in other learning situations, then there is little chance that they will acquire the sense of being worthy and having the creative, inventive and critical capacities that David Hargreaves believes *should* be the main aim of schooling.

Focusing on the Essence of Subjects

If we can ensure that students become well-versed in a range of different subjects then why can they not have a greater say in what they learn within them? They can and they should, if learning that goes on in schools is to be valued, relevant and – more importantly – theirs!

It is to the work and ideas of Jerome S. Bruner to which I would now like to refer, and what he considered to be the very essence of every single subject that appears within the school curriculum. He posited that all subject disciplines have structures which represent and incorporate a series of core ideas and particular methods of learning, and it is these core ideas and enquiry tools that offer a golden opportunity for schools to help students to understand every subject discipline more deeply, fundamentally and meaningfully. He maintained that once students are able to grasp the essential structure of a subject, then they are enabled to understand it sufficiently well so as to allow many other things to be related to it in meaningful ways. Bruner argued that through learning the structure of a subject, the learner is allowed to relate it to other subjects and types of learning. As he said:

"The teaching and learning of structure, rather than simply the mastery of facts and techniques, is at the centre of the classic problem of transfer.

(Bruner: 'The Process of Education', 1960)

In his work, Bruner describes how student interest and enjoyment of learning can be enhanced and heightened through the 'sense of excitement and discovery' that they can experience as the structure of a subject discipline becomes clear to them – the all-important *'A-ha'* moment when students are truly learning, and the proverbial penny finally drops into place. Once students are able to appreciate the structure of a subject then they become aware of its patterns and regularities, and they recognise that certain ideas repeatedly occur in new and different contexts. Once the students are able to understand the way in which a subject discipline is organised or structured then they can more readily transfer what they learn in one subject area to new situations. It is this ability to transfer what has been learnt in one area, to learning in other areas that is sadly lacking in many schools today, as a result of heavily content-laden subjects which are presented to young minds in a ridiculously unhelpful, fragmented and compartmentalised way. The ability to transfer learning in this way is at the heart of the educational process; transfer that contributes to the continual broadening and deepening of knowledge in terms of certain basic ideas. Bruner pointed out that the more basic or fundamental the basic idea that is learned, then the greater will be its breadth of applicability to new problems. So what is it that forms the structural essence of a subject discipline?

As a teacher who is passionate about the subject of Economics, I am aware of the existence of certain key or core concepts, such as 'opportunity cost', 'the margin' and 'nominal' versus 'real' variables, that lie at the very heart of the discipline, and what is more, their application in facilitating the understanding of new situations occurs over and over again. These core concepts represent the essential structure of the subject matter, and they can be applied in simple, as well as complex and sophisticated ways. As Her Majesty's Inspectors of Schools recognised in 1985, in their publication *'The Curriculum from 5 to 16'*:

"Concepts are generalizations usually arrived at through a process of abstraction from a number of discrete examples. They enable pupils to classify and to organize knowledge and experience and to predict. Important concepts need to be identified and understanding them made an important outcome of teaching and learning."

In other words, core concepts help students to make sense of all that they are learning, as well as providing a springboard from which they can dive into, or explore new areas of enquiry and learning.

I am reminded of a conversation that I had with the Head Teacher of one secondary school where I worked when I wanted Economics to be offered as an externally examinable option within the curriculum offered to students working towards their GCE 'O' Levels, in those days. The Head Teacher in question was someone whom I used to fondly describe as a 'lapsed economist' in that he had once taught the subject himself, but a very, very long time before this conversation took place. This usually meant that although he had an affectionate regard for the importance of the subject, he was sufficiently out of touch with its practical delivery in the classroom that he never interfered with what I did in my role as Head of the Economics Department at that time. (For the record, he was a very good Head Teacher and, although his style of management was a million miles away from mine, he was someone who helped create opportunities within the school that helped further my career. I owe him a great deal – thanks James!) My desire to offer the subject at 'O' level, however, was greeted with more than a tad of scepticism when he argued that it was not possible to teach the subject in any meaningful and intelligible way to students 'below' the Sixth Form, where at the time it was being successfully taught to GCE Advanced Level. I expressed my fundamental disagreement with his view in what I recall as a courageously emphatic way, by pointing out that it was possible to teach Economics to a five-year-old. Luckily, he did not take my disagreement as an affront, he simply countered in an incredulously jocular manner by asking, "How would you teach the 'law of diminishing marginal utility' to a five-year-old?" My response was short and straightforward, and I said, "Easy. Just don't call it that."

In short the law of diminishing marginal utility simply maintains that 'the more of a particular good or service you have, the less will be the satisfaction derived from the consumption of each additional unit of that product'. I went on to illustrate how one might explain this fundamental law to a very young child, by referring to cream cakes. Find one child who likes cream cakes, and most do, and ask them how much they would enjoy eating one if they had not had one for a long time. Not surprisingly, they say that they would really, really enjoy it and, thereby, receive a high level of satisfaction or 'utility' by eating it. Then ask them if they would enjoy a second one straight after the first. Of course they would, but not as much as the first one. So what about the third and fourth one? Well, that would become a bit of a struggle as they became increasingly bloated on the sugary and creamy comestible; and so their satisfaction would continue to fall, or diminish from each additional unit consumed. Then ask them how much they would enjoy the fifth cream cake in a row, and they readily confess that it would, in all probability, make them sick, and that my non-economist readers is what is called 'negative utility'! Economics was offered for the first time, in that school, to students as an examinable option within the 14 to 16 curriculum in the following year.

The truth is that the core concepts of any subject are as simple as they are powerful, and students can understand them at an early age if and when they are taught in an intellectually honest way. It is important, however, that when using these key concepts that underpin a particular subject, teaching and learning are organised appropriately, and that what is to be learnt is put into the child's cognitive vocabulary at any given age or stage in their development.

I would recommend that the syllabus for every subject should be presented as simply, but as intellectually honestly as possible, identifying little more than the core concepts of the subject which will form the backbone of teaching and learning, along with the skills and competences that are to be developed and ultimately achieved and displayed. This would then allow the students *to choose their own contexts*, and more specific content and subject matter that relates to an investigation of these core concepts at work within their chosen learning context. Their choice, however, needs to be guided and negotiated with the teacher so that the context chosen does indeed lend itself to a careful study of a specific core concept or concepts at work. The benefit of this greater freedom in determining the specific context and the knowledge or more detailed subject matter to be developed within it, is that it more readily

228

accommodates the different interests and concerns of individual learners. In Economics, for example, the core concept of opportunity cost can be studied in any context where there is a choice to be made between competing alternatives; a choice that involves a sacrifice on the part of the person who has to decide. This provision for student choice of the context also lends itself to more creative and intuitive types of study, with the teacher monitoring and supervising the students' learning to ensure that their study also remains focused on the core concept(s) in question. Indeed, one of the key principles in Bruner's work was the belief that learning should be spurred by the student's interest in the material and where they find the knowledge they are obtaining and gaining increasingly more appealing. This is the antithesis of what seems to be the common practice in schools today, where students are virtually coerced into studying things we feel they should learn, and using punishments, tests and dubious grades that are intended to motivate their learning. This present day practice seems totally uninterested in what it is that students want to learn about, or how, and the hope seems to be that students might come to be interested in the subject matter after they have studied it – another case where current practice can quite generously be described as being arse-backwards.

Bruner went on to argue that each of these core concepts, that explain the essential structure of all fields of knowledge, can and should be revisited in an increasingly more formal way at each rung up 'the educational ladder', a ladder that could become the stairway to an enlightened heaven, as opposed to the forbidding and foreboding steps that nowadays so often lead to the dungeon for individual interest and creativity. This ability and need to keep revisiting the application of the core concepts in ever more sophisticated ways also does much to promote the transfer of learning. In other words, these key issues that have been examined in one relatively simple context can be examined again at a later date, to see how it applies in another, this time more complex situation. Bruner rightly points out that without this integrated base of understanding, few students are enabled to remember the content of their courses of study for very long, or relate what they have learnt at one stage of their schooling to their subsequent learning or, for that matter, to their lives. In short, very few students are currently able to transfer what they have learned in initial contexts to other, later contexts simply because they are not required to, or have not been given the opportunity to do this. Educational research has shown that just because a student can show that they understand something, or that they can display a skill in one context, does not mean that they can apply that knowledge, or use that skill in a new or different context. Today, however, this is how learning is organised: in a linear and unrelated way. The core concepts of a subject provide the contours of an educational clothes-hanger, or the cloakroom pegs on which all learning can be organised, inter-related and made sense of in an orderly and understandable way.

Bruner firmly believed that *with* such a core of integrated understandings most students will be able to do all these things at one time, and much, much more at a later time in their learning. This is very much in keeping with the goals of any educator interested in improving long-term and even short-term educational outcomes. In the current way of schooling young people, we tend to do the exact opposite. We teach each subject in a separate box, totally divorced from any other subject, so it should not be a surprise when we do indeed discover that our students are practically incapable of transferring their learning from one course of study to another – even in closely related fields. For example, students learn all about the three main stages of production (primary, secondary and tertiary) in Geography, and they then study it again if they choose to study Economics. They cannot and do not see the link between the two, such is the power of the hidden message of compartmentalisation when delivering the school curriculum to young people. It should also be equally unsurprising when we find that students who have been taught in a succession of separate subject boxes, also find it almost impossible to think 'outside of that box' in any imaginative, creative and cohesive way. In fact, this explains the need to actually teach students to think outside of the box or laterally, by incorporating other 'subjects' such as *'Thinking Skills'* to overcome the deficiency that the very system itself created and continues to create in the first place.

What is even worse is that, as I have pointed out in earlier chapters, by learning in this way, as they currently do, there is precious little long-term retention of that which was learnt. Once they stop studying one subject or area of knowledge, or when they leave school, they soon forget what they had learnt, although research suggests that they do remember the *ways* in which they learned something, This inability to retain what was learnt at school should not come as any surprise either, because it happens to all of us, and that is because learning is not integrated and inter-related, and so nothing comes along to reinforce what was learned previously, often at such effort and cost, in terms of the sacrifices made. This is why so many young people do not need to wait until they leave school to realize that what they are doing is of no benefit or lasting use to them, and being intelligent creatures, they opt out and prefer to spend their time on things in which they are interested and from which they can derive pleasure, as well as credibility and the kudos of accomplishment, no matter how dubious or anti-social that outcome may be in some cases and circumstances. Decrying this condition, many have argued on behalf of integrating the school curriculum around a common core structure of knowledge, with the contents of all subjects taught as examples of the common core principles in operation. That is a far better way of organizing what goes on in schools around the world.

Such a new approach is very much based on the constructivist theory of education, whereby there is a broad conceptual framework with numerous perspectives, and Bruner was not the only one to argue that schools need to adopt such a framework for learning. Bruner's theoretical framework is based on the theme that learners construct new ideas or concepts based upon existing knowledge. In other words, they are learning by using what they already know to understand what they don't know. In this way, learning has to be a much more active process. Students are required to select and transform information, make decisions and generate hypotheses, and thereby make meaning from the information they gain, and their experiences in different contexts, over time. Furthermore, this type of learning not only recognizes and encourages, but also rewards intuitive as well as analytical thought processes. Indeed, Bruner very much believed that intuitive skills were under-emphasized in the way schools sought to encourage lively and enquiring minds. Progress so often occurs when people take risks and have the courage and ability to make intuitive leaps.

As previously noted, Bruner was keenly interested in motivation for learning, and he felt that ideally, interest in the subject matter is the best stimulus for learning, and he was most definitely not in favour of competitive goals such as the use of grades and class-ranking of students. Student interest provides one very good way to achieve a predisposition to learn, because if they cannot see why they are learning something, they are obviously less inclined, sometimes hostile, to what they see as a waste of their time, and who can honestly blame them for feeling that way? Like Bruner, I am convinced that real learning and problem solving are the result of exploration, investigation and risk taking, and so it is incumbent upon the teacher to maintain and direct a child's spontaneous explorations over time.

Developing Skills-Based Learning

I was once very fortunate to have had the opportunity to work for a large multi-national company in Thailand, in their training department, designing and delivering a range of English language training courses for their senior personnel. I thoroughly enjoyed the privilege of working with so many people who were particularly willing and interested in learning more about the structure and use of the English language. In the office window as one entered the Training Department, there was a galvanizing slogan which read: *"Knowledge is the gateway to success."* I found this very interesting, as in my experience one has to be able to actually do something with, or benefit from, the knowledge that one has acquired from training or studying, if they are going to be truly successful. What, I wondered, does one do, when one wanders through the knowledge 'gateway'? Knowledge which is learned that one cannot apply in the new, different and challenging situations and contexts in which one finds oneself, is surely somewhat sterile and useless. All learners need to not only *know* something, but they also have to really and thoroughly *understand* it and then have the ability to use that knowledge, or be *able to do* something with it. I did suggest to the company for which I worked, that they might consider changing their slogan to read: *"The intelligent application of knowledge within new and different situations is the gateway to success."* Unfortunately, to this day my, admittedly, far less snappy strap-line has failed to take pride of place in their office window, but I remain convinced that all success demands that we can do something meaningful and useful with the knowledge we have amassed, so that we are enabled to act in new, different and hopefully intelligent ways.

What I like so much about a curriculum that is based on developing knowledge around the framework provided by the key tenets of a subject discipline, is that such core concept based teaching and learning in negotiated contexts does so much to promote a more skills-based curriculum. After all, a skill is more than just knowing something and even more than knowing how; it is about action too, in that it is the capacity or competence to perform a task, and a skill involves the application of knowledge to achieve some anticipated outcome. In 1981, The (then) School's Council rightly noted that *'a handful of fundamental skills form the highway to education, and this points to the co-existence of a set of general, transferable skills, in addition to those that are more specific to particular learning experiences or situations'*.

Skill development demands that schools devote more space, time and energy for active and more practical learning, so that students are provided with the opportunity to understand what is required when performing a particular skill. Mastery of a skill necessarily depends upon repeated, first-hand experience and actually performing or practising it. This is no less true for skills which may be termed intellectual or social in nature, than it is for more manual/physical skills, and teachers need to allow students to develop and refine these skills by using them experimentally in a variety of different contexts. In turn, this highlights the need for, and importance of, process-based learning objectives.

The more general, even universal applicability of key skills and core concepts taken together in a variety of different contexts offers the possibility of a more student-centred, active and experiential curriculum, and one that can and should be developed in schools by teachers working together in a collaborative, multi-, and inter-disciplinary way. This is of course, something that they will be largely unfamiliar with doing, but the more pragmatic form of integrated curriculum outlined in the previous chapter might well be seen as an interim stage, leading to this more radical, loosely controlled and far more liberating curriculum for young people in schools.

Awareness, Understanding and Competence

At the moment, however, there is still the need for some form of clear and familiar structure within which the teachers of all curriculum areas could work in their efforts to design a curriculum that systematically allows and encourages the application of the core concepts in increasingly advanced and sophisticated contexts. For this purpose, one needs only look to the GCSE aim of seeking to develop and then assess what students *'know'*, *'understand'* and *'can do'*, but now freed from the excessive reliance on externally-determined, pre-specified content-laden objectives. In other words, the focus should be on firstly developing an awareness of something (something that you 'know'), and then seeking to fully understand it, before demonstrating the competence to be able to use that knowledge in another context, which in turn leads to higher levels of awareness, understanding and competence. In this way, the curriculum does not consist of linear learning that implies an end to the process; instead it promotes the *spiral* development of the core concepts at more and more sophisticated levels of awareness and understanding, and advancing degrees of competence. **As the spiral twists ever upwards, it has if you like an expanding vortex which has the power to suck in ever increasing amounts of subject knowledge and, more importantly, knowledge that builds on itself in a progressive, inter-related and integrated way.**

With the delivery of these new ways of learning, where the student has a much greater say in what they study in terms of **context**, so the role of the teacher will also have to be adjusted somewhat. The role of the teacher will need to switch from being an 'actor/entertainer' and purveyor of agreed knowledge, to become a manager responsible for orchestrating the contributions made by students, as well as an ability to assist in the interpretation of the various learning outcomes. They will need to develop a greater confidence to enable open-ended discussions and debates without becoming anxious about an apparent lack of control (or the need to 'cover' the flood of initiative-stifling, pre-specified learning outcomes that are defined in terms of content).

Other forms of stimulus material, such as role-play activities and simulations, will make greater demands upon the teacher's skills of classroom management and organization. Having said this, if learning is more focused on studying issues and matters of genuine concern or interest to the student, then it is highly unlikely that the teacher will need to waste too much valuable time on behaviour management when responsible for directing and managing the learning of a large group of people.

Another major obstacle to the adoption of new activity-based learning approaches lies in the perception of the learner as to what learning involves and what it is. In schools in which the students' experiences of learning are mainly passive, it is possible that a degree of time and effort will need to be expended helping the students, and again their parents, become more familiar and comfortable with the new methods of learning and appreciate the fact that they are, at least, equally rewarding and effective – if not far more so! This will be especially true, and enormously difficult in schools that are found in South East Asia, where the prevalence of rote-learning is widespread and choking in terms of enabling students to become involved in brainstorming activities, to question and to display initiative, let alone to criticise and analyse.

To illustrate this point I would like to recount an event that happened fairly recently, when I was running a four-day workshop in an international school in Malaysia, with a delightful group of students aged 14 to 15 years. It was an interesting example of their reliance on what can only be called 'spoon-feeding' by the teacher or, in my case, the facilitator of their learning. On the first day of the workshop, each participant was called upon to make no more than a three-minute presentation or talk on any topic that interested them. I then gave them half an hour to prepare what they were going to say. (One of the outcomes of the workshop was to help the participants understand and appreciate that effective presentations rely mostly on spending a great deal of time planning, preparing and practising their talks prior to actual delivery.) The young people involved found this task extraordinarily difficult, and not because they lacked the necessary confidence to stand up and speak. Indeed, all those involved had nominated themselves for the workshop and were serving as school prefects, or members of various clubs and societies which required them to take a lead role.

During the feedback at the end of all these short, preliminary presentations, what emerged was something I had not anticipated. They all said that the most challenging and time-consuming part of the exercise was actually trying to decide what to talk about for the three minutes. The reason they gave for this surprising admission was simply that whenever they had been required to address an audience or deliver a presentation in school before, the students were accustomed to being assigned the topic on which they were required to speak by their teachers. As a result, they all spent most of the preparatory time wracking their brains to try and identify what they were going to speak about, as this task fell outside of, or largely beyond their experiences to date.

To develop the spiral curriculum framework, starting with awareness and then moving towards understanding and competence in any subject area, it is important to begin by drawing on concrete daily life experiences that can be found in the student's environment. These provide exemplar situations out of which the more abstract concepts and principles to be investigated and developed are forged. Using this starting point of the student's awareness or experience of reality to draw out the core concepts, enables the learner to understand more fully that of which they are aware, rather than begin by seeking to apply 'taught' subject-related concepts to reality. This is a significantly better direction from which to engage student interest and promote a greater intrinsic motivation to learn. It is also perfectly reasonable, through the skilful use of a variety of teaching methods, to achieve an educationally beneficial balance between student freedom in the learning process, and prescription. I acknowledge that prescription does have a valid place in the design of this type of learning program so as to ensure that the learner encounters particular experiences which are worthwhile and yet could perhaps risk being missed under a system of totally free student choice, but it is an imperative to avoid the excessive structuring and pre-specification of learning outcomes that prevents students from important activities such as reflecting, questioning, challenging and debating, as well as considering the possible and creative ways of viewing and doing things.

This spiral curriculum framework also has a great deal in common with Whitehead's principle of 'Rhythm in Education' which he saw as an essentially cyclical process in which the most effective approach is to understand the way in which using different but recurring emphasis contributes to effective learning. Within the educational cycle that he talked about, he identified three distinct phases which might be considered to be the methodological counterparts of the three phases or stages within the spiral consisting of awareness, understanding and competence. The three corresponding educational phases that Whitehead identified were called 'romance', 'precision' and 'generalization'.

The romantic stage involves an exploration of the context of that which is to be learned. In Whitehead's own words this means, *"grasping things in the rough, before smoothing out and shaping them through attention to detail."* Romance contributes to learning experiences occurring more in the affective domain, with the student gaining a genuine concern for, and interest in, that which s/he is to learn. Moreover, knowledge is never encountered without the accessories of emotion and purpose, and this stage corresponds to the need for the learner to become 'aware' of subject-related issues and problems in broad outline via a largely experiential form of learning, before seeking to draw out the key concepts that relate to them.

The second stage of 'precision', involves the learner in coming to terms with the detail of what has been experienced, by analyzing the facts carefully and thoroughly. In this stage, as Entwistle (1970) puts it, *"the width of relationship is subordinated to the exactness of formulation,"* and the appropriate methodology may now be a more teacher-led approach, with the learning being exposed to a certain restraint, in order that real understanding can be achieved. Metaphorically speaking, the precision stage of learning, which may involve fairly didactic methods of teaching, enables the student to **'see the wood by means of the trees'**. This recognizes that the stage of precision is barren without the preceding stage of romance, (i.e. that understanding relies on an initial awareness of an issue or problem), and that this precision is a necessary pre-requisite for the third stage in the learning process – that of 'generalization'.

The 'generalization' phase involves the transfer of learning to new situations, and these can be external, real-life situations, or theoretical ones within the school, but this third stage is necessarily founded on an understanding of the issues in question. More precisely, the skills, concepts and techniques mastered at the stage of precision will often come to fruition by initiating another learning cycle, within the same subject area, or, more promisingly, in the interests of achieving more inter-related and integrated learning, in relation to *other* aspects of the curriculum. At this point, the learner can become aware of an access to power, for want of a better word, by being able to see precisely what can be done with his/her new skill, concept and knowledge at this stage of application. Again, this notion of empowerment accords well with the third stage in the development of a subject-based perspective, that of 'competence' and the ability to actually **do** something. The ideas that develop during the more precise form of learning are now utilized, tested and thrown into fresh, new and interesting combinations, thereby countering the danger of inert or barren learning that so often occurs in schools around the world today. What is important, however, about this alternative to the linear style of learning that characterizes the educational diet of many young people at school, is that the activities involved at the 'generalization' stage lead into another stage of romance, or 'awareness', but at a higher level within this spiral process of learning. In other words, the stage of 'precision' is only an intermediary phase in Whitehead's learning cycle and not a beginning and an end in itself. Consequently, teachers involved in this more dynamic process of learning need to be aware, both when planning and then delivering the curriculum, that the precision stage of learning should be conducted with an eye to **transfer value**, with the next stage of 'generalization' in mind.

One of the great advantages that Whitehead's rhythm theory of education, of a learning cycle in which three correlative functions are present, is that it neatly side-steps the 'student-centered' versus the 'teacher-led' debate, or the creation of unhelpful educational dualisms and our seemingly inevitable propensity to regard these as the horns of a dilemma. Instead, the existence of a ***three-phase learning cycle*** recognizes that different approaches are relevant at different stages in the learning process. As a result, this offers us the alternative of educational balance, and one that does not require a dubious compromise between competing approaches.

I should perhaps acknowledge that in his work, Whitehead saw his rhythm cycle of learning happening during the course of a young person's educational lifetime, in which the romance of infancy leads on to the precision of childhood and then the generalization of adolescence. However, he did suggest that this three-phase cycle could well apply, or be introduced to any particular unit of learning, and it is this that more closely matches the awareness, understanding and competence, based on the development of the core concepts of subject disciplines, that I believe could be a better way of structuring the secondary school curriculum.

Under the current regime that is undertaken in most secondary schools, teachers have tended to operate under the mistaken belief that their main pedagogical challenge is how they can translate complex concepts into the language that young people at school will understand, at whatever age. When I taught Economics, therefore, I saw my greatest challenge to be how I could successfully and effectively explain topics such as National Income, Fiscal Policy and the Balance of Payments in an intelligible way to my students of mixed academic ability in the subject. This belief, that the teacher's main task in school is to dilute advanced subject matter into a more easily-digested mulch of knowledge, is erroneously based on the assumption that academic disciplines can only exist and be explored at the level of what Piaget referred to as 'formal operations'.

This attempt to simplify subject matter in order to make it intelligible for young people by dilution is not only really unnecessary, but it is also very unhelpful. It is patently clear that the fundamental or core concepts and principles of any subject discipline are, in themselves, essentially simple, and our approach to the educational process, therefore, should begin by identifying these core concepts and principles, and illustrating them through the simple, concrete, uncomplicated experience of the learner. The educational task then progresses to consider how to apply these key economic concepts to ever more complex, abstract and unfamiliar data.

The notion of the spiral curriculum in the development of any learning perspective has the advantage of suggesting repetition at ever higher levels of difficulty and complexity, rather than returning the learner to familiar subject matter. In Economics, for example, I truly believe that we could design and deliver a curriculum in which the key economic concepts can be acquired at an initial, early stage in the education of a young person – whilst at primary school – and then developed at different stages of schooling not by introducing distinctively new concepts and principles, but by applying the first principles to more difficult and complex material or contexts. In other words, the real task for teachers who are charged with the responsibility of developing an economic perspective to learning is not the simplification of advanced subject matter, but rather the development of an understanding of what is essentially fundamental to the experiences of young people of any particular age group.

To put it another way, introducing any academic discipline to a student should involve an attempt to explain current behavior and experience, and the laying of a conceptual foundation for the understanding of subsequent experiences in the future. In so doing, the spiral framework which adopts a developmental view of the subject matter enables us to avoid another unhelpful and unrealistic dichotomy in education. Again, it was a complaint of Entwistle that:

"The notion of schooling as the enforced learning of adult preoccupations and interests will persist so long as we refuse to entertain the possibility that the key principles of the academic disciplines find exemplification in the behavior of even the very young."

Another important point for teachers, seeking to adopt the approach outlined in this chapter, to address, is that successively reintroducing key issues and generalizations at increasing depth and complexity raises very important questions about how to ensure that continuity and progression is maintained. Given that a young person's development is a continuous process, schools must provide conditions and experiences which maintain and encourage this process. If progression is to be maintained then there is a need to ensure that we build systematically on the knowledge, concepts, skills and attitudes of young people. This will help ensure an orderly advance in their capabilities over a period of time by enabling them to work at a higher and higher level of ability within the spiral framework. This is much easier for teachers in primary school and, to some extent in the first two or three years in a few secondary schools, where one teacher will take one class for all or most of the time. In this scenario, these teachers are well-placed to ensure adequate and challenging continuity and progression in the studies of the young people with whom they work. In most secondary schools, however, this constancy of one teacher taking one class for all or most subjects is rarely the case, largely as a result of the subject-specialist training that they undergo. Consequently, to ensure proper continuity and progression in such situations necessitates a combination of curriculum mapping, strong guidance and support strategies, as well as student participation in formative assessment. Furthermore, to adopt a more negotiated curriculum, which this focus on core concepts not only lends itself to, but also encourages, will enable the individual student (and the school) to recognize the continuity in what they are learning, and the progression in their own work.

Again a thematic approach could be employed to provide a focus for inter-disciplinary and multi-perspective studies, with the aesthetic and creative dimension of learning being given a prominent and central role, for reasons that have already been elaborated upon in previous chapters. This spiral development of the core concepts in all subject disciplines, in which increasing levels of awareness, understanding and competence are developed, also demands that the student is very much at the centre of learning, and that it is their choices in negotiating the contexts in which these fundamental principles are introduced and subsequently revisited. It also focuses so much more on what interests the students in their current existence and relegates the view that schooling should be concerned with preparation for some unknown adult life to a minimal or consequent role, assuming that it is entertained at all. This approach is significantly more concerned with the child's capacity for life as a child. It is in my view a gross mistake, if not frankly silly to think of children as candidates who are merely on the waiting list for recognition as adults, and I much prefer to regard childhood as a stage in life that is also intrinsically worthwhile. From an ethical point of view, this preferred view of what should be going on in school, evokes the concept of human rights against preparation as an educational aim. We must cease this damaging and largely futile practice of sacrificing a child's life in the here and now for the child's own future as an adult, because we can never be sure that the future to which the present is mortgaged will actually ever materialize. Furthermore, the way in which adults (teachers and parents) seek to determine what they want their child to become in the future is a fundamental interference with the right of an autonomous individual, of a unique human spirit, to determine his/her own ends. It is this meddling, often for perfectly understandable, caring and loving motives that leads to people shuffling off this mortal coil with genuine regrets that they have effectively wasted their opportunity to live the life they should have been able to live.

What people and the school system seem to be incapable of grasping is, that since present life merges inevitably and insensibly into future life, the future is taken care of, and that the best way to prepare for adult life is to get the best out of the present, and it would be an act of supreme belligerence to suggest that the way that schooling is currently envisaged even approximates to this ethically more honest standpoint. This is not to say that the future that materializes should be a matter of complete indifference to us, and the notion of negotiated learning contexts between teacher and learner offers the opportunity for exercising some justifiable direction over the kind of growth we encourage in the present.

The chances of teachers being allowed or having the energy to begin developing this more radical alternative to the mindless 'hoop-jumping' in which young people, teachers and schools are required to engage, owing to excessive degrees of accountability to all the wrong people, is remote, as long as the throttle-inducing grasp that the traditional orthodoxy of what amounts to education holds sway. School teachers and managers need to be allowed to express their passion for enabling young people to learn and to fulfil their rich and diverse destinies in life. Freedom for teachers and schools as well as freedom for young minds to learn those things that interest, stimulate and truly engage them is long overdue and desperately needed for all our futures.

That will require school managers to re-focus their minds, and stop spending their time on anything other than the education of young people while they are at school. The current management practice in many schools needs to be rectified if they are truly to be able to adjust their focus in this way. They need to refuse to be an ally to the whims of mindless politicians and their wrecking-balls of different hues and prejudices, because at the end of the day, virtually all of their initiatives are just 'balls'!

Furthermore, those universities who hold the enormous responsibility of training our teachers also need to re-adjust their focus and start to design more imaginative training programs that develop teachers who are not mere technicians, or robots required to undertake duties that are essentially routine, repetitive and administrative in nature, without questioning the educational value that they offer – if any. These issues of school management, teacher training and endlessly interfering and misguided government, will all be my focus in the ensuing chapters.

Section D: School Management and Leadership

Chapter Twelve: Role of Leadership and Management

Clarifying Terms

It is always gratifying and encouraging when the often 'warring' factions involved in education policy-making can see eye-to-eye with one another without there being any rancour or hostile and overly critical discourse. This does happen every so often but, unfortunately, nowhere as frequently as it should if the education that occurs within formal schools is genuinely intended to provide intelligent, empowered and liberated young people – young people full of confidence, interest and specific aptitudes that more closely match their true talents and passions in life.

There is one notable area where Her Majesty's Inspectors, OFSTED, the government and the teaching profession have enjoyed a genuine meeting of the minds, and that consensus ad idem has rested in the shared belief that the function of leadership and management is of vital importance in the creation or development of a really good school – assuming that we can take the definition of 'a really good school' as a given. I know that is a big ask, but for now, let us leave that assumption on the back burner. I do this so as to avoid allowing such a debate to spoil the celebration of the fact that these often conflicting voices all seem to agree on something, because what is of far greater importance is the whole issue of the meaning of the two terms: leadership and management, and their relationship and inter-relationship in actual practice.

Once again, I make no apologies for being utterly predictable by referring to my trusty English Dictionary in order to see what the established wisdom considers the generally accepted meaning of these key terms to be. So often, this lexical starting point is highly illuminating in that the explanations of important terms are either too general in nature, or include words which are arguably rather questionable. Often, our own intuitive definition and perspective is fundamentally at odds with the literal meaning that is given to these terms in the English dictionary.

Let us start with the key term: **'leadership'**. My choice of dictionary (the Collins Cobuild Advanced Learners English Dictionary) maintains that, *"You* *refer to people who are in control of a group or organisation as the leadership.*" Immediately for me, one phrase stands out as deserving of further question or clarification, and that is the precise meaning of the words 'in control'. Well, the dictionary defines 'control' of an organisation, place or system as, "*the power to make all the important decisions about the way that it is run.*" Again, I feel that if those charged with leading an organisation are the ones who make all the important decisions about the way that it is run, then this implies that all key decisions are rightly within their gift to make. I would also suggest that leadership is more about establishing strategy, general policy and the direction in which an organisation is to go, and that it is arguably the role of managers to make the decisions about how to effectively and efficiently chase down that vision and achieve the agreed mission. Yes, it is incumbent upon good leaders to make **_some_** of the important decisions, to exercise **_an element_** of overall control and to shoulder overall responsibility for the organisation, but that is not quite as centralised nor as complete or total as the dictionary definition tends to imply.

In the case of the school, the most important decisions to be made should centre on the best ways of facilitating the learning of young people, and this should be something for professional teachers to determine within the many different and personal contexts that arise in the life of any one school, on any particular day, as well as over time. Perhaps one definition that appears in the dictionary, and one with which I have no real issue or argument, is that leadership, "*refers to the qualities that make someone a good leader or the method a leader uses to do his or her job.*" However, I consider that to identify and recognise these qualities is a lot more productive and useful if we are to clarify exactly what it is that we mean when we are talking about leadership.

The running of an organisation, as far as I am concerned, is really a function carried out by those who are charged with managing it, rather than the person or people holding the leadership function. The dictionary maintains that, "*if you manage in an organisation, business or system, or the people who work in it, you are responsible for controlling them.*" Indeed, the received wisdom regarding 'management', the noun as opposed to the verb, reaffirms the view that it "*is the control and organising of a business or other organisation.*" Once again, both statements contain the notion of '*control*' and I have a real problem with that word because I believe that there is a fundamental distinction between managing something and seeking to control it. Indeed, too many schools seek to overly control or 'manage' what goes on in their organisations rather than leading and giving an overall direction for the various endeavours that seek to provide diverse opportunities which promote the education of young people. Moreover, Warren G. Bennis confirms this view (as does Stephen Covey in his excellent book 'The 8th Habit') when he wrote, *"Failing organisations are usually over-managed and under-led."*

I would go further and say that schools fail to truly educate, as opposed to just 'school' young people, partly because those at the top of the organisation see management as controlling the day-to-day transactions in as much detail as they possibly can. What is even more troubling to me is that it is not only the generals 'at the top' of the organisation who see things this way, but also the foot soldiers lower down in the status hierarchy, such is the power of custom and practice, and that of the traditional orthodoxy. In short, the tendency to over-manage and the concomitant failure to lead, is entirely based upon a fundamental *lack of trust* in one's fellow workmates and the creation of a very unhealthy and counter-productive 'us' and 'them' mentality.

What is more, this twin problem of lack of trust and the schism in the chain of command in so many schools and other organisations, actually feeds the kind of feelings that promote, encourage and falsely justify the need for even more rigid control. I also believe, quite strongly, that this skewed notion of the task of leaders and managers leads to much the same feelings for the need to control what students learn and, more questionably, how they learn it. The hidden messages in many schools also implicitly, covertly and unintentionally communicate this lack of trust, and the divisive 'us-and-them' mentality that the teaching staff perceive, into the experiences of young people and their learning. This *'Daddy and Mummy know best, dear'* paradigm creates the need for a carrot-and-stick approach to how schools are run, and more worryingly, to how students are encouraged to learn, and this manifests itself in the form of complex rewards and sanctions for both teachers and their 'pupils'. The best rewards I have received in my long career to date have always been the feelings invested in knowing that I have done the right thing and done it really well and, therefore, have achieved something really worthwhile. I feel the buzz of personal achievement, often vicarious to the extent that, in common with all teachers (I would hope), my efforts are visible or evident in the success, achievements and accomplishments of many young people, or in some cases, just one. I do not require the incentives of league tables, grades, performance management criteria, bonuses or any other external inducement to motivate me to give of my best. I am my fiercest critic and I reflect upon my own practice, evaluating my successes and my failures, so that I can repeat the former in new contexts and learn from the latter and, thereby, avoid personal disappointment.

Controlling Instincts in Schools

In some ways, things have changed since I was a teacher working in a school at the beginning of my career, but in those days, it seemed to me that school administrators were sometimes overly concerned with making decisions that maintained the status quo, and that necessarily militated against and were resistant to change. There was little, if anything, that remotely resembled risk-taking and experimentation, and even less in terms of having an appetite for effecting school improvement, as this meant a departure from 'the way we currently do things'. Even when I took up my first headships in England, those who were in senior positions, and by definition older members of staff, appeared to be more inclined towards keeping 'the school ship' on a steady course, and preferably one that avoided all storms or ripples that might cause them to reach for the Quells, or incite the crew to question or challenge the course that they were charting, or failing to chart. Continuing with this maritime analogy, the existing emphasis of school management could be best articulated by the expression: 'Don't rock the boat'. In many ways, one might be excused for interpreting the prevailing mood amongst those who were in senior positions (there were rather a lot of them and they had also been in post for quite a long time) as one in which the school was some kind of social club for them; a way for them to guarantee that they enjoyed secure, well-paid and tenured employment until they were ready to retire, which didn't seem as if it was going to be any time soon.

Decisions made were very much on an ad hoc basis, a sort of reactive, fire-fighting role and certainly devoid of any significant claim to be proactive or systematic. In fact the only consistency in the decision making was an apparently overwhelming desire to avoid changing the lack of direction at any cost and continuing to drift peacefully as they had for some considerable time, or so it seemed. Meanwhile, the definitely younger crew who toiled below 'senior-management' deck levels were left frustrated, over-worked and becoming quietly mutinous at the way in which the grandees within the school were taking the crew's labours for granted, whilst strutting around proudly under the guise of their senior status, and enjoying their more substantial, but arguably unjustified, salaries and more generous non-contact time. Furthermore, such senior staff were so often in their elevated positions largely by dint of length of service and (as a generalisation) rarely for reasons of ability, aptitude or qualification. With the benefit of hindsight, I should have perhaps summarised the phenomenon that I encountered at a senior level as, *"Never before in the field of scholastic endeavour has so little been done by so many for so much."*

As far as I could tell, decision making was all too often focusing on notional budgets, staffing levels and administrative matters, often arising due to the lack of effective leadership and systems that were consistently applied once they were agreed. The main reason why there was this lack of consistent application of 'agreed' policies and procedures was that they were not at all 'agreed' in the first place; they were largely imposed as top-down initiatives from those on high, to the minions who worked at the operational level, or if one prefers more anachronistic metaphors, at 'the chalk-face'. I can hear some younger people reading that and wondering what chalk is exactly – yes, I am that old!

These days the emphasis is relentlessly and inexorably being placed upon excessive administration, record keeping and so-called accountability, although it is never at all clear who we are supposed to be accountable to, for what exactly, or why. This erroneous focus is largely determined by external forces, with the government of the day being the major culprit, and it serves no real purpose except to require teachers to expend their time and energies on all the wrong things. I was much moved by the plea from an anonymous teacher (anonymous owing to fears of recrimination one imagines, and doesn't that speak volumes about the state of school leadership and management today) in an article published in The Guardian newspaper (2014) entitled, *'The Secret Teacher – help, I'm drowning in admin'.*

The article begins with a highly pertinent question: *"When did teaching stop being about exciting lessons and giving meaningful feedback, and just become an endless stream of box-ticking and paperwork?"* Now, people enter the teaching profession for various reasons, but the most common certainly at the time of training and subsequent entry, is that it is a vocation for which one has a real passion, plus a desire to contribute to the augmentation of the future life chances of young people. The 'secret teacher' put it this way: *"After all, it's (teaching) all about interacting with people, isn't it? Real, live humans, both young and young-at-heart. I was passionate about teaching and passionate about my subject – in that order."* At the age of 26, our secret teacher deserved a promotion that s/he coveted and landed what s/he described as her/his 'dream job' as Head of Department. I can vividly recall a similar buzz when I first became a Head of Department in a new school at a similar age, as I was responsible for establishing something that I regarded as utterly worthwhile, meaningful and above all else, personally fulfilling. Like me, the secret teacher revelled in being able to lead *"a brilliant team of teachers who, like me, believed that the time we spend with the children is more important than a thousand ticked boxes."* All was well with him or her – at least to begin with. In all honesty, my guess is that judging by the affective tone of the letter, the secret teacher is a female of the species, but admittedly there is a 50-50 chance that I might be wrong in making that assumption.

Then about one and a half years ago, the joy of being a teacher working with talented colleagues and young people all seemed to evaporate, and incredibly quickly. The secret teacher felt that everything went crazy in education (that which takes place in schools). As s/he put it:

"Free periods were no longer about spending time on my classes and the future of our department. After school time stopped being about giving children extra help and running extra-curricular clubs that would nourish their passion for my subject."

Why was this? What happened to detract so devastatingly from our teacher's initial passion and drive, and that made such vital things no longer important? Yes, you've guessed it – administrative irrelevancies and a seemingly insatiable demand for data of dubious use or relevance. In common with many other schools in the UK, as well as many international schools situated overseas, teachers were now required to spend valuable time filling out boxes for each child in the class. These boxes contained simple grades and numbers, matched against National Curriculum attainment criteria, but not helpful and

252

meaningful comments that are designed to help young people make progress and feel good about their achievements over time.

Another distracting and time-wasting, redundant requirement was to produce formal exams for every single year group taught at the end of every term. That means that the secret teacher and her/his colleagues were spending valuable time setting and subsequently marking and grading exam papers three times a year, as well as wasting several weeks in the school year examining rather than genuinely assessing students. In effect, this nonsense meant that the opportunity cost to the students was the loss of a great deal of teaching time every single year, so that they could be seen to be able to jump through largely meaningless 'hoops' called examinations, just like circus-performing animals – an equally inhumane and unnecessary waste of precious time. The secret teacher and 'her' colleagues were also required to do 'work-sampling' every half term, or every six weeks in effect, instead of being professionally **trusted** to manage their department's own carefully designed assessment programme. Hours and hours of time literally squandered for data that allegedly tracks student progress, whereas research into this contentious topic has shown that all this statistical monitoring and recording of student performance in largely irrelevant subject studies does absolutely nothing to enable students to learn and progress more quickly or effectively. In other words, it is all essentially a paper exercise, the worth of which is very marginally of greater worth than the tissue I use in the toilet, to be frank. As our stalwart secret teacher rightly asked, *"Where was the pedagogy in all this?"* There clearly was/is none. The emphasis and focus for both students and their teachers was to provide meaningless data to allegedly demonstrate a spurious and facile yard-stick of accountability for the monetary millions invested in 'education at school'. Instead of really educating young people, the externally imposed system of accountability is doing nothing other than further stressing young people, young people who are already stressed to breaking point in so many cases.

Perhaps the most profoundly honest and straightforward part of the article submitted by this passionate, astute and caring 'secret' teacher, and the part which really struck a harmonious chord with my own sentiments on the changes that have impacted schools in more recent years is as follows:

"I wonder if I'll ever again know the joy of teaching a genuinely great lesson. The kind of lesson when the kids' faces light up and you know they're learning something and having a whale of a time doing it. I don't think I've taught like that in the last year – I certainly can't remember one. I wonder if I'll ever be able to change my plan mid-lesson based on one child's brilliant question, and we'll go off on a wonderful, exciting tangent of learning. It's a bit difficult to do that when you have to keep reciting the doom-laden mantra: 'exam in two weeks'."

That extract demonstrates how the passion-sapping, mind-numbing and spirit-damaging existence of pre-specified, content-laden syllabus requirements, that are externally determined and established, militates so powerfully against what teachers and students should really be doing in schools, wherever in the world they may be located.

How does this reference to the plea of our secret teacher relate to school leadership and management, you may wonder? Indeed, you might expect the teacher in question to embark on a hostile diatribe against the current Secretary of State for Education in the Conservative/Liberal Coalition Government, one singularly unattractive creature – ideologically as well as physically – who (at the time of writing) goes by the name of one, Mr. Michael Gove. In fact, the secret teacher feels that it is the way in which senior leadership teams in schools respond to the puerile, ill-guided and utterly distracting drivel that pours from Mr. Gove's orifice, and I'll let you decide at which end of his anatomy that particular outlet might be found. Instead of standing up against this party-political onslaught on our nation's schools, school leaders adopt a submissive, subservient and knee-jerk posture in the reactive panic that it induces. The secret teacher bemoans the lack of pedagogical and intelligent debate in her/his school that went into the senior leadership team's decision making process when responding to central government's directives and wheezes.

I remember that when I was a serving Head Teacher in the UK in the mid-1990s, I saw it as one of my main responsibilities to act in a role that was more like a type of 'force-field' around the school. My main task in this role was to shield my colleagues, and the sanity of the school, as a whole from the endless interventionist rays of baffledom emanating from central government. In this daring, Dan Dare role, my key task was to act as a filter to identify those initiatives that might offer something that would actually help move the school community forward, and to select those others which we needed to delay, question or discard if at all possible. In most cases, the majority of the partisan political attempts at intervention would serve only to provide a major distraction to our own development agenda and our combined endeavours to make the school a better place for all young people.

Why should the egos of different Secretaries of State for Education, who often enjoy very short tenure of post, be allowed to determine what millions of young people do and are subjected to whilst they are at school. Furthermore, why should schools be required to abandon, subordinate or otherwise 'twist' their own long-term school improvement and development needs and plans for those of central government? This is especially pertinent when one considers that those elected to 'represent' us do not command the majority support of the electorate, given the 'first-past-the-post' peculiarities of British democracy, nor have a significant number of them ever experienced life in a state school – or life in its real and 'raw' state for that matter.

What saddens me more than most things is how these accountability mirages have had a deleterious effect on international schools as well. The tentacles of central control that crush the creative instincts of teachers and students alike have extended beyond the perimeters of the Education Secretary's jurisdiction and permeated the work of those working in and attending schools that are technically free from the legal imperative. In fact, one of the most attractive features of working in international schools for many British teacher émigrés was that such institutions were blessed by being free of the legal obligation to be led up the garden path by British politicians of whatever hue. They were able to cherry-pick, from the battery of education initiatives, those things which the school owners, governors and senior leaders felt were useful to their development, growth and success in their overseas context, and which contributed demonstrably to student learning and school improvement. The freedom to choose in this way also had the corresponding attraction of being able to blissfully ignore the educationally dubious and damaging initiatives that have only served to derail much of the good work that many schools were once doing in England and Wales. Because most international schools recruit expatriate teachers to deliver the particular curriculum model that exists in either the UK, America, Australia, Canada, France or wherever, and because students attending such institutions are very often from those parent countries, it is perhaps inevitable that 'bad' practices from the host country will accompany the occasional good ones.

When I was working in an international school in a South East Asian country, I was mainly responsible for trying to transform a local school that had been offering a broadly British curriculum model into a truly international school. Unfortunately, I was line managed by a local Director who had been at the school for a very long time and had, in all honesty, been responsible for keeping the school going and growing (in terms of the number on roll), but without changing its direction, the nature of the school or the prevailing style of management. To maintain control (that word again), the director sought to micro-manage the staff who were technically under my leadership, and in so doing she was remarkably successful in undermining my authority as Principal through this practice. In fact, I was informed by a reliable senior source that this practice and its effect upon the Principal's ability to lead and effectively manage the school, was the main reason why my predecessor had left the post, before I asked to be released from my contract.

One of the Director's interventions was to task one of my Curriculum Leaders to start the process of tracking individual student progress, as matched against the National Curriculum (NC) requirements of England and Wales. At the time, the school was about to move to a new site and, for a whole host of other reasons was simply not ready for such a challenging initiative, an initiative for which the majority of local staff (who had, in the main, not formally qualified as teachers) did not even appreciate the value or need. The irony of the timing of this initiative was that within a few weeks of the assigned teacher trying to encourage an often reluctant staff to undertake the training and implementation of this monitoring and tracking process, the Department for Education in the UK decided to abandon this requirement owing to its flaws, one of which was that it was highly subjective in nature. In place of this cumbersome system of monitoring student progress, state schools in England and Wales were required, not advised, to devise their own systems of tracking student progress instead. This volte face was remarkable given that individual schools, acting in isolation, were required to find a more effective, valid and reliable system to chart student progress than the machinations of the DFE, with all the resources and expertise at its disposal (an aptly chosen word) had failed to achieve, and by their own admission. What is more, this logically puzzling decision amounts to little more than an admission of how extraordinarily difficult it is to measure student progress in any meaningful, reliable and valid way.

A less obvious source of irony is that, as the Principal, I was not at all convinced that tracking the alleged progress of young learners in this way had any educational merit whatsoever, and even if it did, I considered that following the relocation of the school to a new and arguably 'purpose- built site', the staff of the secondary school needed to focus on a far more pressing developmental agenda: that of developing more relevant, student-centred and active methods of teaching and learning than the traditional rote learning that characterises much of what passes as education in schools in the South East Asia region. (Having said that, the assigned teacher to whom I refer, was a truly outstanding classroom performer, and her willingness, enthusiasm and vitality could have been far more effectively and efficiently harnessed had she been asked to lead teacher development – albeit after the move to the new school site.)

What was even more galling to me, however, was that I honestly believe that this focus on proving that students are making progress for accountability reasons, and as measured against some spurious nationally-determined criteria, contributes nothing whatsoever to improving student achievement in their final examinations or their performance at the time when they are liberated from the externally-imposed drudgery that masquerades as education at the point when they are no longer legally obliged to be at school. When I was a classroom teacher (the best job in any school) I was not really overly interested in teaching just what the GCE 'A' Level syllabus required, as it was always my aim to take students as far beyond that level as it was possible to do, given their interest in the subject and their willingness to devote a lot of time for additional study outside of the chronological confines of a lesson. More importantly, after a very short period of time, in common with my colleagues who taught other subjects, I developed that wonderfully abstract but powerful concept of 'professional judgement'. I was able to instinctively or intuitively identify at what level a student was performing and to extrapolate their effort and progress, so as to predict the type of grade that they might get in the final examination. This did not require me to spend many precious hours assessing the students in some overly complicated and obtuse way, seeking to equate performance with some number or letter grade, or even some graded criteria. Moreover, my professional judgement was hardly ever wrong in terms of the final examination outcome. Instead of seeking to assess performance according to some mathematical benchmark, I simply had incredibly high expectations of what the young people who **trusted** me to teach Economics to them were expected to achieve from lesson to lesson, week to week and for the entire duration of the two-year course. I was not willing to allow them, or me, for that matter, to be constrained by the limitations of the 'A' Level syllabus.

I can understand perfectly well the immense frustration, irritation and disappointment felt by the Secret Teacher in that newspaper article. What that anonymous person felt was that the senior managers within his/her school should have focussed all decisions on one fundamental and pivotal question. That key question is: how, at the end of the day, will the decision to use valuable time in this way, lead to an improvement in student learning, and how does it truly promote life-long, self-directed learning as well as a love of, and a passion for learning? To my mind most of these externally imposed wheezes do little or nothing to substantively improve student performance over time. On the other hand, holding very high, but realistic expectations, and communicating these to the students as a group and individually on a regular basis, is far more effective and allows me to focus my time and energies on what is really beneficial and useful. In other words, please do not ask me to quantify and justify my instinctive and experience-based intuition as to how students are performing, please just *trust* my professional judgement!

Another aspect of managing a school that is very much in vogue these days, to satiate the accountability and quantification brigade that seems to thrive on burying teachers and senior teams under a pile of paperwork, as well as requiring these same dedicated professionals to waste a lot of precious time, is to do with what has become 'performance management'. This requires observing teachers at regular intervals in order to evaluate their classroom performance and identify their strengths and areas for development. This tool is mainly intended to enable senior and middle managers to be fully aware of who are the effective and competent teachers and, therefore, those who merit a pay increment, especially if crossing a salary threshold, and of course, those who do not. Whilst the cynic within me tends to think that this exercise was dreamt up to manage the financial limitations of frequent spending cuts in the government's education budget which, in turn, impact every state school in the land to a greater or lesser degree, the need for a school to 'know' who are its best teachers and, particularly, those others who need development and improvement support is incredibly important. Of course it is; but there are a few points that I would like to make about the need to devote so much time to trying to quantify or measure these people against some highly questionable and equally subjective criteria.

First of all, exposing myself to ill-informed charges of either arrogance or complacency, by those who seek to gain financially and politically from such elaborate systems and procedures, I can honestly say that as a teacher in schools and, later as a Head Teacher, I always 'knew' who were the truly gifted teachers who deserved all the plaudits, as well as the genuinely atrocious ones who needed to find an alternative source of employment. I also 'knew' the vast majority of colleagues who fell into the category of those capable of further improvement through continuous professional development (which was all of them, including me). So how did I 'know' this, in the absence of all this pressing performance management paraphernalia with which state schools, as well as those that claim to be 'international' in nature, have been burdened today? The way to know this as a matter of course is not based on personal prejudice or favouritism; it is based on a number of factors and, undoubtedly, the most vital, reliable and valid of these is to quite simply (but equally importantly) **ask the students**. And if I make a mistake it is unlikely to be any more glaring or detrimental than using questionable performance criteria which omit as much as they include and which are necessarily still largely subjective.

There are, of course, a whole host of other ways in which it is possible to identify and know who are the good teachers in a school by using other criteria

259

that are readily available, such as the more popular subjects that students choose to study when it comes to the options they make for study at GCSE and 'A' Level. Admittedly, this alone is not always a reliable indicator as, particularly in South East Asia but also true elsewhere, certain subjects are 'popular' not due to teacher quality, but the result of parental pressure. In my experience in South East Asia, young people who do not have an aptitude or an affinity for science subjects, are required by their parents to study all three separate science subjects and Additional Mathematics because of traditional mind-sets and the mistaken belief that having good grades in such subjects at IGCSE level augurs well for one's future employment prospects. Arguably, this is true, but this belief is dependent on their children performing well in these 'parent-preferred' subject examinations, which sadly is often not the case. The stark reality is that many students are doomed to three mediocre separate science grades (and often below the 'magical' grade C) rather than one good pass, with time being effectively 'sacrificed' in achieving, at best, mediocrity in science. The educational interests of such youngsters and, I would argue, those who perform well in the three science subjects, would have been better served had they followed a much broader and less skewed educational entitlement, certainly from 14 to 16 years of age.

Again, there are many more reliable ways of assessing who the good teachers are, and these are quantitative and qualitative in nature. Other criteria include the examination success of student cohorts over time, even though the 'success' of the teacher is somewhat vicarious in that it is heavily dependent on the academic ability and natural flair of the students in each year group. This is why value-added initiatives are more reliable indicators of teacher efficacy as a facilitator of the learning of young people.

Furthermore, a lot about teacher effectiveness can be gleaned by walking around the school, assessing the breadth, quality and relevance of student display work, as well as dropping into classrooms and having informal, but nonetheless structured and meaningful, conversations with students. At such times, student books can be checked to see that additional study ('homework' for the press-ganged) is being undertaken, and not necessarily set by the teacher. A lot can be deduced about a teacher by the quality and nature of the interactions that s/he enjoys with students in the different classes that s/he teaches, and how constructive and well-received they are, for example. Observing whose classrooms the students gravitate towards during breaks and lunchtimes, as well as before and after school, is another good sign of a teacher being seen as approachable and respected by students. I am also hugely encouraged to see students wanting to remain in the class discussing the work covered in a lesson with the teacher, long after the lesson has ended – assuming of course that the lesson is followed by a break, lunchtime or the end of the formal school day. It is professionally gratifying to see young people wanting to continue with their learning rather than having it curtailed by the purely administrative demands of the formal timetable that delivers learning in small, bite-sized chunks, which can often do nothing other than further fragment and dehumanise that which should be inter-related, connected, appreciated and fundamentally spiritual in nature.

The type of teachers that I prefer to recruit are those who exceed the expectations that I might reasonably have of my colleagues in school; in other words, those who 'go the extra mile' and whose contributions to school life surprise me – and in a pleasant, positive and encouraging way. In short, there are many teachers in my experience whose effectiveness and overall performance contributes to the unique vibrancy that good schools always seem to possess, and often in abundance. They are the teachers who are the catalysts in developing a united esprit-de-corps within the school, as a result of their efforts 'outside of' and 'beyond' their contractual obligations alone. It is important to note that I am not referring here to the teacher offering an extra-curricular activity (ECA), as this is expected as part of his or her terms of employment, although the popularity of a particular ECA and the number of these that a teacher is prepared to offer is indicative of that teacher's professional standing in the eyes of the student population.

Similarly, many teachers are willing to volunteer to contribute to school improvement by becoming members or leaders of a working group or task force that are set up to promote certain desirous developments in any school that is forward looking and dynamic in terms of what they seek to offer for those young people, as well as others, who cross its threshold. Good teachers are those who consistently apply and adhere to established and agreed school policies and procedures as an unthinking part of their everyday practice and duties. They are the teachers who are proactive and see issues that need to be addressed long before they become problematic or pressing. Such teachers either take it upon themselves to deal with and resolve such issues, or 'seek permission' to address them if its solution lies beyond their circle of influence. Clear, unambiguous and agreed systems, systems that are consistently and doggedly adhered to are the stuff of good and outstanding schools, and this important point is one of many that Peter Hymans makes in his best-selling book 'One out of Ten' when he noted about the school that he used as his main resource material:

"There was a sense of chaos, and of course the school was in special measures. The truth was the school had lost its way in terms of organisational strategies. The problem was not the staff. The problem was lack of organisation."

This pertinent observation confirms what I have argued elsewhere in this book that when things go badly wrong in any organisation, the tendency is to blame someone, rather than accept that the problem arose due a systemic failure that either allowed or actually encouraged the malpractice in question.

The Ascendency of Accountability

The 'secret teacher' referred to above is not by any means the only professional teacher who bemoans the theft of so much time, interest and enjoyment that teaching gives to the dedicated classroom practitioner, as well as the students for whom they are responsible. This obsessive and slavish obedience to ludicrous government demands by school leadership teams, in matters to do with assessment and the tracking of student progress, is disappointing as well as fundamentally and educationally flawed and misguided. It is in the interests and the product of unquestioning compliance to ever-increasing and constantly-changing calls for so-called accountability on the part of schools, and the staff who work in them. More significantly, it is also due to the lack of **trust** placed in teachers by central government politicians and, because of the conspiratorial willingness of the media to broadcast and publish similarly distrustful messages, also by parents and the general public. It is as if teachers are hell bent on doing their utmost to undermine, damage or otherwise thwart the education of young people who attend the schools in which they work. This is, of course, as neurotic as it is fallacious!

Another closely-related area to that of assessment where there has been a further clarion call from government for accountability lies in the issue of being able to measure or assess what constitutes a good teacher, a bad teacher or a truly outstanding one, for that matter. To this end, there has been a great deal of activity and debate about issues such as performance management and teacher evaluations which, as I have already mentioned are usually to justify who should merit an incremental rise in their salary, and who is not so deserving of such extra reward. Again, and I make no apology for repeating myself here, the cynic within me has noticed that the flurry of activity in this area has coincided with severe cutbacks to the budgets that schools have at their disposal, thanks to the miserly attitude of successive governments, and the need to pin the blame for allegedly 'falling standards' on an easy and likely target, namely the beleaguered, yet valiant teaching profession. I would argue that the reason for poor 'standards', whatever these are, is that the goalposts that represent the success criteria for schools have not only been moved on a fairly regular basis, but have also been redesigned or altered in terms of their shape and colour, and this has made scoring anything other than an own-goal quite a tricky accomplishment.

Without wanting to repeat what I have already said in relation to a competent Head Teacher knowing only too well who are the good and bad teachers in a school, or which colleagues are over- or under-performing in terms of expectations, this drive towards quantitatively and qualitatively assessing teachers, is another highly questionable endeavour that governments have required of state schools. I am aware that semantic arguments can be used to illuminate what it is that we are talking about, or they can be used to confuse and obfuscate, so allow me to try and clarify terms that we use so that the former purpose is achieved.

To begin with, to my mind there is, and needs to be, a clear distinction between performance 'management' on the one hand, and performance 'development' on the other, as they are often seen as being one and the same thing. This distinction is crucial as far as I am concerned, as performance management is usually, as I have said, related to assessing whether a particular teacher is deserving of a salary increment, or whether they should be allowed to cross a pay 'threshold'. Such thresholds have become increasingly common in recent years, and they exist to delineate differing levels that constitute many different types of pay and reward structures. When one reaches a particular threshold, at the top of an incremental pay tier or scale, a teacher is usually only eligible to cross the threshold and access further annual increments in salary if they are deemed to be 'worthy' in terms of their degree of competence or excellence. In other words, thresholds act as a financial barrier to automatically being awarded increments year after year without having to justify such financial progression or advancement. In principle, such a concept is one that I fully support for reasons of financial probity and prudence, as well as to offer incentives for teachers to strive to improve. Where I have a real problem with this notion is when performance management initiatives creep into this progression as I do not believe that they are particularly reliable as indicators of competence over time, and they are so often dependent upon dubious benchmarks of what constitutes a 'good' teacher, or a 'good' lesson.

Again, I would prefer to rely on my own professional judgement in determining who is meritorious of a pay increment, taking into consideration the many factors which I have already mentioned in this chapter. To me, this is more reliable, as it is based on a composite picture of the standard of work and contribution made by a particular teacher over time and takes into consideration the views of others as well as casual and formal observations. Above all else, it saves a great amount of time and paperwork that can divert me from my primary concern, and that is seeking to enable the development and professional growth of my colleagues in a somewhat more supportive and collaborative climate. The key word here is 'develop', rather than the 'accountability' which intermittent performance management seeks, and fails, to satisfy. I much prefer spending my time on engaging with colleagues in a formal process of performance development, or teacher appraisal. This is far less threatening and, equally, far more positive, constructive and more likely to engage or motivate, rather than alienate the individual teacher colleague. This process involves the teacher in a dialogue to agree a focus for their professional development, much as effective assessment of a student's accomplishments and achievements should involve the individual learner, but so rarely does in any equal or active way. This focus on development rather than accountability is far more productive in raising the skill-set and knowledge base of teachers, encouraging, as it does, various perspectives on an area of an individual teacher's performance with an essentially analytical and developmental agenda or focal point on each occasion.

I always remember one of many observational gems of one Alun Roberts, a wondrous, much-loved and highly respected tutor at the college of education where I studied for my B.Ed degree over four, highly-enjoyable years. He once remarked to me that there were three categories of teacher: a small minority of truly gifted and talented teachers and an equally small number of members of the profession who were dreadful and should be 'encouraged' to leave and find more rewarding and fulfilling employment in an alternative career. Alun opined that the vast majority of teachers, however, were a mixed ability group of individuals who all had one feature in common: they were capable of being improved and developed over time in a variety of ways. At the time when he casually made that observation, I was not in a position to realise how accurate and perceptive his views actually were. It does not, therefore, make sense to adopt a set of time-consuming, cumbersome and largely irrelevant performance management procedures, simply to provide apparently legitimate and objective grounds to 'get rid of' a relatively small number of unsatisfactory members of the teaching profession. I would argue strongly that it is a far better use of limited time to focus on professional development and growth than on some spurious notion of accountability to the political paymasters of the state school system.

As I have already said, I am aware that claiming to 'know' who are the good teachers in any school where I work, and not necessarily as a senior manager, leaves me dangerously exposed to accusations of complacency and/or even arrogance, if not favouritism. I imagine that the main criticism of relying on my own professional judgement is that it is too subjective, or open to individual prejudice or favouritism. I am inclined to counter this by pointing out that a lesson observation is also subjective, in that it relies on the evaluator's application and interpretation of a teacher's performance, measured against established criteria. Attempts to draw up a set of largely quantitative and objective criteria as to what constitutes a competent teacher have been doomed by enormous arguments in terms of what criteria they contain as well as the hugely relevant and important qualitative element of what it is that characterises a truly outstanding or gifted teacher.

I have been enormously fortunate and genuinely privileged to have been able to observe many different teachers deliver lessons in a large number of schools not only in England, but also in countries around the world. I have seen that the way in which Alun Roberts characterised teachers was indeed very astute, correct and precise. I have also found that although poor teachers tend to have a lot in common, it is nowhere near as easy to identify the common traits in what I would regard to be those of the relatively few gifted teachers that I have been lucky to watch inspire and engage students, as well as the way in which they can act as an enormously powerful catalyst to effective learning. Their impact on learners may be very similar, but the way in which they achieve highly pleasing and impressive outcomes in very limited time tends to be as idiosyncratic and personal to a particular professional, as it is efficient and effective. Again, the problem is that accountability forces us to make a ludicrous attempt to **standardise diversity**, in terms of the behaviour, style and personality of these gifted practitioners. This is as ridiculous as it is absurd and impossible!

At the time of writing I stumbled across a highly pertinent article in the Guardian newspaper online, which is based on a highly critical report of the lesson observations conducted by OFSTED, the school inspection agency in the UK. What makes this report far more newsworthy in a political sense is that it was from the right-wing, think tank 'Policy Exchange', who recommended scrapping lesson observations altogether on the grounds that they found them to be **"neither valid nor reliable"**. Their report also went on to cast serious doubt about the quality of some inspections that are conducted under the aegis of OFSTED. The research that they conducted suggested that there is only a "50-50" chance that an inspector's view of lesson observations will correspond with the progress made by students in the classrooms observed. Jonathan Simons who was the author of the report, and is head of education at the 'think tank' said, *"The evidence suggests that when it comes to relying on the judgement of a trained OFSTED inspector on how effective a lesson is, you would be better off flipping a coin."* Pretty damning stuff, I would venture!

The report made a number of rather worrying criticisms of this august body and its efficacy. In particular, it cast doubt about the role of members of the inspection teams who work for just three private organisations to which school inspections are outsourced. Apparently, these three firms employ about 3,000 staff, of whom 1,500 are actively involved in the school inspections programme. What was more worrying about the report's veiled criticism of the privatisation of the school inspection process is that OFSTED only employs between 300 and 400 staff itself. In its conclusion, the report made it clear that if school inspections are going to be of any use, then the entire system needs to be radically overhauled through a variety of major reforms, including the need to introduce an exam (although I prefer the term 'an assessment') which tests the ability of prospective inspectors to analyse data, before they can be accredited. The report also recommended that all schools should be inspected once every two years with a visit of just one day as opposed to the five days currently. In my view, this is entirely realistic, possible and reliable.

Given this lack of faith in the current system, as well as no guarantee that radical reforms will significantly ameliorate the current school inspection shambles, I reiterate my belief that my own judgement about the competence of teachers, which garners the views of many different stakeholders, and is based on my own observations over time, is far more reliable. This obsession with accountability leads the school system unhappily right 'up the garden path', in that the use of formal lesson observations by untrained head teachers, heads of department once every term to ascertain who are the good, average and poor teachers is a massive waste of time and energy. Indeed, I have already mentioned that I view the opportunity cost of relying on such procedures to evaluate a teacher's competence as being far too high, when one considers how that time could be better utilised on more profitable, valid and reliable alternative and fundamentally more *educational* activities. The most important aspect, therefore, of the recent report by Policy Exchange is that it effectively depreciates the value of relying on lesson observations in the first place, which ratchets up the opportunity cost to an even greater degree. This valid time, and the resource allocated to lesson observations, would surely be better spent on staff training to improve teachers' classroom and behaviour management, as well as how to achieve better pitch, match and relevance in their lessons, and other development areas which are formally identified through performance development initiatives, like staff appraisal.

It is not as if the criticism levelled at the OFSTED inspection process in the report by Policy Exchange came like an unexpected 'bolt from the blue' either, as earlier in 2014, the Association of School and College Leaders (ASCL) proposed that OFSTED stopped using inspectors contracted from the private sector and adopt a lower key approach to inspections. This was reported, again in the Guardian newspaper on 5th March 2014, under the headline: *"Inspection system for state schools has significant problems, OFSTED to be told."* These significant problems were essentially based on the fact that evaluations of classroom teaching observed by OFSTED were considered to be largely inconsistent. It went on to argue that inspectors contracted from the private sector should no longer be used, owing to deficiencies in their quality, due to a lack of training. Perhaps an equally worrying effect of having OFSTED inspections that was raised in the paper written by the General Secretary of the ASCL, Brian Lightman, who is a former school head, referred to some confusion surrounding what it was that OFSTED inspectors were actually looking for during their classroom observations, as well as how school inspections create *"a culture of fear"*, which has the effect of impeding innovation and *"sensible risk taking"*. As I have mentioned in earlier chapters, real learning by students demands that they take risks (not chances) with their learning, so that they can find more imaginative and creative solutions to problems, by entertaining possibility and being willing to learn by making mistakes. Exactly the same is true if we want teachers and schools to work together to learn how best to develop what they do in promoting the education of young people in more interesting, inspiring and engaging ways.

Collegiate management practices which are rigorous and effective are far more likely to foster real school improvement in these areas over time, than the intermittent snapshots that are taken of schools by a government agency in the interests of supposed accountability. In any case, to whom are schools being held accountable? Is it in the interests of the Exchequer or the Treasury, or is it to parents and other stakeholders of particular schools. I would suggest that effective governing bodies, along with active and supportive Friends' Associations, working with school leaders, managers and teachers are far better placed to ensure that quality in schools is maintained and developed in a positive, constructive and dynamic direction. This is especially true when there is a Local Education Authority (LEA) working to offer support and guidance in all aspects of what is conveniently referred to as 'quality assurance'. In short, I believe that interfering governments have a lot to answer for by seeking to emasculate, if not eradicate or eliminate LEAs under the false pretences of giving power to individual school leaders and parents, whilst cynically clawing even more direct control back into the politically jaundiced arena of central administration. What I believe to be the hugely detrimental and damaging impact of government meddling in education and schooling is something to which I propose to return in a later section of this book. For now, I want to look a little more at school leadership and management, as well as ways in which the lack of trust that appears to dominate the political discourse which foments these largely irrelevant and diversionary demands for the so-called 'accountability' of schools, can be more effectively addressed and overcome.

Chapter Thirteen: Leadership and Management

Dream a Little Dream

In my admittedly limited experience, many schools in which I have worked or visited as an adviser or inspector, sometimes fail to place the curriculum at the very centre of the overall process of their development planning, as almost the starting point. That is not to say that they don't do it at all, or that they don't try, but they find reasons and sometimes seemingly plausible excuses for not being fully able to design and deliver a broader and more enriching curriculum for the many young people they serve. In some cases, they just lack the imagination to offer so much more than that which is seen as traditionally acceptable and normal within the largely academic and historically staid school curriculum.

Some of these reasons or excuses could be argued to represent rather defeatist claims that certain combinations of subjects cannot be easily accommodated within the school timetable, or cannot be included at all. Once again, the agony of choice rears its ugly and sacrificial head, and this is made worse owing to the fact that the curriculum is made up of lots of separate, heavily-content-laden subjects, with little or no real attempt to link what they teach into some kind of coherent whole. Once again, the International Baccalaureate does much more to avoid this criticism or accusation by making serious attempts to show the inter-relationship of knowledge across different subjects.

Other excuses for not being apparently able to provide a more diverse, enriching and stimulating curriculum offer, also tend to sound eminently plausible and reasonable. For example, arguments such as the school does not have the space, or the right sort of specialist premises and rooms to make certain types of learning possible. Issues, such as the financial constraints of the school budget, are claimed to prevent the necessary expenditures in equipment, new books and other resources, and this is used to explain inaction or an inability to provide a more exciting and challenging curriculum. All of these excuses, arguments, issues and constraints, call them what you will, are often justifiable in the short term, in that they are technically true, but the real danger is that such a 'can't do' mentality serves to excuse the school from trying to do much, if anything at all to seriously overcome or otherwise deal with these obstacles and limitations over the medium, and longer term.

I am a fervent apostle of the notion that creativity and using one's imagination can make virtually anything possible or achievable in schools, and of the view that 'where there is a will, there is a way'. The trouble is, that the necessary will to accomplish the 'impossible' is all too easily buried under the weight of the apparent difficulties outlined above. For example, engaging in various ways of income generation is one way to increase the funds that any school has at its disposal. Such additional sources of finance could be devoted to developing or implementing imaginative solutions to the problems of lacking the necessary space and buildings that are needed to bring about many changes to the curriculum that have hitherto been considered impossible or, at least, out of reach and unattainable. Furthermore, this process would be so much easier to accomplish if schools were to adopt a truly community outlook.

I have been directly involved, as a teacher, adviser and leader of schools, in many such income generating initiatives; obtaining funds from government agencies such as the Central Bureau and its tremendous Schools Unit, as well as from the business world and agencies, such as the Sports Council and Arts Council. Indeed, there are publications that specialise in listing educational trusts and other sources of extra finance from a whole host of agencies that are available to promote specific types of project, initiatives and ventures, especially in education. All it takes is an idea with a vision that meets (or matches) the funding agencies' aims and objectives as well as those of the school, college or university. So, thinking hats on!

As I have already lamented, the curriculum of so many schools is usually designed around such things as available premises, the number of teachers currently employed and their specialist subjects and interests, and/or the budget available. Budgets, in particular, are such dreadfully restrictive, limiting and constraining factors, which paralyse, inhibit or otherwise preclude creativity and getting actively involved in planning and undertaking that which has previously been regarded as either not viable or risky, or even impossible. The hidden message that such inertia communicates in schools around the world, is that the school curriculum is not really why we are all here, as we are almost obliged to do that which is certain, possible, or, perhaps, easier. It is often considered to be preferable or better not to 'rock the boat' or to challenge the traditional orthodoxy that informs existing practice in so many schools, rather than strive to break free of, or overcome these sometimes rather lame excuses for inaction.

The alternative starting point is to be more daring, more radical and even more rebellious, and seek to throw off the mental shackles that inhibit our propensity to 'think outside of the box' in any significant, imaginative and courageous way. As an aside, I like the idea that I once heard from a stand-up comedian, (and I apologise for not being able to recall his name, but it was a 'he') who said that we shouldn't be so obsessed with thinking outside of the box, instead we should be doing our utmost to ensure that we never get into the box in the first place. But then schools are guilty of doing so much to put us in a box, or series of boxes, as quickly as possible via the schooling that we receive, as opposed to the education and learning that mankind so desperately needs, if it is to solve the problems that it faces in an alarmingly accelerating way, largely by dint of its own actions and inactions.

Why not start by asking all teachers, students and other stakeholders to *'dream'* about what they would really like to be able to do, to achieve in their various areas of operation, and to arrive at and agree upon a truly liberating mission statement and sense of direction for their school, or their centre for learning? And whilst dreaming, for a change, everyone involved should be encouraged to liberate their thinking, in much the same way as we would ideally like to do for the students who are legally obliged to attend school, and to entertain possibility, rather than being impeded in our thinking by mundane and surmountable issues such as those which are customarily assumed to be affordable, impracticable or acceptable.

If good intentions are not to be thwarted, and to make sure that one's dreams become a dawning and living reality, we have to absolutely ensure that once we have come together to arrive at an imaginative and amazing curriculum, as well as how it will be implemented, delivered and modified over time, then it is incumbent upon us all, collaboratively, in a spirit of genuine partnership, to find the resources to achieve it. This may involve building or modifying school buildings and finding the personnel that are needed to achieve our new and, hopefully original goals in both their construction and delivery. We have to seek to guarantee that we can truly make it happen. In short, the resources (in cash or in kind) need to be secured via whatever legal means by increasing student intake, where possible, and from income generating activities in which the necessary finance is raised and provided by the school's many community partners and stakeholders acting in a collaborative and aligned way. More importantly, involving all stakeholders as widely and fully as possible in this way, in the 'dreaming' process, is a vital and, I believe, essential ingredient in enlisting their fulsome support in ensuring that the funds and other resources are acquired, made available and put to use in making our shared dreams become a waking reality. Through this process, there is also an increased awareness that 'a school' in not really about the buildings at all, but a community of teachers, students and other partners or stakeholders, who work together, both on and off the school premises, and who share the joys, the fun and the challenge of learning, with young people very much at the heart of the entire endeavour.

The Need for Transformational Leadership

Earlier in this book, I argued that there was a really important and pressing need for schools to seek to transform society rather than to abide by the detrimental, anachronistic and restraining traditional orthodoxy that leads us all to reflect and act according to current and age-old societal mores, attitudes and paradigms. I also feel that school leadership and management teams also need to try and break the mould that has determined and shaped the way in which schools have operated and been run over many, many years, by adopting more transformational approaches to developing, improving and moving schools forward. This is absolutely vital if schools are to be radically transformed or changed, and a liberating breath of fresh air is to sweep through the dusty, dark and dingy corridors of power and everyday practice.

To do this requires transforming the way in which formal leaders in schools treat and manage their personnel or colleagues. 'Management' is **not** synonymous with 'control' at either the school or classroom level. We need to liberate teachers once they are aligned or 'married' to the school values and committed to the direction the school is taking to achieve the agreed mission and vision. Sadly, this issue of values is rarely talked or thought about in most schools, which is why I shall return to it in more detail in the next chapter. It is impossible to liberate the learning of young people if the schools they attend are manacled to ancient practice, established custom and out-dated mind-sets. Schools also need to liberate staff to think, take risks and experiment in far more imaginative and creative ways.....that is, to make mistakes occasionally. The tendency to seek to control must be swept away as schools see the wisdom in pushing decision-making as close to the operational level of the classroom as is possible, so that those charged with the responsibility of actually doing the core job of facilitating student learning can make their own decisions on how to develop and move forward in new, better and more effective ways.

I like to apply the elements of the acronym regarding the 'CORE' business of schools to staff as well as students; after all, each and every one of us is, or should be, a lifelong learner. All staff and not just the teaching staff need to be **challenged** to give of their very best at all times and to seek to do the impossible or, at least, to surprise themselves in terms of what they are capable of achieving over time. Moreover, in order to enable them in rising to this challenge, they will need some guidance as to what it is that they are all trying to accomplish, in terms of some agreed **outcomes**, although these need to avoid being overly prescriptive and pre-specified if they are not to put a brake on the over-riding need to think and act creatively, and in new and exciting ways. Additionally, school staff need to be required to take far greater **responsibility** for their own work, their own learning and professional development, in just the same way as students should be enabled and encouraged to do. Furthermore, but not finally, all teachers, support staff and, to a lesser extent, all key stakeholders, should have very high, but realistic **expectations** of themselves in terms of their performance, conduct and effectiveness while at work. Again I say that transformational leadership needs to create an atmosphere in which all learners are required to take risks (not chances) in what they do, and be willing and able to entertain the notion of possibility rather than acting defensively by being overly interested, obsessed even, with certainty, exactitude or 'rightness'.

I accept that there are risks involved with pushing decision making closer to the operational level of the individual classroom, and the main one is that the school as a whole is not acting or moving forward with a united purpose, but in a relatively confused, chaotic and misaligned manner. Clearly, something needs to be done by school leaders and managers to ensure that all stakeholders have some common reference points, or a clear and firm foundation upon which to base their work, individually and collectively. There have to be some compass points capable of providing direction and tying all the many individual activities together in a unifying, coherent and cohesive way, so that schools can develop and nurture the synergy of learning that is only really possible when all people are working with an approved, aligned and focused mind-set. It is here that identifying, clarifying and agreeing upon core values is absolutely vital, but before we look at why these are so crucial, there is another element that is also essential, and that is clear, unambiguous and consistently enforced school systems, procedures and policies. In practice the two elements are highly inter-related, but I want to begin by looking at the latter.

In his best-selling book, 'One Out of Ten', Peter Hyman identified two tests that we can apply to identify the real essence of good leadership. He calls the first of these *"the bread and butter test"* or the consistency test, which is to see if a school has adopted sound systems and procedures that all people in the organisation adhere to, and which lead to high standards day after day. This, of course, begs the question of what 'standards' we are talking about and what they look like in actual practice, so that we will know when we are achieving or observing them. The second essential test is what Hyman calls, *"driving an agenda"*. He rightly points out that it is all too easy to become a problem-solving Head Teacher. This is one who spends most of his or her time 'putting out the fires' that have an alarmingly high propensity to combust when schools do not appear to have, or share, a clear sense of collaborative achievement and common purpose. This kind of behaviour is the antithesis of being the type of Head Teacher who is really driving an agenda, and in many ways this is in line with the advice of Stephen Covey who recommends starting with the end in mind, so that everyone knows where they are going, and when they have arrived. Hyman makes the very good point that being an agenda-setting Head Teacher enables him or her to avoid being swept along with the trivia that can prevent schools from focusing everyone's energies on raising the quality of student learning.

Hyman refers to the work of Jim Collins who, in his book 'Good is Great' examined several hundreds of companies so that he was able to identify what causational factors were responsible for transforming an otherwise good organisation into a truly great one. He pointed to the leader possessing a combination of both personal humility and professional will as being the key ingredients. These two ingredients are so important because this duality of being *"modest and wilful"* or *"humble and fearless"* is the main characteristic of great leaders – those who are able to match their humility with a relentless focus on outcomes and goals. In other words, such great leaders are those who direct their individual egos into the organisation rather than using it for self-aggrandisement and personal satisfaction. They understand only too well that it really does not matter that much which person or group gets the credit for something, as long as the organisation as a whole achieves its stated goals and accomplishes them efficiently and effectively. Henry Ford expressed this key point in a similar way when he opined that great leaders are not the ones who stand in the spotlight and receive the applause; they are the ones who stand in the limelight and lead the applause. I could not agree more with such wise words.

I am of the firm belief that there is no real place for trying to tell people what to do, or by seeking to control them as if they were raw materials on a production line. Transformational leadership is about recognising, trusting and liberating the inner giftedness of teachers just as much as it is to do with doing exactly the same for younger learners. Failure to appreciate this is why so many schools fail to perform at their best because it is difficult for them to break away from the old traditional models and attitudes that many people perceive as representing effective leadership.

This very problem was wonderfully illustrated in another article which appeared in the Guardian newspaper in the UK on 7th November 2013, entitled, *"Teachers have no respect for authority, warns chief schools' inspector"* (CSI). My immediate thought was that this accusation could be levelled against the **students** in many schools, as well as their allegedly rebellious teachers, and for very similar reasons. The CSI was reported as holding the belief that this lack of respect on the part of teachers was hampering and undermining the attempts of schools to raise standards, owing to *"a pervasive resentment of all things managerial"* by some members of staff. He might be right, although I would argue that such resentment is provoked and fuelled by some very understandable causational factors. Indeed, during his address at a conference organised by the Westminster Education Forum, Sir Michael Wilshaw, the Chief Schools' Inspector went on to say, *"Some teachers simply will not accept that a school isn't a collective but an organisation with clear hierarchies and separate duties."* I must admit to being a little bemused by such an archaic viewpoint, as schools are very much about undertaking collective actions and endeavours, and achieving collectively agreed goals. Sir Michael then harked back to some apparently left-wing conspiracy in the 1970s and 1980s when he added, *"Even today, too many teachers still think that school leaders do not have the right to tell them how to teach or what to do."* Well, they can try to tell them, but I doubt that any free-thinking individual is going to be motivated by some dictatorial know-it-all.

The big chief schools' inspector went even further to extend and justify his authoritarian credentials and prejudices when he said, *"The staff room, in their minds, is just as capable of deciding the direction a school should take as the senior leadership team."* Yes, of course they are, but a better way to move forward is for leaders to work **with** their 'foot soldiers' (a term chosen just for Sir Michael) so that they feel a sense of ownership in terms of what it is that they are trying to achieve together, as opposed to 'being told'. After all, if people do not fundamentally understand, appreciate and believe in the direction the school is going, then no self-respecting individual is going to be a willing employee – or foot soldier, for that matter. Teaching staff are again to be treated like students: told what to do, and then through the systematic use of rewards and sanctions they are made to do as they are told. There has to be a better way than this and, of course, there is!

As I continued reading this intriguing article my worst suspicions about Sir Michael were quickly confirmed when it was reported that he had warned head teachers not to try and *"curry favour"* with their staff. Instead of such inclusive behaviours, the illustrious CSI recommended, nay demanded, that school leaders should not worry constantly about staff reaction or to fear that *"they cannot act without their employees' approval"*. Well, Sir Michael, if the staff do not agree, believe or share in the direction in which the leader is trying to take them, then their approval is largely irrelevant; quite simply it is not going to happen, or not without a lot of tears, tensions and conflicts. I honestly thought that we had come to abandon the kind of leadership that led to the charge of the Light Brigade into the Valley of Death, but apparently not in Sir Michael's case!

In fairness to this relic of a bygone era, he did go as far as to acknowledge that a leader *"should consult with staff"* and try to explain, but *"never to confuse consultation"*, whatever that means. In that, I assume that he meant that a leader needs to make sure that teachers do not fall into the trap of confusing 'consultation' with 'negotiation' as, in my experience, teachers do not always appreciate the subtle distinction between the two terms. **'Consultation'** is used to explain change to staff in a reasoned way but, at the end of the process, school leaders and managers have the authority to accept or ignore the feedback they receive. Leaders have to do what they believe to be right. **'Negotiation'** is when leaders work with the staff (and others) to discuss and thrash out the best way in which we can collectively achieve our stated aims. Such a distinction is important, and it is incumbent upon leaders to always make it clear when they are consulting and when they are negotiating with their colleagues. The definition of a colleague is someone **with** whom one works.

Sir Michael was not done, as he went on to say, *"We must take the staff with us at all costs, the misguided head would say. No, you mustn't. Not if it means leaving the children behind."* It seems as if he does not understand or appreciate that the two things are not incompatible. As a leader it is surely eminently and arguably more sensible to not only 'take' the teaching staff with you, but also to make sure that no child is left behind at the same time, and it is also perfectly achievable in practice, as one thing assures the other, in my humble, non-knighted opinion.

Nonetheless, according to the article, Sir Michael obviously felt that he was on a roll, when he argued that what was good for the goose was equally beneficial for the gander, by maintaining that teachers, in turn, should also be bold enough to exert their authority and remind *"pupils"* (another old-fashioned term) who is *"in charge"*. What he actually said was, *"There is absolutely nothing wrong in my view in saying to youngsters 'do as I ask because I am the adult – I am older than you – I know more than you and, by the way, I am in authority over you."* His arrogance is wonderfully indicative of someone who believes that the thinking that got us into a mess in the first place is just what we need to change the behaviour of both teachers and their students in order to extract ourselves from the doggy-do.

I feel that the above article suggests that there is an urgent need to distinguish between involving and explaining requests to teachers and students on the one hand, and strictly enforcing what we have all agreed upon or been employed to achieve, after it has been agreed and understood, on the other. One is about effective leadership and the other is about competence, order and discipline. They are not really the same thing.

Shortly after I had read the 'wise' words of Sir Michael, another article in the same august journal made me feel equally despondent about the wisdom of those who might be expected to feel less dictatorial and more egalitarian in their approach to leading a school, but no! On the 15th January 2014, the then Shadow Education Secretary, Tristram Hunt, was reported to be 'talking tough' on classroom discipline by promising that every school in England and Wales will have a teacher dedicated to maintaining order – assuming, of course, his party gets elected sometime soon and he sits in the Education 'hot-seat'. His idea of having *"specialist discipline teachers"* (SDTs), in theory sounds most welcome, but I cannot help but feel that it is not going to be very effective in practice. This is in common with nearly every other central government wheeze when it comes to how schools are managed. In fact, instead of sounding mildly doubtful and sceptical, I would go so far as to say that his ideas are pure hogwash and motivated more by appeasing middle class voters and 'out-Goving' Michael Gove than it is about really helping teachers in schools deal with disruptive and disengaged students. As I have already argued in earlier chapters, the reason for so many young people being disaffected by what happens in many schools is that the curriculum is not relevant to them in the here and now, and does little or nothing to really motivate or inspire them to want to learn in the first place. As a result, Mr. Hunt is following the 'sticking plaster' approach of sticking his finger in the dyke, rather than addressing the egregious deficiencies of schooling, which in so many cases does nothing to really educate young people. In fact, the words 'deck-chairs' and 'Titanic' come very much to my mind when I think about the irrelevance of his vacuous promise. Having said this, the issue of behaviour management in schools is important, and this is something that I shall return to in the section on Teacher Training.

Chapter Fourteen: The Vital Importance of Values

The Effect of Beliefs on Action

When I worked in a recently-established, large comprehensive school with students aged from 13 to 18 years, I always marvel at the fact that although it was arguably the most successful school in the Local Education Authority, and certainly one blessed with wonderful facilities, the staff were far from united, in that they possessed and were informed by one of two very distinct, different and competing educational philosophies. Although I have referred to this before, I wish to repeat it here so as to explain why it was such an obstacle to achieving staff alignment in terms of ensuring all staff members were pulling in the same direction in a collaborative and collegiate way.

On the one hand, there were those who, like me, believed in the comprehensive, all-inclusive ideal of offering a high quality educational entitlement to each and every young person, regardless of their existing academic ability. We believed that we were charged with the responsibility of challenging all students to give of their best and to raise, if not maximise their level of achievement in the subjects that we taught by facilitating their learning through the application of various differentiated teaching approaches, whilst encouraging, supporting and seeking to inspire them. On the other hand, however, there were those colleagues whose attitude to education was more akin to one that would have been more at home within a grammar school environment. Their outlook on education was that they could not reasonably be expected to teach their subject in any academically honest way to students unless they (the students, not the teachers) were academically able. My feelings towards such colleagues were those of frustration, mild annoyance and an element of professional disdain. It was my view that all students were effectively 'academically able', albeit at differing levels at any given moment in time, and I still hold to this perspective. What these 'other' colleagues believed was that it was unrealistic to be expected to teach their subject to students who were incapable of anything approaching relatively high academic achievement, or at least this was the reason they gave when asked to explain the poor external examinations results achieved by some students. In all honesty, such colleagues simply didn't want to teach students of lower academic ability at all, although this was oddly and noticeably out of place in a comprehensive, community school, and could not be stated in such stark terms.

In short, the beliefs and philosophies of the staff who worked in the school were fundamentally misaligned, in an environment where the two conflicting sets of principles and beliefs were effectively forced to coexist in an uncomfortable attempt at professional harmony. The reality was that this dichotomy of fundamental perspectives had the effect of undermining the potential achievements of the school as a whole, as the two camps were effectively pulling in almost opposite directions. I can remember the Head of Modern Foreign Languages fiercely maintaining that German could only be taught in an intellectually honest form to academically more able students, something that at the time I knew to be utterly defeatist nonsense, but as a young and relatively inexperienced teacher, I had no real evidence base upon which to draw in order to try and disavow him of his partisan, misguided and educationally dangerous belief. Later in my career, when I was working as an LEA adviser, I was marginally involved in a project at a school that catered for the special needs of children with severe learning difficulties, and it provided me with the first-hand experience capable of effectively countering if not dismantling the rather elitist view of that teacher of German.

The school in question was set in a small town in the Peak District of Derbyshire, and the Head Teacher and her staff did a wonderful job in providing a rich, varied and suitably differentiated variety of learning opportunities that engaged, enthused and inspired a delightful group of young people, many of whom had Down's syndrome. I was fortunate to become involved with the school as the General Adviser with a specific responsibility for developing the cross-curricular theme of economic awareness and business education in schools within the LEA. The Head Teacher kindly sought my guidance and assistance in setting up a mini-enterprise project whereby the students would learn about business by marketing and selling the flower bulbs they were growing as part of their school's partnership work with a local farm that was run by a nearby college of further education.

I thoroughly enjoyed my limited role in this initiative, and succeeded in enlisting the support of a local High Street bank where the manager became hugely instrumental in enriching the whole project by offering the conference room at his bank's branch for meetings of the students and became actively involved in helping the young people learn about banking, even acting as the chairperson for some of the meetings that were subsequently held at the bank's premises. The mini-enterprise went on to become a huge success, both educationally and financially, so much so that using the profits generated from the sale of their bulbs at local florists, augmented by sponsorship offered by local firms, the school arranged to take the students to Holland so that they could visit the tulip fields and see another version of what they were doing, albeit on a far grander scale. Before they undertook what turned out to be a highly successful and enjoyable educational visit, the school arranged for the students to learn several Dutch words that they were able to use when in the Netherlands.

When I heard of that part of the splendid initiative by the school's Head Teacher and her amazingly dedicated staff, I wanted to go and find the aforementioned head of modern foreign languages and take him to see children with Down's Syndrome learning and speaking Dutch, admittedly not to the level required to pass a GCSE examination in the subject, but in an intellectually honest and relevant form nonetheless.

It is undoubtedly true to say that all organisations are fascinating in nature, and schools are no less interesting and complex in nature. It was the late Harold Sydney Greenen, who was a very successful businessman and one-time president and CEO of the International Telephone and Telegraph Corporation in America, who pointed out that every company consisted of two organisational structures: a formal one that is written on the charts and another more complex dimension that is the relationship between the people in the business. It is these relationships which define the business or school as a culture, a culture that is always special and unique to that particular organisation. This culture both represents and determines the behaviour of individuals who live and work in that organisational community. Furthermore, as a result of the coexistence of these two organisational structures, it is eminently possible for the hidden message in the way that we do things to run counter to the formal structure of the school, and to some extent this was the case at the school in which I once worked.

In other words, it is vitally important that schools identify and recognise, in action and not just in words and assuring platitudes, the central and essential importance of values in determining the behaviour of those who work within the school or organisational culture. It is important that school leaders are aware of this process and treat the issue of values with the seriousness that they deserve. Moreover, leaders must work to ensure that these values are understood and agreed upon by all stakeholders, but especially the teaching and support staff in the school, so that their behaviours are aligned and pulling in broadly the same direction. In short, values are a significant and key part of the hidden majority of the mass of the behavioural iceberg that lies below the surface of observable conduct. They underpin, inform and explain the way in which people think and act, and this explains why they are so important and should definitely not be ignored or left to mere chance or good fortune.

In his book, 'The 8th Habit', Stephen Covey makes the key point that an organisation's values and vision need to be shared with all employees as a precursor to their willingness to accept and adhere to the structures, systems, policies and procedures that embody them. He argues that if people share and accept the values and vision of an organisation then discipline and order are achieved without the need to otherwise demand or supervise people to ensure that they act in accordance with the organisation's preferred policies and procedures. This is a very, very important point as it ensures that the vision is achieved without excessive layers of accountability, supervision and oversight, as people are committed to the values that inform the organisation's vision and mission statements. Moreover, as previously noted earlier in this section of the book, Covey goes on to argue that people cannot be held responsible or accountable for the outcomes of their actions if they are not allowed to *determine* the way in which these results are to be achieved, but are given the methodology by their line managers and 'superiors' instead. This is also a very, very important point to note – which is one reason why I have repeated it here.

Moreover, this view resonates greatly with me as when I was a Head Teacher, I always used to tell my colleagues that I did not want them to come to me with the problems that they faced at work, unless they had a solution, or solutions, that they wished to share and discuss with me. During such discussions, I might occasionally express some doubt about the wisdom of their chosen solution, in terms of its likelihood of solving the problem it was supposed to overcome or ameliorate, and I might even offer a few alternative ways of dealing with the difficulty or challenge that they faced, for them to consider. If my colleagues had any reservations about the other ways forward that I might suggest on such occasions, they would often feel the need to reluctantly agree to my suggestions, despite feeling that their solution was better. Although such professional conversations sometimes led to colleagues finding my ideas as the better ones to follow, there were occasions where some of my co-workers were tempted to abandon their ideas in favour of my less convincing options, to their way of thinking, largely because I was 'the boss'. When such situations arose, I always told my colleagues that they should follow their own instincts and proceed with their own idea(s), and not simply bow to the authority of my higher rank in the school's chain of command. After all, it was their problem, their job and they were responsible for finding the best solution to overcome the particular challenge that they themselves faced. However, should their solution not go according to plan and fail to have the desired outcome, then I would expect them to be accountable to me and explain why. I am pleased to say that in most cases where a colleague went ahead with a method or solution with which I might have expressed serious doubt or scepticism, the outcomes were usually achieved quite satisfactorily, at the very least.

One of the greatest mistakes that is made when schools determine their mission statement and the priorities that arise in their strategic plan is that they are written or developed by the people at the top of the school's hierarchy. This is due to what Covey refers to as the myth that people at the top *"know best"* or are more experienced and better placed in terms of being able to decide the future direction and goals of an organisation. Having said this, when working in schools in England, I had absolutely no idea what the core values of the school actually were and that is because they almost certainly did not have any such fundamental reference points to provide the essential guiding principles for all members of staff. This is such an important oversight or omission, as it enabled teaching staff to behave and act according to their own values, with no unifying purpose or belief system to align everyone's efforts to achieve the aims of the school.

In more recent times, schools have been required or expected to have a set of core values and a mission or vision statement, which in turn informs the strategic direction and priorities of the organisation as a whole. To date, I have never been involved in the process of agreeing upon the core values of an organisation, although I have been responsible for formulating the strategic direction of schools. Without agreeing or being sure that there is a consensus with regards to the core values which we should all be following, the strategy is arguably not one upon which all staff colleagues can unite and strive to achieve. This is like a castle built upon unsettled sands, if ever there was.

When working in schools more recently which have previously published core values as well as vision and mission statements, I have always been surprised by how ignorant all stakeholders tended to be about the belief system upon which they are all supposed to be acting and behaving. Most staff, let alone students, governors and parents have no real interest in knowing what the core values of the organisation are, and they rarely, if ever, have much idea what these core values should look like in everyday practice. This is usually because the core values have been agreed by those at 'the top' of the organisation (invariably in the past and by different leaders), usually at the time of establishing a school and have not, therefore, involved any of the staff or other key stakeholders of the whole enterprise. Stephen Covey rightly points out that, *"Without involvement or strong identification, there will be no commitment."* That is the most vital point to remember whenever the core values of any organisation are being determined.

I find Stephen Covey's views on leadership so exact and full of rectitude when he explains its essential function so simply by viewing it as the process of, *"creating an environment in which people **want** to be part of the organisation, and not just work for the organisation. Leadership creates an environment that makes people want to, rather than have to"*, and this is perhaps even truer in a school context, given the potential impact that a young person's education can have upon their entire life chances. But how to achieve this simple concept in everyday reality is clearly more challenging, although not excessively so. If school leaders adopt a more liberal, less autocratic style in the way they not only decide upon the school's core values, as well as its mission and vision statements, but also do likewise in the way they plan strategically to achieve these grand goals in practice, day-by-day and over time, then it is quite possible to liberate the inner giftedness and individual strengths of all colleagues to achieve the school's aims.

In short, leaders do have to take their teacher colleagues (as well as others) with them, regardless of how much the draconian and 'sabre-toothed' Sir Michael Wilshaw might wilfully denigrate such collegiate and inclusive notions of leadership and management. It is pretty obvious to my mind that if leaders work with colleagues and other stakeholders in helping them understand the school's goals and fundamental ambition, and also involve them in the decision-making process, then everyone is more likely to be inclined towards doing their utmost to ensure that these shared and clearly understood goals are achieved in actual practice.....or am I missing something?

I am a firm believer that schools need to address the issue of the core values that the school fundamentally believes in and which inform the school's vision, mission and strategic plans more explicitly and seriously; doing so is not synonymous with irrelevant, 'pie-in-the-sky' contemplation of one's collective navel. Furthermore, it is absolutely vital to engage everybody in the organisation in the formulation of its values, vision and mission, as well as its strategic goals, so that everyone has ownership of what they are seeking to achieve together, and can share a determination and real commitment to make it happen. In this way, there is a greater likelihood that teacher colleagues will 'buy into' the route the school intends to follow in order to successfully and fully achieve its values and strategic goals. There is also a significantly reduced need for spurious notions of accountability, with the demotivating, demoralising and time-wasting effects that it tends to mean for professional teachers and school leaders alike, as well as the knock-on implications of these unhelpful sentiments on the young learners in the classroom.

In his book, 'The 8th Habit' Stephen Covey also makes a rather obvious point, but one that is often overlooked as a result, and that is that the essential ingredient of any good business is, *"the quality of the relationship between customer and supplier"*, or in the case of a school, between the school (represented by the teachers and support staff) and the parents or guardians, who represent the students or young learners. Covey goes on to develop this rather obvious statement by saying that, *"To be able to really solve the needs of your customers in a way than is more than just a cosmetic pat on the head requires you to deeply **understand** the different stakeholder needs."* In that sentence, however, there are several very important or key issues that schools really do need to heed and take account of, if they are to really strengthen the quality of the home-school partnership. First of all, there are the many different people and groups who have an important stake in the success and the work of the school – the students, their parents, the governors or Board of Directors, the teachers and the support staff who keep the school clean, tidy and well administered, as well as other schools, local community groups, businesses and voluntary organisations. This begs the question of, to what extent is a school able to cater for the diverse needs of these different stakeholders, when the educational interests of the student population should be paramount? Do schools really seek to *"deeply understand"* the needs of all stakeholders so as to see if they are overlapping, compatible and similar in nature? And, of course, does any school really have the time, let alone the inclination, to attempt to do this?

Clearly, if Covey is right in his identification of the importance of this extensive needs analysis exercise, then schools really do have to try very hard to find a way to discover the needs of the students as well as those of many other interested parties. However, as I have argued in previous chapters, I do not feel that schools really have much of an inkling of the fundamental educational needs that are central to the personal and social development of the young people for whom they cater. Is knowing the causes of the French Revolution or any other externally-determined subject matter really meeting the needs of all the children who attend secondary school, even if it might be relevant to one or two of the students in any particular year group? This is highly doubtful, at best.

Nonetheless, if schools involve representatives of all key stakeholder groups in the process of identifying the core values of the institution, as well as its vision and mission statements, then there is something that can definitely bind the diverse interests of all stakeholders together, and ensure that everyone is pulling in broadly the same direction and working towards offering young people a truly stimulating, liberating and empowering curricular entitlement. It will also go a very long way to ensuring that the formal and the hidden curriculum experiences of young people and others are working in concert with each other and contributing to the same ends.

Of course, one potential problem of seeking to ensure such a wide-ranging meeting of minds and needs, is that the members of the various stakeholders of the school, perhaps more so than many other types of organisations, are not static. They are always changing as older children leave the school and younger ones join, and the same is true of the teaching and support staff, as a result of labour turnover and retirement. It would seem as if this dynamic situation requires schools to review their core values at regular intervals, although this is really not at all necessary in actual practice. Let me again refer to the excellent work of Stephen Covey, when he wrote the following in relation to business organisations:

"Customers will change and so strategy must adapt, but if your values are tied to changeless principles, you will have a centre pin on which you can anchor yourself through all the inevitable changes."

What is also needed, of course, is to ensure that when a school recruits new staff, particularly teaching staff, it needs to seriously address the core values of the institution during the selection process, from the advertisement and subsequent application stage to the final interview for those candidates who are shortlisted. Having said this, when I reflect upon applications and interviews in which I have been involved, as either a candidate or as a member of the selection panel, I cannot recall a situation where my values or those of the school have ever been directly addressed at all, let alone being the subject of serious and explicit scrutiny. I now know that this was a grave omission. It is extremely important that new members of staff share and can personally identify with the core values which guide and inform the behaviour of all stakeholders within the organisation, to a greater or lesser extent.

It would be inordinately easy to incorporate an exploration of values within the selection process by asking questions which require candidates to explain why they think certain key values, such as 'integrity', 'respect', 'honesty' and 'loyalty', for example, are important, and/or ask them to illustrate what they look like in practice. Similarly, the mission statement of the school should become part of the professional conversation between the selection panel and the applicant. Again, this could be accomplished in a relatively straightforward way by unpicking key terms such as 'cultural sensitivity', 'lifelong learning' and 'self-directed learners'. Such questions and considerations are probably far more relevant and necessary than whether or not one is capable of using new technologies in the classroom when teaching a particular subject, for example.

By such means, it is eminently feasible to effectively and efficiently address important matters such as the core values, vision and mission statements of schools. This process is essential because once all stakeholders of the school deeply share the content and sentiments of a mission statement and strategic plan, either by involvement in their determination, or by identification during the appointment and admission process for staff and students respectively, then it is far more likely that these statements of intent and plans will be effectively executed in practice.

At this stage, the emphasis can now shift towards making things actually happen in the way intended, with colleagues and others feeling empowered to do what has been agreed, and in an aligned way. Now, school leaders can go about focussing on structure and making sure that the right people are allocated the right tasks to undertake. The leaders and managers can then shun all notions of crude control and offer, instead, the encouragement, support and assistance required by those working at the operational level, and more importantly by 'getting out of their way' and allowing them to make the shared organisational dream a living reality. Warren G. Bennis in his book *'Organising Genius: The Secrets of Creative Collaboration'* puts this vital point more boldly and grandly when he said:

"Too many companies believe people are interchangeable. Truly gifted people never are. They have unique talents. Such people cannot be forced into roles they are not suited for, nor should they be. Effective leaders allow great people to do the work they were born to do."

The core values need to be reaffirmed by management and evident in the behaviour of those who lead the school, as well as the various teams within it.

Even the class teacher must act as a role model for the school's shared values at all times, in both formal and informal contexts within the school, and it is for this reason that the detail of each core value needs to be clearly understood by everyone, with each person knowing what it looks like when translated into the daily behaviour of all different stakeholders. For example, all parents of children in the school need to be fully aware and cognisant of the behaviours expected when addressing members of staff and dealing with their children at home, so that what they do and how they behave does not run counter to, and undermine, those expectations that apply when their children are at school. A tall order? Perhaps, but it is certainly something that we should definitely all strive to aspire and achieve. Let us not ignore it simply because it is going to be challenging in practice, but we also have to accept that we may not achieve perfection in this regard

Communicate Effectively or Fail!

It is important to recognise, however, that if we are all to 'live' the core values of the organisation or school, then we must be both willing and able to communicate them effectively, especially as membership of the different stakeholders groups changes over time. If we do not do this well, then we will fail to live the mission statement and achieve the strategic plan either individually and collectively. Moreover, whilst this all sounds perfectly sensible, wise and correct, one needs to realise that effective communication is notoriously difficult to achieve in practice, in spite of our good intentions. It was George Bernard Shaw who astutely recognised that the main problem with communication was the illusion that it has occurred. In other words, most people seem to believe that speaking or pressing 'send' when using email is synonymous with effective communication. It was Sidney J. Webb who wisely noted that people often use the words 'communication' and 'information' in an interchangeable way, as if they also mean the same thing. Nothing, however, could be further from the truth. On the one hand, 'information' means giving out, whereas effective 'communication' means actually getting through, in that what I have in my mind before I speak or write is identical to what you have in your mind after you have listened or read. In reality there are many filters through which a message has to pass during the process of 'getting through' which can seriously distort or alter what it is that a person is seeking to effectively communicate.

291

If I had a pound or a dollar for every time that I have heard teachers in schools complain about the absence of effective communication between them and the 'senior management team', then I am pretty confident that, although I would not be a millionaire, I would be considerably wealthier than I actually am today. When I was an adviser and inspector of schools, I frequently heard teachers bemoan poor communication between "them' (the management) and "us" (the teachers working at the operational level). Whenever I heard that familiar refrain, I would always ask those complaining, what they were doing to rectify the alleged lack of communication, and they almost always seemed rather nonplussed by this apparently strange (to them) question. On such occasions, I would ask the complainants what information it was that they felt was not being communicated to them, and invariably they were unable to offer anything of any substance. I would go on to make the point that communication is, in fact, a **two-way** process and not simply a 'one-way' transaction and, therefore, if they felt they were the victims of poor or no communication, then it was incumbent upon them to ask the senior management team questions to elicit the information they felt was being withheld for whatever reason. Very often, however, the tension was being created not by any lack of communication per se, but by a lack of involvement or consultation with teaching staff over matters that affected their working practice, their welfare or their morale, as the result of a controlling leadership style adopted by those 'at the top' of the school, and supposedly accepted by those 'lower down'. This is more an outcome of no attempt to communicate rather than any deficiency in the communication or involvement that should have taken place when solving problems and making decisions, for example. It is for this reason, and others, that I maintain that 'effective communication' should itself be a core value, or at least a central tenet that all schools adopt.

This collegiate approach to agreeing and communicating the core values, the mission statement and strategic plan, was also well recognised by Peter Drucker. He made the point that mankind has been trying to communicate 'downward' within more autocratic leadership structures for centuries, but *it simply cannot work*, no matter how hard or intelligently we might try to do so. He also made the point that such an approach fails because the communication is conceived as passing from me to you. Drucker went on to say that communication can only work when it involves going from one member of 'us' to 'another'. To some extent, therefore, effective communication is something that involves people in a community knowing each other and working openly and effectively together.

Furthermore, Peter Drucker said that the most important thing in communication is to hear that which is not being said, and that means reading the body language of the speaker and attempting to ascertain what, perhaps, they might want to say, but are guarded or unwilling to speak their mind. Again, this tends to highlight the importance of having a good community spirit so that members of the collective group feel safe and comfortable in saying what they think, and expressing how they feel, as well as what they might want to see happen.

The views and ideas of Warren G. Bennis in relation to what constitutes leadership and management are well known and, rightly, highly regarded. For example, he made a very succinct comment on leadership when he wrote that, *"Leadership is the capacity to translate vision into reality."* To do this effectively demands that those who lead are capable of articulating and communicating their vision for the organisation to the employees and also to all of the other stakeholders. In the case of schools, the vision must be understood and 'owned' by the teaching and support staff, and also by the young people who attend the institution. All too often, however, little or no attempt is made by leaders to communicate the vision for the organisation to the students and, again, the outcome is to send the hidden message that these core stakeholders are passive in nature and simply have to accept that that which the leaders and the staff choose to do for them is definitely in their best interests. Where this lack of communication occurs it is a massive oversight in my view, as the behaviour of students is central and vital in helping to make the school, as a community of people, successful in terms of achieving its vision and mission.

Furthermore, Warren Bennis once said that he defined leadership as, *"communicating to people their worth and potential so clearly that they are inspired to see it in themselves."* In this way, his views are at one with those of Stephen R. Covey who refers to helping people finding their own voice in his best-selling book, *'The 8th Habit'*. The people who fulfil this leadership role are not simply those who have been appointed to such a position by some selection panel, but those who *choose* to become leaders. In this way, it is possible for anyone to choose to become a real leader. For me, one such person was the late, great Alun Roberts, who was my Economics tutor when I spent four years training and studying to become a teacher. His influence on me was considerable and so effortlessly exerted. He was the first person to really believe in my potential as an academically-able student, bearing in mind my below average achievements at both GCE 'O' and "A' Levels. I can vividly remember him telling me what he believed to be my worth and my potential, and that experience was one that lifted me emotionally and inspired me to prove him right. In this way, I have often said that he was like a second father to me during those four important and defining years in my life and career. Effective communication really is clearly pivotal and crucial in the skill-set of every potential leader. Furthermore, Alun Roberts was and is truly, genuinely and fully deserving of such plaudits, as even the students who never had the pleasure of his guidance as a tutor, instinctively spoke well of him and recognised his immense qualities as a teacher, guide and human being – God bless you Alun!

Developing True Community Schools

There was a time in education in the UK when so-called 'community schools' were seen as a good way of harnessing the power of the various stakeholders within the school community in educating its young people as well as the other stakeholders themselves. It was, in my opinion, a truly great and exciting concept, but one that sadly failed to live up to its true potential for two main reasons: those of a party political nature and a failure of communication by its proponents, which led to the whole initiative being something of a damp squib in terms of its failure to achieve its potential for becoming a fabulous reality.

Early on in my career, as I have mentioned before, I was lucky enough to work in a newly-opened school, and one that boasted tremendous facilities and with the word 'community' in its title. The potential of the school to develop into a thriving community school in which all stakeholders were actively involved and benefiting from its existence was really very exciting. Unfortunately, the school suffered in microcosm from the same two constraining and deleterious factors as befell all intending community comprehensive schools. Margaret Thatcher became Prime Minister in the same year that I joined the staff of this

13 to 18 secondary school, a mere three years after it had opened with just a Year 9 as its first cohort of young people or students. It was unfortunate, nay, perilous timing indeed!

I think what has preceded this section of the book will make quite clear the contempt, the ideological hatred and sheer disdain that I felt for that particular Conservative Party leader, and others since then as well as now in the form of one David Cameron. To say that she represented and pursued so much of what I consider to be truly evil in a modern industrial society would be a massive understatement. For her, there was no such thing as 'society', there were only individual men and women and families plus, of course their own selfish, self-interest. As a result, the whole concept of 'community education' came under a powerful ideological attack, along with the sniping, naïve but mendacious ridicule that such collectivist notions engendered within her Cabinet and many of her back-bench supporters no doubt. Community education was effectively regarded as a left-wing conspiracy and was decried as a creeping socialist cancer within the world of education and schools. It stood no chance of gaining the support and credibility that its potential for outstanding educational achievements rightly justified. For Mrs. Thatcher and most of her viciously illiberal Cabinet, it was a totally alien concept and was undermined by all those in government and her lackeys in the allegedly 'free' press. It never really got off the starting blocks, and I often wonder how things might have been different had there been a Labour government in power under the leadership of genuinely good and decent people, like Neil Kinnock, John Smith or Dennis Healey, for example.

Under Margaret Thatcher, and the influence of right-wing zealots such as Keith Joseph, even the very notion of 'social sciences' came under a sustained attack that ridiculed the very idea of any study of human behaviour, using scientific methodologies, whether it be sociology (or 'social engineering' as the lunatic fringe on the right of the political spectrum preferred to see it), economics, psychology or anthropology. They were politically-infected lunatics indeed, not to mention just plain silly and seriously dangerous in their attempts to besmirch areas of study and knowledge that they were both incapable and unwilling to even think about, let alone entertain in any critically-constructive way. Community education had no chance in such a hostile, prejudicial and truly malevolent political climate, especially in view of the fact that it would have required more money to be spent on schools and education in order to enable it to live up to its glorious ideals of involving and harnessing the talents of many different groups within a school's local community. This was, remember, a time when the only way for such government expenditures was into, what the business news fraternity nowadays like to denote as 'negative territory'.

Having said this, there was still a chance that had the potential for community education been truly understood, realised and demonstrated in practice by a few schools, then it might have been more difficult for the 'restraining-right' to have resisted demands for more resources to be devoted to such an admirable cause. Sadly, however, schools such as the one at which I was working, with its massive head-start in terms of the opportunities offered by splendid new facilities, were not up to the challenge. In fairness to such schools, the whole concept of community education was very new, and that novelty meant that leaders in schools, who are also victims of their own past, autobiographical career experiences, simply did not fully appreciate that they had a wonderful goose within their midst. As a result, the wondrous golden egg never saw the light of day and as a result, and somewhat inevitably, stood no chance of hatching.

Why was it then that schools such as the one at which I was working, failed so dismally to recognise the opportunity and potential for being designated 'community schools' by some more visionary figures in certain local education authorities? For example, during my twelve years at the school, the powers that be only really managed to turn it into a dual-use facility, with various groups using the extensive playing fields and specialist sports premises such as the swimming pool and sports hall when the school was out of session. There was also a Theatre Association which actually did a great job in using the splendidly designed and equipped auditorium in out-of-school hours as a venue for professional and amateur musical and dramatic productions, often by some notable and very high-profile performers – such as Rowan Atkinson and Richard Curtis (together with Mark Goodall), which was a very memorable show!

Apart from such dual-use initiatives, there was no great drive or impetus that sought to link the learning of young people with individuals, business organisations and others within our local, national and international communities in any kind of systematic and structured way. Sure, there were the usual school events such as outside speakers, work experience and occasional school visits, excursions and student exchanges, as well as mini-enterprise activities and such like, but nothing that sought to systematically involve local and wider community agencies in the daily teaching and learning that took place in classrooms within the various faculty areas in a structured way.

I have long believed that schools need to adopt both an 'outside-in' and an 'inside-out' approach to building curriculum-led community links, partnerships and networks that enable us to extend, enhance and enrich the work of teachers in and out of the classroom, and the learning of our young people. We should encourage all stakeholders to see learning and education as something that does not just happen in classrooms, or only within or under the jurisdiction of schools for that matter. We should be designing curricular programmes and building inter-related structures that promote the school as just one community learning resource, rather than as *the* place for learning.

Such an attitude to educating our young people, as well as others in our community, demands that schools take the lead in promoting, encouraging and enabling such programmes. They need to be far more creative in the way in which they structure and timetable the opportunities for learning to take place, and that requires something far more imaginative than between the hours of 9am and 4pm, so that others can become involved in educating our young people. One example of this is to timetable the school curriculum and a range of community education learning programmes and activities over three sessions – morning, afternoon and evening. Older students could then learn alongside adults other than teachers during evening sessions, with unemployed and part-time working adults learning alongside students during the hours of the 'traditional' school day.

This 'session three' concept also opens up the possibility of other positive outcomes, such as the opportunity for flexible employment contracts for teachers. At the moment, teachers are effectively employed to work for ten sessions in one week, i.e. two sessions a day (mornings and afternoons) from Monday to Friday. Session three means that the school will need learners (not necessarily those in compulsory education) and learning facilitators for fifteen sessions each week, or fourteen, if the traditional objection to working on Friday evenings persists when there is this more flexible pattern to working and school life. Full-time teachers would still be required to work ten sessions a week but, in theory, could be timetabled to complete their contractual quota in various ways, such as mornings and evenings, or afternoons and evenings, or the usual mornings and afternoons. The point is that this potential for more flexible employment patterns offers single and working parents, as well as others, like me, who hate getting up early in the morning, more opportunity to work full-time or part-time, as well as overtime.

Furthermore, the flexibility of having a fifteen-session week also offers greater opportunity for adults other than teachers to become learning resources for school-age people and fellow adult learners after they have finished work, for example. It offers the opportunity for new facilitators of learning to be discovered and to become involved, including teachers who no longer want to work full time in what is a physically, mentally and emotionally draining profession. The potential for increasing and developing the pool of talented learning facilitators, as well as the number of people wanting to learn, is considerable, and these ideas are just some of the possible new avenues for a type of working and learning that is far more inclusive, embracing and promising than anything that is currently available.

The potential is enhanced even further when one considers that there are people who want to learn and engage in various activities during weekends and at other times when the school is officially 'closed', for example, during holidays. As an economist, I learnt a long time ago that to have fixed assets – such as school buildings, facilities and learning spaces – and not to use them for twenty-four hours a day if possible, is incredibly inefficient. The reason for this is that the fixed resource is lying idle for a lot of the time and adding no value. The total cost of utilising fixed assets on a full-time basis does of course increase as well, but fixed costs are usually significantly higher than the variable cost of additional labour, electricity, heating, etc. In other words, to use fixed assets more fully increases outputs (or outcomes, in the case of education) less than it increases total costs, in cases where the majority of the assets of an enterprise are fixed, as opposed to variable. In other words, average costs, or costs per unit decrease as the scale of the operation increases.

If schools were to be seen more as a permanent, community learning resource, rather than a place which occupies young people for five days a week, over roughly two-thirds of the year, then even greater possibilities for community learning and increased employment become available to a mouth-watering degree, assuming you are passionate about education in its broadest and most inclusive sense. Just imagine having schools open at weekends and during the school holidays so that all kinds of other learning and leisure activities could take place. The premises and facilities could be utilised by local people who want to run part-time enterprises in food technology, the arts and crafts or ceramics and textiles, for example. Schools could become business education centres, using the auditorium and meeting rooms to run conferences for small and medium-sized enterprises. In such cases, the premises will usually have cafeteria and kitchen facilities that could be used to service such conferences and training programs, again offering employment opportunities to local people, or school students and their teachers. I firmly believe that once such approaches begin to blossom and generate income, so the 'school' would be able to attract more investment from local businesses and other agencies with lottery funding and such like, for projects that might extend and enhance the facilities and accommodation available, as well as the educational potential of its premises and personnel.

When I worked at the community school for those twelve years, I did a lot to run more interesting and enriching learning activities, as well as events that made good use of the facilities that the school was incredibly (but rightly) fortunate to have at its disposal. My motivation for running such additional activities was to enrich the curricular experience of students at my school, as well as other schools in the local education authority. I organised and ran conferences for sixth-form students extending their work in Economics by inviting speakers from local universities and the national media. I worked with the local careers service to run conferences such as 'Insight into Industry', which involved speakers from local industry and commerce, as well as local trades unions and professional associations. These conferences were a national initiative that was born out of the desire to encourage more academically-able students to consider a career in industry and commerce, rather than in the professions, such as medicine, law and accountancy. The target audience was usually students in the 14 to 18 age range, and although these conferences were always well received, they were seeking to persuade if not seduce into an industrial career, a group of young people who had made up their minds about intended careers a long time before. The time to forge a more positive attitude towards a career contributing to wealth-creation in an industrial setting would be during the primary years of schooling, when attitudes of mind are still impressionable or malleable, for want of a better word....assuming it is desirable at all!

Before continuing, and in the interests of all modesty and perspective, these activities, events and initiatives which I recall here, are not included in order to suggest that I was some kind of pioneer or extra-special in terms of my efforts in any way. I readily acknowledge that **many** of my colleagues in the schools where I have worked, and in other schools around the country were similarly engaged and active. These examples, taken from my own experience are incorporated for the benefit of those who are not aware of the extraordinary and additional efforts that so many teachers willingly devote to their calling or their vocation, as well as to remind others who have a tendency to either overlook such devotion or to simply, and casually, take it for granted. These illustrations are also included here in order to show what can be done, relatively easily, to involve a school's stakeholders in the education that takes place in schools, if the will is there. Furthermore, they are included here in order to make what is perhaps a rather obvious point about the way in which society is inclined to perceive education as something that is the sole responsibility of schools; the truth is that all community partners need to be involved in some way, to a greater or lesser extent, even at different times perhaps.

When working in my second teaching post in England, I was immensely fortunate to succeed in getting the school selected as one of a small number of educational establishments nationally, who were to take part in a ground-breaking school exchange programme with partner schools in the, then, Soviet

Union. The whole project was possible following an inter-governmental agreement between Gennady Yagodin and Kenneth Baker, the Education Secretaries in the USSR and the UK respectively. This wonderful initiative was well managed and successfully developed by The Schools Unit of the Central Bureau in London, and the involvement of 'my' school was something that blossomed into an immensely successful and ongoing exchange programme with The Moscow Technical Lyceum Number One. It was also developed and extended over time into a business and wider cultural partnership programme between one of the main districts of Moscow and the Local Education Authority and the Chamber of Commerce in the school's local community.

Just the school exchange programme part of this broader partnership project involved a tremendous community dynamic. When the students from our school travelled to Moscow for the first leg of the exchange, they only had to pay for their own air fares and any incidental expenditures in the USSR. Once they stepped off the aeroplane, they were hosted in the homes of their student partners and the cost of all transport and the many excursions that were planned were met in full by the Soviet Education Department, Sadly this was not a reciprocal funding initiative, as the cost of the return leg, when all the students and accompanying staff came to visit us in the UK, was the sole responsibility of our school, whilst the generous British Tory Government funded absolutely nothing.

As a result of this typically parsimonious attitude of the Conservative Government, who had helped to broker the entire programme in the first place, it fell to our school, the students and our local community to bear the cost of offering our guests a similar degree of hospitality, along with a variety of interesting visits, excursions and activities during their two-week stay. Just the cost of transporting all their students and teachers, as well as an equal number from our own school who had gone to meet their friends at London Heathrow, involved hiring a large coach and financing the ferry fare from the mainland across to the Isle of Wight. This sum was not exactly trifling in size. The two-week programme involved local visits and excursions, as well as a two-day trip to London to meet the Prime Minister, Margaret Thatcher, go shopping in Oxford Street and Harrods, as well as see a popular show in the West End. The cost of all of this, plus overnight hotel accommodation in

301

London, was considerable indeed. The total cost of the whole two weeks was met as a result of sponsorship from local companies, the goodwill of local firms, organisations and venues, and from a series of fun-filled, fund-raising events that involved the students and staff of our school taking part in variety shows, a staff version of a comedy play, and the generosity of many parents and other people in our local community, offered in cash or kind. It was a massive example of enterprise education that involved us all in our common aim to offer a great stay to our very dear friends from Moscow.

The experience which I have attempted to outline above was an example of a community school in action, but it was confined to those initiatives that a few staff like myself sought to embark upon. There was, however, no real community vision from the senior team in the school, until a new Head Teacher was appointed who, in his infinite wisdom, appointed me as a third Deputy Head to lead developments in the area of the curriculum and community. This led on to other initiatives, with teaching staff attending leadership and management courses that were run by local business firms for their employees, as well as sixth-form students joining young business managers on outward-bound courses organised by local businesses, free of charge. These are just a few small and simple examples of what is possible if schools look for ways to find out what local stakeholders can offer, and then link this where at all possible to educational needs and different ways of enhancing, extending and enriching the curriculum entitlement of young people.

In many schools, however, there is no significant precedent of such community partnership initiatives, owing perhaps to a lack of vision on the part of school leaders. In all fairness, however, their agenda these days is dominated by seemingly endless accountability measures, dreamt up and subsequently demanded by know-it-all, interfering governments. This externally-set agenda must have the effect of sapping the energy of the most able leaders and school staff, as well as effectively crowding-out more meaningful and educationally sound developments, on which they might otherwise like to focus, or have the time to consider. It also goes a very long way to explain why I emigrated from the UK some 20 years ago!

In the 'community school' at which I worked all those years ago, I was always amazed by the deficient membership of its governing body. There were, of course, the elected representatives of the teachers and parents of the school, as well as the local education authority, and a good number of well-selected, co-opted personnel from the world of industry and commerce who could offer much needed expertise in certain areas, such as marketing and finance. But what about student representatives to help determine the general policy of the school; they were one set of stakeholders who were either ignored or overlooked for whatever reason.

When I was a Head Teacher, I broached the subject at meetings of the governing body, but the response of the 'adults' present was always rather negative. Their unwillingness to seriously entertain students acting in such a capacity was usually due to the fact that it had not been done before, and some governors added that they felt that students were unqualified to serve, as they were only 'children'. I have always found the views and ideas of students – especially senior students – to be incredibly perceptive, interesting and thought-provoking, as well as creative, imaginative and incredibly sound. In schools where there are students elected to act as head girl or head boy, or as president of the student council, would it not be a good learning opportunity for them, and I dare say the adult governors, if they were allowed to participate in the actual decision-making processes at their school. They are certainly mature enough and often more insightful and intelligent than many of the local politicians who claim to serve their local communities, the electorate and the students in question. Furthermore, it seems eminently sensible and reasonable to me that students should rightly be represented and directly involved in all decision making processes within their school. Obviously, there may be some occasions where they need to withdraw from meetings where matters of a confidential nature are to be discussed, such as staff disciplinary and competence procedures, negotiations of their contracts and grievance procedures – although even that is a moot point.

If we are to have true community schools, there is a genuine need for their physical boundary to be far more permeable to all of the main stakeholders and community partners such as local people, government agencies, voluntary and community groups, as well as other schools, colleges and universities.

However, such a possibility must take full account of health and safety issues, so that the welfare of students and teachers is duly protected and safeguarded. This is not going to be an easy task, but it is, in my opinion, one that we truly need to undertake with great effectiveness and efficiency. The reality is that the achievement of anything that is truly worthwhile is only ever accomplished by being resilient, determined and courageous in dealing with the many difficult obstacles that inevitably stand in our collective path; such is the stuff of achieving those goals that the fainthearted often consider to be beyond them in this ambitious quest.

Schools need to be seen more as just **one** learning resource for all people and organisations in the local community, as I have already said, and they should be a key part of a network of learning which brings together others who have a contribution to make to the development of their local community. This role should be extended to link all potential learning resources in not only the vicinity of the school, but also with the national and international communities. To do this has become much easier and more feasible with the tremendous advances in information and communication technologies, and it would be ultimately beneficial if young people were to be encouraged and required to use them in more creative, constructive and imaginative ways other than to merely occupy their consciousness with relatively trivial pursuits. The potential for a synergy of learning is enormous, if used wisely, carefully and intelligently.....but then I am swimming against a popular counter-culture of 'gentling the masses' when it comes to such optimism.

The interests of real education for all young people and others in our local, national and international communities, demand that we do as much as we can to identity, implement and develop the potential of these community aspects of every school. If we fail to strive to do this in a more substantive, serious and extensive way, then it seems as if the hidden message of schooling is that it is really only something that teachers do for young people, if not to them. It will continue to be seen as an exclusive rather than an inclusive or partnership endeavour.

With the unfortunate reality of continually contracting budgets facing state schools in England and elsewhere, or the imperative of the need to make a profit or a financial 'surplus' in international and public (i.e. privately-owned) schools, all institutions are becoming increasingly focused on making money and managing the budget. I would suggest that in many cases this financial imperative takes on an excessively dominant role, when it comes to decision making and ways to manage and develop the school. Mammon has become all powerful and absorbing of human interest generally, and schools are no exception.

We live in a highly, and some would say unhealthily excessive, materialistic world, where acquisition and financial gain is an over-riding goal. Money, for many, is seen as a goal in itself, rather than the means to an end, or a variety of more altruistic, meaningful and beneficial outcomes. In international education, owners establish schools sometimes for altruistic motives, but for many they see the school as 'a business', and one that should yield a return in the medium-, if not the short-term. Even in schools that proclaim to be non-profit-making, there is doubt about the legitimacy of such claims, as many international schools, for example, do not produce transparent final accounts. Secrecy, under the guise of confidentiality, is the name of the private game. In my view, anyone who sets up a school as a profit-making venture is beautifully misguided, as there is notoriously no 'big money' to be made in the education world – well not legitimately and in a morally sound manner. It is a merit good with elements of being a public good and, as such, is best delivered by the state and funded from general taxation. All forays into the private sector are at best a delicate balancing act between making money on the one hand and, on the other hand, offering a genuine education for the young people with whose education these schools are largely entrusted.

Having worked in international schools that are primarily run for profit, I have found that financial gain is very much a 'chicken or egg' issue in terms of means and ends. Schools which focus overly on the 'bottom-line' and make decisions that are largely determined by raising revenues and/or decreasing costs, in order to maximise returns, usually come unstuck. This is not to say that the financial health of the school should not be a matter of concern, as that could be equally threatening to its survival; it is just that the financial 'cart' should not be put before the educational 'horse'. It is a question of what the main focus of a school should be. In other words, I believe that the best way to ensure a sound financial footing and return is not to be overly concerned with it.

A better approach is to strive to serve the true educational interests of young people. If the focus is on the core business of a school and doing the utmost to enable students to accomplish amazing things and to thrive on the joy of their learning in a safe, happy and challenging environment, then the school is almost absolutely assured of success. Financial security and well-being are then automatically taken care of as a result. Warren Bennis put the same thing as follows: *"Leaders keep their eye on the horizon, not just the bottom line."* In any case, what is profit other than value added, and the focus should be on maximising the value added in terms of children's accomplishments during their time at a particular educational institution, whether it be a school, a college or a university. The late Nicholas Murray Butler, an American philosopher, diplomat and educator, who was once the president of Columbia University and a recipient of the Nobel Peace Prize, made the point more starkly than Warren Bennis when he said, *"Businesses planned for service are apt to succeed; businesses planned for profit are apt to fail."*

Before reaching the end of this section of the book, I do not wish to be seen as having conveniently side-stepped commenting a little more on the distinction between leadership and management. I think most people accept that there is necessarily a considerable inter-connection, if not an overlap, between these two very important functions.

A great deal has been written by many learned and well-informed people, both business leaders and academics, and it is not my intention to rehearse their views or their findings here, as one is quite able to direct one's own study of the literature. However, allow me to briefly refer to two very simple ways of clarifying the distinction between the two terms, by giving the way in which two writers have neatly encapsulated the difference.

Warren Bennis makes the distinction by stating that leadership is all about, "doing the right things," whereas he saw management as being more concerned with, "doing things right." Although this is quite a catchy play on words, it only sheds a partial light on the difference between the two because it does not really say what these two roles involve in terms of the type of job or function that they perform, if you will. As a result, therefore, I prefer the way in which John Marotti illustrates the distinction by portraying those who lead as **'architects'**, and those who subsequently manage being seen as the **'builders'**. I consider that this is far more helpful in describing in very simple terms what the two functions involve that is different, as well as their essentially complementary and inter-related roles.

As for me, I feel much more at home in the role of the architect than the builder, being interested, as I am, in vision and what is possible, rather than being the one who is charged with making it happen. That is not to say that I lose interest in the building because I will want to make sure that the construct put in place at least meets the vision that I had, or exceeds it when others can also see what could be done and take it upon themselves to make the shared dream come true in some spectacularly ingenious ways.

Chapter Fifteen: Transformational Leadership Revisited

Trust and Accountability

One of the most serious ailments that besets the education that schools purport to be seeking to promote, is the malaise of accountability from interfering governments, regardless of their political leanings. This drive of almost endless attempts for finding ways of making schools accountable to their political overseers leads to the senior teams in schools to obediently or submissively agree to jump through whatever accountability 'hoops' that are pressed upon them. All of these usually misguided and time-consuming measures are allegedly designed to prove to the taxpaying public that they are getting 'value for money', and that the government is making schools more accountable for raising standards. As I have said before, what is never really explained or enlarged upon is what standards schools are being required to raise, and how the additional work-load that this quest for increased accountability places upon schools – the teachers and the students – is supposed to lead to this vague and ambiguous outcome. Indeed, when more students achieve good grades in external examinations, the political paymasters are quick to allege that this is due to making the examinations too easy, and so they take retrograde steps to reduce this growing success on the part of so many schools. A cynic might be inclined to deduce that the real or hidden agenda that lies behind most government policy forays into the educational arena are really thinly veiled attempts at enforcing schools to act in ways that support their own political ends. In the case of the Conservatives, most attempts at accountability are a smoke-screen for expenditure cuts and claiming greater control over what teachers teach in schools. If this is not the case, then I find it hard to see how their actions do not simply amount to privatisation by stealth, and ensuring that the middle classes can still steal an advantage when it comes to finding a school for their children. How else does one explain the mendacious push for more 'free' schools, academies and the like? They really represent a panoply of ways of maintaining the divisions in society despite attempts to increase social mobility through more relevant, comprehensive and inclusive forms of education.

308

Schools really do need leaders who will be more militant, courageous and determined to claw back political power and to stifle, as best they can, misguided and politically-motivated attempts by central government to 'know better' than the trained professionals that populate most schools, regardless of one or two less competent members of the profession who do need to be got rid of. Let's be honest, all occupations and workplaces will from time to time find themselves with incompetent and misplaced individuals who are clearly in the wrong job, or grossly under-prepared for the demands and rigours of their occupation. Schools are no different to any other workplace in this respect – so please everyone, develop a sense of realistic perspective!

All of these layers of unnecessary accountability are indicative of a fundamental lack of **trust** by politicians in the work that teachers do to try and educate the young people who present themselves at school – assuming they feel inclined to obey the legal mandate to attend. This lack of trust is really all due to the fact that the whole edifice of schooling is systemically as well as substantively and pedagogically flawed, in that we are still sticking with an outdated, irrelevant and confused modus operandi, with a fragmented, standardised and inert curriculum structure that may have arguably met the needs of young people and society back in the 1880s, but has been rapidly overtaken by events of the last 130 years. As a result, what now masquerades as the education of young people is really little more than a systematic attempt to maintain an outdated status quo, so as to prop up a defunct traditional and conservative orthodoxy.....I am wondering if I should have used a capital letter to begin 'conservative'?

What is needed is a form of transformational leadership that adopts more modern, creative and engaging approaches to the work that goes on in schools. This would also be greatly enabled if governments acted as good leaders and managers seek to do, and that is to support, enable and encourage those who are actually charged – and professionally trained – to stand in front of a large group of highly inquisitive minds that abound with a multitude of diverse and largely untapped talents and potentials. To do this requires **<u>trusting</u>** the professionals and allowing them to do their jobs, within a broad range of professionally determined parameters, so that there is a general agreement among all stakeholders of what represents acceptable behaviour in its broadest sense, and what is not. And this does definitely not involve governments seeking (and failing spectacularly) to dot all the 'i's and cross all the 't's of what schools across the country do on a day-by-day basis. In short, governments and school leaders should stop trying to be both the architects and the builders, and trust those who have been trained to teach to do the detailed construction work. As Warren Bennis also said, *"Trust is the lubrication that makes it possible for organisations to work."*

Again, I feel compelled to refer in some detail to the work of Stephen R. Covey, for what he says is to be done by anyone who finds themselves in a leadership position, in this writer's opinion, is a much more superior way for those in schools and business organisations to proceed, if we are really to better liberate the talents of all stakeholders, but especially the students and their teachers. More importantly, it simply has to be built upon a genuine, sincere and a profound sense of **trust**.

When asked if there was a formula for becoming a transformational leader, Covey put forward four imperatives, the first of which is to inspire trust – what a surprise! The way in which this is achieved is by building relationships of trust, which leaders demonstrate in their own behaviours and which send feelings of trust towards others. This is very unlike the relationship that customarily exists between governments and schools and, increasingly between school leaders and their staff. In other words, one can inspire trust in others, or one can transmit one's distrust of them. It is vital to demonstrate to those you work with that you have real and genuine faith in their capacity to live up to certain high expectations and that they can fulfil promises made and act in ways that move towards achieving clarity on key goals within the strategic plan. One sure fire way of failing to inspire trust is by micromanaging and trying to predict and frame the actions of others. Such behaviour will send messages of distrust and suggest that 'daddy always knows best'.

The second imperative to being a successful leader, according to Stephen Covey is to clarify purpose, and this is poles apart from distrustful, micromanaging behaviours. What great leaders should do, as I have already mentioned, is to involve people in the communication process that is involved in creating and, subsequently achieving, the goals that the school or organisation is seeking to reach, so that there is a real ownership and agreement of the core values upon which the shared mission, vision and strategy are founded.

Once there is trust and a clarity of purpose, the next imperative of leadership that Covey identifies is to move to a more practical level and assure an **alignment** of systems in the organisation. In essence, this means that there should be no discrepancy between what the organisation says it sees as its **core values**, beliefs and what it is all about on the one hand, and what **actual practice** shows to be true. In other words, there should be no *misrepresentation to its stakeholders about what it claims to be seeking to do and how it does it*, when it comes to observing and measuring the daily reality. For example, many organisations claim that people and their development is all important, but the truth is that the way in which the organisation is organised and run demonstrates that they are an expense and a cost, rather than seeing them as an essential asset.

The last imperative that needs to be met if an organisation is to really have a transformational style of leadership is the outcome of the first three, and that is to literally liberate the diverse talents of its people, and not just the students, in the case of a school. This is all about empowering people by creating a climate of mutual trust, where stakeholders understand and share a common purpose, with the organisation operating with aligned systems and procedures. When these three imperatives are in place, then the organisation is able to benefit from unleashing the inner giftedness of its people in terms of their individual and combined aptitudes, as well as their intelligence, creativity and resourcefulness.

What I also feel is even more important is that these four imperatives of **trust**, **common purpose**, **alignment** and **liberating inner giftedness** apply just as powerfully to the way in which all teachers lead the learning processes of the students in the school. They do not apply exclusively to the nature of the relationship that is developed and enjoyed between the leader or leaders of a school and the teaching and support staff who work with them. In many ways, there is even more to be gained from focusing on leading the students in this

311

way, than there is from doing it only in relation to the organisation's employees.

In this way, leadership really becomes what Stephen Covey calls the 'enabling art', in that bad leadership in schools inevitably leads to a poor quality education. Having said this, however, Covey rightly makes the point that all organisations need both leadership and management – they are co-dependent and inextricably linked in practice. The reason for this is that it is patently silly to think that the material resources of an organisation can be led, as the truth is that **only people** can be led and empowered. On the other hand, **things** need to be managed, and managed effectively, as they do not have the power or the freedom to choose. Seeking to manage staff is largely pointless, although many schools try to do this, which is probably why Warren Bennis observed that most organisations are over-managed and under-led, as I mentioned earlier.

In his book, 'The 8ᵗʰ Habit', Covey offers a 'whole person organisational model', at the centre of which is the need to recognise *'spirit'* or *'conscience'* and, according to Covey, this is because organisations that lack the essential imperative of mutual trust are bedevilled by, *"back-biting, in-fighting, victimism, defensiveness, information hoarding and defensive, protective communication,"* or in other words, they will be doomed to be ineffective and *failing institutions*.

In addition to the spirit, or conscience, Covey's whole person organisational model also talks of the importance of considering and involving three other aspects of a human being, namely the *'mind'*, the *'body'* and the *'heart'*. According to this interesting model, it is the 'mind' that provides a common or shared vision for the organisation. In short, this means that unless people are led to agree upon a common value system, then organisations will suffer from political game playing, based upon hidden agendas, and no common criteria being applied when it comes to decision making. All of this will, therefore, result in, *"an ambiguous and chaotic culture."*

The need for leaders to pay real attention to *"discipline and the body politic"*, as Covey calls it, or in other words, the systems, policies and procedures that are designed and necessary to enable the organisation to meet its priorities and goals, is vital if all personnel are acting in an essentially aligned manner, according to the core values, the mission and organisational strategy. If this essential discipline in the organisation is missing, then the resultant misalignment will mean that the organisation will fail to harness the full potential or talents of its people. This misalignment is problematic in that it can lead to a significant number of negative consequences, such as an even lower level of trust, people playing political games to achieve their differing outcomes, as well as competition between different sections, departments or cliques within the school.

This increased rivalry and obvious signs that the organisation is not operating in a coherent way and, thereby, failing to meet its priorities and goals, will lead to management imposing more and more rules, policies and procedures in order to try and get the school 'back on track'. Unfortunately, this leads management to feel a partly understandable desire to take **control**, but this is not the right way to proceed because greater control will limit and inhibit the initiative of staff. **Empowerment will be subordinated to increasing bureaucracy**, more and more rules and regulations, and a more hierarchical structure with the need to seek approval, if not permission to act from the senior team, if not the Head Teacher, herself, or himself. People will be treated just like things and considered as if they were liabilities on the financial balance sheet of the school, and not the talented assets which are the key investment that can drive the organisation towards real accomplishment, success and value added. (Does this not very closely describe the nature of the relationship between central government and schools these days and, also, within many schools between school leaders and their teacher colleagues?)

This organisational inertia, due to ineffective and deficient leadership in the first place, causes formal leaders in the school, or the senior team, to adopt further inappropriate measures that seek to *'control the school towards its vision and mission'*. Such a response is bound to fail, as it creates a dependency culture amongst the staff, who get used to being told what to do and, in some cases, how they should do it, instead of creating a liberating organisational culture, which empowers staff to take initiative in, and responsibility for the jobs that they do. Our colleagues will always work best when they feel intrinsically motivated to achieve what the organisation overall is seeking to accomplish. But, the misalignment that leads to staff failing to feel empowered, will lead to increased passivity, as they become accustomed to, if not almost fearful of, not acting until they are instructed so to do by those at the top. This results in what Covey calls a *"carrot-and-stick"* approach to managing the organisation, where bureaucratic and autocratic leadership styles are employed. He expresses this most succinctly when, he says (in 'The 8th Habit') that the formal leaders, when finding themselves in this position, will, ***"eventually carrot-and-stick, motivate, control and even bring down the iron fist when necessary – passivity justifying external motivation and control justifying more passivity."*** These behaviours become a self-fulfilling prophesy, or a vicious circle of failed organisational leadership and management, because this excessive management-by-external-control does nothing to inspire people to perform at the highest level of their capabilities. Their talents are stifled, or imprisoned within a system that prevents them from finding and exhibiting the real passion or 'voice' that drives them. People are only ever willing and able to **volunteer** this passion; it can never be simply demanded, ordered or required by formal leaders. This is why Sir Michael Wilshaw is just plain wrong when he tells formal leaders never to be afraid to **"tell"** staff what to do, and not to feel as though they have to take their colleagues with them, as they seek to realise the school mission.

As Covey puts it, to be truly effective, leaders must pay attention to, and take account of both the 'spirit', the 'mind', the 'body-politic' and the 'heart' if the problems above are to be avoided and the organisation is to function in a seemingly effortless way. This issue of the 'heart' is also crucial, because if our colleagues in school are unable to, or prevented from finding and unleashing their inner passion, the organisation is never going to realise its own full potential. Stephen Covey again makes this point in a very powerful and cautionary way when he says:

> *"If you neglect the heart, there will be no passion, no emotional connection to the goals or work, no internal volunteer enthusiasm or commitment inside the organisation – leading to a profound disempowerment of the people – and in turn, moonlighting, day-dreaming, boredom, escapism, anger, fear, apathy and malicious disobedience."*

For me, like many of my colleagues in the past, teaching has never been 'just a job' that I do simply to make a living and to survive. For me, work has to make me feel 'alive' and that what I am doing for most of my adult life is not only worthwhile and valued, but also challenging, enjoyable and stimulating. For me, being in a position to lead and facilitate the learning of others, particularly young people (and specifically teenagers), has the proven potential to enable and empower me to achieve all of these things, but if the leadership style of the organisation is inappropriate, then I am deeply unhappy and will do all I can to extricate myself from that unhappy context. In short, I would rather be temporarily unemployed than accept being controlled and mismanaged by those who are in a position to exert power over me. It can be a costly matter of principle, but unlike some others I have known, I feel that life is too short to spend the majority of one's lifetime in a job that is unfulfilling, where one just goes through the motions to 'keep one's nose clean' to keep the monthly income stream flowing (or trickling, given the sums involved) into the bank account. The fact that I am biologically unable to father a child is something of a blessing in disguise, as I am sure that if I had children of my own, then I might not have been able to follow my own instincts in such an honest and timely fashion.

Stephen Covey makes a very important point about leadership, and that is the distinction between what we might call 'formal leaders' – i.e. those who are appointed or elected to a position – and the existence of many leaders who choose to act in such a way, owing to their belief in what they are doing, and the feeling that they are valued as people in the same way as their efforts are valued. As a result, they take it upon themselves to act as 'architects', and also, very often, as the 'builders' in ensuring the organisation moves towards its goals in an aligned manner as a result of the passion and intrinsic motivation that all people can demonstrate and feel. In short, they really **believe in** what they are doing together and want to ensure that their **shared vision** is informing, if not enshrined in their everyday practice.

Where fundamental problems exist in a school or other organisation, Stephen Covey offers solutions upon which formal leaders should focus and act. Admittedly, as with lots of other concepts, they are much easier to articulate in theory than to achieve in actual practice, but that in no way detracts from their 'rightness' as an effective, remedial plan of action, or way ahead. For example, where an organisation suffers from a *lack of trust*, the formal leaders

315

need to concentrate on modelling being trustworthy, or, in other words, practising what they preach in order to achieve this leadership imperative. As was the case at the school where I taught for twelve years where a conflicting set of values co-existed in occasionally considerable discomfort, the solution is to go back to find a set of values in which all people believe, can agree upon and with which they feel eminently and justifiably comfortable.

In situations where people in the organisation are seemingly all pulling in different and often competing directions, without a sense of agreement or consensus about what and where the eventual destination lies, or looks like, then there is a definite need for measures that seek to achieve a greater alignment of all personnel by focusing on outcomes and the organisational structures, systems and ways of actually achieving the shared or mutually agreed goals according to the vision and values of the organisation. Finally, and once these other issues have been addressed, if the people in an organisation are feeling adversely affected by feelings of disempowerment, then the formal leaders need to home in on devolving the authority to do things to those who are closest, if not right at, the operational level. In the case of schools, this is to all team leaders and every member of their respective teams. After all, if they are all passionate and in agreement about what they are trying to achieve and, therefore, all pulling in the same overall direction, then their actions should inexorably lead to meeting the priorities and outcomes established in the strategic plan, and to successfully achieving the organisation's mission over time.

Changing Leadership Paradigms

The way in which we do things in life, at both the individual or organisational level is always informed by what I have called the traditional orthodoxy, or the behaviours and reactions that are believed to have stood the test of time and, therefore, should never be challenged and changed. That is one of the main results of conservatism with a small and a big 'c'. It is no accident that whenever the UK has been 'blessed' with a Conservative government, they seem to be hell-bent on taking us back to a time where Victorian values were de rigueur. What they do not also tell us is that such an outmoded, backward and retarded approach will inevitably lead to the corresponding life styles and most of the social conditions as well. It is no surprise to me that, at the time of writing, the current Conservative government in the UK has managed, through its anachronistic and intellectually-, and morally-deficient austerity economic and social measures, to successfully reintroduce welfare pain and food banks – the modern-day equivalent of the workhouse, perhaps?

In his book, 'The Affluent Society', John Kenneth Galbraith identified that the stranglehold which 'conventional wisdom' exerts over intellectual debate, before it even exerts its pernicious influence over different, more effective and context-related behaviours, is, to all intents and purposes, complete. No end of intellectual argument will be able to effectively challenge the status quo and the established and time-honoured ways of doing things and making decisions. This smacks of Einstein's definition of insanity largely because it is…..well, insane. That is, because we keep doing the same things over and over again, and in virtually the same way, and yet expect to see different outcomes or results. That just is **not** going to happen, simply because it can't! Why is it that a large segment of the electorate have still to figure out this pretty obvious fact for themselves? To my mind, social, political and economic conservatism is pretty much a recipe for inertia, if not stagnation, stepping backwards instead of forwards, and the triumph of an outmoded and backward-looking past over a future, exciting and forward-looking reality.

The most effective way to break away from the failures of past strictures is not to believe in more of the same. What is needed is radical and progressive thinking and subsequent action, to learn by doing and making frequent and beneficial mistakes. It is not as if the problems facing mankind, and not just national governments and its peoples, are trivial – global terrorism, global warming and the seemingly inevitable depletion of natural resources, to name just three pretty big ones; or poverty combined with religion, the burning of fossil fuels, and capitalism which are, arguably, the causes. So far, mankind is not even seriously addressing **any** of these problems because, as a species, we are in a state of utter impotence, if not complete denial.

Paradigms are models which explain how things work or how things can be produced, and most of the existing paradigms are no longer relevant, dangerously outmoded, and in need of a radical overhaul and fundamental change. Conventional wisdom makes the concomitant need for change and new approaches unpalatable if not unnecessary, and keep us all prisoners, victims even, of outmoded mind-sets which have had their day, and are no longer applicable. In short, we both need to, but at the same time are prevented from, effecting significant or real change in the way we see and do things, so that we can move towards more relevant and desirous outcomes in a modern-day context. If the circumstances in which we find ourselves change, then Darwin's theory of evolution and Alice Heim's definition of intelligence need to be taken to heart and truly and genuinely acted upon because that is what adaptive and intelligent creatures do. Indeed, it is what they have to do if they want to survive, to be blunt. Sadly, it appears as though the conventional wisdom, or the ruling paradigm can only be effectively challenged when force of circumstance (usually severely adverse or desperate in nature) demand that we manage our affairs somewhat more prudently, relevantly and differently. When one considers what is going wrong within the education that takes place in schools, I believe that there is a huge need to change the dominant paradigm that has prevailed for more than one hundred years….and I am not alone by any means in thinking this!

In the area of leadership and management styles, the need for a more radical and enlightened modus operandi is increasingly vital and long overdue. Although there are a few attempts to change the way things are done, the power of the ruling paradigm makes it incredibly difficult for new approaches to be taken seriously and even more challenging to give them the time and space to prove themselves. It is here where Stephen Covey makes a particularly valuable contribution in helping us to understand and appreciate the fact that times change whilst paradigms remain fixed, which leads to a **conflict** until a new paradigm becomes the dominant force and is consistent with the changes in society and people's attitudes, outlooks and expectations. This may well be why there is such conflict over, if not downright hostility to the way in which successive governments think is the right one for schools and centres for education to pursue.

Covey refers to the ruling paradigm which informs the current leadership and management behaviours and ways of doing things. He argues, rightly in my view, that we operate businesses and, therefore, our schools *"in a controlling Industrial Age model that suppresses the release of human potential"*.

318

However, we now live in a Knowledge Worker Age which requires new approaches in order for us to fully utilise the talents and capabilities of people, which are inconsistent and irrelevant under the dominant but outdated and outmoded Industrial Age paradigm. Although Covey does not refer directly to schools, as his focus and main concern is the business world, he does refer to the way in which this old-fashioned and defunct way of behaving spills over into our family lives. The controlling way of doing things leads to us dealing and communicating with our partners and children in such a way that we *"try to manage, motivate and discipline"* them. This is true of what we see going on in many schools today, where there are daily attempts to 'make' children do things in which they have no real interest. When they rebel, which they are provoked so to do, we then seek to 'make' or to force them to behave and conform to the demands and wishes of those who are unwitting agents of a failing paradigm.

The simple truth is that one cannot effectively discipline children, or any other person for that matter. They can only learn to discipline themselves, so that they behave in a responsible and acceptable fashion. In the same way, one cannot motivate another person easily, if at all; one can only create an environment or context in which the other person feels intrinsically motivated to act and give of their very best. Unfortunately, as Covey argues, the old Industrial Age mind-set causes us to manage people in the same way that we treat things. As a result, we fail to capitalise upon the innate motivations, talents and genius of young people in school, just as business leaders do in respect of their staff in their organisations, and this quite literally provokes them to feel alienated and insulted. In other words, what we do, and the way in which we do it in schools **'insults the intelligence'** of staff and more worryingly, our young people. We need to adopt new ways of doing things that enable people to find their own voice (our staff) so that they are able to help the students discover theirs!

What we need, therefore, is genuine, transformational leadership that involves formal leaders showing the way in taking huge steps to move what we do, and the way in which we do it, towards the new Knowledge Age Worker paradigm, and this will involve recognising the need to effect change at three different levels. These are the level of the organisation as a whole, the level that concerns itself with the nature of relationships within the organisation, and the individual or personal level.

At the moment, in many organisations, what Covey calls the *"Thing Mind-set of the Industrial Age"* is dominant and needs to be swept away so that instead of seeking to **control** people as we do things, we truly **lead** and **manage** our people in a way that inspires **trust**, recognises the importance of releasing the **passion** that lies within everyone and that seeks to **align** our combined efforts so that people feel **empowered to act**. We need people who do the job, and the students in the classroom or learning environment, to be able to take control and responsibility for their own work and their own learning. What is needed are highly imaginative and creative ways to break the stranglehold of the traditional orthodoxy that is the legacy of the Industrial Age, controlling philosophy.

Today, the dead-hand of the old paradigm is felt also at the relationship level within organisations. It creates a dependency culture where people are either unwilling and/or unable to settle their differences in really lasting and effective ways because of the lack of trust at the organisational level. It creates competition and not collaboration, and indeed, those in the Conservative Party who espouse the magic of competitive market forces which they have tried to foster in schools via league-tables and open enrolment of students and other such similarly divisive and hare-brained ideologies, perhaps in order to further their agenda of 'divide and rule'. The changes they make tend to reinforce the irrelevant and unworkable Industrial Age paradigm, rather than to understand and embrace new and original ways of operating. Their initiatives are little more than very old, incredibly stale and unpalatable wine being decanted into highly expensive new bottles in the form of 'free schools' and 'academies' that are largely run by private business organisations which are propelled by the short-term imperative of the profit motive rather than genuinely having the longer-term education of future generations at, and in, their heart. The cancer of the control philosophy is leeching into the lifeblood of all schools so that they are encouraged to compete with one another, instead of cooperating, and this spreads into, or literally infects the way in which teachers and students within the school relate to one another.

320

Stephen Covey refers to what I call people being victims of their own life experiences when he says that the way in which schools and other organisations are run creates this lifeless culture of dependency, *"the problem is compounded by the fact that so many people have been raised being compared to others at home and competing against others in school, in athletics and in the workplace."* He goes on to say that, these powerful influences cultivate a scarcity mentality, so that many people have a hard time being genuinely happy for the successes of others. These are incredibly astute and accurate observations that he makes, and they go a long way to help explain a lot of what is wrong with the way we school our young people.

Schools that are operating according to the Industrial Age paradigm also experience frustrations and other tensions at the personal level. Despite the staff being highly talented, intelligent and creative people, they are unable to contribute and work as they would like. They feel undervalued and uninspired, as well as being trapped and strait-jacketed within an organisation which has created a culture of co-dependency that effectively prevents individuals from doing anything that might change things for the better. Again, whilst these observations that Stephen Covey covers in some depth in *'The 8ᵗʰ Habit'* are related to employees in such organisations, the same malaise and lost potential is true also for students in schools. **Disaffected staff who are waiting to be told what they should do are hardly the best people to lead the learning of our young people in a way that is inspiring, creative and refreshingly different.**

This problem of an outmoded and outdated mind-set, which is the ruling and dominant paradigm demonstrates that which I have stated several times before, and that is when things go wrong in an organisation, we tend to blame people in order to find convenient scapegoats, but this is a malicious fallacy. In most cases of organisational failure, the problem lies within the system that allows, encourages and does little or nothing to prevent such deleterious events or actions occurring. In most cases, it is completely disingenuous and dishonest to sacrifice an individual on the altar of organisational incompetence and anachronistic leadership and management practices.

Henry David Thoreau once wrote: *"There are a thousand hacking at the branches of evil to one who is hacking at the root."* I love this quotation as, in many ways, it encapsulates the main theme running through this book. School leaders are often too busy seeking to deal with and find solutions to what are really only the symptoms of what is fundamentally wrong with the current methods of education that occurs in schools, so that they are side-tracked or otherwise distracted from tackling the root causes of the problems that arise. These root causes are the powerful hidden messages that we send unintentionally and covertly through our formal actions, statements and behaviours that run counter to, and undermine, what we profess to be trying to achieve in our school brochures and mission statements.

The challenges which formal leaders in schools really have to address are not easy to solve in isolation, as they are so deeply entrenched within the old-fashioned dominant paradigm and a more holistic solution is needed, namely one that addresses the way in which people are trained to become teachers, and the almost incessant spate of new initiatives emanating from central government. It is these two major areas that are the focal points for the next two sections of this book.

To overcome all the issues that hold schools, their staff and students back, regardless of the country in which they are based or the curriculum that they follow, is going to require change that is root-and-branch in nature. This change will necessarily require similarly radical changes in the way in which teachers are trained and how the government works with schools and those professionals who give their lives to facilitating the learning of our future – our young people!

Chapter Sixteen: A Forethought as an Afterthought

Introduction

In February 1998, after I had left the school system in the UK and was working as a teacher of English as a Foreign Language in Denmark, I decided, for reasons that escape me now, to write an analogous outline statement which attempted to illustrate what I considered to be the key characteristics of a great, as opposed to a good school. I thought that I might include that statement here, leaving it unchanged from the time it was written, except that I have **highlighted** a few words which I feel are so important to the integrity of that which I wrote some seventeen years ago. I don't believe that my current thoughts are in anyway very much different to those that drove me to write the following outline all those years ago:

It's Not Noise It's Music

The characteristics of a great school are essentially the same as those of a great orchestra. Such an orchestra is comprised of a group of **talented** people who are all playing the **same** music. Each member of the orchestra knows what the entire piece of music sounds like, intricate and subtle, bold and brash, though its individual parts may be different. They also know when they have to play and when they have to listen – following the performances of the other musicians. After all, not every musician can play every instrument to a sufficiently high standard – even if they know and can appreciate the sound that each instrument makes.

In a great orchestra, the individual musician may only play for some of the time – and not always with gusto. Sometimes s/he may be required to **lead** from the front, whilst at others be prepared to work in support of the lead musicians or simply to listen, in order to know when next to play. Nonetheless, it is understood that the contribution of each musician is of **equal value and worth**........even the occasional strike of the triangle.

All musicians want to play with **passion** and to perfection in order to ensure that the entire piece of music is played as never before. They are prepared to evaluate their own performance in a reflective and critical way and to accept the comments made by others (praise, positive feedback and constructive criticism) in the mutual search for high quality, if perfection is perceived as idealism as opposed to realism.

The great orchestra is, therefore, fundamentally about **teamwork**. It is necessarily about encouraging and allowing individual expression, experimentation and virtuoso performances by soloists as well as particular sections of the orchestra at the appropriate time.

The cement that holds the whole thing together, and miraculously transforms otherwise random noise into beautiful (or at least interesting) music is the fact that **everyone knows the overall musical score**. They are all **playing the same tune**, directed and inspired and coordinated by the **leadership** of the conductor – an individual who may now be unable to play any of the musical instruments in the orchestra, but who understands the **potential** of the piece of music and the performers assembled in front of him or her.

The conductor's task is not to perform on behalf of others but to **empower** each musician to express himself/herself as they wish, so long as it contributes to the quality of the overall sound. S/he has to offer advice, guidance and support – perhaps in concert with others – and to be a critical friend. To achieve a top quality orchestral performance will take time and individual musicians will necessarily make **mistakes** from time to time – and so they should, provided that they admit to, and **learn** from them. In the meantime, the conductor may improvise and re-arrange the piece of music in such a way that it plays to the strengths of the individuals, and provides time to overcome any weaknesses that we all have – as long as the integrity of the piece is not compromised!

The conductor, however, has to ensure that there is a base line, which constitutes an acceptable level of performance by everyone. This is because the orchestra has a duty to perform exceptional music – music of beauty and/or inventiveness – to stimulate and challenge the listeners, whilst taking

324

account of the existing level of musical appreciation of which the intended audience is capable. The aim is to enthrall, to please, but also to raise the musical appreciation, understanding and wonderment of the audience to new heights – as well as to extend the size and range of the audience. To achieve this should satisfy the sponsors of, and other stakeholders in the orchestra and to achieve critical acclaim from those who take it upon themselves to assess the standard of the work produced!

Encore!

Section E: Teacher Training

Chapter Seventeen: Becoming a Teacher?

A Much Maligned Profession?

I want to begin by going on the record to say that, in my opinion, teaching is undoubtedly the most grossly maligned profession of all, in the way that so much of what masquerades as government initiative and media bile is focused on seeking to make schools, and teachers in particular, accountable – the new and exigent buzzword for the public services. There seems to be a constant barrage of attack guns focused on pounding the teaching profession into submission as its members are endlessly required to justify everything that they do and to prove their collective and individual competence, following virtually every salvo of criticism that is rarely, if ever, constructive in nature. I find it difficult to fathom why 'education' (or really, schooling) is always seen as such an easy and desirable target for these unwelcome, unhelpful and politically-motivated assaults. Furthermore, the havoc and disenchantment that these onslaughts create is not something that is the preserve of Conservative governments, as New Labour under the morally questionable leadership of Tony Blair was equally prone to mess around with things of which they understood very little and, apparently, valued even less. My feelings on this are so strong, bordering on hysterical anger that I am being sorely tested in holding my own fire on this topic until the following section of this book, but I will endeavour to follow the structure that I originally established for this personal perspective on what I believe is going badly wrong in schools, and has been for a very long time now.

At the outset, I also wish to make it abundantly clear that my view is that, in the main, teachers are a group of individuals who are deeply dedicated, incredibly hard-working and utterly 'professional' in the way that they approach their work which, for many, is a vocation, rather than merely a source of employment and income. After all, if someone wants to earn a really good salary during their working life, then they are hardly likely to view a career in teaching as a good bet in that regard. As for the popular myth that teachers are fortunate to enjoy long holidays, spending their exorbitant salaries on world cruises, enjoying sunning themselves on exotic beaches in faraway places or otherwise lazing about doing precious little is nothing more than misguided, fallacious and dangerous bunkum. Whilst I am loathe to judge others by my own standards, I am not alone when I say that I have always spent most of my precious 'down-time', from what is an immensely demanding and challenging job, preparing materials and myself for the next school term or year. Moreover, even had I been less conscientious and wanted to follow a more hedonistic lifestyle, my income level made such dreams the stuff of fantasy rather than reality.

Why is it that teachers, and the teaching profession as a whole, are such an easy target for demonization by successive governments and the popular press, which in turn infects the thinking of the general public, from which the parents of school students emerge? Or is it the other way round? Is it because parents and the public at large harbour feelings of considerable resentment or dissatisfaction with the work that schools do, so much so that this concern is reflected in government interference and the hostility of the allegedly 'free' press? Or, has the whole issue become such a popular and everyday political football that identifying cause and effect has become impossibly blurred? Whatever the answer to such questions, I honestly believe that governments and the public are collectively doing what happens when things go wrong in an organisation: they look for scapegoats in the form of people to blame, rather than realising that the root cause of the problem is once again systemic in nature. Schools, and the work that teachers are required to do, are impossibly trapped within an outdated and traditional paradigm that is a complete anachronism and, as a result, people blame the practitioners rather than focus on what is fundamentally at fault and in need of radical and progressive overhaul.

I honestly believe that many teachers know full well what is wrong with much of what passes as education in schools, but they lack the power or the means to do things differently. They are the victims of the system, if you like, which causes them to become inert and 'fatally' transfixed like rabbits in the headlights of an oncoming political car, which itself is directionless and largely out of reasonable and balanced control. More on this in the next section of the book, as I now wish to turn my attention to the possible systemic weaknesses in the way in which we train those who are to be responsible for facilitating the learning of young people, and how calls for greater

331

accountability have resulted in the work that teachers do becoming more akin to that of a 'technician' than a trusted and respected 'professional'.

A Personal Reflection

There is absolutely no doubt in my mind that the four years I spent at Kingston-upon-Hull College of Education were the probably the most enjoyable, stimulating and personally liberating years in my life to date. This is partly due to the fact that Hull was (and still is) a truly wonderful city for a country boy like me to inhabit at such a momentous time in his life, and partly a result of an amazing college life and curriculum, in its widest sense. It felt as though the world had really become my oyster and, in virtually every way, I had the time of my life!

To begin with, my choice of Hull as my destination for the pursuit of Higher Education was undoubtedly one that destiny had pre-ordained. It was not the most attractive or appealing of places to be a student, if one was to believe the erroneous 'Hull, Hell and Halifax' saying of the times, but I chose one of that infamous triumvirate as the place to study for my Bachelor of Education Degree. I am so utterly and immensely glad that I did, as Hull was (and is) a wonderful city which, at that time, had more of a village mentality and culture, and it was one with which I felt immediately and consummately at ease. It was a gloriously empowering time for me, as it offered so many opportunities for me to extend, enrich and challenge myself thanks to its relatively small size, the excellent teaching faculty that it boasted and some great fellow students who heralded mainly from the north of England – from Leeds, Newcastle, Liverpool, Barnsley and Todmorden (a town that famously straddles the two 'proud' counties of Lancashire and Yorkshire). God's country indeed!

It felt like the wisest choice right from the time when I first travelled by train from Somerset to North Humberside, as the East Riding of Yorkshire had largely become known, courtesy of local government reorganization. It was a long journey in those days by any mode of transport, and taking the train took virtually the whole day, although I cannot recall the route that I took, but I can remember feeling a notable sense of relief when the locomotive trundled into the terminus that is Hull Paragon station in the early evening, and the dark. The journey, and the uncertainty that it necessarily entailed did not end as definitely as the train had managed, as I still had to find my way from the station to 'Stan's Guest House', as my father seemed to think was a humorous way of referring to St. Anne's Guest House, where he had booked me a room for the arrival night. It had been recommended by the College as one of a select few affordable and delightfully pleasant places to stay, and an excellent recommendation it was too.

My father had given me very little money for this life-changing trip, but enough to accommodate an evening meal and a taxi from the station to Stan's place. I boarded a taxi at Paragon station and told the driver where I wanted to go. Remember, this was my first major trip away from home all on my own. I could not have been in better hands. The taxi driver immediately guessed what I was doing in Hull. "You are here for an interview at the College of Education?" he enquired. "Yes," I replied in a somewhat surprised state. He continued, "Do you know where you have to go tomorrow for the interview?" What he was effectively asking was did I know the way from the guest house to the college, which I had to undertake early in the next morning and, as a novice in Hull, I had not the faintest clue. I admitted my ignorance readily, with which this truly genuine and generous man offered to drive past the guest house and show me the way up Newlands Avenue and Cottingham Road to the College of Education. Suddenly, I was a little concerned, as I did not have the funds to pay for a taxi journey to my destination for the following morning, and then back to Stan's. I nervously made the helpful taxi driver aware of the fact, and he responded by assuring me that he would switch off the meter as we passed St. Anne's Guest House and the amount displayed at that time would be all that I would be asked to pay. I agreed, and he was a man of his word. He drove past the guest house and told me to pay attention, as I needed to remember the route the following morning when I would retrace the vehicular directions on foot, and in relatively disorienting daylight.

When we got to the College, he actually drove into the grounds and showed me the door in the actual building that was the admissions office, to which I had to report early the next day. In this act of spontaneous but wholly natural generosity, that man eliminated a huge chunk of my pre-interview nerves. He was a real gem, and I wish I had asked his name so that I could record it here – my historical oversight, I'm afraid. After the unexpected, kind and generous

333

detour, I was driven back to the guest house and paid what the meter said was my fare from the station and, as you can see, I have not forgotten that 'good Samaritan'.

But there is something else that I have not forgotten, and that was the number of effortlessly natural times that he said to me, "Eee, you'll like Hull, it's a nice place." That welcoming phrase turned out to be the mantra for the whole of my highly enjoyable visit, as I heard it from so many people during my preciously short, first time in the city that became my alma mater. The next person who uttered those words was the landlady of the guest house as she ushered me to my room; it was as though all the people I met that day had previously gathered together in order to agree a common approach to ensure we accepted our places at the College, assuming that we had successful interviews. I was intrigued to learn that amongst the other guests that night were a few other interview hopefuls, and the members of the Ivy Benson Band, whom I knew only as my father had talked about them at some time in the distant past, but in a way that caused me to make the connection at this much later date.

Over dinner at the guest house, I met the three other interviewees who were also to appear at the College the next morning, although they were seeking places for courses other than those for which I had applied. We decided to team up and visit some local hostelries that evening in order to sample the local ales and meet some local folk. It was an evening that was interesting and highly enjoyable, as everywhere we went, we were met with the same hospitable refrain: "You'll like Hull, it's a nice place." And their certain and most definite optimism proved to be a massive understatement in terms of its accuracy from my point of view. I really did have the time of my life, although it did require me to get used to the malodorous stench of the dockside, fish-meal factory when the wind blew inland from the North Sea, which it did with un-fragrant regularity. However, that minor unpleasantness was a small price to pay for an otherwise joyous four years; in fact it became part of the appeal of the city – in time!

I can vividly recall, to this very day, the enormous pain that the wrench of having to leave my student life in Hull at the end of those four, fantastic,

334

nurturing and enriching years had upon my emotional state. I had to leave the City and many good friends that I had made, as well as the places that had become part of my new 'home from home'. My last full day in the City was a desperately distressing one for me, so much so that I remember how much I cried, almost uncontrollably at times, at the thought of probably never being able to repeat the immense pleasure of the myriad of all my experiences in Hull, a place which still has a very special place in my affections. I have tears in my eyes as I seek to recount those overwhelming sentiments in writing here (and as I re-read them now in the stages before eventual publication of this 'book').

I have taken a little time to reflect on those salad days for three main reasons: to applaud the fact that Hull has recently become the 'City of Culture' in the UK, an announcement that was met with a mixture of disbelief, amazement and even a touch of derision by many (possibly as a result of envy); to give some colour to my views about the replacement of the B. Ed route of becoming a teacher by the shorter and less demanding and rigorous PGCE alternative, and to offer a long-overdue vote of thanks to the people of Hull at that time, and the many dear friends and 'interesting' characters that I had the pleasure of knowing, for four fantastic years – it was as close to perfection as I can imagine a young man's life ever being, and for so many different and diverse reasons. (In addition to the many tutors that made a huge and lasting impression on me, I would like to record my thanks to people like David M. Pugh (as he liked to be called), Steve Lord (the most genuinely and hysterically funny man that I have ever met), as well as many young and beautiful young women that I knew – especially Medina Wintle, Christine Gee and Wendy Crosland!

I also want to take time to refer to the scandal that is the 'double-whammy' of tuition fees and student loans that have been introduced to penalise young people wishing to experience higher education, due to the squandering of national income and wealth by successive governments. The worst culprits were the Conservative Governments of Margaret Thatcher, when the once-in-a-lifetime bounty arising from North Sea oil revenues, plus additional income from selling the family silver, in the form of the mass privatisation of state utilities, was utterly wasted by an ideologically-twisted and morally bankrupt government. The huge funds accrued by the Exchequer during that time from these income streams were effectively used to finance the mass unemployment caused by the incredibly damaging monetarist economic policy dogma, which successive Thatcher governments pursued with reckless, almost joyous abandon. In Norway, a far-wiser government used the funds from North Sea oil to invest in a form of social investment fund, with the interest payments arising every year being generated in perpetuity for future generations and constructive social purposes. Far-sighted policy makers indeed, unlike the short-sighted, politically-blinkered and socially nasty and divisive government in Britain, under the leadership of a Grantham grocer's daughter.....and now (sadly and depressingly) by a manifestly evil, ignorant and socially divisive pack of 'Bullingdon Club Boys'!

Do Teachers Need to Be Trained at All?

Before examining why I honestly believe that the more specific and longer-term B. Ed route to becoming a teacher is far superior to the Post-Graduate Certificate of Education (PGCE) that has replaced it, I do not want to be accused of simply assuming that those who are to teach young people need to be trained in the first place. This is a serious point, as there are many people (usually Tory government ministers with dismantling the state infrastructure and slashing the role of government firmly embedded in their ideologically-twisted minds) who revel in reminding everyone that there are people who, without specific training, can effectively engage young learners, whilst there are trained 'professional' teachers who are far from being as effective in stimulating and promoting student learning in the schools where they work. This is not, therefore, an unimportant issue!

As a result, I would like to briefly consider whether or not those people who are to be responsible for directing, managing and facilitating the learning of others need to be trained at all, and if so, how they could perhaps be better trained to undertake such a vital role in influencing, affecting or otherwise helping to shape the life chances of young people. More broadly, there has been a little anecdotal evidence that seems to question whether or not those who work in some other professions actually need to be fully trained as well. However, I believe that we would all agree that in matters of life and death, such as health care, then it is essential that the practitioners in such areas are

336

properly trained and fully qualified. Nonetheless, there have been notable cases where unqualified individuals have managed to prove exceptions to this general rule, although they do not disprove the general case for, preferably, possessing the right credentials. For example, there are cases where people who are untrained, have managed to land aeroplanes in emergencies, deliver babies and save lives. There are also, less common situations where an individual has masqueraded as a qualified professional for many years and escaped detection. I can recall the case of a man in Leicestershire who served for many years as a family doctor, or GP (General Practitioner), and yet it was not until after he died that anyone discovered that he had absolutely no medical qualifications whatsoever. What was even more amazing was that a posthumous investigation into his actions, to see whether any of his patients had suffered death or permanent injury as a result of his untrained dabbling, concluded that there was no evidence of serious malpractice.

That is not to say that there were no cases where his lack of medical training had led to minor problems. For example, some of the prescriptions he had written were somewhat questionable, to say the least, such as creosote for sore throats and suppositories to be taken orally. This latter fact was something I recall only too well thanks to the hugely talented Paul Merton, who could not let it pass when it was raised on the BBC Television programme 'Have I Got News for You.' He surmised that had he been the patient who had been told to swallow a drug best delivered as a suppository, then he would have gone back to the doctor after a couple of weeks to complain that, *"For all the good these have done me, I might as well have shoved them up my a**e."*

Clearly, training for any job is probably a very good idea, and in cases of life and death I doubt that anyone would suggest otherwise, but what about teachers? In my view teaching, and the education that **should** be taking place in our schools, is a matter of extreme importance because it has a direct bearing on the life chances and attitude formation of our young people. There are those, however, who argue that formal training is not necessarily a prerequisite for practising teachers and, in fact, the employment of untrained teachers is quite a common practice, especially in independent schools, or the private sector.

Schools in the non-maintained sector are not required to follow most of the strictures that are laid down by the Secretaries of State for Education of successive governments in the UK. This begs one obvious question, of course, and that is, "Why not?" Surely, the education of the children and adolescents attending those establishments is of equal importance as those who go to state schools, so why the discrimination? The obvious answer is that independent schools are de facto outside the public sector and concomitant government control and, therefore, free to do as they wish, although this does not prevent the government granting them preferential financial treatment which is not (quite literally) afforded to other private businesses. (In later sections of this book, I wish to return to the inequity of private education and private health care, both of which should be eliminated in my opinion.) After all, should the life chances of the already 'better off' be subject to the preferential treatment that private education and health care offers, thereby giving them a further advantage in the 'game' of life? In my view, this is not only iniquitous, but also grossly unreasonable and unfair. So much for living in a genuine meritocracy!

So, do those adults, who are charged with the responsibility of facilitating the learning of the young people who attend school, really need formal training, or are good 'teachers' just people with a passion in their subject or area of expertise and experience, and who are also capable of 'infecting' the learner with a similar degree of enthusiasm and interest?

I recall very well, during my very first year of teaching in a highly-successful, well-managed and effectively-structured state comprehensive school in Essex (England), when I was literally 'head-hunted' by the Head Teacher of an independent school, in the same town, that had recently 'lost' their teacher of Economics. The subject was quite popular in what was a relatively small school, and so it was essential that they found a suitable replacement to offer 'late-afternoon' classes for their 'A' Level students. I was, more or less, able to state my hourly rate, and so I asked to receive a payment that my professional association maintained to be the level of remuneration for part-time tuition. The only 'rider' that I attached was that the gross pay had to be sufficiently higher so as to ensure that my hourly *net* income was the same as the recommended figure. This was no problem whatsoever, and so I also asked to be paid a small additional sum to cover the cost of having to catch the train home, as staying after my full-time job had formally ended meant that I missed my 'lift' home with one of my older colleagues who lived in the same town as me, and could also afford his own transportation, despite being a humble teacher.

I thoroughly enjoyed the year that I spent working with those young people, whose parents could afford private education, and in very small classes – classes that would not normally have been financially viable in a state school. This was one major advantage that those students enjoyed – a significantly smaller class size – so that I was able to provide the delightful students with a far more individualised and personal service. Those who claim that private education offers no distinct advantage for the students who attend such schools are clearly deluded and talking nonsense. That was beneficially evident during my year offering late-afternoon classes twice a week throughout the year in which I held that 'additional' post. Furthermore, if private education did not offer significant advantage to the students (real or perceived) then why would any parent pay extra for the same service as that offered at the local state comprehensive school in which I worked on a full-time basis? Please don't be so offensively silly! Of course it bestows a considerable advantage on young people of all ability levels, and the school also had entrance examinations that ensured they only admitted students who were of above-average academic ability, so as to ensure their prestigious status, and to justify their additional expense in the form of fees payable.

Before I actually started to teach the students 'deprived' of their previous teacher of Economics, I asked to meet the substitute member of staff who was taking their classes during the timetabled time during the main school day. I was directed to the school staffroom (or was it the Senior Common Room?) to meet the designated teacher so that he and I could coordinate the work that we were going to do with those 'A' Level students. It was an interesting meeting. The designated person was sitting in an armchair in the staffroom (yes, an armchair and not the plastic-covered, foam seats that adorned my school's equivalent space), and he was dressed in a track-suit and looking somewhat dishevelled and tired. I assumed that he had been running an after-school sports activity, but my guess was only partially correct.

339

I introduced myself and I shared my initial assumption with him, and he said, with a delightful Welsh accent, "No. Actually, I am the PE teacher here." I was marginally confused. Perhaps he was one of those 'unusual' people, in those days, who taught two, unrelated subjects, but no. During our brief conversation, it transpired that he had just started studying 'A' level Economics at a local college of further education. His view was, and I quote, "Well, it's only a matter of staying one step ahead of the kids, isn't it?" In the interests of fostering a positive working relationship with the school, I took his utterance as a rhetorical question, and we decided that during my after-school sessions with the students I would reprise the entire 'A' level syllabus. It was a very enjoyable venture, even though it was not a particularly lucrative one, but then, as I have already noted, you definitely do not choose a teaching career if pecuniary reward is your main goal.

Although I had serious misgivings about the somewhat naïve, rather than cavalier attitude of the replacement teacher the school had assigned to cover the Economics classes that is not to say the PE teacher was not doing a reasonably good job. However, my time with the students did suggest that my doubts or concerns could have been well founded. The man was undoubtedly doing his level best to meet the demands the school had unreasonably placed upon him, but it was not enough to prepare a well-motivated and academically able group of young people for their pre-university examinations in the subject.

So as not to appear to be using anecdotal evidence entirely in a negative way, I have experienced a few more situations where schools have appointed people who have not received any formal teacher training (I am seeking to avoid using the pejorative, misleading or ambiguous term 'unqualified' here) and they have been able to achieve quite satisfactory outcomes with the students for whose learning they were responsible. I honestly believe that although there are people with a passion for an area of learning who are capable of engaging, interesting and involving young learners by sharing their passion with them, such individuals would be so much better at what they do if they were to receive specific teacher training. In other words, I remain to be convinced that a love or a passion for one's subject matter alone is enough in itself to make one effective as a classroom teacher, but it is clearly a very, very important and fundamental factor.

My scepticism is due to the fact that 'teaching a subject' alone is not in itself education owing to the apparent disconnection of what is learned in one context to other areas or dimensions of learning, and this something which I have attempted to articulate in preceding chapters of this book. The process of facilitating the learning of others in an inter-disciplinary or more integrated way, so that a real synergy of learning is created with alternative perspectives in different contexts, requires teachers to be able to help manage and direct the overall experience. This is something that requires some formal study or training and which develops over time as the practitioner acquires a greater depth and breadth of experience. I am also fairly sure that the initial teacher training programmes that are currently offered by universities or colleges are not, in themselves, always that relevant to being able to act in this facilitating role. This is something to which I shall return later in this chapter.

Furthermore, the knowledge and skills required to help direct and manage the learning process are brought into sharper focus if learners are to benefit from working with adults other than teachers (AOTs) who, as I have already acknowledged are both necessary and capable of engaging and stimulating young people. When AOTs are used in a relevant and timely way, in other words when they are needed, they can do so much to enhance, extend and enrich the learning of young people in ways that the class teacher alone cannot possibly hope to offer.

Another reason why the right kind of formal training to be a teacher is necessary is, quite simply, because it can make such a huge difference to those who want to become classroom practitioners. In-service training of teachers raises their skill and knowledge base in demonstrable ways, especially if the training is contextual and/or team-based. Let me explain this point in a little more detail.

When individual teachers are sent on external courses, it is very difficult for them to effectively put what they have learnt into practice if others in their school have not been fortunate enough to have had the same experience. 'Cascading' what one or two people have learned from attending a professional development course is not impossible, but it is extraordinarily difficult. Such good intentions almost always fail to materialise, unless the senior team has been involved initially in determining the need for the course, selecting the individual(s) who are to attend, and then becoming *actively* involved afterwards, by supporting and managing the so-called cascade process, so as to ensure the intended organisational impact is actually achieved in every day practice. As I have mentioned before, a better way to ensure the desired outcomes are achieved in actual practice is to bring an external trainer into the school to train a group of teachers or the whole school staff, as necessary. This is far more likely to impact the organisation because it not only eliminates the need for cascading, but it also allows a group of staff to learn together in a specific and known context, relating the subject matter to their own school and its unique culture. In-service training is a vital component in an efficacious process of continuous professional development, and this fact affirms the need for aspiring teachers to receive some type of formal, pre-service training.

B. Ed vs. PGCE – which is better?

Now, I know that everyone is inclined to favour the way in which they became a teacher, and unless one has encountered and experienced the alternative route into the profession, then it is very difficult to assess the relative merits and demerits of the two main pathways an intending teacher can pursue, namely a specialist Bachelor of Education degree, on the one hand, or a Post-Graduate Certificate of Education, on the other. What is more, I am not seeking to disparage the PGCE route into the teaching profession, but I do feel that the B. Ed offers a more specialist and extensive training program, not least in terms of the amount of time needed to complete the programme.

There is absolutely no doubt in my mind that had I not spent four thoroughly enriching, stimulating and enjoyable years at teachers' training college, I would not have become as good a classroom teacher, and trainer, as I believe I have become. Maybe my innate abilities would have led me to a similar degree of competence over time, but it would have taken far longer without those four joyous and fantastic years. And the time one takes to study is significant if it is well spent, focused and rigorous, and it must surely allow more knowledge to be acquired and a greater range of skills to be developed, assuming we are talking about a conscientious student.

During my four years at Kingston-upon-Hull College of Education, I was incredibly fortunate to be pleasantly exposed to all kinds of interesting pursuits in addition to a comprehensive, wonderfully stimulating and truly educational teacher training programme. Although I was a student of Economic Studies and Commercial Subjects, two main elective subjects that comprised the 'Secondary Specialist Commerce' curriculum, most of my contemporaries thought that I was actually studying Drama or Physical Education. This was quite simply due to the fact that I was willingly 'sucked into' a range of pursuits that involved me in compering and acting in the annual staff and student variety show; being cast in the leading role for several plays that were staged by the college Drama and Literary Society. I even had a major acting part in the Drama Department's annual Shakespeare play that was staged first at the college and then for two weeks on the 'Fringe' at the Edinburgh International Festival. I was also a drummer for a short time in a rock band with four students from neighbouring Hull University to which the college was affiliated. It was an immensely joyous time indeed, not least because for the first time in my life, I was actively encouraged and allowed to follow my innate talents rather than expected to follow a largely parentally-determined learning program. Oh that I had realised this fact at the time!

I was so incredibly lucky to have had so many opportunities to explore and give vent to my innate talents, despite my formal studies taking a somewhat different direction. I can vividly recall with great affection and considerable gratitude English classes with Don Ward and working with the Head of Drama, Tom Martin and a superb cast on Shakespeare's 'Winter's Tale' which we performed in both Hull and Edinburgh. I remember very well being asked to compère the variety show by Chris Rowe, and helping Bill Turnbull (who was in overall charge of the Commercial Subjects elective that I followed) with the box office and accounts for another year's Shakespeare production. The two of us would escape for a beer together at a local hostelry whilst the first half was underway, before returning to sell ice creams and other refreshments during the interval. This was all 'extra-curricular' to the main aim of actually being responsible for the accounting role for all ticket sales and box office receipts – thanks Bill! And then there was the immensely influential and much-loved Alun Roberts to whom I owe so very much, as I have mentioned many times before.

I was also very lucky to have been part of a relatively small college which also had a family-like, community feel to it as a result. It is largely true to say that everyone knew each other to a greater or lesser extent, and this was partly enabled for each annual intake because the college rules made it obligatory for all first-year students to stay in one of the halls of residence, which were also on the attractive campus. I was equally lucky because at one time the college had admitted only female students, and whilst it eventually opened its doors to young men, males were significantly outnumbered by the more glamorous and opposite sex – even though their hair was often significantly shorter. I had the pleasure and privilege of mixing with and becoming friends with many of my fellow students, and the joy of those four years is partly due to them and their companionship. It was a time for me, a boarding school boy until sixteen years of age, to branch out and really find myself. I owe so much to some great fellow students whose names I feel obliged to repeat, especially Dave Pugh, Steve Lord and Richard Sales, for their friendship and their influence, as well as their provocations and the good times we experienced together, both at work and at play. They were all instrumental in helping me mature and develop during the four years that we were together, and I am proud to still be in regular contact with some of them. They had a major role in making me the person who I have become over the years – their influence lives on in so many ways, even if only due to their indelible imprint upon my grey matter.

Having said all that, it would be disingenuous to say that every aspect of the college was positive, enriching and joyous. There were notable exceptions, such as some far from effective lecturers, especially those responsible for the philosophy of education curriculum, and the fact that Commercial Subjects required me to attend typewriting classes every week. The latter was a nightmare for me, largely owing to the fact that I had no absolutely no interest in it whatsoever and that my short, fat stubby fingers and huge palm meant that I was as well suited to typewriting as I had definitely not been at playing the piano in my childhood. I have come to learn keyboard skills at a later date and with more high-tech, efficient and user-friendly apparatus. Nonetheless, I experienced four years during which my personal and professional development was considerable and leveraged to a huge extent thanks to the influence, support and guidance of so many staff and fellow students alike. I cannot thank all of the people I should thank at this juncture for reasons of memory, the pain of unintended omission and sheer space.

Up to now, I have spent a lot of time reminiscing on the social aspect of those four years, but I have to admit that the formal curriculum was immensely enjoyable, incredibly useful and relevant, as well as a fantastic grounding for anyone who wanted to grow into an effective classroom performer. The first advantage of the B. Ed programme is that all students have made a decision, or their parents have, that they are going to train to become a professional teacher. They are not going to study for an academic degree and then, subsequently, decide to do a PGCE after their under-graduate three years.

The course I experienced was not only highly academic, but also incredibly practical. In addition to lectures, seminars and tutorials in the two main elective subjects, I was also immersed in the philosophy of education, the history of education, the psychology and sociology of education throughout the four years. Consequently, I had many lectures and other formal sessions that I had to attend for five days a week, and occasionally on Saturday mornings, which constituted a judicious balance between the need to attend formal training sessions or classes, and free time. I say this because I had not really learnt the skills and attitudes that enable effective self-directed study, having had a strictly regulated, secondary school boarding experience followed by the other extreme of a very laissez-faire learning environment whilst taking my 'A' levels at Technical College. What I had really needed was an intermediate experience which was a 'half-way house' following my time at boarding school, when what I did for virtually every waking moment was mapped out for me and directed by a predictable routine, that was determined and timetabled by others. Being thrust into a college learning environment which required me to possess the self-discipline and knowledge needed to make optimal use of the opportunities that were available to me to perform well at 'A' level, was possibly too much of a 'new world' for someone with such a background. So, to find that half-way house whilst training to be a teacher was a real godsend, and I thrived during my time there. In fact, it is hard to think of anything that could have

345

been anything other than such a positive and advantageous experience for me......I literally learned so much!

I think one of the greatest strengths of the B. Ed route over the PGCE alternative is the way in which *theory* of education is combined with the *practice* of education over a number of years, in what is essentially a 'sandwich-type' of course. After a few weeks of my very first term as a student of the 'Secondary Specialist Commerce' programme, I was required to spend three weeks on teaching practice in a school. Furthermore, the college rule was that this first practical immersion in an actual school had to be in an institution catering for students from a different age range to the one for which one was specifically being trained. As Hull City had a system of primary, middle and secondary schools, I spent three fascinating and challenging weeks at a junior high school where the students were aged between nine and thirteen years. Talk about being 'dumped' in the deep end, but I had a college tutor to come and observe me and offer advice and, as I recall, a Mr. Bewick who was the Deputy Head Teacher, and who effectively ran the school. He was an incredibly helpful man, who also taught Mathematics, and one who gave me a wealth of good advice that enabled me to not only enjoy my first teaching experience, but also to make a relatively competent teaching contribution to the school.

To say that I learnt a lot would be a massive understatement. Amongst other more intended things, I learnt that I was to feel privileged as a mere student teacher, as the teaching staff had agreed that I could be invited into the small staffroom at breaks and lunchtimes. This meant that I did not have to spend such times in a cupboard somewhere in the school. Although I was honoured to be allowed into the professional teachers' inner sanctum, I also had to quickly learn that I was not allowed to sit in certain seats as those were the preserve of named, individual members of staff – those were the days of deference and 'knowing one's place'! Nonetheless, when those three weeks were over, I felt motivated to want to learn as much as possible during my college course in order to further develop my nascent skills as an aspiring teacher.

Towards the end of my first year, the time came where those who wanted to graduate with a B. Ed degree had to put their names forward for consideration and approval by the academics who had worked with us during that time. The alternative was to spend two more years, and then leave with a very creditable Certificate of Education, as opposed to a further three years of study to leave as a graduate with a Bachelor of Education degree. I must admit that, given my pretty undistinguished academic career to date, for a whole variety of different reasons, I was unsure that I had what it took to graduate. Nonetheless, I put my name forward for the B. Ed options with more than a little hesitation and self-doubt, and this was something that the amazing Alun Roberts sensed almost immediately. I can remember very well his verdict on my decision to put my name forward for the degree course and three more years. He was a real gem of a man, as you may have deduced given the number of times his name appears in this book. He told me that I could very easily take a straight Economics degree at the university next door and expect to be very successful. Perhaps he saw some latent ability within me, or maybe he was simply trying to boost my self-confidence – or both. I was massively taken aback and pleasantly surprised, as this was really the first time in my life to that date that anyone had told me I was actually suited to any form of academic study. And so it was that I continued into my second year which was the preliminary B. Ed degree course of study and, from that day, I was determined to prove that Alun's faith in me was well founded.

During that second year, I had a second teaching practice, this time in a High School in a pleasant suburb of the city of Hull. It was called Kelvin Hall High School, and I enjoyed a five-week practice there, teaching Accounts and Commerce, as well as some Economics. Oddly enough my memories of that interesting five week period are of amusing incidents with the students, which I feel obliged to share with you, if only to show how you can learn a lot from them, and why teaching can (and should) be a lot of fun as well.

The first of these arose partly because I used to walk to and from the school from the house where I was staying, and on the way I would strike up some pleasant conversations with students of the school who were also on route and, like me, on foot. One student who seemed to go out of her way to 'bump into me' on the way was a young woman who was in what would now be

347

termed Year 10 in the UK. She was from a working-class family, something which gave her the confidence and self-assuredness to engage me in conversation during the chilly morning and more balmy evening journeys to and from school.

One day at school, when I was carrying out a lunch-time corridor supervision, one of the routine responsibilities of being a teacher, I saw the same girl in the corridor, and so I decided to go over and talk to her. She was leaning with her back semi-arched against the corridor wall, and we chatted for a minute or so, before I bade farewell and carried on with my dutiful perambulation. Later that day, as I was on my way home after school, lost in reflections as to how my day had gone, this same girl came running up behind me in her eagerness to talk with me again. I was flattered, of course, as she was an attractive and engaging character. "Thanks, by the way, sir", she said, somewhat breathlessly. I was confused to say the least and so enquired what I had done that required her gratitude. The ensuing conversation revealed that when we had talked together in the corridor that lunch-time, she had been smoking a cigarette, which she had in her hands, wafting behind her back. At that time, I was a smoker myself and so did not detect the smell, and her casual manner and simple cunning meant that she escaped detection by me with considerable ease. She was indeed a **very clever** young woman and, again, I wish I could remember her name!

The second amusing event which is still etched in my memory involved a first-year, sixth-form class to which I had been assigned to teach Book-keeping and Accounts. It is still a cause for much relived embarrassment to this day. The class consisted of about sixteen or seventeen young women of roughly the same age, who were considered to have a more vocationally-oriented educational need. To say that they were a lively and flirtatious group would be a serious under-statement, but they were always an interesting and interested class of learners.

I decided that in order to make their work in book-keeping and accounts more relevant and interesting, they should start up their own imaginary company so that we could relate their work in a more practical way to an 'actual' business. They liked the idea and so I asked them to meet after the class to decide, amongst themselves, what product their company would sell and to give a name to their imaginary business. At the following class, they informed me that their company was going to make a range of different coloured and patterned tights and stockings, and they had all agreed upon a suitable name: **'Naughty Nylons'**. Inventive I thought, but soon my attempt at making their studies more realistic back-fired on me in a possibly predictable, but definitely spectacular way, albeit with the benefit of hindsight. As soon as they had informed me of their decision, one of the more forthright young women cheekily, but very directly and luridly asked me, "Does a woman wearing black stockings turn you on, sir?" My response was immediate and one of immensely uncomfortable embarrassment, which I signalled by blushing profusely and uncontrollably, whilst attempting to give an honest reply by mumbling something about all red-blooded males, perhaps, find such attire alluring, although I was unsure about the psychological basis that might explain why this might be so. Ahem!

They all thoroughly enjoyed my obvious and immensely cringing discomfort, having been angled, caught and well and truly landed, hook, line and sinker. There could not have been a more difficult moment as a young student teacher, I reflected, later that day, and even to this day. How wrong could I have been? It got far worse for my rouging sensibilities, as when the next lesson arrived, the entire class came attired more like a younger female cast of a St. Trinian's film, wearing black stockings or tights beneath their skirts just to enjoy my further and even more extreme discomfort. I learnt my lesson the hard way – never again!

During my first and second teaching practices in my first two years, I was fortunate to have helpful visiting tutors from the college, who came to watch me teach and to meet with the contact teachers in the schools, who were also always very supportive and allowed me to learn the craft of being a competent classroom performer. The advice and guidance I received was never negative and only ever offered if my various mentors felt that I would benefit from their experience, and the better knowledge that they possessed of the students that I was required to teach.

My third and final teaching practice was longer than the first two, which led to me spending seven weeks with a much fuller teaching timetable in a large comprehensive school in the dockland area of Hull. This practice was also the only one that was formally assessed so as to either 'pass' or 'fail' the student teacher, and so there was considerably more at stake. The school catered for a truly comprehensive intake with a significant number of young people whose behaviour and attitude could best be described as 'very challenging', but I had a really enjoyable time finding various ways to initially entertain and then to teach them something supposedly worthwhile. As I have said before, I find challenging students much more fun to teach than those who are well motivated intrinsically, because their needs are arguably greater and if one can gain their respect and, more importantly, their **trust**, then it can be an immensely rewarding experience.

In my final practice, I taught Economics and Accounting in what was a very well-established and competently-staffed department of Business Studies. In fact, while I was there, one of the teachers whose classes I taught had been a trainee teacher at Hull College before me. He was a tremendous help and I think I learnt more from him (Johnny Butlin) in those seven weeks, and his Head of Department (Mike Parrot), than from any other teacher during all of my teaching practices before, but then that is to be expected as it was a carefully-designed, progressive and developmental, practical learning programme.

As usual, I had my visiting tutor from college who came several times in order to make the final assessment, and if one was either in line for a 'distinction' or a 'fail' then the college tutor was compelled to invite an external tutor, from another university or teacher-training establishment, to come and observe said trainee teacher, in order to confirm the final assessment or verdict. It was, rightly, a sort of fail-safe, which is only fair if facing a 'fail' grade after spending virtually three years at college. What is more, distinctions had been awarded in very few cases over several preceding years, and so achieving one was also something that needed a valuable second professional opinion. Needless to say, I was absolutely delighted when my visiting tutor told me to expect an external tutor to accompany him on a visit during my last week of teaching practice at the school. Strangely, I was not at all nervous at the prospect;

indeed, I was somewhat unusually really looking forward to the opportunity of being assessed as someone worthy of a possible distinction. The day in question was not announced, as I was told to expect them to drop into one or two of my lessons in the following week, which they duly did.

Sadly, I cannot remember a great deal about that actual Accounts lesson that they chose to visit, except for the very beginning, which is an event that is deeply etched in my memory, notwithstanding the passage of time since that day. The background is that when I arrived to start teaching at the school, there were two girls in the class who were known to be particularly challenging in terms of their behaviour and attitude to learning. They customarily sat together towards the back of the room with an empty seat between them. The vacant place was reserved for another female student, who was an habitual truant and, as I had been informed by the usual class teacher, was a key figure among the group as the one whom most of her peers looked to as the one to set the 'mood' of the class. In short, she was what was termed 'a *difficult* student' who enjoyed an elevated peer-group status for being the class ring-leader. By the time she was eventually 'encouraged' to return to school, I had already established a reasonably good rapport and working relationship with virtually all class members, but I had my work cut out to maintain such a relatively positive environment when this forthright and dominant personality re-joined the fold, so to speak.

Without wishing to go into too many details, so as not to inadvertently disclose information of a fairly confidential nature, after a short period of re-establishing boundaries and enforcing them, I managed to not only maintain a positive learning attitude among the class members, but I also succeeded in forming a genuine working relationship with the young woman in question. In fact, she became one of the best allies a professional teacher could ever ask for when facing a potentially confrontational group of teenagers. I still consider the forming of that relationship, and one based on genuine mutual respect, as one of the major achievements in my teaching career to date.

That delightful student often acted as a second teacher or classroom assistant, given the way in which she would help me maintain order so that I could focus on what it was I was seeking for them all to learn (or was it, what I had to teach?). She was occasionally known to tell others in no uncertain terms to behave themselves and concentrate on what it was that *"sir"* was trying to explain or ask them to do. I include this anecdote partly because it was a memorable time for me, and I would like to think it might have been for her as well – I remember her and her name to this day. But I also mention it here because I honestly doubt that I would have been able to manage that challenge had my teacher training at that time been truncated into a couple of academic terms under that which today constitutes a PGCE preparatory programme for professional teachers. The continuous and progressive infusion of theory with practice, and vice versa, over a relatively long period of time had the effect of unconsciously endowing me with a greater understanding of pedagogy and methodology. I am unable to prove this sentiment or belief, as it is something that I intuitively feel to be true, but I do trust my intuition.

Anyway, as the lesson was due to commence and I began to settle the class in readiness, in walked the two assessing tutors, and proceeded unannounced to take up two seats towards the back of the class for observational purposes. At the same time, the three wonderful female students (or 'The Supremes' as I now sometimes refer to them) quickly moved to take up their seats at the front of the class, right in front of the teacher's desk. (Over the preceding weeks, they had 'negotiated' their geographical relocation within the teaching group.) As they sat down, the trio's and class ring-leader looked at me, smiled and slowly mouthed the words, *"We'll be good."*

I was suddenly somewhat thrown, as it had taken me a lot of time and a variety of teaching and learning tactics (or tricks) to establish a productive working relationship with the three young women in question and the rest of the class, and my methodology for the lesson had taken into account that they would be as challenging as usual. I need not have worried, however, as the lesson went swimmingly, and the two observing tutors were suitably impressed to feel that I merited a distinction for my Teaching practice – an achievement of which I still feel immensely proud.

However, I do feel obliged to point out that this favourable outcome was the result of real team work. My support team over those three years consisted of the students in the classes that I had taught during my three teaching practices, my tutors at college as well as the teachers who took a pastoral responsibility for me when I assumed responsibility for the classes that they usually taught on a more challenging day-by-day basis.

As I have already admitted, it is true to say that having followed the longer-term, sandwich-style B. Ed course myself, as opposed to the short-term, crash-course PGCE method of achieving qualified teacher status (QTS), I am inevitably going to be slightly biased in favour of the former training programme. Nonetheless, I do try to view both routes to obtaining QTS as objectively as my autobiographical experience allows, and I am convinced that the B. Ed is **by far** the better option for the reasons given above. I think it speaks volumes that one spends four years studying a broader-based training programme with the specific intention of becoming a professional teacher. Its greater length, as well as its breadth, afford far more opportunities for the trainee to develop his/her skills and knowledge base, as well as to learn how to combine these two elements to achieve and demonstrate professional competence in actual practice.

It is for these reasons that I have become increasingly concerned that the B. Ed option is all but extinct nowadays, with the PGCE enjoying more or less a monopoly status in the teacher training market, and this has caused me to reflect on why it is that this lack of an alternative and, arguably, more enriching choice has arisen. I find it hard to think of many sound educational, methodological or pedagogical reasons to justify the current state of affairs, except that it is *quicker* and, therefore, *cheaper.* It is clearly less expensive for both the providing university departments of education as well as the trainee, although the one-year PGCE programme does follow-on from a three-year specialist academic course of study, leading to preliminary graduate status. It does have the advantage of offering the trainee the advantage of having a specialist degree to 'fall back on' if, after completing the PGCE course and acquiring QTS (following an initial year of service), the trainee decides that teaching is not really the right career choice for them after all.

What is also something of significant concern for me, however, is that the number of teachers who leave the profession after a very short period of time is rising, as is the fact that a sizeable proportion of successful PGCE students

353

decide not to even enter the profession, having *'enjoyed'* the challenges that they sometimes or often encounter when undertaking the teaching practice element of the course. It seems as if many are put off entering the classroom as a career option when they face a demanding group of young people and much of the increasing administrative work-load that is frankly, utterly irrelevant in the main. Perhaps the allegedly and allegorically long and frequent holidays that teachers are stereotypically supposed to enjoy, when they can have endless overseas vacations on the generous salaries that they receive, is not as much of an attraction or benefit as is generally perceived by those who have had the experience of both sides of the 'chalk-face' – unlike so many of the other stakeholders.

Perhaps another explanation for this significant drop-out rate of people who have followed the PGCE course of study is that they are saddled with enormous debts after four years at university, courtesy of the utter, total and absolute **scandal** of student loans. In actual fact, their salary expectations in the teaching profession are such that they do not see much of an opportunity of paying back all that they owe in a reasonable period of time. Furthermore, the additional fact that no repayments are required if one's salary falls below a certain minimum level is unlikely to offer a great deal of fiscal comfort, as most people would like to repay what they owe as quickly as possible, so that they can work safe in the knowledge that what they will earn is for them to dispose of as they wish, at least in theory. Having an unpaid debt hanging around one's neck in virtual perpetuity does little to promote highly motivated classroom teachers, especially when not being able to know when the loan will be fully repaid or written off, and one's ultimate employer is determined to severely limit levels of public-sector pay.

Digression: 'The Double Whammy of Student Loans'

I must confess to being one of the lucky ones, in an historical sense, because I was fortunate to have attended higher education in the days when students and their parents were able to access a means-tested system of government grants to cover not only the cost of tuition, but also a subsistence allowance to take care of fundamental issues such as accommodation, food and a little left over for essential entertainment. I qualified for a maximum grant for three of the four years at Hull College of Education, and I managed to survive my time at college of education thanks to this financial support from the state, which was routinely supplemented by a bank overdraft as each term progressed. In those days, it was also easy for most willing students to find holiday employment which enabled me to settle my negative bank balance by the time each new term was due to begin. Furthermore, I was also extremely fortunate to have had a fantastic bank manager at the Midland Bank on Beverley Road in Hull, not too far from the college. If I remember correctly, his name was George Heathcoate, and he was a wonderful bank manager – a real gem – who understood the financial pressures that students customarily created for themselves during term time. In fact, he and I were on first name terms due to the number of times we had met when I went to my bank branch to agree temporary, unplanned and regular overdraft facilities. The last time we met was when I was leaving Hull and I needed to agree repayment terms of my overdraft at the end of my final summer term. As always, it was a constructive, positive and friendly conversation. His wonderfully memorable and incredibly witty parting comment was that he looked forward to the day when I would be able to start banking with the Midland Bank, as it was in those days, instead of them banking with (or was it 'on') me!

Yes, I readily admit that my family and I were particularly fortunate to have been able to rely on government support which allowed me to attend my wonderful four years in Hull at minimal cost to me and my parents, and to leave with qualifications that set me up for a career in teaching and education. Moreover, when compared to those who follow the same path to higher education these days, I do feel incredibly lucky to have been a recipient of a government student grant. I feel incredibly aggrieved for those young people attending university and college these days, for whom the financial ladder of opportunity that I was able to benefit from has been hastily pulled up by successive governments and replaced with the exact opposite: personal and individual indebtedness! Why and how has this ludicrously unfair and discouraging switch of fortunes been allowed to happen?

This parsimonious, negative and erroneous move has been justified with a far from ingenious argument by the proponents of the current system in which students have been required to pay for their tuition and the subsistence costs during their time in higher education, by incurring considerable debt. The argument, as I understand it, goes something like this: because graduates are supposedly going to end up in better-paid jobs and occupations than those who do not go to university or college, it is only reasonable that they be expected to effectively indemnify the state by shouldering the cost of their individual and collective good fortune and benefit. This is such utter piffle and mendacious logic that it hardly stands up long enough for an intelligent person to knock it down – graduate or not!

This perverse notion that it is only 'reasonable' to contribute to one's higher education owing to the higher salary one may or may not eventually receive is at best a highly partial view of the financial costs and benefits involved for two significant and key reasons: the concept of opportunity cost and the existence of academic inflation. Let me briefly examine these two fundamentally important, additional factors that should be taken into consideration when making a proper and more comprehensive cost-benefit analysis of student loans.

Opportunity cost is one of the core concepts within any study of Economics and is defined as, 'the cost of a good or service as measured in terms of the next-best alternative foregone'. In other words, when I go into a shop and buy a new mountain bike for $600, the real cost to me is represented by the home theatre system that I could have spent my limited income on instead. The $600 is simply the real cost to me measured in monetary terms. After all, money as a medium of exchange or a store of value is simply a means to an end, and is most definitely not an end in itself. Similarly, if I spend five or six years studying in further and higher education beyond the official school-leaving age, then the real or true cost of that option is the income that I could have earned instead, as well as the other non-monetary benefits that I might have accrued had I been in full-time employment during that period. When I attended Technical College for three years, followed by four years at College of Education, training to become an eventual teacher, those seven years involved me in a quite considerable loss of potential income. Indeed, by the time that I had started my teaching career, my friends from the village where I had spent most of my childhood and teenage years, already had a house and mortgage, a car and, very often a wife and family. I had an overdraft that I had to repay, no savings, but with a supposedly and potentially rewarding university degree!

As far as I am concerned, that opportunity cost was my way of 'funding' my way through higher education in the hope that I may end up with greater job security and job satisfaction; I certainly did not end up with more money than many of my friends who earned income whilst they served as apprentice plasterers, plumbers or electricians, for example. The reality for me, however, was that I had effectively chosen not to earn an income immediately, thereby deferring from current consumption in order to spend my time investing in my future. This sacrifice or opportunity cost was the 'price' for spending my time studying for my 'A' Level examinations and, subsequently, my Bachelor of Education degree, beyond the formal school-leaving age, as it was in those days.

Students leaving university and college these days have effectively been required to pay twice for their higher education – once in terms of the income from employment that they have sacrificed, and a second time in the form of the huge debt incurred from the honour of receiving a student loan. And yes, the government and other proponents of student loans argue that there is a failsafe built into the system, in that there is a target income that triggers the need to begin repaying the amount owed thanks to the illusory financial largesse of their student loan. In other words, until one reaches the target income, there is no obligation to begin repayments and, whilst that may be true, the debt still remains, hanging over the one-time student like a financial version of the Sword of Damocles. That must cast a whole new light on the decision as to whether or not to take out another huge debt in the form of a mortgage in order to buy one's first house….assuming of course that one can afford to get onto the 'housing ladder' in the first place. After all, one is unlikely to have enough money for the deposit even if a mortgage is a realistic option in actual practice, thanks to rocketing house price inflation during the years spent in higher education.

In short, I would suggest, that the real reason for the introduction of student loans was just, yet another fallacious, argument put forward by successive governments to effectively justify taxing people, albeit retrospectively, in order to help reduce government spending, and eliminating the one-time government spending in the form of student grants. What serves as a double whammy on the student population and, indirectly, their families, conversely and wonderfully conveniently acts as a double benefit to the Government Exchequer.

Furthermore, rather than viewing the cost of a student attending university as a cost or an expense, it should be recognised for what it really is – an investment; an investment on the part of the individual concerned as well as an investment for the country and society in general. After all, those people who do leave higher education and go on to earn large salaries, also go on to pay more in income tax and sales tax, as well as being far less likely to ever be a claimant for social security payments from the government. In effect, that is a third way in which participants of higher education are paying for the cost of student grants.

Perhaps government should treat other forms of investment in an equally pernicious and egregious manner. Just imagine the outcry from the corporate sector and their well-funded lobby groups, if private business organisations were similarly levied when seeking to invest in order to assure sound and enhanced future prospects for themselves. The reality for such businesses is that they usually receive the opposite treatment in the form of tax breaks, government grants or preferential treatment in order to actually encourage them to invest in the future prosperity of their organisations, as this also is expected to benefit the national economies of the countries in which they are located. What is good for the goose is also good for the gander, after all. Having said this, however, such corporate giants are quick to find ways of avoiding central government taxes, thanks to the smart accountants whom they often poach from the HMRC once they have been trained in all aspects of taxation at the government/taxpayers' expense, of course. This is especially true in the case of multi-national companies who have overseas subsidiaries through which their finances can be 'managed' so that they pay little or no taxation to the Exchequer in the country in which various taxes are levied. To threaten (and in the case of student loans, 'threaten' is the right word) them with what amounts to a tax on their investments would possibly lead to them moving their operations overseas to countries who do not seek to penalise them in such a counter-productive and negative way.

Another significant problem that has been caused by the move to a system of student loans and indebtedness, is that there is now a big incentive for any new teacher to seek a better-paid teaching post overseas in a region such as the Middle East and certain parts of South East Asia as soon as they have finished their initial teaching year and acquired qualified teacher status (QTS). Of course, there is no need for teachers who are so minded to actually serve their initial year to obtain QTS. Instead, they can go straight to work overseas, especially if they are thinking of committing themselves to a career worked outside of the UK, and who would blame them for thinking in such a self-serving way? When one works in one of the countries in the Middle East, the salaries offered are generously competitive to those a teacher might earn in the UK, and this is made even more attractive by the fact that they are often tax-free, which is a considerable benefit.

In addition to a salary which is the same in both gross and net terms, teachers are also likely to receive free, furnished accommodation which means that they do not need to concern themselves overly given the fact that soaring house prices in the UK may well result in them being unable to get onto the 'housing ladder' – that is yet another ladder of opportunity that has been pulled out of reach for many aspiring teachers. Moreover, teachers working in countries such as Kuwait, Qatar, Saudi Arabia and Bahrain are not only going to have nice accommodation provided, but also their employer will offer to pay their utility bills, for such things as gas and electricity, so no need to worry about the astronomical charges levied by such privatised utilities in the UK (which are owned by foreign companies). They will also usually receive free return flights to the UK each year as well as international medical insurance cover, which affords them a high standard of health care without having to worry about long waiting lists. The only real expenditure they need to incur, if they are going to be on an equal footing as if they were working in the UK is to make provision for some form of private pension as they will not be making superannuation payments towards a government scheme.

Having said that, the situation in the UK is that superannuated teachers are being required to contribute more to their government pensions, as well as being expected to work longer before they can receive any benefit from them, and then see their pension payments taxed by the beneficent state at an even higher rate. Furthermore, an important, non-monetary benefit is that the weather is almost always sunny and hot, and this is usually most agreeable when one has been able to acclimatise, unless one is likely to miss the changeable nature and freezing winters of predictably unpredictable British weather.

I first moved to work in the Middle East in 1999, after a couple of years teaching English as a Foreign or Second Language in Italy and Denmark, and I found that my net salary was almost the same as I had received when working as Head Teacher of a large, state secondary school in England, after all statutory deductions had been taken into account. In fact, my standard of living and quality of life was demonstrably and significantly higher as a classroom teacher in Kuwait than it had been as a school leader working in the country of my birth, and for that I am almost uncontrollably angry and despondent.

It was also far less stressful, and yet another major blessing was that I no longer had to kow-tow to the endless avalanche of central government initiatives that have been bedevilling English education for many years now, and there is precious little sign of that abating, let along ceasing. It was a real joy to be able to focus all my energies on 'just' teaching and learning. In fact, if I were a newly qualified teacher in the UK today, then the decision as to whether I should begin my career in England or move overseas, especially in a country offering some or all of these levels of remuneration, would be what is these days referred to as a 'no brainer'.

Having given my own view as to the potential impact of opportunity cost of student loans, the second reason why the imposition of student loans is a complete and utter folly is related to the existence of what has been termed 'academic inflation'. Again, using my background in, and knowledge of Economics, it is true to say that price inflation has the effect of reducing the value of money in terms of its actual purchasing power, or what it enables

360

people to buy. It is equally true to say that the currency of all academic qualifications has also been devalued in terms of what additional benefit they bestow upon those who acquire them in the jobs market. This is because the number of people reaching the required levels to qualify has increased over many years, which in some ways is indicative of the good work that teachers in schools and the academic staff in colleges and universities have achieved. Nonetheless, this does not prevent the detractors of state education, usually on the 'Right' of the political spectrum, from proclaiming that "standards have fallen", and "need to be raised". Exactly what world is it that such idiotic political commentators inhabit?

The truth is that having a degree these days no longer guarantees a graduate a job, let alone one that rewards them with a premium salary that is sufficient to trigger the repayment of their student loan. The argument, therefore, that graduates usually receive better jobs and higher salaries has also been devalued and there is a strong case for a return to a means-tested system of student grants, especially if governments are genuinely committed to increasing and enhancing social mobility which will increase opportunities for advancement and the elimination of poverty to which they have eternally proclaimed to be committed – or is that just political 'smoke and mirrors'?

One final argument against the abandonment of the 'grants approach' to higher education, as well as the imposition of tuition fees which, along with subsistence needs are now funded by student loans, is that the impact has been, directly and indirectly, to affect the number of home students seeking university places. As a result, this has led to institutions of higher education having to market themselves in order to attract a compensating number of overseas students.

To be able to attract a large number of students from other countries also represents a significant boost to the revenues of higher education institutions, because they not only enhance the numbers attending, but such students also pay higher tuition fees for the 'privilege'. Whilst this may appear to be a sensible business decision as far as the universities and colleges are concerned, at a national and international level, this effectively amounts to investing in the human capital of other countries rather than our own. To me, this does seem

361

to be a rather perverse situation when our national governments frequently bleat about the need for the UK to compete more successfully with the academic standards that are achieved by students in other countries, even though such international comparisons are more superficial, spurious and questionable because they also assume the pre-eminence of academe over the development of more practical and, arguably, relevant learning outcomes such as creative decision-making and problem-solving skills.

As far as I am aware, there has never been any form of serious quantitative and qualitative cost-benefit analysis to determine whether there is any net advantage or disadvantage to the UK that arises due to this practice of offering Higher Education places to overseas as opposed to domestic students. I would argue that such a study really does need to be undertaken so that we might be able to determine whether or not this substitution of domestic for overseas students has a positive or deleterious impact upon our nation's ability to compete internationally and hold its own in the world as an economic power.

A careful cost-benefit analysis would also need to examine the political, social and cultural element of welcoming so many students into our country's colleges and universities. For example, overseas students do make good friends with their British counterparts whilst in higher education, and both sets of students may possibly go on to become senior personnel in private and public organisations. Such friendships can then be developed into business contacts which would be to the mutual, economic and financial benefit of the UK, as well as the overseas countries in question. These are but a few of the issues that such a study would hope to highlight and quantify, especially to counter any xenophobic sentiments that offering university places to overseas students might engender in a traditionally conservative country such as the UK.

Regardless of the findings of such analysis, however, there are serious drawbacks with the tuition fees issue and the accompanying student loans system that suggest that it is seriously undermining attempts to increase social mobility, and I for one would welcome and celebrate a return to the availability of means-tested student grants to young people aspiring to further develop themselves through **investing their life time** in higher education.

If we are serious about creating professional teachers, then we really do need to at least reintroduce the option of doing a specialist three or four-year initial teacher training course under the aegis of University Departments of Education, or at specialist teacher-training colleges. Furthermore, all young people who wish to advance their personal development by going to university or college to benefit from higher education, must again be able to apply for a means-tested student grant from the government. This would be fairer and more just, in view of the arguments I have put forward under the headings of 'opportunity cost' and 'academic inflation', and it would also play a central role in promoting genuine social mobility which, in turn, would surely enable the country to benefit from liberating the talents, aptitudes and abilities – the undoubted potential and inner giftedness – that rests within every living soul. To do otherwise is pernicious, wasteful and simply and utterly foolhardy.

Should the government abolish tuition fees now? Put quite simply, the government cannot afford not to!

Chapter Eighteen: Technicians or Professionals?

Training Technicians Instead of Professional Educators?

I have already raised the poisonous issue of the way in which teachers are being held accountable through excessive documentation and bureaucracy which has the effect of detracting from their main professional duty, namely facilitating the learning of young people. Accountability is, of course, important, but not if it becomes unreasonable and excessively time consuming, as a result of the dual pressures of performance or 'league' tables of examination results and also seriously undermines if not destroys the morale of the teaching profession, whose members are the major and irreplaceable resource in the formalised education process. There is also the question of to whom schools are to be held accountable, and for what?

The growing obsession with spurious measures that are introduced under the guise of accountability is becoming, or has already become, tantamount to a catalogue of professional intrusion and disrespect. There are signs that the senior managers of some schools feel sufficiently pressured to adopt what can probably be described as extreme and appalling measures to scrutinise the work that their teaching staff undertake. On 20th April 2014, The Guardian newspaper reported on a survey that had been conducted by the NASUWT, one of the main professional associations which represents practising teachers, into the highly-questionable way in which CCTV is being used in some of their members' schools.

Before going into the gory details of this emerging scandal, it is important to recognise the legitimacy of using closed circuit television systems to improve and assure the safety of students and teachers in school, as well as to help protect school premises and resources. Indeed, when I was a Head Teacher in the UK, I was responsible for introducing CCTV cameras into the school corridors and around the perimeter of the school for these very reasons, especially as the school was situated in an area of notable social and economic deprivation. In such an environment, it was of course a sensible precaution to use CCTV, especially as the school had been broken into on a frequent basis in the evenings and during other school closure periods, with the loss of computers and other valuable teaching resources.

As with all technology, however, it is important to regard it as a tool that has to be used in appropriate circumstances and contexts. In other words, there is a risk that the users are unable to use it wisely, sensibly and in acceptable ways. In much the same way that teenagers need to be discouraged from spending most of their waking lives sat in front of their computer screens, smart-phones and televisions, schools also need to ensure that CCTV is used cautiously, judiciously and only where it is appropriate. A line clearly has to be drawn somewhere, and it seems that some schools have already crossed that line by applying the technology in excessive and some rather dubious ways.

The aforementioned NASUWT survey discovered that CCTV is now being installed in the classrooms with its main purpose being to observe teachers and in some cases to directly monitor their performance. In the schools where CCTV had been installed in classrooms, the teachers concerned pointed out that they were unable to turn the cameras off and were being recorded constantly. In these cases, 55% of teachers said that the recordings were monitored by head teachers and other senior members of the school administration, with 41% claiming that the recordings were used in judging staff. The newspaper report included an actual quotation of one teacher who said, *"In my school it has been used specifically with newly-qualified teachers that the senior leadership team think are not performing well."* In my view, such use of CCTV is not only highly inappropriate, but it also constitutes totally unacceptable and unprofessional behaviour. As Chris Keates, the general secretary of the NASUWT, rightly pointed out, teachers were already being observed by Ofsted and other school inspectors and visitors, and he went on to make an interesting comparison when he said, *"Lab rats have more professional privacy"* than the teachers who were subject to this excessive, unreasonable and counter-productive scrutiny.

The growth of this ridiculous and cancerous degree of accountability, along with the endless, almost constant bombardment of hare-brained, politically-motivated central government initiatives, based increasingly on the whim and prejudices of individual Ministers of Education, is seriously undermining teacher morale as well as their effectiveness as professional educators. They are increasingly being required to act more like technicians who jump through another set of hoops, much like the students are expected to do, without really questioning why they are doing it, and how it benefits anybody very much, if at all. The issue of the value added by such measures really does need to be carefully assessed in order to gauge their efficacy or effectiveness.

Furthermore, there is a concern that this powerful trend is exerting undue influence over the way in which teachers are initially trained, as well as their subsequent in-service training. Teacher training is in danger of having more to do with turning out very effective classroom technicians than with helping to develop creative and imaginative professional thinkers with the capacity to radically and progressively transform what is done in schools so that young people are truly educated as opposed to simply being schooled. Technicians are far less likely than professional educators to possess the flair, the talent and skill-set needed to enthuse and inspire young learners in new, different and exciting ways.

According to my dictionary of choice, the most apt definition of 'a technician' is *"someone who is very good at the detailed technical aspects of an activity."* It seems as though the way in which the tasks expected of a teacher have changed mainly in the interests of irrelevant notions of accountability, suggesting that 'good' teachers are those who do exactly what is required of them by their superiors. Moreover, the same degree of obedience is required of, and from, senior team members due to the externally-driven pressures of government initiatives which are readily enforced and checked upon thanks to the careful and dutiful ministrations of the ever-watchful and increasingly interventionist Ofsted Inspectors.

Completing spreadsheets and checklists, or jumping through administrative 'hoops' does not require a great deal in terms of preparatory training. Of course this may well go a long way to explain the demise of the more specialist Bachelor of Education degree courses, and the concomitant growth of the much shorter-term PGCE teacher-training programmes. In teacher training, much like in schools for the students, the motto of 'horses-for-courses' seems to be an apt way of expressing what is most needed from our august training providers. Thankfully, most university institutes, or departments of education appear to still endeavour to do a little more than this when it comes to readying men and women for a possible career in education. Nonetheless, the short time scale and the more intensive nature of the PGCE route into teaching does seem to be inadequate to more fully prepare such good people for what lies in store for them in the classroom, as I alluded to in the previous chapter.

On the other hand, I feel that teachers need to be considered not just as mere technicians, but as dedicated professionals. My trusty dictionary maintains that, *"professional people have jobs that require advanced education or training,"* and the key word there is that of 'advanced', in terms of the training that teachers require if they are to be treated, regarded as and become real professional workers.

I recently stumbled across an interesting article in the 'Bangkok Post', one of the two main English language daily newspapers, published in the Kingdom of Thailand, which was entitled, *"Teachers must start careers fully trained."* It, naturally, caught my eye, given that its sentiments match my own on this fundamental issue. The author of the article was Joe Nocera, a New York Times columnist, and he was referring to several very interesting books that had recently been published on the theme of education, especially the most recent publication, *'Building a Better Teacher: How Teaching Works (and How to Teach it to Everyone)'*, by Elizabeth Green. Although the book, and the article relate to the experience in the USA, given the manner in which successive UK governments have sought to ape the testing and accountability trend that abounds in America, the same comments ring true in England and Wales, as well as in many international schools.

The article acknowledges that, in the last ten years or so, reformers and teachers' unions have locked horns on the best ways to improve student performance in the school classroom. As I have already noted, this clash of views is typified by the reformers demanding greater *accountability* on the one hand, whereas the opinion of the unions, on the other hand, focuses almost entirely upon greater *autonomy* for the classroom teacher. The former school of thought sees the best way of raising standards in schools, although they rarely explicitly state what 'standards' they are referring to, is by the extensive use of student testing and frequent on-the-job, teacher evaluations. Those who, like myself, believe that a return to greater autonomy is definitely required, maintain that teachers are professionals and should be treated (and paid) accordingly. The common denominator, however, to both of these competing approaches is that teachers are basically left alone in the classroom to figure it out for themselves, as Elizabeth Green points out in her book.

In the USA, as in England and Wales, the increasing reliance on shorter, more intensive, initial training programmes leaves relatively inexperienced teachers in front of a classroom full of young people on the first day of their professional life to do the best they can on their way to eventual success, hopefully. In her book, Green argues that whilst many good souls do manage to achieve this, it does take time, during which there is a significant risk that students in schools are being short-changed by rookie or novice teachers. Moreover, she claims that this is the best case scenario, but with a worse-case situation, a mediocre (or worse) teacher might never really figure out what it really takes to bring the learning of young people alive.

I have also read articles and heard many people, including many of those in the teaching profession, espouse the belief that the best teachers are 'natural-born'. This is as erroneous, ridiculous and harmful as saying that birth-right bestows the ability to be creative upon us, a belief which then allows others to live their lives believing that they are incapable of being similarly new and original. Both views are patent nonsense of course.

According to Elizabeth Green, what it takes to be able to become a competent teacher is for a person to be able to manage a discussion and determine which problems and issues are most likely to get the lesson content across. It is also extremely important to understand how students make mistakes, and how they think, so that a teacher is able to know how to respond to these fundamental variables. She goes on, rightly, to point out that such skills and abilities are easier for some people than others – such is the stuff of human diversity and talent, of course. However, it is vital to recognise that such things can be taught, even to those who don't instinctively know how to perform them, or to behave in these ways.

In her book, one of Elizabeth Green's central characters is a woman who began her career as an elementary, or primary school teacher and eventually became the Dean of the University of Michigan in the USA. Green quotes another person who eloquently noted that watching this person teach was akin to *"listening to chamber music"*, in that it was inspiring, moving and beautiful, I presume. Having said this about her ability as a professional teacher at the time of writing, this skill was something that did not come immediately or easily. According to Green, this now gifted teacher struggled a lot as a young teacher, but over time she improved her pedagogical proficiency and began to codify, initially in her own mind, the practices that made her successful. Not surprisingly, this eventually highly successful teacher asked herself why she hadn't learned any of this before she was left alone in the challenging and vital environment of a classroom.

I firmly believe that this understanding is something that virtually all teachers gradually acquire, and some more quickly than others. For me, I recall very well this process developing within me during my four years as a trainee teacher, something that has matured since that illuminating time. This might explain why, when I started teaching, I was able to prove a highly effective teacher of GCE 'A' Level in both Economics and Law, despite many colleagues, within the school, where I became a fully-fledged teacher, actually telling me that they did not think that 'probationary' teachers, as we were then called, should be allowed to assume responsibility for teaching students who were taking such advanced-level studies.

Now that this more fully-developed teacher, who features as the central character of Elizabeth Green's book, is now the Dean at the University of Michigan, she is seeking to redress what she sees as a central flaw in teacher training in the USA. This central flaw lies in the belief that schools of education tend to value things other than the actual teaching of teachers. She is actively promoting what seems to be a rather obvious approach of ensuring that teachers possess the tools and the skills of teaching before they walk into a classroom on their very first day. In effect, this approach is moving teacher training into a situation where it has more in common with other professions and areas of life, where one must be able to demonstrate proficiency **before** one is able to get a licence to practise. The Dean of the University of Michigan argues that hairdressers and civil aviation pilots are given a level of training that teachers simply do not receive, namely that they should genuinely know how to teach effectively by the time they become practising members of the teaching profession. Learning on the job should simply not be seriously entertained any more, and I would argue that there needs to be a resurgence of the B. Ed route into teaching, as the PGCE is not sufficiently fulsome, substantive or focused on the real job of teaching teachers to become fully capable and competent facilitators of student learning.

More comprehensive and focused, pre-service, initial training would do a great deal to not only better equip intending teachers before they start their careers and ensure that they are fully competent beforehand, but also give greater credibility for teaching to be properly regarded as a profession, in common with those of medicine, law and accountancy, for example.

Furthermore, the teaching 'profession' needs to start acting like they really are a profession in the true sense of the word. To begin with, the teachers need to be in a position to control entry into this vital occupation, by being allowed to determine the entry criteria and set the professional examinations that need to be passed before people can become fully certified teachers. (To be perfectly honest, anyone who wants to become a professional teacher these days, definitely does need certifying.) It should not be something that we leave to the vacuous vagaries of politicians who form successive governments in the UK. After all, their track record in seeking to improve the status of teachers and the efficacy of state education is hardly one that is adorned in glory, as the next section of this book will seek to illustrate.

In the same way as The British Medical Association and The Law Society control the training and admission of doctors and lawyers into the medical and legal professions respectively, so a similar body needs to be established to fulfil a similar role on behalf of the teaching profession. The Institute of Chartered Accountants also has control over the training and admission of potential members into their profession, and so what is so problematic about allowing teachers a similar right. These other professions, by having the ability to control or limit the number of people being granted admission as members over time are effectively exercising control over the levels of remuneration that they are able to command in the market place. The pay levels of doctors, dentists, chartered accountants and other professional workers are such that they are able to earn a degree of what economists call 'economic rent'. Let me explain this economic concept for those who are unfamiliar with the term.

In the interests of economic efficiency, the theory suggests that it is uneconomic and wasteful to pay a person more than they could earn in an alternative job that matches their skills, abilities and aptitudes. Instead, employers should seek to pay workers just enough to keep them in their current job, so that they are not enticed by better levels of remuneration in another occupation or organisation for which they have the necessary ability and qualifications to undertake. This is effectively another application of opportunity cost which is the real cost of choosing one course of action over the next best alternative which one necessarily has to go without. Such is the agony of choice!

To illustrate this, if a person decides to work overtime on a Saturday morning, for example, then they are effectively sacrificing an equal amount of leisure time. They are prepared to do this because they value the benefit they can derive from the additional income from the overtime at work to be worth the cost of foregoing or sacrificing the time they could spend with family or friends, or just relaxing. Similarly, if I am prepared to work as a teacher for a given salary, then it can be safely assumed that the monetary and non-monetary benefits I receive from such an occupation are greater than those I might be able to gain from another job for which I am appropriately qualified or suitable. To keep me in that current occupation, therefore, I must earn just enough money, and/or gain sufficient job satisfaction to dissuade me from changing my job – not a penny more and not a penny less. This level of financial remuneration is known as my transfer earnings, or that which I must earn to stop me from transferring to another job.

In many occupations, however, like the aforementioned professions, the admission criteria are sufficiently restrictive that their governing bodies can create a relative shortage of such personnel, thereby earning their members a scarcity value in excess of their transfer earnings. This surplus is considered economically unjustified and wasteful, as people are being paid more than is

371

necessary to keep them in their current occupations. Having said that, however, those benefiting from such 'excess' are not exactly complaining about their good fortune and, arguably, teachers should be able to benefit similarly, if they are to become true professionals, in every sense of the word.

Becoming true professional workers is a far cry from the recent trend of turning teachers into lower-paid technicians. The teaching profession, as I shall optimistically and prophetically continue to call it, is in danger of accepting a role where teachers do little more than jump through accountability hoops that are put in place by non-professionals. In this role, teachers will be increasingly judged according to their technical skills and their ability to perform them, rather than being developed as individuals who together have a really deep understanding of what teaching and learning should and could become, and how to unlock the inner giftedness that I believe lies within every young person for whom they share a joint responsibility to educate. This involves knowing how to expose the innate talents, dreams and passions with which every person is endowed, so that they can become that which they have the inner giftedness and potential to become. This also involves appreciating that intelligence can be expanded in everyone, if we accept that there are many different types of intelligence, rather than trying to force every young person through the academic 'sausage machine'. All types of intelligence need to be treated as having equal worth, as society and humankind need people with diverse abilities and talents to contribute to the greater welfare, well-being and wealth of us all. Until schooling corresponds more closely with the real education of every individual then teachers cannot really expect to be paid in line with other professionals.

Working increasingly as technicians in this way, teachers are becoming more adept at 'schooling' young people, given the way in which these otherwise professional educators are merely being required to follow established procedures in an attempt to achieve largely externally-set, pre-determined and pre-specified objectives or ends. Alternatively, we could choose to see professional teachers as real learning facilitators who seek to truly educate, enlighten and enable the individual learner to discover their innate talents and destinies in life – diverse as these necessarily will be. In schools today, this is especially important for young people who are not particularly academically able or inclined, and who are, therefore, not really interested or suited to academic pursuits.

What is more, it could be that some young people are genuinely academically able and inclined, but are simply not interested in the knowledge or selected content within a particular learning area or subject that they are required to study in order to meet the requirements of a pre-determined program of learning. In other words, what they are required to study in no way resonates with, or awakens, their innate talents, passions and interests. This is effectively tantamount to a lack of individual freedom. If they do decide to undertake their studies in such situations, then they are adopting a largely mechanical approach to learning in order to negotiate the hoops in order to satisfy the mundane, uninspiring and dictatorial requirements of what we might call 'credentialism' – acquiring pieces of paper to prove that we all possess the necessary 'qualifications' or credentials for whatever we choose to do in life. This is schooling, pure and simple, and has precious little to do with genuine education!

Acting as technicians in this way, teachers are akin to worker drones, slavishly following a pre-determined routine in order to support the colony – the school or learning organisation – so as to perpetuate the system by reproducing others in their own image, so to speak. In this way, technicians are the 'builders', whereas the 'architects' are the professionals who are more interested in leading the process of constructing new ways of learning that match the needs, talents and interests of the young people attending school. These professionals are responsible for creating, reinventing and renewing the ways in which young people can learn. They are responsible for finding new ways to inspire, to facilitate and promote; to encourage, support and develop the learning experiences of the students with whom they work in a professional partnership, along with other community partners or stakeholders.

This demanding, more creative and extensive approach to learning is something that should ideally be incorporated into all initial teacher training programs, showing prospective professional educators how they might be able to develop and manage a network of different learning facilitators and community partners. As I have already mentioned, the potential for such community education ventures to create an extensive and exciting synergy of learning – with the school as a focal point – is considerable and yet to be fully and honestly explored. Such a networking arrangement must seek to genuinely encourage, enable and embrace the involvement of many other people and agencies who have a passion, skill or talent to share with the young people who are interested to learn. This is the best way of utilising those people who have the ability to inspire, engage and enthuse school students of all ages, rather than seeing such others as a serious replacement for a fully-trained, professional educator, who is trained to become adept at managing and directing the learning of young people by linking the natural curiosity of young minds to a wealth of learning avenues and opportunities both inside and outside of the 'school' as a building or place. In this way, schooling has the potential to become more synonymous with genuine education in that learning can take place anywhere and almost at any time.

Other Important Themes for Initial Teacher Training

"Teaching is a creative profession."
"Teaching properly conceived is not just a delivery system."
"We must individualise teaching and learning."
"Curiosity is the engine of achievement."
"Instead of curiosity, we have a culture of compliance."
(Sir Ken Robinson)

I am a huge admirer of the work that Sir Ken Robinson has done for education – for his views, his protestations and his great sense of humour and perspective. For this reason, I felt obliged to begin this section with a handful of some of his most astute observations about what goes on in schools, in the name of education, and how it is high time that this is radically revised and changed. Sir Ken and many others have long since been arguing that schooling is almost the antipathy of true and genuine education, but still the stranglehold of traditional orthodoxy maintains its vice-like grip on the vital business of liberating the diverse talents of our young people, which would otherwise be able to breathe new life into the stale corridors of what we call 'schools'.

Initial teacher training obviously has a massive role to play in this process of much needed and long-overdue transformation of what young people are currently forced to endure during their compulsory years of 'education'. To begin with, courses looking at the philosophy, history, sociology and psychology of education need to refocus themselves to begin by seriously re-examining why young people need to attend school to learn anything that is really useful to them as current and future citizens. This would represent a much better starting point than simply assuming that the status quo is unquestionably worthy of rightfully being the best environment in which young people can learn new, interesting and useful things, because it clearly isn't. Furthermore, if we conclude that there are benefits to be derived by attending a formal school environment, then surely we must rethink the fundamental nature of what goes on in such a context, so that it arouses, ignites and captures the imagination of those who are expected to learn and be developed, personally and socially.

So what specifically should universities and colleges who purport to train aspiring teachers be focusing on and developing within PGCE students, if they are not already incorporating these things within their initial teacher training programs? One key area that seems to stand out, according to media reports and the like, is in the area of behaviour management, so that teachers are better able to deal with low-level disruption in classrooms, as well as the more serious behavioural issues that can occur between students and those that also impact adversely upon the relationship that teachers have with the young people at school, such as verbal and physical abuse.

Sir Michael Wilshaw, head of the British Government's Ofsted (Office for Standards in Education) or school inspectorate, has again made his feelings known about what he claims are the poor behavioural standards that exist in many schools in England and Wales. In an article entitled *'Headteachers too soft on unruly pupils, says Ofsted chief Sir Michael Wilshaw'* (The Guardian newspaper, 25 September 2014), the illustrious chief school inspector is reported as warning that Head Teachers are failing to adequately enforce school discipline. His claims this time centre on the view that these wayward school leaders are guilty of blurring *"the lines between friendliness and familiarity"*, that leads them to tolerate unruly *"pupils"* (that old-fashioned word persists in his lexicon despite its pejorative overtones implying subordination or inferiority), whose behaviour – such as humming and fidgeting – he alleges disrupts lessons and takes up valuable teaching time.

As one might expect, Sir Michael's latest broadside on the teaching profession, especially its leaders, has been roundly condemned by not only the professional associations that represent teachers, but also by many representatives of Head Teachers themselves. Their most effective counter seems to be that Sir Michael's utterances on this matter run contradictory to Ofsted's own findings, in which school inspectors rated 83% of schools as good or outstanding for behaviour and 'pupil' safety in the most recent year (2013-14), compared with 88% in 2012-13. Just to be clear, that leaves 17% as either satisfactory (meeting expectations) or unsatisfactory or poor, unless I am mistaken?

What puzzles, or more precisely, bothers me, however, is why this issue of student behaviour whilst at school has dominated public and professional debate for so long – in fact, many decades, at least! It was an issue when I first started teaching, and it seems to have become increasingly more pronounced, even more intensely pressing, since then. But why? I would suggest that these types of arguments are guilty of missing the point pretty substantially and being more concerned with effects rather than root causes. Surely, the most important question to be asked is *WHY, WHY, WHY* are students so inclined to behave so badly or indifferently whilst at school, if Sir Michael Wilshaw is to be believed?

Perhaps a more constructive question to ask instead is, why are students not so interested, engaged and immersed in what it is that they are supposed to be learning at school, that they come to resent the sound of the end-of-lesson bell or announcement, rather than literally yearning or longing for it? Why are we apparently viewing the students attending school more as conscripts, or unwilling members recruited by a statutory 'press gang', demanding or forcing them to submit, subordinate or suppress their natural, innate talents, interests and abilities to the more dictatorial and seemingly dulling demands of compulsory schooling? Again, it was Sir Ken Robinson who rightly pointed out that when people spend time doing what they like to, then that will help them (and others) identify what are their real talents and capacities in life. Why are schools not focusing more on how to achieve this, as opposed to finding ever more coercive ways of making young people behave whilst following a curriculum largely determined and assessed by undisclosed and unidentified others, instead of by the learners themselves? Once again, the answer would seem to be simply because that is the way we have been doing it for over one hundred years – good old custom and practice!

Perhaps initial teacher training should begin by fundamentally questioning why students need to attend school at all and, if there is a justifiable and substantive need (as I think there is) for this, what is it that they should be learning when they are there, as well as how best to deliver and achieve this more student-centred requirement. This is surely far more worthy and justifiable than subjecting young minds to the boring, predetermined and anachronistic sabre-toothed curriculum that schools have been following for far too long already. Clearly, times have significantly, radically and progressively changed during the last 150 years, so why are schools still soldiering on in such a dull, outmoded and irrelevant way? Well it is obvious isn't it? It is common sense; it has stood the test of time, and so there is no need to fix something that clearly isn't broken. Don't make me laugh!

I also believe that it would be very useful to include elements of educational leadership and management in initial teacher training programs as well. This is because all teachers are effectively managers and occasionally leaders of others, even when they are not formally in senior roles in schools. The concept of leadership has been extended to acknowledge the fact that organisations need lots of people to act as leaders at different times and in different contexts and circumstances. It is, I feel, a major mistake to leave such things until teachers have begun their careers and find themselves, as I did, accepting leadership roles after only one year of teaching when I went from being a teacher in the Business Studies Faculty at my first school, to becoming the teacher in charge of Economics within that broader team, as well as in charge of school fund raising initiatives, which was essentially a whole-school responsibility in a very large comprehensive school in Essex, England. Leading and managing such important ventures should not be left to chance or sheer force of personality. Furthermore, my elevation on the pay scales was largely due to being a good classroom teacher, and because in my first year, I had taken the initiative and organised a highly successful and entertaining sixth-form variety show, and to this day, I cannot remember why I decided to undertake such a task.

I also think that it would be useful to train pre-service teachers in other leadership matters such as whole-school development planning and managing change, as well as encouraging more teachers to see change as an opportunity rather than a threat. After all, schools are dynamic places, even if most of the change leaves the fundamental and traditional issue of how schools determine the curriculum and its delivery largely unaffected; the ruling paradigm stubbornly persists to hold sway. During my nearly 40 years in education and training to date, I have seen a multitude of new initiatives, mainly as the result of government legislation and executive orders, and yet the way in which the curriculum is packaged and delivered has somehow survived the gales of such imperatives; perhaps they were only diversions after all, or just wind instead of gales (pun most definitely intended). I also think that aspiring teachers, who are usually and rightly required to be actively involved in whole-school development initiatives, whatever their source, need to be prepared to understand and appreciate the processes involved prior to actually becoming involved in them. This might make change more meaningful for them, more effective for the school and focused more specifically on aiding and promoting student learning, above all else. They might also be universally more willing participants in the development and change process, especially if school leaders actively involve them in the associated decision making.

Moreover, in this process of whole-school improvement, development and the concomitant change that this involves, trainee teachers should also be exposed to the fundamental issue of values and how these can either support or inhibit, if not prevent, desired and beneficial change. After all, the thrust of whole-school development must, I believe, involve and elicit the views as well as the support of all stakeholders, and not only that of the teachers involved. The process must, therefore, begin with an exploration and reaffirmation of the values that are vital if the alignment and deliverability of the change or improvements are to be assured in actual practice.

I have already provided my views on the importance of two other topics, both of which I feel should feature more prominently in initial teacher-training programs, and they are community education links, ventures and partnerships, as well as that of how to introduce more opportunities for creative learning

378

within all subjects. It is these two very important themes to which I would now like to turn, albeit briefly.

Aspiring teachers ought to be exposed, in the nicest possible way, to the considerable potential for broadening, enhancing and extending student learning that is offered by establishing and subsequently developing genuine community education initiatives in schools. It is not glib, trite or twee to quote the old adage that 'it takes a whole village to educate a child'. It is certainly true, and a potentially powerful concept, and I refuse to accept the negative retort that the villagers are all too busy right now to become involved. Student teachers need to both understand and appreciate the huge potential of such ventures, not only in the way they can impact upon student learning in such a vital and powerful way, but also in the way in which they can bring communities together, communities that have been fragmented by extensive specialisation, geographically, occupationally and by process within one productive unit. Schools can be vital community hubs that network all the various community partners, and advances in information and communication technologies have made the huge potential of such initiatives eminently possible and relatively easily to set up, maintain and maximise. One very easy way to illustrate this point is by referring to the way in which the teacher training institutions and universities themselves rely a great deal on considering, exploring and forging such community links and networking arrangements in delivering their research and learning programs. Furthermore, student teachers could, perhaps, be asked to evaluate the use made of community links and partnerships by the schools where they undertake their teaching practice, and to recommend ways in which their range and scope could be developed in order to more fully realise their potential impact upon student learning, as well as school finances and resourcing.

Doing this would require considerable ingenuity, or creative thought, careful analysis and individual and collective imagination, and this, in turn, demands entertaining, considering and applying possibility rather than playing it safe by always seeking certainty. This is where cognitive creativity comes into play, in addition to the aesthetic and expressive forms of learning which should be at the heart of every school curriculum. In other words, teachers of the various 'subjects' or 'disciplines' which together constitute the traditional school curriculum, need to be taught how to be more creative in their thinking when it comes to devising programs of study, schemes of work and individual lesson plans, so that they can incorporate more cognitive creativity into their planning and preparation for teaching and, more importantly, also into student learning. If this was done with passion, determination and persistence, perhaps we might prepare our young people to use different methods of thinking than those that have led to the problems of today, and overcome our seemingly inevitable and insane propensity to keep repeating the mistakes of history over and over again whilst hoping for or expecting different results or outcomes.

The Fundamental Importance of Effective Communication

Another key skill that simply must be one vital element in all teacher-training programs is that which many theorists see as being of prime importance in leadership and management, and that is the ability to communicate effectively. In my experience, people do not really understand how tricky effective communication can be when they speak and, especially when they write. Teachers, I have found, are no exception. It is a strange irony that so many teachers, who are supposed to, and need to be excellent communicators, are often so bad at communicating effectively with students, with school leaders, with parents and other stakeholders (actual and potential) in the wider community. If you don't believe me, ask any teacher to stand up and deliver an inspiring, engaging and memorable assembly for the school's students, or to speak in public for that matter. In common with other skills, the ability to communicate effectively can be learnt following training and lots and lots of actual practice.....much of which should feature as part of their preparation for entering the teaching profession, especially if they are going to help develop the very same skills in the student populace. They too can learn by doing!

Communication is as much about listening as it is speaking, or reading being just as important before writing and responding. Teachers need to be trained to listen more effectively to their students and be more willing to learn from their interactions with their younger learning partners. This is especially important, if not crucial and pivotal in ensuring that teachers really do facilitate young people to learn that which they – the students – feel is what really motivates, interests and inspires them. In short, teachers have to be trained and encouraged to be significantly more receptive to the needs of the younger learners, so that they learn a great deal themselves. In particular, teachers need to be encouraged not to merely assume that they should treat and interact with students in the way that such relationships were conducted when they were at school, however many years before they take on this influential professional role.

Teachers today, I feel, need to be genuinely, profoundly and keenly interested in the young people whose learning they are endeavouring to foster, facilitate and maximise over time. Teachers must learn to treat young people in a manner which reflects less on where they are now, socially and educationally, and focus instead upon where they could go next, with their options kept open for as long as possible, until they are able to discover their true interests and have a clearer, initial direction in life. Clearly, these current and future contexts need to be inter-related or linked in a realistic, concrete and practical way so that the present merges imperceptibly into the future in a seamless and meaningful way – and meaningful to the individual learner. Teachers, or the facilitators of learning, need to really know and understand – or try to – where their students are coming from, and to be able to do this; and to do this, it is absolutely essential for them to devote a great deal of time listening to the learners to discover what it is that interests, motivates and stimulates their curiosity and willingness to learn, and this needs to be very much an ongoing discourse or process.

In the service of this key process, teachers need to work to negotiate the targets to which the individual learner should aspire so that they are challenged to rise to high and realistic expectations. This would be perfectly reasonable and feasible if the subjects featuring in the school curriculum were only required to develop the core or fundamental concepts of the discipline, without all the pre-specified content or clutter that unknown 'others' deem should be taught, as I argued in an earlier chapter. It is important to note at the outset, however, that if this is to be an achievable proposal, then these targets need to be ones that the learners not only understand, but also want to accomplish, no matter how odd or out of the mainstream these may seem. This is streets better than externally setting the students targets that the teacher, in cahoots with the examination or curriculum 'authorities', dictates are the ones which young people should be required to achieve or accomplish. Because, by definition, 'negotiation' involves mutual agreement and a degree of acceptable compromise, and this is a far better, more relevant and intrinsically motivating modus operandi than students being faced with a pre-determined fait accompli, which has been dictated or determined by those in positions of authority and power, and whose agenda for selecting certain specific content is unknown and potentially open to accusations of indoctrination either intentionally or by default. In the process, students would learn the skills involved in effective negotiation, which are very important in life, whether at home or in the workplace.

In general, teachers need to be more alert to what drives young people as individuals, and to understand them more personally and more profoundly as creatures of emotion and ambition, and I believe that this is particularly true when dealing with students in their so-called 'troublesome' teenage years. I must confess to being in professional awe of those colleagues who take responsibility for the personal and social development of young people who attend kindergarten and even primary school – 'ankle-biters' as they are often described by those like me, who may find them adorable, but equally if not inordinately more menacing, unruly and challenging. Having said that, I have met many such teachers who also willingly confess to being similarly petrified at the prospect of having to be responsible for the schooling of (who they perceive as) terrifying and truculent, even treasonous teenagers. As someone who believes in the perfect-ability of human nature, I genuinely believe that all young people are inherently good, as well as talented, interesting and aspiring individuals, and so it is our professional duty to do our utmost to help them realise these qualities, develop their innate talents and release their inner giftedness over time in their current and future lives.

In order to fulfil this enormous responsibility, I also believe that we, as teachers, must be trained so that we can learn more helpful and natural ways of showing real interest and genuine understanding and appreciation of the daily circumstances as well as the social environment of the young people with whom we work. We need to make a serious attempt to understand what it is that young people are endeavouring to deal with, and how they are often trying to come to terms with the apathy, ignorance and even the hostility of others (usually, but not exclusively) that challenges them and affects their daily behaviour. It helps, therefore, if aspiring teachers are recruited from all walks of life and with as wide a range of life experiences as possible, so that they can empathise with the environments and associated feelings of teenagers especially. This argument also adds further weight to the need for more meaningful and widespread community education, which has the effect of enlisting the support of stakeholders who can play an important part in broadening, deepening and enlarging this pool of adults with diverse backgrounds, knowledge and skills.

Similarly, professional teachers need to share in and celebrate the triumphs, successes and gains, however diverse and multitudinous they may be, as well as share with them their mistakes, failures and losses, so that they see these as the necessary stepping stones to learning things that are really worthwhile. We need to really help young people understand that these set-backs are in no way a reflection of their worth as people, so that they maintain their drive and determination to succeed as well as their confidence and self-esteem. Being fundamentally interested in our students as people rather than receptacles of dubious, if not irrelevant knowledge, will also enable us to enhance their chances of achieving this positive mind-set, even in the face of temporary adversity or difficulty. They need to learn that sometimes it takes many wrong answers to arrive at the right one to a particular challenge. After all, learning not only involves asking oneself questions, but also asking oneself the 'right' questions!

In short, we need to communicate with young people through our everyday behaviours as professional teachers that we care for them and their achievements, and demonstrate in a powerful way that we are partners in their learning, and that we have a vested interest in seeing them aspire and fulfil their hopes, their ambitions and their dreams.

Delivering Stimulating and Effective Lessons

Teachers are increasingly being observed and evaluated in the pressing and pernicious interests of accountability, and yet there is a need for trainee teachers to be well versed in the features that mark out a good lesson, and one that will arouse, maintain and develop the interests of the many different students whose learning they will become responsible for facilitating, helping to manage and occasionally direct. I have been enormously privileged in my career to date, to have had the opportunity of observing many teachers practising their art in classrooms in several countries on different continents, and I honestly believe that good or outstanding lessons are always those that are essentially founded on four main principles, namely *'pace'*, *'pitch'*, *'match'* and *'progress'*. Allow me to explain these a little further by taking each one in turn, although it is important to note at the outset that all four are necessarily and highly inter-related, inter-linked and inter-dependent in actual practice.

As the term implies, *'pace'* is about the speed with which the lesson is conducted in order to cover the intended content and achieve the learning objectives that the students are hoping to meet or achieve. Occasionally, teachers deliver a lesson during which the pace that they adopt is too slow, insufficiently demanding and occasionally pretty much constant for the whole time the students are supposed to be on task. In my experience, the pace needs to be the opposite of this in virtually every case, in that it should ideally be varied, challenging, rigorous, and yet manageable. Learning activities need to be organised in a progressive, continuous way and linked in an active and dynamic sequence so that each section of the lesson is completed successfully in the minimum amount of time needed for each student – a form of educational efficiency, if you like. That is not to say that good lessons are to be rushed through, as that would be akin to students believing that completing the task is more important than learning something worthwhile by working through the steps needed to reach the right or a desired conclusion or outcome. It does mean, however, that given the finite nature of time, it is in everyone's interest to make good use of this limited and precious commodity and not waste it. Indeed, one of the main challenges facing teachers is that young people in the main have not yet come to fully appreciate the significance of their own mortality and, as a result do not perceive any real need to be economical in their use of their life time.

During every lesson, the level of work also needs to be *'pitched'* at a level which is challenging and has high, but realistic expectations of each young person in the class, and this is where the skill of knowing how to do this, and being able to differentiate teaching and learning is so vital. This is why the teacher needs to really know the students that they teach, so that they possess a full and accurate understanding of each student – their preferred learning styles, their ease with the subject matter and their current level of learning. It would be true to say that the art of effectively differentiating teaching and learning through the use of appropriate methodologies and various resources, as well as the judicious use of remedial, reinforcement and extension activities, for example, is the one that all teachers find the most challenging and, even troublesome. Clearly, differentiation by outcome alone – that is by using different test or assessment scores to measure student attainment – is simply not acceptable, as by that stage it is obviously too late to affect student outcomes through timely interventions during the learning process itself.

In addition to pace and pitch, professional teachers need to be able to *'match'* the teaching and learning that they are orchestrating to the specific needs and interests of the young people in their classes. This is potentially extraordinarily difficult owing to the fact that most syllabuses are heavily content laden, with quite specific and pre-specified learning outcomes being given for the teacher and the students to accomplish in, very often, extremely short time spans. How then, can teachers be realistically expected to match the learning materials to the needs of students if there is no freedom of choice over, or negotiation of the subject matter that is presented to the learners. Moreover, how can teachers be expected to match a standardised subject matter to the needs of so many different individuals in any one class? This goes back to one of the central tenets of this book: how is it logically and logistically possible or feasible to standardise diversity?

If only teachers were required to teach their separate disciplines via the core concepts alone, so that they could negotiate the learning context with each student or groups of students, then it would be much easier to introduce a greater sense of meaningful match into the teaching and learning process in a way that captures and motivates the learner(s). Unless this kind of approach is introduced, it is always going to be a major challenge for the teacher to try and find ways to match something that is prescribed and externally-determined to so many different individual needs or individuals. This would require, among other special skills, the teacher to have a detailed understanding of each and every student's preferred learning styles, as well as what s/he is passionate about, and her/his talents and disposition to learning. That is asking quite a lot, he says with more than a soupçon of the English art of under-statement. Doubtlessly, there are teachers who can do this very well, largely, perhaps, through force of personality, for example, but how much more fulfilling it would be if teachers and students could agree together upon the contexts and specific content in which core concepts could be explored, investigated and understood. How truly exciting and genuinely worthwhile that really could be!

For teachers to be able to perform such a task, however, would require them to be trained as real professional teachers, rather than mere technicians, and then given the latitude and greater responsibility to take risks (not chances) with the way in which they help facilitate the learning of every young person, rather than being required to treat them as a largely misunderstood, truculent and disinterested homogeneous blob that is to be recipient of the strictures and diktats of transient government ministers and their often perverse and partial political prejudices. Teachers need a stable playing field upon which to work their 'magic', and not one that is constantly shifting and being brutally shaken, stirred and confused by seismic, party-political whims.

At the end of the day, the most important characteristic of a good lesson is that by the end of any unit of learning, regardless of its duration, students are seen to have made *'progress'*, and progress that is in line with having the highest and most realistic expectations of every single, individual learner. And who said that being a teacher is easy? It is a challenging, positively stressful and potentially immensely rewarding way of spending one's precious lifetime – if only teachers could be trusted, allowed and empowered to act as professional educators and not akin to circus animals who are required to jump through an ever-increasing number of meaningless, diversionary and irrelevant performance hoops, at the bidding of the political ring-master (mistress) of the day, all in the interests of spurious and facile notions of accountability.

Teachers need to be trained to be negotiators of learning with the students they teach. They need to be trained to identify, encourage and sustain the interest of a diverse group of young minds and characters, and they need to be trained as professional educators and not as cheaper, functional technicians and, subsequently, paid accordingly!

As I have claimed in earlier chapters, people are required to live lives that others have mapped out for them. As a result, there are obvious instances when people who become teachers, in common with others in different occupations, find themselves trapped in a job which they do not enjoy and in which they feel no sense of real job satisfaction, let alone any genuine enthusiasm, excitement or passion. To be a professional teacher is to genuinely regard the task as a vocation, rather than 'merely' a means of employment and income, particularly at times when other forms of employment are increasingly hard to come by which, when Tory governments are in power, tends to be the rule. If people feel that they have a true vocation it means, *"They have a strong feeling that they are especially suited to do a particular job or to fulfil a particular role in life, especially one which involves helping other people."* (Collins Cobuild Advanced Learners' English Dictionary) In other words, there is a feeling of altruism that motivates one to seek such a job or role in life and, according to the same source, that key word means, *"To have an unselfish desire for other people's happiness and welfare."* I should, perhaps, point out that the use of the word "unselfish" in that definition should not be used as a reason, or excuse, not to pay people such as teachers and nurses a decent living wage that reflects their value to society, rather than a simplistic view of market value, which is necessarily lower it seems, owing to the number of people who are driven by such noble and honourable motives exceeding the demand for them. Perhaps the market also fails in that it under-estimates, under-values and even penalises the contribution that so many altruistic people make towards our collective social welfare and progress!

What is clearly evident, however, is that whoever decides to pursue a career in teaching these days, faces a demanding, challenging and difficult job if they are to inspire, motivate and facilitate the learning of many young people, who are increasingly uninspired, demotivated and uninterested in much of what is supposed to educate them whilst they attend compulsory schooling until the age of 18 years effectively. This growing trend of disenfranchisement and disillusionment among the school population is hardly surprising given that the learning opportunities they face emphasize the almost unique pre-eminence of academic pursuits over all other forms and types of learning, and that they will be graded and sorted in terms of how well they fare under the 'one-model-fits-all' inevitability of an outmoded, fragmented and partial school curriculum entitlement. What is surprising, however, is that so many young people – who are experiencing the 'fish trying to climb a tree' metaphor – are willing to apply themselves to such a standardised and dull daily educational diet to a greater or lesser extent – or at all!

During their training, aspiring teachers need to be helped to understand that the old, traditional paradigm desperately needs to be radically changed and that they are victims of this masquerade by schools that they are really educating young people, in that they have also been through this failed system. They are victims of the same system, although as those who have performed quite well under this process of standardised and predictable conditioning, they are less inclined to question its validity or consider real, exciting and more embracing alternatives. There is a danger in this of what might be termed 'smug quietism' on the part of these successful victims of the traditional school system, which has survived largely intact after nearly two centuries during which it has quite literally failed so many millions of young people. As Sir Ken Robinson pointed out, *"Reforming is trying to fix a broken model."* What is needed is not reform, therefore, but a fundamental paradigm shift leading to sensitive, courageous and radical change.

Creating more fertile territory for such radical and progressive change could be partly achieved if trainee teachers were encouraged to think outside of the box when learning their craft, so that they would be more willing and able to recognise the deficiencies of the traditional orthodoxy, and to think more critically and creatively. In this way, they might invent or otherwise find better ways of making what they do in the learning environment more educational and less about schooling or shaping young minds. Better still, it would be a smart move to encourage them to ardently and fervently resist 'getting into the box' in the first place, although chances are, their life experiences have ensured that is exactly where they already find themselves. To show how little has changed, consider the following extract taken from 'Deschooling Society' which was published in 1971, in which the author, Ivan Illich, made a hugely relevant observation which remains even more vital, pressing and urgent:

"I believe that the contemporary crisis of education demands that we review the very idea of publicly prescribed learning, rather than the methods used in its enforcement. The dropout rate — especially of junior-high-school students and elementary-school teachers — points to a grass-roots demand for a completely fresh look. The "classroom practitioner" who considers himself a liberal teacher is increasingly attacked from all sides. The free-school movement, confusing discipline with indoctrination, has painted him into the role of a destructive authoritarian. The educational technologist consistently demonstrates the teacher's inferiority at measuring and modifying behavior. And the school administration for which he works forces him to bow to both Summerhill and Skinner, making it obvious that compulsory learning cannot be a liberal enterprise. No wonder that the desertion rate of teachers is overtaking that of their students."

I defy anyone to say that those words do not apply on an even more magnified and intense scale today, compared to over forty years ago; what has really changed?

I feel very strongly, as I approach my 63rd birthday, that one effective way of improving the thinking of practising teachers is to welcome back to the classroom, those of us who had once, idiomatically crossed the Rubicon into senior leadership roles, and who now want to disprove the old adage that there is no going back. After all, age is merely a trick on the eyes, and life expectancy and longevity are increasing and governments are becoming less able to afford the welfare concept of retirement at the age of 60 or 65 years. I have met and know many 'old' young people as well as a smaller number of 'young' older people. I like to think that I remain physically and mentally fit and agile, as well as being a person who feels a burning passion still to teach Economics again.

Sadly, I have encountered a strong and almost insurmountable reluctance by many schools to entertain such a figurative return journey across that legendary, Italian river for people who are more senior in years, especially in international schools, where most of my recent experience lies. What is more, in many countries nowadays, such as China and Brunei for example, new recruits over 60 years of age (and 55 in Brunei) are legally prevented from obtaining a work permit, due to 'ageist' visa regulations. As a result, my desire to relinquish senior leadership roles and prove that there is a lot of life in the relatively old dog yet by returning to an active teaching role has been thwarted by legal and prejudicial laws and attitudes that still would rather see a younger and, arguably, less experienced person standing at the electronic whiteboard.

However, as if to prove that persistence pays off and that there are still open-minded individuals working in schools in some parts of the world, after scores of applications for teaching posts that have been advertised internationally, I have secured a fantastic opportunity to fulfil my dream and teach Economics again, and even as a Head of Department once more. In the next few weeks, at the time of writing this, I shall be relocating to a different continent to show that such a leap of faith in my talents has been well founded and that I can still engage, inspire and truly try and educate young people. I will certainly give my all to prove that the offer of employment was a smart move and not an unnecessary risk. I feel incredibly lucky to be able to spend the next two years at least doing what I have always loved most of all, as well as express my gratitude to those who have given me this wonderful opportunity once more in my lifetime!

Section F: Interfering Government

Chapter Nineteen: Impact of Government Interference

The Long Arm and Dead Restraining Hand of Government

Nearly 30 years ago, I experienced a sudden and urgent desire to work for the Head Teacher of a particular school in Cambridge; I wanted to work for the person who had the wit, the refreshing honesty and courage to write a job advertisement, that was so poignant, direct and to the point. I really would dearly have loved to have worked for the man or woman who was the author of the short piece of persuasive and enticing prose in question.

It happened back in 1986, during my weekly perusal of the Times Educational Supplement, using the staffroom copy in school at a time when I was beginning to consider a move from a Scale 4 (in those days) to become a Deputy Head Teacher. I came across this literally outstanding advert that evoked a veritable series of different emotions within me, from out-loud laughter to an overwhelming desire to share what I had read with all of my colleagues at the time, given its laudable honesty and its succinct ability to summarise the mood, if not the predicament of most teachers in schools at that time.

The fact that it appealed to my own sentiments so perfectly can perhaps best be demonstrated by the fact that I copied the advert onto an overhead projector acetate sheet for possible use in subsequent training, and also lest I forgot its impact upon me. The following is the full version of that advert which had been placed by, I assume, the Head Teacher at Impington Village College in Cambridgeshire:

"Required for September, Deputy Head (Group 11) to join forward looking management team at this 11-18 Village College. Experience of walking on water and doing the impossible by yesterday desirable, but will settle for a highly energetic mortal with commitment to Community Education, and belief in the perfectibility of human nature. Role will be flexible to suit individual talents but will particularly include primary liaison and lower school curriculum."

Needless to say, I was gutted by the last sentence which precluded me from applying, given my specialism in upper secondary schooling and education.

Today, as I write this, I am again considering how much has really changed in terms of the 'mood' of school teachers worldwide, but especially in the UK, in the face of seemingly endless and usually mindless intervention by central government. It is really worthy of some serious and careful consideration in order to assess how much has really changed over the last 30 years, since that advert was published. If anything, the words could apply equally and more powerfully today, although I can imagine that the motivation to be as humorous in today's educational climate may well have been long since eroded away, as a result of the cumulative effect or weight of government and external initiative fatigue on members of the teaching profession, at all levels.

Disillusionment, Demoralisation and a Deficiency of Love

It is commonly understood that the government of the day in Westminster, London – once duly elected – has a mandate to take a leading role in the direction in which state-funded education should proceed, and that means they have the right to set policy and pass laws which prosecute this responsibility and, more questionably, their particular political agenda, which may or may not be in the best educational interests of the young people who attend such state-sponsored institutions. It is not for me to argue that there is anything particularly amiss with what is regarded as part of a fair and democratic system, of course, even if those who are most immediately and directly affected by the educational policies of central government – the students – are in no way involved in selecting these elected political representatives. It is their parents, as well as millions of other citizens who have reached and passed the age of majority who are responsible for electing a government to hold the reins of power at any given time.

Given the fact that most people who vote probably never bother to read the election manifestos of the competing parties and, given the generality of party support, it is fair to say that voting for a particular political party does not mean that one is necessarily in agreement with every policy that the government of the day claims it intends to implement. Nonetheless, the elected government does have the right to 'inflict' its partial will on the entire population in every sphere over which it has a legitimate constitutional responsibility. Since the Great Education Reform Act, passed when Margaret Thatcher was Prime Minister, which heralded a virtual avalanche of endless central government initiatives in education, there has been no discernible let-up in this interference from Westminster in the broad thrust or behaviour of successive governments, regardless of whether these were those of the Labour governments presided over by Tony Blair and Gordon Brown, or the Conservative-Liberal Democrat coalition, recently re-elected as a 'majority' Tory government – heaven help us! (I make no apology for being so openly hostile and fundamentally opposed to anything on the political right, other than 'One-Nation' Conservatism perhaps.)

As I have already mentioned, under the Blair government, the ruling mantra was, *"Education, education, education"*, or to perhaps put it into more accurate language: "Interference, interference, interference!" (It is interesting to note that an anagram of *'Tony Blair MP'* is, somewhat ironically: 'I'm Tory Plan B'!)

Before I get into the more specific problems that I have about this ongoing, invasive and mendacious trend, I want to turn your attention to the overall, general and cumulative damage that its impact has had, apart from almost totally destroying the goodwill of a highly-dedicated teaching profession, upon the education and welfare of the children who have been the involuntary guinea pigs of this central government 'interest' and interference in predominantly state-funded schools. Let us not forget the important fact that the government has precious little influence or control over privately-funded schools, and so such schools are largely able to avoid the pervasive and often egregious barrage of educational initiatives emanating from Whitehall.

I was fortunate to come across another very interesting headline in the Guardian newspaper which appeared on Monday, 30th September 2013. It immediately captured my attention as it was entitled, *"Love has disappeared from state education"* by the Education Editor at the time, Richard Adams. The article refers to a *"wide-ranging assault on the policies of successive governments"* by Tim Hands who, as the Head Teacher of Magdalen College School, was about to become chairman of the Headmasters' and Headmistresses' Conference (HMC). He took advantage at the 2013 AGM of this elite and esteemed group to claim that excessive interference by, and the obsession of governments with infamous and almost universally loathed league tables had, *"emasculated the education system of this country"*. Strong words indeed! He went on to claim that love had long since deserted state-run education and that children were unwitting victims of government's, *"long arm and dead restraining hand"*.

His far from complimentary comments were made at the time when one Michael Gove was secretary of state for education, and he did not exactly mince his words when he went on to refer to the education department as *"the office of the Supreme Soviet"*. Such an attack from someone in such a senior and prominent position within the private-school system is both refreshing and worthy of celebration in equal measure, especially when such schools are (in theory) able to avoid most of the accountability nonsense emanating from the Secretary of State.

Tim Hands, not being content with calling into question the wisdom of, and motives for such central government interference in education, went on to simultaneously identify and bemoan the additional and more surreptitious privatisation by stealth of state education when he pointed out that education, *"is increasingly in the grip of central government and, worse, increasingly at the mercy of much-favoured commercial providers who would like to expand their operations."* Yes, the Tories' true motive for the minimally stealth privatisation of state education is writ large in government policy, so that fundamentally important state education can finally be handed over to private operators as profit-making business ventures, by hook or by (literal?) crook!

Indeed, the article pointed out that the government's construction of new schools, academies and free schools, whilst promising independence from the government, is an Orwellian trick of language that serves mainly to obscure the state's strengthening grip. Hands even suggested, *"There is a real danger that, promised an educational treasure house, adults end up deceived by a shameful political thesaurus."*

But perhaps the most worrisome and fundamental point that Tim Hands made was when he is reported to have said, *"the story of the last 50 years is.....the intrusion of government and the disappearance of the child. More radically put, it is the intrusion of the state,* **and the disappearance of love.***"* What is even more persuasive in Tim Hands' survey of education policy over recent decades is that the time frame he chooses to comment upon results in his evaluation being non-partisan in nature; he appears to condemn all political parties equally. He criticised the misguided drive on academic standards which successive governments since the 1980s based on the mistaken belief that making a child happy was <u>not</u> the first priority of a school. They argued and apparently believed that academic success itself was the route to the inner happiness of a young person attending school, and this perverted logic was evident, according to Tim Hands, in the *"flawed mechanics of league tables"*, and *"the increasing obsession with the curriculum, and especially a curriculum which is prescriptive not liberal; functionalist, not humanist."* On a more positive and directly-related note, Tim Hands pointed out that the less-messed-about independent schools retained a belief in cultivating the moral and spiritual elements of childhood that, in state schools has been replaced by the misguided results-driven agenda of governments over the years. Indeed, according to the article in the Guardian, Tim Hands concluded that:

"Children and childhood are too precious to be abandoned to the anonymous and impersonal guardianship of the state. The state is not currently suitable to direct education unaided or unchallenged because it does not understand the child."

I would go further by suggesting that the state – as represented by different governments over time – does not really know much about schools and what goes on in such establishments, and really does not understand the purpose and true nature of education, as it relates to young children and adolescents, let alone under-graduate adults who attend further and higher education institutions for that matter. For these profoundly fundamental reasons, the state should **listen rather than profess**, should **support rather than enforce**, and should **enable rather than direct or dictate**. After all, we like to pretend that we live in a democracy, where the rights of the individual within society are paramount and to be cherished, as well as upheld. It follows, therefore, that if such a cherished aim is to be more than mere pretension, then those basic rights should be thrust to the fore of all educational initiatives emanating from central government, and not subordinated and/or negated by the political whim of a cabal of government ministers and their private enterprise acolytes, supporters and lobbyists.

Sheer Wrong Bloody-Mindedness

If government is to direct educational policy initiatives in schools with real wisdom and in the interests of the whole country, then there is a preceding assumption that those in government know what they are trying to achieve, as well as what is meant by 'education' when they talk about schools and their collective endeavours. In other words, what are the government (in their infinite political wisdom) and successive secretaries of state seeking to achieve, and how do they know that their 'view' is 'right' for millions of individuals, who inevitably possess a multitude of diverse talents and abilities in a range of currently known and unknown types of intelligence and aptitudes. Quite simply, they do not and cannot know – therefore, they should tread softly and cautiously if they are not to do more harm than good! Furthermore, how can they be so incredibly arrogant as to assume that they do know? What do they mean by 'improving' or 'raising' educational 'standards', and what standards is it that they are talking about – standards in what, for whom, why and measured how exactly? We have to stop being so easily seduced by such bland educational soundbites, or utterances of such little substance, real meaning, or intelligent and relevant explanation.

For example, there was an article in the Guardian entitled, *"OECD: English pupils are 'more practical than academic',"* which was published on 1st April, 2014, claiming that teenagers in schools in England are among the best in the world when it comes to solving problems, according to the first international study of its kind, involving some 44 nations. The study concluded:

"Students in England perform significantly above the OECD average in problem solving (scoring 517 points compared to an OECD average figure of 500). England ranks above the top-performing European countries."

This result was good enough to put England in 11th place in the international table!

Now, you might be forgiven for feeling that such a finding should be the cause for some celebration, but then again, it depends on who you are it seems, as well as what you consider to be the pinnacles of human achievement. Personally, given my belief in the need for a far more creative curriculum, I have to applaud such a finding and ask that it be further promoted and enhanced. This is so that those of us who work in schools can really help to nurture young people who are able to think differently, more imaginatively and laterally, so that we are better placed as a species to intelligently manage our collective affairs with a greater degree of equality in the distribution of income and wealth, as well as positively and sustainably in terms of our environmental impact or footprint. Furthermore, this would do so much to help us all find new and better ways to ensure our very existence in peaceful, individual and collaborative coexistence, where natural justice prevails.

Moreover, my personal view regarding the relative success of our young people being adjudged to be among the very best in the world at problem solving seems even more justifiable when one compares them to the somewhat disappointing results of the previous year's PISA study, also by the OECD, which measured the performance of 15-year-olds internationally in reading and mathematics. That earlier study indicated that literacy and numeracy standards in the UK had shown little or no improvement for some three years. This it seems was despite repeated government initiatives and their myopic emphasis on developing these fairly fundamental abilities over many years before and during the period in question. In fact, students in the UK were ranked 26th in mathematics and 23rd in reading, out of some 65 nations. So much for marks out of ten for successive governments' endless initiatives in terms of raising literacy and numeracy standards in the UK, then, it would seem! (By means of a minor but relevant digression, it might be useful to offer a brief explanation of PISA for those who are not familiar with yet another piece of educational jargon. PISA is the abbreviation for the OECD's Programme for International Student Assessment, which seeks to evaluate educational systems worldwide, by testing students aged 15 years in key subjects, including problem-solving.)

Rather than joining me in celebrating the success of UK students for their success in problem-solving, the Right Honourable Michael Gove, who was Education Secretary at the time, sought to pounce instead on the negative findings for literacy and numeracy that had been published the year before.

Being a typically adversarial politician, he took the opportunity for a rather pointless and childish swipe at the record of previous Labour governments, when he claimed that standards had fallen during their time in office, adding, *"The last government failed to secure the improvements in school standards and (failed) our young people desperately."*

It is sad, but such comments serve little other purpose than to highlight the unhelpfulness of the chronically adversarial political system in the UK, especially in view of the lack of any form of proportional representation in the electoral system that might otherwise promote a degree of consensus. Wouldn't it be so much better if political parties could seek to work together for the benefit of everyone, by focusing on discovering that which unites them, in terms of policy formulation in a whole host of matters political, economic, social and educational, rather than trading in petty insults and pointless point-scoring, by preferring to revel instead in that which apparently divides them?

So it was, then, that a politically-blinkered, or should it be politically obsessed, Mr. Gove moved to introduce a shake-up of tests and exams by making them much more difficult, and concentrating on core knowledge, plus spelling, grammar and punctuation within the national curriculum tests for 11-year olds. This was made an even more regressive and retrograde step by announcing an increasing emphasis on terminal, or end-of-course examinations, rather than coursework. It is important that the reader does not interpret my distaste for all things Gove, within the educational arena, as if I regard matters such as spelling, grammar and punctuation as unimportant; nothing could be further from the truth. They are extremely important indeed, but not at the apparent expense of skills in problem-solving and the eradication of the learning benefits and more reliable assessment afforded by coursework. In fact, Michael Davidson, of the OECD, warned against this kind of 'either-or' response that Michael Gove seemed to prefer when he said: *"It will obviously be important not to squeeze out all opportunities there are to develop problem solving skills now among 15-year-olds."*

Russell Hobby, the general secretary of the NAHT (National Association of Head Teachers) took a more forward-thinking, constructive and intelligent line when considering the OECD's findings, by correctly and wisely identifying that PISA's study into problem solving demonstrated three noteworthy points, the first of which being that such activities are becoming increasingly important if individuals are to achieve real success in their lives and work. Secondly, Russell Hobby rightly deduced that schools can make, and are making, a real difference in developing this vital aptitude within a person's life skill-set. His third and final comment was, perhaps not surprisingly, more robust and motivational, as well as being in stark contrast to that of Mr. Michael Gove, when he rightly celebrated the fact that British schools were performing significantly above average in developing these key problem-solving skills in young people, by saying: *"This last fact is of immense credit to our schools and challenges us to discover how we can do even better."*

Furthermore, Russell Hobby took a more balanced and inclusive line than the combative Education Secretary when he went on to correctly point out:

"It seems that the answers lie both in what you teach and how you teach. Core skills in maths and literacy matter greatly as does knowledge of particular domains. However, it is also important to build an inquiry-based, problem-solving style of learning on top of these foundations."

Well said, Mr. Hobby!

The article in the Guardian to which I refer above, went on to examine the important role that a subject like technology can play in the development of problem-solving skills, by reporting the views of Mike Griffiths, the Head Teacher of Northampton School for Boys, one of the country's most successful state schools. He commented on the school's belief that a strong emphasis on the teaching of technology was fundamental and essential to developing the students' aptitudes and abilities in problem solving. Evidence of this commitment is provided by the fact that 'his' school seeks to encourage all of its students to study the subject up until GCSE, at the age of sixteen years. The rationale for this is succinctly put by Mike Griffiths when he said: *"That's an area where they're always being confronted by design problems and issues like 'how are you going to do this?' It really should pervade all through the curriculum, though."* He went on to also talk about the 'core' subjects of maths and science by saying, *"It's all very well to teach about quadratic equations but it's using them and knowing what you're going to do with them that gives you the kind of practical skills that the British always seem to have had."* I couldn't agree more. If academic studies

402

were to be reinforced by skills and aptitudes more easily identified, nurtured and developed in the technological, aesthetic and creative learning domains – with the latter being the central element of the curriculum, then it could literally *"pervade all through the* (academic*) curriculum"*, as Mike Griffiths says – then graduates from universities might find themselves more employable, assuming that this is rightly one of the main aims of the education that takes place in schools in all countries.

What was also interesting, and encouraging, from the OECD findings in relation to problem-solving, was that boys were found to be better at problem-solving than girls – six percentage points ahead, in the case of English schools, to be precise. Now before I am accused of any misogynist tendencies, please note that I say this only because it tempers and counters the fact that girls are out-performing boys in terms of the more academic curriculum – as a generalisation, of course. Mike Griffiths believes that the success of the students at Northampton School for Boys offers a sound degree of proof to support the view that, *"problem solving is an extremely important skill, rather than just concentrating on rote learning, which may well be necessary for learning the basics."* The importance of arousing and reawakening the creative instincts with which all individuals are naturally endowed at birth, he went on to say: *"We need also to encourage pupils to be innovative and come up with solutions to get round a problem,"* going on to add, *"I would like to think it is something that the British are still very good at."* I believe that we are still good at that, but that we could be so much better still if teachers were allowed to follow their instincts, based on empirical data, and determine the nature of the school curriculum, rather than be confronted by politicians, following their political prejudices instead......and it is a confrontational style that schools generally seem to face in their dealings with central government.

In short, yes, maths, science and English are crucially important, but not at the expense of other, equally valuable types of learning experience. After all, who is to decide what is 'valuable' learning, and by what yardstick of value. I would argue that it is the students who should decide what is valuable to them in their learning, and when, as well as why. If these things are entrusted to the learner, then young people are more likely to be intrinsically motivated to learn them, and learn them well – as well as in context – rather than having them exclusively rammed down their throats at the behest of some other individual, who might possibly be driven by some dubious political motive.

The kind of mutually exclusive mentality that we have been examining above, sadly seems to pervade the thinking of many other politicians. For example, I can recall a comment made by David Cameron, the Prime Minister of the UK, shortly after a fairly recent visit to China, where he was actively seeking to promote business and trade links with that country, rather than perhaps more publicly castigating the Chinese government for its appalling record on human rights, let alone its expansionist tendencies in the region, and the despoliation of the environment, to name but two. Upon his return to the UK, he was reported to have said, understandably full of post-visit bravura, *"Learn Mandarin and not French – the language that will seal tomorrow's business deals!"* I was immediately struck by what seemed to me to be a rather facile, narrow-minded and dictatorial comment to make, especially as he was, in my view quite wrong. Why? Well, because it was again an exclusive and arguably simplistic response; after all, why should students not learn **both** languages or, indeed, choose the language that interests them, and best meets their needs, rather than those of the British economy?

Moreover, if one is going to learn Mandarin, or the less commonly spoken Cantonese for that matter, rather than French, why can it not be motivated by a love of such a splendidly tonal language, or to better understand the country's culture, its music, its food, its people and their customs, rather than for purely mercenary economic reasons? What is more, focussing on these other, more intrinsically rewarding, diverse and interesting reasons for wanting to learn Mandarin, might also then lead on to the development of greater trading links between the two countries by more genuine default. In fact, such an indirect approach may better serve the laudable commercial aims of the Prime Minister, rather than crudely approaching things just to make money, whereby cause and effect (or means and ends) are effectively and inadvertently juxtaposed.

Messrs. Cameron and Gove, in common with some other right-wing politicians, seemed obsessed with emulating all things educational which relate to China, especially when it comes to justifying their limited views on the nature of the subject-based curriculum, and all things American in relation to the drive for even greater testing of students and the accountability of members of the teaching profession. In this respect, such government politicians seem to be more akin to human cushions, in that they bear the imprint – or bum print – of the educational philosophy of the country that last sat on them during one of their expensive overseas junkets, and all at the expense of the tax-payer, not to mention young people and teachers in schools.

At the moment, then, for the likes of Cameron, Gove and other education ministers, it is an obsession with emulating all things Chinese when it comes to what goes on in schools, and like all things obsessive, they can be to the exclusion of all other things of worth, value and importance to individuals and society alike, in much the same way as an obsession with alcohol or gambling can be degenerative, damaging and dangerous for individuals and their families.

As you may have gathered by now, I am an avid reader of The Guardian newspaper in the UK, but I also read quite extensively from a range of sources, both online and in publications. I just find what I read in most other sources, deeply at odds with my own values, or my own belief-system, that means reading them simply confirms the rectitude of my own position as being fundamentally opposed to all forms of social injustice and harmful discrimination, particularly in matters relating to schooling and its antithesis of what would constitute a liberating, enlightening and personally challenging view of education. In view of the Conservative government's current obsession with all things Chinese and mathematical, and my own predilection for rational and relatively independent thought, I inevitably found an article entitled, *'For Britain's pupils, maths is even more pointless than Latin'*, written by Simon Jenkins in The Guardian (18th February 2014), quite compelling as an invitation to read on. It was a brilliantly crafted and argued article, in which the author focussed on the fact that government ministers seem *"gripped by the cult of maths"*, and that what goes on in the classrooms of China's schools, does not hold the key to the future of the British economy.

His article was prompted by the intended visit of Elizabeth Truss, the education minister at the time, to China to discover why Chinese students are apparently so good at maths. Indeed, his opening sentence read: *"There are lies, damned lies and statistics, but worse still are maths statistics."* Quite so!

One of the important points in Simon Jenkins' article was where he referred to research in 2010 by the London Institute of Education which had made it quite clear that Chinese school performance had little to do with the country itself, in that even in the UK, *"Chinese pupils from families in routine and manual jobs perform better than white pupils from managerial and professional backgrounds."* So why the need for a visit – or junket – to the Peoples' Republic of China one might wonder. Jenkins referred to the *"mesmeric appeal"* of a system that Gove and Truss both appear to view more like a state religion than just one particular type of learning experience. In his article, Simon Jenkins went on to explain that, *"The appeal of school maths to control-minded politicians is obvious: it is easy to test, and thus to measure, unlike vague, slippery humanities."* As a result, he went on to make a key point when he wrote: *"British governments gripped in the vice of targets, crave quantification. They have thus made what is measurable important, rather than what is important measurable."* That is such an accurate and honest appraisal of what recent government interference in state education has come to be about.

He cited the importance that the government attached to what Jenkins referred to as *"the OECD's rubbishy but much publicised PISA tables, which put China "top" in maths in 2012."* He continued by commenting on the inherent danger of attaching too much importance to particular sets of statistics, when he pointed out that figures did not refer to China as a whole, as they were based on data from *"booming Shanghai"*. Indeed, the other 'countries' cited in the PISA report were Hong Kong and Singapore – which are effectively *"de facto city states.....shorn of their poorer hinterlands"*. As Jenkins concluded, Elizabeth Truss might just as well have been impressed with comparisons made between *"rural China"* and *"the cities of London and Westminster"*. So what is it about the intellectual allure of performance in mathematics, as opposed to other forms of human endeavour, achievement and learning that make such questionable data so attractive? I found much merit in Simon Jenkins' own admission that he learned maths and had found it to be both personally challenging and enjoyable. Indeed, he admits that *"Algebra, trigonometry, differential calculus, logarithms and primes held no mystery, but they were even more pointless than Latin and Greek,"* in that only a small minority of his contemporaries found much subsequent practical use for, or value in, such topics when it came to living their lives. He further opined that he was not aware of any evidence that could prove *"a causal link between maths and national success or happiness"*. Indeed so. After all, I am very happy in my life these days, and yet I was frankly rubbish at maths, to put it bluntly – or to perhaps more closely paraphrase what numerous maths teachers of mine have told me in the dim and distant past.

The current and dangerous obsession of current government ministers, and most middle class parents it would seem, with the educational efficacy of mathematics is nothing new. Back in those halcyon days when Margaret Thatcher was Prime Minister, her government was driven by its false belief that Britain needed more mathematicians and scientists, rather than better and more creative ones, and this led to skewed spending priorities in favour of such a misguided – or incredibly partial – policy aim. This manifested itself in the government increasing funds for universities for science subjects and research, whilst simultaneously cutting it for the arts. Teachers who decided to teach these favoured god-like subjects were given salary increments as a reward for their sacrifice of the arts subjects – in some kind of twisted and perverse logic that infected the policies and actions of subsequent governments led by John Major and 'Tory Plan B'. Despite this determined push by successive governments, students acted according to their personal preferences, talents and values by choosing overwhelmingly arts-based subjects instead – and as Simon Jenkins rightly points out – the British economy boomed nonetheless.

These misguided and failed spending priorities by a series of governments were predicated upon a false premise and a belief that what had apparently led to their success as government leaders and ministers, supported by legions of equally schooled civil servants, would obviously be the 'right' treatment for future generations of young, less cynical and ambitious minds. Rote learning ruled, as did student disaffection with what passed as education at school. In Simon Jenkins article, he closes by what he refers to the wisest comment on all of this misdirection and wasted effort (as well as money) which was made by South Korea's former education minister, Professor Ju Ho Lee, who, looking at the highest youth suicide rate in the world, declared that *"test scores may have (once) been important in the age of industrialisation"*, but that today that is a long-outdated and irrelevant paradigm which fails to take into account that a paradigm shift has since taken place. Alternatively, he argued, schools must focus their attention on creativity and social and emotional capacities, which are those most appropriate, relevant and necessary for the future.

Fundamental, 'root-and-branch' change is essential, pressing and long overdue, but politicians are stuck with conservatism and are victims of their own outmoded experiences whilst at school. So why should we allow them to continue to proceed with their collective heads firmly buried up their rear ends? Please allow those who are to be directly responsible for promoting the learning of young people, and especially the young people themselves, to decide what it is that should constitute the education that takes place in schools. Better still, would be for the government ministers 'responsible' for education, to work together in tandem with the teaching profession, supporting, offering advice and generous funding in achieving a truly student-centred education for young people at school. Such team-work would enable us all to accomplish so much more, rather than operating in the increasingly distrustful, parsimonious and dictatorial manner which has so adversely impacted upon school students as well as members of the teaching profession at large. More on the damage that such an adversarial, arrogant and archaic centralist approach has caused, as well as how we might achieve a more united stance, will be addressed later in this chapter.

It seems as though the arrogance of government education ministers has a tendency to spill over into indirect nationalism, especially when deciding how to 'raise standards' and allegedly 'improve' the education that is supposed to be taking place in the nation's schools. For some time now, there has been a growing belief in the fact that a broader, less narrowly focussed curriculum would more easily accommodate the learning needs of young people, and I agree with such a sentiment. Personally, I favour the International Baccalaureate program from the early years (PYP), through the middle years (MYP) to the Diploma program (for students usually between 16 and 18 years of age). It is a superior program in so many respects, and the fact that many schools in the UK follow the Diploma Program, alongside the long-standing and more narrowly focussed GCE 'A' Level programme of study, bears testimony to such a belief. So, if government ministers see the merit in encouraging schools in England and Wales to move in such a direction, then why not formally adopt the IB program. It is, after all, a tried and tested program of learning which students and their teachers tend to regard as being of greater educational value. But no, government ministers and others suggest that we should effectively 'reinvent the wheel' by developing our own **English** baccalaureate, or EBacc, don't you know. To be perfectly honest, given the track record of past governments in the field of education, I wouldn't trust them to sit the right way on a toilet, let alone devise a new curriculum and associated methods of assessment.

Putting arguments about such nationalistic tendencies to one side, however, there remains the issue of what might be the best way of going about developing such an ambitious alternative and less Anglo-centric programme of study for our nation's school students. There is/was another excellent article in The Guardian, entitled *'English baccalaureate: another dog's dinner of a plan for exam reform'*, written by John Bangs (an honorary visiting fellow at Cambridge University), published on 17th September 2012. He began by rightly pointing out that in 2005, Mike Tomlinson wrote a wide-ranging review of the external examination system which all young people (14 to 18 years of age) currently experience whilst at school, and he succeeded in achieving an almost impossible consensus between all interested parties on the way to proceed. Unfortunately, this notable achievement was to be, *"blown out of the water by a general election in which neither the Conservatives nor Labour wanted to be seen as the party about to scrap 'A'-levels."* That old chestnut keeps rearing its antiquated head, as successive governments are fearful of being seen as educational saboteurs by the aspiring middle-class, who are enthralled by the educational rightness of those very exams that served them so well, after all; or did they? Instead, the government of the day put forward a proposed English baccalaureate, before having undertaken a serious review of either the current GCSE system at 16 years of age, or thinking to consider the finer details of the new EBacc proposal.

At this point, I do not wish to get bogged down in the detail of the current examination system or the merits of the new English Bacc; instead I want to refer to the way in which the government came up with this new examination and curriculum structure. As John Bangs rightly notes, when Michael Gove entered government, he declared that he would liberate teachers (long pause for ribald and well-deserved laughter). Consequently, this new examination initiative was cobbled together by the two coalition parties (Conservative and Liberal Democrats – an unholy alliance of two fundamentally opposed political philosophies, if their titles are to be believed, namely conservatism on the one hand and liberalism, on the other – what could possibly go wrong?). They concocted this proposed and major piece of educational reform entirely on their own, without any serious attempt to consult the teaching profession, that is the very people who would be charged with its implementation and, no doubt, subsequently castigated should this grand initiative fail to meet the trumpeted political aims that it had inevitably been expected to achieve. More to the point, there was no serious attempt to consult with, or seek any meaningful input whatsoever from the other major stakeholders of state education, namely academics, parents and perhaps, most importantly of all, the young people who might be expected to take the new examination.

As John Bangs so rightly pointed out in his article, ***"In no other profession would such a significant reform be imposed in such a way."*** Please take time to reflect on what that short and accurate quotation is actually saying!

He went on to suggest that the reason why this important initiative might have been formulated in such a way, was because it was mainly intended to act as a form of Trojan Horse, if you will, to move schools away from the fairer, more reliable and valid criterion-based exam system that students experience currently, and return to one that is based on norms, with each grade having a quota of passes allocated to it. Michael Gove and his Tory friends, in cahoots with their Liberal Democrat coalition partners who were probably just happy to be in government for once, have hardly hidden their dislike for the academic inflation that has led to more students getting high grades particularly at GCSE. The government clearly wanted to return to the good old days when the majority of students have to fail so that the minority can continue to rule the waves, so to speak, much as they did before. Such an approach is elitist, dangerous and educationally backward. As John Bangs pointed out, *"Would the same criticism be allied to a rising percentage of people passing the driving test?"* Clearly not – but education, in the Conservative lexicon, is all about identifying 'horses for courses', driving us instead up a dead-end, and precious little else.

It is such a backward (or conservative) approach for any government in the world today to pursue a policy which drives down the percentage of high achievers by reverting to norm-based examinations which, as John Bangs rightly says, have another pernicious effect: *"the possibility of maintaining standards over time is undermined by arbitrary quotas that obscure a consistent picture of what young people can do."* In persisting with this flawed educational nonsense, the coalition government was going in exactly the opposite direction in terms of successfully introducing effective educational reform. In Singapore, one of the city states whose PISA outcomes so readily impress Mr. Gove, arrived at their examination system following an extensive system of consultation with teachers, parents and industry, and an approach that resulted in real consensus as to the right way of proceeding. Another shining example, where student drop-out rates in relation to secondary schooling or education are unheard of, is Finland, who also determine their ground-breaking, evolving and immensely successful state education system as a direct result of cross-party **consensus**, as well as starting with a mind-set that truly values its education system, rather than acting as if it was a political vehicle to achieve twisted, outmoded and partisan 'Victorian' conservative values, based upon everyone 'knowing their place'.

This iniquitous approach to education was evident in all that Michael Gove sought to do when Secretary of State for Education, it seems. He was obsessed about grade inflation at A-level as well as at GCSE level, and called upon OFQUAL (the educational qualifications body) to undertake a crackdown on this pet hate of his. This leads to a very real danger that recent, and genuine, improvements in the examination system at 16 and 18 will be undermined by retrograde action to eliminate coursework, as well as the practical elements of some subjects which are such an essential ingredient in order to give students exposure to the way in which theory can be applied in actual practice. One case in point was OFQUAL's idea to seek to have the performance of students in science practical experiments and laboratory work separately reported so that they could have no impact or effect upon a student's headline grade in 'A' level physics, chemistry and biology. This was based on the belief that students were picking up 'easy' marks in practical exams, and eliminating these from

411

the final award would help to achieve the desired and sought after reduction in 'academic inflation'.

Fortunately, government-appointed Sir Mark Walport, who is co-chairman of the prime minister's own strategic science advisory body, the Council for Science and Technology (CST) was vehemently opposed to such a backward and detrimental step, so much so that he was reported to have warned David Cameron that such a step would further downgrade practical skills at a time when Britain was participating, in what the Prime Minister himself referred to as a global race for economic success. It would, he argued, also be sending a hidden message to schools and colleges that scientific theory was all that mattered in order for students to obtain a good grade in science examinations. This was particularly worrisome given that members of the CST were already of the view that students were not being well enough prepared for undergraduate science courses, and this new proposal would adversely affect students' skill base in the sciences at 'A' level. As another member of the CST, Sir John Tooke (Head of the School of Life and Medical Sciences at University College London) said: *"Experimentation is core to the scientific method. There is a clear sense that reducing exposure to practical classes that are designed to inculcate the requisite skills, rigour and approach would damage the student's understanding and development."* According to The Observer newspaper, he went on to say: *"To achieve these aims practicals need to be more than 'recipes' but rather challenge students to pose research questions and design and execute the means to answer them."*

This is further evidence of how government actions can potentially lead to adverse outcomes in the field of education, albeit indirectly, owing to the prosecution of questionable political fancies, if not fantasies, such as the desire to offset the effects of grade inflation, in this particular case. When The Observer sought a response from the Department for Education, they were told that the issue was a matter for OFQUAL to decide, as if this quasi-autonomous body was genuinely free from political interference. If that were the case, then why would Sir Mark Walport have to raise the issue with the prime minister, one might ask, assuming that the article in The Observer was accurate, of course.

412

I have previously referred to my own involvement in the murky waters of government-inspired educational review and change, when asked to temporarily join the working group that was charged by the Economics Association, at the behest of the Thatcher-led Conservative government, to review the content of all 'A' level Economics syllabuses. My extreme anger and disappointment with the political interference that seemed to prevent that group from offering a more meaningful course content for future Economics students lasts to this day, not least due to the fact that I have now returned to teach the subject again in a school, and in what some may regard as the 'twilight' of my career. I felt partly vindicated at being so annoyed with such a lost opportunity at that time, when I came across an article by the eminent economist Robert Skidelsky, entitled *Economics faces long needed upheaval as students demand right to dissent*', and which was published in, yes, you guessed it, The Guardian, on Wednesday 18th June 2014. Well, let's be honest, it was not likely to reported in right-wing rags like the Daily Mail, The Telegraph or Daily Express, let alone the once mighty Times, before Murdoch got his grubby little hands on that one esteemed title.

The article referred to a manifesto published by economics students at the University of Manchester who are advocating a different approach to the teaching of the subject, and one that *"begins with economic phenomena and then gives students a toolkit to evaluate how well different perspectives explain it."* They succinctly and accurately justified this break from the traditional orthodoxy by arguing that, *"The mainstream within the discipline (neoclassical theory) has excluded all dissenting opinion, and the crisis is arguably the ultimate price of this exclusion. Alternative approaches such as post-Keynesian, Marxist and Austrian economics (as well as many others) have been marginalised."* The students said that the aim of the new approach they were advocating should be to, *"bridge disciplines within and outside of economics,"* so that economics is not divorced from psychology, politics, history and philosophy, for example. I could not agree more firmly with such a sensible and superior approach, and when I taught and teach economics, I have always sought to incorporate these elements as much as possible to bring a practical and theoretical richness to the understanding of the subject matter by the students. This was, and is, in my mind absolutely the right and most vital thing to do, to bring the subject alive, and to give it greater meaning, relevance and usefulness to the lives of the learner.

413

All I can say to this determined new approach to economics by the students at the University of Manchester, and elsewhere, is a big thank you. I fervently hope that it serves to act as a much-needed thin edge of the wedge that leads to a more enlightened, balanced and inter-disciplinary approach to the teaching of the subject at all levels – it is critically and painfully long overdue. In fact, I always find it deeply disappointing when people tell me that they once studied economics but hated it because they found it to be incredibly boring and 'dry'. My answer to such expressed sentiment is always the same: well, it must have been very badly taught, in that it must have been delivered in a dangerously single dimensional way, and almost certainly focused on teaching positive economics, to the exclusion of any normative considerations.

What a Waste!

Before I move my focus onto the effects of misguided, partisan and detrimental government intervention in education, in the way they have currently sought to determine and subsequently steer the debate, I want to briefly talk about the wasteful irrelevance of faddism is education, especially the most costly and ongoing fad of all and that is 'technology in teaching and learning' in schools. I always recall a conversation with Alun Roberts, in the days when I was a trainee teacher, when I asked for his opinion on the use of television and audio visual equipment in the classroom – heady stuff, eh? His response was typically well contemplated, to the point and student focused. He felt that if the use of such technologies improved the motivation of students to learn, then they were to be welcomed, but that they should not, and could not be seen as a realistic alternative to the presence of a well-trained, effective and engaging teacher. In other words, such resources should not be seen as more important than the human element in the teaching and learning dynamic, but merely as a tool, and, like any tool, they need to be utilised appropriately, wisely and carefully, if they are not to prove excessive or counter-productive.

His words, as well as my own reservations and sentiments regarding the current fad for a greater use of information technologies in the classroom, were brought to mind when I read an article which reported that Russell

414

Hobby, as general secretary of the National Association of Head Teachers (NAHT), was dubious about the use of technology as a teaching aid in non-IT lessons (The Guardian, 19 January 2015). Indeed, he went on to say that schools should stop wasting money buying i-Pads and other *"shiny gadgets"* for students and use the funds instead on employing more teachers – hear, hear, I say!

The funds that are being spent on this latest fad are by no means meagre, in that according to BESA (the educational suppliers' organisation) a quarter of a billion pounds sterling a year is being spent on computers in schools. That is a colossal sum and, as an annual figure, it is frighteningly excessive, I would argue. Furthermore, according to Mr. Hobby, that amount of money would be sufficient to pay the salaries of more than 8,000 teachers or build 40 secondary schools, and that is a classic and considerable illustration of the economic concept of opportunity cost, especially in times of extreme economic austerity measures. Russell Hobby seems to share my belief on alternative uses for such vast sums of cash when he was reported as saying: *"I think we'd be better spending the money on recruiting and training great teachers and sticking them in front of old-fashioned blackboards."* Well said, sir!

What I particularly enjoyed and appreciated was his reference to "old-fashioned" blackboards, as I found using blackboards eminently more practical and flexible as a teaching tool. It is a shame that I have to use the past tense of 'find' in the previous sentence, as these days classrooms are adorned instead with whiteboards and 'smart' boards' which, although I use, I find inferior as an efficacious and environmentally-friendly teaching aid.

Let me just make a somewhat tongue-in-cheek comparison of the whiteboard with its photo chromatic opposite, the blackboard, as an example. I find the blackboard a far superior teaching aid than the whiteboard for some pretty basic, if not mundane reasons. If I want to draw a graph, for example, then the trusty blackboard affords the user a greater degree of surface friction. This enables me to draw a straight line with some degree of exactitude. precision and ease, unlike its white counterpart, where the relative lack of friction leads to drawing the axes of a graph, let alone straight-line supply and demand curves, something more akin to a hesitant drunken stagger than a confident and sober swagger. Moreover, the glare from natural or artificial light serves only to highlight what I have drawn on the blackboard, as opposed to obscure or detract from the display on the whiteboard. Also, if I have a box of chalks, preferably of different colours, then I know that I can write or illustrate more or less whatever I want on the blackboard. On the other hand, however, if I have a bag full of whiteboard markers, I cannot be as confident that they will allow me to write clearly, if at all, as the markers evidently have an unhelpful half-life, where they can write, but not sufficiently clearly, before they finally expire, dry out and effectively 'die' altogether.

Additionally, I have always found chalk to be more environmentally friendly than whiteboard markers. Chalk is a natural substance that occurs in abundance, whereas whiteboard markers are made out of metal with fibre tips, and once they have dried out, the habit is to throw them away. This is surely less cost effective than using chalk, and they are more expensive to purchase in the first place. And before anyone talks about the health problems of chalk dust, marker pens are usually spirit based, and this can give the user quite a buzz when breathing in the fumes, and so the health cost-benefit is far from conclusive either way.

Yes, I can imagine that I am laying myself open to taunts from technology lovers that I will be advocating a move back to the classroom use of slates and chalk before long, for the individual student to use. If you are inclined to tease me in such a way, then allow me to refer you to the use of individual white boards in many classrooms today, which are nothing more than a more expensive, and less environmentally friendly equivalent of their even more ancient predecessors – slates and chalk. So there!

The final word on this should, perhaps, go to Russell Hobby when he said, *"We need a suggestion, a goal, not a glossy brochure or shiny gadget. And preferably not a goal suggested to us by a purveyor of shiny gadgets, but one that already existed before we spoke to them. Too often, technology is a solution in search of a problem."* This comment was echoed and supported by Louis Coiffait, of NAHT Edge (part of the NAHT which represents aspiring heads – the fools) who said, *"Billions of pounds are being made by private investors and companies out of education hardware and software"*, and this should make one question the way in which Conservative

416

governments are ideologically introducing more and more ways of introducing private enterprise and the profit motive into their educational initiatives. This adds even further question marks over the nature and extent to which central government muscles in on the genuine improvement of learning opportunities for young people at school, with measures designed to line people's pockets rather than educate a future generation of students.

Enough is frankly enough, when it comes to the recent history of governments becoming increasingly more interventionist in the area of education and schooling. The repeated meddling has largely been counter-productive and has a hugely damaging impact upon student welfare and learning, as well as a massively deleterious effect upon teacher morale and, in turn, the recruitment and the longevity of service of truly professional teachers. I am a classic case in point. Having seen the way things were going and the worrying portents in the writing on the wall, so to speak, I left the UK to live and work overseas back in 1997. The privilege and joy of working with young people, the camaraderie in the staffroom and the generally positive, supportive and constructive relationship between school leaders and their colleagues have all been systematically eroded over many years, and for very little obvious gain.

I have already referred to the most welcome wise words and perceptive views of Dr Tim Hands, the chairman of the Headmasters' and Headmistresses' Conference who, although the leader of the organisation representing the top independent schools, has been highly critical of the damaging effects that endless government interference in education and schooling have undoubtedly had. In September 2013, he voiced *"deep scepticism"* about the wisdom of letting politicians run the country's education system. The way he captured the prevailing mood in schools, and actually articulated this scepticism was beautifully put when he said: *"It would be good if there was a cross-party agreement on issues arising from a consensus among interested parties rather than chucking everything out every five years."* His comments were largely driven by the impending reforms to the examination system at 16 and 18 years of age, which he clearly felt were ill-conceived and, as he put it, the government was attempting to fix a model that wasn't broken, and all that was needed to improve the system was a little 'fine-tuning'. Although I personally believe that what is needed is a radical, root and branch change to the system of schooling, I accept that within the

417

ruling paradigm of traditional orthodoxy regarding education, it is hugely counter-productive to waste the time and effort of the teaching profession on unnecessary reforms. Furthermore, he rightly argued that the timetable and the means by which the changes were being determined, were questionable and unwise, when he said, *"Too few of these exams are capable of being piloted before their introduction – and too much of what has been agreed for the syllabus has been agreed behind closed doors. It would appear some people's personal imprints are on these curricula – the most obvious being history."* He was, of course, obliquely referring to the influence of Michael Gove, who had taken a keen personal interest in the redrafting of the history syllabus, where he wanted more weight attached to British history and a chronological approach to the way in which the subject was to be taught.

Arguing against the changes that Mr. Gove was proposing, he said that, *"GCSEs and A-levels are good tests – if you teach pupils more than just the syllabus."* I could not agree more with that statement, as I have always instinctively sought to do just that when teaching Economics at any level, but especially at A-level. I have always felt a compelling urge to teach beyond the strict confines of the set syllabus, and the students whom I have been fortunate to have taught, have benefited from that compulsion in the main, of that I am quite sure. I feel enormously vindicated by what Dr. Hands said about doing just what I had always felt a natural and intuitive inclination to instinctively do......because it just felt 'right' somehow. In other words, he was referring to the restrictive effects of a subject syllabus as well as expressing the educational merit of not being confined by the prescription alone. Well, just imagine the advantages to be gained by allowing students to choose their own contexts in which to develop their understanding and application of the core concepts of subjects in an inter-related and inter-disciplinary way.

Dr Tim Hands gave an interesting example of such extension and enrichment studies from his own school, (he is the Head of Magdalen College School in Oxford) where every student would spend one period in eight learning something which was not on the syllabus. During these sessions, students would receive lectures from top people in the fields of, say, economics and medicine, and write up their own university style projects that were subsequently reviewed by an adjudicating panel. Dr Hands was reported to

418

have said, *"The commitment to that kind of extra-curricular activity is sometimes not there in government schools because of the pressures they are under."* He is undoubtedly correct, and this is the educational penalty under which all students suffer, and largely in the name of accountability and ill-defined standards. As I have already mentioned, I used to run Economics A-level conferences, attended by students studying the subject at four other local schools, when I was Head of Economics on the Isle of Wight, involving university academics, eminent newspaper journalists and captains of industry, but I am not at all sure that I would be allowed the latitude, or feel that I would have the time and energy to do likewise in one of today's state-run secondary schools. I am so glad that I 'got out' in time, before the trend that was already beginning under Margaret Thatcher's governments gathered momentum and became even more of a cancerous tumour that threatened young people's education.

Dr Hands was reported as saying, *"Sir Keith Joseph, Margaret Thatcher and certainly Michael Gove promoted academic, academic, academic as their curriculum; a national curriculum so we can test you and test you again and then put you under more pressure."* He also went on to say, back in 2013, that if he were to achieve one thing as a result of his year as chairman of the HMC it would be that he, *"would like there to be a proposition that the child is at the centre of education,"* adding that this was something that *"government over-interference in education in the post-war period had regrettably neglected."* A laudable and long overdue aim Dr Hands – thank you, sir, for having the courage to say such things!

Chapter Twenty: Initiative Fatigue

Instead of *'academic, academic, academic'*, a term used by Dr Hands, or *'education, education, education'*, the mantra used by newly-elected Tony Blair back in his day, which I interpreted as *'initiative, initiative, initiative'*, perhaps a more summative and all-encompassing mantra would be: **'pressure, pressure, pressure'**! After all, the cumulative effect of endless government initiatives, apart from sheer initiative fatigue, is to create an educational environment of which a well-heated pressure-cooker would be incredibly proud, if not envious. In short, the end product of all this government intervention, interference or alleged interest in education, call it what you will, has been to destroy the love of learning for learning's sake for children and students alike, and this is totally inexcusable.

Government Failing Students

In October 2014, more than 400 children's writers, parents and teachers sent a signed letter to The Independent newspaper, expressing their concern over the sheer stress levels experienced by students attending the increasingly pressurised environment of *"exam factories"*, or schools in their more everyday vernacular. The signatories of this letter expressed increasing concern at *"the pressure that is being placed on our children"*, particularly as a direct result of the government's apparent love of a regime which involves seemingly endless testing. According to The Independent newspaper (3rd October 2014), the concerns expressed in the afore-mentioned letter had tapped into a storm of debate over the nature of schooling, following John Cridland's call (as director general of the Confederation of British Industry, the CBI) for the *"exam factory"* model of schooling to be replaced by a process that allowed students to receive a more *"rounded and grounded"* education, for their own sakes, and for that of the economy. The signatories of the letter cited their main complaint as being the adverse effects on children and teachers alike of the avalanche of examinations and tests that are increasingly being crammed into school time. They were referring to the greater consequent anxiety and stress levels that students were experiencing, and which were also being felt by head teachers who were increasingly afraid of being dismissed because their schools were failing to meet minimum government targets.

The letter to The Independent went on to state: *"We are concerned to hear of children crying on their way to school, upset that they will not be able to keep up: of parents worried that their four-year-olds are 'falling behind' or their six-year olds scared that 'they might not get a good job'……And we wonder what has happened to that short period in our lives known as 'childhood'."* As Richard Garner, who wrote the article in The Independent rightly pointed out, young children are already required to take a mandatory reading test, after only one year in school. Furthermore, as if to add to the pressure, with effect from September 2015, children aged four or five years of age will be required to undergo a baseline assessment when they arrive at school to identify such skills as counting, and letter and picture recognition. This then leads inexorably on to their later childhood when they will experience the mounting pressure inherent within three consecutive years of external exams in the form of IGCSEs, AS and A-levels. How the hell are schools expected to instil in young people the joy and the thrill of learning in the here and now, let alone lifelong learning, when forced to operate under this kind of externally-imposed madness, all at the behest of an elected government whose members profess to know better?

In late 2013, the Conservative coalition government announced yet another wheeze to eliminate the genuine rise in student achievement at GCSE examination level in the UK, which is often, somewhat unfairly, referred to as 'grade inflation'. The government is, not surprisingly, seeking to revert to the old 'horses for courses' purpose of testing and examining student performance, by wanting to adopt a new, numbered grading system for GCSEs which will make it easier for universities and employers to select high-flying (academically able, that means) students. Indeed, OFQUAL almost boasts that the new system will enable *"greater differentiation"* at the top end, with nine number grades replacing the current seven letter grade pass system. Yet again, the entire school 'education' system is serving one purpose only: to fail a greater majority so that universities can more easily single out the 'brightest' students for popular courses. In short, the government seems anxious to fail (even if in only relative terms) more students, whilst belittling the past achievements of a greater number of young people who had studied hard and deserved their examination successes. This is quite frankly a disgraceful exercise in pure snobbish elitism, and is a million miles away from what I understand to be the true purpose of education, which is designed to enable young learners to discover their true passion and talents, so that they can lead diversely rich, successful and fulfilling lives, from which we all stand to benefit greatly.

If I am perceived to be a little harsh on Mr. Gove, let me refer to a newspaper article ('GCSE exams to be replaced by EBacc', The Guardian, 17th September 2012) which reported Mr. Gove proudly announcing to MPs:

"Critical to reform is ending an exam system that has narrowed the curriculum, forced idealistic professionals to teach to the test and encouraged heads to offer children the softest possible options. It is time for the race to the bottom to end. It is time to tackle grade inflation and dumbing down. It is time to raise aspirations and restore rigour to our examinations."

You have to admit this is a well-crafted piece of grandiose rhetoric, which does little more than to confirm that a larger number of students will be leaving school without any qualifications. If that is the government's view of a successful state school system then I joined the wrong profession. I also wonder if Mr. Gove might have reflected on who might have been responsible for the 'narrowing of the curriculum' and "idealistic professionals teaching to the test", other than government ministers over the years, and the Tories' love of an academic national curriculum (pretty narrowing I suspect) and league tables of school performance, which promote competitive comparison. Enough already!

Rigour, high expectations and excellence are definitely important qualities, but why must this always be achieved at the expense of not allowing all young people to experience worthwhile success at school, in other types of learning apart from the purely academic, and for these achievements to be celebrated with an equal degree of fervour and genuine praise? What was interesting was that in the article referred to above, it was also noted how, the now, Lord Baker, who was the education secretary in Mrs. Thatcher's government of the 1980s, had raised some concerns regarding Mr. Gove's intentions, somewhat puncturing the latter's posturing as the saviour of education in the UK. Lord Baker warned, *"It's vital that schools and colleges provide education which develops practical skills and personal qualities as well as subject knowledge."* I must admit, I found this 'shot across the academic bows' of Mr. Gove's intended reforms utterly refreshing and equally interesting, especially when one considers that both Mr. Gove and Lord Baker were contemporaneously regarded as dangerously misguided and interventionist when in post. Perhaps this minor disagreement is further evidence of the drift to the right on the political spectrum in both Conservative policy making and educational 'reform', although going backwards is a rather odd interpretation of any genuine or progressive notion of reform. I also find myself in unfamiliar territory by being in agreement with Lord Baker, for once! To steal a little from William Shakespeare, an apt expression might be: **'Hubble, bubble and Tory trouble; testing mounts and children crumble'**.

It certainly seems as though it is open season for loopy ideas from the political right, when it comes to possible initiatives to improve state education, or maybe to win a general election might be more accurate. Prior to the last general election in the UK, when the Conservative-Liberal Democrat coalition was replaced by a majority Tory government, unencumbered by the modifying tendencies of their previous minority partners, there was yet another brilliant idea reported (by Felicity Morse, 30 January 2014) on how the Conservatives might win the majority vote in a newspaper article entitled: *Longer school days, shorter holidays and 45-hour weeks 'could be the perfect manifesto to win the Tories the next election'*.

I breathed a sigh of vicarious relief, on behalf of teachers in England and Wales, when I realised that this seriously worrying idea had come from a former policy advisor to Number 10 Downing Street, Paul Kirby, and not the education secretary. It seems as though Mr. Kirby had lost none of his zeal for brilliant ideas, despite being a partner at accountancy firm KPMG at the time of coming out with this cunning plan. He was suggesting, I assume seriously (as it was not the 1st April), that as from September 2016, all state-funded schools would be required by law to provide 45 hours of education per week for 45 weeks of the year. One must admit, it did have a certain numerical symmetry to it, even if was a bloody silly idea. Given the current negative, disaffected and disenchanted attitude that many students seem to have towards attending school for a currently smaller percentage of time, one can only wonder what the practical consequences would be if they knew they were to become compulsorily obliged to spend even more time each day, and for a greater number of weeks in every year in school, as it is currently envisaged. It also seems a universally-firm non-starter in the minds of teachers who are already leaving the profession in their droves due to massively increased work-loads and stress levels, which is just one of the major consequences of past and present government initiatives. I shall deal with this very worrisome trend in a moment, when I look briefly at how successive government actions have effectively sabotaged a once very worthwhile and spiritually rewarding vocation in life for many of my fellow professional teachers.

To be fair to Mr. Kirby, the motives behind his election-winning idea were not all entirely bad, especially as he argued that the longer school day would enable extra-curricular activities to be provided within the school day, so that all students could access them. He also argued that the idea would allow more women to enter the workforce, which would give economic growth a boost, which would be a most welcome and very worthy outcome. What is more, despite saying, *"the role schools play in our national and family life is far too important to leave to teachers"*, he felt that in time, teachers would soon see the benefits of his plan, because the extra time would provide the opportunity *"to explain, to repeat, to explore."* He also argued that increasing things like PE lessons would mean teachers would not have to be in class constantly, as they would have more free time to plan – and PE teachers, as we all know, need no time whatsoever to plan the activities that they offer to our young people, they just kick balls and such like.

I would like to recommend that government ministers and their policy advisors, like Paul Kirby, be compulsorily required to spend a reasonable period of time as teachers in schools, before they are deemed in any way qualified (theoretically or practically) to profess they know how to improve the quality of education that goes on in schools – something that could and should be done without increasing the overall quantity of it. What is required, as I have argued elsewhere, is for a radical overhaul of how we structure and deliver the learning experience. Can I please suggest that such a policy, although it might not win an election, could result in a lot of people voting for the party who made it an essential pre-condition to hold political office? Also, whilst on the topic of qualification for public office, how about suggesting that all ministers of education send their children to state schools, that all ministers of health and their families make use of the National Health Service exclusively, that all ministers of transport use public as well as private transport, and that they are also qualified to drive a motor vehicle as well as ride a bicycle? If we were to insist on this type of eminently reasonable qualification to hold political office then perhaps the post-holders would reap what they sow, and become more aware of the need for change or improvement and how best to bring it into effect.

Needless to say that Mr. Kirby's 'pie-in-the-sky' wheeze to make the Conservatives more electorally popular, also led to some pretty contrary and dismissive comment from people such as the General Secretary of the National Union of Teachers (NUT) and child psychologists, who represent the best interests of both teachers and school children respectively. The former representative, Christine Blower (of the NUT) pretty well demolished Mr. Kirby's plan when she said, *"For many children spending such a long period in school will be counterproductive. Primary school pupils in particular will find it very difficult to concentrate or even stay awake for such long periods."* I can also imagine it would be equally testing for many teachers as well. She did go on to correctly point out to Mr. Kirby that, *"Teachers already work some of the longest hours of any profession with many putting in 50 or 60 hours a week. There needs to be a balance to ensure that both teachers and pupils have time to recharge their batteries."* The article in 'The Independent' newspaper also included the views of eminent psychology professor, Dr. Peter Gray who has called for childhood *"to be given back to children"* and he called for a greater amount of time for play, when children can learn what they want to learn in a more discovery mode of learning.

I would not wish to call Mr. Kirby a sycophant, but his idea to increase the time that students spend in school was more of an echo of Michael Gove's call for longer school days, which was made back in 2013. At that time, Mr. Gove told the Spectator's schools conference that, *"in most successful East Asian education systems"* (here we go again) *"school days are longer, school holidays are shorter."* However, in the newspaper article, Dr. Peter Gray pointed to the work of scholar and author Yong Zhao, who is an expert on schools in China, who said that a common Chinese term used to refer to the products of their schools is *'gaofen dineng'*. What this basically means is that students end up performing very well in tests but badly in virtually everything else. The reason for this is that the young people in China spend nearly all their time studying and, as a result, have precious little opportunity to be creative, to discover or pursue their own passions or develop physical and social skills. Furthermore, following a large-scale survey carried out by British and Chinese researchers, it was found that Chinese schoolchildren suffer from extremely *"high levels of anxiety, depression and psychosomatic stress disorders, which appear to be linked to academic pressures and lack of play."* Sounds good; let's have some more of that effective child abuse if not torture for young people in the UK – blow education, let's just school them a lot more!

Government Failing Teachers

When I started teaching, I was most willing to work long hours in order to be fully prepared to teach both Law and Economics at A-level in the 6th form, as well as CSE and O-level classes for students aged 14 to 16 in subjects like Social Economics and Commerce. The types of qualification and some of the subject titles betray how long ago that was, back in the mid-1970s, not to mention how old I am. The fact that I had experienced the joys and rigours of a four-year B. Ed degree, with three full-time stints undertaking the practice of education in Hull schools, meant that I was under no illusion as to what would await me in my first post, and I eagerly rose to the challenge. I worked every evening and most weekends and holidays, leaving nothing to chance and doing my utmost to facilitate and manage the learning of a large number of students. I thrived on the hours of preparation, and gave all too willingly to my chosen vocation, even to the extent that it was a contributory factor leading to the breakdown of my first marriage. Sorry Claire!

Now that I have returned to the classroom to teach Economics again, I find myself once more working many hours in a week, but with a greater sense of having achieved a healthier work-life balance. I estimate that I now work on average at least 50 to 60 hours a week, and that does not include the time when I am thinking about school and my students when doing other things, especially indulging my other passion of cooking international cuisine, and trying to sleep at night. There are three fundamental reasons, however, why I have never begrudged the hours that I have given my job as a teacher and educationist in various roles.

The first reason is that the work that I do is largely self-directed, in that I can choose what I wish to spend my non-teaching hours working on, although the accountability and assessment trend, which has begun to affect even schools outside state systems of education, has started to intrude into my professional role. I have come to resent that a little, as some of the additional duties that I am required to perform are highly questionable in terms of their educational value or value for money, in terms of the time taken to complete them as is required. Being able to trust my own professional instincts and intuition, based on my experience and observations of other teachers over the years, provides me with enormous intrinsic motivation to work hard. It is almost a pleasure to do this, because I am confident that it will aid the learning of the students with whose education I am partially entrusted, and that they will appreciate my efforts to a greater or lesser extent. As I have mentioned before, education is and should be about profound care, and a love for the young people with whom we are fortunate to work.

The second reason can best be summarised as: 'If you can't stand the heat, get out of the kitchen.' The role of a professional teacher is an incredibly important one in terms of the personal and social development of young people, and if one is not prepared to work the hours that are needed to do one's level best at all times, then my advice is to urgently look for another source of employment. After four years at college of education, I knew what to expect, in terms of the demands on my time, as well as the challenges of managing the learning and behaviour of young people – well, teenagers to be precise. It seems reasonable to me to say that the whole raison d'être of teenagers is to 'test the boundaries', the parameters and expectations placed upon them, either by circumstances, by their parents or guardians or by society at large. It is quite literally a testing time for all concerned – parents, teachers, family members and others with whom they come into contact. In short, being a teacher involves a lot of stress, usually positive and ultimately rewarding, in the spiritual sense of reward, not to mention a lot of hard work in terms of the physical and mental energy expended – it goes with the territory, so to speak.

The third reason for being prepared to give so generously of my time is quite simply that I enjoy working with young people, and so I love the work that I do. In fact, I am driven by a strong personal belief which is that life is too

427

precious and too short to quite literally waste one's lifetime by working in any form of employment that one does not enjoy and for which one feels no real passion. Over the past forty years, near enough, I have occasionally and willingly made what might be called a career change, or I have resigned my job and moved to do something else, on the grounds that I was not enjoying what I was doing. This was usually due to not being able to perform the job that I was charged, required or expected to do in my own way, within the framework of policies and procedures of my employment, without being micro-managed or expected to tolerate unacceptable professional behaviour by my employer. The latter issue is particularly common in international schools, in my experience, where there are some real charlatans in positions such as school owner, director or senior manager.

I gave up my role as Head Teacher in the UK because I was no longer enjoying what I was doing – or not sufficiently anyway. Similarly, I have more recently made the decision to stop being a senior manager in an international school setting, as I felt that I was a little past my sell-by date, especially in relation to having to deal with the politics that such posts necessarily require. I am again doing what I have always loved most, and probably because I am better at it, and that is being a classroom teacher, and Head of Economics, working in a school which is located on an exciting, vibrant and developing continent. In all honesty, my ability to move locations and posts has been made much easier by having a loving and supportive wife, as well as my not being biologically able to father children, which has limited my familial roles and responsibilities. Being childless is both a blessing and a curse, but I cannot say which is greater because if one is dealt a hand then one has an obligation to make the most of it. I often say that as one door closes in life, so several others will eventually open up, and there is no time to regret past choices and events, only learn from them. In any event, the past is over and cannot be changed, so harbouring regrets is really little more than a waste of time and one's mental energy.

The one thing of which I am absolutely certain is that I would not be able to work in a school back in the UK, given the way in which successive governments have trampled most good practice underfoot, having swamped schools with misguided, unhelpful and really unnecessary and damaging initiatives and demands for change....and rarely for the better. I would not be

428

able to work in the UK, because I am absolutely sure that I would not enjoy the role of being either a senior manager or a classroom teacher much, if at all, these days.

The speed and magnitude of suffocating, politically-driven initiatives emanating from central government, have not only increased the stress levels that students feel, but they have also seriously eroded, undermined and, in some cases, eliminated the goodwill of members of the teaching profession. The insidious way in which the morale of teachers has been systematically undermined by this avalanche of political drivel has led to serious recruitment issues. Who in their right mind would want to be a teacher in a school in the UK today? Furthermore those who have made the choice to either train or enter the profession, are not staying in post for very long, assuming they stick with it after what they encounter during their all-too-brief initial teacher training. This professional desertion in itself is a most worrying and growing trend, and when one considers the indirect impact that this must inevitably have on young learners in schools, it becomes a major and alarming crisis!

The truth is that teachers are becoming just as disaffected and demotivated as are the young people who inhabit many schools today, and this is leading to a growing number of teachers leaving the profession after a very small number of years in post. One only has to read the newspapers to read of a catalogue of disaffection, disillusionment and the virtual destruction of the morale of teachers, and their declining willingness to try and withstand the way in which government initiatives require them to perform largely meaningless tasks of seriously questionable value, and all in a vague drive to 'improve schools' and 'raise standards'. The educational landscape has been scarred by governments and the whims or prejudices of education ministers, who don't seem to have the first idea of what education is, let alone what teaching involves, or how to introduce and implement effective change for that matter. What is more, many of these educational initiatives are undertaken against the background, or as a smokescreen to disguise the reality, of reductions in education spending, either in school budgets or in the way in which teachers are initially trained, as well as to further privatise state schools by stealth, in cahoots with a heavily-politicised Ofsted inspectorate.

I have read, with a growing sense of despair and concern, the views of dedicated teachers who have had enough and are either thinking of leaving the profession, or already have. At a more senior level, a newspaper article on the 3rd May 2015, by Sally Weale, summarised the findings of a survey that was conducted by the NAHT (National Association of Head Teachers) which revealed that schools were finding it incredibly difficult to recruit senior teachers. More precisely, it was reported that almost 62% of school leaders were found to be struggling to recruit teachers on the upper pay scale, with 14% claiming to have been unable to recruit deputy heads and some 20% failing to fill posts for assistant heads. Schools are effectively suffering from an exodus from the profession owing to concerns about three main things, namely workload, the level of pay and conditions of work. All of these problems are not only directly caused, if not determined by government policy, but they are also within the gift of central government to alleviate if not solve, assuming the will was there, as well as the wit to know what really needed to be done. No one is claiming that throwing money at the problem, to use a political utterance favoured to excuse inaction and parsimony, will solve these problems, but if the government could and would just **STOP** meddling in education, then things would begin to get a whole lot better. Furthermore, if the government really wants to improve education in schools then they should listen to, and work with members of the teaching profession, rather than viewing them as another 'enemy within', to borrow a term from the late Margaret Thatcher.

The survey referred to above, involved 1,110 head teachers across England and Wales, and was carried out at the beginning of the academic year (or school year as I prefer to call it). It also highlighted the growing concern of those surveyed over the quality of newly qualified teachers (NQTs) upon whom schools had to rely in order to fill vacant posts, and deliver the curriculum. A third of senior respondents claimed that the NQTs they had recruited in the past two years, *"were not well prepared to start working in a school."* Their particular concern was that these beginning teachers were not sufficiently able to control and focus student behaviour in formal lessons, with 73% of head teachers worried about deficient classroom management skills among new recruits. This goes back to the relevance of my comments regarding the dilution of the quality of initial teacher training, due to government policy and budget cuts, not to mention government initiatives to allow adults other than teachers to take classes in schools – it is cheaper you know, and 'cheap' is a good epithet to attach to recent government actions in the public sector of the economy.

Another newspaper article published on 31 March 2015, reported on figures disclosed at the previous day's Association of Teachers and Lecturers conference which revealed that only 62% of teachers were still in the profession a mere one year after achieving QTS (Qualified Teacher Status). To put this another way, nearly 40% (four out of every ten) of teachers decided to quit the classroom after one year of service. Such a figure is both alarming and scandalous, not least because it represents such a waste of money in training those leavers in the first place, as well as painting a pretty damning portrait of the state of British education today. It is patently clear who is accountable for such an appalling waste of public money, not to mention the difficulties which it inevitably poses for schools who wish to deliver the entitlement curriculum. The article estimated that the cost to the taxpayer of training this unhappy 40% of NQTs to be a little under **one billion** pounds sterling. Successive governments and politicians are clearly the major culprits in this national debacle – no one else; they are to be held accountable, to use one of their favourite words!

Speaking at the conference, Dr. Mary Bousted, general secretary of the ATL, said: *"It is sad but true that students and newly qualified teachers are being told by teachers they meet during their training that with current workload, inspection and training this is no career to enter."* She went on to add that, *"too many school leaders drive their teaching staff to do things which add not one jot to the quality of teaching but to bureaucratic work, filling forms, inputting data and using three different coloured pens for 'deep marking' and so on."* She also spoke about the fact that in addition to the problem posed by the 40% who quit the profession prematurely, there was a growing trend of serving professional teachers who were leaving their posts before they suffered from the greater likelihood of ill-health, mainly because teaching has become a profession which is incompatible with a normal life.

Teaching in the UK is a profession in crisis and Mark Baker the ATL's president rightly pointed out that teachers today face, *"so much bureaucracy driven by mistrust, driven by an unquenchable thirst for data but so utterly pointless."* This is so much more than a financial waste, but also a waste of incredibly passionate and talented individuals who decide that teaching is just not for them. In her speech, Dr. Bousted said that it was the *"wrong time"* for the profession to face an exodus of staff as schools were facing a *"tsunami of curriculum and qualification reforms."* These reforms were being undertaken at the behest of OFQUAL, the exams regulator, which Dr. Bousted said was, *"staffed by fundamentalists – true believers who worship the exam,"* because they are convinced that written examinations completed under strict timed conditions are the best way to test a student's knowledge in a subject. (As I mentioned in the section of this book on assessment and testing, such an approach is backward and omits so many other and more important types of human achievement and accomplishment than it seeks to include and measure.) The article reporting on the ATL conference also included the experience of a 45-year old English teacher who admitted to having left her secondary school in order to quite simply get her life back.

Another, earlier newspaper article (30th August 2014) referred to the short teaching career of another opt-out individual after a mere three years in the profession. The article was entitled: *A teacher speaks out: 'I'm effectively being forced out of a career that I wanted to love'*, and reported on the experience of Sam Burton who had also had enough, and decided to leave the teaching profession. He cited the seemingly pointless nature of the administrative burden of his job which was compounded by the unrealistic hours of work that he was having to undertake. More worryingly is the way in which teachers often feel almost victimised by senior managers in their schools, rather than supported and aided in their endeavours. Sam Burton talked of the one thing that the three head teachers he had worked with had in common and that was their apparent inability to change things, largely because their hands were also tied by the same external demands for accountability and good data, demanded by an increasingly out-of-touch government. This is such a sad indictment of successive education secretaries and their part in the effective destruction of such an important profession, and vocation for so many decent men and women.

Successive governments have evidently got it all wrong, as numerous newspaper articles written by outstanding teachers who are leaving, or have already left the teaching profession illustrates. This amounts to what can best be described as a catalogue of ministerial shame. What is more, I can tell that these individuals are/were outstanding teachers from the way in which their articles are written and how they explain their approach to working as a teacher; this fact shines through the disappointed, often very angry but remarkably restrained prose. Furthermore, the fact that they feel motivated to write and explain why they are leaving, perhaps with a sense of personal defeat, bears testimony to the fact that they are professionals who really care about teaching and learning, as well as the way in which the state-school education system is being ruthlessly undermined and wrecked by ignorant politicians, who are driven by ideological motives with little or no regard to either the young people who attend those learning institutions, or the teachers who work there. Central government needs to heed the old saying that rightly suggests when finding yourself in a deep hole, the best policy is to stop digging – and enough really is enough already! The time for a time-out, a rethink and a new approach, or a return to the original way of running (as opposed to ruining) children's education that existed before initiative fatigue became initiative overload and eventually systematically encouraged an exodus of teachers from such a vitally important profession. When one considers how Jeremy Hunt and the Cameron Tory government are treating junior doctors working for the NHS currently, one might be forgiven for thinking that the government are actually deliberately trying to destroy state provided education and health care, whilst appearing to be seeking to improve such vital services. In short, depress the state providers, ruin and seek to discredit the publicly provided systems, whilst simultaneously allowing private operators to open 'for-profit' academies and private hospitals.

Out of all the many depressing articles that I have read about new government initiatives which illustrate the dogmatic ignorance of so many education ministers, the one that really stood out was from one of the aforementioned outstanding teachers (*'How Michael Gove's reforms drove me out of teaching'*, The Guardian, 5th August 2014). Her name is Liz Palmer and she admitted to being a 30-year old outstanding teacher who had just left the profession and moved to live in France to run a ski chalet with her husband, another disaffected ex-teacher. What she had experienced and how she felt about effectively being professionally abused by relentless government interventions in education was beautifully and powerfully articulated. I just wish I could include the whole article here, as it encapsulated the cumulative emotions of so many dedicated professional teachers. She is undoubtedly a major loss to the teaching profession. As she says, from the sanity of her new life, *"The damage to education has been done and will take a long time to fix."* For sure!

Before giving up teaching altogether, and for reasons that she describes as self-preservation, Liz Palmer even opted to take a reduction in her pay as a result of deciding to work part-time. She wrote:

"According to all the different criteria against which I have been judged, despite constant shifting of goalposts, I have been outstanding. I worked hard; I delivered engaging yet academically challenging lessons – despite us all being told that these two concepts were mutually exclusive; I assessed pupils in rigorous detail against ever-changing marking schemes; I completed fatuous administrative tasks within all deadlines. I was at the top of my game. I should have been seeking promotion opportunities. Instead I found myself, along with my pupils, becoming increasingly insignificant. Now the school to which I gave my twenties is haemorrhaging good and outstanding teachers."

Her article can hardly be dismissed as purely anecdotal evidence because it is one of many such articles, and the desertion rate of teachers from the profession illustrates an obvious groundswell of disaffection and disillusionment. I feel that it is long overdue to re-visit and revamp Sir Kenneth Baker's statement made at a Tory Party Conference, and say, **"For far too long, education has been in hands of political ideologues and needs to be returned to the loving, caring and intelligent hands of the teaching profession,"** assuming it is not too late already, given the seemingly perpetual damage that has been wreaked upon it. I shall close this section by incorporating a few more snippets from Liz Palmer's article, a person who I intuitively feel would make an excellent minister of education!

"I also cannot work in a system that prioritises political gain over the good of our young people."

"….yet again it was the children who suffered the fallout of a politically motivated decision. They had worked hard to meet the rules of the game that they were playing, then those rules were changed."

"While trying to teach young people, I attempted to gain their interest and meet their individual needs. This is the point at which my educational philosophies diverge irreparably

from those of the government: I see children as individuals; today's ministers see them as a mass that must be trained."

"The public throughout the years of the coalition government, has been empowered to distrust teachers. But it is this government that has failed pupils."

"We now have a generation of pupils who have been trained that their individual opinions and skills are invalid, that reading is only worthwhile if the text was written by a white, British man; we have a generation of disaffected teachers, who are woeful about the notions of change (even if it is sometimes for the better); and a generation of school leaders that has been told that managing teachers must involve distrusting them. Politicians may be transient, but attitudes are not. The rot has set in, its effects will be felt for years."

Again, I say that one might be forgiven for cynically believing that the previous coalition government and the present majority Conservative lot are hell-bent on completing an effective dismantling of the public sector, and the wholesale handing over of the state system of education – well, at least the bits that can be privatised and subsequently exploited to make nice healthy profit – to the private sector. In the process, there are numerous illustrations of the government contradicting itself in terms of the nature of various initiatives, as well as having to reinvent the public sector machinery, or wheel that once existed to manage schools – by which I am referring to Local Education Authorities (LEAs).

The last few years in the UK have seen a rash of new types of school being allowed to open, and OFSTED inspections have arguably become a political weapon, whereby otherwise good schools are abruptly deemed to be unsatisfactory, leading to them being recreated as academies or free schools, which are effectively privately operated. As a result, in November 2013, it was reported that Michael Gove, who was still education minister at the time, was to appoint a new layer of bureaucracy to oversee the burgeoning number of new, privately-run schools (*Michael Gove to appoint new regulators to oversee free schools and academies'*, The Guardian, 20 November). It is worth remembering, at this point, that it was the public-sector hating Margaret Thatcher's governments that led to the demise and reduced role of LEAs in the first place, with the Greater London Council being eradicated for entirely political reasons. Londoners now have a flaxen-haired buffoon and self-publicist as

435

their Mayor to represent them instead – another improvement in representative democracy perhaps.

The newly-publicised plan is to appoint powerful school regulators called chancellors, by a Government who finds regulation an ideologically abhorrent idea, who would then work within eight geographical regions that would be created, operating separately from local councils and LEAs. Each new regional area (oh, what to call them?) was to be supervised by a new body to be known as a Head Teacher Board (HTB) with the new post of chancellor to oversee each of them. This need to create a middle tier between individual schools and the Department for Education (DfE) in Whitehall was apparently the result of months of wrangling following the difficulty the DfE had been experiencing in overseeing this glossy array of new educational institutions, which had been largely set up in order to replace state-run schools.

I am not in the least surprised by the need, although the reason for it suddenly becoming apparent smacks of ministerial incompetence in terms of not having a long-term plan for the establishment, management and oversight of these new creatures, which were themselves the product of government initiatives after all. It would seem as if ministers blunder from initiative to initiative, depending on the political wind, or wheeze, of the day, dealing with the 'fallout' using sticking-plaster measures as and when they become necessary. 'Badly thought out' is a phrase that springs to mind here. I know that Mrs. Thatcher was the daughter of a grocery shop owner, but her heirs seem to have precious little idea about how to manage a business, especially once the grocer's shop has become a national chain.

Any school student of Business Studies will know full well that centre-periphery models of management cannot be expected to work efficiently or effectively if there are a large number of peripheral units emanating from the hub or centre that have to be controlled and overseen, much in the same way that centrally-planned economies cannot control all enterprises from central government due to factors such as distance, communication problems and sheer cost. Think of the enterprise as a wheel, with the DfE representing the hub at the centre of the wheel, and the spokes representing the separate links which join the centre to each and every individual school across England and

Wales. At the time of writing, since 2010, more than 3,444 schools – including over 50% of secondary schools – have, for one reason or another, become academies or free schools. Such new-found status allows these institutions to operate largely outside the supervision of LEAs, and bestows upon them greater freedoms over the curriculum, as well as teacher's pay and conditions. Correct me if I am wrong, but it seems a little odd and lacking in forward planning that if these new schools are allowed greater freedom over the curriculum, then why did a previous Conservative government introduce the very concept of a National Curriculum in the first place? Another inadvertent contradiction, perhaps, and further evidence of government pronouncements on education being little more than the whim of individual education ministers, which hardly allow schools to plan ahead and seek to effect long-term improvement.

It seems somewhat incongruous that if this new bureaucracy were to be put into place it would create a two-tier-system of schools – those academies and free schools that fall under the aegis of this new regulatory network, and the remaining secondary schools which remain loosely allied to LEAs. The way in which the political tide is turning is pretty clear for all to see, and all justified under the notional opportunity of individual choice. Uhm.....

I leave the final word on this initiative to Russell Hobby, the general secretary of the NAHT who understandably gave the move a cautious welcome when he said: *"Opinion is pretty united on the fact that there ought to be something between schools and the secretary of state."* Even GCSE Business Studies students concur with this view. Mr. Hobby continued, *"The idea that we should have some organisation with local knowledge and insight operating between the two is right, but we need to know the detail."* I would suggest that we already have this necessary intermediary in the form of existing LEAs, and this point was diplomatically alluded to by Russell Hobby when he said: *"In particular, we need more information on how local authorities would fit into this new structure, since **we would want to avoid duplication** and **90 per cent of primary schools still look to their local authority for local oversight.**"* (The highlights are mine, and I would hope for reasons that are pretty obvious in light of what I have said above regarding the political agenda and central government seemingly figuring things out as it goes along.)

I make no apologies for referring to so many newspaper articles as I have not been working in schools in the UK since 1997, something which I celebrate, as it has largely enabled me to avoid being sucked into the sorry state of affairs that we call the state-sponsored education that goes in schools there. I have attempted to use admittedly anecdotal evidence, but all very much from the horse's mouth, with the horse being a collective term referring to teachers, head teachers and senior managers, and journalists who seek to report the facts, so as to avoid legal action.

For a number of years now, we have seen endless initiatives emanating from central governments of various political beliefs, and this unfortunate trend has had some pretty major outcomes to date. To begin with, they have collectively taken education, particularly the curriculum and how we assess student achievements, out of the hands of professionally-trained and experienced teachers and wilfully handed this over to politicians, civil servants and, often, unqualified others. I would go on to argue that such initiatives have been based more on political fancy rather than any substantive reason, especially when one considers that after so many years of government intervention, there is precious little evidence that state education has improved very much if at all. This evidence is clear because the governments still feel the need to continue to interfere, with apparently no over-arching blue-print, other than politically-driven prejudices. These initiatives have tended to focus on the symptoms of alleged under-achievement rather than the root causes – which I have attempted to outline in previous sections of this book. In particular we are still all operating within an outmoded and traditional paradigm, which has led to very little substantive change to what schools seek to do, or how they do it, for more than one century.

Furthermore, government initiatives have ignored or been blind to the fundamental and immensely powerful, but essentially 'hidden' messages that are communicated through the way in which we structure, or package, and subsequently deliver the education that goes on in schools, with the outcome that they seriously undermine our stated aims, as well as most – if not all – initiatives that are introduced to be put into effect. A further indictment is that these central government initiatives have clawed power to the centre, whilst pretending that they are extending and enhancing 'choice', which is more a notional opportunity to choose rather than any real, genuine personal freedom. This is especially true when it comes to the right of the learner, the individual student, to choose what they wish to learn, when, how and with whom. What about devising a system that truly honours and genuinely bestows the right of self-expression and self-determination upon our young people, for example?

Education Interruptus

The reason why this litany of central government failure has come about is due to the political obsession of successive Conservative governments which seeks to shrink the role of the state. It is an ideological belief and has absolutely nothing to do with ways of improving the education that occurs in our nation's schools. In common with the failure of schools to truly educate young people, successive government actions have in the main had nothing really to do with school improvement, as they both suffer from the same basic flaw, and that is the fundamental arrogant belief that adults and politicians know best, and so the correct way forward is to tell others what to do, as well as how to do it in many cases. As Stephen Covey's work, among others, has powerfully argued, such an approach is doomed to fail as we are not enabling the individual child, or the individual school, for that matter, to find their own voice. I would argue that before all this centralist nonsense began in earnest, with the Great Education Reform Bill, back in 1985, schools were doing very well in finding their own voice, and experimenting with ways of designing a more liberating and engaging curriculum that would hopefully help more young people discover their individual and collective voice. This was enabled by the work of many good LEAs who largely sought to work with schools, rather than against them (with some notable exceptions), in sharing interesting and good practice, as well as supporting in a variety of ways school improvement, through professional development initiatives in the form of in-service training for teachers.

I feel it is important to acknowledge that not all government initiatives, from Labour and Conservative governments, have been wrong headed and ill thought out, and having solely negative outcomes, but the way in which they have failed to always have the desired outcomes has been mainly due to not

439

properly understanding schools or, indeed, how to effectively and efficiently implement change over time. Also, due to the failure of initiatives in practice, this has given greater impetus to the increased politicisation of the initiatives, and the belief that the failure was down to schools seeking to thwart government intent. This incorrect view may go a long way to explain the introduction of greater accountability measures, in the belief that compulsion might effectively force schools to do the centralist bidding enshrined within government policy on education. Unfortunately, instead of having the desired effect, the barrage of attempts to 'up the ante' in such a way has led to the alienation of the very practitioners who were supposed to implement these often conflicting orders emanating from Whitehall, and the expensive loss of so many valuable members of the teaching profession in the meantime.

I would argue that the failure of government initiatives to improve education in schools can be attributed to several fundamental factors or errors on the part of the government. The first of these lies in a stunning lack of clarity in terms of what each particular initiative was designed to achieve in everyday practice, and what it would look like if successfully implemented in schools – that is, in terms of actual behaviours and concrete outcomes. In short, too much political rhetoric and a fatal lack of practical realism. Secondly, the party political motives of some initiatives have tended to over-shadow and detract from the educational benefit that they are intended to accomplish, vague though these so often are, other than simplistic soundbites like 'raising standards'. Thirdly, and allied to the previous points, it is quite clear that successive governments were grossly unaware of the steps that they should take in order to effect the desired improvements in relation to how they should actually manage change. This has led to an increasing emphasis on seeking to dictate and virtually force change to happen, rather than adopting an approach which would be more likely to succeed. Such an alternative way forward would have necessitated consultation and negotiation, or processes which would involve listening to and involving teachers at all stages of the proposed change, beginning with what it is that we are collectively trying to improve and why. Admittedly, this would have taken more time, a commodity of which politicians seem desperately short, due to the nature of the adversarial party political system. As a result, politicians are in too much of a hurry to be seen to do something to justify being in office that they rush through the implementation of half-baked ideas which are almost bound and pre-destined to fail, and when they do, the need is to find a scapegoat – the truculent teaching profession and the unions. If one were to believe what some government ministers say, you would think that teachers are a bunch of lazy individuals whose sole motive is to undermine or even destroy the education of young people who attend school. Whilst I would accept that teachers could be better trained and more focused on facilitating learning rather than teaching the syllabus, the reality is that the vast majority of the teaching profession are dedicated and caring individuals who devote a vast amount of time and energy to the personal and social development of young people, and for relatively little financial reward, especially if one were to calculate their pay for each hour actually spent on school work, either in school or at home.

Another reality that is essential to the successful management of change is institutional readiness, in terms of getting the key change agents to perceive the need for change in the first place, and then possess the intrinsic willingness and ability to effect it in their everyday practice. In this regard, individual schools and the teachers who work therein are just like individual learners – they are very much a 'mixed ability' group, and so a good starting point would be to recognise and understand this, and then act accordingly.

In his incredibly insightful book, 'One Out of Ten', Peter Hyman, the one-time educational adviser to Tony Blair and the Labour government who eventually taught in a school, refers to the 'School Improvement Reports' which was edited by Tony Attwood. These reports, based on actual school improvement in practice, rightly acknowledged that the power to effect change exists within each and every single school itself. Hyman and Attwood admitted that this was something of a radical perspective at a time when the real power in education has been shifting away from teachers, and towards central government, and for such a long time – a trend that has continued and become more harmfully acrimonious since the publication of their work. In other words, individual institutions or schools can only develop and grow when the teachers (including head teachers) who work within them recognise the need for improvement and decide to take steps to achieve what they themselves know to be right. School improvement does not and will not happen by dint of anything imposed from without, whether that be government initiatives or league-tables, simply because those who will be required to effect the changes do not see the need; in short, they do not 'own' it or, as the Americans say, 'buy into' it, and so they have precious little incentive to make it happen, regardless of external accountability measures and the threat of sanctions being imposed upon them should they fail to achieve the externally-imposed agenda. In fact, such an imposition is likely to result in genuine hostility among those who are required to implement change, as we have seen in the earlier part of this chapter. The agenda for change must essentially, fundamentally and necessarily arise from **_within_** the organisation!

Such a view makes obvious sense when one accepts that schools are all different, at different stages of development, in different areas and with their own different and unique culture. Consequently, their individual needs are all going to be different and, where they are similar, one school may have progressed further with the desired improvement than another, and in a totally different way. On this veritable sea of individual difference a government initiative ship is launched which has been christened with the politically-attractive name 'One Policy Fits All', imploring, urging or demanding all individual ships' crews to do the same thing, at the same time and expect them all to reach the same port of destination. Good luck with that philosophy; it isn't going to end well, and with press-ganged, as opposed to enlisted crew members those ships are heading for the rocks marked 'mutiny' or at best 'desertion'.

If I may be allowed another analogy – that of doctor and patient. Different patients, even those suffering from the same ailment, have different physiologies, are of different ages, live in different types of environment with differing degrees of opportunity, and perhaps suffer from different other maladies. No cure-all regimen prescribed by their doctor is going to be very effective in achieving an overall recovery success-rate. All change or improvement necessarily occurs within a very specific context, environment or set of circumstances. One initiative most definitely does not fit all, in much the same way that one curriculum model cannot possibly be expected to meet the needs of every individual learner – it is unrealistic madness to think that it might. All change must begin with where the learner actually is at any moment in time, and not where one would like them to be, or thinks that they are. Change is, if nothing else, fundamentally contextual in nature.

What is even more worrying is not only that externally imposed agenda for change are destined to fail, but also that their impact is to, as Peter Hyman puts it, *"throw existing school development off track because the school feels obliged to follow the orders from above."* Such externally-imposed obligations can sometimes carry the force of law, implying sanctions for those who do not seek to obey or live up to the mark. I am reminded of one such legal obligation which was designed to fulfil Margaret Thatcher's governments' desire to impose 'The Six Rs' upon state schools (which was a rather inaccurate mnemonic for reading, writing, 'rithematic, right, 'rong and religious education), and that was 'the daily act of collective worship', which also had to be broadly Christian in nature. When OFSTED came visiting, I had to be able to offer plausible explanations justifying why the school where I was Head Teacher was not following this statutory obligation, imposed by the Tory government. I remember my excuses very well, and the first one was that, as a confirmed atheist, I considered it might be a tad hypocritical, if not a little disingenuous of me to lead such an assembly, and there were no other members of staff who felt both willing and able to lead such a daily event. Finally, as a school of some 750 students, we had no space where we could accommodate a gathering of us all, and the playing fields in mid-winter, when it was blowing a gale and with rain lashing down were probably not a venue that was conducive to such a celebration for those of faith. Fortunately (or unfortunately), we did not obviously have any students who had alternative religions and faiths, which would have provided another logistical, if not ideological problem. I went on to say that as a school we did ensure that the main Christian events, such as Christmas, Easter and Harvest Festival were celebrated in style, inviting members of the local clergy, as well as other members of our school community to lead and attend respectively. I thankfully managed to avoid prison for the school's almost inevitable legal infraction in the circumstances.

Another reason why government initiatives have largely all failed is due to the fact that there are too many of them at any one time and they are often too contextually vague for the individual school to act upon, even if they wanted to. Additionally, the change the government seeks may be at odds with the

443

school's own development or improvement plan, or even their mission and vision statements, and the reason why schools have such statements is due to previous government requirements. Also, please note, I believe that these were good and right-minded requirements as part of the need to devise school development or improvement plans that would avoid the institutional inertia which would have an adverse effect on student learning over time. Added to the sheer number and incredible vagueness of government initiatives, especially in terms of how they would alter actual practice in schools, failure is also often a result of the fact that initiatives and external requirements change far too frequently. This is not only due to the fact that governments change, according to the political party or parties elected and taking up power, but also because education secretaries or ministers of education change even more often, with each individual seeking to make their political mark – or leave a nasty stain, might be a more apposite phrase.

As I have already explained, the priorities of central government, because of their universal intended application, can often, quite literally supplant those that the school stakeholders may consider to be more pressing in their own collective context. As a result these unrealistic and general external demands placed upon schools may not accord with the pressing and specific development and improvement priorities which an individual school has identified, and which they are already seeking to implement as part of their own agenda of continual institutional growth. If that is even partly justified as an explanation, then it is hardly fair to blame or victimise schools, the teachers who work there and the communities that they collectively represent, for failing to 'score' when not only are the political goalposts being moved, but they are placed on a seismic political playing field that is frequently being relocated, if not sold off to the private sector!

Yet again, the intrusion of what I call 'hidden messages' goes a long way to explain why government initiatives have largely failed to achieve their often vague and politically-motivated outcomes in schools across the country. The whole issue of initiative fatigue, with their individual and collective foci on symptoms of perceived problems rather than the actual root causes, not to mention the inappropriate lead-in times or the inadequate time-scales for their successful implementation, along with little or no training and inadequate

444

budgets with government-determined strings attached, is one that is inevitably bound to falter, if not fail. The hidden message of all of this is that governments are better placed to know better than professionally-trained teachers, in partnership with students, parents and other stakeholders what is needed, even if it is solely intended to prosecute their own personal or party political prejudices.

Alternatively, and if you wish to cling to a less cynical perspective than the one I have just put forward, you could perhaps argue that politicians are essentially victims of their own schooling, who with their own, often privileged experiences who therefore, inexcusably confuse action with effecting real change, development and school improvement – thereby creating more heat than light – or that they are simply untrained, politically motivated people who are ignorant as to what should and ought to be done, who subsequently confuse action with achievement. They simply know that education or schooling is important, and so like caring parents, they are prone to do all of the wrong things for all of the right motives or reasons.

In Peter Hyman's book, he refers to Sir Michael Barber's use of the analogy of a computer to illustrate the three types of reform. Firstly, one has the **hardware** which is the funding, the capital for building works and the qualifications framework, and then there is the **operating system** which consists of the performance management framework, as well as choice and diversity and, finally, there is the **software** which contains the strategies for teaching and learning. I like this analogy, despite the fact that Sir Michael is a top-down strategist in favour of government involvement in education. However, in terms of these three types or stages of reform, my own view is that the government's role is primarily at the hardware stage, with perhaps the exception of the qualifications framework, which I prefer to see as a professional responsibility and, therefore, falling under the jurisdiction of the teaching profession.

In conclusion, it would be wonderful if we could achieve a development framework in which the government were to act as the determined accomplice of individual school improvement rather than its assassin, by working with the teaching profession in a spirit of genuine and equal partnership, with little

445

regard as to who should take the credit for successful outcomes – unless it is a celebration of student accomplishment and achievement.

If real school improvement is a genuine aim, then I am convinced that team-based approaches are far more likely to result in eventual success than if one of the team members, or team leader acts in a manner more fitting of a dictatorial bully than a genuine collaborator, or comrade in arms, if that is not too leftist a term for the more politically right-leaning reader.

I feel that the following quotation is a fitting summary and conclusion to this chapter:

"We trained hard, but it seemed that every time we were beginning to form up into teams, we would be reorganised. I was to learn later in life that we tend to meet any new situation by reorganising.....and a wonderful method it can be for creating the illusion of progress while producing confusion, inefficiency and demoralisation."
Petronius Arbiter 27-66 AD

Are we really learning the lessons of history, or acting in abeyance of Albert Einstein's definition of insanity?

(Note: In the interests of fairness as well as possibly accuracy, it should be recognised that Wikipedia, among others, says that this apocryphal quotation is spuriously attributed to Petronius, but was actually written by Charlton Ogburn in 1957 about his experiences in the British army. Either way, it is still sufficiently dated to indicate that not much has changed!)

Chapter Twenty One: Inappropriate Funding Priorities

Once Upon a Time

In days gone by, Britain was often and rightly referred to as 'the workshop of the world', given the nation's considerable economic might when it came to importing raw materials to be combined with the skills, inventiveness and ingenuity of the indigenous labour force in order to produce a plethora of much sought after manufactured goods for sale around the globe. Those were perhaps the golden days in terms of Britain's ability to generate income and wealth that led to rapidly rising living standards for most people, albeit to a greater or lesser extent, as well as a justifiable sense of general economic prosperity and a pride in our national collective identity.

Economists, however, recognise that there are phases in the nature of economic activity and development, over time, as countries inevitably develop out of predominantly agrarian, land-based production into more industrialised landscapes, where the emphasis shifts inexorably towards manufacturing and construction. This process of ***industrialisation*** is typical as countries grow and develop, as they are able to produce adequate foodstuffs which frees up scarce economic resources that can be reallocated into the production of consumer and investment goods, which offer a higher productive potential.

What is equally well understood, however, is that this secondary stage in the economic development process will eventually lead to ***deindustrialisation***, whereby manufacturing and construction become more fully mechanised and automated, leading to a rapid growth in employment in tertiary or service industries and, eventually, the knowledge-based industries. But this shift does not necessarily mean that each stage completely replaces the old order so that we abandon primary production for secondary, or secondary for tertiary. There are many successful economies where the balance shifts somewhat, but they are still able to sustain reasonable levels of agricultural production of foodstuffs and/or raw materials, whilst also maintaining prosperous manufacturing productive capacity and developing a vibrant tertiary sector which provides the bulk of gainful employment for the populace. This is the ideal development model and one that the UK economy has signally failed to implement or sustain, largely due to a misguided, failed and extraordinarily destructive economic and political agenda imposed by governments, mainly (but not exclusively) from the extreme right of the political spectrum, particularly since the 1980s.

A stark and shocking illustration of the damage that was wreaked upon the UK by mendacious Thatcherite Conservative economic policies, (and to some extent in the USA by similarly misguided Republican policy measures approved by Ronald Reagan), lies in a statement that was attributed to the Right Honourable Dennis Skinner M.P. who still represents the people of his Bolsover constituency in Derbyshire. One day, in the House of Commons he pointed out to Margaret Thatcher that the economic and industrial policies of her Tory government had succeeded in inflicting substantially greater damage to British manufacturing industry than had been achieved by Adolf Hitler and the Third Reich during the Second World War.

Strong stuff indeed, from the veteran Labour politician, and a statement that at the time was considered to be so offensive and distasteful that the Speaker of the House of Commons had him ejected from the Chamber as a form of punishment. The truth of the matter was (and is) that Mr. Skinner's observation was factually accurate, and his statement has since been supported by official data and empirical evidence regarding industrial production in the period 1979 to 1982.

During the Thatcher 'experiment', which was based on discredited and historically failed economic dogma, the UK was 'transformed' into what might be accurately described as an anorexic economy, one that had been systematically starved of any notable sustenance from much in the way of manufacturing industry. Consequently, since that time, the British economy has become imbalanced and effectively forced to rely almost entirely upon what are rightly termed 'invisible' earnings, derived from the operations of speculative and highly dubious financial markets, for its very economic survival – and we all know how much the financial markets are concerned for the economic wellbeing of the real economy upon which they feed like voracious parasites.

I accept that this sounds harsh, but I am not alone in my loathing of the behaviour and effects of 'the banks' who were wrongly deemed "too big to fail", so that governments used taxpayer's money to bail out and rescue those institutions that had failed so spectacularly – socialising the cost of the profligacy emanating from their private and ill-gotten gains. In his outstanding book, *'Austerity – The History of a Dangerous Idea'*, Professor Mark Blyth reflects upon these global events in an immensely interesting and refreshingly honest way. He admits that, at the time, he was in favour of the bailing out of the banks, but argues that he (and many others) may have been wrong in their support for the financial largesse so generously afforded to the banking sector by the taxpayers and governments of all countries affected. Mark Blyth writes, *"Having pumped and dumped every asset class on the planet, finance may have exhausted its own growth model."*

Professor Blyth goes on to offer some evidence that such a claim may not be too wide of the mark, nor as outlandish as it may seem on first reading. He points out that, recently, banks almost everywhere are reducing the extent of their financial speculative instruments, which will in turn reduce their lending, restrict their growth and the volume of business that they are able to conduct. Moreover, whilst this 'shrinkage' is occurring, Professor Blyth adds, *"what growth there is seems to be on the retail rather than the investment banking side. But retail depends more directly on the real economy (involving the production of actual goods and services) which is shrinking because of austerity."* He concludes this point on a rather worrisome note when he writes, ***"In sum, we may have impoverished a few million people to save an industry of dubious social utility that is now on its last legs."***

If Professor Blyth's conjecture is proven to be correct, even partially, then it will have massively grave implications for the British economy and its unhealthy reliance on the financial sector for its prosperity, because successive governments have foolishly surrendered (if sabotaged is too strong a word) too much of the truly-productive, real manufacturing economy. This is particularly foolish when one considers that consumers worldwide still display an apparently insatiable appetite for spending vast sums of money on acquiring consumer durable and non-durable goods - in other words, buying 'stuff'. I intend to return to the issues of Britain's economic ***deindustrialisation*** and the impact of material consumerism in the next section, when considering how schools alone cannot be expected to transform society, even if they were politically allowed, encouraged or enabled to do so, when it is the bigger picture of society as a whole that must also be re-thought and radically transformed, and so I will not dwell further on such issues here.

The rise of high finance, with its emphasis on monetary gain, which is usually short-term in nature, is effectively in the hands of the rabidly-driven politically right-wing ideologues who have dominated government in the UK over the last forty years. This pursuit of short-term financial return, preferably as high as possible, is rampant, rife and ruinous, but has been generously supported by Conservative governments who do all they can, while in office, to line the pockets of the financiers and their supporters in the City of London and big business. After all, how else can one honestly justify wave after wave of privatisation of public sector industries, institutions and agencies which are sold off, primarily to financial institutions (directly or indirectly), at well below their true asset worth. Such actions simply enable the buyers to sell them on again for their true, and usually significantly higher, market value and reap an easy and highly lucrative capital gain, and all at the taxpayers' expense.

Another Tory Party obsession has also been with severe cutbacks in the public sector by slashing government spending in an attempt to reduce, if not eliminate borrowing needs. This has also entailed cutting income tax in ways that tend to be highly regressive, leading to the greatest burden falling mainly on the poorest members of society, as a proportion of their income. *'Private sector good, public sector bad'* is their myopic, elitist and far from egalitarian agenda, or mantra. As a result, the last forty years have seen draconian reductions in levels of public expenditure on state education in real and per capita terms. 'Real' terms means after allowing for changes in the value of money due to inflation, and per capita spending means the sum of money expressed in terms of for an individual school student. Per capita spending has also been adversely impacted by rising school populations. This right-wing agenda has also seen an erosion, if not elimination of the power of local education authorities in the sphere of state schooling and an unsavoury politicization of the government inspectorate. The latter phenomenon is being used, and this stands repeating, and has led to a notable rise in the number of once good schools suddenly and mysteriously failing their OFSTED inspections, and being reborn as privately-run and privately-funded academies and free schools instead. This is the further privatisation of state education, with the purse strings being tightly held by the private paymasters and their quest to make a financial gain out of other people's education at school.

It seems as though, in these days of the ascendency and dominance of high finance, with maniacal financial services effectively propping up the UK economy, since the demise of Britain's manufacturing industries, the old adage of 'he who holds the purse strings, calls the shots' rings starkly true – even if I might have re-invented the phrase somewhat. Nonetheless, it is certainly true to say that those who control the purse strings of state education systems effectively determine most of what goes on in schools in the broader, macro sense. This more indirect form of government interference in state education, although less visible than endless statutory measures and government directives emanating from the Department for Education, has the effect of further undermining the tremendous work, to which the vast majority of professional teachers quite literally devote their lifetimes. They do this in order to provide young people with the best possible start in life, despite all of the odds stacked against the teaching profession, usually emanating from outside of the school gates in the form of pushy and ignorant parents, societal disintegration and mendacious central governments.

The Devolution Con!

It is no exaggeration to say that education is very much what is called a 'political football', to which previous chapters in this section of the book bear powerful testimony. Because political parties, regardless of their leanings or hue, have a relatively limited period of time in office, during one term of government, so it is that they are understandably forced into looking for what can amount to 'quick-fix' solutions when it comes to most of their policy decisions in those areas over which they exert a modicum of control. In other words, they seek to do the right things or, at least, be seen to be attempting to do the right things in order that they might be re-elected, although such actions are unlikely to always be in the best interests of the country, by which I mean all people, regardless of their income, background and potential voting habits or inclinations. Well, that's the theory I guess!

Over the last thirty or so years, one of the devious ways in which Tory governments in particular have sought to deflect if not avoid the political flak, or fallout if you prefer, of endless public expenditure cuts in general, but in particular political hot-potatoes such as state education and the National Health Service, is by devolving the funds earmarked for such provision to the actual providers. It is a brilliant wheeze, although if managed in a more beneficent and generous manner, does have the potential of providing individual schools and hospital trusts with considerably greater freedom to operate more independently.

As with all such initiatives, the use of devolved budgets for individual schools to manage has potential benefits as well as possible drawbacks, in that they can be a blessing or a curse depending on a variety of factors, financial and contextual. It is worth examining some of these if we are to consider some of the many ways in which the government can be accused of inappropriate funding priorities when it comes to education and schooling.

By means of an introduction, this financial practice dreamt up by Thatcher's Tory government is designed, if we are to believe the political rhetoric, for central government to bypass local education authorities (LEAs), and allocate the Treasury's budget for the purpose of state education directly to schools, on an individual school basis. The amount that each school receives is determined by a formula which focuses on the number of students on a particular school's roll as well as the age of students in each year group. In other words, it is essentially a per capita amount, whereby the schools with a greater number of students on roll receive a larger amount on total income. Of equal importance is the age of the students in each year group, as the formula ensures that older students receive an incrementally increasing per capita sum.

This results in secondary schools receiving a lot more money per head than their primary school counterparts, and those secondary schools with a sixth form (i.e. students aged 16 to 18 years) receiving the largest per capita sum. This, of course, explains why such schools are so desperate to hold on to their cherished sixth-form status and resist attempts by either central or local government to reorganise educational provision and create local specialist colleges of further education, which means their students leave school at 16, with a corresponding and significant loss of income in their devolved budgets. My views about the unequal levels of funding received by primary as compared to secondary schools under this arrangement is something to which I will return, later in this chapter.

To begin with, let us examine some of the advantages, perceived or actual, that local management of schools and devolving budgets to individual institutions are supposed to offer, before we look at some of the potential and very real disadvantages.

First of all, giving greater autonomy to schools allows head teachers and their governing bodies, of community stakeholders and co-opted members, greater freedom over how they decide to spend their budgets and allocate their funds to different types of expenditure. After all, no two schools are identical, for a whole host of cultural, environmental and contextual reasons, and so individual financial freedom appears to be decidedly reasonable, sensible and particularly attractive.

What also needs to be realised about devolved budgets under the LMS scheme (the 'Local Management of Schools', as the government called it), however, is that each school was now responsible for the dispersal of its entire budget, which is to fund all aspects of its daily operations and functions. This means that the school staff are no longer solely responsible for their 'core business', which is one way of referring to the processes of teaching and learning and the delivery of a relevant, broad and balanced curriculum, but also for the overall management of a whole host of additional budget headings or responsibilities.

Previously, these additional financial and managerial responsibilities fell under the aegis of the relevant local education authority (LEA) who, in theory, were just a phone call away for advice, assistance and guidance. Now, however, each school was to be responsible for managing and financing such things as cleaning and caretaking or site maintenance as well as grounds maintenance (e.g. tending the gardens, mowing the playing fields, marking out the various games boundary lines, etc.). The individual school was also now responsible for security matters, such as CCTV and perimeter fencing, minor building works like fixing leaking roofs and, of course its catering arrangements (the euphemistic, but very important, 'school dinners' – albeit eaten at lunch time). Only a few areas of responsibility, such as provision for special educational needs and major capital building works were retained by, and fell under the discretion of the increasingly marginalised LEAs.

In terms of the school's core business, its curriculum, one potential advantage was, as previously mentioned, to be given greater freedom to innovate, experiment and prioritise, as well as use its spending plans over time in a manner which enabled heads and their staff to bolster, support and implement the aims and objectives of their individually-determined school development or improvement plans. I largely applaud and acknowledge this benefit, as it allows schools to offer a greater diversity of educational provision, notwithstanding the legal obligations imposed by the ever-changing National Curriculum, which seemed to be largely determined by the political whims, prejudices and values of the Education Secretary in the government at any moment in time. Indeed, I would argue that it was rare for sound educational reasons to be the rationale or driving force that under-pinned the frequent amendments, new directions and legal imperatives that constituted various versions of the government-imposed National Curriculum, and this was a great shame as well as a wasted opportunity, not to mention a massive waste of teachers' time and efforts.

LMS and devolved budgets also amounted to a blessing in disguise in that, to a very large extent, it liberated individual schools from the actions and directives of politically-motivated LEAs, thereby allowing schools greater independence and autonomy in meeting the educational and development needs of its human constituents, primarily the students and their teachers. I could refer to one local education authority in the south-east of England who, in my experience, could fairly be accused of favouring certain schools in particular areas that fell under its jurisdiction when it came to managing the funding of all schools in its county. Let me illustrate this by recalling the regional preferences that I witnessed in Tory-controlled Essex County Council when I was working there in the past. One only needed to visit schools in the leafy, middle-class towns like Brentwood, Colchester, Billericay and Chelmsford, for example, to witness at first hand the effects of discriminatory levels of financial provision that were, quite literally, afforded to the schools in those places, compared to other towns like Basildon, Harlow, Dagenham and Barking. These latter areas could perhaps fairly be described as those experiencing a greater degree of social and economic deprivation, as well as being populated by a majority of less discerning, usually working-class, parents when it came to the quality of the schools attended by their offspring, and for quite understandable reasons….or that was actually the perception of the LEA.

On the other side of the coin, these advantages were also accompanied by some real and potential pitfalls, drawbacks and disadvantages, many of which created considerable angst and stress to head teachers, governing bodies and teachers. The opportunity to take control of one's own budget is undoubtedly a major attraction to ambitious head teachers who, when managing their 'own' money, so to speak, will be motivated to find savings in some areas in order to finance innovation and expansion in others. However, having this financial autonomy is only really a true blessing when the size of the budget being devolved to the individual school is wholly adequate and reasonably generous, which it should be, given the fundamental and central importance of education to the wellbeing and growth of our nations. Sadly, however, when head teachers were given control over their own budgets, the funds that were allocated were largely insufficient to maintain current expenditures, let alone fund new and exciting directions in curriculum design and delivery, for example, due to year-on-year reductions in the amount of money that central government afforded state education. These cutbacks were usually 'real' reductions, which diminishes the purchasing power of the actual money figure, after taking account of increases in the annual rate of inflation, although there were occasions when these budget trimming measures also led to an actual fall in the money income that was made available to schools. Falling money income is effectively a double financial whammy in times of rising inflation, which was a feature of the economy at the time.

As a result of this fiscal parsimony, the tables were turned on head teachers who received these devolved budgets and were politely instructed that they had to live within the meagre means afforded to them, as setting a deficit budget – that is where planned expenditure exceeds planned income – was illegal. As annual budgets invariably shrank, this responsibility was often the source of considerable personal and institutional stress. This was most definitely the case under consecutive conservative governments in the 1980s and 1990s, and it remains true even today under the austerity programmes of George Osborne, the particularly obnoxious and pompous Chancellor of the Exchequer in David Cameron's Conservative government. If funds are falling in real terms, year on year, then head teachers are inevitably going to be shackled, inhibited and prevented from expending their energies on effecting real school growth, development and continual improvement. Instead, they are going to be forced to focus upon the negative and far less exciting, but equally challenging agenda, namely protecting their schools from severe rationalisation and down-sizing. In view of the fact that schools are necessarily labour intensive organisations, some 80 to 85% of their overall budget is customarily spent on staffing, mainly teaching staff, but also ancillary personnel in the form of administrators, classroom assistants, and so on. It follows, therefore, that schools will logically look for 'savings' – a less pejorative term for 'cuts' – by reducing this largest expenditure element, in the form of staff lay-offs. I intentionally avoid using the word 'redundant' as that means the staff lost are no longer needed for the efficient and effective operation of the institution, and that is something that was quite simply not the case.

456

This virtually enforced requirement to rationalise the human resource, especially a reduction in the number of quality teachers employed, will obviously have a particularly serious and damaging impact upon school morale and the range of learning experiences that can be offered to students by specialist and suitably-qualified teaching staff. Well-trained, suitably-qualified and inspiring teachers who, together, are capable of offering an exciting, challenging and dynamic curriculum to their students, are the life blood, the most vital and essential ingredient of any high-performing school. Falling or inadequate budgets will place a severe and painful burden on the head teachers of any school that is seeking to offer the very best education to its young people, rather than to merely stay afloat on turbulent and troubled waters, after the plug has been pulled out.

During periods of dreaded rationalisation, it is impossible for head teachers and their governing bodies to protect teachers from the negative emotions that these cutbacks necessarily involve. Either my colleagues or I face losing our jobs. I am likely to have to deliver the same curriculum to students with fewer quality teaching and learning resources. We will find it impossible to invest in expensive information and communication technologies, plus relevant software packages for learning, in order to provide variety and a more modern learning environment.

Tough decisions will need to be made, with some older and, arguably more experienced teachers feeling an obligation to accept voluntary redundancy or voluntary retirement packages in order to protect the employment of their colleagues, especially those with young children and a family to support. Those who remain will inevitably feel the additional pressure of having to take on increased workloads, and the additional stress that this involves, to compensate as far as possible for the negative educational impact that losses incurred through staff and resource reductions will obviously involve.

For those who are left to deal with minimizing the detrimental impact of enforced cutbacks, thanks to this mixed blessing of devolved school budgets, it will be difficult for senior managers to prevent the onset of a pervasive mood of negativity and pessimism, if not extreme cynicism, adversely affecting staff morale. This will be especially challenging when the expectation is that in a little under twelve months' time, everyone will be once again be trying to find the least harmful ways of effectively reducing expenditures whilst endeavouring to maintain high-quality provision.

What is more, local management of schools and devolved budgets raise important issues regarding the prudent, efficient and effective management of such key responsibilities for senior managers and governing bodies. This issue is especially acute when one considers that most head teachers were not trained in financial management, site maintenance and the provision of cost-effective and nutritious school lunches, let alone cleaning, school security and marketing, among other additional and new responsibilities. As a result, there is the need for relevant, focused and detailed in-service training for all staff, but especially the key financial decision makers, and this needs to be a prerequisite that precedes the responsibilities involved in the local financial management of schools.

Unfortunately, political expediency and urgency often result in the government putting the cart before the horse, so to speak, by devolving responsibilities to schools before adequate training is put in place to ensure those involved can effectively discharge their new, additional responsibilities. I can recall grappling with understanding and knowing how to design and implement the outsourcing of the many new, non-core areas of business that I faced as a new head teacher, such as cleaning and security, so that I was not unnecessarily and directly encumbered by too many tasks of secondary (excuse the pun) and lesser importance.

Before becoming a head teacher, I had been very fortunate to have worked for two years as a general adviser and inspector of schools for Derbyshire LEA. My introduction to the advisory service was a baptism of fire in some respects owing to the fact that one of my first responsibilities was to accompany a more experienced colleague in visiting several primary schools in order to check the accuracy of the budgets being proposed by the head teachers and their governing bodies. For some reason, primary schools were to deal with the move to local financial management before their secondary school counterparts. Perhaps the Tories thought that the initiative should follow the same route as the children.

458

What made this inaugural experience a fairly harrowing and sobering one for me was the fact that most of the primary schools we visited were small in size with a modest number of students on roll, and a correspondingly limited core of highly-dedicated and hard-working classroom teachers. Moreover, although most of the head teachers had received a minimum of training to ready them for their newly-acquired responsibilities, they were totally unprepared for the harsh realities that they were about to experience in actual practice. I can vividly recall meeting with, mainly female head teachers, who had successfully managed to draw up their school budget, but who experienced real distress when they explained to me and my colleague the human and educational costs involved in achieving a legal outcome, given the limited and reduced sums of money at their disposal. It was no easy task to be confronted with highly competent primary school head teachers who were reduced to tears when they presented their budget proposals and highlighted the number of teaching colleagues, co-workers and friends, that they would have to 'lose' in order to meet the financial strictures imposed on them by a mindless, Tory-controlled central government.

The last school we visited during this emotional and painful process was a larger primary school, with a healthy number of students on roll, as it was situated in a more inner-city area with a larger population for whom they had to cater. First impressions were very encouraging in that the head teacher (the only male head among our allocated schools) appeared smartly dressed in a snappy, business-like suit and with an air of assured confidence and of being in total control. He took several copies of his school's proposed budget for the forthcoming school year from a well-organised filing cabinet, and presented them to us for our perusal. His confidence was well-placed, it seemed, as it was the first where there was a slight budget surplus that had yet to be earmarked to one of the many budget heads, and meanwhile languished under the heading of 'contingency', or funds that were available for unforeseen events during the coming year.

It soon dawned on me and my more experienced advisory colleague that the staffing costs in the proposed budget statement had been incorrectly calculated. My colleague politely took the initiative and asked the rather dapper head teacher how he had arrived at the total salary costs for his teaching staff, which we felt were somewhat on the low side, given the number of staff the school currently employed, and who were all to be retained in the next financial year. The head teacher confidently said that he had used the agreed salary scales that were published by his professional association, from which it was possible to identify what any one teacher would be entitled to receive as his or her annual gross salary.

My colleague and I exchanged a quick and seriously concerned glance at each other before we asked the head teacher whether or not he had taken into account what are known as **'on costs'**, when calculating the actual cost of employing each teacher to the school. This figure is far in excess of the amount that the individual teachers can expect to receive as their gross income on a monthly or annual basis. This is because schools were now the actual employer of their teaching and other staff. This meant that they now had to include in their calculations additional costs which have to be paid by the school, which are sums of money over and above that paid to the teachers each month. To begin with, the school has the responsibility to find from within its devolved budget sufficient funds to cover the school's or employer's part of each teacher's overall National Insurance contribution. The employee or individual teacher has an amount, which is their contribution to National Insurance, deducted from their gross salary, **and** the school, or employer, has a statutory obligation to supplement this sum from within their own overall budget.

This was not the only omission in the proposed school budget for the next financial year. There was also the significant matter of the employer's contribution to each teacher's superannuation or pension fund. As with National Insurance contributions, employees have to pay a chunk of money each month to their individual pension fund before receiving their net monthly income, **and** a similar amount has to be contributed by the employer out of their own funds or budget. So it was that the head teacher suddenly realised his massive, but understandable error, and it was an experience I will never forget, nor want to witness again, to see his very impressive, initial self-confidence quite literally and visibly drain from his face and overall demeanour.

460

As a result of this oversight, our meeting with him went on to take a very different emotional and substantive turn. When we incorporated these two 'on costs' that the school alone has to shoulder, and which are not included in national teacher pay scales, instead of finding a healthy surplus in the form of a contingency reserve, the school had to find a way to significantly reduce its planned expenditure for the next school year. We spent a great deal of time advising the head teacher on how he could explain to his teaching staff that a sum equivalent to the salaries of six of his valued colleagues would now need to be found in order to live within a significantly reduced budget allowance. The spectre of actual teacher redundancies was one that was to loom large over future staff meetings.

It is hardly surprising, therefore, that many bigger (usually secondary or high) schools and those with the financial means, find it necessary to find the funds to employ full-time school business managers or bursars to relieve hard-pressed head teachers from these additional duties and their potentially fiscal pitfalls. The employment of these additional, non-teaching administrators and managers in itself represents an additional financial cost to each school, but they are necessary if only for their expertise in preparing financial reports, dealing with the outsourcing of peripheral aspects of the school's 'business' such as security, catering and cleaning, which involves preparing contract service agreements, tendering for potential providers and subsequently helping to decide which contractor offers the best service and value for money.

The alternative is for the school to directly employ their own cleaners, security officers and catering staff, but this increases the onus of having to secure, supervise and manage such additional personnel. This is why outsourcing is often preferred, although the school has no direct jurisdiction or control over the staff provided by external contractors. Some schools actually decide to spend some of their devolved budget to buy back services from their LEA, as I did when I first became a head teacher. Although our school decided to outsource these peripheral services and tasks, the LEA acted as our business manager by taking over the whole management process, and being directly accountable to me and the governing body.

The two alternatives above have the advantage of allowing schools and head teachers to retain overall responsibility for these non-teaching services and budgets while being free to concentrate their professional energies and focus on improving teaching and learning by enriching, extending and enhancing the curriculum offer, so as to "litter the paths of young people with quality learning opportunities". That is and must always be the unquestionable core business of every successful school or learning institution!

As an economist, as part of the syllabus, I help students discover that competition is inherently wasteful as it necessarily involves the duplication of scarce and finite resources. For example, instead of having one factory producing a particular good or service, competing firms will each have their own productive unit with similar production facilities and personnel, and some of them may not be operating at full capacity, which means some of their resources are not being efficiently utilised, which is, again, wasteful given that economic and productive resources are scarce. This waste is effectively the opportunity cost of consumers being able to have a choice between competing brands of the same product.

To digress briefly, I can recall very well the interesting and challenging comments, views and perceptions offered by a group of students from *The Moscow Technical Lyceum Number* 1, in the days of the Soviet Union, when they visited the Isle of Wight as part of my school's official participation in the ground-breaking UK/USSR school and student exchange programme, back in the 1980s. (Full credit goes to Kenneth Baker and the Conservative Government for negotiating such a worthwhile and immensely educational initiative.)

When they visited us, we took our party of Russian students, and their hosting British students, to a large supermarket in Newport on the Isle of Wight, so that they could see the very different type of shopping that British people were able to enjoy. I believe that we did this based upon a somewhat arrogant assumption that the Russian students would be amazed and impressed in equal measure at the stark contrast to their very drab, small specialist shops with long queues of customers waiting patiently outside the shop before being able to enter to see if any goods were left for them to purchase. I remember three very thought-provoking comments by some remarkably intelligent Russian students, which were hardly expressions of being impressed and envious, although they were occasionally amazed, but not by what we might have rather smugly anticipated.

Several students asked us, with more than a little incredulity, why exactly we felt that we needed such an excessive degree of choice for fairly mundane things like breakfast cereals, which occupied one lane or aisle of the spacious supermarket. As far as they were concerned such excess was very much OTT (over the top) and wasteful. Upon honest reflection, I think they were spot on. One of the boys, Sasha (the diminutive for Alexander), asked me how we, as a society, justified having one whole lane of the supermarket devoted to a diverse array of different pet foods, doggie snacks and treats, when one considered that some people in our own country were unable to afford a decent meal for themselves and their families. It was also a very fair observation to make. Perhaps our resources could and should be better and differently allocated as a matter of meeting other, more pressing and basic priorities.

By far and away the best observation, made by a couple of Russian students, came later in the day as we all sat together conversing and reviewing a busy day of local visits and excursions, one of which had been to the aforesaid supermarket. When it was casually pointed out to our guests that one positive feature of our shops when compared to theirs, was the absence of long queues of people waiting patiently outside of their premises, their response was one of measured amusement and surprise at our limited observational powers. They rightly pointed out that our shops also had queues. To explain this they referred to the number of people standing at each one of the numerous check-out tills in the supermarket. If we asked them instead to form just a single line, then we too would have a very long queue. Another Russian student laughed politely and said that the only real difference was that in Moscow, people queued to get into the shop, whereas in the capitalist West, we make the customers queue up inside the shop waiting for us to allow them to pay, once they had selected the goods they wished to purchase!

To return to the matter of the local management of schools, we have seen how it became necessary for each school to have their own bursar, business manager and human resource personnel, for example, and how this is also incredibly wasteful, as it involves the unnecessary duplication of limited resources, which could arguably be better utilised elsewhere. In a large local education authority area there might be say one hundred schools, and we now have each one with its own array of ancillary or non-teaching staff, instead of having an LEA at County Hall, or in Regional Offices, with a much smaller team of financial managers, human resource and security officers. The latter arrangement would be far more cost effective surely, as well as having the advantage that these teams would have detailed, specialist knowledge of their respective areas and could, therefore, offer more detailed, precise and accurate information, advice and assistance to individual schools under their jurisdiction. They can also undertake a lot of the more peripheral non-teaching tasks for the school, leaving the head teacher and teaching colleagues to more fully devote their time and energies to improving the quality and effectiveness of teaching and learning.

Despite having some advantages in certain situations, generally speaking it is true to say that competition is wasteful, largely due to this duplication of resources in the form of ancillary staffing needs in each school, instead of having a smaller team of managers and administrators in the locally elected and locally accountable LEA. Arguably, LEAs are better placed and more qualified to look after budget management, staffing costs, grounds maintenance, security, catering and so forth, rather than having each school with their own staff to perform the same duties. Economies or savings from large-scale production are lost in the devolved model, making it much more expensive overall. It also diverts much needed financial resources to purely administrative, non-core functions, which obviously means less remains from a given budget for providing quality learning opportunities for students. So why have Conservative governments been so much in favour of this more wasteful notion of devolved budgets and the local management of schools?

In many ways, the answer to this question lies in the whole competition versus collaboration dilemma and debate. By prising individual schools away from local political control and making them more autonomous as individual institutions, they become more susceptible and vulnerable to not only being more easily controlled by central government diktat, and that is certainly a trend we have seen since the Great Education Reform Bill in 1985, but also to being far easier to 'persuade' or 'bribe' into leaving the state sector and becoming privately-owned academies and free schools – a form of privatisation by stealth. They also give greater impetus to the competitive use of school league tables, again in a way of separating the 'wheat from the chaff' and identifying winners and, by default, losers.

On the one hand, I understand and appreciate that some head teachers prefer this autonomous, even privatised status for the schools that they lead and manage for the reasons given above, especially the greater freedom to manage their own affairs more independently, and this also confers upon such heads significantly greater power, prestige and feelings of enhanced importance. On the other hand, however, I fear that this more competitive system forfeits some of the real benefits and advantages that arise when schools collaborate and work together in some form of tacit or formal relationship. For example, I find it interesting how international schools often form franchise-type organisations or other types of formal networking arrangement so that they can reap the benefits of various economies of scale in their management and operation. Such partnership approaches also create an environment where schools, by which I mean the senior leaders, the teachers, the support staff and the crucially-important students, are able to work collaboratively, sharing interesting and best practice, something that is very unlikely under a system where schools are encouraged by the government to be in competition with one another.

My final comment on what I have called the 'devolution con' is to mention the very important party political advantage that local management of schools and devolved budgets gave to the Conservatives in central government, by helping them to implement a series of swingeing financial cutbacks to the overall budget for state education whilst simultaneously absolving themselves from any political blame, flak or negative political fallout. It is a brilliantly cynical and patently dishonest way of escaping responsibility, or blame, for the increased class sizes, poorly resourced schools and plummeting teacher morale that was the direct result of reduced levels of funding over time. The message from Conservative central government, reinforced by the politically complicit and notoriously right-wing media, including a politically neutered and once independent BBC, is that they are giving adequate financial resources to education, and so for anyone unhappy with the education their children are receiving, then that is the fault of the individual school which is simply "not managing the budget we gave them in a sufficiently efficient or effective way" – so take it up with the head teacher and not with your local member of parliament, thank you very much!

This is a brilliant wheeze, and one that the Tories have very successfully replicated with the National Health Service and the individual hospitals managed by hospital trusts, who also have devolved and dwindling budgets taking account of inflation and the spiralling costs of medical treatments as a result of improved techniques and technology, as well as improved and more advanced, efficacious and life-saving drugs. Even in times when the government will correctly claim that they have increased the central budget for the NHS in real terms, that is in line with annual rises in the cost of living or retail price index (RPI), this is yet another cynical way to abrogate any real political responsibility for being refused the treatment one needs, increased waiting lists for surgical procedures and cancelled or repeatedly postponed operations. This is particularly cynical because raising allocated budgets in line with increases in the RPI fails to take account of the fact that the inflation in the price of advanced medical equipment and new medications is notoriously well above changes in the RPI which only takes account of changes in the price of a representative sample, or 'basket' of goods and services bought by a 'typical' family. How many families do you know who include an MRI machine in their 'basket' of goods? This argument used by government involves significant budget reductions, benignly paid for by an ignorant general public, who are also skilfully misled by complicit media organisations.

In this section dealing with my belief that the funding allocated to education is insufficient, misdirected and unevenly distributed, there is a far more profound issue which explains my claim that the funding priorities exhibited by governments, central and local, ***regardless of their political leanings*** have been seriously misguided, wrongly targeted and wholly inappropriate in nature throughout recent history, and it is this issue which I now want to address.

466

The Vital Importance of Early Years Learning

I may be an experienced secondary school teacher and senior leader, but I have long felt that there is a fundamentally serious educational error that has traditionally been made in relation to the amounts of money that are spent by government on secondary education at the expense, and to the detriment of schools in the early years and primary school sector. I also believe that this lies at the heart of why formal schooling largely fails young people in terms of truly educating, enlightening and liberating their innate and creative instincts, which represents a massive loss to humankind as a whole. The spending priorities of central government are fundamentally wrong!

This persistent bias demands that excess attention and the lion's share of the education budget is directed towards funding initiatives that exclusively involve secondary education, as if the prevailing perception is that secondary schools are the only place where 'real learning' or 'real education' actually happens. Furthermore, even within the largesse afforded to secondary schooling, the age-weighted, per capita spending within secondary schools favours students in the 14 to 18 age range, as I mentioned earlier in this chapter. The key question is what is the reason that explains this financial discrimination in favour of secondary schools and even the older students within these institutions? The answer is simple and has been either stated or alluded to elsewhere in this book, so allow me to re-state the obvious reasons and make explicit those which can be inferred by 'reading between the lines', so to speak.

First and foremost is the flawed premise that the over-riding function of state schooling is to prepare young people for some notion of adult and working life that they will experience at some time in the future, rather than really focusing on educating young people while they are at school, and in their lives, in the here and now, as the present merges imperceptibly and seamlessly into the future.

As a teacher of Economics and Business Studies, I was delighted by the funds given to various initiatives, usually dreamt up by Tory governments who tended to be less inclined than more progressive Labour governments to the

467

concept of 'education for education's sake', which sought to promote the link between school and the world of work. Even within the broad spectrum of the world of work, there were frequent attempts by governments to encourage academically and otherwise talented youngsters to seriously consider a career in industry, rather than culturally and instinctively being drawn into the professions. Of course, these attempts by government tended to ignore the fact that the main reason why students expressed this preference for the professions was twofold. The first was that the same Tory governments that wanted students to opt for employment in industry and manufacturing, were also systematically following economic policies that were highly effective in destroying the industrial and manufacturing base of the economy which provided those very jobs and opportunities. The second reason was that the levels of pay and remuneration packages for employees in the professions were always far higher and superior to those offered by manufacturing industry.

If one thinks about this for a nano second, if industry is being systematically and wantonly destroyed by inappropriate and politically motivated economic policy measures, then this will inevitably both curtail the supply of jobs suitable for employees of any calibre, and lead to a reduced demand for industrial labour which will inevitably lead to lower salary levels and career opportunities for all employees in that sector of the economy. This is hardly compatible with wanting to increase the supply of new entrants seeking (rapidly disappearing) industrial jobs, or trying to enhance the attractiveness of a career in industry to those school students who are skilled, academically able and, therefore, much sought after and who are also more likely to aspire to the significantly more financially rewarding employment in the professions.

In any case, the initiatives of central government, usually Conservative administrations, were almost exclusively focussed on trying to change the attitudes of young academically able students in the 14 to 18 age range, particularly those closest to the school-leaving age, namely the 16 to 18 age range, who were soon to go on to university or possibly learn to appreciate the potential excitement and professional development opportunities of a career in a more industrial setting as engineers, leaders and managers, for example. This age bias inherent in new government initiatives was bound to fail, simply because they were targeting entirely the wrong age group.

In my experience, this type of age and ability focused initiative was doomed to fail long before it 'got off the drawing board' and was effectively 'sold' to secondary schools through the offer of incredibly generous central government funding, albeit with strings attached as to how the money could be spent, and on what. Nonetheless, such initiatives rarely, if ever, had the desired impact on the attitudes and career intentions of those young people who became involved, or participated in them. The main reason for this failure was largely because this type of initiative was essentially motivated by political and not truly educational considerations. To begin with, they target the older secondary age students, such as the once 'Insight into Industry' initiative which was designed for students aged 16 to 18 years and who would be taking their A-level courses of study in school sixth forms or colleges of further education. The students involved had already made their career decisions some time before, and so despite enjoying and being interested in such awareness-raising events, they did not lead to any students that I encountered changing career intentions at such a late stage in their schooling.

Leaving things until they are too late is, in fact, a very considerable and fundamental problem when it comes to central government expenditure earmarked for state education, especially in terms of the weighting that is attached to the age of the students in schools. As I have already explained, per capita spending is age-weighted, with the older students attracting increasingly larger sums of money. This necessarily means that primary education attracts significantly less generous funding than is granted to secondary education. The hidden message of this intentional discrimination is quite clearly saying that the foundation learning undertaken in the primary sector is also of significantly lesser importance, and absolutely nothing could be further from the truth!

It is for this reason that I have long since held the view that this financial discrimination is completely the wrong way round, and that primary schooling should receive the largest tranche of state school funding and, the younger the student, the greater should be the per capita amount that their learning attracts. Ever since I can remember, the reality has been that the largest share of the overall education budget, whether taken over the state school system as a whole or within a particular school, is most definitely **not** allocated to that

469

stage of education where basic skills, values and attitudes are formed, and where the most essential, fundamental and pivotal learning actually occurs, or should do, and that is during a young person's nursery and primary school years. So, how and why has this utterly miserable, contrary and educationally deficient state of affairs been allowed to not only come into existence in the first place, but also why has it been allowed to persist for so long, largely unchallenged?

I am certain that an educational historian would be able to explain this more precisely and accurately than me, but I feel obliged to hazard a couple of potentially pertinent and fundamental possible explanations. To begin with, the main problem is political in nature, and has a great deal to do with the fact that governments have relatively short periods of time in office before they have to face the electorate once again and be judged on their record whilst in office, before possibly being given yet another fixed term in power.

It is, of course, the nature of the political beast that any new government wants to quickly be seen to begin changing things, and hopefully for the better, and this compels them to devote precious little time to preparatory research, planning and consulting, so as not to delay the actual implementation of their wondrous new policy measures. This is especially true in view of the fact that it takes time to actually implement new policies and then for such policies to have the desired effect, if indeed they ever do. This political expediency means that those in power are inclined to want to see positive results, and as quickly as possible, please. This understandable urgency, coupled with the belief that the main function of schooling is to prepare young people for adult and working life, steers politicians to focus on outcomes, especially those that are evident at 16 and 18 years of age.

To invest more funds and policy effort during early years and primary schooling would take way too long to reach fruition and become evident in terms of increased employment opportunities for school leavers. The short-termism associated with the political cycle, on the one hand, and the dynamic and long-term nature of effective educational change and improvement on the other, are diametrically opposed to each other in terms of the time spans and motives involved. They are contrasting rather than corresponding or complementary in any compatible way.

It is perhaps also fair to suggest that this negatively skewed funding in favour of secondary schools has a lot to do with the fact that, given the pre-eminence of academic learning, it is perceived as the absolute pinnacle of worthwhile achievement. Also, given that this type of learning becomes more acute and intense when young people reach their later years at secondary school, politicians who are responsible for determining the allocation of the state education budget, can perhaps be forgiven for this misallocation of the financial resources at their disposal. I am sure that it would also be equally true to suggest that successful academics, many of whom find themselves working in the civil service advising government, are also guilty for this financial neglect of younger learners and primary education. This is hardly surprising when one considers that those who are pulling the political strings have done very well as a result of their educational qualifications, which are almost exclusively academic in nature.

This inappropriate funding priority in favour of secondary education needs to be radically overhauled and reversed, with the lion's share of the education budget going to primary schools. This is where the really crucial learning, as well as the key personal and social development takes place. Remember the saying: "Give me the boy until he is seven (years of age) and I will give you the man!"

I am certainly not recommending anything that one might deem to be hare-brained or dangerously subversive in making this plea for radical change. A long time ago, an ally in the form of the Royal Society of the Arts (RSA) strongly recommended that the 'pupil-teacher' ratio in schools should be calculated using a far more appropriate and educationally-sound formula. This formula is based on taking the average age of the students in a class and multiplying it by a figure of two, with the result being the optimal number of young people there should be per one teacher. Therefore, if the average age of the children in a class is five years, then there should be no more than ten students per teacher. At the age of 11 years the maximum class size should be 22 students, and by the time they are 16 years of age the correct figure would be 32 young people per teacher. This is exactly the opposite to the way in which funding is allocated and how class sizes are determined in actual practice today and in the past, for as long as I can recall. What is more, this ratio would arguably negate the need for classroom assistants who are employed to assist the class teacher struggling to engage and inspire a large group of, often, over 30 young minds, which would represent a significant and highly cost-effective saving.

Although I have been professionally steeped in the secondary sector of state schooling, I have refused to be trapped within it in terms of educational thinking and beliefs. For a very long time now, I have been convinced that the RSA formula for calculating class sizes is eminently sensible, educational sound and wholly relevant. Why? Well, because once children have developed the ability to direct and take greater responsibility for their own learning, and they have learned the art and skills involved in '**how to learn**', they will hopefully have discovered the joy to be gained from genuine self-initiated and self-conducted enquiry and discovery of knowledge, as well as having the capabilities to rely less and less on interventions by the class teacher. The teacher will increasingly become redundant as the facilitator, director and sole manager of the individual student's real learning and their genuine education. Furthermore, students will learn the importance of identifying other learning facilitators in their local and national communities to assist them, giving a real impetus to, and justification for genuine community education initiatives, for which I have been an advocate in an earlier chapter of this book.

As an aside, I have always found it quite depressing that when schools are not legally encumbered by the demands of central government and are, therefore, largely free from the impedimental fetters of state education compulsion, such as independent schools, international schools and academies (in the UK), they fail to take the opportunity and use the power arising from their autonomy to do things in a radically and substantially different way. They too seem to have become trapped within and seized by the traditional educational orthodoxy, or the notion that: "That is not the way we do (or have done) things in this country." And so nothing really ever changes.

472

Secondary schools need to relinquish their favoured financial status and governments need to begin a process leading to a reversal in the current funding priorities, so that most money is spent where it will really do the most good, assuming that the learning of young people really is the intended goal. It is also true to say that we need to almost revere the work that goes on in primary schools and view education and learning as a dynamic and not a linear experience. Secondary schools have such a great deal to learn by really adopting the best practice of teachers working in primary schools – working with classes bulging with sometimes more than 30 youngsters and with miserly budgets which force teachers to spend large amounts of additional time designing, preparing and producing their own materials to promote teaching and learning. When one considers these handicaps, then secondary schools really are favoured, not least because their teachers have far less contact time – the actual time in a week spent in the classroom teaching – than their primary colleagues. This provides secondary teachers with the relative luxury of time out of the classroom, during school time, to plan lessons, assess student assignments and provide feedback and occasionally make new teaching materials rather than relying on published learning resources that they can afford to purchase courtesy of their more generous capitation allowances.

I also find it of considerable fascination that the language we employ when talking about the primary-secondary interface, which is an artificial dichotomy when it comes to learning, suggests that the learning process which young people experience is linear in nature, as opposed to its highly dynamic nature in reality. For example, I can often recall secondary head teachers talking about their *'feeder'* primary schools, whenever they referred to the primary schools that effectively *'supplied'* them with their student intake. The casual use of such terminology really does indicate that even professional head teachers see education as a linear process, which really is rather worrying. This bizarre notion of 'feeder' schools was more common admittedly in the days of school catchment areas, which was basically a system whereby your child had to attend the local school nominated by the LEA, and then students from a particular cluster of primary schools would 'go on to' a designated local secondary school. This highly formalised and structured system pre-dated the concept of open enrolment, which was introduced by the Conservative government in the interests of allowing parents 'freedom of choice' when it came to selecting the right school for their offspring.

Fortunately, the epithet 'feeder', as applied to primary schools, has become far less common or relevant as a result of open enrolment, but as a secondary head teacher in the UK with a clearly defined catchment area, I always referred to our *'partner'* primary schools, as it was a better description of the nature of the relationship I felt that we should be forging with them; they were our partners in educating local children at various stages of their personal and social development. This notion of partnership was, for me anyway, based on the legal definition of a partnership, as stated in statute law in England, as: *"Where two or more people come together to carry on a business in common with a view to making a profit".* This corresponds fully with a situation where a secondary school and its partner primaries work together to carry on a business in common, namely the education of a group of young people, which is designed to add value to their personal and social development during their time in compulsory schooling. 'Adding value' is, of course, synonymous with making a profit in the legal definition of partnership, and learning is all about adding value!

Our partnership work involved a range of initiatives which focussed on making the geographical and institutional move from the primary to the secondary phase of education as seamless, natural and constructive as possible, so that it was relatively stress free for young people in terms of getting used to a new environment, new fellow students and different teachers, for example. This collaboration involved developing joint schemes of work in the core subjects particularly, but not exclusively, temporary teacher swaps for our teachers to get to know their future students before the 'move' and vice versa, as well as 'taster days' when the primary students would come and spend a week following a specimen of the classes that they would experience during their first year at secondary school. These types of initiative were hugely beneficial educationally as they helped to ensure that student learning would not regress when the time came for them to officially make the move and join our school.

474

A vitally important time in my career to date was when I experienced two years as a General Adviser and Inspector working for an LEA before becoming a head teacher, and this gave me a lot of practical exposure to working closely and constructively with a group of primary schools for whom I had a 'pastoral' responsibility, as it was described. That exposure was incredibly beneficial for me, and perhaps the most important thing that I took away from it was that secondary school teachers have so much to learn from primary school teachers in terms of how to develop, differentiate and manage teaching and learning, and much else besides. This was definitely instrumental in my wanting to forge collaborative ventures, especially teacher exchanges, with our main partner primary schools.

It also explains an interesting reason why I signed up to attend a highly enjoyable, nationally advertised, two-day Primary Head Teachers' conference in Leeds when I was in my first headship. It seemed perfectly natural for me to want to join such an event as it provided me with an opportunity to broaden my experience of, and exposure to, interesting primary school practice, and to keep up-to-date with recent developments and issues which were affecting and impacting upon them, and me. When I went to the registration desk on the first day, it soon became obvious that I was something of a rarity amongst the delegates. As far as I can recall, I was the only male in attendance and definitely the only secondary head teacher who had bothered to give up two days of their time. The latter point was certainly a huge surprise for me, as it was for the primary head teachers present. In fact, they all remarked – more than once during the two days – that it was astonishing and the first time they could recall when one of their conferences had been attended by an 'interloper' from the secondary sector. What is more, they considered it a very positive, sensible and beneficial thing for me and for them, and they expressed a strong desire that more secondary heads would follow my example. I am sure that in the intervening years between then and now, their expressed wish has become more commonplace and standard practice, or I certainly hope it has. In many ways, as a direct result of the loss of catchment areas and designated partner primary schools following the move to more open enrolment, such practice has become even more important and valuable, if secondary heads and primary heads are to work together and learn from one another. However, another direct result of this loss of a cosy number of catchment schools is that it has become far more difficult to work collaboratively in this way, as the intake for a typical secondary school could well involve students drawn from an even greater number of potentially partner primary schools.

This illustrates yet another way in which Conservative government initiatives, such as open enrolment and increased competition between schools have made collaboration, cohesion and coherence between schools in the same phase of education, and certainly between schools in different phases, much more difficult to accomplish, with the concomitant loss of the considerable benefits to be gained from sharing interesting practice and generating a much more beneficial synergy of professional learning between teachers.

Putting Things in Perspective

Throughout this section of the book, I have given my own views regarding what I perceive as the pervasive, largely unhelpful and often destructive effects of government interference and intervention in state education directly and, indirectly, the influence that these interventions have also had on international and independent schools. For the sake of balance, however, I should perhaps concede that there are some initiatives that I have already acknowledged, welcomed and applauded, such as the requirement for school development plans, and measures which have opened up *'the secret garden of the curriculum'* thanks to schools being required to publish a school brochure or prospectus, including their values, aims and objectives.

I also feel that being required to demonstrate greater accountability to stakeholders and to be assessed by qualified others, such as LEA or OFSTED inspectors, is only right and proper, as long as extremes of party-political pressures and prejudices are kept well away from the process. So, whilst I acknowledge that government intervention is perfectly reasonable, as well as right and proper in principle, in practice the approach should be one of partnership and not pressure, collaboration between government agencies and schools rather than coercion, as well as sharing and celebrating good practice and not stressing, shaming or otherwise denigrating the efforts of professional people who are willing to give their all to the service of what is a very demanding and incredibly challenging function of government, and their job.

476

In other words, government influence could be a force for the good of education if politicians **listened** more intently, carefully and genuinely to education professionals and academics, rather than their lobbyists, political pressure groups and vested interests. Government could indeed be a force for good if our elected representatives in power exhibited trust and respect for teachers, school leaders or managers and governing bodies, rather than undermining their autonomy through ill-conceived and politically motivated accountability measures. As Einstein once said, *"All things that count cannot be measured, and not all things that can be measured count."*

Government could also be a force for good if they were prepared to promote collaboration, coherence and cohesion between schools and their stakeholders rather than naked, wasteful and selfish competition. We are seeking to educate **all** of our country's young people, rather than just some, or at least I hope that is what we are trying to achieve. Sadly, for most of the last thirty years, government intervention has largely failed to achieve any of the above and so deserves to be condemned as being divisive, derogatory and detrimental.

What is more, previous sections of the book have examined the negative hidden messages that are sent as a result of a lot that goes on in the name of education and argued that the system of state education is more about mere schooling and in need of a major and radical paradigm shift if it is to break free from the shackles imposed by the persistent practice of the last 180 years or so.

Reform alone is not enough, as that implies tinkering around with the current system. But that system is indeed broken and mending something that is outdated and no longer serving the needs of generations of young people would be pretty pointless. The whole edifice needs to be discarded and replaced with a more relevant, fulfilling, student centred and liberating model which is based on partnership, teamwork and mutual benefit, as well as one that actively promotes education for education's sake, and not for some purely utilitarian notion of moulding young people for the world of work and adult life generally.

As an 'old' teacher and someone who passionately believes in the concept of society and social cohesion and development, it is understandable that with such a perspective I might be highly critical of the current model of schooling, as opposed to genuine education. However, if we were honest, there are others who are supposedly beneficiaries of the existing system who are equally critical and condemnatory in their comments and views about the current 'broken' system, and who are calling for it to be replaced and not merely fixed.

As an illustration of this, I will refer to yet another article published in The Guardian newspaper in the UK, entitled *'School system "shameful" says CBI boss'*, which reported views expressed by Richard Lambert the then Director General or head of the most powerful group that represents business leaders in the UK. What makes this even more interesting is that Mr. Lambert expressed his views during the time of the last Labour government and so one might expect someone in his position to be critical of a left-wing administration but, as we will see, he was condemning the failures of largely Conservative governments before that time.

In the article, based on an interview he had with The Guardian, Mr Lambert said that money was being wasted in English schools, which had some of the most generous funding in the world but examination results that were beginning to trail behind competitor countries. Ignoring the fact that his only real yardstick of successful education rests upon results in external examinations and global competition, he was reported as saying that the education system is failing young people from poorer homes because it was producing exam results which *"we ought to be ashamed of"*. He went on to claim that the problems in state schools were a product of a *"culture of low aspiration"* that predated the then Labour government and included the longer period of Tory administrations. To quote him from the article more directly, he was reported to have said:

"If you look at all the data you see as a country we spend a lot on educating kids, but the outcomes aren't great. There's a very long tail of under-performance. I think this is more than an educational issue, it's a social and cultural issue as well.......Part of the story is the correlation between deprivation and poor academic outcomes, which are more marked in

this country than we ought to be able to contemplate. We ought to ashamed of the numbers."

His comments were perceptive and saw the problems as being largely external to schools themselves, which makes one wonder why government intervention seems to have always focused on school problems rather than the bigger societal picture. To be more precise, he said, *"There is an absolutely straight correlation between GCSE results and free school meals, a straight line so the most deprived get the worst results."*

Furthermore, I think it is extremely important to note that his comments were not negative about the work of schools in general, in fact he acknowledged from first-hand experience that he had visited *"lots of amazing schools"* and seen *"amazing teachers doing amazing things"*. As a result, he rightly and sensibly recognised that there must be some other cause of the academic under-performance, which he attributed to, *"social, cultural pressures; aspirational gaps."*

In saying this, Mr. Lambert was being very genuine and honest and, in my view, utterly correct. Schools alone, no matter how well they function and perform, and for whatever reason, cannot be held up as the scapegoat for a much wider and more challenging social and economic malaise that also requires a radical change before, or in tandem with, the essential paradigm shift that must be allowed to inform our country's education and school system. Consequently, it is to this *'bigger picture'* that I now wish to turn and examine what some of those social, cultural pressures and aspirational gaps, to which Mr. Lambert referred, might actually be, how they have arisen, as well as how they might be addressed and rectified.

Section G: The Bigger Picture

Chapter Twenty Two: Meritorious Meritocracy!

'The Slippery Slope'

Willingly risking a little repetitive tedium, throughout this book I have often made reference to an English dictionary to begin or introduce various sections or ideas by examining the generally understood meaning of important words which we use in an attempt to entertain and communicate core concepts whether they be concrete or abstract, in conversation, argument, discussion, negotiation, etc. Indeed, the English language is veritably incredibly rich, endowed as it is with an extensive, comprehensive and often fascinating vocabulary. We have at our disposal a huge number of words, phrases, idioms and metaphors which provide us with the means to express our ideas, our feelings and emotions, hopefully with linguistic accuracy, in a whole variety of different situations and contexts.

More often than not, we usually learn new vocabulary in a contextual way by listening to others speak, by reading books and newspapers, through conversations at work and with our friends, families and so on. Consequently, and I imagine surprisingly often, we use words in a somewhat clumsy way, perhaps without fully understanding their meaning or truly grasping the fact that one word can mean subtly different things in different circumstances, and to different people. Ask anyone, for example, to define the meaning of a word that they might use on a regular basis and see how difficult and frustrating they can often find the task of adequately completing such a seemingly simple request, without actually using the word itself, of course. But we really do need to share a greater clarity of what key words and concepts mean if only because this mutual comprehension forms the basis for a common dialogue and, subsequently, allows us to achieve a shared understanding of what it is that we are seeking to communicate – thereby facilitating a true meeting of the minds!

Semantics, the branch of linguistics that deals with the meaning of words and sentences in isolation can, therefore, be used to clarify what we want to say, as well as to cloud and confuse communication. In an attempt to pursue its former and more helpful application, let us take the meaning of the word '**power**', for example – a word that has enormous significance and is frequently used by those interested in politics with a small and a large 'p'!

Too often, the word 'power' is taken to mean a situation where somebody is in a position to exercise a lot of control over other people and their activities. In this sense, its manifestation is something that is done unto others, with two sets of protagonists, the controllers and the controlled – or, theoretically, and perhaps somewhat naively, in the context of our democratic system, the politicians and the electorate. Rather than representing the electorate, politicians take it upon themselves to know better and to take control over the life-styles, if not the life chances, of so many people. As a result, too many people discover that, in reality, they are actually quite unable to influence or control things or events themselves – things and events that impinge upon their lives and those of others. Sure, they can exercise a degree of control over the mundane matters of life, such as which channel they are going to watch on television, but what about the truly fundamental and crucial aspects of their existence and welfare?

Napoleon Hill in his celebrated book, *'Think and Grow Rich'* says that Man was designed for accomplishment, engineered for success and endowed with the seeds of greatness. How true! We all have the latent skills, talents and aptitudes to be successful and truly happy in our lives so why is it that such a tiny percentage of our citizens ever manages to *'reach the top'* – to fulfil their innate potential and become really active players, if not real 'winners', in the game of life?

Henry David Thoreau said that most men lead lives of quiet desperation. So why is it that people prefer to sit it out on the substitute's bench, living vicariously through the ones who are actually doing it, consoling themselves that they could have been contenders if only they had had the breaks, the luck, the right parents, education, environment, talent, etc.?

We are all rapidly becoming 'couch potatoes' and arguably we have already reached that end; a spectator nation that increasingly spends its precious leisure time watching others doing things that we would really like to do, if of course we even believe that we could. Our adulation of our sports stars and the vast sums of money that they can earn – assuming that they win their team or individual game or event – turn these mere mortals into highly marketable and 'valuable' celebrities, with all the physical, spiritual, mental and moral pressures that this somewhat perverse system generates, whilst the rest of us sit back and savour the gladiatorial contests that are televised for our entertainment. These days, it is the worship of Mammon that is the ultimate divinity which our athletes and sports personalities are programmed to practise and covet.

I have been criticised for my cynicism regarding the way in which winning at all costs has become a highly malignant tumour which is eating away at the very fabric of sporting and human endeavour, destroying the joy of participating in an avaricious quest to win at all costs. In this way, our celebrities are being manipulated by the system and the people who also stand to gain from their success; they are no longer really in control owing to the power that such forces exert over their thinking, their behaviours and their actions. The very pressures that our sports men and women are placed under by our – and their – lust for victory (if not for glory) are immense and often unbearable. Very often these pressures and stresses grow to the extent that they too, quite literally, lose control over their own lives.

The Olympic spirit was supposed to be enshrined in the belief that it was the taking part and not the winning that was all important. This supreme ideal has been effectively substituted by the maxim of 'win at all costs', even if that means taking illegal substances, fouling, bribing, deceiving, cheating and anything else that meets the often unrealistic expectations of the paying public and 'the sponsors'. Cast your mind back to the plight of Ronaldo in the Soccer World Cup Final of 1998 – allegedly pressurised into playing for Brazil having just suffered some sort of fit. Did he choose to play? Was he, even with all his income and wealth, truly in control of his own actions at that time?

Consider, also, the 1998 Tour de France which was bedevilled by the infamous doping scandal. Surely, the French police were quite right to treat the riders involved as drug-takers and pushers just like any other addict. The cyclists complained that the police were treating them like 'common criminals'.....well, if the (cycling) helmet fits.....! Where was the outcry by the 'innocent' cyclists when illegal drug-taking by some of their fellow competitors was alleged and admitted to by so many of their rivals and, often, team mates? I would have been outraged had I, after months and years of dedicated, hard training and personal sacrifice been in competition with others who were then found to be cheating to gain unfair advantage – wouldn't you? Why, then, did so many of the other riders, when asked if they too had ever taken illegal substances to 'enhance their performance' (linguistic garnish for 'cheat'), reply not with an emphatic and reassuring denial, but by saying that they had "never tested positive"? In other words, "I have never been caught," Is that really an adequate defence? Perhaps, the prize for sheer hypocrisy should go to cyclist Lance Armstrong, who went even further when looking straight into the camera lens and insisted, on numerous occasions, that he had "never doped", let alone never tested positive.

The truth of the 1998 Tour de France is that it was finally rumbled that drug-taking was endemic – as well as an epidemic. Instead of condemnation by fellow riders we witnessed their collusion, collaboration and support in the form of demonstrations against the actions of the French police, and attempts to be assured that no other riders would have their hotel rooms searched. Some teams withdrew rather than risk such treatment – methinks they did protest too much!

The traditionally wonderful spectacle of the Tour de France became a mere side-show to the doping debacle. The event itself was threatened by the actions of the riders who were basically saying to the organisers – leave us alone or else there will be no completed Tour de France this year. The money, quite literally riding on the event for the organisers and their sponsors was too great to lose. The certain, adverse reaction by the French public to any cancellation or further dilution of the event would have been potentially terminal to a once great sporting competition. Indeed, it seems as though the vast majority of the loyal spectators were in sympathy with the alleged and admitted cheats because of the harsh punishment meted out to them in accordance with the rules of the competition and the laws of the country. Where are we going? Is anyone really in control of this nonsense – apart from the offenders, or those who aid and abet them in one way or another?

What will happen in the years ahead to avoid such awful diversions in this and other international competitions? Perhaps we will see a more rigorous testing of riders followed by the most severe of penalties for those who are found to have cheated and otherwise broken the rules and codes of good conduct. Alternatively, we can expect the ruling bodies of various sporting competitions to admit defeat and simply deem currently illegal, performance-enhancing drugs to be legal. Indeed, in some sports this has already happened. In American baseball, players are already allowed to take certain types of performance-enhancing drugs, or steroids that are prohibited in other sports – sports whose governing bodies are merely thinking of joining their colleagues on this infamously slippery slope.

What will be the response to this? Surely, all that will happen is that new (unauthorised) drugs will be developed to enable athletes to steal an advantage over their rivals – the financial and other rewards associated with winning are an ample incentive under such 'market' forces. Winning will increasingly become a question of who has the best chemist!

More and more athletes will run the risk of severe and serious health problems in mid-life, even premature death, for their moment of glory. Will we try to stop and turn the clock back when an athlete dies during the tournament as a result of prolonged or careless use of some legal/illegal substance? Or will it be claimed that it was an accident because the deceased person was just not in control of her/his newly enhanced 'diet'?

I feel that my observations and comments above are entirely justified when we look at the most recent (at time of writing) revelations regarding doping in sports, namely the outrageous scandal that is the state-supported and systematic doping in Russian athletics which, according to the investigators, almost certainly involves not only other sports, but also will be found to have become common practice in several other countries as well. Furthermore, as if the unfolding problems of the IAAF were not enough to have to contend with, there are also the on-going and yet to be concluded investigations into FIFA. In short, in sport, corruption is rife and the athletes and victims of doping are often coerced or duped into doing the bidding of their corrupt coaches, administrators, governing bodies and now, seemingly, governments as well!

Implications for Schooling and Education

So how is all or any of this really germane to the central theme of this book, or how is the above relevant to the way in which I believe schools so often fail young people, rather than it being juxtaposed and expressed instead as young people failing at school, which is the manner in which this unfortunate system of schooling is portrayed in the media and public consciousness? Well, it should be abundantly clear from what has gone before, that my genuine and fervent belief is that the major aim for schools is to enlighten young people, to energize and empower them in the process of helping them to discover their true talents and their passions. Striving to attain that goal may then form the catalyst that powers and drives young people to fulfil their destinies as individual men and women, and make their positively indelible mark upon their families, their communities and societies, as well as their nations and even the world. Moreover, the process of striving to make one's mark may enable young people to feel a true and lasting fulfilment in their current and future lives. A somewhat idealistic or romantic vision perhaps, but what a worthy goal if we are genuinely seeking to maximise the potential of our people – young and older!

To achieve this will require not only root and branch changes in how we perceive, structure, operate and fund schools – assuming, of course, that we keep such institutions, at least in the medium term – but there will also have to be a fundamental change in the way we conduct our societies at large and in microcosm. There is absolutely no point whatsoever, to liberate and enlighten our young people if they are then to leave school and live and work in societies that seek to control them and exert external power over them, in the interests of larger organisations, business corporations or others generally. For example, the pernicious way in which endemic cheating and defrauding in sport is undermining fair competition, is sending all the wrong hidden messages to our young people. Of far greater concern to us all should be the effect that this reckless behaviour, exhibited by hugely powerful role models, has upon our children and young people. Already, some young people are taking illegal substances in an attempt to make them something they think they could be or ought to be. Others have openly admitted that they would take performance-enhancing drugs if they thought that others, with whom they were competing, were likely to be doing the same thing. This smacks of a modern day version of 'fighting fire with fire'.

This frightening scenario is already fast becoming a reality. Why be surprised? After all, little or nothing has been done to stop young people and children aping the loutish behaviour of some tennis players, and most footballers for example, who seem to persistently question and verbally abuse the umpires and referees with impunity. Go to virtually any school or other amateur soccer fixture and observe the same delinquent behaviour on the part of the players, let alone many of the spectators. It has become almost a ritual and most definitely part of the culture of the game, and an unwanted part at that. In the USA – currently the most powerful role model for the rest of the world (sadly) – it is a growing problem, with verbal and physical fights breaking out among spectator parents at school sporting fixtures, for example. Perhaps we are losing the fundamental plot?

If we were honest and took a 'time-out' to think long and hard about the way we live our lives and the 'choices' we make, we might consider that things are not as we would like them. I ask again, are we really in control? After all, we can choose to take control over our own lives, or allow ourselves, often unconsciously, to be controlled. We can try and choose our own goals and then make plans to achieve them, or we can simply become part of someone else's plans. The question is are we going to become courageous leaders or meek followers?

Two famous quotations spring to mind at this point, both of which relate to living our lives and following our inner dreams so that we do not die with the bitter taste of regret tainting our final moments. Both quotations are from people who are no longer with us, as they passed on not that many years ago, and the first is attributed to Dhirubhai Ambani, who was the successful business tycoon who founded the Reliance Industries in Mumbai. He said:

"If you don't build your dream, someone else will hire you to help them build theirs."
And, as if working as a double act, the late Emanuel James 'Jim' Rohn, a successful American entrepreneur, author and motivational speaker added:

"If you don't design your own life plan, chances are you'll fall into someone else's plan. And guess what they have planned for you? Not much!"

As a nation, I maintain that we are literally losing the ability to exercise any meaningful control over most aspects of our lives. Many people have entirely lost this fundamental human right already, and are either unaware of the fact or feel unable to do anything about it. In short, more and more people are coming to discover and, more worryingly, accept that they are impotent – the feeling that they have no power to influence people or events, even their own lives and the forces that shape their lives and basic existence. This, I believe, goes a long way to explain that the disaffection felt by so many members of the electorate with the efficacy of the democratic process is such that they do not even bother to vote at General Elections.

The practical application of 'power' as some control that is exercised over us, is very much the one that characterises our lives in the UK, and probably in most countries in the World. The marvel is that this power is often exercised in such a covert and inconspicuous way that many of us are led to actually believe that we **are** in control. As President Nelson Mandela notes in his autobiography:

"Laws stripping people of their rights were invariably described as laws restoring those rights."

Consider again the 1988 Education Reform Act, steered successfully through a Conservative dominated Parliament by the then Secretary of State for Education, Kenneth Baker. This was heralded as a great reforming piece of legislation that transferred power in education away from the so-called 'Educational Establishment' and back into the hands of the consumers – sorry, the parents. To begin with, the real 'consumers' of education are surely the students who may also be represented by their parent(s) or guardians. The central importance of meeting the needs of the young people who represent our future is something that we should never lose sight of, and yet how rare it is for teachers and parents, let alone local or national government to really canvass the views of these important young individuals. Far too often they are being patronised as being too young to know what is good for them. But in

490

any case, the 1988 Act was a brilliant piece of divisive and typically devious legislation on the part of the Tories. Whilst proclaiming to be giving power to parents, the Act effectively bestowed upon the Secretary of State for Education literally hundreds of additional powers, many of which were originally the gift of Local Education Authorities and schools working in partnership with parents within the context of their local communities. This was effectively transferring power in education away from the 'Educational Establishment' and handing it to the 'Political Establishment' in the shape of the traditional and ruling elite in Parliament in Westminster.

The real effect of that piece of legislative trickery, that statutory sleight of hand – ably assisted by the largely Conservative controlled 'free' Press – was to throw education into highly damaging and inappropriate competition rather than collaboration; encouraging schools to work against, rather than with one another. Conflict was to replace harmony with no tangible benefit to the schools, parents and students, as far as I could see.

I am not the sad victim of so-called conspiracy theorists. The reality, if only we were prepared to be honest about what really goes on all around us, is that there has been a big increase in the dominant, top-down, application of power accompanied by a corresponding reduction in our ability to do things for ourselves, or to take control. Real power is bestowed upon people when they have <u>both</u> the **ability** and the **resources** to take control over their lives, and to determine things for themselves.

It is considered rather trendy to talk about 'empowering people' so that they have the authority or power to do something for themselves, either at work or in their personal lives. Again the reality is that people who seek to rubbish the notion of genuinely empowering people in this way, or perhaps pay mere lip service to it, are usually those who have most to lose in terms of their loss of controlling, dominant power as a result of giving people the means to achieve something for themselves. To give people power in such a way is to bestow upon them genuine status in a particular situation which, through a sense of personal achievement, fosters a feeling of legitimate self-esteem and self-worth.

Living in a Meritocracy

It is often said that we live in a meritocracy – a society in which people get status or rewards (or both) because of what they actually achieve, rather than because of their wealth or social position. Although this is a highly desirable state of affairs, in the context of the UK it is unfortunately what may generously be described as being more of a myth or an illusion than a genuine reality.

The myth that we can all achieve success and happiness by dint of our own initiative and efforts alone is a dangerous concept in that it provides us with an excuse for doing nothing, or precious little, to sweep aside or eliminate the enormous and often multiple obstacles that so many people face – even before birth – in their attempts to lead successful lives. Social position, privilege, income and wealth are so inequitably distributed that most people face considerable, if not insurmountable, barriers in their attempts to achieve success, with the result that many talented men, women and children silently and unconsciously surrender their aspirations, or seek to achieve them in ways which run counter to the mores or guiding principles of the society that so effectively constrains them and keeps them 'in their place' in the first place, and then punishes them for their deviant and maladjusted actions and behaviours. In this way, by failing to design their own life plan, such people fall into the plans of central government, and guess what they have planned for these people – not much!

Has the way in which 'schooling' been traditionally envisaged, structured and delivered robbed so many people of being either willing or able to have power over their own lives, thanks to the objective of 'preparation for adult and working life' holding sway, as reinforced with the chimera of endless material consumption as the glittering prize for their endeavours?

To begin with, huge amounts of inherited wealth for a minority of individuals immediately belie the notion of our society being a true meritocracy. By accident of birth, some individuals immediately inherit enormous advantage over the vast majority of their fellow citizens in the 'competition' of life today. The point that I make here is not necessarily that this practice is wrong and should be outlawed (although I do believe that it needs to be regulated, and its effects minimised or seriously compensated for), rather that it is a complete contradiction to argue for maintaining the current system of inherited wealth whilst insisting that we live in a truly meritocratic society. Surely, to do so is just plain dishonesty, or misguided and hypocritical thinking at least!

Inherited wealth would be no problem or obstacle if we were all able to inherit roughly the same, <u>unearned</u> sums of money and property – or initial advantage. To allow this state of affairs to continue in such a generous, skewed or lopsided manner in a society where there is also a huge disparity in the distribution of <u>earned</u> income and wealth, however, is to add insult to injury for the disadvantaged, and to grant more power to those who are already unduly powerful in our society. Or is it 'their' society?

So, if we do not live in a meritocracy and we genuinely want to make the most of the potential of every member of our national community, then we need to address issues such as the way in which income and wealth is distributed, and the effect this has upon individual and collective opportunity, particularly for those whose life chances are seriously restricted if not actually damaged by the growing inequality that Nobel Prize-winning Economist Joseph Stiglitz brilliantly reveals and analyses in his aptly entitled book, *'The Price of Inequality'*. Let's be honest, the way in which income and wealth is distributed largely determines, or at least has a dramatic impact upon, the distribution of health, education, housing and other factors which vitally affect life chances and the very concept of social mobility for individuals and groups within society. In addition to affecting the distribution of these fundamental human rights, the distribution of income and wealth also plays a major role in determining the <u>quality</u> of such provision.

The life chances of a significant number of people are adversely affected by a deficiency in these basic amenities even ***before birth***. Some people – children and young people even – are discriminated against when applying for a school place or a job simply by the post code that identifies the area where they live in the UK. Moreover, to face a deficiency in one area such as housing is handicap enough but, unfortunately, such impoverishment or deprivation tends to be multiple in nature, with many people suffering from a lack of access to several areas of basic, decent social provision. To make matters worse, these multiple deficiencies tend to be inter-related. This means, for example, that poor housing can have a seriously deleterious effect upon the health of those who have little or no alternative but to accept their lot. A pregnant mother living in squalid circumstances, unable to afford a sufficiently nutritious diet, either because of lack of funds and/or the transport essential to access cheaper food sources in out-of-town supermarkets, is more than likely going to give birth to an underweight child with less than perfect health. This is a well-documented fact and yet it remains a persistent and, arguably, growing problem for a worryingly large and increasing number of people in our 'advanced' industrial and 'developed' society.

In our highly dubious and skewed notion of a meritocracy, a very small minority of people are bequeathed vast amounts of wealth, which is tantamount to a massive and veritable head-start in life, whilst a much bigger minority, thanks to their limited and limiting 'inheritance', face multiple and compounding disadvantages from birth. Such a negative and disadvantageous legacy not only amounts to something more onerous than 'an uphill battle', it is also massively unfair and wholly unjust. In between these two extremes lies a vast, 'grey' territory populated by contestants, in the life-long, erroneously named, game of *'Meritocracy'*, who start to play their role with hugely differing degrees of advantage/disadvantage, or *'Chance'* cards!

In virtually any other game, especially those favoured (and afforded) by the more affluent members of society, such as golf or squash, when a player of considerable skill is matched against someone of inferior ability, in order to make the contest fair and the competition meaningful, a system of bestowing 'a handicap' is introduced. This practice is something of a misnomer, in that it actually involves giving the weaker player a head-start or advantage – in terms of points won, for example. This is in a fair and just recognition of his or her relative lack of ability. The **outcome** is that there is almost always a winner, whereas the handicap allows the game to commence with both parties having roughly an **equal opportunity** or chance of winning. Why, then, in the all-important *'game of life'*, when there is no chance of a replay at a later date, do we adopt the opposite and more commonly used meaning of handicap – namely bestowing, accepting or compounding deprivation and disadvantage?

494

To insist on any contest taking place without such an initial levelling process at the outset is to court a 'walkover' or, worse still, a 'white-wash'. Of course, there is always the outside chance that the weaker player may win as the result of a fluke – as opposed to any real skill – or because the more skilful player lets the other contestant win, by deliberately having an 'off-day'. The same outcome is occasionally the case in the game of life in that a very few people with a negative handicap at birth go on to be remarkably successful. Admittedly, this is in part due to their drive, their talent, their ingenuity, their innate skills and other personal qualities and abilities, but it is also the case that many of these definitive examples of 'exceptions to the rule' are just plain lucky. Their success may simply be attributable to them just being in the right place at the right time with the right idea; they happened to pick up the right 'Chance' cards as the game got underway. The worst thing about this is that such people, or tokens of bucking the system, encourage others to think that they too can be successful if they just try hard enough, and this is a damnable lie.

I remember being at a conference of 'professional' people when a keynote speaker began by remarking that we were all successful people....of course we were......because of our own efforts and initiative. Whilst it is always nice to accept sole responsibility for our achievements (the opposite tendency to blaming others for our shortcomings), I felt duty bound in the name of all due humility and honesty to interrupt in order to qualify the speaker's somewhat smug assumption. Much of my success was a result of having had remarkably supportive parents who not only believed in me, but were also willing and able to allow me several chances to find success in life. Whilst I didn't know what I didn't know, and could have easily become a professional lay-about, (or arguably a highly successful musician, actor and entertainer had I had control over the educational choices made in my name) my parents had higher expectations and aspirations. Their enormous generosity in terms of time and money gave me real opportunity, or at least enabled me to take (and re-take) opportunities that may have already been there even when my indifferent attitude and truculent, adolescent behaviour made me somewhat undeserving and unworthy of such personal sacrifice on their part.

In many cases their actions and kindness served to compensate for an education system that sought to fail me at the earliest opportunity. They encouraged me to try by telling me that I could and should, whilst others, the overlords and agents of 'The System', were guilty of the ultimate crime – conditioned as they were by the dominant social and political hegemony – of insisting that I could not or should not and, if I did, then I would not!

'Horses for Courses'

I remember being quite willing to accept my failure in the 11-Plus examination as being a sign that I was not as 'bright' as the minority that went on to the grammar school. I was destined to take inferior examinations in an (obviously) inferior secondary modern school, along with the concomitant closure of many doors (or windows) of opportunity, and all on the basis of a very narrow, written examination taken on one day in my life. No account was ever taken of my other achievements because there was no historical or broader method of assessment, only that single terminal one just as I approached the age of ten years! Furthermore, nobody really bothered to explain what was happening to me. I just came to meekly accept that grammar school was for the 'brainy' kids who also seemed to constitute only a surprisingly tiny minority of my contemporaries.

How can we seriously say we live in a democratic meritocracy – or is it a meritocratic democracy – when the same opportunity for academic success is not afforded to everyone, especially in a society with such an elitist view of academe, when we effectively write-off the majority at such a ridiculously tender age, especially when it comes to issues such as the incredible degree of maturation that occurs later on, during one's adolescent years?

What is more, during the phased introduction of assessment procedures under the National Curriculum, the extreme right-wing fools who populated the inappropriately termed 'think tanks' that advised the Tory Party seriously entertained the idea of formally assessing children (only applicable in State schools, remember) at the age of seven years. They felt it was important that children of such a low chronological age were allowed and aided to discover the extent of their limitations as soon as possible.

496

More to the point, we now *do* assess those of such tender and early years, and the previous Tory coalition with the Liberal Party went even further by proposing tests should be introduced for five year olds. This, despite the mass of evidence, brilliantly exposed by Guy Claxton in his book '*What's the Point of School? Rediscovering the Heart of Education*', that shows how this mania of holding schools and learners accountable to the Exchequer through more and more testing is causing untold stress for young people in schools. These pressures of being endlessly held to account are contributing to alarming and well-recorded incidence of increasing mental illness, depression and even suicide for young people at school. As if the world they live in and which they are inheriting is not already stressful enough!

Although I failed the 11-Plus, thanks to the ability and willingness of my parents to just about afford a private education, subsidised by H.M. Royal Navy, I eventually went on to gain a first and second degree from 'reputable' universities; there is, after all, a pecking order within the elite world of academe itself. I was able to prove myself to be a late developer in an academic sense because I was lucky enough to be given <u>several</u> and <u>repeated</u> chances to do so. To have been denied this number of false starts or aborted attempts, as was the case for many of my contemporaries, would be akin to refusing people a driving licence if they do not pass a compulsory driving test, allowed to be taken only once after having reached their 17th birthday. Such an idea would be preposterous, except of course in the educational world where it was, and is, seen as the right and proper thing to do.

Moreover, the number of children who were 'selected' to attend the grammar school was determined ultimately by the number of vacant places at the local grammar school rather than the number of young people who reached any established baseline or benchmark of academic achievement. Open another grammar school and more people could and would pass. Open lots of grammar schools and then everyone could go! To continue my chosen analogy, this is like limiting the number of people who pass their **one** chance at the driving test to the number of cars currently in ownership in their area unless, of course, they can afford to move to another part of the country where the number of cars in circulation exceeds the size of the local population. Just plain daft!

497

In the UK, those who failed the eleven-plus could get the opportunity to take the thirteen-plus exam, with the successful ones then being transferred to the grammar school at the age of 13 or 14. The reality, of course, was that having followed a more technical and practical curriculum at secondary modern school, not one student to my knowledge was ever able to reach or match the academic standard attained by their contemporaries at the grammar school, who were following a different type of curriculum. This was not because they were not as 'good', but because the system was cynically failing to truly compare like with like. This cosmetic and largely fallacious 'opportunity' also served to apparently (and artificially) reinforce the reliability of the original assessment at eleven, given that virtually no one can recall anyone transferring schools after success in the thirteen-plus examination. Indeed, can you recall ever having even heard of that particular exam?

Additionally, in the UK, perhaps because independent schools are perceived as inherently better, by dint of their private sector status and more generous per capita funding, the benevolent government would identify a few academically gifted high-fliers and, at the tax-payers' expense, subsidise their 'escape' from the inferiority of the state sector (for which successive governments were responsible) so that they might attend some of the superior, prestigious public schools. This discriminatory *'assisted places scheme'* served to impoverish the state schools which lost these students – effectively robbing Peter to pay Paul!

It's hardly surprising that independent schools tend to perform better in academic league tables when they can select the most academically able students via entrance examinations, and then 'steal' the nascent academic elite of the state schools to boot. This is before one considers that they can afford smaller class sizes, better resources and offer higher salaries to attract supposedly 'better' teachers. Once again, so much for claims of living in a meritocracy when a minority of individuals are selected for such limited and privileged treatment.

All of these token schemes are designed to appease the masses with the attempt to prove the efficacy and fairness of 'the system'. After all, if the tokens can do it, then so can anyone, and so can you! What a crazy and inequitable system it is – one that effectively fails the majority of its young citizens (its future) in order to identify the minority, a relatively small academic elite, who will go on to fill the places at university as well as, eventually, the seats of 'power', one presumes.

Some people can beat the system and go on to achieve success in their lives in a variety of different areas of endeavour. The number of people who failed the eleven-plus and yet have succeeded in all walks of life is testimony to this fact. How have they managed or succeeded to do this? Certainly, for many, it was due to hard work and sheer, personal determination. For others, it was parental support and direction while, for others still, there was perhaps an element of luck.

It has been said that 'luck is merely preparation meeting opportunity', but all such opportunities have, first of all, to arise. Then they have to be spotted or recognised, taken and hopefully maximised or exploited – to make the most of them. Sounds simple, doesn't it? But handicaps prevent many of us from even seeing the opportunities that present themselves in the first place, let alone take them. It was once said that many people trip up over opportunities in life only to get up, dust themselves off and walk away as if nothing had happened. To be prepared to take an opportunity, or to be 'lucky', is a great deal to do with having the resources that are necessary such as financial or human skill, talent, self-esteem and self-belief. In either case, the maldistribution of resources, and the inequality in the area of education, as well as low self-esteem due to apparently repeated failure, can present formidable obstacles even when people are trying to 'make their own luck' in life. Similarly, another resource that may be needed to take full advantage of an opportunity, of course, is the time to take it. Many young people, in the UK and, especially in many developing countries, simply do not get the luxury of that space in time as they have jobs to do after school in order to supplement their family's income. This debars them from having the time to be actively involved in valuable learning opportunities that are often called 'extra-curricular' or, in the USA, 'co-curricular' activities.

Notions of Equality and Inequality

499

If we were prepared to be entirely honest with ourselves, and with others, we would admit that there is an undeniable need to make structural and more significant compensations for the unfair way in which income and wealth is distributed, and seek instead to offer much **greater equality** of opportunity. Some people are led to believe that 'equality of opportunity' is espoused by people who want everyone to be the same. This is, of course, utterly trite in its naivety and cant complacency! *'Equality of opportunity'* is most definitely not the same thing as **'equality of outcome'**. To believe otherwise is clearly a nonsense and flies in the face of the inevitable reality that we are all inherently unique individuals. For the 'powers that be' to devalue the notion of the former, by implying that it is synonymous with the latter, is just one way in which I believe we are effectively controlled.

It is only natural that in a world of diversity of need and talent there will always be those who succeed more than others in any given context and at any given time. But such disparity is only acceptable, and morally just, if everyone has been given the same chance (or opportunity) to be 'more successful' than others at the outset. When I refer to 'success', this may, of course, result in some individuals earning more, but it is to debase the true meaning of success to assume that it must always be financially rewarding. That incredibly narrow and limited assumption is just another way of 'controlling' the actions of others. It also places the acquisition of income and wealth as the sole reason for effort, enterprise – even life – often without regard for how it has been earned.

Real success can be (perhaps 'should be') spiritual as well as material in nature. In fact, it might be that the reason why so many people who are so materially successful and financially 'blessed' often appear to be so dreadfully unfulfilled and unhappy in their lives. Nonetheless, they still act – by working harder and longer – as if the acquisition of even more money and possessions will eventually bring them to that elusive Nirvana. They inevitably fail in this misdirected quest for real happiness, perhaps because it is impossible to square that particular circle. But then who sets the agenda? Who is it (or what is it) that equates the two things when they are so often, if not always, mutually exclusive? Stop and think for a minute, and if you can figure it out, do please let me know your thoughts!

500

In the game of life, the sensible goal of equality of opportunity is spurned in favour of (or substituted for) exactly the opposite scenario. Enormous inequality of opportunity is perpetuated by the massively, and negatively, skewed distribution of income and wealth. The truth, as we all know only too well, is that income and wealth are grossly mal-distributed not only within the UK, but also between the so-called 'developed' and 'developing' countries, worldwide. Some believe this to be a natural state of affairs, an immutable law in the game of life, where there have to be 'winners' and 'losers'.

There is, of course, nothing 'natural' about it. In the world of nature, most things are distributed along a normal distribution curve, like physical height, for example. There are a very small number of midgets at one end of the scale (those who are deemed to be 'vertically challenged') and a very small number of giants at the other (I guess they should be termed the 'vertically blessed'). Most people find themselves of around the average height or, as I would like to say, the median. In other words, line up all the people in the country in order of physical height, with the tallest at one end and the shortest at the other, the median would be the person standing in the middle. The reality is that most of us would be in this average position or, at least, very close to it. The average and the median height would be one and the same, more or less. Most things in nature approximate to this statistical reality. Not so for the way in which income and wealth are distributed!

It is hardly surprising, therefore, that those who are the most ardent supporters of 'free' markets are those who speak out against a fairer/more equitable distribution of income and wealth. As an economist, I am infuriated by the lengths that these people and their accomplices go to, to construct bogus economic arguments to maintain, if not strengthen, the status quo. They put up all kinds of unsubstantiated, often fallacious arguments to prevent the elected government of the day taking the necessary steps to eliminate poverty within our so-called 'advanced' industrial nation, via progressive systems of taxation and intelligent government expenditure programmes. These bogus arguments and dubious theories deserve a careful and lengthy dissection at another time and elsewhere, but a limited critique is perhaps relevant at this juncture.

501

Although all economic systems around the world are mixed economies, we refer to 'free-market' economies and planned economies as the two theoretical extremes at either end of the spectrum of competition and individual ownership/control over the resources used in producing income and wealth. Neither of these two extremes can exist in the real world, which means that all countries adopt a mixed economy solution to the economic problem, with varying proportions of private and public ownership and control over the means of production.

In the USA, we have an example of a market economy, but it is far from being a 'free' market economy, as the government intervenes in a whole host of ways. To begin with it has a public sector, where resources are owned and controlled by the state. The government also implements a range of macroeconomic and microeconomic policy measures designed to modify the workings of the private sector, in which private individuals own and control the means of production.

The old Soviet style economy was essentially centrally planned. Decisions about what to produce and in what quantities, how and where to organise production, and how to distribute the income and wealth generated, were made by a Central Planning Bureau (CPB). Nonetheless, there still had to be elements of a market economy in that system. Private individuals were allowed to own and control some resources and, because it was not possible to 'own' the resource of labour in the production process, workers were encouraged to move to different jobs (and away from others) by means of wage differentials, or market-style incentives, even though these were determined by the state in an attempt to try and direct the allocation of the human resource.

The fundamental criticism of, or flaw in, this type of planned economy was that the goods and services that were produced were those that the CPB decided were the ones that consumers either wanted or should have. This means that the decision of what to produce and in what quantities was made by a few individuals, with resources subsequently being allocated or directed accordingly.

502

Now, whilst there are many other criticisms of both types of economic system, this loss of consumer sovereignty in deciding what to produce is the one on which I wish to focus. After all, how can the members of the CPB possibly know what all consumers taken together desire? Hence, in the former USSR, there were unwanted stocks of some goods and acute shortages of others – something that could never happen in superior market economies, of course.

The better alternative is to allow consumers to determine what is to be produced by giving them the freedom to exercise their demand in the 'market place'. The combined market forces of supply (of producers) and demand (of consumers) will ensure that the goods and services that consumers really want are produced in the right quantities, with the result that maximum satisfaction is derived from the allocation and consumption of our scarce resources, at least in theory.

Market economies are claimed to be 'better' because private, individual consumers can affect the nature and pattern of production via their combined market demand. They get what they want, in other words. **BUT** (yes, this is a big 'but'), market demand is more than just a want for something. It has to be a want that is backed by income, so that mere desire can be expressed as <u>effective</u> demand. The problem is that the promotion of unfettered, or free, market forces always results in the massive negative skew in the distribution of income and wealth, previously referred to, with the result that many, many people simply cannot exercise their free choice because they do not have the money needed to flex their economic muscles.

Thus, it seems entirely logical and sensible that those who advocate the supremacy of market forces in ensuring the best allocation of resources, would want to ensure that income and wealth were re-distributed, if not equally, then in a far more equitable fashion, so that the market failure of negatively skewed income distribution does not prevent the market from achieving its theoretical objective of maximum, or optimum, consumer satisfaction. Fat chance!

The Acheson Report on Health Inequality, set up in 1997 by the Labour Health Minister, is an extraordinary survey of the condition of the disadvantaged British. It may seem obvious, but the Report finds it necessary to remind us all that the main cause of poverty is that ***poor people have no money***. What a stunning revelation! Consequently, if we are ever to tackle the problem seriously, we must have welfare reform which unambiguously deals with this most fundamental cause of the problem. It is a diversionary tactic simply to expect the poor to somehow help themselves, by pulling themselves up by their bootstraps, when they are denied the means to do so. We have a collective obligation to achieve one of the cornerstones of any society that claims to be affluent, advanced and developed, let alone civilised, decent and compassionate, which is the elimination of grinding and disempowering absolute and even relative poverty - surely!

The Report chronicles the multiple handicaps that constitute the wider definition of poverty. Will Hutton summarised these so starkly and wonderfully well in his article in the 'Observer' newspaper (29.11.98) that I include them as written below:

*"The poor are unhealthy. They live less long; they suffer more from lung cancer, coronary heart disease, strokes, suicide and violent accidents than their richer peers – inequalities that have steadily been getting worse over the past twenty years. They are more likely to have their cars stolen and their homes vandalised. They eat less iron, calcium, dietary fibre and vitamin C. They are fatter. Their homes are colder. The schools their children attend have poorer results and they will be less well fed, with their mothers going without to achieve even that, and they are less likely to have enjoyed any pre-school education. They will have less access to child care, which, in any case, is the most expensive in Europe. The list goes on. There is one over-riding reason for their circumstances. They are not morally depraved, work-shy or single parents who have malevolently chosen to have a litter of children they cannot afford. What binds them together is **lack of money**."*

In his Report, Acheson reminds us that the social welfare payments that we offer to these, our fellow disadvantaged citizens, is simply too low to live on. Worse still, many of those entitled to benefit payments, do not even claim them, due to the stigma and loss of dignity associated with the means-testing that so often precedes this meagre out-pouring of state largesse, (although if one were to believe the evil misrepresentations of the Tories and their media pals, they are all a bunch of dependents and scroungers, which of course, excuses them from further reductions in such payments).The penalty, inherent in these two easily avoidable factors, impacts most seriously upon young, pregnant mothers and children under the age of two years, totally innocent children, in the form of an inadequately nutritious diet. Such a reminder, and from such an eminent source, powerfully counters and shames smugly misplaced notions that we all live in a real meritocracy!

The publication of The Acheson Report just so happened to coincide with the release of the findings of a sixteen-year-long study by the Medical Research Council into the effects of poor nutrition on babies in the last three months of pregnancy and around the age of two years, when brain growth is at its most pronounced. The results provided clear evidence of a huge loss of cognitive potential due to poor nutrition. If the government of the day is serious about significantly improving literacy and numeracy levels of children in school and, subsequently, the population as a whole, it would do well to raise benefit levels to those that would enable the brains of these seriously disadvantaged babies, and embryos, to grow as nature intended and stand a much better chance of fulfilling their true potential. The increased expenditure needed to provide impoverished, pregnant mothers with an adequate diet will clearly be a lot less than the cost of compensatory measures after the birth of the child. Doing this also avoids another, currently overlooked, failing of the wonderful capitalist system.

In his Report, Acheson referred to the evolution of what he called 'food deserts' in the context of many poorer housing estates, which describes a situation where shops selling fresh food and vegetables have literally ceased to exist. This forces our poorer citizens to travel in order to purchase their basic means of survival, at a time when the cost of public transport has rocketed in the wake of its privatisation and/or de-regulation. In South Yorkshire, for example, de-regulation led to a 250 per cent increase in bus fares. Private gain at public expense seems arguably to be the true motive behind all privatisation. The attitude of the Tory government towards our more disadvantaged and deprived citizens, as well as public sector employees who won't do as they wish, seems to be one of, "Fuck you! What are you going to do about it?" (My apologies for resorting to such base language, but then it is a totally justifiable summary, I would argue, especially today, when I hear that Jeremy Hunt has announced in Parliament that the government will enforce their new and highly-contentious contract on junior doctors, because of the two sides being unable to arrive at a consensus.)

In his wide-ranging Report, Acheson argues that the government needs to work on a broad front if it is really serious about dealing with this unacceptable level of human suffering and disadvantage within the boundaries of our 'great' nation. This would, in turn, require increasing social payments and putting right the detrimental and destructive effects of the massive and sustained cuts in government expenditure, on such things as housing and education, undertaken by the Thatcher and subsequent Tory governments towards the end of the last millennium, which were vigorously renewed under the previous, malevolent Conservative/Liberal coalition government, and now more forcefully and perniciously by the 'True Blue' Tories and their own 'majority' government. They really are an uncaring, selfish and self-serving bunch of spoilt brats!

If anything meaningful is to be done to alleviate the lot of what is conservatively estimated (no pun intended) as nine million adults and two million children living in the circumstances and at the time described by Acheson, then we have another compelling reason for a more equitable distribution of income and wealth. Before this can happen, there will have to be an acceptance, on the part of the majority of the electorate, that this is at least necessary, if not long over-due.

Perhaps the most dangerous legacy of the Thatcher years, and the hardest one to overturn, is that naked self-interest, intolerance and greed are now seen as the tenets of a decent society. Indeed, a whole generation grew up at a time when this particularly nasty ideology was the only obviously apparent show in town. Perhaps this explains the sadomasochistic belief that continued austerity policies are the only way to ensure sustained growth, which is the pernicious, parsimonious and pusillanimous mantra that we hear from Thatcher's Tory heirs in the form of Cameron and Osborne. It is unbelievable that these clowns are inflicting irreparable, long-term damage to the productive potential of the British economy, let alone increasing the inequality and depths of disadvantage of millions of people, and being allowed to convince the general public that things are apparently getting better. This is not only far off the mark, it is also a blatant lie for the vast majority of British citizens for whom it is anything other than 'apparent'.

'Where Power Really Lies?'

The reality is, however, that all politicians are becoming increasingly powerless to act in the interests of those they are elected to serve, due to the huge countervailing power wielded by the large multinational corporations. These organisations are possibly the greatest threat to true democracy and the delightful diversity of national cultures that we face today. These corporations essentially have the power to benignly approve or actively veto any government policy measure, whether these be social, economic or environmental in nature. We need look no further than the USA to see how quickly the supreme marionette, George W. Bush, acted to appease his presidential paymasters in the energy giants and power utilities. The so-called 'leader' of the country in which 6% of the world's population collectively produced over 25% of all greenhouse gases, effectively ripped-up the Kyoto Treaty on global warming, an international agreement designed to make very modest reductions in the rate of growth of these environmentally destructive and life-threatening industrial emissions. He repeatedly sought to open-up the Arctic National Wildlife Refuge to oil-drillers, retracted his presidential campaign promises to protect forests, and moved to weaken the requirements on mining companies to clean-up after themselves. Not bad for starters, and it only cost those vested interests US$47 million in *tax-deductable* campaign 'gifts'.

These corporations operate across national boundaries and owe no allegiance to any one country, or anyone, other than themselves. They pursue that myopic and potentially terminal goal of profit at almost any real cost. How can we expect a government anywhere to take steps to redress the aforementioned inequalities in income and wealth, when this will require us all to make a contribution in the form of higher-tax payments to the government of the day? Under progressive systems of taxation, it is those with the greatest earnings and accumulations of income and wealth that will be called upon to make the greatest contribution because, quite simply, they can afford to. But any attempt to raise (as opposed to reduce) the tax rates on these global giants results in their threatening to close-down or scale-back their operations in the country in question, with all the devastating potential knock-on effects that such an act would have upon employment and national prosperity. This happens everywhere. In Germany, for example, the income from corporate taxes has fallen by 50% in the last twenty years, whilst at the same time the profits of these organisations have increased by 90%. Similarly, any attempt to impose what are called 'green taxes', which are an incentive to encourage corporate giants to take steps to act in a more environmentally-friendly manner, rather than to generate income for redistributive purposes, is also met with the same moral blackmail.

We, the people, appear powerless and governments are also evidently powerless, which is precisely why we need to act on a united front to protect ourselves against such naked abuses of power. In the same way that workers need to combine together and form Trades Unions, so world governments must form supra-national bodies if they are to stop being blackmailed by these distasteful and self-serving multi-national corporate bullies.

These multinational corporations have been given excessive power by the very governments that they now can hold to ransom. Margaret Thatcher's and the Conservatives' inherently unfair and skewed notion of economics led her to denounce monopoly trades unions and then effectively seek to emasculate, if not destroy, them. Her motives were rooted in her determination to wage and win a class war – why else horrendously and arrogantly refer to striking miners, trying to protect their livelihoods and their long-established communities, as *"the enemy within"*? At the same time as seeking to hide these true motives behind flimsy economic theory (and that is being generous), she was more than happy to turn a blind eye to a literal festival of mergers and amalgamations, take-over bids and buy-outs, which resulted in a huge increase in the concentration of industrial production in the hands of a much smaller number of producers. Monopoly producers good; labour monopolies bad! What blatant and transparent hypocrisy!

We have to at least regain real control over our lives, assuming that we ever really had any of course. If not, then we must at least stop any further erosion of our self-power, by seeking to ensure that our national governments can make the decisions needed to achieve that which they were elected to do for us, the electorate. When domestic, party politics resembles a 'Punch & Judy' show, and when large corporations wield countermanding amounts of economic and political power, is it at all surprising that the electorate questions the validity of bothering to make the walk to the polling stations. For many, have they already thrown in the towel?

There are many people who may well agree with some of the above but are resigned to the fact that it will survive in perpetuity, or until conventional wisdom is quite literally overthrown by demands for change, and at the point where the damage may be permanent even if the recognition of the overwhelming need for change is finally in the ascendency. Others still may believe that it is now apparently *impossible* to seriously entertain the necessary and urgent radical and progressive surgery that is desperately needed if we are to transform our disfigured political economic system into something that more effectively meets and resembles the needs of every individual citizen, man, woman, child and student in life. But then, I am reminded of the boundless optimism and realism in the following quotation attributed to the late David McClure Brinkley, an American television newscaster who said:

"Impossible is just a big word thrown about by small men who find it easier to live in the world they've been given than to explore the power they have to change it. Impossible is not a fact. It's an opinion. Impossible is not a declaration. It's a dare. Impossible is potential. Impossible is temporary. Impossible is nothing."

We need to enable and empower our young people to develop the skills, the values, the knowledge and the talents needed to regain control so that they can truly exercise power over, and in, their lives so that they can accept the dare to which David Brinkley refers and explore the potential of the currently impossible. They need to be endowed with fortitude, self-confidence, resilience and much else besides, such as creative brilliance, if they are to resist, counter and successfully overcome the brickbats thrown at them in their ambitious and vital quest and, achieve a better society for us all by again heeding the wise words of David Brinkley:

"A successful man is one who can lay a firm foundation with the bricks that others have thrown at him."

Chapter Twenty Three: Cohesion, Collaboration, Coherence

Society Does Exist!

I make no apologies for having what others may wish to call socialist beliefs and values in life, as I recognise that society does indeed exist and that it explains how we are all bound together despite being a collection of individual beings. Unfortunately, the reality is that our society is under a sustained attack by those whose individual interest runs counter to those of us taken together.

A society that functions effectively is one that recognises and encourages individuality and independence whilst seeking to build collaborative networks of industry, effort and personal interest so that there is more than a semblance of cohesion and coherence to our collective actions. Such aims are the very antithesis of competition and conflict that naked self-interest actively encourages, promotes and even worships. In many respects, these notions of collaboration, social cohesion and coherence are contrary forces to the impotence and powerlessness that are a result of the societal fragmentation, referred to in the previous chapter.

What is more, it is this very fragmentation which is one of the root causes of what leads us to possess feelings of individual impotence and powerlessness. After all, *'divide and rule'* is a wonderfully effective concept for keeping us in our place, so to speak. Politicians and leaders frequently, if not always, resort to this highly effective tactic to achieve, maintain or strengthen their power base. The successive governments presided over by Margaret Thatcher, for example, used this tactic with remarkable skill and aplomb, especially in breaking the power of the public sector unions, taking on one group after the other.

In essential service areas like health and education, the sheer professionalism and dedication of the work force produces, within the staff, a natural reluctance to take any form of what might loosely be called 'industrial' action that might hurt patients or students respectively. It takes a lot to provoke such groups into withdrawing their labour, but provoked they most definitely were, and under the current, anti-public sector Cameron government, this process is being continued with renewed vigour and extreme right-wing political zeal and zest.

Recently, the UK temporarily managed to avert a highly damaging strike by junior doctors, whose goodwill, conditions of work and working conditions were being substantially undermined and worsened by a bunch of Tory ministers who understand the price of everything and the value of nothing. Their political agenda is to squeeze blood from the human stones who are our dedicated junior doctors and classroom teachers, with the result that record numbers are quitting both professions in order to restore some sanity in their lives in terms of achieving a sense of a more human and realistic work vs. life balance.

The unwillingness to take strike action, and in some cases any type of 'industrial' action, among certain sections of the work force leads to some teaching unions, and their members, supporting strike action with others seeking a less, or non-confrontational approach. Instead, they seek to rely totally on trying to negotiate with a government that frequently admits its total unwillingness to concede ground or compromise in any way. There was, after all, *'no alternative'*, as Margaret Thatcher was so fond of telling us, which is, of course, blatant stupidity!

These varying degrees of union militancy have led to the teaching unions adopting a divided and disunited stance. The government and its supporters in the media have made and continue to make much of this, setting one group against the other, in schools and hospitals around the country. This also presented another dimension to the 'divide and rule' winning formula, the alienation of the public whose very welfare structures were actually being attacked, diminished, if not effectively dismantled and destroyed.

In the past, the general public tended to side with the government, despite the fact that their children were sent home and the 'baby-minding' service offered by schools and the teaching profession had come to an end. There is no chance of mounting effective resistance to the onslaught of a government that was prepared to win at all and any cost. They are willing to vilify teachers, doctors and nurses who take any action that might threaten the welfare of those they are supposed to serve. This occurs despite the fact that the unions were protesting about deep spending cuts, and intolerable conditions that were doing far more damage to patient care and the life chances of our young people in the longer-run than the short-term inconveniences of poor 'industrial' relations. Under Margaret Thatcher and successive Tory governments, the protests duly came to an end with inferior conditions of work and a demoralised work force, heralding a hollow victory to the government, and leaving deteriorating public education and health services that will probably never be able to fully conceal the scars that such wilful assault and neglect has inflicted over so many years.

If we really want to be honest about this, one has to admit that to turn a traditionally conservative and Conservative work force, like teachers, into an intensely militant and hostile one, suggests that the government was doing something fundamentally wrong, either substantively, or through the way in which the change was being implemented.....or both!

It is as true today as it has always been – 'united we stand, divided we fall'. Today, being united is probably even more of an imperative if the interests of the ordinary world citizen are to be protected, promoted and enhanced. We need to stand firm against the might of multinational companies and extremist governments, no matter how neatly they disguise their true self-interested intent, and to make them do **our** bidding, and not vice versa. The odds are massively stacked against us, however, as there are many other causes of the growing fragmentation that underlies our increasing powerlessness, and all in the name of 'progress'.

In days gone by, the industrial revolution extended the notion of the division of labour beyond its geographical and occupational application and into the division of labour by process, where one worker produces one small part of a product, never getting to see the result of one's collective, productive effort. It is no accident that the term involved is the word 'division'. For generations our production processes have fragmented the work force more and more, cutting the people off from their 'species being', as it was called by Karl Marx.

512

Now, before you switch off completely, having read the name of a radical thinker, recognise that whilst you may not agree with the general stance of the radical Marxist school of thought, that fact does not render every word that Marx ever wrote extremist nonsense, and dangerous extremist nonsense at that, in the eyes of so many who know little, if anything of his work. To do so is to fall victim of one of the classic ways of protecting vested interests, namely the emotive rubbishing of any alternative viewpoint, without having given it any serious critical examination or thought. If you are interested in an immensely readable, informative, entertaining and up-to-date account of the increasing relevance of the work of this radical thinker, you would be well advised to purchase a copy of *'Why Marx Was Right'* by Terry Eagleton, or borrow one from your local library......if it has not already been sold off to some supermarket chain, of course, in the name of *'sound public sector finance'*.

Karl Marx referred to the concept of ***alienation*** of the work-force under modern production methods adopted by the capitalist system. One way in which this happens is by dividing the production process into a large number of mundane, repetitive tasks that an individual worker can perform without skill, training or initiative. This fails to recognise that human beings are essentially social creatures who need personal interaction with each other to retain their spirituality, dignity and creativity, as well as to develop fully as a species being. This need is inversely related to the division of labour by process. We become more fragmented and isolated at work, as well as less creative, with the extension of this method of organising the productive process.

It baffles me as to why we have for so long envisaged the main aim of schooling to be all about preparing our young people for adult and working life if this is the divisive shambles into which we wish for them to be assimilated and accommodated. This is especially true if we are to really harbour any real hope that they will lead lives of self-determined fulfilment, where they have the power to shape their own destinies and to make their unique and lasting mark on society as a whole, no matter how large or small their individual contribution may be.

513

If only young people were more inclusively able to discover the joys of learning and genuine education in matters which they find intriguing, interesting or fascinating, and at times of their choosing rather than being fed the disjointed pap that constitutes the curriculum of most schools, then perhaps they would be genuinely equipped and enabled to learn collaboratively, and to enjoy a true and immensely creative synergy of learning with others. Perhaps then people would be able to identify, shape and follow their true destinies in life, rather than live lives as pawns in the game of life that is increasingly set for us by corporate giants and the invisible hands that manifest themselves in the ways we run our political, economic and social affairs.

We need to question, take control and live our true lives, and do something eminently and spiritually worthwhile with this unique gift that is mine, yours and ours and, most certainly, not spend our existence in trivial monetary, materialistic and unfulfilling pursuits that we are persuaded to believe is what life is all about!

Cancerous Competition

For as long as I can recall, education, like most things in life, has been fundamentally predicated upon one big, massive assumption that the best way of achieving anything worthwhile is through the creation of competitive environments, or one that inevitably and necessarily creates 'winners' and, therefore, by definition, 'losers'. Perhaps there was a time when competition was relevant in mankind's somewhat chequered development and evolution, but if we accept the notion that individual and societal harmony is what we should now be seeking in most areas of life, then perhaps the time is long overdue for us to question the very assumption that competition is king. This is especially true if we are serious about unleashing (if not merely promoting) real learning and the development of self-confidence and self-esteem in the personal and social development of our young people now, and in the future. But this is not what schools as they are currently envisaged, structured and operated are really seeking to achieve, or, if they are, then they are going about things in completely the wrong way. Perhaps we should triumph collaborative success, achievement and advancement in the place of this competitive mantra or panacea which demands 'winners' and losers' as its over-riding modus operandi?

In his book, *'Creating Tomorrow's Schools Today – Education – Our Children – Their Futures'* (page 33), Richard Gerver argued, very perceptively in my view, that **"in many schools, classrooms and learning are like casinos"**, going on to point out that, **"the thing is, we don't gamble with money but with self-esteem"**. It is my view that, in most cases, unless used very selectively and in the right contexts, competition is a cancerous growth, and a highly malignant one at that, which eats away at, and eventually destroys individual and collective achievement rather than promoting and encouraging it across the board, as is so often customarily and unquestionably taken for granted.

At this point, I should perhaps recognize my acceptance of the fact that competition is perhaps the best way of promoting *individual* success and achievement; that is without doubt, it seems to me, as the litany of historical examples testifies, but when it comes to how to nurture, engender and assure *collective* or *societal* achievement, I fear that it has exactly the opposite, and far more negative, worrisome and destructive effect or outcome, which no longer serves us as a species, or a planet for that matter, in any long-term, positive and constructive way.

In my quieter moments, when I have time to rue the pre-eminent and overwhelming assumption that competition is a positive force and the way for human advancement, I reflect on what I feel the world really and honestly needs today in the face of our feelings of increased powerlessness, disenfranchisement and unhappiness, not to mention greater fragmentation, alienation, global conflict and environmental destruction, and that is an epidemic of collaborative togetherness as well as individual and international cooperation.

As I have said several times before, I am a firm believer that when things go wrong in an organisation or situation, it is not usually the fault of individuals, rather it is a systemic failure. In other words, it is the way in which we organise our affairs and actions that allows or encourages anti-social, damaging or unwanted outcomes, or does not incorporate checks and balances to ensure that they cannot and do not arise in the first place. But our whole society seems to be all about 'winners' and 'losers' (after all, the former necessitates the latter), whereby one person's or group's success requires or demands another person's or group's diminution, loss or failure. It seems to me that this is such an incredibly deleterious, divisive and wasteful construct if we wish to accept and recognise any desirable notion of society, community or common humanity, whether that be organisational, institutional, local, national or global in scale and nature!

It follows, therefore, in my train of thought, that if we are to radically rethink the way in which we organise formal schooling so that it becomes more synonymous with genuine education, then we cannot expect this to happen or have the desired outcomes if it occurs in some splendid isolation. In other words, (and in another world), if schools are to be radically and progressively revamped, re-structured and remodelled to promote the kind of interdependent learning that promotes rather than undermines collaborative and collective achievement, then we also need to seriously consider doing the same with the way in which we organise and operate our societal systems, in order to achieve mutually supportive outcomes.

My step-mother and I, when I was a teenager, used to argue repeatedly about whether mankind as a species is innately competitive in terms of hereditary codes, or whether it is the system that forces mankind to engage in such selfish and self-interested behaviours. Needless to say, I always adopted the latter perspective in our never resolved 'discussions'. It was as though she had accepted selfishness over selflessness, whereas I was romantically attached to the notion that mankind could and should rise above such self-centredness, once we came to recognise that it is in everyone's interests for us all to strive to be successful, content and inter-dependent. I cannot and will not accept that it is universally and naturally inevitable that a species that is essentially creative, imaginative and social in nature innately craves a behavioural credo that is based upon an inherently wasteful and highly destructive philosophy of 'dog-eat-dog'.

The competition that is absolutely vital, central to our advancement and the force that drives us forward should be less about the detrimental and counter-productive inter-personal variety, but the one that is far more individual and personal in nature. That demands and requires setting oneself new, ambitious

516

and challenging aims and goals, followed by then charting a course that is designed to actually achieve them. Such a beneficial process can also be undertaken collectively in groups or teams, as well as (not instead of) individually and independently. If each member of a functioning team seeks to excel individually then the dynamic generated by the subsequent synergy that it creates will be exponentially greater than that which one might hope to achieve when operating all by oneself, and in combative competition with all others. Let's face it, all individual achievement is always the result of a team effort; if you don't believe me then just ask Usain Bolt!

When thinking of more concrete and anecdotal examples of why and how this concept of collaboration is so much more positive, constructive and developmental, I often reflect on an article I recall reading in the 'Times Educational Supplement'. If my memory serves me right, I believe it was written by Professor Ted Wragg, when he recounted a weekend he had spent renovating an old wooden gate that formed the entrance to his newly-acquired house in the countryside. He admitted to not being at all practical in nature but that he had set himself the task, and a very demanding and challenging one it was for him as he was not particularly experienced or skilled in such matters. Nonetheless, he was determined to achieve what he foresaw was going to be a fairly daunting DIY home task. I know how he felt!

He began the task one weekend by planning the materials and tools that he considered might be necessary to complete the task that he had envisaged in his mind's eye. He then went to obtain these additional resources from his local DIY store, returned home and commenced his two-day task. During the course of the weekend, he was forced to make repeated trips to the DIY store to supplement, replace or augment the various tools and materials he found that he actually needed, as a result of initial underestimates as well as his lack of prior experience and skill.

By the end of two very busy, challenging and difficult days, he eventually completed the planned task, much to his delight and satisfaction. This was a feeling most definitely derived both from a sense of personal accomplishment and having saved a lot of money that the alternative of hiring a professional carpenter to do the job for him would necessarily have required. So pleased was he at having achieved something that had initially seemed almost implausible, if not impossible for him, that when he had finished the job, he crossed the road to stand opposite his house so that he could admire his handiwork from further away, much as one would do when approaching his home.

One can understand just how good he must have felt about what he had achieved, especially if like me, you are also someone who dreads having to undertake such practical and technical assignments, partly due to the incompatibility afforded to me by being left-handed in a world full of tools designed for right-handed users. The best part of his story, which he wrote in an honest but amusing way, which was very much his trademark, was his admission that even several days and weeks after having renovated his drive-way gate, on his journey home from work each day, he would find himself pausing for a while on the opposite side of the road to further appreciate and enjoy his sense of personal accomplishment, and the greater dexterity, skill and knowledge that the learning process had allowed him to acquire and develop.

However, he then went on to point out how he might have felt if, at the same time as he undertook this domestic challenge, his next door neighbour who, for the sake of argument was a skilled carpenter, had completed a similar task on his own driveway gate. In such an imaginary situation, it is abundantly clear that Ted Wragg would have felt quite differently about his own accomplishment, as he would inevitably be placed in a situation where he would have compared his achievements with those of his appropriately and more skilled and experienced neighbour. Such a scenario would have completely and seriously undermined the self-confidence and self-esteem that he rightly felt as a result of what he had done, purely as a consequence of being forced into making an unhelpful competitive comparison.

In schools, surely we should be endeavouring to allow, enable and empower all students to operate in a learning environment where they can sense, measure and see their own personal and professional development and growth over time, rather than always comparing their results with those of their contemporaries, so that the greater self-esteem that such accomplishment inevitably generates, motivates and drives them into feeling much more confident about setting themselves even more challenging and demanding tasks in the future. Such a way forward is not only in the best interests of each and every individual learner, but also those of society as a whole.

In short, it is my fervent belief that although competition may indeed bring out the best in a *few* individual people, team work and collaboration is far more likely to bring out the very best in us *all*, leading to a significantly greater pool of human accomplishment, attainment and achievement.

Competition and Inequality

Competition can be a highly negative force given that it necessitates comparison, envy and obvious inequality of outcome, and so the way we envisage society as a whole is also desperately in need of a paradigm shift so that issues of inequality of opportunity, which are becoming increasingly more marked in all countries, do not destroy the essential cohesive fabric that constitutes a stable society.

The French economist, Thomas Piketty, in his outstanding book, *'Capital in the 21ˢᵗ Century'* documents the glaring inequalities in income and wealth in most countries that are becoming so enormous that they are increasingly threatening social cohesion. I do not intend to go into the details of his work here, but the message of his book is one that all politicians and sociologists need to heed and act upon. What I do want to consider, however, is that unless these issues of considerable inequality are addressed and mitigated to some extent, expecting schools alone to right society's wrongs is nothing but a pipe dream. We simply must address glaring issues of inequality if we are to give young people real opportunities in life.

I stumbled across an article, published in the "Bangkok Post' (an English newspaper published daily in Thailand) of all places, entitled, *'Inequality is about more than being short on cash'*, written by Lawrence H. Summers (a former World Bank chief economist, former US Treasury secretary, former US National Economic Council director, former president of Harvard University and currently the Charles W. Elliot professor at Harvard University). His article, which referred to the work of Thomas Picketty, made some fundamentally important and seriously worrying points that society as a whole needs to address, and urgently. Summers rightly acknowledged the need to distribute income and wealth more equitably by increasing the progressive nature of direct taxation, but he went on to note that important aspects of inequality are unlikely to be transformed just by effecting a limited income redistribution.

He went on to highlight the vital importance of, what he called, *'two fundamental conditions of life'*, namely health care and the ability to provide opportunity for children. He noted that over the last two generations, the gap in educational achievement between the children of the rich and the children of the poor has doubled. To support this statement, he identified that, *"while the college enrolment rate for children from the lowest quarter of the income distribution has increased from 6% to 8%, the rate for children from the highest quarter has risen from 40% to 73%."* A stunning and frightening statistic, which more than highlights my assertion that transforming schools alone will achieve little, if society as a whole does not address issues that more profoundly undermine opportunity and that are created by basic inequality.

Summers acknowledges that many factors will have driven this divisive trend, but in his article he refers to one very crucial factor, by noting that the average affluent child (in the USA, I assume) now receives 6,000 hours more enrichment activity – such as being read to, taken to a museum, coached in a sport or other kind of stimulation provided by adults – than the average poor child, and this gap has greatly increased since the 1970s. What is more, he concludes the article by correctly noting that the observations he reports on health and the ability to provide opportunity for children suggest that the differences between the rich and everyone else are not just about the amount of money that one has, but concern things that are far more fundamental and important. His verdict is not only to call for far more progressive direct tax regimes, whereby those with the greatest means pay a larger share of their income and wealth to the Exchequer, but also to move towards a society which is more "just and inclusive". He argues that it will be necessary to craft policies that address the rapidly increasing share of money income going to the very rich.

Such calls as those being made by Lawrence Summers and many, many others, are not wish lists that can be achieved at some later date, and they are not purely theoretical or recent in nature. They are pressing, practical, urgent and long overdue!

Let's move from the general to the more specific, and consider some more real world, everyday evidence of how this inequitable distribution of income and wealth is seriously eroding the good work of schools in the UK, and has been doing so for some time now. Let us remind ourselves that it was the kind, caring and inclusive Prime Minister, Margaret Thatcher, who extolled the virtues of returning to "Victorian values", when Britain was allegedly 'Great', when it came to the right way to ruin…..sorry, run….the economy. Furthermore, let us not forget how, at the time of writing, UK society is again suffering the onslaught and ravages of a right-wing, Conservative political and economic agenda that is continuing the misguided, mendacious and egregious policies that are effectively designed to eradicate any semblance of inclusion and fairness by destroying all forms of social welfare, social support and greater financial equity in terms of the distribution of income and wealth, not to mention opportunity.

To provide a classic example of how this divisive and selfish agenda is being ruthlessly pursued in the UK, the Guardian published an article entitled, 'Children living in Victorian conditions, say teachers' (5th April 2015), which reported on the findings of a survey commissioned by the NAS/UWT (one of the teacher professional associations). According to the survey, 60% of teachers said they had seen students arriving at school hungry, while 80% had witnessed youngsters turning up in clothes that were inappropriate for the weather, as well as similar percentages reporting children arriving in unwashed, damaged or frayed clothing. Furthermore, 78% of teachers said that they had seen pupils attending school without the right footwear, and 55% had seen students whose families were simply unable to afford the traditional and customary school uniform. All of this, the article concluded, was not due to neglectful or uncaring parents, but a direct result of a continuing squeeze on family finances thanks to a neglectful and uncaring Conservative government – well, what's new?

The NAS/UWT warned that the lives of many children and young people are being, *"blighted and degraded by poverty and homelessness"*, but then of course, it is much easier to blame schools and teachers for their educational failure while at school, isn't it? The report was full of shocking observations and anecdotal evidence of youngsters going to school with no socks or coat, and how an increasing number of families were depending on 'food banks' to feed their children. Cases of pupils in need of medical attention attending school because their parents are not able to take them to the doctor, optician or dentist, very often because of the loss of income of having to take time off work to do so.

The findings of the survey were even more worrying when it was reported that about a third of teachers said that they had experienced students either joining or leaving a school halfway through a term because their families had been forced to leave their homes. A similar proportion reported teaching children who were living in temporary accommodation, with 22% saying they were aware of cases where youngsters had lost their homes due to money pressure, but then of course, it is much easier to blame schools and teachers for their educational failure while at school, isn't it?

Many teachers added that they had noticed how financial pressures at home were impacting youngsters in the classroom, pointing out that many students in such circumstances were less able to concentrate, more likely to be absent or late for school, as well as understandably show behavioural problems and be lacking in self-confidence and self-esteem, but then it is much easier to blame schools and teachers for their educational failure while at school, isn't it?

The general secretary of the NAS/UWT, Chris Keates, summed up these truly shocking statistics and the seriously detrimental effect of government cutbacks on young people's life chances by referring to how poverty and homelessness do indeed take a very real and physical toll on children. *"They often cannot concentrate when they are in school because they are tired and hungry, have no space to do homework and have to travel long distances to get to school from temporary accommodation. They are more likely to suffer more ill health and absenteeism,"* she said, but then it is much easier to blame schools and teachers for their educational failure while at school, isn't it?

Just for the sake of perspective at this point, I am of course referring to the UK, which is supposedly one of the leading (and assumed 'advanced') industrial democratic societies, and the plight of an increasing number of young people – and people generally – who are finding their life chances and their futures damaged, restricted and severely curtailed by the combined pressures of economic and social deprivation. We are not talking about young people who cannot afford foreign holidays with their parents or the latest hi-tech gadgetry, or even having reasonable expectations of one day being able to afford their own home without the additional worry of the burden of huge debt incurred as a result of their higher education. We are, however, talking about children who cannot afford adequate food, shelter and clothing, which are most definitely considered to be among the very basic necessities of life. And all this in a country which boasts considerable wealth in every sense of the word.

Moreover, I can hardly be accused of scouring the media for isolated examples of worrying information and evidence of hardship, as a result of these deliberately partisan government economic and social policies, as another later article (the Guardian, 11 September 2015) loomed large with the headline *'Scotland's child poverty levels so severe teachers are sent advice on spotting malnourished students'*. The piece explained that new guidance and advice from the Educational Institute of Scotland (EIS) had been distributed to their schools and colleges, warning them that the issue of hunger (yes, a basic lack of adequate food) among pupils was, *"moving from the exceptional to the commonplace,"* as families were struggling more and more to make financial ends meet. This was the very first time that the EIS had ever felt the need to issue such advice!

The guidance from the EIS stated the following: *"Pupils may appear pale, fatigued, irritable or lacking in concentration, or complain of headaches or feeling unwell."* Now, I appreciate that elsewhere in this book I have admittedly acknowledged that the curriculum and essential nature of schooling in the UK and wider world is so outmoded, irrelevant and drab for so many students (well, all of them actually, although some do play along with the system and successfully jump through the performance hoops laid before them) that finding young people who are switched off, are mentally 'elsewhere' or are complaining that their brain hurts, and such like, may not be just attributed to pangs of hunger. The EIS, however, had taken this into consideration before issuing their advice to schools when they went on to acknowledge, *"While there can be other reasons underlying such signs, for a growing number of children and young people.......today, the reason will be hunger."* So what to do?

The article included some of the helpful advice to teachers who suspect that a child may be going hungry by suggesting that they should include such youngsters in morning 'breakfast clubs' and post the details of nearby 'food banks' on school notice boards and websites, so their families can seek the necessary help. The EIS identified that more than 222,000 children in Scotland could currently be described as being in poverty, and went on to warn that this shocking number would continue to rise if the Government's *"austerity agenda"* continued. This fear of growing deprivation led the EIS to publish a 20-page booklet entitled, *'Face up to Child Poverty'* giving practical advice to teachers which might allow them to *"poverty-proof"* their classrooms. The booklet also sought to help teachers deal with other poverty-related challenges that faced a growing number of parents and families, such as the cost of school uniforms, field trips, homework and basic class equipment. This was deemed necessary, if not vital information for teachers, given that some young people were effectively forced into attending school wearing the 'wrong type' of clothes, due to being unable to afford the cost of stipulated uniform items and such like, and the negative stigma that accompanied this led them to feeling uncomfortable about telling their teachers the real reason why they were 'breaking the rules', so to speak. Mind you, if anyone is 'breaking the rules', then it is the Conservative Government in 10 Downing Street led by its privileged leader, David Cameron.....a good Scottish family name too!

It is worth asking, however, whether or not such tasks really should fall under the daily remit of a typical professional teacher in the first place, when the very same government feels the need to continually add to the teachers' daily workload in the highly dubious interests of fairly meaningless, unhelpful and professionally obstructive accountability measures? No wonder so many thousands of teachers are quitting the profession now in order to restore some sanity into their lives by seeking a healthier, more enjoyable and productive 'work-life' balance!

I was also delighted to note that the above article referring to the latest EIS guidance, included a quotation from Iain Gray, the **Scottish Labour Party opportunity spokesperson**. My delight was largely due to the very notion of seeing that the Labour Party actually felt it was sufficiently important to give one of its political representatives such an important area of responsibility as 'opportunity'. Wonderful, I thought, although his rightful indignation and anger was well expressed when he referred to the *"damning picture"* that the new EIS advice painted of the gruesome effects of basic poverty on schools and future generations of young people, by saying *"In a well off 21ˢᵗ century country some of these findings are shameful, but will not surprise anyone who deals on a day to day basis with the growth of food banks and the impact of the Tory government's welfare reforms."*

None of this should really come as any real surprise to anyone, however, as the warning signs of the Tory government's increasingly wicked, pernicious and elitist agenda have been growing ever since the election of Margaret Thatcher effectively discarded any notions of a more inclusive and just 'One Nation' Conservatism.

What is more, it should come as no surprise either to hear on the world media news, broadcast by both the CNN and BBC World networks over the festive period of 2015, about the way in which diseases once associated with poverty during Victorian times in England are now making a big comeback, most notably tuberculosis (TB), scarlet fever and whooping cough. What is more worrying is that some of these diseases, most notably for TB, are becoming more far more challenging to treat owing to the emergence of drug-resistant strains of the disease. The world news media also reported a marked increase in the growth rates of 'Victorian' ailments like cholera and even scurvy, although the number of sufferers in the UK is still quite small in comparison to the 'headliners' mentioned above. How can we have a Conservative government in the UK that talks about economic and social progress and growth when in such basic issues as human welfare, health and education, the evidence is of a movement in exactly the opposite and backward direction for an increasing number of its citizens? The answer must surely lie in the ignorance of the electorate, an outdated and anachronistic political system and the willing complicity of the Conservative-owned and controlled media who support their political 'friends' in power.

Equally, it should come as no shock to anyone that over Christmas 2015, the media baron and owner of the infamous News Corp empire, Rupert Murdoch, had a drinks soiree or social at which the Conservative Prime Minister and his wife were among the very select group of guests.......notably the Labour leader, Jeremy Corbyn was not invited, and would probably have refused the chance to be present even if asked to attend. Let's remember that this is an organisation that, apart from being involved in phone tapping and similarly disgraceful breaches of an individual's right to personal privacy, controls large swaths of print and broadcast media in both the USA and the UK. Yet this does not prevent Tory government ministers still holding meetings with discredited News Corp personnel before deciding to place further restrictions on the growth, future operations and finances of the state-owned and funded British Broadcasting Corporation, which Murdoch would doubtlessly love to see become extinct, in furtherance of his own business interests.

We Need Real Social Mobility

If we are to create a society in which there is real opportunity for our young people to develop their talents and contribute to our overall social welfare, then we desperately need to take serious steps to increase social mobility, and this cannot be undertaken without also addressing the chasm of increasing proportions that exists in the distribution of income and wealth in all countries. Young people and their families must be genuinely enabled to improve their lot in life, without having to overcome monumental obstacles that militate against such social advancement. Indeed, the shrinking of the middle class and its economic well-being, which is a process that has been underway for some time now, fundamentally undermines any realistic chance or hope of increasing social mobility. The work of economists like Picketty and numerous others bears startling testimony to the fact that the middle class is indeed being squeezed out of existence as a direct result of the way in which we have been conducting our economic, social and political affairs, particularly for the last 40 years.

In November 2013, The Guardian published an article *('Sir John Major: do more to boost social mobility')* in which the former PM, from the marginalised sanctity, privilege and safety of the House of Lords, criticised the dominance of privately educated and affluent people who occupied what might be neutrally described as the upper echelons of power. In fact, Margaret Thatcher's successor as Tory PM was fairly forthright in his criticism, describing this dominance by the privately educated and affluent middle class as *"truly shocking"*......well, better late than never, Sir John!

In some ways, such welcome and long overdue remarks from Sir John Major could be interpreted as a sideways swipe at Eton-educated David Cameron, given that his Tory predecessor in 10 Downing Street actually attended a south London comprehensive school, and left with a hardly impressive haul of three GCE O-level passes. Consequently, he is well placed to be critical, and his comments were hardly tempered when he claimed that the *"affluent middle class"* dominated *"every single sphere of British influence"*, so that their interference and privileged position in schooling is all ultimately designed to perpetuate the system for people like Mr. Cameron and many of his Cabinet colleagues. Sir John was specifically very clear when he commented that *"hard graff"*, or individual effort and talent was not enough in today's society for state-school educated young people to reach the *"upper echelons of power"*. The clarity in calling for the government to genuinely address and improve measures to promote social mobility was exemplified when Sir John was quoted as saying, *"We need them (young people) to fly as high as their luck, their ability and their sheer hard graft can actually take them. And it isn't going to happen magically."*

In effect, Sir John's comments argued strongly that we need to take steps to promote the type of 'meritorious meritocracy' that I referred to in the previous chapter, although I admittedly went somewhat further in offering practical steps about measures that might be needed if this is to stand any realistic chance of being achieved in practice, although they were measures with which I doubt that Sir John would be comfortable. In fact, he offered remarkably little in terms of how greater equality of opportunity might actually be achieved, other than commenting on its growing deficiency and the concomitant unjustness or unfairness of such a situation. After all, there was a time when he could have actually done something about the imbalance that has existed since time immemorial in the way in which real power is distributed within society as a whole. Furthermore, the earlier in life we begin to seriously compensate for such inequities that young people encounter is a particularly acute point that demands immediate action, as it has been well documented that deprivation, and the restrictions that this disadvantage places upon opportunities for social mobility actually and inevitably increases as they grow older.

This was well documented in another Guardian article back in February 2010, which reported on the findings of a Millennium Cohort Study of 15,000 children and their performance in motor skills at the ages of nine months and five years. The study highlighted the fact that children who do not reach key development milestones by the time they are nine months old are increasingly more likely to experience difficulties at school as they grow older, with more limited cognitive development and an increased likelihood of developing behavioural problems by the time they reach the age of five years. This Millennium Cohort Study by the Sutton Trust charity found clear evidence that children from the poorest homes are more than one year behind their peers from more affluent families in such key skills as the acquisition of vocabulary by the time they reach school age. This type of evidence clearly demonstrates the cumulative impact that financial or material deprivation and limited opportunity has upon the personal and social development of children from the youngest of ages. Such youngsters are, therefore, effectively handicapped and disadvantaged for life as a result of the way in which income, wealth and subsequent opportunity are so **intentionally** and unfairly distributed.

What is even more disturbing is that the problem of poor education and its effect on limiting genuine social mobility, where people can advance and improve themselves, is not just about poverty, real though the problem of insufficient money and opportunity really is. A report published by the House of Commons select committee in June 2014 (The Guardian, 20 June 2014), demonstrated that only a meagre 32% of white, working-class children leave school with the 'league-table benchmark' of five good pass grades in their GCSE examinations, whereas nearly double as many children from a poor Indian background manage it in British schools, as do more than 75% of children from poor Chinese backgrounds in the same country. These are very concerning statistics indeed, as they suggest that a lot is going wrong in our schools if they are truly supposed to be educating, enabling and empowering our current and future generations. What is the reason for this surprising and concerning trend?

Graham Stuart, the Conservative chairman of the select committee explained this by saying that poor white British children, *"do less homework and are more likely to miss school than other ethnic groups."* He went on to admit that the report did not shed any light on whether or not this, *"underperformance was due to poor attitudes to school, a lack of work ethic or weak parenting."* Such a view tends to suggest that the select committee chairman was looking for an explanation that blamed poor character for this lack of aspiration, rather than poor educational and social provision. In the Guardian article, however, written by Deborah Orr, one highly plausible alternative was put forward to explain this lack of aspiration towards the education that takes place in the name of schooling, and that was something much more pervasive and debilitating, namely a lack of aspiration about life itself, perhaps.

Deborah Orr argued that, these days, the middle and upper classes are motivated by the fear of them, and their children, losing their privileged status and advantage in society that they are striving to achieve. Furthermore, people who have no real advantages at all are actively afflicted by a fear of losing what little they do have, and such people are thereby forced into believing that mere survival is the best they can expect from, or manage in life, rather than any real hope of personal and social advancement or improvement. What is even more worrying, she said, is that politicians of the 'right' see the creation of fear as the *solution* to low aspiration, and not the root cause of this problem of under-achievement. As a result, they seem to see the solution to be one of frightening people into aspiration, by cutting their welfare and social benefits and punishing them by whatever means they devise. This appears to have been the strategy for the last 30+ years, Deborah Orr claims, where we have seen successive governments taking away job security, taking away and reducing real wages so that people struggle to meet their financial obligations in life, as well as taking away social housing and other forms of welfare provision.

This perverted form of attempting to motivate those with low aspirations has, of course, exactly the opposite effect, as the more you take away from people, the less they have to lose in the first place. As Deborah Orr rightly points out in her excellent article, therefore, deprivation does not serve to make people aspirational, it only acts to make them feel, and be, deprived. Expecting people who are affected this way to buy into middle class values and work harder to lift themselves out of the mire of low opportunity, disadvantage and even deprivation, is unlikely to be a very successful approach, it seems to me.

In the article, Orr refers to another report, that was published in the same week as the select committee, by the Poverty and Social Exclusion project which found that the number of people falling below minimum living standards was more than double the level it had been thirty years before, despite the fact that during the same period of time, the size of the economy had actually doubled. The report also found that, *"the majority of children who suffer from multiple deprivations live in small families with one or two siblings, with both parents, have at least one parent who is employed and are white."* This finding shows that it has become ever more difficult to even be aspirational and this, coupled with the effects of academic inflation, has made achieving and living what might reasonably be called a 'normal' or 'ordinary' life a far more challenging prospect.

The significance of how the last thirty years in the UK has seen a diminution and erosion in the opportunities for social mobility is highly relevant, as it has been the period when the once 'social contract' was quite literally torn up and discarded by the deliberate economic and social policies of mainly Conservative governments, and one deeply disappointing spell in the clutches of 'New' Labour and Tony Blair. In this crucial period of time, we have experienced a concerted, cynical, and systematic attempt to shrink the size of the public sector (the state) coupled with a persistent application of failed, austerity-style economic policies, which have exacerbated the inequities in the distribution of income, wealth and opportunity, as well as the shrinking of the middle classes. These years have seen a massively increasing disparity in the distribution of income and wealth and an economic society where opportunity and individual aspiration to believe, achieve and succeed has withered away, along with Britain's manufacturing, the country's real economy and the employment opportunities that it once afforded. Employment and the opportunity to really participate in the process of economic growth are vital to seriously increasing the notion of social mobility in actual practice.

When I started teaching back in 1976, school leavers could reasonably expect to find gainful employment producing real goods and services that people in the UK and around the world wanted to buy. As the country had been experiencing the social contract and a commitment by consecutive governments to full employment as an over-riding macroeconomic policy objective, so school leavers were effectively assured of being able to walk into gainful employment, finding a job and acquiring the means to live a normal or 'ordinary' life. The mood then was one of optimism, high aspirations and genuine opportunity for social mobility, with governments acting as willing conspirators in the process. But that was all about to change!

In 1979, and the election of the first Conservative government under the leadership of Margaret Thatcher and her brood of hawkish right-of-centre political acolytes who were wedded to what effectively amounted to a class war and failed neo-classical economic policies of an extreme and uncompromising variety. So the country embarked upon an economic programme which demanded a systematic dismantling of the state, slashing public expenditure on infrastructure and merit goods such as education and health care, a reduction of taxation for the wealthiest members of society, and a meteoric rise in levels of unemployment, lost opportunities and an alarming increase in levels of poverty, deprivation and crime. Since that time, the economic compass has seen very little course adjustment to ameliorate the damage that was being done to social cohesion, let alone the country's real economy. If anything, after a lost opportunity where the country flirted with a rather abstract social agenda under 'New' Labour, we have seen an accelerating rate of austerity-style economic policy, rising social inequality, and lost opportunity for many of our young people especially.

Soon after I began my teaching career, we entered the 1980s, when students leaving school soon learnt that if they were to have any realistic chance of securing one of the rapidly dwindling number of jobs, then they would need to achieve at least five good pass grades at GCE O-level – the forerunner of today's GCSE examination – including Mathematics and English. As unemployment soared from around 700,000 in 1979 to nearly four million in a massively destructive two-year period, so jobs in the private and public sectors virtually vanished. This raised the level of competition for employment to a greater degree, so school leavers soon discovered that instead of five good GCSE passes, they now needed at least eight, or even two or three GCE A-levels. At the same time as this process was in play, there was also an increase in the number of students obtaining pass grades at O-level and A-level, and with improved grades. These two phenomena created the grade inflation that so many school leavers had to contend with, a sort of pincer movement involving curtailed employment opportunities due to economic decline and deindustrialisation, and more school leavers with better job qualifications or credentials.

Students who find academic studies interesting, engaging and enjoyable and who have the capabilities to pass brain-numbing and creativity-devoid external examinations, were able to obtain the higher entry requirements for employment and university in the form of examination grades with relative ease. For the majority of students who must necessarily obtain the lower, less attractive or fail grades, the chances of social mobility were seriously eroded and, over time, this lack of opportunity inevitably whittled away at the hopes, dreams and aspirations of young people and, very often, their parents. A pervading sense of hopelessness began to develop among young people while at school, and certainly when it came to leaving and searching for a way to make a living, so that they would not be dependent on government welfare payments. To make matters more hopeless, the government was reducing welfare payments to those unable to find employment which were also being reduced in real terms (i.e. their purchasing power) or the entitlement criteria for such government assistance were being inexorably tightened, mainly to limit the cost of this increasing pool of unemployed youngsters on the public purse.

One delaying tactic devised by 'New' Labour was to increase the number of new universities so that more school leavers could access and attend higher education, despite having somewhat inferior examination grades. This was largely pointless as it was simply 'kicking the can of eventual unemployment and frustration further down the road' as they say. That is why today, we see an increasing number of university graduates who are unable to find employment of any kind, let alone a job that makes full use of their capabilities. This has led to increased pressure on school students to choose certain types of courses, such as the sciences, mathematics and technology in preference to the arts and humanities courses, which makes a mockery of the notion of the joy of learning for learning's sake, and following one's own passions and dreams in life!

In view of this understandably myopic approach to choosing a university course of study, it was so refreshing to read an article in The Observer newspaper (8th June 2014) written by the Education Editor Richard Garner entitled, *"Universities are 'not just for getting a job,' says one of Britain's leading academics."* The leading academic in question was Professor Sir Christopher Snowden who was defending the idea of education for its own sake, as well as the importance of research to the economy, by criticising those trying to promote higher education for placing too much emphasis on vocational skills simply to secure a job and to make money. Sir Christopher, who is also vice-chancellor of Surrey University, argued that students should not be taught to limit themselves to studying only what will benefit them in their future careers because he believed (as do I) that there is a lifetime benefit to be gained from going to university. Sadly, the financial pressure of having to repay one's student loan incurred during higher education makes it much more difficult to follow Sir Christopher's advice, as one will need gainful employment to be able to afford the cost of reimbursing the government. This loss of a system of means-tested student grants limits a student's freedom of choice over their university course of study and eventual career, and represents yet another nail in the coffin of increased social mobility, and living a life that is personally rewarding, meaningful and fulfilling.

When politically perverse, ignorant and/or malicious governments are responsible for creating an economic and social situation in which opportunities for education, employment and opportunity have become so scarce and expensive to take, as a direct result of their own mean spiritedness, economic incompetence or wilful neglect, then is it hardly surprising that school students are given little reason to harbour high aspirations of being able to live an ordinary life, without unnecessary obstacles and barriers being put in place to thwart their endeavours, not to mention their innate talents, passion and spiritual calling?

It remains as true today as it has been for generations, that access to opportunity, income and a reasonable degree of wealth depends increasingly on an outdated, unfair external examination system, which discriminates against so many talented young people. It discriminates against those who may not be suited to or engaged by a programme of increasingly narrowly-focussed academic study, where the knowledge and skills to be acquired or developed are determined not by the learner but by politicians or faceless others, and where most of what is 'learnt' is of little or no obvious use or interest to the learner in their existing or future lives — but it is what the system dictates.

We cannot continue to ignore and waste the genuine innate passions, aspirations and dreams of young people by forcing them through a school and examination system which in no way meets or serves the needs of the majority who are obliged to attend through legal compulsion and punishment should they choose not to do as they are required to by the system. Would it not be infinitely better to have a series of truly educational opportunities that young people of all ages passionately wanted to pursue or from which they could see real merit to them as individuals, as opposed to being coerced to attend school simply because they have to do so, under threat of some external sanction. That might be a better way to raise student aspirations, as well as those of the same young people when they reach adulthood, one might reasonably argue. Instead, consecutive governments persist in seeking new ways to enforce involvement in a largely failed, irrelevant and wasteful system of compulsory schooling. No wonder that 'home-schooling' is becoming such an attractive proposition to the parents of many children.

The Solution – Barking up The Wrong Tree!

If all young people are going to become intrinsically motivated and possess a genuine desire to learn, and if the world of work is to be equally attractive, then both need to become an enjoyable means to an end, and not a demoralising and unfulfilling end in itself, as Melissa Benn rightly argued in an article entitled, *'Education's culture of overwork is turning children and teachers into*

534

ghosts' (the Guardian, 16 April 2014). We need to be equally clear that creating a culture of overwork does precious little to stimulate aspiration, effort and opportunity which, in turn, will act as a catalyst to greater social mobility and optimism.

Unfortunately, this culture of overwork has been adopted by successive governments to schooling and education, where the participants' lack of effort is demonised and blamed for the problems in our system, whilst the authorities disregard or blindly overlook the root cause which is, as Melissa Benn identifies, *"decades of inequality in provision and under-investment"*. The government's solution has been more of the same, an intensification of inter-personal competition and devising new forms of punishment or sanction for the slackers and mutineers. Not so long ago I read an article (Guardian, 18 June 2014 – *'White working class boys do worst in school, claims major new report'*) in which the draconian, chief schools inspector Sir Michael Wilshaw was seriously advocating that head teachers be legally empowered to impose financial penalties, in the form of fines, on parents who failed to ensure that their offspring are not late to school or fail to complete their homework. He was also reported as saying that poverty was often used as an **excuse** for children from working-class families failing at school, whereas in my book, poverty and deprivation are the root causes of under-achievement, and Sir Michael should, instead, excuse himself from making such banal educational comment in the future. Let's be honest, such a wheeze as fining parents is more likely to switch them off even more from the education of their children and, if they are poor, Sir Michael, surely it would be logical to assume that they are unlikely to be able to afford the fines even if they agreed with the reasonableness of the solution you propose in the first place?

The government seems equally blinkered and determined to charge up the wrong path altogether in its attempts to rectify what is essentially a failed system of state schooling. In her article, Melissa Benn makes a very important observation when she observes how the government's solution is to promote more of the same. Educational reform now has taken on the mantle of what she describes as intensive schooling, which includes such things as early-morning catch up classes, after-school clubs, longer terms, extended school days, more testing and more homework. Melissa Benn argues that the human body and human communities do not flourish through being flogged to death, and families do not relish or respond well to being rushed: *"They simply forget who each other is, or could be, which is where the real problem begins."* She goes on to rightly point out that over-tired children don't and won't learn in such a repressive environment, they will more likely switch off, rebel or simply fall asleep and otherwise occupy themselves.

In short, we are not going to achieve a great deal if we revamp and re-invent the nature and purpose of state schooling, as opposed to merely reforming it, unless we radically rethink the 'bigger picture', namely the type of society we wish to create so that it truly encourages the individual effort of **all** its citizens in such a way that our collective welfare is at least recognised if not enhanced and enriched.

Some time ago, The New Economics Foundation proposed that we should, as they put it, *"make part time the new full time"*, by which they meant that instead of a smaller number of people working harder and longer, we share employment through measures such as job rotation and job-share. Such a new and radical approach would guarantee everyone an income of some sort, not to mention create more time for everyone to do the things that make us human, like spending time with our family and friends, reading a book or going for a walk in the countryside, rather than forcing us to behave like automatons or machines operating on a production line.

I feel obliged to comment on two other wonderfully insightful suggestions that Melissa Benn included in her article back in 2014. The first of these is where she reminds us that in some of the most impressive education systems in the world, children do not actually start formalised learning until they are seven years of age, and they then experience school days which are notably shorter. This is very much at odds with the urgency that so many parents, in the UK and in international school communities overseas, seem to feel which leads them to enrol their children at school at the age of two or three years, and then hope to see them kept there until late in the afternoon. Moreover, Melissa Benn also noted that visitors to some of the Nordic countries, including Finland which is renowned as having the highest-performing system of education in Europe, often comment on the fact that it appears as though the students are not actually doing a great deal when in the classroom; instead the educational conversation, as she puts it, *"is about deep flourishing, enjoyment, stimulation of a different kind."* Perhaps, in this way, it is more akin to successful examples of home schooling!

In the final section of this book, I shall return to look in a little more detail at the very different and far more positive and effective school system in Finland, as it offers a great deal of evidence that shows our frantic and single-minded obsession with content and academe is more than seriously flawed.

Melissa Benn also referred to the work of the education philosopher John White who has long argued that, *"schools (should) be mainly about equipping people to lead a fulfilling life."* She also refers to Anthony Seldon, the master of Wellington College, home of the much celebrated *"happiness lessons"*, and the movement for what can best be described as *"slow education"*. She explains that slow education emphasizes, *"The importance of process over pushing, and quality over endless quantifying."* This concept or notion of *"slow"* helps nurture and engender intensity of understanding and appreciation, allowing students to learn how better to reason for themselves, rather than being dependent on having everything explained to them or for them.

I would prefer a more relaxed and discerning approach to the whole process of learning, with far less importance placed upon success in academic examinations in as many subjects as possible. This game of sitting and succeeding at examinations – and it is largely just a game – is designed to suit a particular type of person, one who is, *"thorough, plodding, uncreative, capable of taking in great mounds of received wisdom and regurgitating them, undigested, unquestioned, unprocessed in three-hour bursts of neat handwriting"* (Lucy Mangan, the Guardian newspaper, 16 August 2014 – 'Sitting exams is a game, and the game is rigged'). In this article, Lucy Mangan used her own life experience to conclude that the exam system, although it clearly worked for some types of young person, such as herself, seriously discriminated against and limited the hopes, aspirations and opportunities of many others. As she put it, the exam system may not exactly be broken, but it is hardly fit for purpose if we are serious about wanting an education system that, *"instils a love of learning and grants access to the joy that brings, or that brings out the best in each child and finds a meaningful berth for each one at the end of it."*

In conclusion, while attempting to fix the many structural, procedural and operational aspects of schooling as it is now envisaged and practised, so that we might seriously tackle and rectify the deficiencies that limit, restrain and confine the greater potential diversity of human achievement within the status quo, then there also needs to be a radical overhaul of our political, economic and social policies so that they offer a far more honest and genuine degree of true social mobility. In other words, the bigger picture of society as a whole and the way in which we organise our affairs must also be seriously addressed, and urgently, if we are to staunch the loss of human talent, human passion and the dreams of every boy and girl that we currently squander by failing to offer genuine opportunity to succeed and develop once they actually leave formal schooling. It would be almost cruel and inhumane to do otherwise!

Chapter Twenty Four: Reality vs. Make-Believe

In the previous two chapters of this section of the book, I have tried to outline why I believe that radical change is needed in the way in which we organise society if we are to make the most of the diversity of innate human talent that we possess. To do this we must provide abundant opportunities for this talent pool to be developed and grown throughout the life of every individual citizen, by encouraging everyone to work more collaboratively within a more inclusive and just environment, rather than being encouraged to compete and beat others. In such a way, I believe that we would all have a far better opportunity to live fulfilling lives and eventually to die with little, less or no regret. Sadly, I believe that there is another major obstacle that prevents us from being able to achieve this, perhaps, more idealistic version of life, and that is the way in which our economic system is founded upon a simplistic and unfulfilling version of competitive capitalism that inexorably compels us to spend our lives and our limited resources simply acquiring stuff, rather than focusing on our inner spirituality.

The Menace of Materialism and Consumerism

It would surely be true to say that the lives of most people, if not all of us, have become more and more material rather than spiritual in nature over the course of the last sixty years or so. Unfortunately, these two forces of materialism and our human spirituality seem to be mutually exclusive given the way in which the exigent former has come to dominate and subjugate the latter, rendering it a marginal force at best.

Whilst I admit to have been powerfully seduced by the lure and novelty of living a highly material life, such is the power of the capitalist economic system and the prevalence of a consumerist society, I remain fearful about the impact it has upon our individual and collective existence. This fear is based on the superficial way in which it forms the basis of our existence, and the fact that the notion of perpetual economic growth, upon which it is founded, is simply unsustainable, owing to the finite nature of natural resources, combined with its severely deleterious impact upon climate change and environmental degradation. My fears are such that I feel immensely relieved that I have no children of my own, but that does not stop me from feeling a genuine concern for the future welfare and well-being of our young people and future generations. After all, young minds seem to be more susceptible to, and easily seduced by such powerful forces.

I do not intend to write a treatise on my concerns regarding such forces, but I would like to refer to how I am not alone in feeling a sense of foreboding and genuine sympathy for what a continuation of this consumerist tide presages for the future of our species and our planet.

The collective consciousness of our children and teenagers is being swamped in the most insidious of ways by the 'hidden' messages that shape us as human beings. Moreover, we are almost totally unaware of, and incapable of countering, this attitudinal, psychological and behavioural indoctrination and damage which by being so essentially subliminal is, of course, why it is so powerful, so lasting and so much a matter of really serious concern.

I first had my own concerns affirmed and heightened a few years ago now, when I read about an author who was also seriously alarmed and worried by these processes, so much so that it had prompted him to write a book about them. In his book entitled *Britain on the Couch – Why We Are Unhappier Compared With 1950, Despite Being Richer'* (2010), leading psychologist Oliver James discusses this very issue in a very eloquent and persuasive manner. He talked at length about the effects of television – in those days – on the psyche of our youngest citizens; its content, the length of viewing and the lack of parental supervision that accompanied that viewing. James described the television as having become a sort of 'electrical nanny', keeping the kids quiet and 'occupied'. But as he pointed out, *"It keeps them quiet now, but a diet of glossy wannabe fodder from the box may seriously impair teenage mental health."* Of course, despite the fact that his book was first published a mere five years ago, the five years since that time have seen an inexorable rise in information and communication technologies to include far more plentiful and effective ways of occupying our waking hours, such as the swamping pervasiveness of Smart Phones, social media websites and the other gadgetry which offer an even more extensive and troublesome dimension to the validity of James' point above.

Back in 2010, he argued that the TV blurs the differences between viewers and the wealthy, successful, attractive people, and the celebrities, who largely fill the screens, inviting inappropriate upward comparison. Instead of being able to learn from people in superior positions to us, in terms of looks, career or life-style, James argued that the democratic levelling process inherent in TV makes us feel that we too could have what they have, regardless of their hard work, good looks, good fortune, connections, and so on.

Taken together, TV and the new technologies exist primarily as a means of selling the advanced capitalist dream, and of poisoning our waking reality. And in whose interests is this psychic holocaust? The pressure to create an endless supply of new consumer needs, and to sustain unprecedented, rapid economic growth, has been relentless since the 1950s, and TV, now accompanied and reinforced by other information and communication technologies, is the engine room. Along with other, more traditional media, such as magazines and newspapers, James argued that this process encourages dissatisfaction with what we have got, and a longing for new commodities, jobs, bodies and even identities to make us feel better. In fact, it has been claimed by other social commentators that the unattainable and irresistible consumerist appeal of always wanting something bigger, better and newer, also goes some way to explain why, in the same time period, we have seen the tandem development of increases in divorce rates and a weakening in other forms of inter-personal relationship ties.

James posited that only if we are made to believe that our inner lives, as well as our material ones, will be improved by consumption of new goods can this growth process continue and strengthen over time, and he continued by warning that the increased profits, new markets and growth in the economy are, however, tumorous for our psyches. James also felt that television's job of spreading this cancer had been made all the easier by a related development, namely that our personal identities had also become much more plastic. He argued that our identities were once ascribed at birth, but today they are 'achieved' by educational, occupational and economic activity and through open competition within a supposedly meritocratic system. The 'achieved self' is defined by reference to inner feelings and thoughts rather than to externally pre-ordained roles, such as kinship ties and the execution of associated roles like 'mother and son'. The goal of the achieved self is to express itself, whether through hedonism, achievement or consumerism. To be fully realised, it must break away from ascribed family ties to become a separate person. The achieving adolescent must seek out new social networks through school, university and occupation.

He continued by making the point that, by contrast, in the collectivist societies of the kind we had in the 1950s, and which still predominate throughout much of the developing world, identity was ascribed on the basis of kinship ties that were pre-ordained at birth. Consequently, the goal of the ascribed self can be seen as putting one's own interests to the group first, by a willingness to feel and think what others are thinking and feeling, to absorb this information without being told, and to **help others satisfy their wishes and realise their goals**. Moreover, the erasure of hedonistic and selfish desires is valued as part of the successful execution of social roles and obligations, with the cardinal virtue being sensitivity regarding the potential impact of one's actions upon the common fate. Furthermore, ascribed adolescents are not encouraged to cut loose from parents and family. On the contrary, the goal of parents is to inculcate obedience, reliability and proper behaviour, and of children to obey.

James went on to argue that it was a much easier task for marketing and television to sell this vast array of stuff to people who have achieved rather than ascribed identities, making the point that although achieved persons are more introspective, like depressives, they are also far more likely to look nervously outwards for definition, constantly checking to see how they are performing in relation to others. As a result, they can be easily lured into the excessive and maladjusted social comparing that TV deliberately nurtures, using its market research to identify and target their vulnerabilities. In this way, it encourages the viewer to observe the life-styles, bodies and psychologies of others, to long for them and to define who they are through what they buy. Identities are so weak that they can change with the fashions, to provide a ready market for the steady flow of new products that are essential for this puerile form of economic growth.

I remember feeling when I read about James' work, that if he was only partly right in his analysis then it was wrong for politicians to blame the breakdown of families and social cohesion upon teachers, schools, parents and other convenient scapegoats, whilst wilfully promoting the unchecked, unmodified extension and acceleration of the very process that is the real disease, or culprit. No wonder they need to 'dumb-down' society, in order to prevent people from challenging and seeing through, let alone beyond, the convenient and woolly rhetoric of politicians and the demons that they create to justify their simplistic and wholly inappropriate remedies.

If there is to be an alternative way of managing our economic lives, then its starting point must be the realisation that we are easily affluent enough as a society. We need, therefore, to find and develop ways of making that affluence work for, rather than against, our emotional and spiritual well-being. For a start, we need a truly radical alternative and one that goes far beyond merely managing the status quo more efficiently than 'the last lot' in government.

Alternatively, or additionally, we would do well by developing indicators of our declining quality of life that would help persuade and convince the voters to forget about economic growth. Surely, we have reached a time when there is no longer such a pressing, urgent and relentless need for our companies or our national economy to grow, as we are already quite rich enough, in material terms.

I have long since felt that with more equitable distribution of wealth and less stimulation of our competitive and comparative instincts at the expense of the co-operative, altruistic ones, we could concentrate on the only thing that really matters, that of enjoying each other and ourselves amidst our unimaginably great affluence, whilst avoiding the incredible psychological and social damage that the process of economic growth and materialism at all costs has involved.

Furthermore, this long-held belief that I have was better articulated in an article in The Guardian newspaper, written by the ever-readable George Monbiot, entitled *'Materialism: a system that eats us from the inside out'* (9th December 2015), the main argument of which is that buying more and more stuff is directly associated with depression, anxiety and broken relationships and, it has the power, therefore, of being both incredibly socially destructive as well as self-destructive.

Monbiot refers to an impressive body of psychological research which suggests that materialism, which the researchers involved define as, *"a value system that is preoccupied with possessions and the social image they project"*, adversely affects both the rich and poor in a manner which is not only socially destructive, but also self-destructive. Materialism, they argue, destroys the happiness and peace of mind of those who are seduced by it, as it is associated with envy, anxiety and depression as well as broken relationships. What is perhaps more important in Monbiot's article is that he refers to recent research which has shown that a long recognised and observed correlation between materialism and a lack of empathy and engagement with others, not to mention unhappiness, can now be said to be an actual cause of these social afflictions. By way of an example, he refers to a series of studies published in the journal 'Motivation and Emotion' earlier in the year that emphatically noted that as people become more materialistic, their wellbeing, in terms of sound personal relationships, autonomy and a sense of purpose in life for example, actually diminishes. The converse was also noted, in that as people became less materialistic so their actual feeling of wellbeing increased.

In a related study, referred to in Monbiot's article, the psychologists involved examined the impact, over time, of Iceland's economic collapse on the general population. What they found was that some citizens focused a lot more on materialism, in the hope of perhaps regaining lost ground during the depression, whilst others responded by becoming more interested and concerned with matters related to family and community life, as opposed to acquiring or obtaining more money. Again there was a perceived contrast between the levels of wellbeing experienced by both groups, with the level diminishing for the first group and rising for the second group of citizens.

What I found to be of even greater interest in Monbiot's essay was his reference to a second paper, published in 'Psychological Science', which found that people in a controlled experiment who were, *"repeatedly exposed to images of luxury goods, to messages that cast them as consumers rather than citizens, and to words associated with materialism (such as 'buy', 'status', 'asset' and 'expensive')"* led to them experiencing *"temporary increases in material aspirations, anxiety and depression."* The study also found that these people became more competitive and more selfish, demonstrating reduced feelings of social responsibility and tending to avoid participating in demanding social activities. This finding is of real concern to me because it shows a strong, but not really surprising, link between the unsavoury aspects of competition and materialism, with them both feeding on and off each other.

One final piece of research which George Monbiot included in his article was, somewhat paradoxically, published in the 'Journal of Consumer Research', and studied the behaviour of 2,500 people over a six-year period. It found a two-way relationship between materialism and loneliness in that, not only does materialism generate and engender social isolation, but also people who feel socially isolated and cut off from others gravitate towards the acquisition of possessions and materialism. What is more, this attachment to materialism leads to a crowding out of social relationships, something that was also identified in Oliver James' earlier work. Again, we find that despite having known about the detrimental and carcinogenic nature of materialism on social welfare and social cohesion, which is reliant on and perpetuated through the pursuit of endless economic growth, absolutely nothing has been done to arrest this process and change the way we conduct our lifestyles and materialistic obsessions. This lack of remedial action to prevent, reverse or minimize the continuation of these obsessions, and the social atomisation that they create in their combined wake is also the result of the vast financial and political vested interests that are heavily invested in the traditional orthodoxy of maintaining the status quo. This impotence to even recognise this socially destructive trend, let alone reverse it by radically rethinking and re-prioritising our lifestyle goals, is much the same as how we seem incapable of radically reformulating what goes on in our nation's schools, in the name of education.

Monbiot concludes his article by stressing the harmful relationship between materialism and social cohesion and wellbeing, due to the way in which the former forces us into a largely meaningless and irrelevant comparison with the possessions of others, and that this material pursuit of self-esteem inexorably reduces one's own feelings of personal self-esteem. Because I agree wholeheartedly with this conclusion, that is why I felt it necessary to devote a

545

section of this book to encouraging people to radically re-think and re-shape not only the goals of schools and the education of young people, but also the goals of the society in which they live and the system that they will inherit. Moreover, if we are serious about re-creating schools that actively promote and nurture the development of young people's self-confidence and self-esteem, then it seems insane to try and do this in a society predicated on, and obsessed with, generating (unsustainable) endless economic growth that ensures the effective worship of an unavoidably destructive form of consumerist materialism. The two are mutually contradictory in nature!

George Monbiot's final sentence in an excellent and thought-provoking article reads as follows, *"Worldly ambition, material aspiration, perpetual growth: these are a formula for mass unhappiness."* Would it not be so much better and more enriching and fulfilling if we were to create a system which promotes and rewards young people who aspire to realise their innate talents, dreams and passions in life rather than jump on the materialist treadmill that demands the mindless acquisition of the latest and newest 'stuff'?

In any case, the whole system is rigged in favour of an incredibly small minority who are the holders of huge amounts of income and wealth. For example, it has been reported that the four members of the Walton family, who own Walmart, have a combined wealth of $145 billion which is greater than that of the bottom 40 per cent of Americans, some of whom are employees of Walmart and paid very low wages. Such disparities in the distribution of income and wealth, apart from being extraordinarily unfair, engender undesirable emotions of envy, not to mention economic hardship for many at the bottom of the income and wealth index. When we consider the glaring and increasing inequality in the way in which income and wealth are distributed within the most developed capitalist economic countries, a situation which is not only unjust but also far from inclusive, how can we seriously describe countries like the USA or the UK as being, in any real way, democratic?

Until societies seriously tackle the obsession with materialism and the perpetual acquisition of stuff, as well as genuinely redistribute income and wealth more equitably, the aspirations and opportunities for young school leavers are going to be adversely affected, and we will continue to see young people who lack self-esteem and self-confidence that is so vitally important if they are to believe that they can achieve and succeed in life. Radically reformulating formal schooling, which is a big ask in the first place, is unlikely to be enough to create the opportunities needed for young people to go on to live fulfilling lives and to promote individual and collective feelings of wellbeing if we do nothing to change the way in which the bigger picture of wealth distribution and obsessions with economic growth and consumerism are also seriously and radically addressed.

I felt that it might be relevant to conclude this short chapter by including the message written by Jimmy Carter, the then President of the United States of America, to explain the contents of the space-exploring Voyager 1 craft. I have intentionally highlighted the parts that I thought were the most honest and pertinent to what I have written about the twin dangers of economic growth and obsessive consumerism if only to remind us all that we need to try a great deal harder if we are to achieve those aims (the highlighted sections have been added by me):

"This is a present from a small distant world, a token of our sounds, our science, our images, our music, our thoughts and our feelings. ___We are attempting to survive our time so we may live into yours.___ *We hope someday,* ___having solved the problems we face___*, to join a community of galactic civilisations. This record represents our hope and our determination, and our goodwill in a vast and awesome universe."*

Section H: The Solution

Chapter Twenty Five: Regaining Control

I had initially intended that this final section of my thoughts on why schools fail students, as opposed to why students are considered to fail school, would be a little shorter, and slightly less substantive, than most of those that have preceded them. However, as I came to write these closing chapters, I found that the length of this final section could not be abridged, as intended, although the substantive element would still be significantly less prescriptive and detailed in nature.

There are three major reasons for this, and the first is that a lot of the issues that I believe lead to this sorry state of affairs in schools and need to be challenged, changed and completely overhauled have been stated in what has gone before in other key sections of this book, where I have made recommendations as to possible alternative ways of doing things, or not doing such things at all.

The second reason is one of simple honesty and humility. Where I have not offered clear or definite solutions, I can explain this by admitting that it would be foolhardy, arrogant and silly of me to claim that I have all the answers myself, even though I may be highly critical and, occasionally, cynical about a lot of what passes as current practice in the education and schooling of young people, as well as having made some fairly strident comments.

Allied to this is the third explanation for the absence of definite solutions, which is that no one person could (nor should) be expected to devise a new educational paradigm that will overcome the deficiencies and failures of the current system, by replacing it with radically new ways of thinking about, structuring and delivering state education, so that the end result is something that ignites the interests of our young people, and provides the spark that ultimately liberates their innate talents, passions and dreams. To undertake such a process will demand a massive team effort and a pooling of the diverse creative instincts and imaginations of as many people as possible, ideally. We need people who are themselves willing to entertain possibility and to take risks through a willingness to try things out, to experiment, so as to effect desired change. I hope that I have already made it patently clear that tinkering around at the periphery with piecemeal and micro-level change which is still predicated on the current flawed anachronism that is state education, will simply just not do anymore.

Such a team approach will be enormously beneficial due to the dynamics that arise from collaboration and which, in turn, lead people to feel that they have a stake in what we proceed to do. This is called the 'ownership of', or 'buying into' something that has been designed and devised collectively, rather than merely adopting some 'top-down' model where a few individuals undertake these tasks on behalf of those who will be ultimately responsible for making it a successful reality in actual practice. It is believed that there is a great deal to be gained from involving as many key stakeholders of education in this process, at various stages perhaps and in different ways, simply because it allows us to canvass their views and ideas as well as to harness their expertise, efforts and creative energies. Well, that is the theory anyway, in very loose terms admittedly. (In fact, I came across yet another excellent quote, attributed to Albert Einstein, whilst reading Ha-Joon Chang's outstanding book entitled *'Economics: The User's Guide'*, which I recommend to everyone in the interests of greater economic literacy and education for lay-people, as well as for established teachers of the subject. In discussing the difference between theory and practice, Einstein succinctly said: *'In theory, theory and practice are the same. In practice, they are not.'*)

I include the above simply to say that we must do our utmost to ensure that our joint endeavours in designing and creating a new theoretical model of schooling, and one that is truly synonymous with the education of young people, result in a situation where the actual practice and concrete outcomes closely mirror the abstract version. Building ownership into both the theoretical and practical stages, I believe, offers us the best possible chance of proving Einstein wrong! And how about *that* for a challenge?

Recent history has shown us that when we slavishly kowtow to government's top-down innovations, new ideas and wheezes, then the result is what might aptly be described as a pig's breakfast, where even the pigs come to find the offering inedible or unacceptable. We, and by 'we' I mean mainly the education and teaching profession, need to regain control and wrest the vital process of education out of the grubby hands of politicians, who really must learn to work with us rather than persistently against us. The achievement of a consensus ad idem is much needed by way of working collaboratively, rather than being constantly in competition and at odds with those responsible for the theory of education and classroom practice.

Autonomy over Accountability

The teaching profession must regain control of the process of designing and delivering education in schools, although they need to think differently, by thinking outside of the box and not act as the victims of their own experiences of school and schooling. The ancient and out-dated mould needs to be broken, and we must urgently forge a new and modern template for compulsory education. Once the teaching profession regains control of schooling and education, the sooner teachers' autonomy will be restored and we might be left in relative peace to develop far better and more relevant practice that will truly engage our young people. To achieve this autonomy will also require us to decide to whom the teaching profession should really be accountable, and then retain those measures that we currently have which successfully serve that end, and sweep away the bilge that simply obstructs, distracts or detracts from what young people and their teachers really should be doing in schools.

A good starting point would be to simply get rid of the raft of meaningless assessment and testing that floats upon the bilge water that has drained down through the corridors of power in Westminster and eventually been discharged into the once calm sea of education. Anything that promotes competition over collaboration and which sets people against each other is, for me, deeply suspect and should be seriously questioned, if not eliminated altogether. To use an old school expression, we need to 'wipe the slate clean' and say a far from fond farewell to the current and centrally imposed nonsense of league tables, examinations and testing, testing and testing which are the greatest cause of intolerable levels of stress that are being heaped upon our young people. Education should be a joyful experience and one that is also challenging, accompanied by high expectations of oneself and of those with whom we work in a spirit of collegiality and collaboration. Let us by all means create what I call positive stress, an atmosphere which arises from a sense of real challenge combined with the excitement of rising to meet such high expectations, and eradicate those forces and events that simply create negative and harmful stress.

The education system in England and Wales, the one with which I am most familiar, is obsessed with external examinations, especially of the type that relies on terminal assessment and testing, and their ultimate requirement of identifying the 'winners' and 'losers'. I was delighted to read a newspaper article, which I really should have sent to the current British Prime Minister and old-Etonian David Cameron to read, entitled *'Eton headmaster: England's exam system unimaginative and outdated'*. Hear, hear!

Tony Little, the then Head Teacher (but he still called himself 'headmaster') of Eton College wrote an article published in the Radio Times in which he said: *"There is a lot more to an effective and good education than jostling for position in a league table"*, and he was spot on. In fact, he was highly critical of the British government's obsession of seeking to copy the excessively academic schooling offered in areas of the Far East, such as Shanghai. This was something described as ironic, given that the schools there were, at the same time, looking at the value of giving children 'a more rounded' education. As Tony Little put it: *"We seem intent on creating the same straitjacket the Chinese are trying to wriggle out of."* He went on to warn that we should be *"wary of emulating Shanghai"* at a time when they were considering the value of the *"liberal values"* associated with a broader and more all-encompassing curricular entitlement, which is *"something we have traditionally been good at."*

Perhaps the most telling and refreshing thing that Tony Little said, when explaining why he felt that England's exam system was unimaginative and outdated was when he argued that it: *"obliges students to sit alone at their desks in preparation for a world in which, for much of the time, they will need to work collaboratively."* This is perhaps why he claimed that the exam system was little changed from Victorian times and, in reference to working collaboratively, I assume, he said that as a result, it fails to prepare young people for modern working life. To be honest, I did wince a little when I read that part, but not wanting to look a gift horse, such as the Head of Eton, in the mouth, I decided to overlook the 'preparation for working life' part and convince myself that he could easily have said that it failed to prepare students to work collaboratively, successfully and harmoniously for a lot of the time at school, as well as being a part of their families and wider communities in the here and now.

What I also liked about what Tony Little said in the article, referred to above, is the fact that he offered his support to a Lancashire primary school which had sent a letter signed by the head teacher Rachel Tomlinson and Amy Birkett, a year 6 teacher, when the ten-year olds had received their SAT (standard assessment test) results. The letter from the two of them was designed to inform their students that they were proud of their efforts during the tests, but added that they should also be aware that the tests they had sat most certainly did not assess all of what contributed to each of them being *"special and unique"*. Sheer class!

The steady narrowing of the curriculum in most state schools has been something that is of grave concern to me, given my unshakeable belief in seeking to litter the paths of young people with as many quality learning opportunities as possible whilst they are of school age, and not necessarily when they are just 'in school'. The former phrase accommodates and incorporates the significant benefits to be gained by community education, with the school acting as the most-important centre of learning, but most definitely not the only centre of learning. As the late Al Capp, an American cartoonist and humorist once was alleged to have said, *"Any place that anyone can learn something useful from someone with experience is an educational institution."* This is why my understanding of a true community school, which acts as the hub for a community network of 'educational institutions' of the type described by Al Capp, must necessarily be both *'outside in'*, as I call it, as well as *'inside out'* – as I argued initially in Chapter 14. This simply means that these community-based 'educational institutions' need to work with teachers and students actually in schools and on the school premises in various ways and, similarly, school students and their teachers must go out, away from the physical confines of the school site to other places where they 'can learn something useful'.

At this point, I should perhaps point out that I am most definitely not advocating teachers being replaced by other adults of experience who can clearly offer additional experiences, knowledge and skills that will be of benefit to young learners. What I am calling for, however, is a practical model whereby the boundary of the school is permeable to the influences of, and exposure to, the type of educational institutions to which Al Capp referred, and these lie within the school itself (other students, other teachers, parents, support staff and teacher assistants) as well as those that can be found in the wider school community beyond the school gates.

I feel the need to make this important clarification because recent governments have been promoting, allowing and/or turning a blind eye to the worrying practice of students actually being taught by non-specialist teachers, something that is becoming increasingly prevalent in primary schools. Unfortunately, this dubious practice is inexorably spreading to secondary schools, which is possibly a panic measure by government to compensate for the fact that schools across England and Wales are bleeding qualified teachers at an alarming rate, as well as finding it increasingly difficult to recruit qualified others to take their place, especially in the 'core' subjects of mathematics and the sciences.

An article which appeared in the Observer newspaper (5 July 2015), written by the education editor, Polly Curtis, reported on the biggest independent inquiry into primary education in the last forty years. It was based on 28 research surveys, 1,052 written submissions and 250 focus groups. The process was conducted by 14 authors, 66 research consultants and a twenty-strong advisory committee at Cambridge University. The whole comprehensive process was led by Professor Robin Alexander, described as 'one of the most experienced educational academics in country'. Its main conclusion was that schoolchildren should not start formal lessons, or formal schooling, until they reach the age of <u>six</u> years.

In summary, the study was reported as a damning indictment of the education record of, please note, the Labour government since 1997. It claimed that successive Labour ministers had intervened in what went on in school classrooms on an unprecedented scale, and this included controlling the very precise detail of how teachers teach. The report also said that this level of interference had *"Stalinist overtones"*, as well as having the effect of exaggerating student progress and narrowing the curriculum by crowding out timetable time for other, equally important subjects like history and, of course, music and arts. The report went on to recommend that SATs should be scrapped in order to relieve the negative stress and damaging pressure that young students face, all for the sake of competitive league tables.

The teaching profession really does have to regain control of education, and that includes notable academics such as Professor Robin Alexander. Such a process or change requires government to butt out of directing the process, and accept that they don't know their educational arse from their political elbow. It was hardly surprising that although the review's conclusions were supported and agreed to by all trade unions/professional associations in the country, it was rejected by know-all government ministers, who were rightly accused of, and condemned for rejecting the findings of very extensive research that was both independent and rigorous. As we all know, and only too well, politicians and their civil service enablers can never lose face by being wrong, and fundamentally, extensively and spectacularly wrong at that! It was once said that God created mankind with two ends: one to think with and the other to sit on. In which case, the government should stop talking out of the one designed for sitting on!

Not only were the decisions and subsequent actions of politicians severely criticised, but also, so were the very processes by which these hare-brained decisions were made. To be more precise:

> "The report notes the questionable evidence on which some key educational policies have been based; the disenfranchising of local voice; the rise of unelected and unaccountable groups taking key decisions behind closed doors; the 'empty rituals' of consultations; the authoritarian mind-set, and the use of myth and derision to underwrite exaggerated accounts of progress and discredit alternative views."

I would venture that such comments could rightly be described as being pretty damning indeed, as well as being very apposite, accurate and essentially truthful, in view of what has passed in the last 30 to 40 years.

As a result, Professor Alexander argued for a *"rolling back of the powers of the state"* and a *"reversal of the centralisation"* which had begun to interfere in how teachers actually conduct their day-to-day teaching. In short, the interfering and interventionist tentacles of central government could be found to be adversely

557

affecting and polluting not only the types of schools and how they are funded, but also all aspects of the curriculum, even to the extent of the types of classroom methodology employed. This might be more palatable and reasonable if civil servants and education ministers were required to undertake an intensive teacher training course, including a stint in front of some of the more challenging school students, so that they might come to understand and empathise with what the school dynamic is like, and how demanding teaching is as a vocation. Otherwise, government should retract its tentacles and start to listen, work with and praise teachers on the good work that they do, whilst being willing to fairly point out where a school or a teacher is failing to meet the professional standards that are needed to perform their vital function of facilitating student learning.

A return to an over-riding culture of autonomy is essential if we are to overcome the educational quagmire that is causing young people, their parents and teachers at all levels of the profession untold levels of negative stress which is poisoning the whole notion of state education. In the findings of the review conducted by Professor Alexander, it was quite clearly stated that there is a growing *"pervasive anxiety"* about children's lives, with teachers and parents concerned about the pressures that students experience with frequent SATs, which clearly undermine learning which is designed and intended to be a student-centred, self-directed and intrinsically stimulating, worthwhile and rewarding experience.

The report of this very extensive review of primary education also made another extremely important and frightening finding. This was the damaging effect that starting formal lessons at the age of four years was having on a lot of students, particularly boys. This highly detrimental first experience of formal schooling was so acute because the young students were found not to be ready to read and write. The importance of acquiring these basic skills which we, as adults, take for granted and rightly regard as being the cornerstones of having the ability to learn in a formal way, is why parents are, wrongly, pressuring their children to start this process even earlier, as if that will overcome the problem. This shows why teacher autonomy is so vital and needs to be regarded as a positive force for good and to be trusted, as long as it is undertaken by fully-trained, professional teachers (and by what I mean by 'fully' trained, please refer back to the section in this book on Teacher Training).

Professor Alexander's review also noted that in many other countries, young children do not start academic lessons until they are around six or seven years of age, and they are not in any way handicapped by this later start, mainly because it has been shown that their performance actually overtakes that of their counterparts in England at some point, as they grow older and mature. Indeed, this issue of maturation is something that is vital to consider, as its rate varies in different young people, depending on a whole host of factors like gender, social and domestic pressures, prior learning experiences and hereditary differentiation. It makes absolutely no sense, therefore, to once again try to standardise individual diversity by starting all young people on the academic treadmill at the same age, and certainly not before they are ready. In fact, it is definitely going to have the opposite outcome to the one intended in theory. For any learning to be successful, one has to start by taking account of what every individual student in a class already knows, understands and is able to do, as this will affect their ability to learn and their capacity to develop, by building on their existing and differing abilities.

In essence, the answer to the question of when will a child be ready to begin formal schooling is a very simple one: when they are ready! As Gillian Pugh, who was the chairwoman of the review warned: *"If (children) are already failing by the age of four and a half or five, it's going to be quite difficult to get them back into the system again"*. Furthermore, in the process of 'getting them back into the system', once their nascent self-confidence has been potentially bruised, if not shattered by premature schooling, then it will very much be a case of 'once bitten, twice shy' as far as the student so affected is concerned.

My final reference to this huge piece of research into primary education goes a long way to confirm the views I expressed in the previous section, regarding 'the bigger picture', which deals with the undeniable link between educational achievement and poverty, and remember we are talking about England in the 21st century, and primary education. The review concluded that this link is the biggest problem children face in their personal and social development, by saying, **"What is worrying is the persistence of a long tail of severely** *disadvantaged children whose early lives are unhappy, whose potential is unrealised and whose future is bleak."*

One of the additional and major problems faced by state schooling that can largely be attributed to the increasingly interventionist and authoritarian nature of government interference, which has been persistent, pernicious and parsimonious over too many years, is the flood of serving, qualified and professional teachers that are leaving the profession. They are either leaving in their droves due to the pressures of intolerable accountability measures that have repeatedly undermined their efforts, and adversely affected their work-family life balance, causing extreme levels of negative stress, or due to their preference for the (quite literally) richer pickings and better working conditions that can be found in the private sector and in international schools. The employment opportunities for disaffected teachers from the UK are far better in the blossoming and booming international school sector.

This bleed of qualified personnel is deeply worrying as it is creating a significant shrinkage in the pool of qualified teachers from which schools in the UK are able to recruit, not to mention a dilution of quality. What is more, fewer graduates are considering a career in the challenging school environment, and so the supply of suitably qualified teachers is failing to meet the increasing demand. This is made worse when one considers how few people are signing up to train to teach specialist and government-determined core subjects, like the sciences and mathematics. This is turning a headache for head teachers, on the look-out for suitably qualified teachers, into a veritable and severe migraine. After all, having suitably able individuals standing in front of every class, and for every subject on the curriculum, is pretty basic, important and essential.

This ongoing and worsening shortage of qualified teachers is one that central government has to recognise, understand and remedy if state schools are going to ever be expected to flourish in terms of their contribution to enabling and inspiring young people to maximise their potential at any point in time. Unfortunately, the signs are far from rosy in this regard; governments have instead sought cheaper, quicker and consequently educationally unsound solutions, mainly in an effort to convince the electorate that all is well in the schools to whom many of them entrust their children. Nothing could be further from the truth, but then truth is not a currency in which the majority of politicians, and certainly those in senior ministerial positions, trade.

One such diversionary wheeze to distract a worried electorate is to allow inadequately trained, non-specialists to teach what are called 'shortage subjects', especially in the core areas like mathematics. It is fascinating, in fact, to witness how we have developed our vocabulary to quantify the severity of these shortages. The truth – politicians please note – is that there are veritable shortages for teachers of **all** subjects, which is why it has become necessary to further grade the severity of these deficiencies as being either 'acute' or 'chronic'. This worsening problem with the reform of teacher training by government was commented upon in the Observer newspaper (5th July 2015), and far from favourably.

The main thrust of the editorial was to comment on the fact that an increasing proportion of young people is being taught mathematics by non-specialists, a situation it described as *"deeply worrying"*, not least in view of an OECD study into the teaching of maths worldwide, which showed that the UK was placed at a derisory and *"deeply worrying"* 26th in the global ranking. Verdict: Could do better!

The editorial was very well informed, especially when it emphasised that the quality of teaching is the most important difference between what may be considered a 'good' school, as compared to an 'average' school. The commentary rightly noted that a truly great teacher is one who possesses not only a genuine passion for what they are teaching, but also someone who simply must have the ability to explain it to learners of any particular age, and then to really inspire them. To be competent in doing this, the teacher has to possess real skill and expertise as well as a deep understanding of their subject. That is not to say that the teacher must have a doctorate in their subject to be considered qualified and suitable to teach primary students, for example, but they do need to have considerable authority in what they are teaching, and that comes from being fully trained and qualified, so that they can be seen as authorised to teach, say maths, for example.

Again I find myself referring to the wise words of the genius Albert Einstein who was reported to have commented: *"If you can't explain it to a six year-old, you don't understand it."* This echoes the sentiments of Bruner, referred to earlier in the book, who maintains that the key concepts of any academic discipline are as simple as they are powerful, depending on the context in which they are developed. The inverse of what Einstein said is also true, in that if you are to be required to explain something to a six-year-old, then you must properly understand it yourself. As a teacher of economics and economic awareness, who has taught students of all ages, I have discovered this to be profoundly accurate, partly because one can never predict the problems that all individual learners might encounter in understanding something, nor the potential questions that their inquisitive minds might prompt them to ask. You certainly have to be 'on top of your game' to be an effective classroom teacher, without any shadow of a doubt!

I fully concur with the views of the Observer's editorial when it said that this **trend** – which in itself implies a worrying longer-term practice – of having maths taught by non-specialist teachers is one that is, **"unfolding against a troubling backdrop: a general shortage within the profession and government reforms that have watered down teacher training and scrapped the need in state-funded schools for a teaching qualification".** Acknowledging the fact that some teachers are born brilliant, the editorial confirms what I, and many other have also maintained, and that is, for the majority of aspiring teachers, *"the ability to educate is a skill that needs nurturing".* The editorial concluded by warning that the government's attempts to reform Britain's system of teacher training are based upon a *"flawed premise"* that the country is blessed with *"an abundance of naturally outstanding teachers"* who are merely deterred by the inconvenience of the need to be properly and fully trained, will not only fail to *"address shortages",* but will also seriously *"undermine the profession's status".*

Hand Back the Reins of Power

It should by now be abundantly clear that in every sphere of state schooling and education in which the government has interfered, the end results or improvements are rarely, if ever, those that the government had promised to achieve at the outset, with the actual effect being mainly adverse, negative and thoroughly damaging to the whole system. Their fearsome tentacles have not had the Midas touch, that is for sure, as most things that they have touched have turned to stone, from which they then seek to try and extract blood.

They have created confusion and havoc in areas such as the content and delivery of the curriculum, with the creative and aesthetic dimensions of learning being squeezed out altogether, or shuffled off into the twilight hours of after-school activities. Methods of assessment and testing have been reinforced with layer after layer of additional stress-inducing new tests and demands for the measurement of student performance against very specific and narrow outcomes, not to mention the ludicrously counter-productive moves to test students from the earliest of age, and at very frequent intervals. It seems as though some government ministers, responsible for education, change their demands as often as their personal underwear.

Governments have sought, in effect, to micro-manage the ways in which schools and even individual lessons are run, as if they always know best – the arrogant fools! Their initiatives have constrained the ability of head teachers to manage their schools in the manner which they believe is right and proper in their individual contexts, starting with where they are already, as well as the people with whom they work. As any school inspector or casual visitor with a modicum of observational intelligence will tell you, every school is very different to all the others, even those within the same locality. It follows, therefore, that a 'one-size-fits-all' approach to launching new initiatives for schools to follow and adopt is seriously flawed in terms of their design from the very outset, and long before they reach the implementation stage. They are destined to fail, and to fail miserably, as it is an act of utter folly to try and standardise the diversity of so many schools that represent such a diverse range of different communities, with differing resource levels, different student intakes, varying quality of school premises, and diverse social and economic conditions which the children experience in their daily lives.

What is more, government seems to think that education operates within a bubble that is totally disconnected to, or with, the bigger picture of the societies they represent, not to mention the ways in which the government is operating mutually exclusive or contradictory initiatives when it comes to the economic and social agenda that their policies are seeking to address. For example, for the government to expect schools to churn out more young people, eligible to enter the world of work, at the same time as its economic policies are decimating British industry, will obviously be frustrated as a direct result of a significant curtailment in the range of job opportunities on offer.

Perhaps the hope is that new jobs will arise in the future. If that is the optimistic vision, when automation and the increasing use of robot technologies are rapidly reducing the need to employ human beings, how are schools to know what type of jobs will exist in some unknown future, and jobs that will be able to offer our hopeful school leavers a challenging and fulfilling working life – and preferably one that matches their passions and talents – thereby providing each and every one of them with a real chance in life?

Repeated government intervention has had the cumulative effect of demoralising and over-burdening the teaching profession, as well as the young people who are those who really suffer from this perpetual barrage of mindless meddling. The result of this has seen students becoming as demoralised as their teachers, with increased opting out in the form of increasing truancy by the students, as well as the considerable number of teachers that are leaving the profession, year on year.

Furthermore, the training period that an aspiring teacher can be expected to receive is being shortened, and new ways of qualifying 'on the job' both inevitably mean that those entering the profession cannot possibly be expected to be fully prepared for what awaits them. As if to add insult to injury, incompetent governments with their short-term political needs are allowing unqualified personnel to become teachers and take the enormous responsibility of facilitating or helping to manage and direct the learning of young people in a more negotiated way. It would be so much better if teachers found themselves working with young learners in a more collaborative way, rather than forcing them to jump through increasingly irrelevant, esoteric and pre-specified educational hoops which have been set in place by our confused and partisan political masters and mistresses.

All of this because the government does not trust the teaching profession, whilst the teaching profession seems to have lost all faith or belief in a government that subjects them to unnecessarily increasing workloads, which are largely administrative in nature, and then holds them accountable for undertaking fairly meaningless tasks and meeting spurious outcomes that prove to be very little of a truly educational nature.

What is more, these changes that have been forced upon schools have usually been utterly contradictory in nature, with each new initiative or, as I prefer to call them, political wheezes, rarely being given adequate time to be understood in schools let alone acted upon and outcomes observed and evaluated, before another over-lapping and new set of central demands are decreed, and which schools are expected to obey and follow within ridiculously tight and unrealistic deadlines. Recent history of central government involvement in education powerfully demonstrates that the politicians and civil servants who are pulling the strings, or pulling the levers of power and control, have absolutely no real understanding of two fundamentally important things: firstly, to know what is actually going on in schools and how they function in an everyday reality, and secondly, to be able to manage change effectively, which must start with ensuring a professional consensus and readiness for such change, to enhance the likelihood of meeting intended goals and outcomes.

The fine and bold rhetoric of governments is one thing, but they have utterly failed to deliver in reality. It has often occurred to me, and I'm sure to many other suffering teachers, especially those who have not done what I did and emigrated to avoid the pernicious influences of endless Conservative governments, to ask why is it that the performance of politicians and education ministers is not assessed and evaluated by identically exacting daily standards or expectation that those same politicians endlessly impose upon hard-pressed teachers and school leaders, as British education languishes in the doldrums and lower echelons of international 'league tables'.

It also occurs to me that if the huge amounts of time, as well as physical and mental effort that schools – and by that I mean heads, teachers and students – had instead been spent doing what they inherently knew to be right, then I feel secure in saying that schools would have achieved so much more over the last 30 or so years, with student progress being more substantial and relevant to **their** needs. And let's face it; meeting their needs in the here and now is inevitably going to meet the needs of the future, as they are the future!

Politicians and civil servants are not superior beings, much as they might like to think that they are, and so it would serve them well to be a little more modest, humble and circumspect in the way they collaborate with the teaching profession if they seriously wish to help the latter effect more effective and relevant education which will have exciting outcomes. They also need to understand that, with regard to their current ways of operating, they are in a fairly cavernous educational hole, thanks to their endless initiatives or wheezes, call them what you will, and the best advice for anyone in such a predicament is that they should simply stop digging and continuing to make matters worse, in the pursuit of genuine educational gain. The time has most definitely come to return the reins of power and control to those who are qualified to hold them. I refer, of course, to the teachers, head teachers, the schools and the all-important students, who are then rightly accountable to the parents and local education authorities, or the equivalent democratically elected and representative bodies. These authorities are then accountable to central government for the ways in which taxpayers' money is being allocated and spent.

To be perfectly honest, it seems to me to be an act of sheer folly for an elected national government to seek to marginalise, if not exterminate locally-elected government bodies. Thatcher began this hypocritical trend by getting rid of the Greater London Council. Norman Tebbit, her right-hand man, seemed to suggest that this was a good thing and, therefore, perfectly reasonable and justifiable because they were an extreme left, Marxist style organisation. That was possibly quite true, but then I would not recommend abolishing a Thatcher or Cameron style Conservative government, run as extreme right-wing organisations, much as I might personally like to, simply because they too were democratically elected, and under the same unrepresentative electoral system.

If we are even going to salvage the state education system in England, then the government needs to agree to put their faith in the teaching profession to take the lead role in the process of curriculum design, as advised by academics, Her Majesty's Inspectorate, and democratically elected bodies such as LEAs which are, by definition, accountable to a local electorate within their local area. More specifically, I am convinced of the over-riding need for the teaching profession to be allowed to regain the power to be responsible for the overall design and structure of the education that is to take place in schools, and as soon as possible. Indeed, I believe that this is paramount if we are to see any shift away from the harmful straitjacket of a narrowing curriculum, something to which Tony Little referred (above), and if we are to reverse the damage that has been done to the professional standing of teachers and reverse the collapse in morale that has been allowed to continue unabated, as far as the effects of central government's actions are concerned. In fact, consecutive governments have, either intentionally or unintentionally, as a result of recklessness or neglect, made matters worse in this respect by continuing to pile on new rules and regulations in the form of new initiatives. At the same time, they have then ruthlessly denigrated the understandable pleas and requests from teachers to 'lighten the load' of their ever increasing administrative burden, thereby allowing them the time and energy to focus on that which should be their sole responsibility: facilitating the learning of young people to the very best of their ability. (Exactly the same folly on the part of an arrogant and bullying Tory government is being repeated in the case of junior doctors, with what seems to be a deliberate sabotaging of the wonderful and rightly cherished National Health Service.)

Central government needs to begin by being honest enough to admit that they don't really know that what they are doing will do much, if anything, to improve the education of all our young people because they are motivated by political values and rarely, if ever, by truly educational ones. What is more, virtually all of their new initiatives are bound to fail for all children because they are predicated upon the utterly false assumption of believing that it is possible to standardise the diversity of human talent and needs, as well as failing to take account of fundamental issues like the differing rates of maturation and progression that will affect children's learning at different ages and stages in their life in compulsory education. The teaching profession must be allowed to regain control of what goes on in schools, subject to certain safeguards in the form of appropriate checks and balances in the system, to ensure that this newly regained power is not abused.

The pyramid of school management needs to be inverted so that once the key stakeholders have agreed the overall direction in which the school will proceed and have formulated a school development plan, then subsequent decision making and management should take place at, or as near as possible, to the operational level, which is in the classrooms or individual curriculum teams. This type of 'bottom-up' model casts head teachers as having the main task of supporting and enabling the needs of the operational level, whilst supervising and making sure that the work of different teams are all aligned, according to the school's mission and vision statement, and the core values of the institution.

In much the same way, a better role for central government to adopt would be to work in a spirit of genuine collaboration with all educational professionals and their representatives, with the aim of supporting, facilitating and enabling the initiatives that individual schools and LEAs themselves have decided are right for their own institutions at any given time, and for their students. The government needs to return the reins of power of state education to the rightful owners, and people who, however imperfect they may be, are better placed to know what they are doing and what needs to be done, when and by whom, and with what, as well as where. To achieve this more productive and harmonious modus operandi, central government needs to work collaboratively with the educational professionals and other stakeholders to agree on a long term educational development plan, and then stick to it. This process would also have to include representatives of all political parties, so that whoever is in power at any one time can continue with this long-term and agreed plan, and teachers in schools and colleges can continue with their own growth and development according to their own long-term plans, without endless changes of tack and additional tasks being imposed by meddling and micro-managing central government.

What would have to cease would be the incessant squabbling between the major parties when they are in power, owing to our peculiar adversarial system

568

of politics, which is characterised by destabilising, detrimental and damaging tit-for-tat bickering, much like silly kids in the playground taking it in turns to claim that "my Dad is bigger than your Dad". Political parties would have to learn anew, a different and far better way of operating in this planning process, and that would be to find the areas and things that unite them, which I believe would be considerable, rather than preferring instead to focus on exaggerating and highlighting those points that divide them. After all, this is surely the kind of approach that teachers are supposed to follow when helping young children to appreciate the need to cooperate, to bury their differences and work together in a positive and constructive manner. Politicians have obviously forgotten such things since they left school, and so they should perhaps return for a refresher course of counselling and study.

Operating under this far more united and collaborative way forward would mean that no one interest group would be allowed to exert undue influence on the decision-making process, and this may, therefore, take some of the illusory power away from the 'pushy' middle class parents, with education being far more representative and able to serve the needs of everyone within society. In this, it should be the students, their diverse talents and interests that take greater precedence, which involves clipping the wings of pushy parents who need to be carefully and politely re-educated as to what education is really for, why we need it and what it should be seeking to achieve for all young people.

There was another very interesting article in the Guardian, written by George Monbiot (9th June 2015) which ran with the headline *"Aspirational parents condemn their children to a desperate, joyless life"*. I could do nothing other than read what he had to say, especially as he is one of my favourite regular contributors to the newspaper, although this favouritism is not slavish in nature, as I don't always agree with him on all points that he makes in his writing. The invitation to read was heightened by the 'strapline' that followed the headline which was: *"Surrender your freedom, avoid daylight, live to work, and you too could join a toxic, paranoid elite."*

His article begins by contemplating the way in which we willingly believe that the people who wield power actually know what they are doing, and we cling to this tacit belief, or perhaps more of a hope, that there is some form of *"guiding intelligence"* as he calls it. Despite this tenuous belief to which we cling, Monbiot claims that we are all aware that our conditions of life, or our quality of life, are deteriorating. He justifies this pretty gloomy view by pointing out that due to declining incomes, a shrinking middle class and exorbitantly-inflated property prices, young people face a fairly bleak prospect when it comes to owning their own home or renting a decent one, as an alternative. He goes on to rightly point out, in tones that echo my own views expressed in the previous section on 'The Bigger Picture', by saying:

"Interesting jobs are sliced up, through digital Taylorism, into portions of meaningless drudgery. The natural world, whose wonders enhance our lives, and upon which our survival depends, is being rubbed out with horrible speed. Those to whom we look for guardianship, in government and among the economic elite, do not arrest this decline, they accelerate it"

He goes on to point out that the political system that delivers these outcomes is sustained by aspiration, which he defines as being a real belief that simply by working more and trying even harder, people will eventually be able to join the elite themselves. But, as he rightly points out, this aspiration is set in stark contrast to the fact that living standards are declining and that social *__immobility__* seems to have become set in stone. This is the ridiculous inconsistency in government policies in the macro sense, where one set of policies in education for example, runs up against another set of policies on managing the economy and the role of the welfare state (assuming there is to be one at all) that operates to limit job opportunities and the prospects of earning a decent income, as well as to further curtail any real apparatus to encourage, promote and assure social mobility and genuine attempts to achieve egalitarianism.

Monbiot talks about how the world of work for the aspiring individuals has become increasingly competitive, feverishly pressured and massively stressful. In his article he refers to the content of a note, which was leaked to the press, from an analyst at Barclays' Global Power and Utilities group in New York, and which was to be sent to all students who were to begin a summer internship. The leaked note makes for pretty worrying reading in that it introduces the young participants to what they call the '10 Power Commandments', which includes a list of ludicrously demanding and almost slavish expectations. These ridiculous 'commandments', by which the potential interns are expected to live or die, include expecting each one of them to be the last to leave the office every night, and being urged to take a pillow with them to work as it makes sleeping under one's desk more comfortable. The internship is summed up as really being a nine-week commitment at the desk, and there is not going to be any real down time, a fact that is made perfectly clear.

George Monbiot questions what sort of young person is going to want to live by such a high-pressure and stressful set of commandments or expectations. He suggests that there are potential candidates, however, who are used to living under these intolerable and life-curtailing rules. Monbiot refers to an article in a recent edition of the Financial Times newspaper which talked about the emergence of a new form of employment as a 'nursery consultant'. These new consultants charge high hourly rates to help pushy parents – which in my mind are definitely not the same as the majority of discerning parents, which is a much more agreeable and helpful category – find their very young children a suitable nursery school which will help put them on the right track that will result in them eventually gaining admission to an elite university.

By way of a couple of examples, the article in the FT talked about one set of parents who had already decided that their six-month-old son would eventually go to Cambridge University and then get a job working for Deutsche Bank. A second example of such parents cited a couple with a two-year-old daughter who was already being 'hot-housed' with tuition two afternoons each week from private tutors in maths and literacy, in addition to weekly phonics and reading classes, drama, piano, beginner French and swimming. As if that was not enough, the young girl's parents were also considering topping that little lot up with some tutoring in Mandarin and Spanish. The FT article concluded by saying that the poor little girl *"was so exhausted and on edge she was terrified of opening her mouth."* Again, to my mind that also represents treatment, or a form of mental torture, that is tantamount to child abuse!

Of course, in the USA they like to go that one step further than we Brits, which is why in New York, according to Monbiot's article, people now work as 'playdate coaches' who charge a modest $450 per hour to train young children in social skills that will enhance their chances of gaining admission to the most prestigious of private schools. This even involves them being taught how to hide traits that could suggest signs of autism, in case it limits their high ambition regarding securing a place at an elite school. Monbiot describes these kinds of stress-inducing and twisted notions of pushy parenthood in the following terms:

"From infancy to employment, this is a life-denying, love-denying mind-set, informed not by joy or contentment, but by ambition that is both desperate and pointless, for it cannot compensate for what it displaces: childhood, family life, the joys of summer, meaningful and productive work, a sense of arrival, living in the moment." He is again, to my mind, entirely correct in such a condemnatory and damning description of these developments, and this explains why parent education is also a vital component of any new system that is going to be more inclusive and canvass the views, as well as enlist the support of all stakeholders in education.

What is perhaps more worrying is that if this kind of practice were confined to an elite group of pushy parents that would be bad enough in itself, but it seems as though they are the pace-setters and guiding stars for the rest of us. Monbiot illustrates this apish tendency when he rightly notes that, *"as if assessment regimes were too lax in primary schools, last year* (2014) *the education secretary announced a new test for four-year-olds"* – yes, **four-year-olds**. And, where the education secretary does not fear to tread, schools obsessed with meeting ridiculously obtuse accountability targets, so that they climb or maintain their positions on the slippery slope of performance league tables, feel compelled to follow. This explains why a primary school in Cambridge felt the need to begin streaming their four-year-old students into classes according to their perceived ability, **not** their **actual** ability (which, in itself, would be bad enough at such a tender age) but on their **perceived** ability. I wonder upon whose perceptions this process was to be based?

The opportunity cost, or sacrifice, of this excessive, unrealistic and harmful competition to join a shrinking elite is, as Monbiot explains, very expensive in terms of the impact that this kind of schooling – it is not education in any sense of the word, as far as I am concerned – has upon the mental health of those exposed to this sheer madness. The potential damage should be assessed by governments, as it once was, when they surveyed the prevalence of children's mental health issues every five years. This would be a very responsible measure to take given the tender age of those beginning to run on the schooling treadmill towards limited opportunities for success, a process which involves weeding out an increasing number of 'also rans' from the field, so that those with their noses in front can continue to compete at even higher levels for places at the best universities. Well, it would be a very responsible measure if such a survey had not been abolished as long ago as 2004. As Monbiot points out, imagine the public outcry if the government were to adopt a similar opt-out from collecting and publishing data on the incidence of childhood cancer for example, and from this one may *"begin to understand the extent to which successive governments have chosen to avoid this issue"* of children's mental health and wellbeing. In short, Monbiot concludes from this, and with more than a little justification, *"if aspirational pressure is not enhancing our wellbeing but damaging it, those in power don't want to know"* – so kill the messenger and stop collecting mental health data for our young people at school.

Despite the government's abdication from fulfilling such an important duty, there has still been a lot of education research conducted by many reputable bodies and academics, like Guy Claxton, which has monitored this vital aspect of children's mental health and wellbeing. Monbiot includes a handful of other examples which offer an insight into the mental health damage that is being inflicted by these unrealistic expectations of pushy parents, complicit and uncaring governments and obsequious schools that feel obliged to undertake whatever hare-brained scheme comes along to stay 'on top' of the competitive dung heap, or to try and grow into a rose that blossoms atop the steaming pile.

Here are some of the statistics and indications that George Monbiot includes in his article, and which are borne out by people like Guy Claxton. First off, the number of mental health beds for children in England increased by 50% in the fifteen-year period from 1999 to 2014, and yet that increase still failed to meet the demand for such essential opportunities for treatment and help. This shortage has led to children having to be placed in adult wards in hospital, due to the lack of specialist places for youngsters, or in some cases left in police cells, and one can only begin to imagine the potential dangers and damage that such a desperate practice entails for those young minds subjected to such casual disregard by an uncaring and penny-pinching government.

Additionally, data collected independently indicates that the number of children admitted to hospital because of self-harm, like cutting themselves as if to relieve internal pain through inflicting personal physical damage, has risen by 68% in 10 years, and at the same time, the number of young patients with eating disorders, such as anorexia, has almost doubled in three years. As if this was not indictment enough and a shocking stain upon the record and concerns that a government should have, in order to be ready and able to exercise an appropriate duty of care towards ensuring, maintaining and improving the mental health of our youngest citizens, we have governments who continue to pass measures that exacerbate rather than abate, alleviate or eliminate the causational factors that are fanning the flames that have led to such a parlous state of affairs for so many young people in the first place.

Monbiot continues to offer further evidence in his article when he refers to the charity Young Minds who have found that the number of young people receiving counselling for exam stress has tripled in the previous year (2014). What is more, there was an international survey of children's wellbeing which found that in the UK, where the kind of pressures to which Monbiot refers are peculiarly intense, Britain ranked 13th out of 15 countries surveyed for children's life satisfaction. What is worse is that the UK was ranked 13th for children agreeing to the statement, "I like going to school", 14th for children's satisfaction with their bodies and bottom of the pile for self-confidence.

That is truly shocking on the one hand, but hardly surprising on the other, when one considers the perpetual avalanche of misguided and highly damaging initiatives that schools have been legally obliged to follow, or to which they have been subjected, thanks to the partisan and partial political agenda of a particularly right-wing series of Conservative governments. In conclusion, Monbiot closes with a suitably chilling message about the *"toxic culture"* to which he refers, when he writes:

"In the cause of self-advancement, we are urged to sacrifice our leisure, our pleasures and our time with our partners and children, to climb over the bodies of our rivals and to set ourselves

against the common interests of humankind. And then? We discover that we have achieved no greater satisfaction that that with which we began."

When I read such words, my belief in the need for a more cohesive, collaborative and coherent society, rather than one founded on increasingly stressful, harmful and wasteful types of manufactured or artificial competition, is strengthened and confirmed. I feel a greater sense of confidence that I am right in calling for such a more humane, inclusive and just society for all people.

In any case, what chance do young people with such pushy and unrealistically aspirational parents have when they are incapable of deciding their own destinies in life, by following the instinctive nature of their innate talents, their dreams and their passions. What miserably unfulfilling lives these young people are going to be forced to endure, thanks to their parents' unrealistic and abusing mind-sets. Someone once said that *"freedom is the opportunity to make decisions"*, and the young people that are subjected to these parentally-directed and pre-determined lives are far from being free in any such way, which implies that they are slaves to their parents' demonic and particularly selfish, pre-determined plans. As Judy Garland was quoted as saying, *"Be a first-rate version of yourself, not a second-rate version of someone else."*

That is what we should all – teachers, parents and other stakeholders – be seeking to achieve for each and every one of our students, children and young people, so that they can live fulfilling and self-determined lives. If the alternative is for some children to be fed into a pre-determined road-map for life from which they are not allowed to deviate, then they are either going to drop out, or resist and become disobedient (hear, hear, I say), or have their passion in life crushed beneath their parents' alternative, life-chance threatening jackboots. It has also been said that nothing great in the world has ever been accomplished without passion, so there is precious little hope that the aspirations of pushy parents are likely to be compatible and synonymous with the passions in life that their offspring should have the right to discover for themselves. As John F. Kennedy said, *"We need men* (and I assume he included women in that single-sex reference) *who can dream of things that never were."* Or as the greatest boxer of all time opined, *"Champions are made from something they have deep inside them – a desire, a dream, a vision. They have to have the skill and the will. But the will must be stronger than the skill.* "Wise words indeed from Mohammed Ali, but ones that are going to fall on deaf ears when it comes to the pushy parents who inflict their own dreams and visions upon their poor children, and from the very youngest of ages.

Lest I am accused of contradicting myself by advocating, on the one hand, an accountability of schools to their key stakeholders, such as parents and, on the other hand, warning of the harm that can be done to student wellbeing by unrealistically pushy parents, I need to perhaps point out that most parents may be discerning, but they are not unrealistic in their expectations of their children, at various ages and stages in their personal and social development. Most parents want their children to be in a school where they are safe, happy and encouraged to give of their best at all times.

Pushy parents, such as those described above are, at least for now, very much in a minority, and even they, if encouraged and allowed to enter into a regular and ongoing professional discourse with autonomous teachers and school leaders who are allowed to run their own schools, can be 'educated' to moderate their excessively unrealistic and vicarious ambitions. After all, if schools are to become more inclusive of all stakeholders, as well as to develop into institutions that actually educate people, then that education also becomes inclusive. Schools should be seeking to educate and develop the learning, the thinking and the attitudes of **all** their stakeholders, and not just the student population, as they are inter-related and inter-dependent in a more collaborative and cohesive social context. And, in any case, if excessively and persistently pushy parents cannot be educated, then autonomously-controlled schools can respectfully suggest that they look for another school for their children. At present, the economic system that we operate, and the ever-expanding control of schools by central government, means that unrealistically pushy parents are listening to, and being seduced and even motivated by, the ruthless dictums of competitive market forces, while listening to the ill-informed and partisan prejudices of politicians who really are not qualified to speak on such matters with such absolute authority.

Governments must stop being passive, if not willing partners in this conspiracy against allowing young people to discover and then set about achieving their own dreams, passions and ambitions in life, and go even further by acting to protect young minds from such harmful and mindless moulding by ill-informed, and not particularly intelligent, parental influence. To do this requires less competition and greater collaboration in and between schools, by returning the power to determine what goes on in the name of education in the nation's schools to the teaching profession, and by giving genuine power and opportunity to people from all walks of life or social class to be afforded genuine social mobility so that we can begin to claim that we live in a truly meritorious meritocracy.

In short, governments with interventionist, interfering and politically partial intentions should be politely told to "butt out" and leave education and schooling to those who have a truly vested interest in it, namely the teachers working with their students and being accountable and in close communication with the parents of such young people, as well as locally elected or appointed representatives of the local community who sit on governing bodies, and work within LEAs. The government also needs to operate policies across all areas of its influence, whether this be social, economic or environmental in nature that are wholly consistent with what it is doing in other areas – especially those as important to the life chances of our young people through the direction and funding of state education.

We need schools that work for **all** young people, and not just the few, and we need schools to be radically reorganised and restructured so that they are capable of truly educating our young, and not just occupying some whilst indoctrinating others to do as they are told, so that a minority can go on to achieve a particularly narrow form of success that is purely academic in nature. So how do we achieve such a massive paradigm shift that is not only extremely urgent and vitally necessary, but also long, long overdue in state schooling and the education of our youngest citizens?

Chapter Twenty Six: A School for Now and the Future

If Only…..

I have long harboured a desire to 'put my money where my mouth is', and I am using the term in a figurative, not a financial sense, owing to my limited pecuniary means, and set up a school based upon my general beliefs and ideas about how we might better design and organise the curriculum and the learning of a group of individual young people. A school to which students want to belong, to attend and where they feel able and encouraged to discover and then begin to fully explore their innate talents and really learn. A school that is fundamentally committed to acting as perhaps the main focal point in a truly community education venture, networking with other people, organisations and agencies to take full advantage of the knowledge, wisdom and skills of so many others, by adopting the 'inside out' and 'outside in' model to which I referred earlier. A school that is an enjoyable and successful environment for all young people who attend it, so that they are given every opportunity to show what they can do well and build their self-esteem and self-confidence. In other words, a school that eschews dullness, pointless repetition and mundane mediocrity, by avoiding a purely mechanical approach to learning that promises the tedium of endless, predictable routine and little else besides. A school that offers an integrated and thematic-style curriculum so that there are no artificial boundaries or 'walls' erected between different areas of knowledge or subject disciplines, and then negotiates the contexts in which individual students will explore the world, new ideas and areas of personal interest by basing their learning upon acquiring a greater awareness, understanding and competence in the core concepts which define the different perspectives on learning. Remember the very wise words of Albert Einstein when he said, *"relativity teaches us the connection between different descriptions of one and the same reality."* These core concepts will form the central platform of the curriculum, instead of a content-laden syllabus which, by being necessarily selective and partial, as well as externally determined (external to the school and, more importantly, the individual student), must by definition exclude far more areas of considerable interest than it can possibly hope to incorporate and accommodate. A school which places great store upon recreation for health and fitness rather than pure competition. A school which encourages students to learn together in a spirit of genuine collaboration and partnership, which discourages them from making inter-personal comparisons of ability and progress, by focusing instead on individual achievements and advancement over time, so that everyone can be a 'winner' in their own right, and on their own terms. A school that promotes choice when it comes to what one learns and how, rather than being obliged to follow a prescribed and standardised course of study, which offers little real opportunity for self-expression and the discovery of knowledge that is of particular interest to the individual learner. A school that builds character and courage, where students feel no fear of failure or making mistakes, displaying instead resilience and a commitment to keep trying until one achieves one's goals, which will promote feelings of self-worth and value. I could go on, but will leave it there, hoping that what I have included gives some idea of what I envision a school based on some of my own ideas, thoughts and beliefs might look like, in part at least.

Now that I am in my 63rd year, I am sure that if I ever had the means and the opportunity to form such a learning institution, I would not see myself as the head or lead teacher. I would much rather be on the advisory board having been involved in appointing a group of individuals who want to take a similarly exciting risk with their work, and whose interests and values are broadly in line with those that I have sought to outline above, and elsewhere in this book. I also envisage the school being formed, organised and operated along cooperative business lines, with one person entitled to one vote, no matter how much their individual financial stake in the enterprise might be. In other words, a much more democratic way of operating any enterprise. The members, or shareholders, would be the students, the teachers, the parents, community stakeholders or partners, and others who sit on the school's governing body. In such a way, the school would be better able to be sure of truly serving the individual and collective educational interests of the young people, rather than the selfish political and financial needs of powerful vested interest groups and lobbyists.

The school of which I dream would be founded on the principles above and would necessitate recruiting and enlisting the support of a diverse range of others – specifically teachers, support staff, local community institutions, agencies and other bodies – to build a powerful team of individuals who would be encouraged to pool their ideas, energies, interests and aptitudes and create the finer details of the structure of the curriculum, and its delivery, from the outset. This team would also be responsible for formulating and agreeing the policies, procedures and systems that would be necessary to ensure that the nascent school is set upon a firm foundation, enabling it to get off to a successful and orderly start, and a start that inspires confidence, as well as a sense of excitement, in its stakeholders, current and future.

This team would, in effect, shape the school, and everyone's view would be considered as initially having equal value, worthy of serious and joint consideration by the steering team. This would enable the team to begin developing a real dynamic that, in turn, would create a potential synergy of exciting proportions, enabling it to pass through the stages of Forming, Storming and Norming, with one clear leader, or Head Teacher, leading the overall venture and team-building process, ensuring all the while that the essential values of the school remain intact and 'owned' by all team members. The overall model would be one in which people listen, reflect, assess and discuss before acting, paying specific attention to the views and needs of the central group of stakeholders – the students themselves!

The Importance of Ownership

During this formative process, and as the school grows, learns, develops and improves itself over time, especially in terms of extending the range of learning opportunities that are afforded to the students, the notion of assuring feelings of genuine ownership of the venture, and its future direction, must be maintained, broadened and deepened. This is not as difficult as it sounds, as long as there is effective communication between all partners or stakeholders and decision making processes are transparent and well understood, as well as being founded on the core principles of the new school model and what it is seeking to achieve that is different. There would have to be a Head Teacher and a senior team to support the day-to-day running of the school, as well as staff teams being fully involved in the decision making processes at both the micro and macro levels. There would also have to be a carefully formed Governing Body with elected representatives who would act as channels of communication to their respective stakeholder groups. Ideally, all meetings would be considered to be open meetings, so as to allow interested parties (which would necessarily include the students) to see how decisions were formed and arrived at. Ideally, there would be only a very few exceptions where closed meetings might be deemed to be needed, when matters of personal sensitivity were on the agenda, which might necessarily involve discussions of a highly confidential nature, for example.

The school must most definitely not adopt or practise a traditional top-down model of management, as the strategic decision making would need to be fully informed by the needs of, and issues faced by, those at the operational level — in other words, the teachers and students working and learning together. And student representatives would also have to be extensively involved in the running of their school, and they would need to be as fully involved as possible in appropriate ways. By this I mean that in addition to having an elected student council with real powers, there would also have to be elected student representatives who serve as full members of the governing body, and who possess voting rights in common with other representatives.

The school would utterly resist any notion of an 'us-and-them' mentality between the students and the teaching staff, as well as other AOTs (adults other than teachers). There could be no 'out-of-bounds' areas to students, except in cases where student safety is paramount, such as in science prep rooms where dangerous chemicals are stored. In this spirit of common ownership of the school, there should be no separate social room for staff or discrete social areas for the student population at breaks and lunch times, for example. Instead, the school would have a combined or separate dining area for meals and a cafeteria with comfortable seating where staff (teachers and support staff) and students could relax and socialise together. The multi-media resource centre would also have designated areas where staff and students could undertake preparatory work or complete learning assignments. Furthermore, these social and work areas could be used by other stakeholders, such as parents and community partners who offer external learning opportunities as part of the agreed curriculum.

In determining the new style school curriculum, this would again have to be a team effort, pooling and sharing ideas, as well as exhibiting a willingness to take risks, which avoid accusations of recklessness or being dangerous because they are calculated experiments to try new things based upon a genuine willingness to entertain possibility on a par, at least, with a traditional reliance on certainty. Central to this new curriculum would be teacher and, above all, student autonomy, with accountability based upon a process that fully involves those who are being held to account. It is vital that subject content and context arise from the student body in negotiation with their teachers, and that accountability for one's actions, both individually and collectively, is related to the school's mission, its values and agreed school development or improvement plan. What students learn, and how stakeholders are held accountable should be consultative and constructively critical, in the main, and not rely overly much on data measurements and statistical analysis. To remind ourselves of what Einstein said: *"Not everything that can be measured counts, and not everything that counts can be measured."*

The need is to be willing to consider and incorporate the more subjective, qualitative aspects of performance when evaluating success and identifying areas where further development and improvement is needed. As Gerver rightly noted in his book (Page 41), ***"You cannot develop a meaningful and powerful education system around data outcomes; the quality comes from the process and not the product."*** This wise advice reinforces what Guy Claxton said about the fact that young learners at school usually forget **what** they learn very soon after the experience is over, but what remains with them is **how** they learnt things, and that is the processes that were used to discover or access the requisite knowledge and to develop transferable skills.

Furthermore, this fundamentally important point provides the power that enables the teams of stakeholders to arrive at a school structure, curriculum and development plan in which they have a real sense of ownership, which means it is theirs, as opposed to something that has been externally determined and imposed, with threats of accountability and possible sanctions, including school closure, being done to them by people who are not stakeholders and have no real knowledge of the culture of the school, its past and future plans – apart from what they read in selected documentation and by talking to people. These methods of discovering what has gone on before, and what is planned for the future, have one important limitation: their inability to get a real 'feel' for the human emotion invested in past actions and future plans.

As I mentioned elsewhere in this book, one of the few central government initiatives that I welcomed and applauded, and still do, is the requirement that was placed upon every school to formulate school aims and objectives, as well as an institutional development plan, with an emphasis on the process of continuous school improvement. In our school of the future, our stakeholders would continue to use this vital process instrument to move the school forward, and it should welcome and include the contributions of all stakeholders, and not just the teaching staff and students. Nonetheless, the overall planning process must once again place real decision-making power in the hands of the professionals, supported, aided and abetted by the many other vitally important stakeholder groups.

By involving *all* interested parties in the process of formulating the institutional development plan, with its complementary components of curriculum development, personnel development, learning resource and premises development, community or stakeholder development and financial or budgetary development, there is a far greater chance that those involved will have bought into what they are collectively trying to achieve, and will possess a real determination to see the plan successfully executed. In seeking to adopt a new educational paradigm, it is the process of designing the plan that far outweighs the content of the finished document, if combined intentions are to truly become a collective and exemplary reality. This process of formulating the plan fosters a deep sense of genuine ownership – it is ours and not 'theirs' or 'someone else's' – which acts as a far more powerful motivational force when it comes to the very challenging stage of actual implementation and the realisation of collective ambitions and dreams.

There are also secondary benefits or spin-offs from following such an inclusive design and implementation process of school improvement, one of the most powerful being that it offers a very effective and fairly effortless and inexpensive school marketing dimension. (It is important to note that when I refer to 'marketing' the school, I am not talking about schools becoming involved in any form of ruthless or open competition, merely making potential parents and other stakeholders aware of what the school aims and objectives are, and to provide a window into the school's facilities and unique culture. In short, the promotional element of the marketing effort should be wholly informative and not at all persuasive in nature.) The truth is that the most effective form of marketing is 'word-of-mouth', rather than the more 'hit-or-miss' use of expensive advertising campaigns in the media, or the school spending a substantial chunk of its budget commissioning and printing glossy publications which tend to sell 'an' image, but not necessarily anything approaching the reality of what really goes on, and what the school is really about.

Someone once said that marketing is much more a way of thinking rather than anything that somebody (like a marketing manager and team) actually decides to do in order to specifically 'sell' or, as I would prefer to call it, 'raise awareness' of the school. The involvement of a range of school and wider community stakeholders in designing the school and formulating, as well as jointly implementing, subsequently evaluating and re-formulating the rolling development plan, leads them all to become the owners or custodians of this shared intention. This means that they possess a strong and shared vested interest in ensuring its success in terms of outcome. What is more, they will also be able to bask in a sense of real, worthwhile achievement that such success rightly bestows on all participants, no matter how great or small their own, individual contribution may have been. That is what team effort looks like!

It should be noted that the most numerous and arguably vociferous and passionate advocates for the collective endeavour should be the students of the school, as it is 'their' school after all, and they are the reason why everyone else is involved in the first instance. But other important stakeholders would be the teachers, the governors, parents, the community partners who help in the delivery and resourcing of the community-based curriculum, and the extremely important support staff. That is why it is important to involve the cooks, the cleaners, the grounds maintenance staff and others in the school development planning process. They too will inadvertently market the school and feel that important sense of genuine ownership and equal value.

584

All stakeholders will have partners, friends, relatives, work contacts and more casual acquaintances, such as the person at the check-out till at the supermarket and the general public walking the streets. All of these people will either hear the words of the stakeholders in formal and casual conversation as well as observe the behaviours of the young people when they are at the movies, in the shopping malls and in other social settings. I can remember when I was training to become a teacher, sometimes deliberately travelling to and from my teaching practice school by public transport (on the bus), as opposed to walking, where this was a reasonable proposition. I did this because none of my fellow travellers recognised me, and so I was able to sit and eavesdrop on the conversations of fellow travellers sitting nearby, and I discovered a great deal of general information about the social issues surrounding the school, as well as the truthful gossip about what people thought about various schools along the route. It was a fascinating experience. When attending interviews for jobs later on in my career, I would always walk around the neighbouring streets – loitering almost – in the vicinity of the school in question, as the students were walking to school. I walked alongside listening to their honest and casual observations about various people who taught them, as well as what they thought about their school. I liked to see how many gaggles of students would gather to have their final cigarette before proceeding to school, and see how they wore their school uniform before actually being checked out by their form teachers. It was all very revealing and gave me a tremendous and reliable feel for the school in which I might find myself working. I like to enter into things with my eyes fully open – who doesn't?

Passionately positive utterances of all stakeholders and exemplary and courteous, considerate behaviour from the students in particular can become naturally infused into the mind-sets of those involved in the collaborative venture, and marketing an appropriate and accurate image of the school is virtually automatic and assured. And all this, without expending a great deal of forced or untypical energy on special events like 'open days' and the like, or allocating funds that would be far better devoted to improving teaching and learning, rather than excessive expenditure on the publication of printed prospectuses and brochures.

Whilst a school brochure is also an important document to provide a written and factually accurate portrayal of the school, the 'word-of-mouth' and other more informal evidence will confirm that what one sees and reads in print is what really goes on. In fact, the 'word-of-mouth' marketing adds considerable weight to, embellishes and enhances not only the image portrayed, but also the reputation that the school possesses, which is far more important. This is because if the image portrayed in the publications and media statements is not compatible with the reputation that the school already has in the local community, then no one will believe the image. The image must be totally consistent with the reputation for it to have any effect in convincing those who are not 'in-the-know' about what our school is really seeking to achieve as a collective venture.

The Importance of Trust and Mutual Respect

It is evident from what has gone before that the quality or value of trust, as well as that of mutual respect has, to a significant extent, been lost in schools and certainly between most schools and their government or private sector employers, in the case of academies and to a notably lesser extent, independent schools, who are somewhat a law unto themselves – as, indeed, it should be! To try and operate anything worthwhile in an atmosphere of accountability and a lack of trust in teacher autonomy on the one hand, and disrespect either real or perceived on the part of the two main protagonists (central government and individual schools and teacher professional associations) is doomed to result in failure or breakdown, sooner or later. Where feelings of total mistrust and mutual disrespect exist, this offers no foundation for being able to run an effective educational service for our young people and society. Being in a state of endless warfare and open hostilities based on adversarial political and educational standpoints is a recipe for a war of attrition with everyone losing out. It is, in the terminology of effective negotiations, a definite 'lose-lose' scenario, so why do we persist with such utter madness? It is clearly no way to run anything successful, let alone something upon which the life chances for many young people are going to be determined!

Conservative governments seem to have become ever more supercilious and arrogant in their approach, with both the teaching profession and now, at the time of writing, with the junior doctors who work for the National Health Service (NHS) in the UK. The latter are facing an identical ideological battle with a right-wing administration that is seeking to further privatise the NHS whilst worsening the conditions of work of the junior doctors. In recent pronouncements, despite the two sides being at complete loggerheads with each other, the Prime Minister, David Cameron has effectively warned the junior doctors not to prevent the 'changes' in the NHS, although I believe Cameron used the phrase 'development' of the NHS. So the 'changes' or 'developments', call them what you like as it makes no difference because they are still detrimental to the service and the morale and wellbeing of the junior doctors, are expected to be steamrollered through and forced on those people who are supposed to be key players in making or delivering these 'changes' in actual practice? That demonstrates a laughable degree of sheer ignorance regarding how to effectively manage change. It also provides overwhelming evidence of the current Tory ideologues' utter and crass incompetence as a government for the people and by the people. They ought not to be allowed anywhere near the nation's health or education services, but then a politician needs no formal qualifications or specialist knowledge to stand for office do they? Compare this with the pre-service and in-service training that teachers and doctors are required to undergo before being declared competent and fit to serve. In stark contrast, government ministers conduct reckless politically-motivated initiatives without listening to the professionals or even attempting to negotiate a mutually beneficial 'win-win' outcome. Instead they simply profess to know better than the professionals who actually run the service. This is astounding arrogance, an astonishing display of assumed and unabashed superiority, which is utterly detrimental, extremely worrying and most definitely bound to fail us all!

This lack of trust and the way in which the government pursues its partisan agenda through the use of fear, propaganda and an absence of reasoned argument, relying instead on 'brute force and ignorance' supported by the law, which it also largely determines, is utterly disrespectful and a symptom of irresponsible intolerance and sheer bloody mindedness. That is no way to run an organisation, and I recommend that the Tory ministers take some time to read books by people like the late Stephen Covey, such as *The 7 Habits of Highly Effective People*' and the even better **'8th Habit'**, to which I will refer again in a short while. But then, as J.K. Galbraith once said in a radio series he presented, there is a thing called 'Carter's Law' which states: *"The trouble with radicals is that they only read radical literature, whereas the Republicans (right-wingers) don't read anything at all."* Consequently, I shan't hold my breath and expect the Tories in the UK to do any mind-broadening reading anytime soon!

It is absolutely vital, therefore, that schools try to run their operations in a totally different way from the central governments that we have been forced to endure over the past 40 years in the UK. In other words, the school of the future must ensure that we **trust** our students, give them genuine responsibilities and treat them with the utmost respect. After all, we must be the ultimate role models of such essential values and attitudes, so that we lead by excellent example. In my experience, these three very important issues are not always explicitly or implicitly modelled in some schools as well as they may be, and I stress that I am drawing only upon my own, relatively limited exposure to various schools in an active and advisory capacity. Let me illustrate what I mean by referring to two occasions where I encountered a reluctance on the part of teachers, including my senior colleagues, to treat all students with this virtuous trinity of **trust**, **responsibility** and **respect**. They both occurred at the same school during my first time as a practising head teacher of an 11 to 16 comprehensive school, one that was effectively a failing school, located in an area which could fairly be described as economically and socially deprived.

The first instance occurred during the time we were restructuring the school curriculum, staffing, management structure, the premises and the school budget to fund improvements in teaching and learning resources and the quality of the environment in which students and teachers worked and learnt together. We decided that visitors and guests to the school ought to be greeted by students at a newly constructed and fairly plush reception counter which we had built outside the main school office, with a sliding glass window and a door linking the two so as to allow for adult supervision of the students in their new role, should it be necessary.

We decided that we should draw up a rota that required three students each week to serve at the reception desk, after some initial training, so that all Year

9 students would get the opportunity to take on what was a highly responsible and important role in their school. Perhaps not surprisingly, this idea ran into some initial resistance before reaching the implementation stage, as some of my more senior colleagues and fellow teachers felt that there were certain students, whose attitude and behaviour in school might best be described as challenging, if not extremely truculent, disaffected and often downright discourteous, who should be excluded from the weekly rota, at least until their undesirable conduct and fairly negative attitudes were considerably tempered, if not entirely eliminated, which was highly unlikely to happen any time soon, not without some pretty powerful, remedial experience.

I felt an immediate animosity to this exclusion proposal, primarily because it was based entirely on the argument that only after these students started to behave responsibly in school generally, should they be considered suitable to be trusted in such a potentially important role of responsibility. The student receptionists would, remember, be responsible for welcoming parents, current and prospective, LEA officials, the community policeman, governors, angry parents, OFSTED team members and lead inspector, as well as a host of other visitors – all of whom were equally important as marketers of the school and the improvements that we were seeking to put into effect.

After some fairly heated discussions my allies and I managed to persuade those with reservations to allow all students to be included in the rota, and not to debar some individuals based on the doubting arguments of others which were in favour of such limited, restricted and exclusive involvement. My argument was essentially that the students could not just be assumed to behave responsibly, when in their lives to date, both in and out of school, they had been given no real opportunity to display responsibility which would enable them to learn something as basic as how to behave appropriately in any given situation.

The upshot was that our faith and our trust in these more challenging youngsters was more than justified, In fact, we all subsequently agreed that some of these 'unlikely candidates' performed their roles with considerable aplomb and style, and very often far better and with more confidence than their more easily biddable and generally better-behaved peers. Our faith in

589

such students showed that we trusted them and believed in them equally, which is tantamount to showing them unexpected and, arguably, unearned respect. It is essentially the 'chicken and egg' question, although with a far simpler answer. By believing in all our young people, we enabled them to believe more in themselves, giving them a degree of self-esteem and self-confidence, as well as an experience of behaving responsibly, and gaining respect for so doing.

This important lesson was one that informed the second example at the same school, but on a much larger and more ambitious scale, and one on which I look back with considerable pride, not just for being bold, but because my faith in the school population was totally vindicated, with their behaviours meeting my high expectations of them all, bar none.

It occurred on the occasion of the Remembrance Day event to mark fifty years since the end of World War Two, on the 11th day of the 11th month. The Royal British Legion with whom we had forged a curriculum project in languages and the humanities, with students meeting men and a few women who had participated in the war to hear of their experiences and to write poems which sought to empathetically capture their mostly diverse, but commonly unhappy experiences. Those who came into school (AOTs) were all people from the local community, but rarely known to the students largely due to the age difference I would imagine. In our meetings with these fascinating and immensely interesting people, I met one man who had been a prisoner-of-war (POW) who handed me a poem provided by the British Legion entitled, "Why Wear a Poppy". There was also a request that the entire school observed a **two-minute** silence (longer than the usual one minute due to the importance of this 50th anniversary). I felt compelled to oblige and so called a meeting with my senior colleagues in order to plan the event.

Being from a 'military family' and having been to naval boarding school, I feel a strong, emotional and unquestioning belief in the need to honour the sacrifice of so many people, even though I have never been able to fully comprehend the need for wars or why so many people were prepared to enlist to fight the war at the sharp and lethal end. Amazing duty, astonishing courage and unswerving loyalty to one's country – people and values which we must

590

rightfully honour! I am not sure that I would be equally dutiful, courageous or loyal, but then I have never been put in the position of those brave and unfortunate souls. Luckily, I have never been tested in such a context, and that is largely due to those who fought and even paid the ultimate sacrifice so many years before. My background and value system convinced me that we must remember them in an honourable manner!

At our planning meeting in my office, my willingness to have a whole-school assembly to mark this event culminating in a two-minute silence, was met with polite opposition from my colleagues who put forward various reasons why, in their opinion, it was not a good idea, even though they acknowledged the significance of the event. The first obstacle put before me was of a logistical nature: the school hall was not large enough to seat some 750 teenagers all together. No problem, I countered with the solution of using the sports hall, which was just about large enough to accommodate all of the students sitting on the floor, with the teachers sitting on benches on three sides of the rectangular space. The second problem raised was that it would take a long time for all students to enter and sit in their respective year groupings, with year 7 (the 11 year olds) at the front, and year 11 (the 16 year olds) sitting at the rear of the hall. I felt sure that we could overcome this through careful planning and briefing of class and form tutors beforehand.

And then a more emotive and possibly legitimate reason for the serious doubt expressed by my senior colleagues became apparent, very loud and clear. In essence they were worried that it would create an opportunity for the disruptive minority to sabotage the solemnity and importance of the event. The views aired I remember very well, and went something along the lines of: the time taken for students to enter, be seated and settle would make them restless and when it came to the two-minute silence, all that would be needed was for one student to fart (the word that was actually used) and the assembled mass would collapse into uncontrollable laughter.

I interpreted this, rightly or wrongly, as if my colleagues simply didn't **trust** the students to behave in a sufficiently **responsible** and **respectful** manner. I more than understood their reservations, but my instinct was to test the competing views by taking the risk of holding the assembly in the sports hall.

I made an executive decision and decided that we would go ahead as I had outlined. In doing so, I simply asked my senior colleagues if they had ever tried something similar before, so that they could reasonably evidence their reservations upon actual past experience rather than imagined portents of a potentially fearful outcome. They could not do so, simply because they never had tried before and, like a Mexican toilet, had very little to go on!

The day of the event arrived, and the students filed into the sports hall in their usual and relatively noisy way, sat in their respective year groups with the youngest at the front and oldest at the back, and there was something more than a buzz among the assembled school community. Once everyone was in place, I entered and stood at the front, as was expected. The plan for the assembly was fairly simple. I would say a few, hopefully choice words to introduce the special assembly, then the aforementioned war veteran from our local community would briefly talk to the students about his experiences of active service in the Royal Air Force, being shot down and spending the rest of the war as a POW. He was a good choice, speaking to them in a vernacular that they understood and to which they could relate. When he had finished I had wanted him to read the poem, "Why Wear a Poppy", but he declined the offer, expressing a preference that I should read it, as he believed that I would do it more eloquently than he.

Before he spoke I talked to the students in a fairly improvised way as, somewhat uncharacteristically, I had not really planned my input, mainly because I was concerned that the predictions of my senor colleagues might become an unwelcome and highly embarrassing reality. When I spoke, it occurred to me to make my words relevant to them in the here and now whilst, at one and the same time, linking it to the massive event that was the Second World War. In essence, I asked them to imagine that the war had broken out that very day. I explained to the students in Year 11 that they would be called up to join the armed forces upon reaching the age of 16, and that during the rest of the war, the same would happen to the younger years, with Year 7 being called into action towards the end of the war, when they too would have reached 16 years of age. I went on to inform them that many of the teachers sitting around the assembled throng in the sports hall would also be called into action to fight the war effort, and that by the end of the war, it would be possible for us all to hold our assembly in one of the school classrooms, rather than the significantly more spacious sports hall.

It struck a chord with everyone present, I know, given what eventually transpired. I invited the veteran to speak to them all from his first-hand perspective, and informed the students that once he had finished I would read them the poem that had been given to me. I also said that when I completed reading the poem, I would bow my head, and invite them to join me in a two-minute silence to remember the fallen and those who experienced the horrors of war. We proceeded as I had explained to the students and staff, and then came the 'acid test' of the two-minute silence; could they prove their doubters wrong? The time ticked past in complete silence. So quiet were they that you could have heard a pin hit the ground (as, for the purists, you cannot actually hear a pin 'drop') had we not been able to hear delightful bird-song from outside the sports hall. I looked down, anxiously eyeing my watch to ensure that we managed exactly two-minutes silence, and when the time was up, I simply looked up, with tears in my eyes and body hairs standing to attention and said: *"Thank you everyone. Now I know why I became head teacher of this school – you have made me very proud of you all."* At which point I left through a side door, briskly made my way to my office to seek a tissue with which to dry my eyes, before thanking my co-presenter once more for his wonderful speech.

In all honesty, that Remembrance Day assembly was the one event which filled me with the greatest pride I think I have ever experienced in a long and varied career to date. Why was this, and what did it teach me? It proved to me that we should **trust** students to give of their best, and we should put them in positions, individually and collectively, to justify the faith or trust placed in them in advance. We must take risks and challenge our young people by holding high expectations of them and not allow them to disappoint or fail, either because we make the mistake of setting low expectations of them at the outset, or because we do not give them the opportunity in the first place. If they do disappoint, despite the trust and the respect we hold for them, by behaving irresponsibly, then that presents an unmissable learning opportunity, and one that will contribute to their personal and social development or growth. **Trust** is everything, and schools should be places of mutual trust, respect and responsibilities among all stakeholders, including central

593

government, who disappoint by failing in all three areas in an almost willing, but definitely spectacularly indifferent and arrogant way.

The 'Meat of the Matter' – Curriculum Cornerstones/Principles

Thus far I have tended to skirt around the detail of what the curriculum would be, and for good reason. This is because it really must be a team effort involving people who share the values advocated in this book – as I do not have the expertise to devise an entire school curriculum; I am fallible after all! But it should seek to avoid certain bad practice and adopt interesting, radical and progressive ideas about education, and I would like the following to be used as food for thought.

First of all, as a huge admirer of the work of Stephen Covey, I would like to propose that we seek to enable everyone (students, teachers and other stakeholders) to find their own 'voice', as he puts it, by first of all finding our own 'voice' as an educational institution.

In his excellent and tremendously apposite book, 'The 8th Habit', he makes a very interesting reference to a Harris interactive poll which was a survey of some 23,000 US residents who were employed full time in key industries and key functional areas – in other words people of some note in terms of their employment status. The findings of this Harris Poll were quite revealing, and could even be described as startling. So interesting were the findings, I feel that I must list them here in outline, by referring directly to the original text. <u>The findings revealed that only</u>:

- ➢ 37% of those surveyed were aware of their organization's aims and overall rationale for being;
- ➢ 20% were found to be enthusiastic about their team and company goals;
- ➢ 20% were able to see any link between the goals of their team and those of the organization;
- ➢ 50% of employees felt a degree of satisfaction at the end of the week with the work that they had accomplished;
- ➢ 15% felt that they were in a position where they were enabled to execute key goals, assuming that they were aware of them in the first place;

> A similar and miserly 15% felt that they worked in a high **trust** environment;
> 17% felt that their organization fostered open communications and was respectful of different views and ideas;
> 10% felt that their organizations held people accountable for results;
> A mere 20% fully **trusted** the organization for which they worked;
> 13% of those surveyed felt that they had high **trust** and highly cooperative work relationships with other groups or departments within their organizations.

Such findings are devastatingly different from the kind of environment that we must be seeking to create in our school(s) of the future. It is patently obvious how vitally important the value of mutual and shared **trust** really is, and how it must be at the very centre of everyone's individual and collective endeavours.

Taken together, the formal curriculum and what is known as the 'hidden' curriculum must be consistent if they are to mutually support each other, as opposed to the hidden curriculum messages being seriously at odds with the stated and explicit aims and objectives of the school, and the way in which it operates on a daily and longer-term basis. Together, they form the school curriculum, or the entitlement curriculum of every young person, and I fervently believe that it must incorporate the four dimensions of everyone and what they come to learn. These are, as Covey maintains, not just people's mental or cognitive intelligences and capacities that we traditionally tend to regard as the only important one, which we affectionately call our 'intelligence quotient', or IQ, but also three other equally important intelligences and capacities. Our IQ includes our ability to analyse, to reason and to think abstractly, using language to visualise and comprehend.

Additionally, there is the vital component of intelligent behaviour that is called our EQ, or emotional quotient, which includes the essential capacity of possessing self-knowledge, self-awareness, and, with that, social sensitivity, empathy and an ability to communicate with others, as opposed to merely talk to them. EQ is also very much about having the courage to acknowledge our own weaknesses, as well as those of others, and to express and respect differences. EQ is equally about using one's brain holistically, drawing upon and uniting the left brain capacities of analytic, linear thinking, language, reasoning and logic, with the capacities of being creative, intuitive and being able to think holistically in order to see and sense, that are attributed to the right brain. I am a firm believer in, and I rely heavily upon intuition in my work and my life, because as Dr Jonas Salk said, *"Intuition will tell the thinking mind where to look next."* I am inclined to feel very confident in his qualification to make such a great statement, as he was an American medical researcher and virologist who discovered and developed the first ever vaccine for polio!

The third vital component required to truly find our own 'voice' is perhaps somewhat beyond our own ability to control directly, as individuals, and that is what Covey calls our 'physical intelligence', or PQ. This is mainly concerned with what the body does without conscious effort, automatically taking control of our respiratory, nervous and other vital systems. We often hear the idea that a healthy body is vital for a healthy mind, and that is what I believe Covey means, and he readily acknowledges that the body can heal itself, often with the assistance of medical assistance to remove the obstacles to this process. He also points out, however, that medical intervention can actually create obstacles to our body's ability to heal itself if it works contrary to our own body intelligence.

Finally, Covey draws our attention to the central and most fundamental of all intelligences, the one that acts as the source of guidance for the other three elements or capacities, and this is spiritual intelligence, or SQ. In other words, in school we need to nurture and help young people develop their whole selves by devising a curriculum that highlights and harmonises the mind, the body, the heart and the spirit of the individual learner when operating either independently or interdependently, in collaboration with others.

What I also found immensely encouraging, on a professional level, were the two alternative life paths identified by Covey that are available for people to adopt and follow, and he refers to these as the *"quick fix"* road and the *"sequential process"* road, and they effectively describe the old, traditional paradigm to life at work, at school and in general, and the new, more liberating and relevant alternative paradigm, respectively. I would refer the reader to

596

Chapter 9, in which I included a detailed reference to Covey's brilliant work in this regard, although it warrants a reprise in this closing chapter.

The 'quick fix' road adopts what Covey calls a cultural 'software' approach, which leads to mediocrity and straitjackets human potential, as people follow a short-cut approach to life, with people *"living out the cultural 'software' of ego indulgence, scarcity, comparison, competitiveness and victimism."* The way I interpret Covey's work in this regard is that this former approach to life creates the inevitable winners and losers, with people having various degrees of choice, or notional opportunity within a fixed, top-down and fairly rigid social system.

The choices that people have are largely shaped by whether they flourish within the system, on the one hand, thanks to advantage, opportunity and high aspirations, as well as an element of luck and personal aptitude perhaps, or whether they are held back by experiences of failure, lack of opportunity, disadvantage and deprivation. The winners tend to have different degrees of response to what they experience at work, school and in life in general, ranging from a mere "willing compliance", where they are prepared to tolerate and go along with the way they are treated, through feelings of "cheerful cooperation" and "heartfelt commitment", right up to "creative excitement". Those who are the losers and the people handicapped by the system tend to choose behaviours which are less desirable, such as "malicious obedience" or, worse still, deciding to either "rebel or quit" altogether and opt-out of the games that they are simply unwilling or unable to play. A more succinct version of these choices could be summarised by the fictional, Doctor Gregory House's advice to his new budding doctors during the competitive selection process, when he said they could, *"Be good, get good, or quit."*

The alternative paradigm of a sequential process is founded on what Covey describes as a "creative force approach" to life in various social, economic and political contexts. He argues that this road leads to greatness because it not only unleashes human potential, but it also enables its realisation. He described it as a process of sequential growth from the inside out, starting with identifying and developing innate human talent. This encourages and enables people to rise above the negative cultural influences, which tend to constrain and limit our ability to find our true 'voice', and to choose instead to become the creative force in our own lives.

It is vital, therefore, for schools to become places that actively promote the creative force approach offered by the sequential process life path. This means that we must put the needs of students above those of any other stakeholder, otherwise we are at risk of returning to the quick-fix approach which is inherent in the cultural 'software' of being schooled, as opposed to truly and properly educated. This undesirable approach is the one that is wonderfully demonstrated in the way in which central governments have literally deprived teachers and schools of their professional autonomy as educators. They have also displayed an utter lack of any real understanding of the need for long-term planning and consistency in the vital work that schools do, or should be doing. This ignorance has led to contradictory initiatives that have led to an enormous waste of teacher time in seeking to make the changes demanded by government, only to be told shortly afterwards that they can abandon some aspects or all of those initiatives and return to something that teachers were offering in the first place.

This point can be effectively illustrated by referring to an article in The Guardian newspaper, entitled, *'Scrap history lessons in primary, says study'* (Polly Curtis, education editor, 8 December 2008). The article referred to the presentation of plans, back in 2008, by the most senior adviser on primary schools, Sir Jim Rose, who was calling for an overhaul of education for five- to 11-year-olds. He believed this was something that really needed doing, as a matter of some urgency, because he claimed that a "bloated" curriculum, as he called it, was making children's knowledge and understanding shallow. As a result, he was proposing that traditional lessons in history, geography and science should be removed from the primary curriculum, with students taught their essential content through the development of cross-curricular themed classes. Hurrah, I thought, when I read this, but then I wanted to ask why limit such a sensible approach to just the primary school curriculum, as the secondary curriculum suffers from exactly the same malaise, and students would encounter a fairly dramatic change in their learning if they were to follow a completely differently structured curriculum once they left primary school and went to the 'big school'. It seemed somewhat obtuse to leave the design, and method of delivery of the secondary curriculum unchanged following this fairly notable change in primary practice.

The curriculum that Sir Jim Rose was proposing was to eradicate rigid subject areas but to place, instead, a central requirement on teachers to foster and nurture the social and emotional wellbeing of students, which was to recognise that schools should be seeking to try and help alleviate, if not eliminate, some of the "social ills" that society was having to contend with, and still is! Again, it crossed my mind whether schools could and should really be expected to make much of a difference when 'the bigger picture' issues that I have already referred to, are sending incredibly powerful messages that explain the persistent existence of these social ills in the first place.

Under his fairly radical new curriculum plans, the proposal was to replace the existing 13 subject areas that were found in the curriculum with a reduced number of a mere six areas of understanding, which were identified as: understanding English, communication and languages; mathematical understanding; science and technological understanding; human, social and environmental understanding; understanding physical education and wellbeing, and understanding the arts and design. What I found to be rather ironic, these are virtually the same as the learning experiences identified by HMI back in the 1970s – so back to square one again after a government-inspired walk up the proverbial garden path in the secret garden of the curriculum. The proposal to use themed projects to cover the same material instead of having discrete lessons in separate subjects was also a return to the direction that the teaching profession had been taking before the government decided to intervene with a National Curriculum back in the 1980s.

What was interesting about the stance taken by Sir Jim Rose was that he could hardly be considered as being someone from the radical school of thought, as he was a former director of inspections at Ofsted. He even went as far as to admit that the curriculum had been allowed to grow *"by stealth"* over several years, and he was quoted as saying, *"There is confusion in schools about what they do and don't have to teach"*. As a result, he felt that schools would benefit greatly from being given *"greater flexibility and freedom in how they teach"*. He explained this view by pointing out that, *"schools are telling us there is too much prescription. It does put considerable time pressures on schools".*

The article by Polly Curtis illustrates how much wasted time and effort has been allowed to occur, simply because in matters of the curriculum – its design and delivery – the government has ridden rough-shod over the teaching profession and prescribed not only what should be taught, but also how it should be taught, which in my professional opinion is the responsibility of the schools and the teaching profession, rather than ill-informed, and unqualified politicians or Whitehall mandarins. It has all been so unnecessary, and the educational fallout from this blundering around and 'control freakery' by central government has been wrongly and unfairly laid at the door of those whose powers have been subsumed by less-qualified others. It is worth mentioning that one of the late Stephen R. Covey's nuggets of fundamental advice is, **"seek first to understand"** before seeking to advise, to intervene or to act. Central government rarely, if ever follows such a sound maxim, failing to even listen to the teaching profession and academics sufficiently closely – and I mean 'listen' and not merely 'hear' – as a fairly basic prerequisite needed to understand the context and the culture into which they are seeking to become the most active or key player.

Looking Elsewhere for Inspiration and Ideas

It has also occurred to me, on many occasions, why it is that the British government has been historically so obsessed with the American model for state education and, more recently, by the way in which the Chinese run their schools, instead of looking elsewhere for inspiration and 'new' ideas about how to run state schooling in the UK. The government would be well-advised to follow the lead and example that has been given by schools in Finland, for example, where their government has been radically reforming the way in which children are taught and in a manner which meets with the approval, rather than the chagrin of the teaching profession there.

Essentially, what the Finns have decided to do is to scrap traditional *"teaching by subject"* in favour of *"teaching by topic"*. In all honesty, that does not sound particularly radical to me, given that such an approach in primary schools in England has long since represented common and good practice, until the disease of subject specialisms began to creep down from the secondary sector, supported by the misguided mind-set and lack of sound educational thinking that tend to seriously underline central government interventions. I can only assume that our political lords and masters (as well as dames and mistresses) have been labouring under the mistaken belief that the sooner young people start to learn in separate, academic subjects, the more likely it will be that they will be more successful by the time they reach secondary school and, eventually, when the time for external examinations arrives. Nonetheless, for a country's government to realise the folly of such naïve and sloppy thinking, and to the point that they see the best solution as a radical reorganisation of state schooling, rather than a little bit of further tinkering, then this is indeed remarkable and deserves to be loudly applauded.

This huge change that is being undertaken by schools in Finland was reported in a Guardian article entitled, *'Finland schools: Subjects scrapped and replaced with 'topics' as country reforms its education system'* (Richard Garner, 20 March 2015). As an example of how this might work at a secondary level, however, the article reported that subject-specific lessons, such as an hour of history in the morning, followed by an hour of geography in the afternoon, were already in the process of being phased out for 16-year-olds in Helsinki's upper schools. Breaking the mould that had been originally cast back in the 1880s, the students attending schools in the Finnish capital city were, instead, receiving *"phenomenon"* teaching, which was effectively the same as teaching by topic. So, a teenager studying a vocational course, for example, might experience classes in "cafeteria services", which would necessarily include, integrate and relate elements of mathematics, languages (so that the learners are able to serve foreign customers), writing and communication skills, but all located in a very realistic and everyday context.

Students with a more academic bias or aptitude would be taught in a similar fashion, again using topics that are fundamentally cross-subject in nature. An example, given in the article, would be to study the European Union, which would necessarily link elements of economics with the history of the countries involved, the languages they speak, as well as their geography. This is so easy to do and has such considerable educational benefit because it overcomes the artificial separation of knowledge by using topics, which demand examining

601

real-world situations, using different perspectives (of one and the same reality) and encouraging the application of knowledge learnt in one 'subject' being applied automatically and quite naturally in others. Such an approach promotes and develops the transferability of skills, as well as explores more fully and meaningfully the way in which knowledge is utterly, essentially and necessarily interdependent and inter-related in the real world which the learner inhabits.

Apart from the design and structure of the emerging school curriculum in Finland, there are also obviously beneficial changes in the way in which classes are organised, which are also incredibly simple to implement in everyday practice. The traditional format of having rows of students sitting passively, looking forward at a class teacher who is traditionally standing at the front of the class, waiting to be called upon to become involved, is finally being replaced with a far more active and collaborative approach to learning. As a result, students experience working in smaller groups, solving problems together in teams and, at the same time, further developing their communication skills. Collaboration wins over individually competitive, stifling and unnecessary inter-student competition, and this can only be a good thing if we are genuinely interested in seeing all students discover their talents and taste real success whilst at school!

The one thing, however, in the article, that made me cringe a little, with a modicum of professional discomfort, was when Marjo Kyllonen, who is Helsinki's education manager, was quoted as saying: *"We really need a rethinking of education and a redesigning of our system, so it prepares our children for the future with the skills that are needed for today and tomorrow."* The reason for my doubt about such an admission or statement was again related to the notion of 'preparing' young people for some uncertain and unknown future, rather than enabling them to deal with their current lives in the here and now, so that they grow seamlessly and relatively effortlessly into the future as self-directed, and more fully 'prepared', lifelong learners who are no longer dependent on the direction, the constant support or input provided by a classroom teacher. I found solace in the acknowledgement of preparing students with the skills that are needed **_today_** and tomorrow, as the former merges imperceptibly into the latter as time passes. In short, we need to focus more on developing intelligent young people who are adaptable and flexible, as well as creative, aware and knowledgeable, so that they are able to comprehend the essentials in a given situation and then respond appropriately to them, as Alice Heim might have expressed it.

What was more encouraging was that Marjo Kyllonen admitted, *"There are schools that are teaching in the old-fashioned way which was of benefit in the beginnings of the 1900s – but the needs are not the same and we need something fit for the 21st century".* The article went on to note that the reforms being introduced in Finnish schools are very much in line with demands in the UK from the Confederation of British Industry, as well as the Labour Party's Shadow Education Secretary Tristram Hunt, as he was then. These somewhat unusual bedfellows, in the political sense, share one thing in common, and that is, they are calling for schools to promote and develop personal qualities such as character and resilience, as well as communication skills, rather than just serving as *"examination factories"*, whose sole aim is to try and force as many young people as possible to jump through fairly meaningless, external examination 'hoops', as though that is their sole raison d'être.

Getting teachers and heads in secondary schools to change their role, as is the case in Finland, can be challenging in itself because both groups are victims of their own experience of a subject-based, academic education, from which they themselves obviously emerged as relatively successful individuals. The system worked for them, let's be honest, to a greater or lesser extent. But what was encouraging to read in the article, however, was that, following training for teachers in Finland, on how to make this all-important switch from a subject-based to a topic-based curriculum, the experience of those involved was entirely positive. Some evidence of this was offered by Helsinki's development manager, Pasi Silander, who believed that the switch, although challenging for teachers and heads, had been a success. He said: *"We have really changed the mindset…….it is quite difficult to get teachers to start and take the first step…..but teachers who have taken to the new approach say they can't go back."* This does not surprise me in the least, as it supports my view that secondary teachers have so much to learn from studying how their primary school counterparts and colleagues deliver such vibrant, attractive and effective classroom teaching and learning methodologies, to which students respond with a far greater sense of enthusiasm and eventual success.

What is even more encouraging about the new approach to curriculum design and delivery in Finland is the fact that, according to the article, early data has shown that students were benefiting a great deal as well. In fact, in the two years since the new teaching methods were first introduced, student *"outcomes"* – a term they prefer compared to fairly traditional talk about nebulous 'standards' – had also improved. Once more, I have to say that this does not come as much of a revelation or a surprise to me, as it seems pretty obvious that integrating subject specialist content in real-life contexts, is bound to enable young learners to make the fundamental connections that are the essence of the seamless cloak that is knowledge. They are also actively encouraged to see the different perspectives of one and the same reality when studying in this more realistic and natural manner. In fact, it effectively 'forces' students, in the nicest possible way, to explore the inter-connections between otherwise discrete subject disciplines, avoiding the fairly pointless academic learning of subject-specific content that traditionally occurs in splendid isolation.

Whilst such alternative models of school organisation like those in Finland are definitely and urgently needed, there is also a more fundamental shift needed in the way in which the education that goes on in schools is able to become far more student centred and focused on the needs of the learner, and not the whims of central government, examination bodies, pushy parents or the teaching profession, for that matter. There is most definitely a long-overdue paradigm shift in education that is even more radical, progressive and revolutionary – and please recall how I define such often denigrated and rubbished epithets. It is to this complete re-design of the system of education to which I now wish to turn to conclude this book.

Chapter Twenty Seven: System Redesign

David Hargreaves – Educational Guru

> *"Education must provide the opportunities for self-fulfilment; it can at best provide a rich and challenging environment for the individual to explore, in his* (or her) *own way."*
> (Noam Chomsky)

Most, if not all of this final section of the book has, so far, looked at empirical and anecdotal examples of what might constitute far better ways of approaching, designing and organising the education that is intended to be the aim of state schooling. I have also wanted to make it abundantly clear that I am no more an educational 'guru' than any other professional teacher, which is why the school of the future, in its practical manifestation, must be the product of a team effort, involving a diversity of dedicated, qualified and risk-taking professionals. But the time has come to consider very carefully the more philosophical and theoretical arguments of someone who justly and rightly deserves to be viewed as a truly genuine educational guru, at least as far as I am concerned, and I am referring to the ideas of Professor David Hargreaves, whose brilliance was first brought to my attention when I was a trainee teacher at the wonderful Hull College of Education. This may be due to the fact that this academic's only real school-teaching experience was confined to three years in a grammar school in the great city of Hull!

It seems somehow fitting that the wise words, meticulous and (actually) beautiful thinking of David Hargreaves, who is now well into his 70th decade of life, should become a significant part of the closing chapter of this book, just as it was during my early learning as a budding classroom practitioner back in the 1970s. His influence upon me has never really gone away, I am pleased to say, even though I have not read many of his publications, nor really been consciously aware of any of his public utterances, since those formative years, for me, in Hull. Having said that, however, the effect of reading his outstanding book, *'The Challenge for the Comprehensive School'* (1982), has most definitely never left me. If you are a teacher, or an interested other, and you have not yet read this outstanding publication, then I recommend it to you as a highly worthwhile and interesting read – the man is a real gem, if not a genius, in my humble opinion!

If one wishes to more fully appreciate his contribution to, and knowledge of education, then one needs only to be aware of the many different roles he has undertaken during his life, and how he has always been willing to take risks by taking on posts for which he was perhaps not an obvious candidate, for various reasons. However, in the interests of brevity, I shall not provide a potted curriculum vitae for such a great man, when one can easily check this for oneself, and be equally, as well as rightly, impressed.

Peter Wilby wrote an excellent article all about David Hargreaves's latest ideas and proposals regarding how to redesign state schooling back in September 2009 (*'Intellectual guru seeks 'system redesign' of secondary education', The Guardian*), which was introduced with a summary sentence that said, *"David Hargreaves has recently finished his work on the curriculum and, if he has his way, secondary schooling could be transformed."* Unfortunately, it seems perfectly clear that even the logic and reasoned argument of someone as able and visionary as David Hargreaves cannot, on its own, at least, lead to the much needed transformation of state schooling, so that it becomes truly synonymous with real education. This is especially true given the fact that all existing stakeholders seem to believe that simply continuing the current seriously flawed system is the obvious way ahead. As I have said before, they are victims of their own past experiences, labouring under the severely limiting misapprehension of the traditional and comforting notion of 'better the devil you know than the devil you don't', which is, of course, a recipe for crushingly devastating inertia and stagnation.

The article by Peter Wilby centred upon Hargreaves's call for a complete *'system redesign'*, by saying that every aspect of secondary schooling as we currently understand it – lessons, classrooms, subjects, tests, year groups, the role of heads, the authority of teachers – has been fundamentally challenged by Hargreaves' latest thinking. No tinkering at the periphery for David Hargreaves, only a wonderfully complete, radical and progressive overhaul of virtually every cherished, quaint and assumed notion of what it is that schooling should be, especially if we are truly serious about educating our young people, rather than merely occupying them with stories of the past,

606

delivered within fairly randomly packaged knowledge in a variety of convenient, familiar and discretely-delivered academic subject disciplines.

David Hargreaves was reported as saying that his 'system redesign' was, *"more exciting than anything I've done in my career before."* For me, I find the fact that he continues to display a seemingly undiminished zeal for effecting the real growth, development and improvement of secondary schooling not only truly amazing and wonderfully impressive in someone of his age, but also so utterly refreshing and incredibly encouraging and motivational. Moreover, to find myself on the same page in so many ways with someone of David Hargreaves' outstanding academic and practical pedigree, gives me a sense of genuine optimism that the point at which I now find myself, after 40 years in education and training, although radical, is not one of a fool, hopeless romanticist or incurable cynic.

Back in 2004, David Hargreaves was seeking to help the last Labour government transform education by focusing on what was referred to as 'personalised learning', which was definitely a move in the right direction if one is serious about overcoming spurious and facile attempts to standardise the immensely diverse talents of individual learners, whereby the focus of schools would be firmly placed upon *"individual learning styles, motivations and needs".* Fortunately, someone like David Hargreaves is never satisfied with 'nearly there', as he is clearly driven to fully deliver on his pledge to *"transform"* education. Hence, he has moved on a long way from merely personalised learning to system redesign, and that is a big, and much needed leap forward. Thank you, David Hargreaves, sir, I feel vindicated in believing in what I have written about over these last few years, and which has culminated in this book!

Peter Wilby's article refers to Hargreaves' vision for 21st-century schooling by identifying four key areas where the degree of proposed change is not only delightfully radical, but is also entirely correct in my humble opinion. The first of these radically different proposals rightly begins with the students themselves. They should be the ones who should inform the school on matters such as how information technology should be incorporated into the learning process, as they are usually several steps ahead in such areas when compared to some of their teachers, especially many of the older ones, such as me.

Hargreaves believes that even more power should be given to the learners, individually and collectively, as it should be their responsibility to establish standards and determine learning objectives, as well as assess their own work and that of their peers. Furthermore, the learners should also be enabled to devote whole or half days to projects which are collaborative in nature, and Hargreaves says that they should sometimes also be allowed, perhaps encouraged, to work at home. And why not? After all, if they are determining their own learning outcomes, and assessing their own work, then they are clearly going to be heavily invested in ensuring that they achieve these self-determined goals and their own success. This is far more likely to include and promote intrinsic motivation on the part of the individual learner, and they will want to achieve their own learning outcomes and achievements.

Another area where David Hargreaves envisions radical change is in the role of teachers in school. Instead of being the 'fount of all knowledge, direction and wisdom' for want of a better and more apposite phrase, teachers should become mentors and coaches who help negotiate student learning, and then offer constructive and beneficial comment on the work of students, rather than being required to grade or, even worse, rank it. What is more, David Hargreaves argues that traditional subjects should be re-defined as *"essential learnings"*, such as communication, thinking or social responsibilities, or *"competencies"* such as how to manage information, or how to relate appropriately to people in different contexts or circumstances, using the right tone of communication depending on the status and communication preferences of those with whom one is in contact.

Finally, and this is yet another area where I could not agree more with what David Hargreaves was proposing, and that is how schools desperately need to change. In the article, Peter Wilby said that David Hargreaves believed that schools should become part of a series of networks – working collaboratively with other schools and colleges (which necessarily and definitely means not being in petty competition with them), as well as sometimes outsourcing the work of whole departments. This latter proposal fits with what I have argued, and also eliminates or reduces the need for every single school to have specialist or dedicated facilities, which in themselves can be hugely expensive or difficult to afford or acquire, when community resources can be safely and conveniently accessed or shared by students at school.

One of the reasons why I greatly admire the thoughts and ideas of David Hargreaves, is that he is his own man. Yes, he might work for politicians, but only on his own terms and without diluting or abandoning his own beliefs. He is no one's lackey, that's for sure. His thinking is always moving on, which is why he has come to prefer the term *"personalising"* learning over his original brief of 'personalised' learning, simply and, again, rightly because the former implies a continuing process, which is precise and correct, whereas the latter term suggests that there is some definite end to the process, some notion of a finished product. Then again, as Peter Wilby explained, David Hargreaves felt the term 'personalised learning' has been politically hijacked by the Labour Party as a term which they could use as a *"clothesline on which to hang existing policies"*. This is yet another reason why central government needs to butt out of such a crucial and critical process that is the education of our young people, and leave it to 'the professionals'. Please!

Where I find myself in even closer unison with David Hargreaves is where, although he is clear about what needs to be done, he insists that he himself is unable to provide any blueprint of what exactly should be done. Instead, like me, he sets out what needs to be done to make schooling equate with genuine education. Hargreaves rightly believes that the impetus for the detail of the change must necessarily come from below, by which he means that heads and teachers together need to rethink how we should go about secondary education. Not government, not academics and not examination bodies. To be more precise, David Hargreaves was reported to have said: *"We are not talking about a new model of schooling, handed down from above."* And he goes on to say: *"The notion that there should be or can be a standard model is dead."* He is just so, so right!

The reason why David Hargreaves believes in an educational model based on the work of teachers, schools leaders and individual schools, is based entirely on his first-hand experience over the years of what is described in the newspaper article as *"numerous examples of mind-boggling innovations from the grassroots"*. In exactly the same way of trusting students to know what they want to learn, and allowing them to direct their own learning, in negotiation with their teachers, so teachers, working individually or more collaboratively in curriculum teams, will be encouraged to rely on their collective talents and experience as professional educators to take risks in their own teaching and learning, once they are freed from the shackles of the stultifying and blind obedience to central government diktat in the form of mostly moronic new initiatives and impossible quick-fixes.

To help explain this paradigm shift towards allowing students to determine the curriculum – i.e. that which they learn, how and why – David Hargreaves says that the necessary changes are comparable to that which occurred in the industrial world during the 1980s, when there was a move away from the mass production of a standardised product for everyone, into mass customisation instead. He illustrates this by referring to, *"People like Michael Dell came along and, instead of customers going into a shop and choosing between three models of computer, he said: tell me what kind of computer you want, and I'll make it for you."* He went on to relate this to schooling by saying, *"Now customers actively contribute to innovation. Producers seek people's ideas for improving something. It becomes a partnership between producer and consumer. That's the way schools will go."* I sincerely hope that he is right on that change of direction and in the modus operandi of schools.

The system redesign, which David Hargreaves proposes, puts the needs and interests of the students, sometimes individually but largely collaboratively, at the very centre of the curriculum, both in its design and its delivery, and rightly so, as the student is the learner, or the ultimate customer, if we are to use business terminology to describe roles, with the teacher as the mentor and critical friend in the learning process. I really cannot understand why anyone could possibly have a problem with such an obviously relevant, clearly-focused and needs-related 'business model'. Hargreaves places what he calls, *"student leadership"* at the very centre of his thinking and proposals, as are the collaborative projects which he believes must be *"co-constructed"*, or negotiated with the student learners, taking *"authentic"* problems, or real-life situations of the students' choosing as the contexts in which the learning is to occur. What could be more intrinsically motivational to the learner than determining their own projects and contexts in which to develop and explore knowledge and to apply skills, values and attitudes? He argues that this is a far better way to motivate young people to want to learn, rather than doing what we do now in schools by merely presenting them with a set of things that they are required to simply memorize, regurgitate when required, when sitting examinations or tests, and then proceed to forget in their inglorious entirety, due to their utter irrelevance to the learner in their current, challenging and troublesome existence. Let's face it, growing up in today's world, beset with seemingly insurmountable problems, is far from being an easy process, and schools should be ensuring that it is as enjoyable, trouble free and success full as possible, rather than making it so incredibly and unnecessarily stressful for so many young people. In this respect, schools are currently failing our students, and failing them spectacularly effectively – excuse the irony.

In his earlier writings, Hargreaves was one of the first to identify what teachers often refer to as the 'awkward squad' of students in school, who are challenging for all the wrong reasons. He explained that such students create a sub-culture within the school, which is akin to a mirror image of the school's dominant and pre-eminent culture of academic achievement. In common with any culture, this undesirable sub-culture forms its own rules or code of conduct, its own language and what the article refers to as "badges of achievement". This undesirable tendency is hardly surprising when one considers that those for whom academic success is not really their forte, or those who simply do not feel inspired or engaged by academic study, are effectively deprived of status in the teachers' eyes, and so the lesser academically able students seek status amongst their peers instead. When Hargreaves first identified this phenomenon it "had the force of revelation", as the newspaper article pointed out, although today it is a fact that we take very much for granted, such is the failure of schools to offer these young people real opportunities for success in other areas of study, and which are celebrated at least on a par with those who reach the pinnacle of academic success.

Some years ago, when I was waiting to take up my post as Secondary Principal at a school in Singapore, I found myself without work for three months, and so returned to the UK to act as a supply teacher in a large comprehensive school on the Isle of Wight, and not the one where I had been Head of Economics and, later, Deputy Head Teacher some 12 or so years before. I was a lodger with a family who are dear friends of mine, and who also worked at the school. It was a real eye-opener for me, as well as a significant personal and professional challenge, after several years as a Head Teacher and General Advisor of schools.

This challenge to my authority was something to which I had never really been exposed to such an extent, and it highlighted the difficulties that 'supply' or 'substitute' teachers face, due to having no real status in the school and, therefore, in the eyes of the students. I also asked the Deputy Head after about one month if he sought to identify the frequency with which particular classes and students were often left without their usual classroom teacher, owing to staff absence, attendance at training courses offered in the school and by external agencies, and such like. When he said that he did not do that, I recommended that he should, as the classes and students that I covered almost every day, and several times at that, were always the same faces, and comprised members of the 'awkward squad' in very large numbers. So challenging was their anti-school behaviour that such classes had full-time teacher assistants assigned to try and help teachers retain control, let alone teach them anything worthwhile. Despite my best efforts, their behaviour in class was appalling, by my standards, although I drew some crumbs of comfort from the fact that I managed them far more effectively than their usual timetabled teacher, according to the teacher assistants present.

Some weeks after I completed my time at that school, I was speaking to another ex-colleague of mine, who had been a Head of Drama, and I confessed at being shocked at how much worse the behaviour of students had become since my time as a full-time class teacher. My old colleague corrected me by pointing out that such ill-discipline and bad behaviour had been just the same when I was teaching, with students offering no respect to the teachers, and responding with negative and anti-social conduct, but the difference was that it was confined to a relatively small and manageable number of individuals within the school population. What had changed, he opined, was that the incidence of such poor conduct had become far more widespread in recent years and had infected a larger number of the total school population. It was this that made it seem as though the behaviour had deteriorated and, of course, upon reflection and due consideration I had to agree with his analysis of the phenomenon that I had encountered. Even students who had academic ability were far from engaged, inspired or otherwise encouraged to stay on task, largely because what they were required to learn was of no real interest or relevance to them whatsoever, and was hardly likely ever going to be otherwise. Schools were quite simply failing students by boring them stiff with acquiring knowledge that was utterly redundant to them, and their disinterest manifested itself in their lapsing into the behaviours of the challenging sub-culture.

David Hargreaves was fortunate, because he was highly academic and part of the mainstream school culture, but in his seminal book, 'The Challenge for the Comprehensive School' published in 1982, he recognised and pointed out in a damning and wholly convincing way that, *"our present secondary-school system….exerts on many pupils…a destruction of their dignity which is so massive and so pervasive that few subsequently recover from it"*. To illustrate this, he provided the reader with an insight into his own schooling and the fact that, although academically able, he was hopeless in gym, games, painting, swimming, running and, above all, woodwork. He mentions in his book how his woodwork teacher would occasionally instruct the class to *"stop work and look at Hargreaves"*, using him as a classic exemplar of how ***not*** to do it at all well or correctly. This led him to imagine the scenario of what he called a *"nightmare curriculum"* which was dominated by compulsory woodwork and the other activities in which he readily exhibited his relative incompetence. The other part of his worst dream ever was that subjects like maths, English and history came in thin slices, and then largely disappeared when he reached 14 years of age, which is of course what usually happens to the expressive and creative arts, as well as the humanities to some extent, in many secondary schools today. This nightmare curriculum prompted Hargreaves to note that faced with such a daunting prospect, and knowing he was doomed to experience persistent failure, would he not also have found a degree of escape or solace in being a truant, subverting the school that he would leave just as soon as it was possible for him to do so?

As a result, as long ago as 1982, David Hargreaves wrote that schools need to broaden the curriculum and litter the paths of young people with diverse quality learning opportunities which would enable all of them to experience success in areas other than *"the dominant cognitive-intellectual mode"*. He went on to argue, **some 34 years ago**, that traditional subjects should be subsumed into an integrated core, which students would experience for a longer time period, such as half of the school day, with examinations at the age of 16 years abolished altogether. He specified that the core curriculum that he envisaged should give the expressive arts a major amount of time because it offers so many different avenues for students to feel a sense of achievement and self-worth or self-esteem; it would give them the bags of confidence that Tim Brighouse said was an absolutely essential ingredient if students were to be successful at school and in life.

During the remaining half a day, Hargreaves argued that students should have the time to remediate skill areas which were deficient and in need of improvement, especially in key areas such as literacy and numeracy, as well as to experience specialist options of limited and brief duration. These options would be specialist and not general in nature, so instead of studying just English, for example, students would be offered "science fiction" or "Romantic poetry". The advantage of this approach is that if a student did not enjoy a particular specialist option, then they would not become alienated to whole subject areas for good. When one considers when this was written and first mooted, it was considered revolutionary and radical, and one can see how he has, more recently, arrived at the point of proposing his "system redesign", which is even more progressive and truly transformational in nature.

During the 1980s when David Hargreaves was the chief inspector of ILEA (the Inner London Education Authority) he was the most talked about educationist in the UK. Although a career academic, this was an opportunity for him to put his money where his mouth was, so to speak. Sadly, although some small parts of his wider philosophy, such as the use of modular course units of study that permit more frequent assessment, managed to find their way into mainstream schooling, at least for a while, most of his ideas were never to find their way into everyday school practice. Why? Again, the answer was the politically-polluted agenda of Margaret Thatcher and the Conservative Party in government at the time who, in 1988 abolished ILEA, and he returned to the world of academe at Cambridge University, until he was brought back into the more practical educational world by New Labour who appointed him as the chief executive of QCA (the Qualifications and Curriculum Authority). The Guardian article about Hargreaves made the point that David Hargreaves quickly came to realise that the radical changes he wanted, *"were not going to come as long as No. 10 dominated the agenda"*, and so he resigned from his post well before the end of his first contract.

His most recent work for the Specialist Schools and Academies Trust (SSAT) has led to his system redesign proposals, and the article questioned whether his ideas will ever see the light of day in terms of the complete transformation of secondary schooling, so that it can become synonymous with offering a genuine education to our young people. Although David Hargreaves was encouraged, impressed and highly enthusiastic about the number of confident, risk-taking people that attended the conferences organised by the SSAT, he doubted whether central government would be sufficiently courageous to allow it to happen at all. He was quoted as saying, *"They say they are in favour of innovation, but it has to be innovation that they approve of. It's as daft as the Department for Industry telling businesses where they can and cannot innovate."* That statement alone encapsulates the reason why I have argued for the teaching profession to regain control of what goes on in schools, and why the government has little or no role to play, apart from helping to support what teachers decide to try and do to educate all young people. This is so that students can find ways in which they can seek to combine passion with talent, in order that they may all experience the joy that comes from achieving and succeeding in something really relevant to them as individuals, something that strikes the right chord within them, and excites them, simply because it is something that is truly worthwhile.

When people such as David Hargreaves, Ken Robinson and many other notable academics and practising teachers have been eloquently advocating the need for a radical transformation of how we envisage everything that schools are currently engaged in and have been so involved in with such persistence over many decades, we really cannot allow future generations of young people to undergo an experience that for too many of them is irrelevant, uninteresting and uninspiring, as well as limited to only really acknowledging success in academic studies as being worthwhile, when that is simply a long-established custom and a falsehood that condemns young people to schooling that is not enlightening, does not fill them with the self-confidence to boost their self-esteem, and does precious little to even prepare them for adult and working life.

The time to act is now, and is desperately long overdue!

For a very long time, it has become a very pressing issue to try something radically different and which genuinely places the learner at the very centre of our joint endeavours. The government needs to listen, fund and support the efforts of the teaching profession, working with education academics, as well as other stakeholders in a community dynamic that entertains the creative capabilities attributed to possibility, just as much as it celebrates the certainty of established fact and existing knowledge. For far too long, education has been in the hands of those who are the least knowledgeable, the least qualified and the least able to implement effective change in the way we design and run our schools from the other side of the 'chalk-face'. The time has come to return education to the educationists and for the government to butt out and stop wasting the time of teachers, school leaders and, most importantly of all, our young people. Education and the life chances of our young people are simply far too important to be left in the hands of politicians – we must act, and we must do so now to really transform schooling!

The Epilogue

I don't really know why, but I feel a real need to include the following quotation in this final section of the book:

"What we do in life, echoes in eternity."

(Maximus, played by Russell Crowe in Ridley Scott's movie "Gladiator")

Perhaps, the need to include this fictional quotation is prompted by my belief that as human beings, we have within each and every one of us, a fundamental desire and a moral or spiritual need to leave our legacy, as proof that we existed and had a reason for being alive at one time. As a result, our job as professional teachers and heads is to build learning institutions that enable every young person to discover their innate talents so that, during their lifetimes, they can follow their true destinies and take full advantage of their inner passions in the various roles that they fill in life, so that they can experience a truly liberating and fulfilling existence.

I have also decided not to include a formal bibliography, and I offer three reasons for this intentional omission. To begin with, I have referenced the work, comment and ideas of notable others in the text itself, and secondly, I consider it to be an academic practice which, in itself, perpetuates the supremacy and pre-eminence that academe enjoys within the arena of learning, despite it being only one key type of scholastic endeavour.

My third and final justification for not including a bibliography is due to the fact that I am learning to be a true Buddhist. I may have been christened shortly after birth, but becoming a member of the Church of England was not a conscious decision that I made at the time, and now I find myself unable to believe in some deity or higher power. I prefer to contemplate the teachings of a man who actually existed and made no claims to be the offspring of some deity.

One of the most often used quotations of Lord Buddha himself is as follows:

"Believe nothing just because a so-called wise person said it.
Believe nothing just because a belief is generally held
Believe nothing just because someone else believes it.

617

Believe only what you yourself test and judge to be true."

Referring back to the beginning of this book, I sought to make it clear that what I have written is where I stand after some 38 years in education and training, and my sole intention was, and still is, to provoke thought by reflecting on the fundamental difference between education and schooling, as well as the nonsense of trying to standardize human diversity when young people attend school and follow a common curriculum diet of set subjects.

I am sure that I will refine some of what I have written, with the benefit of time, and I may even change my mind on some of the less substantive or central issues that I have written about. But for now, I rest my case and thank you for taking the time to read what has taken me quite a large number of years to complete – at least for now!

In Memoriam

This section is the most emotional and difficult one for me to write, as I must acknowledge and remember various people who have passed away, and to whom I owe a huge debt of gratitude. Foremost among these people must be my dear father, Ivor Gilman, my natural mother Betty Georgina Barker and my second 'Mum' (somehow 'step-mother' seems wholly inadequate as a description of the maternal role she offered me) Nina Irene Allen.

I would also like to remember my 'second father', the wonderful Alun Roberts, who was my Economics and Education lecturer, as well as my mentor and later dear friend, who helped me to eventually develop my academic potential, and encouraged me to believe in myself. He never lost faith in me, and if I am a good teacher, then it is only really because he was my role model as a practising educationist. He is mentioned several times in this book by name, and that was as necessary as it was natural. He was simply a delightful and tremendously gifted man!

Additionally, I would like to remember Ekta Sheti and Christopher Bennett. Ekta was a student in Year Nine at the British School of New Delhi who tragically died suddenly on the playing fields whilst practising for sports day. Losing a student in that way, at such a tender age, is something I can never forget, such was the immense pain that I felt as Secondary Principal and the sense of loss that it caused the whole school community, but especially her wonderful family and closest friends.

Chris Bennett was my Vice Principal when we were preparing to open Day Waterman College, a new boarding school in Abeokuta, near Lagos in Nigeria. In the week before the school was due to welcome its first ever intake, Chris (and his wife Khwan) both contracted malaria. Whilst she eventually made a full recovery, Chris died one week after diagnosis. He was a dear, dear man, and although we only worked together for a very short time, everyone thought that we had done so before over many years. Such was the closeness of our professional regard for each other, as well as our friendship. I miss him to this day, and without him, I left the school shortly after his passing.

Finally, my thanks to the three people who were my Head Teachers from 1976 to 1982, all of whom were very different in their style of leadership, but who always recognized my abilities and promoted me during my time working with, and for them: Arthur Lingard (at Billericay School), the dear James Archer and his successor, Chris Evans (at Medina High School), all of whom have sadly passed away. I am indebted and eternally grateful to them, and remember them with considerable fondness!

This book is dedicated to all of the above, as well as "to the young, in whose spirit the search for truth marches on"!

Printed in Great Britain
by Amazon